1000 Great Guitarists

HUGH GREGORY

GPI BOOKS
An Imprint of
Miller Freeman Books
San Francisco

Published in the UK by Balafon Books, an imprint of Outline Press Ltd,
115J Cleveland Street, London W1P 5PN, England.

First American Edition
Published by Miller Freeman Books, 600 Harrison Street,
San Francisco, CA 94107
Publishers of GPI Books and *Guitar Player* magazine
A member of the United Newspapers Group

Distributed to the book trade in the US and Canada by
Publishers Group West, PO Box 8843, Emeryville, CA 94662

Distributed to the music trade in the US and Canada by
Hal Leonard Publishing, PO Box 13819, Milwaukee, WI 53213

Printed in Hong Kong

Art Direction & Design: Nigel Osborne
Editor: Tony Bacon
Consultants: John Morrish and Paul Day
Research: Roger Cooper

Library of Congress card no. 94-75867
ISBN 0-87930-307-7

Typesetting by PLS Limited, London W1
Print and Origination by Regent Publishing Services

94 95 96 97 98 5 4 3 2 1

THIS BOOK celebrates the music made by 1000 great guitarists, and relishes the fact that the guitar is used as the driving force behind a greater and more excitingly diverse range of music than any other instrument. Our 1000 players come from classical, country, R&B, bluegrass, new wave, western swing, jazz, pop, blues, rock, funk, folk, punk, new age, world music, heavy metal and more, and all share an uncommon ability to turn strings and frets into remarkable music.

No doubt your own list of 1000 great guitarists would differ from ours – that is inevitable. This book is a personal view, drawn from the entire world of guitar playing. We make it clear that in our opinion some players do a better job than others, and with a gentle if purposeful hand we try to steer you toward guitarists and styles of guitar music that we feel you may have overlooked or undervalued.

In the course of the book you will find that we have presented 12 illustrated features on a range of guitarists. We have picked these not as 'the best', but as our own personal selection of living guitarists who together underline the sheer diversity and brilliance of guitar-driven music.

The book is presented in an easy to use A-to-Z format, and each player's entry is headed by personal information and the principal guitar models they use. In the entries, song titles are in single quotes, album titles are in italics, and references to players in other main entries are in bold. The index at the back of the book can be a useful way to cross-reference, and can for example help you to find out the bands and groups in which particular guitarists played.

Naturally we have gone to great lengths to ensure that the information in this book is correct, and the publishers welcome updates for future editions. We would especially like to thank the various record companies who have helped the factual and visual substance of this book, including Ace, A&M, America, Arista, Beggars Banquet, Black Crow, BMG, Compulsion, Concord, East West, Edsel, Ember, EMI, Imperial, MCA, New Note, See For Miles, Silvertone, Sony, Stax, Topic, Trailer, Urantia, Verve, Warner Bros.

Abb-Ada

DREW ABBOTT

Born: January 13th 1947, Detroit, Michigan, US.

■ *Gibson Les Paul; Gibson Explorer; Fender Stratocaster.*

In the mid-1970s one of the best live bands on the US concert circuit was Bob Seger's Silver Bullet Band, boasting guitarist Drew Abbott. Seger, hailing from Ann Arbor, Michigan, had led an eventful career until joining Capitol Records in May 1975 after his previous label had rejected the *Beautiful Loser* album. Capitol snapped him up and Seger embarked on a coast-to-coast tour of the US fronting the Silver Bullet Band, which had been formed in 1974.

The band was a hard-rock/R&B outfit with guitarist Abbott providing the main thrust to the sound. Never a flamboyant soloist, Abbott's guitar work complemented saxophonist Alto Reed and emphasized the melodic qualities in Seger's writing. This was best evidenced by 1977's *Night Moves* album, which demonstrated the range of Seger's songwriting skills and showed Abbott to be a guitarist in a similar style to **Miami Steve van Zandt**, who played guitar with **Bruce Springsteen**.

Later albums, such as *Stranger In Town* and *Against The Wind*, were commercially successful, but Seger's 'big ballads' dominated the proceedings and relegated the group to a supporting role. This was a little shortsighted as 1976's *Live Bullet* and 1981's *Nine Tonight* had shown that the Silver Bullet Band was a fundamental part of Seger's sound.

In 1983, Seger hired session musicians like guitarist **Waddy Wachtel** and pianist Roy Bittan for *The Distance*, irritating Abbott to such an extent that he left the band. While Seger continued to be a major US attraction into the late-1980s, the fire and flair of the Silver Bullet was notably lacking. As for Abbott, he disappeared into obscurity.

JOHN ABERCROMBIE

Born: December 16th 1944, Port Chester, New York, US.

■ *Ibanez Artist; Ovation.*

In the late-1960s Abercrombie, with hornmen Randy and Michael Brecker, was helping the fusion being made in jazz-rock band Dreams. While this gave him an opportunity to develop a driving, Hendrix-influenced style, it sounded all technique and little heart. Through the 1970s as fusion held sway he continued to pursue this course with drummer Billy Cobham's Spectrum, while leading a separate career as a sessionman with arranger Gil Evans and saxophonist Gato Barbieri. By 1975, tiring of fusion, Abercrombie formed Gateway with bassist Dave Holland and percussionist Jack DeJohnette, encouraging him to embrace an altogether softer and more cerebral style. Since that time he has, like **John Scofield**, acquired a melodic yet challenging style that has established him in the vanguard of contemporary jazz guitarists. His collaborations with saxman Jan Garbarek (*Eventyr* 1981) and with multi-instrumentalist **Ralph Towner** (*Sargasso Sea* 1977, *Five Years Later* 1982) have heart coupled with technique, a combination notably absent in Abercrombie's formative years.

MICK ABRAHAMS

Born: April 7th 1943, Luton, Bedfordshire, England.

One of the most appealing aspects of the original lineup of Jethro Tull was the inclusion of Mick Abrahams. Although he only remained with the band for the debut *This Was* (1968) his nimble dexterity on tracks like 'Cat's Squirrel' gave the group its reputation for being blues-based. His departure scotched that, and Abrahams went on to form Blodwyn Pig – while Jethro Tull went on to be Ian Anderson.

With the emergence of a flourishing club and pub circuit in the late-1960s and early-1970s, Abrahams was in his element before small but appreciative audiences where he was able to experiment with his style. Often playing slide guitar, he had considerably more technique at his disposal than other contemporary slide players such as **Jeremy Spencer** of Fleetwood Mac or **Stan Webb** of Chicken Shack.

While neither of Blodwyn Pig's albums (*Ahead Rings Out* 1969 and *Getting To This* 1970) were resounding commercial successes – nor indeed was Abraham's later solo albums – they had a rough and ready charm that illustrated his versatility and gave the impression that here was a man who just loved to play, completely unmoved by record company pleas for commerciality. Consequently, he remains an unsung hero of the club circuit. In 1975 he issued a lively and approachable instructional album called, unsurprisingly, *Learning To Play With Mick Abrahams*.

WILL ACKERMAN

Born: November 1949, Germany.

■ *Kelly Johnson; Guild D25.*

After moving to the West Coast of America in the late-1950s, Ackerman took up the acoustic guitar in 1960. Citing his prime influences as **John Fahey** and **Leo Kottke**, he started the Windham Hill label in 1976 as no other outlet expressed much interest in his work. His debut, *In Search Of The Turtle's Navel* (1976), was sparse and uncluttered and contributed to an early definition of so-called new age music, in which Windham Hill specialized. Over the years his haunting excursions into the subconscious have slowed down as he nurtured younger Windham Hill talents such as **Michael Hedges** and Alex de Grassi, although *Imaginary Roads* (1990) showed little deviation from his established route.

ROY ACUFF

Born: Roy Claxton Acuff, September 15th 1903, Maynardsville, Tennessee, US. Died: November 23rd 1992, Nashville, Tennessee, US.

Roy Acuff was synonymous with Nashville and country music from the 1940s until his death in 1992. Although his instrumental prowess was less noticeable as his fame increased, his guitar work made him a leading role model for aspiring musicians in the country field.

Acuff's career started in a medicine show, and he then went on to form The Tennessee Crackerjacks (later The Crazy Tennesseans), recording titles like 'Wabash Cannonball' and 'The Great Speckled Bird'. In 1938 he changed the name of his group – which now included dobroist **Bashful Brother Oswald** – to The Smoky Mountain Boys. During the war years Acuff established himself with a string of hits which included 'Wreck On The Highway', 'Fireball Mail', 'Night Train To Memphis', 'Precious Jewel', 'Pins And Needles' and 'Low And Lonely'.

After World War II Acuff's popularity declined drastically, but with songwriter Fred Rose he set up the music publishing company Acuff-Rose, and it remains the most successful of all Nashville music publishers. Although he never recovered his early reputation as a ground-breaker, his position as King Of Country remained unchallenged and he continued to perform at the Grand Ole Opry at least twice a week right up to his death. He had also established a museum for his considerable collection of musical instruments at the Opry.

BRYAN ADAMS

Born: Bryan Guy Adams, November 5th 1959, Ontario, Canada.

■ *Fender Stratocaster.*

Bryan Adams remains one of the best live rock acts in the world today, a position he has achieved through non-stop touring, performing a string of self-composed songs that combine the immediacy of pop with the urgency of rock. Although his best-known single is 'Everything I Do (I Do It For You)' (1991), in fact 'Run To You' from *Reckless* (1984) and 'Heat Of The Night' from *Into The Fire* (1987) are much better illustrations of his output. His guitar work provides the core of his group's sound, while his sparring partner **Keith Scott** offers a counterbalance with melodic, tightly structured solos. While Adams' shows are central to his appeal, strong working relationships with producer/engineer Bob Clearmountain and, later, producer Robert 'Mutt' Lange have ensured that there is a sense of continuity and progression to his albums.

STUART ADAMSON

Born: April 11th 1958, Manchester, England.

■ *Yamaha SG2000; ESP Strat-style.*

The twin-guitar-based sound of Big Country was founded in Dunfermline, Scotland in 1981 when Stuart Adamson left the Skids to form the group with Canadian guitarist **Bruce Watson** and the rhythm section of Tony Butler (bass) and Mark Brzezicki (drums). After being signed to Phonogram by A&R man Chris Briggs they were teamed with producer Steve Lillywhite and came up with the novel, swirling 'bagpipe sound' for the two guitars, later emulated by other Scottish bands such as The Waterboys and Simple Minds. Their debut *The Crossing* (1983) featured titles like the anthemic 'In A Big Country' and 'Fields Of Fire'. Both Adamson's and Watson's guitar work, with the former's hectoring vocals punctuated by the trademark 'Shout!', gave the group the identity that many other bands tried so desperately to achieve.

BERNARD ADDISON

Born: April 4th 1905, Annapolis, Maryland, US.

■ *Epiphone Emperor.*

Addison was one of a number of rhythm guitarists of the 1920s and 1930s who underscored the contributions of soloists like Louis Armstrong and Billie Holiday. Appearing on many of the best sessions that Holiday cut at Columbia, he was the vital foil for pianist Teddy Wilson and hornman Lester Young. While he tended to be an adjunct of the rhythm section, his embellishments provided variety and depth, particularly on a 1939 session with Coleman Hawkins that included 'Body & Soul'. Among the other people he sessioned with were Fletcher Henderson, Art Tatum, the Mills Brothers and Red Allen.

JAN AKKERMAN

Born: December 24th 1946, Amsterdam, Holland.

■ *Gibson Les Paul Custom; Framus 'signature'; Roland GR505.*

Akkerman came to the fore in the early-1970s with Dutch band Focus, with whom he recorded the touching guitar instrumental hit 'Sylvia' (1973). Since that brief flirtation with the stardust of rock'n'roll he has churned out clinically perfect albums with any number of jazz and new-age musicians, but none of these records has managed to raise the pulse above comatose. This is mainly due to an apparent indecision about the direction he should follow. His propensity for extended solos for their own sake indicates a preoccupation with the instrument's capabilities rather than aesthetic possibilities. There are those who share this preoccupation and would best be served by checking out two compilations, *The Complete Guitarist* and *Can't Stand Noise*, both of which ably demonstrate his technical prowess.

BERNARD ALBRECHT

See BERNARD SUMNER

OSCAR ALEMAN

Born: 1909, Chaco, Argentina. Died: October 14th 1980, Buenos Aires, Argentina.

■ *National resonator; Maccaferri.*

Aleman would be remembered today as an important jazz guitarist, had it not been for **Django Reinhardt** who completely overshadowed the superficially similar work of the Argentinian guitarist. Around 1930 Aleman's duo was invited to play in Europe, and after the duo split Aleman was taken on briefly as accompanist to music hall star Josephine Baker in France. Later in the 1930s Aleman began recording in and around Paris... at exactly the same time that Reinhardt was making his mark there.

While there are similarities in the style and sound

of the two players, Aleman had a wider technical ability and greater rhythmic diversity, although Reinhardt's natural feel was of course quite magical. Some of Aleman's more exciting recordings made in France at this time include refined solo items like 'Whispering' and 'Nobody's Sweetheart' and trio sessions such as 'Just A Little Swing'. At the time of writing these recordings were not available on CD, and vinyl releases have long since been deleted. Aleman returned to Argentina in 1941 and, despite recording a few sessions locally, he produced little more music until his death in 1980.

JOHNNIE ALLAN

Born: John Guillot, March 10th 1938, Rayne, Louisiana, US.

Johnnie Allan enjoyed a brief spell of cult hero status in 1974 when British DJ, author and label-owner Charlie Gillett picked up and released Allan's rip-roaring version of **Chuck Berry**'s 'Promised Land'. While Allan was formerly a rhythm guitarist and steel player and had a local hit with 'Lonely Days, Lonely Nights' in 1959 with The Krazy Kats, it was this version of 'Promised Land' that still seems to distil the riotous good nature of the very best Cajun music, with swirling accordions propelling the thunderous chords. Anyone who can stand still while it plays has obviously forgotten what legs are for.

RODNEY ALLEN

Born: Bristol, England.

Blue Aeroplanes were formed during the early-1980s as an aggregation of musicians and poets purveying a multimedia act. While their template was that of the Velvet Underground, Principal Edwards Magic Theatre would be a closer assessment. Initially their eclecticism militated against breaking through and the lineup was in a state of constant flux, but after their third album *Spitting Out Miracles* (1987) Allen, who had been an occasional contributor, started to exert more influence. Since then he has become a part of the group's nucleus, appearing on *Friendloverplane* (1988) and *Swagger* (1990) which saw them move closer to the mainstream, emphasizing their new-found orthodoxy, which was consolidated with *Beatsongs* (1991).

LUTHER ALLISON

Born: August 17th 1939, Mayflower, Arizona, US.

■ *Gibson ES335.*

A journeyman blues singer and guitarist, Allison has for years plied his trade on the international festival circuit without achieving the dizzy heights of superstardom attained by lesser players. He was raised in Chicago where he formed The Rolling Stones (no, not that one) with his brother Grant in 1954 and started to play the local club circuit. By 1958, after numerous personnel upheavals and changes of name, the band split and Allison started to gig with **Chuck Berry** and **Magic Sam**.

After moving to the West Coast in the 1960s he started to play the burgeoning festival and college

circuit, and in 1976 came to London to play The 100 Club. The results of this gig were captured on vinyl and issued as *Southside Safari*, a set that illustrates his showmanship and fine guitar work and echoes the Muddy Waters Band of the late-1960s. While Allison's feet are more deeply grounded in the traditional urban blues than, say, **Robert Cray**, there is a suggestion of modernity in his outlook that is best heard on the self-penned 'Luther's Blues' (1974).

DUANE ALLMAN

Born: November 26th 1946, Nashville, Tennessee, US.
Died: October 29th 1971, Macon, Georgia, US.

■ *Gibson Les Paul Standard; Gibson SG.*

Listening to Duane Allman's guitar work 20 years after his death disproves the theory that only black musicians can have soul. In his short career Allman brought a soulful lyricism to the guitar that was only matched by bluesmen like **BB King** and **Robert Johnson**. The enduring irony of it all was that his most celebrated solo was on **Eric Clapton**'s 'Layla'.

Allman's career had started with local bands like The House Rockers, Allman Joys and Hourglass, and he recorded a brace of undistinguished albums for Liberty with the latter. When these bands sank Allman resurfaced as a session musician in Muscle Shoals, working for producer Jerry Wexler and Wilson Pickett sessions.

Duane formed the Allman Brothers Band in 1969 with brother Gregg (vocals) and guitarist **Dicky Betts**, and they were signed to the Capricorn label which was owned by the group's manager, Phil Walden. After a brace of studio albums, the band cut the live *At The Fillmore East* (1971) which included pieces like 'In Memory Of Elizabeth Reed', 'Whipping Post' and 'Statesboro Blues'. These illustrated the rich diversity of Duane's influences and highlighted his particular skills as a slide .player, perfectly complementing the country feel of Betts' style. Significantly, and atypically in a guitar-based band, the relaxed fluidity of each man's style never gave the impression that they were trying to outdo one another.

The follow-up *Eat A Peach* (1972) combined live material with studio tracks and gave the group the commercial acceptance that was long overdue, but while it was being recorded Duane had been killed in a motorcycle accident. Although his death was a major blow to the group, their fortunes continued to spiral upwards for some years under the guidance of Betts and Gregg Allman. However, it was Duane's influence that stimulated the emergence of so-called southern boogie bands such as Lynyrd Skynyrd, Wet Willie, and The Marshall Tucker Band, among others.

TOMMY ALLSUP

Born: Tulsa, Oklahoma, US.

Prior to joining The Crickets, Allsup had led The Western Swing Band. While the sides he cut with Buddy Holly were few, 'Love's Made A Fool Of You', 'It's So Easy', 'Lonesome Tears', 'Heartbeat' and 'Wishing', recorded in summer 1958, were nonetheless the clearest indication of Holly's ability to control his own career away from producer Norman Petty. After those sessions Allsup left, but in January 1959 he rejoined for what turned out to be Holly's last tour, augmenting a lineup that comprised drummer Carl Bunch and bassist Waylon Jennings, a further stab by Holly at autonomy. Unfortunately Holly didn't live long enough to find out whether such a course would work.

LAURINDO ALMEIDA

Born: September 2nd 1917, Sao Paolo, Brazil.

■ *Julius Gido; Takamine.*

The man responsible for introducing Brazilian bossa nova music to North America, Almeida started his career in Brazil as a classical guitarist. Then he visited Europe and saw **Django Reinhardt** play, returning to Brazil only long enough to pack up and move to Los Angeles, where he joined the big-band jazz orchestra of Stan Kenton in 1947. While with Kenton he recorded a masterful piece in 'Lament', and also became one of an increasing number of jazz and classical musicians playing sessions for the movies.

Through his work with Kenton he landed a recording contract with Capitol and started to make a number of eclectic solo albums. Almeida, unlike many others, was able to play jazz or classical equally effectively, with the result that his interpretation of Rodrigo's 'Concierto de Aranjuez', for example, was widely praised by classical critics. Such versatility enabled him to expand and extend his repertoire without becoming bogged down by technique, giving added attraction to his playing.

Almeida's assistance in the popularization of bossa nova started in the late-1950s with *Brazilliance* and sax player Bud Shank, while in 1962 Almeida recorded the wildly influential *Viva Bossa Nova* which included 'The Girl From Ipanema'. In addition to winning a Grammy, the record also opened the door for Stan Getz's experimentation with Latin rhythms and introduced Latin composer Antonio Carlos Jobim's work to US record buyers, who found the music irresistible.

With the passing of the years Almeida has continued to experiment, releasing *Selected Classical Works For Guitar & Flute* with Shank in 1982 and two albums of duets with Latin guitarist **Charlie Byrd**, *Brazilian Soul* (1980) and *Latin Artistry* (1982).

CARLOS ALOMAR

Born: US

■ *Alembic; Kramer.*

For a short time in the mid-1970s when David Bowie flirted with soul on *Young Americans* and *Station To Station*, one of his best moves was to enlist Carlos Alomar, the guitarist from New York soul group Main Ingredient. Alomar's unfussy, sultry accompaniment to songs like 'Golden Years' and 'TVC15' gave *Station To Station* the feel of a proper soul album. While this association with Bowie landed him plenty of subsequent work, he was mainly required to play rock

material which seemed totally opposed to his natural style. No-one seemed to realize that Bowie had recruited Alomar because he was an ace soul guitarist – heavy on the rhythmic figures, light on the extended soloing – and not because he wanted to turn him into a rock guitarist.

ERIC ANDERSEN

Born: February 14th 1943, Pittsburgh, Pennsylvania, US.

In the vanguard of the 1960s folk revival, Andersen operated alongside Tom Paxton, Phil Ochs, Judy Collins, Bob Dylan and Tom Rush on the New York folk club circuit. Purist to a fault, Andersen's style is immutable and has contributed through his songbooks to the rise of young performers like Tanita Tikaram and Mary-Chapin Carpenter, and his lyrical, inventive work on albums such as *'Bout Changes And Things* (1966) and *Blue River* (1973) has a reassuring individuality.

IAN A ANDERSON

Born: July 26th 1947, Weston-Super-Mare, Somerset, England.

One of the most significant interpreters of blues and R&B, Anderson has applied his acumen to a range of traditional British folk material through his inspired use of bottleneck guitar. At first he recorded blues material in the manner of Delta bluesmen such as **Mississippi Fred McDowell**, for example on *Stereo Death Breakdown* (1969). By 1973, as a soloist or in tandem with a group, he brought his considerable expertise to bear on different genres of traditional music: as a solo guitarist (*Royal York Crescent* 1970); with the Hot Vultures (*The East Street Shakes* 1977) as an R&B band; and in the English Country Blues Band (later Tiger Moth) who played traditional English dance music (*Unruly* 1993). Underrated to a fault, Anderson has a knack of knowing exactly what's going in the traditional music world, no doubt helped by his founding of *Folk Roots* magazine.

JOHN ANDERSON

Born: December 13th 1954, Apopka, Florida, US.

Where guitars are often little more than props for many country singers, this 'new country' singer/songwriter's acoustic picking has established him as a guitarist with great potential. Anderson has combined the influences such as the Rolling Stones, Steppenwolf and Alice Cooper with the diehard traditionalism of one of country's purest genres, honky-tonk.

Moving to Nashville in 1972, he performed occasionally with his sister Donna and joined the group Living End, and was signed to Warner Brothers in 1977 where he had a number of country hits with songs like 'Eyes Of A Hurricane' (1985). His best work appeared in 1992 on *Seminole Wind* (including the hits 'Straight Tequila Night', 'When It Comes To You' and 'Seminole Wind'), reflecting his growing ability to adopt the key reference points of honky-tonk without becoming too derivative.

MILLER ANDERSON

Born: Scotland.

The Keef Hartley Band formed around the same time as **John Mayall**'s extended lineup of The Bluesbreakers. The biggest difference was that Hartley allowed a flexibility in personnel and in repertoire which imbued the group with a semblance of spontaneity. Miller Anderson, the guitarist, vocalist and songwriter, contributed the vital spark: his songs were strong enough to support the improvisations of trumpeter Henry Lowther and saxophonist Jimmy Jewell, while Anderson himself tended toward the odd well-placed phrase rather than the extended solo. *Battle Of NW6* (1970), *Overdog* and *Little Big Band* (1971) still retain that spark, due in part to Neil Slaven's acute production. Anderson attempted an abortive solo career, issuing *City Lights* (1972), joined forces again with Hartley in the unexciting band Overdog, and appeared briefly in T Rex, Savoy Brown, and a band called The Dukes.

SAM ANDREW

Born: December 18th 1941, Taft, California, US.

■ *Gibson SG; Gibson Les Paul.*

One of Janis Joplin's longest serving lieutenants, guitarist Sam Andrew backed her in Big Brother & The Holding Company and in the Kozmic Blues Band. Andrew was, thus part of a band who were playing bars one minute and The Fillmore the next, and quite frankly seemed under-rehearsed and overwhelmed by Janis's overnight stardom. But their *Cheap Thrills* album (1968), despite the appalling sound quality, came to be one of the most significant of the epoch, thanks to the blues-rock singer fronting the outfit. Andrew for his part contributed the odd chop to *I Got Dem Ole Kozmic Blues Again Mama!* (1969), but in truth no-one was much interested in his ability one way or another.

ANTENNAE JIMMY SEMMENS

See JEFF COTTON

JOAN ARMATRADING

Born: December 9th 1950, St Kitts, West Indies.

■ *Ovation; Fender Stratocaster.*

A singer / songwriter of some distinction, Armatrading's subtle acoustic guitar work marked a resurgence of interest in folk-based music in the 1970s. Her first successful album *Joan Armatrading* appeared in 1976 with Glyn Johns producing, and the sparse arrangements complemented her reflective lyrics that dwelt on social issues and affairs of the heart. More significantly, her guitar work suggested a warm intimacy that belied the occasional poignancy of the lyrics. While later albums tended to be more elaborately arranged and Joan has flirted with electric guitars, the acoustic bias remained, and songs like 'All The Way From America', 'Me Myself I' and 'Drop The Pilot' retained much of the atmosphere of the earlier albums. Such is her success that a whole new generation of female singers emerged in the late-1980s, such as Tanita Tikaram and Tracy Chapman, who cite Armatrading as a crucial inspiration.

KOKOMO ARNOLD

Born: James Arnold, February 15th 1901, Lovejoy, Texas, US. Died: November 8th 1968, Chicago, Illinois, US.

An underrated blues singer and bottleneck guitarist who recorded during the 1930s and reserved his most impressive performances for duets with pianist Peetie Wheatstraw. After Wheatstraw's death in 1941, Arnold disappeared into obscurity until Elvis Presley covered his song 'Milkcow Blues Boogie'. Although Arnold didn't really earn any cash out of this, it prompted enthusiasts to seek him out and encourage him to make a comeback. This he duly did in the early-1960s, when he gigged at Chicago's Gate of Horn club, before hitting the festival circuit. Despite the rarity of recorded material, Arnold's slide guitar work was an inspiration for **Elmore James**, among others.

ALICE ARTZT

Born: March 16th 1943, New York, New York, US.

■ *Sergio Abreu; Rubio.*

Having studied in Europe with **Ida Presti**, **Alexandre Lagoya** and **Julian Bream**, Artzt has toured relatively widely on the international recital circuit, and recently she has begun to play in guitar ensembles. Her recorded output occasionally wanders from the beaten Spanish track on records such as *Bach & His Friends* and *English Guitar Music*, and Artzt's book *The Art Of Practising* can be recommended for its good advice to players from any sphere of music.

DANIEL ASH

Born: England

■ *Fender Telecaster; Washburn electro-acoustic.*

During his tenure with Bauhaus, Ash was often overshadowed by their opaquely photogenic singer Peter Murphy. After the group's demise in 1983 Ash went on to assemble Tones On Tail, who cut the atmospheric *Night Music* (1987) over a period of three years.

IRVING ASHBY

Born: December 29th 1920, Somerville, Massachusetts, US. Died: April 22nd 1987, Perris, California, US.

■ *Stromberg; Gibson Super 400; D'Angelico.*

In 1951 pianist Oscar Peterson, in association with Norman Granz's Jazz At The Philharmonic, formed a trio that was loosely based on the Nat King Cole Trio. Unlike Cole, Peterson was no songster – but he certainly knew how to pick sidemen. The first trio comprised bassist Ray Brown and guitarist Ashby, who had replaced **Oscar Moore** in Cole's trio. While Ashby remained with the Peterson trio for only a couple of years, his interplay with the pianist established a role model that later trio members

Barney Kessel and **Herb Ellis** would emulate, and Ashby's delicate **Charlie Christian**-influenced phrasing on standards like 'Autumn Leaves' and 'The Shadow Of Your Smile' provided an ideal counterpoint to Peterson's flamboyance. After leaving the trio, Ashby worked sessions for film companies such as MGM and Paramount.

JOHN ASHTON

Born: November 30th 1957, London, England.

Despite their brief flirtation with celebrity in the mid-1980s, John Ashton and The Psychedelic Furs were seldom able to replicate their sound beyond the studio, where they were helped by such skilled producers as Steve Lillywhite and Todd Rundgren. Throughout their career the Furs managed to capitalize on a number of pleasant enough singles – 'Pretty In Pink', 'Love My Way', 'Heaven' and 'Ghost In You' – but any enthusiasm they might have had seems to have been waylaid on the way to the bank.

CHET ATKINS

Born: Chester Burton Atkins, June 20th 1924, Luttrell, Tennessee, US.

■ *Gretsch (various); Gretsch 'signature' series; Gibson 'signature' electric-classical; Gibson 'signature' (various); Gibson Country Western.*

If there is any one particular individual responsible for the Nashville Sound today, it is Chet Atkins. His finger-picking style, influenced in part by that of **Merle Travis**, has become a benchmark since the late-1950s.

Atkins' guitar work on solo instrumentals like 'Chinatown, My Chinatown', 'Country Gentleman' and 'Downhill Drag' illustrated the diversity of his technical expertise: on 'Country Gentleman' the sound is more reminiscent of a steel guitar. His striking use of muted, syncopated bass parts, dazzling deployment of the guitar's natural dynamics and an open willingness to experiment with new sounds and effects have combined in a style that has been supremely influential, not only among country players but with guitarists from all musical areas.

Over the years, Atkins also produced or supervised recordings by a host of artists, from the Everly Brothers to Elvis Presley. Among his own hits were 'Poor People In Paris', 'Boo Boo Stick Beat', 'One Mint Julep' and 'Yakety Axe', available on a number of compilations. He has teamed up with **Merle Travis**, **Jerry Reed**, **Mark Knopfler**, **Les Paul** and **Doc Watson** for respective albums of duets, with the album *Me And Jerry* being a particularly impressive offering, and he has helped to design guitars for the Gretsch and Gibson companies.

MIKE AULDRIDGE

Born: US.

■ *Dobro resonator.*

Mike Auldridge, briefly a member of New Shades Of Grass, has become one of a small handful of tasteful, refined session players who, when unleashed in the

studio by himself, turns out some extraordinarily fine records. Primarily a bluegrass style dobro player, Auldridge's understated and melodiously rolling syncopations on albums such as *Eight String Swing* (1988) are as smooth as a satin jockstrap.

RANDY BACHMAN

Born: September 27th 1943, Winnipeg, Manitoba, Canada.

■ *Fender Stratocaster.*

Bachman's enduring contribution to the guitarist's pantheon was a neat fuzz guitar effect on Guess Who's 'American Woman' in 1970. That it was Guess Who's finest hour in commercial terms should not detract from the fact that over 20 years later it still bears positive comparison with much of the post-psychedelic nonsense still being served up.

Guess Who first made their mark in 1965 with a magnificently crude version of Johnny Kidd & The Pirates' 'Shakin All Over' which in contemporary terms could best be described as falling somewhere between garage and thrash. After leaving Guess Who in 1970 Bachman, by now a Mormon, resurfaced with the Bachman-Turner Overdrive in 1973, scoring a hit with 'You Ain't Seen Nothing Yet' to which he added his clear, straightforwardly melodic guitar lines.

On 'Nothing' Bachman pulled up well short of plagiarizing his heroes The Who. Instead of copying 'Won't Get Fooled Again' he skilfully aped its production values: blending acoustic and electric guitars, slinging in the odd cowbell, and rounding the whole thing off with the trademark stutter. Formidably successful everywhere, it provided advertising agencies with an apparently perfect soundtrack to dozens of commercials. All in all, while Bachman may not have been the most original guitarist of all time, what he lacked in finesse he compensated for with initiative. He also has an enviable guitar collection, especially strong in Gretsch models.

JOAN BAEZ

Born: January 9th 1941, Staten Island, New York, US.

■ *Martin.*

Ever since Baez made her first public appearance at the Newport Folk Festival in 1959 she has spawned imitators. Galvanized by the iniquitious inequalities endemic in contemporary America, she became the first and most vocal of all the protest singers of the early-1960s. The folk club circuit was the perfect place for her to air these views and the material, drawn from the repertoires of Pete Seeger, **Woody Guthrie**, Cisco Houston, **Leadbelly** and The Carter Family, was ideally suited to her own acoustic guitar accompaniment.

While her guitar playing range was limited, the chops she had she manipulated with precision, always in support of the song. Baez's association with Bob Dylan culminated with her recording a selection of his songs on the album *Any Day Now* (1968), but as the 1960s moved to a close her attempts to be commercial were artistic tragedies, such as the commercially successful but anodyne version of

Robbie Robertson's 'The Night They Drove Old Dixie Down' (1971).

In 1976 she recorded the live *From Every Stage* which showed that she hadn't lost the gift for fine concert performances, and displayed a repertoire that had become even more eclectic and guitar playing that was atmospherically effective rather than accomplished.

Her influence has been formidable. The number of teenagers who have taught themselves a few chords on an acoustic guitar through hearing her records must run into millions. And some of them, like **Joan Armatrading**, have even made a career out of it.

DEREK BAILEY

Born: January 29th 1930, Sheffield, Yorkshire, England.

■ *Gibson ES175; Epiphone.*

A tough earful for the listener used to conventional harmony and shape, Bailey's uncompromising guitar playing has made an influential sound in the avant-garde jazz scene for over 25 years. His academic approach has been partly responsible for British jazz no longer being seen necessarily as the poor relation of its American or European counterparts. Bailey's refusal to be hidebound by the conventions of form and structure have made him as innovative as reedman Ornette Coleman and pianist Cecil Taylor, both staunch practitioners of the harmolodic theory – or, as one wit was moved to observe, the 'play what you like, when you like' approach.

In 1971 Bailey cut *Improvisations For Guitar and Cello* with Dave Holland (better known as a bassist) which illustrates the redundancy of musical classification. In 1982, he gained some sort of formal recognition for his achievements as the solo *View From Six Windows* was nominated for a Grammy. Boldly impressionistic, it represented a tentative flirtation with less abstruse forms. While notions such as accessibility are misleading, his contributions to the guitar will be given greater weight with the passage of time.

GUY BAILEY

Born: London, England.

A good-time booze'n'boogie band, The Quireboys' riotous bonhomie is best captured in concert (*Live Around The World* 1990) where Bailey's powerhouse riffing, echoing that of Keith Richards and Ron Wood, plus Spike's throaty vocals, suggest a debt of allegiance to The Faces and Dr Feelgood. But unlike The Faces' early albums, the **Jim Cregan**-produced *A Bit Of What You Fancy* (1990) lacked an enduring body of material.

MICKEY BAKER

Born: McHouston Baker, October 15th 1925, Louisville, Kentucky, US.

■ *Gibson Les Paul.*

Baker settled in New York in the early-1940s and began playing blues and jazz guitar. By 1953 he had become a member of the Atlantic Records house band, where he contributed crisp punctuation to a spate of hits by R&B artists such as The Coasters, Ruth Brown and Ray Charles. He worked more sessions with other R&B artists such as Little Willie John, Screamin' Jay Hawkins, Earl Bostic and Little Esther Phillips, and started to teach guitar. One of his pupils was Sylvia Vanderpool, whom he later married, and they formed the duo Mickey & Sylvia, scoring a monster hit in 1957 with 'Love is Strange', into which Baker inserted some effective blues licks. At this time Baker also published guitar instructional books, including his popular *Jazz Book*.

After splitting up with Vanderpool in 1961 Baker moved to Paris where he worked with Memphis Slim and Champion Jack Dupree. In more recent years his fascination with different guitar styles has impeded his artistic judgement with the result that albums like *Jazz-Rock Guitar* (1978) are uninspiringly bland.

RUSS BALLARD

Born: October 31st 1945, Waltham Cross, Hertfordshire, England.

■ *Fender Stratocaster.*

Formerly a member of Adam Faith's band The Roulettes, Ballard's songwriting abilities and incisive guitar work enabled the group to have a life of its own – albeit briefly – after Adam Faith had moved on. An even briefer spell with Unit 4+2 followed, before Ballard joined Argent (with keyboardist Rod Argent, drummer Bob Henrit and bassist Jim Rodford).

Argent had a series of strong singles, including such anthemic ditties as 'God Gave Rock'n'Roll To You' and 'Hold Your Head Up' penned by Ballard, but their albums were less consistent. Ballard's subsequent solo career has been sporadic – *Russ Ballard* (1975), *At The Third Stroke* (1979), *Into The Fire* (1981) and *Fire Still Burns* (1986) among others – but the collected works presented on his albums have proved to be a useful portfolio for the songwriter in Ballard: Hot Chocolate, Rainbow, Three Dog Night, Magnum, Little Angels, Kiss and Ringo Starr have all covered his material, often to greater effect than the original versions. As a session guitarist Ballard has worked with artists such as Graham Bonnet, Adam Faith and Leo Sayer.

PETER BANKS

Born: July 7th 1947, Barnet, Hertfordshire, England.

■ *Gibson ES335.*

Banks had left Yes before the band became the quintessential progressive rock band. Prior to forming Yes, Banks and bassist Chris Squire were members of Syn, soon joining Mabel Greer's Toyshop where they met vocalist Jon Anderson. In 1968, with the addition of drummer Bill Bruford and keyboards player Tony Kaye, they became Yes. On the debut album *Yes* (1969) Banks showed a masterful gift for understatement on covers of Lennon & McCartney's 'Every Little Thing' and The Byrds' 'I See You', reinforced by his evocative guitar work on **Stephen Stills**' 'Everydays' on the sequel *Time And A Word* (1970). However, the rest of the band seemed more intent on adopting classical and jazz motifs, and Banks left the group to form Flash and then After The Fire. Banks was replaced in Yes by **Steve Howe**.

DAVE BARBOUR

Born: May 28th 1912, New York, New York, US. Died: December 11th 1965, Malibu, California, US.

■ *Gibson ES5; Gibson ES150.*

Barbour was a fine guitarist of the swing era who, after recording and performing with Red Norvo and Benny Goodman, hit his creative peak in conjunction with his wife Peggy Lee (they married in 1943). Although his contributions to Goodman hits like 'Jersey Bounce' and 'Why Don't You Do Right' (1942) were valuable, his skill as arranger and bandleader for Lee on hits like 'Waitin' For The Train To Come In' (1945), 'I Don't Know Enough About You' (1946) and 'Manana' (1948) showed that he was a natural, tasteful accompanist – yet he lacked the necessary self-promotional zeal to become a first-rate soloist. Some of his best work with Lee is admirably compiled on her Capitol Collector's Series *Volume 1: The Early Years* (1990) that covers the 1945-1950 period. After Barbour's divorce from Lee in 1952 he retired, reemerging briefly in 1962 to cut *BBB & Co* with saxophonist Benny Carter.

DANNY BARKER

Born: January 13th 1909, New Orleans, Louisiana, US.

■ *Epiphone Emperor.*

One of the survivors of jazz's golden age, Barker accompanied such luminaries as pianist Jelly Roll Morton, trumpeter Red Allen, bandleader Lucky Millinder, saxophonist Sidney Bechet, pianist/arranger James P Johnson, vocalist/bandleader Cab Calloway and saxman/trumpeter Benny Carter. Barker has remained rooted in the traditions of New Orleans jazz, his articulate playing style a rare survivor from a bygone era. He now lectures, and published his autobiography *A Life In Jazz* in 1986.

EVERETT BARKSDALE

Born: April 28th 1910, Detroit, Michigan, US.

■ *Epiphone.*

Jazz musician Barksdale started his career playing alto sax and then bass, eventually taking up the guitar. During the 1920s he played with big-band leader Erskine Tate and then spent ten years with violinist Eddie South before working with saxman/trumpeter Benny Carter, pianist Herman Chittison and bandleader Leon Abbey. From 1942 Barksdale worked at CBS TV, performing on *The Arthur Godfrey Talent Show*, but his finest work occurred during his tenure with pianist Art Tatum, whom he remained with until 1956. Tatum's depth of feeling and innate swing found a perfect partner in Barksdale, who proved to be a more than suitable replacement for **Tiny Grimes**. When Tatum died, Barksdale returned to a lucrative career on the session circuit. Much of the Tatum material has been repackaged, with *The Complete Capitol Recordings* showing a fine trio on top-notch form.

James Burton

If it is possible for a session guitarist to become a household name, James Burton is a contender. His past employers, many of whom owe at least part of their success to his distinctive style, include some of country music's most celebrated artists. He has also been a significant influence on such players as John Fogerty of Creedence Clearwater Revival and Robbie Robertson of The Band. Burton first made his mark in 1957, playing sessions with Dale Hawkins: in particular, he contributed a solo in a staccato blues style to 'Suzie Q'. This was followed by a stint with rock 'n' roller Bob Luman and bassist James Kirkland. The following year saw him joining Shindig, the television pop show, as a member of the studio band with Leon Russell and Delaney Bramlett. He also played a crucial part in Ricky Nelson's band; it was on records like 'Hello Mary Lou' that Burton developed his highly individual style of finger picking,

using a normal flat pick, or plectrum, and a single finger pick. In 1964 he left Nelson and started to work with Buck Owens and Merle Haggard, creating the "Bakersfield" sound, which owed as much to rockabilly as to Nashville traditionalism. In 1969 he formed an alliance with pianist Glen D. Hardin, and they were both recruited by Elvis Presley, forming the mainstay of his touring band over the next eight years. In 1972 both started to record with Gram Parsons, appearing on the albums G.P. and Grievous Angel. When Parsons died in 1973, they were enlisted by Emmylou Harris to form The Hot Band. In the early 1980s both returned to session work. Burton has cut two solo albums, Corn Pickin' And Slick Slidin' with Ralph Mooney, and the dire Guitar Sounds Of James Burton, the latter proving that a good session player is not necessarily a good front man.

JAMES BURTON AND RALPH MOONEY: CORN PICKIN' AND SLICK SLIDIN' (Released 1969)

This album, with pedal steel player Mooney, sums up the finger-picking style that was central to Burton's "Bakersfield" period. Guitarists Joe Maphis and Buck Owens had invented the style by cranking up the volume on their Fender Telecasters in the early 1950s, but Burton made it popular. The album was recorded in nine hours.

THE GUITAR SOUNDS OF JAMES BURTON (Released 1971).

Unfortunately, no matter how good a guitarist may be technically, his material has to be up to scratch. This album came about when Elvis cancelled a week's sessions with Burton because he was ill. Elvis's producer Fenton Jarvis suggested Burton use the time. The resulting solo album was rushed and suffers from poor songs, some of them Burton's own. A missed opportunity.

| 1957 | 1958 | 1959 | 1960 | 1961 | 1962 | 1963 | 1964 | 1965 | 1966 | 1967 | 1968 | 1969 | 1970 | 1971 | 1972 | 1973 | 1974 | 19 |

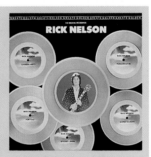

WITH RICK NELSON

In 1958, Rick Nelson formed a band from the nucleus of session men he had used on his album *Ricky*. It included James Burton (guitar), James Kirkland (bass), later replaced by Joe Osborn, Gene Garf (piano) and Richie Frost (drums). Nelson was then a star second only to Elvis Presley. His band provided a musical backing infinitely more sophisticated than the usual teenage material: the singing and the lyrics, however, remained firmly anchored in pop. With Burton's cogent, incisive guitar work heavily featured, the band was an adaptable outfit made up of players accustomed to working on sessions. They were able to work at

speed without written arrangements, which made them stand apart from most session bands of the day. When Ricky's years as a teen idol were over, he had a band that was musically capable of following any direction he chose. That he turned to country music was, perhaps, due to Burton's influence as much as anyone else's, but it also confirmed the link between rock 'n' roll and country. In 1969, Nelson put together his first "grown-up" group, The Stone Canyon Band, featuring steel guitarist Tom Brumley, while Burton joined Elvis Presley's band.

● 1957 Ricky
● 1958 Ricky Nelson

● 1959 Ricky Sings Again Songs By Ricky
● 1960 More Songs By Ricky
● 1961 Rick Is 21
● 1962 Album Seven By Rick
● 1963 A Long Vacation For Your Sweet Love
● 1964 Ricky Sings For You The Very Thought Of You
● 1965 Spotlight On Rick Best Always
● 1966 Love And Kisses Bright Lights And Country Music
● 1967 Country Fever
● 1969 Another Side Of Rick
● 1972 Legendary Masters

WITH GRAM PARSONS

● 1972 G.P.
● 1973 Grievous Angel

After Gram Parsons left the Flying Burrito Brothers, he embarked on a solo career. Among the sidemen for his debut *G.P.* were James Burton, Glen D. Hardin and bassist Rich Grech, formerly of Family and Blind Faith. This was followed by *Grievous Angel*, which featured Emmylou Harris, but Parsons died before its completion and Harris was left to finish it off. Both *GP* and *Grievous Angel* are five-star country classics and they established Burton as the country-rock guitarist.

Jeff Beck Group From the moment of its inception, Jeff Beck had trouble settling on a regular line-up. Initially it included bassist Jet Harris, formerly of The Shadows, and drummers Viv Prince from The Pretty Things and Aynsley Dunbar from John Mayall. By the time the group's debut album *Truth* emerged, the line-up had stabilised, with Rod Stewart (vocals), Ron Wood (bass) and Mickey Waller (drums). Over the next five years, the line-up for each album would differ from that of its predecessor, with Beck often the common denominator. These shifting combinations inevitably weakened the public's perception of the group, and Beck linked up with Tim Bogert and Carmine Appice.

JEFF BECK GROUP (Released May 1972) *Line-up:* See *Rough And Ready*. *Tracks:* Ice Cream Cake/ Glad All Over/ I'll Be Staying Here With You/ Sugar Cane/ I Can't Give Back The Love/ Going Down/ I Gotta Have A Song/ Highways/ Definitely Maybe. *Producer:* Steve Cropper.

WIRED (Released August 1976) *Line-up:* Jeff Beck (guitar), Wilbur Bascomb (bass), Max Middleton (keyboards), Richard Bailey (drums), Jan Hammer (synthesizer), Narada Michael Walden (keyboards). *Tracks:* Led Roofs/ Come Dancing/ Goodbye Porkpie Hat/ Head For Backstage Pass/ Blue Wind/ Sophie/ Play With Me/ Love Is Green.

The Late 1960s After leaving The Yardbirds in October 1966 to form his own band with vocalist Rod Stewart and Ronnie Wood, Jeff Beck was taken under the wing of producer Mickie Most. His first three singles, 'Hi Ho Silver Lining' (March 1967), 'Tallyman' (August 1967) and 'Love Is Blue' (February 1968) were at odds with his live work. In June 1968 the Jeff Beck Group made their debut at New York's Fillmore East Auditorium. The following month Beck started to discuss plans for a group with Rod Stewart and the rhythm section of Vanilla Fudge, bassist Tim Bogert and drummer Carmine Appice. The plans were shelved when Beck was injured in a road accident. In August 1968 *Truth* was issued. This was a significant departure from the rampant commercialism of the Most-produced singles and the ill-judged Donovan collaboration, showing his power and inventiveness as a guitarist. Indeed, many of the Jeff Beck Group albums had this feature: material or production was often uneven, but the quality of his playing was always interesting. In 1973 Beck formed a power trio to end all power trios with bassist Tim Bogert and drummer Carmine Appice.

THERE AND BACK Released July 1980) *Line-up:* Jeff Beck (guitar), Mo Foster (bass), Simon Phillips (drums), Jan Hammer (synthesizer/drums), Tony Hymas (keyboards). *Tracks:* Star Cycle/ Too Much To Lose/ You Never Knew/ The Pump/ El Becko/ The Golden Road/ Space Boogie/ The Final Peace. *Producer:* Jeff Beck & Jan Hammer.

| 1973 | 1974 | 1975 | 1976 | 1977 | 1978 | 1979 | 1980 | 1981 | 1982 |

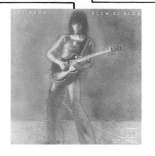

● Gretsch Duo-Jet

BECK BOGERT AND APPICE (Released March 1973) *Line-up:* Jeff Beck (guitar), Tim Bogert (bass), Carmine Appice (drums). *Tracks:* Black Cat Moan/ Lady/ Oh To Love You/ Superstition/ Sweet Sweet Surrender/ Why Should I Care About You/ Lose Myself With Love/ Livin' Alone/ I'm So Proud. *Producer:* Don Nix.

BLOW BY BLOW (Released April 1975) *Line-up:* Jeff Beck (guitar), Philip Chen (bass), Max Middleton (keyboards), Richard Bailey (drums). *Tracks:* It Doesn't Really Matter/ She's A Woman/ Constipated Duck/ Air Blower/ Scatterbrain/ Cos We've Ended As Lovers/ Thelonius/ Freeway Jam/ Diamond Dust. *Producer:* George Martin.

LIVE WITH JAN HAMMER (Released May 1977) *Line-up:* Jeff Beck (guitar), Wilbur Bascomb (bass), Richard Bailey (drums), Jan Hammer (synthesizer), Narada Michael Walden (keyboards/synthesizer). *Tracks:* Freeway Jam/ Earth/ She's A Woman/ Full Moon Boogie/ Darkness/ Earth In Search Of A Sun/ Scatterbrain/ Blue Wind.

BECK'S GUITARS Jeff is best known today for his work using Fender Stratocasters, and in 1991 he was one of a select handful of players to be distinguished by a Signature Edition. A special Custom version made by

● 1976 STANLEY CLARKE *School Days*
BILLY PRESTON *Billy Preston*
UPP *This Way Upp*

● 1977 NARADA MICHAEL WALDEN *Garden Of Love Light*

● 1978 STANLEY CLARKE *Modern Man*

● 1979 STANLEY CLARKE *I Wanna Play For You*

● 1980 MURRAY HEAD *Jokes & Voices*

● 1981 COZY POWELL *Tilt*
AMNESTY INTERNATIONAL *The Secret Policeman's Other Ball*

● 1984 THE HONEYDRIPPERS *Volume 1*
ROD STEWART *Camouflage*
STANLEY CLARKE *Time Exposure*

BOX OF FROGS *Box of Frogs*
PHILIP BAILEY *Inside Out*
TINA TURNER *Private Dancer*
DIANA ROSS *Swept Away*

● 1985 MICK JAGGER *She's The Boss*

The career of Jeff Beck is, arguably, one of the most inconsistent in the history of rock music. Despite the apparent ups and downs, there is at the heart of his work a reluctant compulsion to record and to play the guitar. Often he gives the impression that he'd rather be doing anything other than playing, but the slight, nervy Beck will gradually be drawn back into the studio. What happens then is an extraordinary metamorphosis and the guitar playing takes over. For Beck, more than any other contemporary 'guitar legend', is governed by gut and instinct, with technical prowess not figuring as a consideration. Nonetheless, his playing skills are considerable. It is for this reason that some of his best efforts have been under the watchful eye of seasoned producers like Steve Cropper (Jeff Beck Group) or George Martin (Blow By Blow), both of whom have managed to refine and polish the resulting

sessions, while retaining Beck's innate flair. This reliance on the judgement of others has been responsible for the lack of consistency in his recording career: just after Beck signed to Mickie Most's production company in 1967, Most insisted that Beck should record an instrumental version of Paul Mauriat's 'Love Is Blue'. Hardly an inspired piece of repertoire, and Most was adding insult to injury as he had stopped Beck from singing the vocals to the second single, 'Tallyman'. Beck appears not to mind what anyone thinks about the quality of his work and he doesn't concern himself with tedious details, like whether something is commercial or not. Crazy Legs, his tribute to Cliff Gallup, the guitarist from Gene Vincent's band The Blue Caps, was greeted by critics with comments such as, 'Why did he bother?' The simple answer to that is because he wanted to. Jeff Beck is his own man. Long may he run.

YARDBIRDS (Released July 1966) Line-up: Keith Relf (vocals and harmonica), Jeff Beck (guitar), Chris Dreja (guitar), Paul Samwell-Smith (bass), Jim McCarty (drums). Tracks: Lost Women/ Over, Under, Sideways, Down/ The Nazz Are Blue/ I Can't Make Your Way/ Rack My Mind/ Farewell/ Hot House Of Omagarashid/ Jeff's Boogie/ He's Always There/ Turn Into Earth/ What Do You Want/ Ever Since The World Began.

TRUTH (Released August 1968) Line-up: Jeff Beck (guitar), Rod Stewart (vocals), Ronnie Wood (bass), Mickey Waller (drums). Tracks: Shapes Of Things/ Let Me Love You/ Morning Dew/ You Shook Me/ Ol' Man River/ Greensleeves/ Rock My Plimsoll/ Beck's Bolero/ Blues De Luxe/ I Ain't Superstitious. Producer: Mickie Most.

1963	1964	1965	1966	1967	1968	1969	1970	1971	1972

EARLY YEARS Beck had always wanted to play the guitar, giving up piano lessons and constructing his first guitar out of bits of cigar box and piano-wire. By the time he was 11 he was a more than competent guitarist. After leaving Art School he joined a local band, The Tridents, who began to attract a strong local following. The Tridents drew their repertoire from Chicago bluesmen like Muddy Waters and rock 'n'rollers such as Bo Diddley and Chuck Berry. While the group were by no means exceptional, they started to draw attention beyond the immediate environs. On March 26th 1965 Beck was recruited to fill the shoes of another local Surrey hero, Eric Clapton, in The Yardbirds.

The Yardbirds When Eric Clapton left The Yardbirds in the spring of 1965, Jeff Beck filled the vacant slot in what was fast becoming one of the most talked about bands on the circuit. Managed by Giorgio Gomelsky, the group's R&B roots were gradually being eroded by a series of pop songs like 'Heart Full Of Soul' (June 1965), 'Evil Hearted You'/'Still I'm Sad' (October 1965) and 'Shapes Of Things' (March 1966). Performances at the Richmond Jazz & Blues Festival on August 6th 1965 gave Beck the chance to show his mettle. In April 1966 Simon Napier-Bell took over from Gomelsky as manager and in June bassist Paul Samwell-Smith left to become a producer. His replacement was Jimmy Page. Chris Dreja then took over as bassist, enabling Page to partner Beck on lead guitar. Perhaps the only way to comprehend the impact is to see them playing in Antonioni's film Blow Up. It gave a worm's eye view of how Beck was altering the face of rock. It was apparent that he would not be able to stick endless tours.

BECK OLA (Released September 1969). Line-up: Jeff Beck (guitar), Rod Stewart (vocals), Ronnie Wood (bass), Nicky Hopkins (keyboards), Tony Newman (drums). Tracks: All Shook Up/ Spanish Boots/ Girl From Mill Valley/ Jailhouse Rock/ Plinth (Water Down The Drain)/ Hangman's Knee/ Rice Pudding. Producer: Mickie Most.

ROUGH AND READY (Released October 1971) Line-up: Jeff Beck (guitar), Bobby Tench (vocals), Clive Chaman (bass), Max Middleton (keyboards), Cozy Powell (drums). Tracks: Got The Feeling/ Situation/ Short Business/ Max's Tune/ I've Been Used/ New Ways/ Train, Train/ Jody. Producer: Jeff Beck.

SESSIONS with other artists

- 1968 DONOVAN 'Goo Goo Barabajagal'
- 1969 GTO Permanent Damage
- 1970 SCREAMIN' LORD SUTCH Lord Sutch & Heavy Friends
- 1972 STEVIE WONDER Talking Book EDDIE HARRIS Eddie Harris In The UK
- 1974 BADGER White Lady
- 1975 STANLEY CLARKE Journey To Love UPP Upp

WITH ELVIS PRESLEY When James Burton joined Elvis Presley's band, it was as a member of the touring unit put together in 1969 to revive a career that had dwindled during the years he spent making terrible films. In the week before Elvis opened in Las Vegas, Burton called in Charles Hodge and John Wilkinson (guitars), Larry Muhoberac (keyboards) later replaced by Glen D. Hardin, formerly of the Crickets, Jerry Scheff (bass), Ronnie Tutt (drums), the Sweet Inspirations and the Imperials (backing vocals). Although by now Elvis was emphatically past his best, with a band of this calibre he could still cut it when he climbed on stage. Despite the visual evidence of physical decline, Elvis showed that he was more than capable of meeting the demanding standards established by his band on material dating back to the 1950s, as well as on more contemporary numbers such as 'Suspicious Minds'. James Burton continued working with Elvis until 1977 when Elvis died; between Presley tours he worked on sessions with Gram Parsons, Emmylou Harris and others.

- 1970 On Stage
- 1972 Elvis As Recorded At Madison Square Garden
  Elvis Now
- 1972 Aloha From Hawaii Via Satellite
- 1974 Elvis Recorded Live On Stage In Memphis.

EMMYLOU HARRIS
- 1975 Pieces Of The Sky
- 1976 Elite Hotel
- 1977 Luxury Liner
- 1978. Quarter Moon In A Ten Cent Town
- 1981 Evangaline (guest)

After Gram Parsons' death, Emmylou Harris was encouraged to retain James Burton and Glen D. Hardin and cut her own album. What emerged was *Pieces Of The Sky*, with a bunch of session men who became known as the Hot Band; the line-up included Burton and Hardin, with Byrone Berline, formerly of Country Gazette, (fiddle), Hank DeVito (steel guitar), Rodney Crowell (guitar), Emory Gordy Jr (bass) and John Ware, formerly of Michael Nesmith's First National Band, (drums). This line-up produced a series of albums that reflected interest in a more traditional form of country than that which had been made commonplace by country-rock outfits such as the Eagles and Poco. Harris's tremulous vocals were complemented by Burton's hard-edged finger-picking licks on a wide range of material, including covers of songs by the Louvins, Gram Parsons and Felice & Boudleaux Bryant, as well as new material by new writers such as Rodney Crowell. The Hot Band also backed a variety of other country artists, including Crowell and Jesse Winchester. By 1978, both Burton and Hardin had left the Hot Band (Burton's replacement was Albert Lee, a long time admirer) and returned to session work.

JOHN DENVER
- 1977 I Want To Live
- 1978 J.D.
- 1979 A Christmas Together With The Muppets
- 1980 Autograph

When James Burton finished working with Emmylou Harris's Hot Band and Elvis Presley, he quit touring for the comparative ease of session work. One of his first regular employers was John Denver. Although Denver had passed his peak in terms of the global popularity he had enjoyed at the beginning of the 1970s, he had moved towards the mainstream as an entertainer and celebrity, commanding substantial fees in Las Vegas or on television spectaculars. In order to fulfil these various commitments he needed a strong band and Burton was the ideal man to front the studio sessions. The association started in 1977, when Burton did a TV show with Denver. It must be said that these four albums are unlikely to take pride of place in Burton's musical memoirs as the most satisfying ventures of his career: but they did provide another opportunity to work with some of the most professional players in the business, and no doubt the financial arrangements were entirely advantageous. Since 1980, Burton has continued to play sessions, as well as touring with the Everly Brothers and Jerry Lee Lewis.

BURTON'S GUITARS Most associated with the Fender Telecaster, Burton originally played a 1953 model.

He acquired his famous Paisley Red Telecaster in 1969, when Fender embraced psychedelia by sticking patterned wallpaper to some guitars – a shortlived idea. A new 'signature' James Burton Telecaster model appeared in 1990, with a modern interpretation of the paisley pattern.

SESSIONS (selected)
- 1957 Dale Hawkins – 'Suzie Q'
- 1958 Bob Luman's Band (tours)
- 1964-66 Merle Haggard (sessions)
- 1966 Johnny Rivers (sessions)
- 1968 Lee Hazelwood – Love And Other Crimes
- 1968 Steve Young– Rock Salt And Nails
- 1969 Phil Ochs – Phil Ochs

HIS GREATEST MOMENTS
- 1973-77 Hoyt Axton – Less Than The Song, Life Machine, Southbound, Fearless and Road Songs.

- 1978 Rodney Crowell – Ain't Living Long Like This
- 1982-84 Everly Brothers (tours)
- 1984 Chris Hillman – Desert Rose
- 1986 Elvis Costello – King Of America
- 1987-93 Jerry Lee Lewis (tours)

1976 1977 1978 1979 1980 1981 1982 1983 1984 1985 1986 1987 1988 1989 1990 1991 1992 1993

who had been filling in time since the original plans foundered in Cactus.

Trios And Legs Beck, Bogert & Appice were short-lived. Just the one eponymous album emerged, featuring 'Superstition', the Stevie Wonder composition (Beck guested on Wonder's own *Talking Book* album). After constant touring, Beck, Bogert & Appice split up. Beck's next move was a series of jazz-rock instrumental albums. The success of *Blow By Blow* and *Wired* was irrefutable evidence that Beck was a master axeman who didn't need a

vocalist. In 1981 Beck's performance with Eric Clapton at the Amnesty International Benefit Concert confirmed his position as one of the world's respected stylists. In 1985 Beck released *Flash*, which included Curtis Mayfield's 'People Get Ready' with Rod Stewart handling the vocals, and the Grammy-winning 'Escape'. Later, *Jeff Beck's Guitar Shop With Terry Bozzio and Tony Hymas* also won a Grammy. In 1992 the compilation *Beckology* was released, followed in 1993 by *Crazy Legs*, a tribute to Cliff Gallup, and *Frankie's House*, the BAFTA award-winning music for a TV mini-series.

BECKOLOGY (Released August 1992) A four-CD compilation chronicling Jeff Beck's entire career; it includes material that was previously issued on the *Anthology Of British Blues* (Immediate, 1968), as well as previously unavailable alternate studio takes from the *Beck Bogert & Appice* sessions.

JEFF BECK'S GUITAR SHOP WITH TERRY BOZZIO AND TONY HYMAS (Released October 1989) *Line-up:* Jeff Beck (guitar), Terry Bozzio (drums), Tony Hymas (keyboards). *Tracks:* Guitar Shop/ Savoy/ Behind The Veil/ Big Block/ Where Were You?/ Stand On It/ A Day In The House/ Two Rivers/ Sling Shot. *Producers:* Jeff Beck, Terry Bozzio, Tony Hymas & Leif Mases.

FLASH (Released July 1985) *Line-up:* Jeff Beck (guitar), Rod Stewart (vocals), Jimmy Hall (vocals), Mo Foster (bass), Carmine Appice (drums), Simon Phillips (drums), Tony Hymas (keyboards), Jan Hammer (synthesizer/keyboards). *Tracks:* Ambitious/ Gets Us All In The End/ Escape/ People Get Ready/ Stop, Look And Listen/ Get Workin'/ Ecstasy/ Night After Night/ You Know, We Know. *Producers:* Nile Rodgers & Arthur Baker.

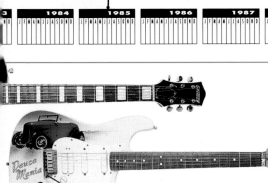

| 3 | 1984 | 1985 | 1986 | 1987 | 1988 | 1989 | 1990 | 1991 | 1992 | 1993 | |

• Fender Jeff Beck Stratocaster Custom

CRAZY LEGS: Jeff Beck & The Big Town Playboys (Released February 1993) *Line-up:* Jeff Beck (guitar), Mike Sanchez (piano & vocals), Adrian Utley (rhythm guitar), Ian Jennings (bass), Clive Deamer (drums), Leo Green (tenor sax), Nick Lunt (baritone sax). *Tracks:* Race With The Devil/ Cruisin'/ Crazy Legs/ Double Talkin' Baby/ Woman Love/ Lotta Lovin'/ Catman/ Pink Thunderbird/ Baby Blue/ You Better Believe/ Who Slapped John?/ Say Mama/ Red, Blue Jeans And A Ponitail/ Five Feet Of Lovin'/ E-I-Bicky-Bi-Bo-Bo-Go/ Blues Stay Away From Me/ Pretty, Pretty Baby/ Hold Me, Hug Me, Rock Me. *Producer:* Stuart Colman.

...der for Jeff with an airbrushed hot-...is shown above. Up to his mid/late...'0s solo albums Beck had been a Les...I man, although his earliest...dbirds playing was on a Fender...uire. Recently, after recording *Crazy*

Legs, Jeff acquired this 1956 Gretsch Duo-Jet (top), very similar to one used by his hero, Gene Vincent's guitarist Cliff Gallup.

• 1987 MICK JAGGER *Primitive Cool*

• 1991 BUDDY GUY *Damn Right I Got The Blues*

• 1993 KATE BUSH *The Red Shoes*
ROGER WATERS *Amazed To Death*
BEVERLEY CRAVEN *Love Scenes*
STONE FREE: A Tribute to Jimi Hendrix

• Music composed by Beck with keyboards player Jed Leiber for a Yorkshire TV programme. This won a BAFTA Award for Best Original Music.

JUNIOR BARNARD

Born: Lester Barnard, December 17th 1920, Coweta, Oklahoma, US. Died: April 15th 1951, Fresno, California, US.

■ *Epiphone Emperor (+ pickup); Gibson ES150.*

Barnard is a fine example of the underrated country guitarist who excels on sessions but never really establishes himself in the minds of record buyers beyond the small type on the back of record sleeves. However, Barnard's single-note jazz style, derived from **Charlie Christian** and **T-Bone Walker**, illustrated the extent to which country music drew stylistic inspiration from jazz and the blues. The best examples of his playing can be found on *The Tiffany Transcriptions* series (1946) as a member of Bob Wills' band The Texas Playboys, which at that time included such luminaries as steel guitarists **Noel Boggs** and **Herb Remington.** Among his most notable recorded work is the version of 'Fat Boy Rag' on the *Transcriptions*. (See also **Jimmy Wyble**.)

GEORGE BARNES

Born: July 17th 1921, Chicago Heights, Illinois, US. Died: September 15th 1977, Concord, California, US.

■ *Guild custom electric archtop; Gibson ES330; Gibson L5CES.*

Barnes suffered a somewhat erratic career, yet his partnership with guitarist **Carl Kress** and the series of duets they recorded in the 1960s continued the developments that **Eddie Lang** and **Dick McDonough** had made in the 1930s. The Barnes/Kress duets (for example *Something Tender*, or collections such as *Two Guitars*) included reworkings of lusty items like 'Someone To Watch Over Me', 'How High The Moon', ''S Wonderful' and 'I Don't Stand A Ghost Of A Chance'. They were lyrical and evocative, never sacrificing themselves to technique, containing spirit and feeling in equal parts, and remain performances of the highest order. Barnes was sometimes criticized for playing in 'down-market' radio orchestras along the way, where he might absorb too much pop influence at the expense of his jazz muse. But on the basis of the duets, Barnes remains one of the best and least acknowledged guitarists of the era.

MARTIN BARRE

Born: November 17th 1946, England.

■ *Schecter; Hamer; Gibson Les Paul.*

After the departure of **Mick Abrahams** from Jethro Tull in 1969 he was replaced by Barre, who's been there ever since. While Barre's technical prowess is undisputed, the material that he has to work with seems uninspiring. While Tull mainman Ian Anderson has penned some worthy ditties in his time – 'Livin' In The Past', 'Witches' Promise' and 'Life's A Long Song' – the pretentiousness of concept albums such as *Aqualung* (1971), *A Passion Play* (1973) and *War Child* (1974) militated against Barre's creative development as a guitarist to the extent that his principal role appears to be that of the performing seal who does his turn every so often. It seems to

these ears a pity that Barre didn't leave Jethro Tull years ago: then his inventiveness might be more apparent.

PAUL BARRERE

Born: July 3rd 1948, Burbank, California, US.

■ *Fender Stratocaster.*

Little Feat were one of the most distinguished bands to emerge in the US in the 1970s. Although much touted as the vehicle for **Lowell George**, this fails to acknowledge the individual contributions of the other band members. Paul Barrere joined the group in 1973, making his recording debut on the immaculate *Dixie Chicken*. While George's compositions and slide guitar work remained the group's distinguishing features, Barrere's resourceful combination of jazz and rock influences and Bill Payne's keyboarding gave depth to the group's sound. *Feats Don't Fail Me Now* (1974) and later albums saw Barrere gaining an upper hand within the group – often co-writing much of the material with Payne – as George's input decreased. In 1979 the band split and Barrere went into session work, eventually cutting a solo album *On My Own Two Feet* in 1983. Barrere was part of the generally successful reformed Little Feat, which debuted in 1988 with *Let It Roll*, with **Craig Fuller** replacing Lowell George.

SYD BARRETT

Born: Roger Keith Barrett, January 6th 1946, Cambridge, England.

■ *Fender Telecaster; Danelectro Standard.*

The early years of Pink Floyd were hallmarked by Barrett's quirky lyrics and the clean spare lines of his guitar playing on tracks like 'Arnold Layne', 'See Emily Play' and 'Scarecrow', echoing bluesmen such as **Lightnin' Hopkins** and **Charley Patton** (the group's name, too, was derived from bluesmen Pink Anderson and Floyd Council), while Barrett's live work on the group's extended, experimental pieces was more exploratory. After Barrett's departure from the group he recorded a brace of equally eccentric albums, *The Madcap Laughs* and *Barrett* (1970), where the electric guitar had largely given way to an acoustic and his style had become altogether more idiosyncratic. Both solo records were produced by Roger Waters and **David Gilmour** of Pink Floyd, the latter being Barrett's replacement in the band.

MANUEL BARRUECO

Born: December 16th 1952, Santiago, Cuba.

■ *Ruck.*

Barrueco moved to the US aged 15, playing his concert debut seven years later, and has become a most versatile and elegiac interpreter of Spanish guitar music, among the best currently working in the field. His arrangement of Albeniz's 'Suite Espanola', for example, possesses an endearing warmth and clarity (the *Spanish Dances* album is superlative), while Turina's 'Complete Works for the Guitar' are executed with aplomb and panache. His

repertoire is inspired, with lesser known composers such as De Visée alongside the great Spanish composers of the 20th century (Tarrega, Castelnuovo-Tedesco, Falla and Granados), and at the time of writing he was about to record some duets with a harpist.

BASHFUL BROTHER OSWALD

Born: Beecher Pete Kirby, Sevier County, Tennessee, US.

■ *Dobro resonator (wooden-bodied).*

Kirby was raised in a family of ten children, his father an accomplished fiddler and guitarist. After learning to play the dobro, Kirby moved to Knoxville, Tennessee and joined **Roy Acuff**'s Crazy Tennesseans who in 1939 became The Smoky Mountain Boys. As Bashful Brother Oswald, Kirby's dobro playing became one of the star attractions of the group as both he and Acuff refused to bow to the trend for amplifying the dobro. While the repertoire was confined to staunchly traditional fare, his contribution to Acuff hits like 'Wabash Cannonball' and 'The Great Speckled Bird' was immeasurable. His distinctive, almost Hawaiian-influenced playing has made him a legend, and he was one of the principal guests on the Nitty Gritty Dirt Band's album *Will The Circle Be Unbroken?* (1970), one of the best introductions to the more arcane aspects of traditional country music.

CAL BATCHELOR

Born: England.

Briefly **Tim Renwick**'s sidekick in Quiver, Cal Batchelor was sidelined when Quiver and The Sutherland Brothers joined forces – a curious occurrence, given that Batchelor was a more eloquent player than either Gavin or Iain Sutherland. While Quiver had never accurately been represented on record (*Quiver* 1971) Batchelor and Renwick's country-style picking had proved a fine addition to the British pub-rock circuit of the early-1970s. Batchelor went on to play briefly with vocalist Kevin Ayers' group 747.

JENNIFER BATTEN

Born: US.

■ *Ibanez 540S.*

A notable addition to the Los Angeles session fraternity, Batten first caught the eye of producer Quincy Jones, who used her on several of Michael Jackson's albums. This led to an unbroken stint in Jackson's touring band, promoting *Bad* (1987) and *Dangerous* (1991). Great work if you can get it... but Batten has the talent to do something more challenging, as she began to prove with her debut solo album *Above Below And Beyond* (1992).

BILLY BAUER

Born: William Henry Bauer, November 14th 1915, New York, New York, US.

■ *Guild.*

Joining the Woody Herman Big Band in the

mid-1940s when it was known as Herman's Herd, Bauer's swinging style was a distinct bonus for the outfit, and although he remained for just two years his solos on titles like 'The Woodchopper's Ball' (orginally recorded in 1939) and 'April Honey' have a fresh, pithy eloquence.

After his spell with Herman, Bauer joined forces with the blind composer and pianist Lennie Tristano, recording 'Night In Tunisia' for the Keynote label, among others.

Bauer's instinctive quest for fresh ideas was suited perfectly to Tristano, who was anticipating the emergence of free jazz by advancing the notion that players might start without a designated key, chord structure or melody. *Crosscurrents* (1949) was among the first recordings of such music, and these early examples of the avant-garde can be found combined on 'Intuition' (also on *Capitol Anniversary Jazz Collection* 1992) which, despite the cacophonous potential, works explosively well – primarily because Bauer didn't know how not to swing.

JEFF BAXTER

Born: December 13th 1948, Washington DC, US.

■ Fender Stratocaster; Roland guitar synth; Baldwin Baby Bison.

In 1972 keyboardist Donald Fagen and bass player **Walter Becker** formed Steely Dan, while under contract to ABC-Dunhill as staff writers. With producer Gary Katz they cut some of the best albums of that troubled decade. Among the session musicians they recruited was 'Skunk' Baxter, who was a full-time member of the group until 1974, appearing on the group's first three albums, *Can't Buy A Thrill* (1972), *Countdown To Ecstasy* (1973) and *Pretzel Logic* (1974). His fluid playing and astonishing melodic constructions on guitar and pedal-steel on songs like 'Reelin In The Years', 'Do It Again' and 'Show Biz Kids' emphasized the laconic, literate lyrics of Becker and Fagen, while the crystal clear production of Katz established a benchmark for later studio personnel.

After leaving Steely Dan, in 1975 Baxter joined The Doobie Brothers (playing on the sublime 'What A Fool Believes') before returning to session work in 1979, working with **Joni Mitchell** and singer Donna Summer among others.

DON BECK

Born: US.

Steel guitarist in The Flying Burrito Brothers after **Sneaky Pete Kleinow** and **Al Perkins** had got fed up with all the tantrums, Beck participated in the tour of Europe with guitarist/vocalist Rick Roberts fronting the band that resulted in *Live In Amsterdam*, recorded in 1971 but not released for another four years. After the band disintegrated, Beck and **Alan Munde** joined Country Gazette for a spell. Since that time Beck has remained active on the Los Angeles session circuit, working with former members of Country Gazette such as fiddler Byron Berline.

JEFF BECK

See also pages 11-13
Born: June 24th 1944, Woking, Surrey, England.

■ Gibson Les Paul Standard; Fender Jeff Beck Stratocaster; Fender Esquire; Jackson; Gretsch Duo Jet.

The guitarists' guitarist, Beck has managed effortlessly to bounce from one style to another without so much as batting an eyelid. Inspired by the great blues guitarists **BB King** and **Muddy Waters**, he joined The Yardbirds as **Eric Clapton**'s replacement in 1965 and immediately demonstrated his experimental style, using fuzz-box distortion and heavy tremolo on titles like 'Heart Full Of Soul' and 'Over Under Sideways Down'. Leaving the Yardbirds after a dispute with **Jimmy Page**, Beck recorded a string of erratic but successful singles.

In 1968 he formed The Jeff Beck Group with Rod Stewart, drummer Micky Waller (later replaced by Tony Newman) and bassist **Ron Wood**, cutting two albums *Truth* and *Beck-Ola* (1968). The former included a stonking version of the earlier Yardbirds hit, 'Shapes Of Things', and the atmospheric instrumental 'Beck's Bolero'. *Beck-Ola* included 'All Shook Up', demonstrating Beck's dazzling prowess on the slide guitar. Both albums became manuals for successive generations of metal guitarists, but the group broke up.

In 1971 he reformed The Jeff Beck Group, but despite success in the US the albums were patchy. In 1975 he side-stepped into what could be best described as jazz-rock with *Blow By Blow*. Despite the suspect reputation of this genre, Beck's technical expertise was highlighted by George Martin's sympathetic production, and Beck played like a man who had discovered the meaning of life. It was followed by *Wired* (1976), again with Martin producing and including a lyrical version of Charlie Mingus's 'Goodbye Pork-Pie Hat'.

With the passing of the years, Beck has continued to become involved with unsuitable collaborators (like keyboardist Jan Hammer) resulting in records of inconsistent quality. But then who cares? Beck certainly doesn't: he plays what he wants and when he wants. Which is the way it should be.

JOE BECK

Born: July 29th 1945, Philadelphia, Pennsylvania, US.

■ Fender Telecaster.

Beck was at the core of producer Creed Taylor's operation during the 1970s, when Taylor's labels CTI and Kudu were at the cutting edge of jazz-funk. Although **George Benson** recorded for the label and **Eric Gale** played sessions, Beck's collaborations with flautist Joe Farrell and, more particularly, arranger and composer Bob James inserted steel into performances that might otherwise have been tired.

Beck's work with vocalist Esther Phillips for Taylor was also notable, including *From A Whisper To A Scream* (1972), *Confessin' The Blues* and *Esther Phillips With Joe Beck* (1975). Briefly he flexed his muscles with **Larry Coryell** and **John Scofield** (*Tributaries* 1979) and with bassist Red Mitchell (*Empathy* 1980). More active on the session circuit

now, Beck lacks the public profile to achieve the necessary credibility for a solo career.

JASON BECKER

Born: 1970, California, US.

■ Ibanez; ESP; Carvin; Peavey; Valley Arts.

After **Steve Vai**'s departure from vocalist David Lee Roth's band in 1989, Becker stepped in. Although his debut with Roth on *A Little Ain't Enough* (1991) was technically good, his playing lacked Vai's range and depth of emotion. A previous solo album, *Perpetual Burn* (1988), had already underlined Becker's ability.

WALTER BECKER

Born: February 20th 1950, New York, New York, US.

■ Fender Stratocaster; Fender Telecaster.

Better known for his achievements as Donald Fagen's co-conspirator in Steely Dan, Walter Becker developed an interesting parallel career as a producer after the demise of Steely Dan. In 1992, he contributed to Fagen's long awaited follow-up to *The Nightfly* (1982), *Kamakiriad*. In the past Becker had concentrated principally on the electric bass, although he had contributed some guitar work to Steely Dan, like the wah-wah guitar phrases on 'East St Louis Toodle-oo'.

During the recording of *Kamakiriad* Becker was brought in to provide the finishing touches – and ended up playing most of the guitar solos as well as producing the album. The fluid guitar lines rekindled memories of **Larry Carlton**'s work on Steely Dan's *Aja* (1977), but where Carlton played with clinical precision Becker had greater suppleness and warmth. Becker's emergence as a guitarist of some skill further underscores his ability as a highly talented all-round musician.

FRANNIE BEECHER

Born: September 29th 1921, Norristown, Pennsylvania.

■ Gibson Les Paul Custom; Gibson ES350.

Despite what one might think in retrospect, when Bill Haley & The Comets emerged in 1954 they were one bunch of wild and crazy guys, getting up to all sorts of tricks on stage. Rudi Pompelli would play the sax lying on his back, and Al Rex would throw his bass around the stage. Guitarist Frannie Beecher, however, was a model of propriety, having played with jazzman Benny Goodman, and his tasteful stage licks and cool image did much to compensate for the lyrical crassness of Haley's records, infusing them with a melodic exuberance that the remainder of the band could only approximate. The guitarist heard on 'Rock Around The Clock' was **Danny Cedrone**, and Beecher was replaced in Haley's band by one Dale Edwards in 1957.

ADRIAN BELEW

Born: c1951, Covington, Kentucky, US.

■ Fender Stratocaster; Fender Mustang.

In common with **Lee Ritenour** and **Robert Fripp**,

Belew has acquired a reputation for technical perfection, for an ability to conjure those sublime solos that mix power and perspective in equal measure.

Perhaps Belew has been more subtle than Ritenour, for example, in determining those whom he should accompany – Talking Heads, David Bowie, Frank Zappa and Ryuichi Sakamoto – knowing that while all are interesting, for sure, none is noted for producing albums that pack heavy emotional punches.

Inducted by Fripp into King Crimson for *Discipline* (1981), *Beat* (1982) and *Three Of A Perfect Pair* (1983), Belew had an opportunity to lock antlers with another player of extraordinary virtuosity. A number of arresting solo albums have also appeared, including *Twang Bar King* (1983) which alludes to his profiency at devastating de-tunings of his Stratocaster via its vibrato arm. However, despite the manifest brilliance of his solos, and a penchant for the application of sheer noise to the stock of sounds at the disposal of the electric guitarist, to these ears at least, Belew's work leaves an unfortunate chill of indifference.

CHRIS BELL

Born: January 12th 1951, Memphis, Tennessee, US. Died: 1978, US.

When **Alex Chilton** left The Box Tops he joined a local Memphis band Ice Water, led by Bell. Changing their name to Big Star, their debut *#1 Record* (1972) was a tight collection of neat melodies and guitar work. However, Bell and Chilton were quickly at loggerheads over the group's direction and Bell left, continuing to play in and around Memphis. He was later killed in a car crash.

MARTIN BELMONT

Born: December 21, 1948, London, England.

■ *Fender Stratocaster.*

During the 1970s a breed of guitarist began to emerge, especially in Britain, without dependence on lengthy guitar solos to make a point; rather, they provided assured rhythmic embellishments that added depth to the songs of writers like Joe Jackson, Graham Parker, **Elvis Costello**, and **Chris Difford** & **Glenn Tilbrook**, among others.

Of these players, Martin Belmont was a prince among boys, and his effortless and economical switching from one style to another remains a joy. As a member of Man and then Ducks Deluxe he exhibited more finesse than most of his compadres, and with The Rumour (both with and without vocalist Graham Parker) he struck an all-time high, appearing alongside guitarist **Brinsley Schwarz** on a string of sadly under-valued albums such as *Howlin' Wind* (1976), *Heat Treatment* (1976) and *Squeezin' Out Sparks* (1979).

Belmont's understated playing brought out the strong R&B influences in Parker's acerbic lyrics and hectoring vocal style, and while Belmont rarely took solos, the lead on 'Don't Ask Me Questions' (*Howlin' Wind*) is a pleasing exception. Since The Rumour

split in 1981 Belmont has had to rely on session work, notably undertaking production and touring duties with British country artist Hank Wangford.

ARIEL BENDER

See LUTHER GROSVENOR

GEORGE BENSON

See also pages 33-35
Born: March 22nd 1943, Pittsburgh, Pennsylvania, US.

■ *Ibanez 'signature'; Gibson Super 400CES; Guild Artist Award; D'Angelico.*

While Benson has established himself in the minds of many as a purveyor of easy-listening soft soul, his reputation as one of the most accomplished guitarists of the post-war generation has been partially obscured. His career started as a vocalist in a Pittsburgh R&B band, until **Grant Green** spotted him and advised him to become a session musician. This immediately paid dividends and Benson started to work with organists Jimmy Smith and Brother Jack McDuff on sessions for the Blue Note and Prestige labels. This led to a meeting with **Wes Montgomery** and being signed by talent scout John Hammond to Columbia.

Early records like *The George Benson Cookbook* (1966) showed his fluency and a willingness to incorporate oblique references to influences like Montgomery. While these albums were commercially unsuccessful they improved his reputation among players, and after Montgomery's death Benson was signed to A&M with whom he started to record contemporary material. His readings of pop songs and R&B material such as 'I've Got A Woman' showed the extent to which his technical prowess was expanding.

After leaving A&M he signed with Creed Taylor's newly-established CTI label, where with a nucleus of stellar sessionmen such as bassist Ron Carter, hornman Joe Farrell and keyboardist Herbie Hancock, over the next half-dozen years Benson cut material like 'White Rabbit', 'Summertime' and 'Take Five', and the excellent *In Concert: Carnegie Hall*.

Signed next to Warner Brothers, he cut the epochal *Breezin'* in 1976. With Benson's relaxed vocals as seemingly effortless as his delicately cascading guitar lines on tracks like 'This Masquerade', it sold more albums than any other jazz album before or since, and won a truckload of Grammies. What has set Benson apart is the quality of his phrasing and his cool, languid style that seems to create so much space in which the other instrumentalists can interact. And that's what jazz is all about.

RAY BENSON

Born: March 16th 1951, Philadelphia, Pennsylvania, US.

■ *Gibson ES5; Gibson ES355.*

Benson's band Asleep At The Wheel have proved to be one of the more durable country-rock outfits thanks to their ability to synthesize some of the more diverse

elements of country music (western swing, Tex-Mex, bluegrass) into a readily accessible and identifiable style of their own. Much of this has been due to Benson's ability as a bandleader, building the group around musicians who excel in different areas. Benson's contribution as the main guitarist is not to be underestimated, best demonstrated on the live *Texas Gold* (1975).

CHUCK BERRY

Born: Charles Berry, October 18th 1926, San Jose, California, US.

■ *Gibson ES350T; Gibson ES355.*

Despite his legendary reputation for awkwardness, Berry's contribution to rock'n'roll and the guitarists' pantheon is assured. From the opening bars of his debut 'Maybelline' in 1955 through the glory years of the late-1950s on songs like 'Roll Over Beethoven', 'School Days', 'Johnny B Goode', 'Carol' and 'Back In The USA', Berry's swashbuckling style cut a swathe through the instruction manuals, and he has inspired virtually everyone who ever thought about playing the guitar.

Berry's style evoked **T-Bone Walker**, boogie-woogie pianists and country music, and he created signature licks that have been copied by thousands of guitarists since. Moreover, the lyrical content of his songs matched the freewheeling machismo of his guitar-slinging pose. His later years were marred by Berry's extraordinary notion that everyone is trying to take advantage of him. As a result even diehard fans like **Keith Richards** have been hard pressed to put up with his bouts of intransigence.

SKEETER BEST

Born: Clifton Best, November 20th 1914, Kingston, North Carolina, US.

■ *Various flat-top; Gibson Les Paul.*

A first-class swing guitarist, Best had his heyday during his tenure with jazz pianist/vocalist Earl Hines. Best made his debut in the 1930s with a local band before joining Slim Marshall from 1935 to 1940. After serving in the US Navy and arranging for services bands, Best worked with bassists Bill Johnson and Oscar Pettiford. Throughout the 1950s and 1960s he worked and toured extensively, cutting *Swingin' The Blues* with saxman Paul Quinichette and *Best By Test* with keyboardist Sir Charles Thompson. Little known today, Best is one of the many guitarists who found his voice as **Charlie Christian** and **Eddie Durham** were asserting the role of the modern jazz guitarist.

NUNO BETTENCOURT

Born: September 20th 1966, Azores, Portugal.

■ *Washburn 'signature'.*

For any metal band the most elusive task is creating a recognizable identity that stands or falls on its own merits. Inevitably, much of a band's distinctiveness lies in the hands of the lead guitarist or the vocal cords of its singer.

Bettencourt has fared better than most with a style

that freely borrows from a bewildering array of guitarists. While his band Extreme's first effort carried with it all the concomitant drawbacks of debuts, it set in motion an approach that could only benefit from practice. The second album *Pornograffiti* (1990) showed that Bettencourt, instead of aping influences such as **Jimmy Page** and **Eddie Van Halen**, was borrowing and then applying his own flourishes. The title track includes a solo that could have cropped up on any Page outing, but Bettencourt made it his own by drawing on the input of the other band members of the group, while his feature 'Flight Of The Wounded Bumblebee' is an outrageous tongue-in-cheek swipe from classical composer Rimsky-Korsakov's 'Flight Of The Bumblebee'. Similarly, 'Li'l Jack Horny' is reminiscent of Van Halen, but goes beyond mere influence, and the big hit 'More Than Words' captured Bettencourt's non-electric guitar work at a time when the acoustic guitar was on a fashionable high. Although 1992's *Three Sides Of Extreme* lacks the consistency of its predecessor, this was due more to the group's lack of experience in effectively editing themselves.

DICKY BETTS

Born: December 12th 1943, West Palm Beach, Florida, US.

■ *Gibson Les Paul.*

The combination of Betts and **Duane Allman** in The Allman Brothers provided one of the finest hybrids of contemporary rock music, with Betts' roots in country music and Allman's in R&B and blues. After making a couple of average studio albums they cut the magnificent *Live At Fillmore East*. Better live albums you just do not find. After Allman's death in 1971 it was widely supposed that the group would disintegrate, but Betts asserted his country roots and pioneered a loose form of country boogie that retained bluesy elements. The Allmans' first post-Duane album *Brothers And Sisters* (1973), with **Les Dudek** in support, included the sublime 'Jessica' and 'Ramblin' Man'. Lyrical and melodic, Betts played as if the spirit of Duane had taken residence in his fingers. And Dudek wasn't bad, either. However, the burden of expectation seemed to prove too heavy on later albums. Having spawned the new genre of country-boogie, like Dr Frankenstein the Allmans became victim of the monster they had created.

ED BICKERT

Born: Edward Isaac Bickert, November 29th 1932, Manitoba, Canada.

■ *Fender Telecaster; Fender Stratocaster.*

In Toronto during the 1950s Bickert developed his reputation by accompanying visiting jazz musicians. Gradually word of his talent filtered back to the US and he was booked to tour with a host of performers such as vocalist Rosemary Clooney, pianist Oscar Peterson, saxman/trumpeter Benny Carter and vibesman Milt Jackson. He made his recording debut with *Ed Bickert* (1975) where his introspective style contrasted markedly with the contemporaneous fad for jazz-rock fusion. In 1979 he joined up with

cornetist Ruby Braff for *Ruby Braff & The Ed Bickert Trio*, where his dexterous style echoed that of **George Barnes**. Bickert has continued touring, and remains a central figure on the Canadian jazz scene.

ELVIN BISHOP

Born: October 21st 1942, Tulsa, Oklahoma, US.

■ *Gibson ES345.*

The Paul Butterfield Band's first major outing for the Elektra label boasted Bishop and **Mike Bloomfield** in the guitar department, but sounded desperately thin, the fault lying with poor production (or, perhaps, non-production). The follow-up was *East West* (1966), and this was magnificent. Bloomfield and Bishop traded licks, anticipating the genus of the bluesy, twin-lead-guitar bands of the 1970s and 1980s. Butterfield sang or played the harmonica, and **Howlin' Wolf**'s former bassman Jerome Arnold and drummer Billy Davenport provided a rhythm section that was tight enough to make you wince. Extended work-outs on 'East West' and Nat Adderley's 'Work Song' were a revelation at the time, with Bishop and Bloomfield drawing from a range of disparate influences. After Bloomfield left the band Bishop stayed with Butterfield to cut *The Resurrection Of Pigboy Crabshaw* before leaving to form his own band. Never a great vocalist, Bishop's band foundered until the arrival of singer Micky Thomas (later of Jefferson Airplane), and they scored with 'Fooled Around And Fell In Love' (1976). Thereafter obscurity beckoned, and Bishop complied.

ERNESTO BITETTI

Born: July 20th 1943, Rosario, Argentina.

■ *Fleta.*

Bitetti has concentrated his recording activities on the great Spanish composers for the classical guitar. His vibrant if somewhat dated style is amply demonstrated on *Ernesto Bitetti Plays*, which features compositions by Turina ('Hommage A Tarrega'), Falla, Tarrega, Moreno-Toroba and Granados, and his readings of Rodrigo's 'Concierto De Aranjuez' and 'Fantasia Para Un Gentilhombre' are flamboyant. Modern composers such as Castelnuovo-Tedesco and Rodrigo have written pieces specially commissioned for Bitetti.

KATE BJELLAND

Born: Woodburn, Oregon, US.

Hardcore outfit Babes In Toyland have initiated the emergence of other all-female bands such as Hole and L7. Bjelland's plangent riffs don't pile on the dissonance in quite the same way as **Polly Harvey**'s, but they are part of a similar school. What both Harvey and Bjelland possess is a rhythmic thrust, propelling the songs organically. Although the Babes' material is far from comfortable, lacking any neat, easy hooks to latch on to, *To Mother* (1991) has a raw power that is comparable in its lack of artifice with the work of avant-garde jazzmen such as Don Cherry and Anthony Braxton.

BOBBY BLACK

Born: 1935, US.

■ *Sho-Bud.*

Formerly a member of Bill Monroe's Blue Grass Boys, Black's stab at immortality came in the early-1970s when he was recruited as pedal-steel guitarist by Commander Cody for the Lost Planet Airmen. This group was one of the most effective live country-rock bands of the era, due to their authentic adaptation of traditional country styles like western swing, Tex-Mex and Cajun. Despite a tongue-in-cheek attitude to this heady amalgam, the instrumental prowess of individuals like Black and fiddler/saxophonist Andy Stein ensured that live performances were well above par. Black's virtuosity was best demonstrated on the 1987 compilation *Commander Cody Returns From Outer Space*, which includes such old classics as Cab Calloway's 'Minnie The Moocher', 'That's What I Like About The South', 'I Been To Georgia On A Fast Train' and 'Hawaii Blues', the latter providing Black with the opportunity to stretch himself. After the band split in 1976, Black played on sessions and cut his own *Ladies On The Steamboat*.

RITCHIE BLACKMORE

Born: April 14th 1945, Weston-Super-Mare, Somerset, England.

■ *Fender Stratocaster; Gibson ES335.*

One of the most accomplished rock guitarists of the heavy metal era, Blackmore came to prominence on the definitive *Deep Purple In Rock* (1970). His snarling guitar work, thunderous riffs and pseudo-classical melodies were highlights of tracks like 'Speed King' and 'Child In Time'.

In 1973 the archetypal blues-based rock riff made its debut on 'Smoke On The Water', and Blackmore's guitar work there has been the inspiration for countless spotty youths who have subsequently hammered out that seven-note riff in bedrooms, garages, school halls and guitar shops throughout the otherwise civilized world.

While Blackmore has to shoulder a portion of the blame for the many imitators he has spawned, he was an imaginative and skilful technician as his work as leader of his own band Rainbow (1975-1983) testifies. Although that group managed to combine the trash theatrics of heavy metal with a tuneful zip, Blackmore's inability to keep a lineup together for any length of time militated against any sense of continuity, and his bombastic adaptation of Beethoven's Ninth Symphony casts a serious shadow over his judgement of good taste. Those misgivings aside, the *Best Of Rainbow* showed that Blackmore still had a fine ear for melody... and that he could squeeze out almost as many notes as **Jimmy Page**.

SCRAPPER BLACKWELL

Born: Francis Hillman Blackwell, February 21st 1903, North Carolina, US. Died: October 7th 1962, Indianapolis, Indiana, US.

In partnership with pianist Leroy Carr, Blackwell was

one of the first successful bluesmen, appearing on 'How Long, How Long Blues' in 1928. His picking gave character and added emphasis to Carr's enigmatic vocals, with the result that they immediately acquired a substantial following on the Indianapolis club circuit, before moving south to St Louis where they cut sides such as 'Prison Bound Blues' and 'When The Sun Goes Down'. Such was the intensity of Carr's work and the delicacy of Blackwell's playing that they established themselves as role models for successive generations of bluesmen. The partnership broke up when Carr died in 1935, and Blackwell left the music industry. With a resurgence of interest in blues in the late-1950s Blackwell resumed his career, but was fatally shot in 1962.

BLIND BLAKE

Born: Arthur Phelps, c1890, Jacksonville, Florida, US. Died: c1933, Florida, US.

■ *Stella.*

A street corner singer and guitarist, Blake's mix of minstrelsy, ragtime and dance tunes anticipated the emergence of the formalized style that came to be regarded generically as the blues. His peripatetic lifestyle, born of an inability to get a regular job because of blindness, caused Blake to cut his first sides in Georgia, before moving north to Chicago in 1926 to record for Paramount. As his influences had been diverse his musical vocabulary was extensive, enabling him to record with musicians from varied musical backgrounds, such as entertainer Gus Cannon, blues singer Ma Rainey and jazz clarinettist Johnny Dodds. His nimble rags and guitar picking were the inspiration for later bluesmen like **Big Bill Broonzy**, **Josh White**, **Blind Boy Fuller**, **Rev Gary Davis** and **Lightnin' Hopkins**. In 1985, the specialist blues label Yazoo issued *Ragtime Guitar's Foremost Picker*, a fair indication of his abilities.

NORMAN BLAKE

Born: March 10th 1938, Chattanooga, Tennessee, US.

■ *Martin; Santa Cruz.*

Blake has been justly regarded as one of the most influential session musicians on the circuit, excelling on guitar as well as dobro and mandolin. His knowledge of traditional styles and expertise in bluegrass enabled him to record an album of duets of Appalachian tunes with banjoist Bob Johnson in 1959, long before interest in traditional music had come into vogue. This versatility has encouraged artists like June Carter, Bob Dylan, Johnny Cash, Kris Kristofferson, **Joan Baez** and **Willie Nelson** to enlist his services, and among the best examples of his work are those to be found on Bob Dylan's *Nashville Skyline* (1969), while Blake's best solo albums include *Home In Sulphur Springs* (1972) and *Fields Of November* (1974).

NORMAN BLAKE

Born: October 20th 1965, Bellshill, Strathclyde, Scotland.

■ *Gibson Les Paul; Heritage H357 Firebird-style.*

Along with Suede, Teenage Fanclub are at the time of writing seen by some as the great hope of a British music industry desperate to build up credibility by visibly signing new and interesting bands. Someone, they figure, has to provide a lucrative recorded inventory that will still be selling ten years hence. Whether either of these bands have that sort of potential is open to question, but both groups do possess a songwriting ability that makes most of the 1990s remixers look like opportunists. Blake's knack for a tune has turned Teenage Fanclub into serious contenders, with a string of albums – *A Catholic Education* (1990), *The King* (1991), *Bandwagonesque* (1991) and *Thirteen* (1993) – that should stand the test of time.

MIKE BLOOMFIELD

Born: July 28th 1944, Chicago, Illinois, US. Died: February 15th 1981, San Francisco, California, US.

■ *Fender Telecaster; Fender Stratocaster; Gibson Les Paul; Kay archtop; custom acoustic.*

With a precocious talent that never properly fulfilled its potential, Bloomfield was a virtuoso before most had acknowledged the scope and the selling power of the electric lead guitar. Many had played the guitar and done outrageous things with it, including **Paul Burlison**, **BB King** and **Clarence 'Gatemouth' Brown**, but in the mid-1960s it was Bloomfield in the US and **Eric Clapton** in Britain who intimated that the lead guitar was the instrument of the era. **Jimi Hendrix** confirmed it.

In 1965 Bloomfield joined The Paul Butterfield Blues Band and contributed to an Elektra sampler, *What's Shakin'*. He was then co-opted to appear with Bob Dylan at the Newport Folk Festival with bassist Jerome Arnold and drummer Sam Lay, and subsequently played cutting Telecaster for Dylan on *Highway 61 Revisited* (1965), including such pearls as 'Like A Rolling Stone', 'Ballad Of A Thin Man' and 'Desolation Row'. While with Butterfield's band, Bloomfield was teamed with **Elvin Bishop** on *East West* (1966), a partnership that produced some of the best white blues of the era, matching landmarks like **Duane Allman**'s 'Whipping Post'.

But Bloomfield got restless and left Butterfield, forming Electric Flag with drummer Buddy Miles, bassist Harvey Brooks, vocalist Nick Gravenites and a bunch of other reprobates. The result was *A Long Time Comin'*, another superbly evocative elegy to the spirit of the blues, featuring **Howlin' Wolf**'s 'Killing Floor', with a spoken prologue from President Johnson that begins, 'I speak tonight for the dignity of man' ... but the remainder is drowned out by Bloomfield's thunderous guitar.

The Electric Flag was a short-lived outing for Bloomfield, who then teamed up with **Stephen Stills** and **Al Kooper** for *Super Session* (1968). Bloomfield and Stills' playing on tracks such as Donovan's 'Season Of The Witch' made a fine marriage of disparate styles, Bloomfield spiky and bluesy while Stills was rhythmic and melodic.

Thereafter, Bloomfield never harnessed his true ability, squandering his talent on half-organized projects that never amounted to much. *Fathers And Sons*, for example, included **Muddy Waters**, Paul Butterfield and any other bluesman unfortunate enough to be around, but suffered from poor production and jaded performances, while *KGB*, with Kooper and Gravenites, was pure bombast. However, in those few short years between 1965 and 1968, Bloomfield was a Cadillac among guitar players. He died in 1981 as a result of his drug habit, aged just 36.

DAVID BLUE

Born: Stuart David Cohen, February 18th 1941, Providence, Rhode Island, US. Died: December 2nd 1982, New York, New York, US.

During the early-1960s Cohen was an active member of the East Coast folk circuit that included other luminaries such as **Dave Van Ronk**, **Eric Andersen** and Phil Ochs. After signing with Elektra, Cohen changed his name to David Blue and began to embrace country styles. A fine guitarist and composer, Blue's career never achieved the recognition it deserved, despite a number of interesting albums, such as *David Blue* (1966), *Stories* (1972) and *Nice Baby And The Angel* (1973). A number of appearances as an actor in Wim Wenders' *American Friend* (1978) and Neil Young's *Human Highway* (1979), among others, subordinated his career as a musician.

NOEL BOGGS

Born: November 14th 1917, Oklahoma City, Oklahoma, US. Died: 1974.

■ *Fender; Bigsby.*

A masterful steel guitarist who nevertheless failed to achieve the celebrity of some of his colleagues, Boggs came to prominence with Hank Penny's Radio Cowboys in 1939 before joining Bob Wills' Texas Playboys in 1945. At that time the Playboys featured some of the best instrumentalists on the western swing circuit, including steel guitarist **Herb Remington**, guitarist **Junior Barnard**, fiddler Louis Tierney and mandolinist Tiny Moore.

Over the next two years Wills helped cut the sessions that became the excellent *Tiffany Transcriptions* series, originally staged for a limited audience of DJs and other industry personnel, which ensured that the recordings were relaxed. These were some of the best sides that Wills ever laid down, and included ageless classics like 'San Antonio Rose' and 'Steel Guitar Rag', as well as jazz numbers such as 'Take The A Train', and 'Basin Street Blues'. Boggs' rippling steel complemented the harsher, more staccato tones of Remington, lending the sessions an airy fluidity that was improvisational in character but controlled in essence. After leaving Wills, Boggs went on to work with Spade Cooley's band and lead his own groups, but he never bettered his Tiffany work.

BOB BOGLE

Born: January 16th 1937, Portland, Oregon, US.

■ *Fender Jazzmaster.*

While their simple instrumental records ceased to sell in the US and Europe over 30 years ago, The Ventures enjoy a success in Japan that continues unabated – they were the first foreign inductees to the Music Conservatory Of Japan in 1972 – and the group carry on knocking out concise cover versions of contemporary pop hits that are short on aesthetics but high on technical expertise.

For the non-expert it is difficult not to be impressed by Bogle, whose clean, bright, melodic, tremolo-laden guitar work on early hits such as 'Walk Don't Run' (1960) and 'Perfidia' (1961) stands out in stark relief against the pulsating rhythm section of bassist Nokie Edwards and drummer Howie Johnston. In 1963 Edwards became the lead guitarist, and Bogle moved to bass.

MARC BOLAN

Born: Mark Feld, July 30th 1947, London, England. Died: September 16th 1977, London, England.

■ *Gibson Les Paul; Fender Stratocaster.*

Initially an acoustic guitarist with a penchant for fey tales about pixies and elves, Marc Bolan reinvented himself in the early-1970s as a guitar-toting teen idol with T-Rex. In the former role he had limited success; in the latter he broke out with a series of finely wrought and exciting singles such as 'Ride A White Swan', 'Hot Love', 'Get It On', 'Metal Guru' and 'Telegram Sam', counteracting the drab pomposity of the prevailing trend among progressive bands of the era. While his guitar work was effective rather than accomplished, the simple chord structures of his songs opened up fresh vistas and inspired what was loosely termed glam rock and, later, punk.

Although this simplicity was roundly denigrated by intellectual snobs everywhere, it appealed to those without any formal musical training (among others) and generated an enthusiasm and vitality about pop music that had been effectively eradicated by the emergence of so-called 'progressive' rock bands. Bolan died when the car he was a passenger in crashed into a tree – and the site in south London has become a mecca for thousands of pilgrims over the years.

EARL BOLICK

Born: December 16th 1919, Hickory, North Carolina, US.

Earl Bolick and mandolinist brother Bill formed The Blue Sky Boys in 1936, cutting Bill's composition 'The Sunny Side Of Life'. Lacking any blues orientation and wholly influenced by a combination of old-time and religious music, their style differed from that of contemporaries like The Delmore Brothers and The Monroe Brothers who were much hotter instrumentalists than the Bolicks. However, the appeal of hits like 'Down On The Banks Of The Ohio', 'Story Of The Knoxville Girl', 'Are You From Dixie', 'Turn Your Radio On', 'Short Life Of Trouble' and 'Kentucky' proved that simple, unadorned acoustic accompaniment could be highly effective. In the early-1950s RCA tried unsuccessfully to persuade them to add an electric guitar to the lineup, and they stopped performing altogether. In the mid-1960s, as traditional styles were once again appreciated, The Blue Sky Boys reformed to play at festivals and on the college circuit.

TOMMY BOLIN

Born: August 1st 1951, Sioux City, Iowa, US. Died: December 4th 1976, Miami, Florida, US.

■ *Fender Stratocaster.*

A fine, nimble-fingered guitarist, Bolin enjoyed a certain amount of fame as **Joe Walsh**'s replacement in The James Gang, and then as **Ritchie Blackmore**'s replacement in Deep Purple. By the time he'd joined, both bands were past their respective sell-by dates, and consequently his talents were not accurately represented by any of the records he cut with either outfit. Prior to these outings Bolin had played sessions for jazz-rock drummer Billy Cobham, appearing on *Spectrum* (1973), and according to some authorities **Jeff Beck** was so impressed by Bolin's fleet fretwork on the record that Beck went on to cut *Blow By Blow*. Apocryphal or not, the story does tend to underline the notion that Bolin's best work was as a fusion guitarist.

CARLOS BONELL

Born: July 23rd 1949, London, England.

■ *Fleta; Rubio.*

Bonell studied guitar and violin as a child, encouraged by his Spanish parents, and soon settled on the guitar as his first love. Recognition by a British arts association helped Bonell's success in early concerts, and since the mid-1970s his emotive, solid sound has been a regular fixture on the international recital circuit. He displays an admirable willingness to collaborate with other guitarists, notably **John Williams** (who taught Bonell at the Royal Academy of Music in the late-1960s) and British jazzman **Martin Taylor**, while his solo recorded work includes the impressive *Guitar Showpieces*, and fine readings of the popular Rodrigo works, underlining his notes to the 'Aranjuez' concerto: 'A synthesis of diverse elements: the rhythms and melodies based on the folk music of southern Spain, the piquant harmonies and modulations derived from Falla, and the poise and elegance of a classicist.'

TONY BOURGE

Born: November 23rd 1948, Cardiff, Wales.

■ *Gibson Les Paul.*

A hard hitting heavy rock band from south Wales, Budgie established their reputation in the early-1970s, doing the rounds of the club and college circuits. Bourge was a later arrival, but his brash riffing, coupled with an unabashed bravado when it came to repeating the same solo, caused him to be taken to the hearts of the group's admirers. Budgie have joined the caucus of long-disbanded, much lamented outfits whose fans seem to grow in quantity annually, judging by the number of leather jackets still seen in Britain emblazoned with Budgie motifs. Bourge left the band in 1978, after playing on *If I Was Britannia I'd Waive The Rules* (1978) and formed Tredegar with ex-Budgie drummer Ray Phillips. Budgie continued until 1987, having cut *Deliver Us From Evil*, their final album, some five years earlier.

DENNIS BOVELL

Born: 1953, Barbados, West Indies.

Despite a reputation founded on his production abilities, Dennis 'Blackbeard' Bovell was one of the best reggae guitarists of the 1970s. With a style that fused elements of **Jimi Hendrix** and **Mike Hampton** with the traditional choppy rhythms of reggae, he formed Matumbi in 1972. Over the next decade he had cut a string of albums, including *Seven Seals* and *Point Of View*, which utilized dub, toasting and lover's rock in a clever, pleasing sonic mix.

MICK BOX

Born: June 8th 1947, London, England.

■ *Gibson Les Paul.*

Despite a succession of personnel changes over the years, Uriah Heep has continued as a band thanks to the sterling efforts of guitarist Box. While his heavy rock guitar work is not exactly free of clichés, it is highly effective and has helped underpin the group's identity through all those shifts.

Formulaic they most certainly are, but Heep's constant touring and a trusty repertoire of classics like 'Gypsy' (1970), 'July Morning' (1971) and 'Easy Livin'' (1972) has enabled Box to keep the band going when other more worthy outfits have long since curled up their toes. The best collection of Box's fiery riffs is *Anthology* (1985).

LIONA BOYD

Born: 1950, London, England.

■ *Ramirez.*

Boyd and her parents moved to Canada while she was still young, and in 1967 she was taken on as a pupil for a **Julian Bream** masterclass in Ontario, later continuing studies with **Alexandre Lagoya**. Boyd has become a very successful and popular classical guitarist, and her collaborations with non-classical artists has done much to popularize the instrument both in America and beyond. For example, she undertook a tour with Canadian singer/songwriter Gordon Lightfoot in the mid-1970s, and teamed up with country wizard **Chet Atkins**, as well as guitarists John Knowles and John Pell, on the interesting *First Nashville Quartet*.

JAMES DEAN BRADFIELD

Born: Blackwood, Wales.

In their short career The Manic Street Preachers have built a reputation for an uncompromising attitude, which seems misleading because they all play like pussycats. Bradfield's ability to whip out a series of knee trembling riffs is matched only by his capacity to adorn acoustic pieces with florid motifs and curlicues that might just make **John Williams** jealous. While many attempts have been made to categorize the group, their greatest achievement is their songs, such as 'You Love Us' (1992), 'From Despair To Where' (1993) and 'La Tristesse Durera', also released in 1993.

HAROLD BRADLEY

Born: January 2nd 1926, Nashville, Tennessee, US.

■ *Gibson; Fender; Martin; D'Angelico.*

Bradley is the embodiment of the highly-efficient Nashville session guitarist. The younger brother of producer Owen Bradley, Harold started his career in Ernest Tubb's band in 1943. Throughout the 1940s he honed his style, working with country-pop singer Eddy Arnold and bandleader Pee Wee King among others before joining the house band at WSM, Nashville's premier radio station and home of the long-running *Grand Ole Opry* show.

During the 1950s, Harold was regularly used by his brother Owen on sessions at the Quonset Hut studios, accompanying artists like Brenda Lee, Patsy Cline, Marty Robbins and Gene Vincent. Although he played guitar like ringing a bell, Bradley never had the opportunity to extend himself, due to the constraints of the two- or three-minute single format. When he broke those shackles to cut his own albums, for example the seriously appalling *Bossa Nova Goes Nashville*, he fell into the usual trap for session musicians of recording unsuitable material.

He had to wait until he worked with **Leon Russell** on *Hank Wilson's Back* (1973) to show to a wider audience just what a nimble picker he was, but once the session was over he returned to turning out the usual tame stuff for artists like Slim Whitman.

PAUL BRADY

Born: Paul Joseph Brady, May 19th 1947, Strabane, Co Tyrone, Northern Ireland.

■ *Ovation; Takamine; Yamaha.*

Paul Brady has been talked of for many years in hushed reverential tones by the cognoscenti (Bono and Bob Dylan) for his immaculate songwriting, causing Tina Turner, **Eric Clapton, Bonnie Raitt, Carlos Santana** and **Dave Edmunds** to record his songs. This facility has obscured Brady's talent as a performer and guitarist.

Initially with The Johnstons folk group and then as Christy Moore's replacement in Planxty, Brady's strong vocals and picking gave Planxty a reputation for being one of the most audacious of all Irish folk groups. After the group broke up, Brady and fellow Planxty man Andy Irvine cut an excellent acoustic album together, *Paul Brady & Andy Irvine* (1976), that was traditional in character.

Brady's solo debut *Welcome Here Kind Stranger* (1978) was one of the finest folk albums to emerge in recent years, mixing traditional material with his own. He also collaborated with **Mark Knopfler** on the soundtrack to *Cal* (1984). His own albums – for example *Hard Station* (1981), *Full Moon* (1984) and *Trick Or Treat* (1991) – have become progressively more rock oriented while retaining a folk quality, and Brady remains an undervalued musician.

DELANEY BRAMLETT

Born: July 1st 1939, Randolph, Mississippi, US.

Bramlett was a reasonable rhythm guitarist who kept such distinguished company that he got completely overshadowed by famous friends – such as **Leon Russell**, Joe Cocker, **Eric Clapton**, **George Harrison** and **Dave Mason**. Nonetheless, Delaney & Bonnie's *Accept No Substitute* (1969) made with his wife, singer Bonnie Bramlett, was a good early example of blue-eyed soul. That it failed to sell was probably due more to the record company's apparent unwillingness to market it than to the album being ahead of its time. It was followed by a tour with Clapton and a modest hit single, 'Comin' Home', but the duo's moment of glory was short. After divorcing, the couple went their separate ways: Delaney cut a few solo albums and Bonnie became a born-again Christian and sang gospel.

GLENN BRANCA

Born: 1948, Harrisburg, Pennsylvania, US.

■ *Modified Japanese budget models.*

A reluctant neo-classicist, Branca has said that he uses the symphonic form to explore the physics of sound through guitars. The *New York Times* has described his music as a mix of symphonic music, free jazz and heavy metal. And while the instrumentation is not confined exclusively to the guitar – *Symphony No 1: Tonal Plexus* was scored for trumpets, French horn, saxophones, drums and four guitars – the tonal potential of the guitar is the catalyst. In that piece all six strings of each guitar are tuned to a single note, at four different octaves, and the net result is awe-inspiring for its ferocity, calling to mind The Jesus And Mary Chain meeting the men from Ministry for a course in harmolodics – not exactly an exercise in calm.

With that in mind, approaching Branca's *Symphony No 7* requires some fortitude. Notable for its absence of melodic themes, it approaches the conceptual properties of harmony with, for Branca, a rare lyricism that calls to mind minimalist composer Steve Reich. His *Symphony No 10* for massed guitars was premiered in London in February 1994: the Festival Hall warned 'this concert will be very loud indeed'. Although his music will never find itself tinkling away in the background at chic dinner parties, Branca's aggressive disavowal of conventional structure is doubtless necessary for what he sees as the continued advancement of contemporary music.

JOSHUA BREAKSTONE

Born: July 22nd 1955, Elizabeth, New Jersey, US.

A good post-bop guitarist, Breakstone's swinging style echoes that of **Kenny Burrell**. Despite gaining a bunch of degrees and studying with Stan Kenton's erstwhile guitarist **Sal Salvador**, Breakstone's playing has seldom been purely cerebral or academic. Instead he has relied on the urgency of guitarists like **Jimi Hendrix** as his source of inspiration, which manifests itself in his ability to improvise and in the graceful clarity of his lines. A fine introduction to his work is *9 By 3* (1991), containing a mixture of ballads and uptempo swingers that fully demonstrates Breakstone's range.

JULIAN BREAM

See also pages 55-57
Born: July 15th 1933, London, England.

■ *Hauser.*

Bream has had as much influence on 20th century music as, say, **Jimi Hendrix**, establishing himself as a master of all classical guitar styles – and the world's premier lutenist.

While it would have been easy for Bream to remain a virtuosic interpreter of the existing guitar repertoire, he has continually widened the picture by commissioning new works and transposing to the guitar material originally written for other instruments. For example, in the 1960s he commissioned a range of works from significant contemporary composers such as Henze, Benjamin Britten and Frank Martin, which was released as *20th Century Guitar* (1967). This brave approach could have seriously foundered, damaging a reputation that was still developing and which saw him cast in the role of **Segovia**'s understudy. But this album established Bream as a grand master with a unique style.

Since those heady days Bream has continued to expand and develop the agenda of the classical guitar, exhorting new talent and stimulating guitarists of all musical persuasions. His recorded output is large, ranging from romantic Spanish music to 'difficult' modern composers such as Takemitsu.

However, if we had to name one special recording from among the dozens and dozens that Bream has made, it would have to be the stunningly beautiful *Music Of Spain Vol 5: Granados & Albeniz* (1982). And from Bream's equally assured lute recordings, *The Woods So Wild* (1972) is probably his finest studio collection.

BRAD BREATH

See ANDY ROBERTS

LENNY BREAU

Born: August 5th 1941, Auburn, Maine. Died: August 12th 1984, Los Angeles, California, US.

■ *Sand; Dauphin; Holmes (all seven-string).*

Little known beyond the nether world of guitar fanciers, Breau was described by funk guitarist **Phil Upchurch** as 'the most innovative guitarist since **Wes Montgomery**, and **Chet Atkins** dubbed him 'the greatest guitar player in the world'. What caused him to be so glowingly remembered was that he played the guitar as if it were a piano with the sustain pedal down. While his finger-work was that of a classical guitarist, he extended his range by using seven-string guitars, and his harmonic and rhythmic knowledge gave albums like the live *Velvet Touch Of Lenny Breau* (1969) a timeless and ethereal quality. Despite the extent of his influence, he recorded little – and those albums that he did cut have long since been deleted. That should be remedied by the relevant record companies. Tragically, Breau was strangled and his body discovered in a swimming pool in 1984.

BILLY BREMNER

Born: England.

■ **Fender Telecaster.**

Bremner is a session guitarist par excellence who has worked with Nick Lowe and **Dave Edmunds**, among others. His finest moment thus far was the guitar work on the Pretenders' 'Back On The Chain Gang', written by Chrissie Hynde as a tribute to guitarist **James Honeyman-Scott** who died after a drug overdose. It is one of the most moving tributes in rock, emotive and full of passion, with Bremner's guitar underscoring every nuance. It may only be rock'n'roll, but it beats the hell out of moping.

POL BRENNAN

Born: Gweedore, Co Donegal, Ireland.

Clannad's Gaelic traditions have tended to form the subtext to a rather more conventional AOR approach. While Maire Brennan's affecting vocals dictated the group's sound on most of their best-known albums and provided them with an identity, their instrumental base, fronted by Pol Brennan and supplemented by Padraig and Noel Duggan, Ciaran Brennan and session guitarist Pat Farrell, has continued to win them admirers in folk circles. Although later albums such as *Anam* (1990) and *Banba* (1993) have broadened their audience, while Maire and Pol have moved on, they lack the haunting, atmospheric charm of early albums like *Dulaman* (1976), *Clannad In Concert* (1978) and *Magical Ring* (1983).

TIM BRICHENO

Born: July 6th 1963, Huddersfield, Yorkshire, England.

Bricheno and vocalist Julianne Regan provided the thrust for All About Eve in the late-1980s. While they were instrumentally indebted to the British 'goth' scene, their hippy-dippy lyrics relating to the tarot and mysticism were redolent of 1960s psychedelia ('Our Summer' and 'Flowers In Our Hair'), with Regan in particular providing a strong folk-rock undercurrent. This conflict resulted in Bricheno's departure to The Sisters Of Mercy in 1990, causing much of the band's impetus to be dissipated. With the Sisters, Bricheno's abrasive guitar work was in its element on *Vision Thing* (1991).

CHRIS BRITTON

Born: January 21st 1945, Watford, England.

■ **Gretsch Country Gentleman.**

Ever since The Troggs' emergence in the mid-1960s their basic approach has garnered plaudits from a variety of more accomplished musicians than themselves. Formed in Andover and signed by impresario Larry Parnes, they first attracted attention with a raucous reworking of The Kinks' 'You Really Got Me' (1965). Chris Britton's guitar work made **Dave Davies**' playing on the original sound

the last word in sophistication. Later singles such as 'Wild Thing', 'Any Way That You Want Me' and 'I Can't Control Myself' (all 1966) established The Troggs as unwitting precursors of the punk movement, aligning them with US garage/punk bands such as The Standells, The Stooges, and Blues Magoos. In later years, after playing the oldies circuit, The Troggs were rediscovered because a private tape of one of their recording sessions came into circulation: littered with expletives, it offered a penetrating insight into the recording process. At the end of the 1980s – by which time Britton had left – they cut *From Andover To Athens* at REM's studios in Georgia.

DAVE BROCK

Born: Isleworth, Middlesex, England.

■ **Ibanez Artist.**

Brock has been at the helm of Hawkwind ever since their inception in the late-1960s around the Ladbroke Grove area of west London. Since then the group's lineup has undergone myriad changes, but Brock's tenuous grasp of reality has been strong enough to ensure the band's survival. While their albums (*In Search Of Space* 1971, *Space Ritual* 1973, *Quark Strangeness And Charm* 1977, and *Space Bandits* 1990, for example) have been erratic over the years, they have pursued their own rather eccentric path, espousing a view of the world informed by science-fiction and pulp novels. Brock's guitar work has remained as effective and unselfconscious as it was when the group began.

DAVID BROMBERG

Born: September 19th 1945, Philadelphia, Pennsylvania, US.

■ **Martin; Fender Telecaster.**

From the late-1960s Bromberg's prowess as a multi-instrumental session musician – he played guitar, mandolin, banjo and fiddle – was sought after by artists as diverse as Chubby Checker, Bob Dylan, Ringo Starr, Gordon Lightfoot, **Jerry Jeff Walker** and Sha-Na-Na. However, it was on his solo albums that the full range of Bromberg's musical knowledge and versatility was displayed for all to hear: the collaboration with country fiddle player Vassar Clements on *Hillbilly Jazz* showed two master musicians at their peak, trading chops as if they were bubblegum cards. Other albums like *How Late'll Ya Play 'Til?* showed Bromberg picking his way through a variety of styles with an easy nonchalance. While failing to achieve the commercial eminence of **Ry Cooder** and **John Fogerty**, he was one of the first to pay homage to and acknowledge his roots by playing and recording the songs of his youth. Since 1980, Bromberg has been making violins.

LONNIE BROOKS

Born: Lee Baker Junior, December 18th 1933, Dubuisson, Louisiana, US.

■ **Fender Stratocaster; Fender Telecaster; Gibson SG.**

A fine R&B guitarist, Brooks has since his debut in 1957 operated on the periphery of celebrity. With his

tough, urgent style, he had a brace of minor hits, 'The Crawl' (later revived by The Fabulous Thunderbirds) and 'Let It All Hang Out'. He toured Europe with blues pianist Willie Mabon before cutting a fistful of albums for Bruce Iglauer's Alligator label, including *Wound Up Tight* (1987), *Live From Chicago* (1987) and *Satisfaction Guaranteed* (1991).

BIG BILL BROONZY

Born: William Lee Conley Broonzy, June 26th 1893, Scott, Mississippi, US. Died: August 15th 1958, Chicago, Illinois, US.

■ **Photographed with Gibson Style O.**

Broonzy's career fell into two distinct periods: before World War II; and towards the end of his life in the mid-1950s.

During his earliest years he accompanied performers like Washboard Sam and Sonny Boy Williamson, as well as pursuing his own solo career. His ragtime-blues guitar work in the 1930s bordered on the virtuosic, and he displayed a mastery and control that has become legendary. Pieces like 'Saturday Night Rub', 'How You Want It Done' and 'Pig Meat Strut' underline his astonishing abilities both alone and in duos. A couple of collections on the Yazoo label draw together some of Broonzy's best material of the late-1920s and early-1930s.

During the 1950s Broonzy traded less on his guitar abilities than his storytelling singing and reminiscences on his early life, along with his reworkings of traditional blues, which struck a chord with college-educated white kids who were beginning to accept that the blues offered potent images of social history which books had somehow overlooked.

CLARENCE BROWN

Born: April 18th 1924, Orange, Texas, US.

■ **Gibson Firebird; Gibson L5 (+ pickup).**

Clarence 'Gatemouth' Brown is a good example of the black R&B guitarist who defies convention by incorporating healthy chunks of country-influenced material into his repertoire. Much of the blame for this 'aberration' has to be laid squarely at the door of Brown's father, who was a country fiddler. Being born in Texas, Brown attempted to lead the life of a good R&B guitarist and follow in the footsteps of **T-Bone Walker**, but try as he might, influences of western swing, Cajun and country kept creeping into his music. While these disparate influences might have smacked of tokenism, they coalesced into a vibrant cocktail that was uniquely Texan in character. His guitar work bore similarities to that of Walker, but was more staccato and punchy. *Makin' Music* (1979) shows his polymorphous tendencies, with a cast that included country singer Roy Clark, percussionist Airto Moreira, drummer Jim Keltner and The Memphis Horns, among others, while 1982's Grammy award winning *Alright Again* was pure R&B.

DURWOOD BROWN

Born: c1915, Stephenville, Texas, US.

Durwood's brother Milton Brown was one of the

Bro-Buc

prime movers in the development of western swing, and it was only his untimely death in a car accident that stopped Milton from becoming as well known as Bob Wills. Milton had formed his first group, The Musical Brownies, in 1932 after stints with The Aladdin Laddies, and The Light Crust Doughboys. Durwood was one of the first recruits, as rhythm guitarist, and provided the setting for virtuoso soloists like fiddlers Cecil Brower or Cliff Bruner, pianist Moon Mullican and steel guitarist **Bob Dunn**. In 1935 they cut some sides for Decca, which included jazz standards like 'St Louis Blues', 'Hesitation Blues', 'Memphis Blues' and 'Mama Don't Allow' and traditional country items such as 'Carry Me Back To The Lone Prairie', 'You're Bound To Look Like A Monkey' and 'Sweet Jennie Lee'. The effect was electrifying, echoing a style that was redolent of the Hot Club of France. The following year, Milton was killed in that fateful car crash and, although the group continued until 1938, the later work lacked direction without his influence.

JOE BROWN

Born: Joseph Roger Brown, May 13th 1941, Swarby, Lincolnshire, England.

■ **Gibson ES335; recently Music Man Silhouette.**

An incongruous notion, perhaps, but England's answer to **Cliff Gallup** in Gene Vincent's Bluecaps was Brown, a chirpy lad with a cheeky grin, raised in east London. His rockabilly styled guitar work on Billy Fury's *The Sound Of Fury* (1960) was fresh and inventive, complementing Fury's impassioned vocals on this collection of self-composed songs. Brown's career with his own group, the Bruvvers, stalled despite a string of country tinged hits, marred by over zealous production. By the mid-1960s Brown's role as the showbusiness token Cockney had become firmly established.

KENJI BROWN

Born: Kenji Chiba Brown.

Rose Royce were formed by Motown producer Norman Whitfield in 1973 as Total Concept Unlimited to back artists like Edwin Starr. TCU consisted of Kenji Chiba Brown (guitar), Kenny Copeland (horns), Freddie Dunn (horns), Henry Garner (drums), Juke Jobe (bass), Michael Moore (horns), Mike Nash (keyboards) and Terral Santiel (percussion). When Starr left Motown they became the road band for Undisputed Truth and for The Temptations. In 1976, Whitfield left Motown to set up his own label, taking the group with him, recruiting vocalist Gwen Dickey, and changing their name to Rose Royce.

Whitfield's first coup was to write the score for the film *Car Wash* (1976), with Rose Royce performing the music and The Pointer Sisters supplementing the vocals. The title song 'Car Wash', along with 'Put Your Money Where Your Mouth Is' and 'I Wanna Get Next To You', gave funk a user-friendliness. Over the next ten years Rose Royce, with Dickey's ethereal vocals (she left in 1981) and Brown's apposite guitar, notched the occasional hit – but nothing they did touched *Car Wash*.

MEL BROWN

Born: 1941, US.

■ **Gibson ES175; Danelectro.**

Throughout the 1950s and 1960s Bobby Blue Bland's mellow baritone graced some of the best R&B records of the era. These records, including 'Further Up The Road' (1957), 'Cry Cry Cry' and 'Lead Me On' (1960), 'I Pity The Fool' (1961), 'Call On Me' (1963), 'Ain't Nothing You Can Do' (1964) and 'If You Could Read My Mind' (1966), were produced by Joe Scott and included the guitar work of Mel Brown (later, and less impressively, Wayne Bennett). While producer Scott was adept at building dynamic backdrops for Bland's voice, Brown's bluesy licks, reminiscent of **T-Bone Walker**, foreshadowed the great white session guitarists of the late-1960s like **Steve Cropper** and provided the ideal foil for Bland. There are few soul albums that can match Bland's *Two Steps From The Blues* (1961) for depth and variety of style.

BOB BROZMAN

Born: 1954, New York, New York, US.

■ **National resonator (various).**

Brozman is one of those guitarists who probably don't sell many records because nobody knows where to look for them in the record store. A ghostly hybrid of folk, blues and jazz (*Hello Central, Give Me Dr Jazz* 1985, *Devil's Slide* 1987, and *A Truckload Of Blues* 1988) Brozman's playing, with its evocations of traditional styles, echoes that of **Leo Kottke** and **John Fahey**. Couched firmly in the vernacular of the contemporary guitarist, he is a fine picker and slider who gets the best from the brash sound of resonator guitars, and who deserves to be better known. But Brozman suffers from the attitude of those who do the marketing: if it can't be pigeonholed, it can't be niche marketed.

TOM BRUMLEY

Born: December 11th 1935, Powell, Missouri, US.

■ **ZB.**

When steel guitarist Brumley left country singer Buck Owens' Buckaroos in 1969 to join Rick Nelson's Stone Canyon Band, he became one of the first country session musicians to embrace the burgeoning hybrid of country-rock – a fusion that was to become one of the most lucrative genres of popular music in the early-1970s. Brumley had joined The Buckaroos in 1963, linking up with **Don Rich** and Owens to give the group the distinctive hard edge that became a trademark of the Californian Bakersfield sound.

After joining Nelson, Brumley's immaculate steel on *Rick Sings Nelson* (1970) and *Rudy The Fifth* (1971) set The Stone Canyon Band apart from most of the contemporary country-rock bands, playing on tracks like the cover of Jagger & Richards' 'Honky Tonk Women', Bob Dylan's 'Love Minus Zero' and Nelson's 'Gypsy Pilot'. In 1976 The Stone Canyon Band disbanded and Brumley worked sessions thereafter, also finding time to build guitars.

JIMMY BRYANT

Born: 1925, Moultrie, Georgia, US. Died: September 22nd 1980.

■ **Fender Telecaster; Magnatone; Rickenbacker; Guild; Vox; Hohner; Stratosphere.**

One of the foremost country-jazz session guitarists on the US West Coast during the 1940s and 1950s, Bryant played on many country and pop records. Along with **Joe Maphis** he became a reference point for the hard-edged, fast-fingered picking style of the Bakersfield sound that emerged during the 1950s.

Originally a fiddler who toured with his guitar-playing father's band, Bryant soon took up the guitar and it immediately became clear that he had an affinity with the instrument and was partial to the speed that had characterized his fiddle playing. He worked as a session player, appearing on records by artists as diverse as Tennessee Ernie Ford (in the 1950s) and The Monkees (in the 1960s).

Bryant's lightning picking was equally at home in a variety of styles that included rags, boogies and polkas, illustrated by a 1989 compilation *Guitar Take Off*. For some breathtaking work from Bryant in tandem with steel guitarist **Speedy West**, with whom he had worked on the country radio show *Hometown Jamboree* and made several other records, look no further than their staggering 1950s album *Two Guitars Country Style*.

ROY BUCHANAN

Born: September 23rd 1939, Ozark, Tennessee, US. Died: August 14th 1988, Fairfax, Virginia, US.

■ **Fender Telecaster; Fritz Bros 'signature'.**

Buchanan was one of the finest guitarists to emerge amid the hype of rock, deploying lacerating solos that incorporated an individual control of harmonics and a peerless sense of melody and economy. His guitar work has proved to be a strong influence on players such as **Jeff Beck** and **Nils Lofgren**.

In the late-1950s Buchanan played with rock'n'roller Dale Hawkins, but after publicity from a TV documentary he signed a solo recording deal in the early-1970s that led to best-selling records like *Second Album* (1973) and *Loading Zone* (1977), and his instrumental verve is finely captured on the classic single 'Sweet Dreams' (from *Roy Buchanan* 1972).

Buchanan was quoted as saying that one note can be as effective as dozens, and his bluesy style was best demonstrated on his later solo albums made with similarly non-career-oriented musicians like singer **Delbert McClinton**, cutting the music that he understood best.

The natural sounding *Dancing On The Edge* (1986, with McClinton) showed Buchanan in his element on songs like 'The Choking Kind' and a revival of **Duane Eddy**'s 'Peter Gunn' – great, fiery solos all.

Buchanan had wrestled with drug and drink problems over the years, and in 1988 he hanged himself in a prison cell after being arrested for drunkenness. He at least deserves the respect of a posthumous retrospective of his recording career, when perhaps his true worth will become apparent and properly appreciated.

PETER BUCK

Born: December 6th 1956, Athens, Georgia, US.

■ *Rickenbacker 360; Rickenbacker 12-string.*

In some ways REM are comparable to another great American institution, The Band, in that they have achieved the unthinkable by generating critical acclaim as well as commercial success. The world weary wisdom of Michael Stipe's lyrics, despite their abstract imagery, coupled with Buck's guitar work, have made REM the band of the 1990s, evoking a vision of America that is contemporary yet romantic. They have deliberately eschewed the showbiz posturing endemic in global celebrity, settling instead for the tranquil backwaters of Athens, Georgia and concentrating on the honing of individual skills.

While Stipe has been the object of media speculation, Buck has quietly gone about his business, demonstrating an instrumental virtuosity and eclecticism that many have essayed but few have attained. Drawing from America's rich musical heritage, Buck uses elements of country, R&B and jazz among others to come up with a style that is uniquely his own. The underlying features are fluency and lyricism; whether picking single notes or playing chords, Buck's guitar is an integral component of the group's sound and the song of the moment. He doesn't indulge in overblown soloing, but rather emphasizes and embellishes every nuance of Stipe's lyrics. *Out Of Time* (1991) and *Automatic For The People* (1992) illustrate the diversity of his musical pedigree.

ROBERT BUCK

Born: Jamestown, New York, US.

■ *Starfield custom.*

Since vocalist Natalie Merchant has embarked on a solo career the fate of her erstwhile band, 10,000 Maniacs, remains to be seen. The group's swansong with Merchant, *Unplugged* (1993), was an elegant summation of their career together. Throughout, Buck demonstrated an equal lightness of touch on acoustic as well as electric guitars. Straddling the divide between folk and country-rock, Merchant's socially aware lyrics often smacked of hubris, but the warmth of the arrangements provided a keen balance. While later albums haven't matched the spartan brilliance of *The Wishing Chair* (1985), *Our Time In Eden* (1992) included the lush 'Few And Far Between', featuring a brass arrangement by Paul Buckmaster.

LINDSAY BUCKINGHAM

Born: October 3rd 1947, Palo Alto, California, US.

■ *Gibson Les Paul; Turner.*

When Buckingham and vocalist Stevie Nicks joined Fleetwood Mac in 1975 they revived the tired old warhorse that had started life as a blues band in 1968. Their arrival was the catalyst for the transition from Just Another Band to Exemplars Of AOR.

Writing together, Buckingham and Nicks contributed songs like 'Over My Head', 'Rhiannon', 'Say You Love Me' and 'Go Your Own Way', and while Nicks' distinctive, slightly nasal vocals complemented Christine McVie's bluesy tones, Buckingham's melodic acoustic and electric guitar playing gave the band an edge over other LA-based outfits. Their dependence on tightly structured songs in preference to extended instrumental noodlings was a departure from the norm, and Buckingham's versatility on a variety of stringed instruments gave extra weight to the group's catchy material.

In the early-1980s Buckingham made a brace of solo albums, *Law And Order* (1981) and *Go Insane* (1984), that bore similarities to his work with Fleetwood Mac. While they gave him an opportunity to extend himself instrumentally, the tightly structured material and tastefully phrased solos were a welcome departure from so many solo albums where self indulgence seems to be the key ingredient.

DENNIS BUDIMIR

Born: Dennis Matthew Budimir, June 20th 1938, Los Angeles, California.

■ *Gibson ES335; Gibson ES347.*

The Chico Hamilton bands have provided a training ground for almost as many musicians as the groups of Miles Davis and Art Blakey. While drummer Hamilton's acolytes have been less innovative, they have consolidated the mainstream as the basis from which others can experiment. Budimir joined Hamilton during the 1950s, and the group's standing was enhanced by their inclusion in the film *Jazz On A Summer's Day* (1958). After a round of session work, Budimir cut *Sprung Free* and *Second Coming* (1961) with bassists Gary Peacock and Bobby West.

SANDY BULL

Born: February 25th 1941, New York, New York, US.

■ *Fender Bass VI; Ovation; Sho-Bud pedal-steel.*

Bull was an eclectic multi-instrumentalist who anticipated the emergence of Eastern styles in Western contemporary music in the early-1960s. While his versatility enabled him to move freely between guitar, banjo, oud and sitar, adapting classical, folk, jazz and Eastern motifs to his own requirements, his precocity militated against any commercial acceptance. Nevertheless he recorded a string of albums for the Vanguard label, including *Inventions* (1965) with drummer Billy Higgins. This featured 'Blend II' on which he foresaw another trend by playing all the instruments himself using overdubs. Although few of his records are still available, Vanguard did issue a retrospective, *The Essential Sandy Bull*, in the late-1980s.

TEDDY BUNN

Born: Theodore Bunn, 1909, Freeport, Long Island, New York. Died: July 20th 1978, Los Angeles, California, US.

■ *Gibson L5; Gibson Super 400.*

Bunn was an inventive jazz guitarist whose skillful solos anticipated **Charlie Christian**'s inroads with

the guitar by some years. His group, The Spirits Of Rhythm, were a ground-breaking outfit of the 1930s, combining swing and comedy. Some of Bunn's finest work can be heard on tracks like 'I'll Be Ready When The Day Comes'. Ultimately Bunn jettisoned his own band in preference to playing with jazz greats like Duke Ellington, Sidney Bechet, Mezz Mezzrow, Peetie Wheatstraw and Johnny Dodds. Seldom lauded today, Bunn's single-string soloing on a non-amplified guitar quickly became commonplace – the difference being that he was one of the first.

CHARLIE BURCHILL

Born: November 27th 1959, Glasgow, Scotland.

■ *Gibson; Fender; Ibanez; Casio.*

Simple Minds built their reputation on a big sound, replete with crashing chords, which slotted easily into the contemporaneous need for bands to sound good in massive stadiums or concert halls. Lyrically, the band touched on themes of social awareness and moral issues, highlighted by Charlie Burchill's abrasive chords and Jim Kerr's hectoring vocals. These two personalities were the nucleus of the band's sound, complemented by a driving but changing rhythm section and rounded out by Mick McNeill's keyboards. Although albums like *Sparkle In The Rain* (1984) were immense commercial successes, as were singles such as 'Don't You (Forget About Me)' (1985), 'All The Things She Said' (1986) and 'Belfast Child' (1989), there was an irritating lack of variety about the group's music.

PAUL BURLISON

Born: February 4th 1929, Brownsville, Tennessee, US.

■ *Fender Telecaster.*

The Rock'n'Roll Trio, formed in the early-1950s, were guitarist Burlison, bassist Dorsey Burnette, and Dorsey's brother Johnny. Burlison had formerly played with **Howlin' Wolf**, and developed a buzz-saw guitar sound that became the Trio's trademark. Although they stayed together for a short time, they cut sides like 'Blues Stay Away From Me', 'Tear It Up', 'Oh Baby Babe' and 'Train Kept A-Rollin' which came as close to defining the spirit of rockabilly as anything else around at the time – and was an early recording of a distorted guitar sound. Burlison left the group in 1957 to run a construction company, and the Burnettes soon went their separate ways: Johnny achieved the adulation of the masses as a teen idol, most successfully with 'You're Sixteen'; Dorsey had a middling career as a country singer and songwriter.

T-BONE BURNETT

Born: John Henry Burnett, 1945, St Louis, Missouri, US.

A highly-rated producer, guitarist and songwriter, Burnett came into his own with a series of impressive solo albums – *Proof Through The Night* (1983), *Behind The Trap Door* (1984) and *The Talking Animals* (1988) – that bridge the gap between white soul and folk. His laconic lyrics, complemented by a stellar array of guests and sidemen, made him one of the unsung heroes of the 1980s, with the self-containment of a troubadour. Among his production credits are Los Lobos and **Leo Kottke**.

JAKE BURNS

Born: Belfast, Northern Ireland.

Stiff Little Fingers' Jake Burns provided the band's cutting edge with a roistering blend of punk and R&B. While this generated an expansive fan base for their live shows, the group's albums – *Inflammable Material* (1979), *Nobody's Heroes* and *Hanx!* (1980) and *Go For It!* (1981) – were anonymous. By 1983 Burns, after a brief dalliance with his own outfit, went to work for the BBC.

KENNY BURRELL

Born: Kenneth Earl Burrell, July 31st 1931, Detroit, Michigan, US.

■ **Gibson Super 400CES; Gibson L5CES; D'Angelico; Epiphone.**

Burrell is one of the most incisive and least provocative jazz guitarists of the post-war era. Influenced by **Charlie Christian**, Burrell got his degree in music at Wayne University, Detroit in 1955, after playing briefly with Dizzy Gillespie's band in the early-1950s.

In 1956, he became a temporary replacement for Oscar Peterson's sideman **Herb Ellis** before moving to New York where he was signed by the Blue Note label and joined the Benny Goodman band. Burrell's wide-ranging experience has enabled him to adopt any style or idiom, although this very versatility sometimes gives the impression of a journeyman lacking a clear identity.

Whether that is true or not, his work has included some impressive highlights: the soulful *Midnight Blue* (1963) with tenor saxophonist Stanley Turrentine includes a bluesy but funky reading of Don Redman's 'Gee Baby Ain't I Good To You?'; *Fusion* (1963) with **Wes Montgomery** has two master technicians at their peak, trading licks with a wonderfully casual informality; and *Guitar Forms* (1965) with arranger Gil Evans includes an evocative and haunting rendition of George Gershwin's 'Prelude Number 2'. Although Burrell's later years have seen him straying perilously close to cocktail jazz with offerings like *Togetherings* (1985) with Grover Washington Jr, his understated eloquence remains a joy.

JAMES BURTON

See also pages 93-95
Born: August 21st 1939, Shreveport, Louisiana, US.

■ **Fender Telecaster; Fender 'signature'.**

One of the most versatile session guitarists of the rock era, Burton's economical style has given many pop songs the extra zip that raises them from the mundane to the superlative. He first demonstrated this ability while working on Shreveport's *Louisiana Hayride* radio show, backing vocalists like George Jones. In 1957, he was recruited by rockabilly singer

Dale Hawkins to play on 'Suzie Q', and while it wasn't much of a hit, Burton's staccato bursts set the tone for later rock guitarists.

With this critical success under his belt, Burton joined Rick Nelson's studio and touring band, replacing the illustrious **Joe Maphis**.

The clinical efficiency with which he unleashed superb cameo solos on singles such as 'Believe What You Say', 'Poor Little Fool', 'Never Be Anyone Else But You', 'It's Late', 'Just A Little Too Much', 'Travelin Man', 'Hello Mary Lou' , 'It's Up To You' and 'Fools Rush In' did much to convince listeners that the solidbody electric guitar was indeed the premier instrument of rock'n'roll.

After his stint with Nelson finished in 1964, Burton reverted to session work before joining Elvis Presley's band in 1969. For the next eight years he was the focal point of Presley's road and recording unit, providing an instrumental astringency that had been lacking in Presley's music since the departure of **Scotty Moore**. Meanwhile Burton played sessions with country-rock singer/songwriter Gram Parsons, being featured on the classic albums *GP* (1972) and *Grievous Angel* (1973).

When Parsons died in 1974 and then Presley in 1977, Burton and pianist Glen D Hardin were recruited by Emmylou Harris for her Hot Band. While Harris's pure, tremulous soprano often sounded neutral, Burton and Hardin gave material like her 'Boulder To Birmingham', Shel Silverstein's 'Queen Of The Silver Dollar' and Rodney Crowell's 'Til I Gain Control Again' a toughness and urgency that was to set Harris apart from the mainstream of country singers.

Throughout his career, Burton's tasteful solos have complemented all whom he has played with... but the less said about his solo records the better.

TREVOR BURTON

Born: March 9th 1944, Birmingham, England.

A founder member of The Move, Burton imbued the band's early work with a wry tongue-in-cheek levity. While his playing showed signs of the handiwork of **Mick Green** (a proto-metal guitarist if ever there was one) Burton borrowed from **Pete Townshend** as well as **George Harrison** and **John Lennon**. The Move scored many hits, and were one of the first groups to be progressive within the constraints of the three minute single. 'Night Of Fear', 'I Can Hear The Grass Grow', and 'Flowers In The Rain', all **Roy Wood** originals, were fine pastiches of any number of disparate influences. Burton moved to bass in 1968, and later that year left the group, joining The Uglys and then The Steve Gibbons Band.

BERNARD BUTLER

Born: England.

■ **Gibson Les Paul; Gibson ES355.**

Suede were formed in 1989 when singer Brett Anderson and bassist Mat Osman advertised for a guitarist, finding Butler, and the three were joined shortly after by drummer Simon Gilbert. Two promising singles, 'The Drowners' and 'Metal

Mickey', led to the group's debut *Suede* (1993). Guitarist Butler has shown himself to have a fashionably retro approach to his raw, melodic guitar parts, blending influences from 1970s players like Blondie's **Chris Stein**, The Jam's **Paul Weller**, Orange Juice's **Edwyn Collins**, and Television's **Tom Verlaine**.

BILLY BYRD

Born: US.

■ **Gibson Byrdland.**

For 13 years Byrd was one of Ernest Tubb's principal accompanists in The Texas Troubadours, contributing the ascending four-note run that became the linchpin of Tubb's sound. After leaving Tubb in the late-1950s Byrd became a session musician, collaborating with **JJ Cale**, and with **Leon Russell** on the affectionate *Hank Wilson's Back* (1973) and its sequel *Hank Wilson Volume 2* (1984). Byrd helped in the design of Gibson's Byrdland model with **Hank Garland**.

Still a strong influence on the more purist of the 'new country' guitarists, Byrd has hopped off the session merry-go-round and only works when the spirit so moves him.

CHARLIE BYRD

Born: September 16th 1925, Suffolk, Virginia, US.

■ **Ramirez; Ovation.**

Best known for his collaborations with saxophonist Stan Getz on *Jazz Samba* (1962), which popularized the Brazilian bossa nova, Charlie Byrd had a versatility that fostered a misconception that he was an easy-listening guitarist. While his records may have been accessible, his nylon-strung acoustic technique was impeccable and enabled him to play jazz, classical and sambas without batting an eyelid. Among his most successful outings were the unaccompanied *Plays Villa-Lobos* (1967), and *Brazilian Soul* (1980) with **Laurindo Almeida**, both of which contributed to the wider acceptance of Hispanic influences in contemporary music. In 1974 Byrd cut *Great Guitars* with **Barney Kessel** and **Herb Ellis** on which he demonstrated his less apparent debt to **Charlie Christian**.

JERRY BYRD

Born: March 9th 1920, Lima, Peru.

When Byrd decided to quit the music industry and move to Hawaii in the 1970s, country music lost one of its most innovative steel guitarists. He grew up in the US and worked as a painter until 1939 when he became a professional musician, joining The Pleasant Valley Boys and then vocalist Red Foley's outfit. With Foley he developed the melodious, rounded sound on the steel guitar that was to become the standard in Nashville. Byrd started a solo career with the Mercury label in 1949, cutting albums such as *Hawaiian Beach Party* (1951), but like many session musicians he needed to be told what to play by his employers in order to produce his very best work.

DAVID BYRNE

Born: May 14th 1952, Dumbarton, Scotland.

■ **Fender Stratocaster.**

Guitarist and guiding spirit of Talking Heads, one of the most influential and artistically correct bands of the 1980s, Byrne, who grew up in the US, provided the group's rhythmic framework with his taut vocals and abrasive chords. Contributing the melodic shadings over the organic rhythm section of Tina Weymouth and Chris Frantz were guitarists like **Adrian Belew** and Alex Weir (of Brothers Johnson) and keyboards player Jerry Harrison.

Never averse to using all manner of influences, from African and South American rhythms to the avant-garde experimental work of Philip Glass and Brian Eno, Byrne developed a guitar style secondary to the expansion of the group's musical vocabulary. But as frontman in the band he helped repopularize the instrument in an era of increasing reliance on keyboard-based synthesizers. *Remain In Light* (1980) had a string of innovative videos for the extracted singles and indicated the degree to which Byrne's approach to music was governed by multimedia.

ALAN CADDY

Born: February 2nd 1940, London, England.

■ **Gretsch Chet Atkins solid; Gibson ES335.**

As a member of Johnny Kidd & The Pirates, Caddy was a key element in the group's rough-hewn dynamism. The Pirates were one of the first genuine British R&B bands back at the end of the 1950s, and Caddy's ringing, tremolo'd backdrop to 'Shakin' All Over' (1960) was much emulated by fledgling guitarists. Caddy left the group in 1960 (after 'Please Don't Touch') and became part of producer Joe Meek's house band, forming The Tornados with ex-Pirate drummer Clem Cattini. Although the Meek-produced 'Telstar' and the follow-up 'Globetrotter' were great object lessons in production technique, they did little for Caddy, and with hindsight have to be viewed as retrograde steps. After his departure from the group in 1965, Caddy disappeared from sight.

CHARLOTTE CAFFEY

Born: October 21st 1953, Santa Monica, California, US.

■ **Fender Telecaster.**

Along with The Bangles, The Go-Go's were one of the best new-wave female groups to emerge in the US in the late-1970s and early-1980s. Reminiscent of Blondie (they shared producer Richard Gottehrer for a spell) they were assembled by vocalists Jane Weidlin and Belinda Carlisle in 1979. Caffey was brought in to supplement the lineup when Weidlin's guitar playing was found wanting. Caffey's plangent chords did much to characterize the tuneful, witty epics of 'We Got The Beat' and 'Our Lips Are Sealed' (1981, from *Beauty & The Beast*) and 'Vacation' (1982), giving the group's sound a vibrant identity that later imitators such as Wilson Phillips found difficult to replicate. After the group split, Carlisle went on to a very successful solo career and Caffey was instrumental in

helping her to complete those awkward first few solo albums.

BUDDY CAGE

Born: US.

When Jerry Garcia's activities in The Grateful Dead became so onerous that he had to give up moonlighting as the steel guitarist in The New Riders Of The Purple Sage in 1971, Buddy Cage was recruited as the full-time replacement. While steel player Cage was a better technician than Garcia, he lacked Garcia's light, airy feel, with the result that his playing, especially after the group's second album *Powerglide*, seemed ponderous. This was probably due to the years Cage had spent working sessions; he was not so accustomed to improvising as was his predecessor. Furthermore, once Garcia terminated his association with the band the material lost direction.

AL CAIOLA

Born: Alexander Emil Caiola, September 7th 1920, Jersey City, New Jersey, US.

■ **Epiphone 'signature'.**

Caiola was a virtuoso guitarist who spent most of his career working with movie and TV studio orchestras under bigwigs like Percy Faith, Andre Kostelanetz and Hugo Winterhalter. Pleasant, innocuous and perfectly formed, his guitar work has probably been heard more frequently than that of **James Burton** or **George Harrison** – not least on the theme tune to the old TV Western series, *Bonanza*.

TOY CALDWELL

Born: 1948, Spartanburg, South Carolina, US. Died: February 25th 1993, US.

■ **Gibson Les Paul; Gibson ES335.**

Along with The Allman Brothers Band, The Charlie Daniels Band and Lynyrd Skynyrd, The Marshall Tucker Band were one of the best southern boogie outfits of the 1970s.

The Caldwell brothers, bassist Tommy and steel/lead guitarist Toy, formed the band in 1971 and were signed by the Allman Brothers' manager Phil Walden to the Capricorn label. Although Toy's playing was not as inspired as Duane Allman's, it displayed a degree of taste and a broad spectrum of musical influences that were often notably absent from most boogie bands of the time.

Tucker's supreme achievement *Searchin' For A Rainbow* (1976) crystallized their range, with Toy demonstrating a tender lyricism one minute and ripping into scintillating runs the next. The extent to which Toy was able to move between the rock and country camps was illustrated by his appearance on the Hank Williams Jr *And Friends* album (1975).

In 1980 the band was split asunder by the death of Tommy in a car crash. While Tucker continued to tour, the records lost their edge, and by 1985 Toy had left for an uneventful solo career, interspersed with the occasional outside session.

JJ CALE

Born: Jean-Jacques Cale, December 5th 1938, Oklahoma City, Oklahoma, US.

■ **Harmony (+ pickup).**

Cale is one of a small number of players who have evolved such a distinctive guitar style derived from the blues, country and rock that he transcends genre. He learned to play guitar while still at school and formed The Valentines, the first of a string of bands, and by 1959 had moved to Nashville to attempt to build a career as a singer and songwriter. But he couldn't penetrate their close-knit community, so in 1964 he went to Los Angeles to seek a publishing deal, where he teamed up with fellow Oklahomans **Leon Russell**, bassist Carl Radle and drummer Chuck Blackwell, cutting 'Slow Motion' the following year.

In 1968 Cale returned to Oklahoma where he built his own studio and started to put together some demos, which eventually saw the light of day as *Naturally* (1971). The lean, languorous lines of tracks like 'After Midnight' and 'Crazy Mama' were so laidback – and Cale was one of the first performers to be so described – that he seemed to be playing by rote. However, his approach was best summed up in the self-penned 'Clyde', despite the bass reference: 'Clyde plays electric bass/Plays it well with finesse and grace/Sits on the porch without no shoes/Picking the bass and singing the blues.'

Over the years Cale has given the impression of recording pretty much when he feels like it, and his output has varied remarkably little in quality. But his influence is clearly detectable in both **Mark Knopfler**'s and **Richard Thompson**'s playing. Furthermore, Cale's total indifference to the exigencies of fame and fortune is legendary.

RANDY CALIFORNIA

Born: Randolph Craig Woolfe, February 20th 1951, Los Angeles, California, US.

■ **Kramer (later).**

Archetypal psychedelic guitarist California first came to attention in Spirit, although the over-wrought pyrotechnics of his later solo album, *Captain Kopter And The Twirly Birds*, bears more than a suggestion of one who has been ingesting hallucinogenics.

In Spirit, California's ability to sound more like **Jimi Hendrix** than Jimi Hendrix disguised a band that would surely have been at ease with the later development of jazz-rock. While tracks like 'I've Got A Line On You' and 'Fresh Garbage' were sufficiently tuneful to chart, the elaborate arrangements of *Clear Spirit* (1969) and *The Twelve Dreams Of Dr Sardonicus* (1970), often bearing California's overblown embellishments, combined jazz, rock and Eastern elements to give the group a distinctive quality that ranked them alongside titans of West Coast rock like The Grateful Dead.

JOHN CALL

Born: John David Call, US.

The Pure Prairie League were one of many country-rock groups to emerge in the early-1970s. They were

Cam-Car

formed in Cincinnati in 1971, with their lineup comprising Call (steel guitar), **Craig Fuller** (guitar and vocals), **George Powell** (guitar and vocals), Jim Lanham (bass and vocals) and Jim Caughlan (drums). After the group's debut *Pure Prairie League* (1972) Call left, returning briefly while 'Amie' was a hit; they disbanded again in 1975. In 1978 Powell and Call reformed the group and, in 1980, Vince Gill joined. They then enjoyed their greatest success, with titles like 'Let Me Love You Tonight', 'I'm Almost Ready' and 'Still Right Here In My Heart'. In 1983 they disbanded for good, with Call working thereafter as a session musician.

GLEN CAMPBELL

Born: Glen Travis Campbell, April 22nd 1936, Delight, Arkansas, US.

■ *Ovation.*

Despite his generally dire taste in material these days, Campbell wasn't always a progenitor of MOR. He was given his first guitar at the age of four and joined his uncle's group, Uncle Bill's Western Band, in 1954 where he developed a jazzy single-note picking style reminiscent of **Merle Travis** and **Jimmy Bryant**. After touring, Campbell formed the Western Wranglers and in the late-1950s moved to Los Angeles where he picked up work as a session guitarist, appearing on the Champs' hit 'Tequila' (1958).

This led to session work with Frank Sinatra, Jan & Dean, Rick Nelson, Elvis Presley and The Beach Boys, among others. Such was his technical prowess and his ability to play in almost any style that he was drawn into touring with The Beach Boys when Brian Wilson lost the plot.

In 1965 Capitol Records signed Campbell as a singer/guitarist and he cut songs like Buffy Sainte-Marie's 'Universal Soldier' and John Hartford's 'Gentle On My Mind'. By 1967 he had started the inexorable slide towards MOR with 'By The Time I Get To Phoenix' and 'Wichita Lineman', among a number of Jimmy Webb songs he was to record. Since then, despite lionizing lesser known writers, Campbell uses his guitar as a prop for his live act and hasn't done anything interesting with it in years.

GLENN ROSS CAMPBELL

Born: US.

In the mid-1960s Campbell fronted a San Francisco-based band, The Misunderstood, and issued a reworking of Bo Diddley's 'Who Do You Love?' and the self-penned 'I Can Take You To The Sun'. The former was a rough and ready version of the song, now well known thanks to Ronnie Hawkins & The Hawks (later The Band) and Quicksilver Messenger Service (who were to include it on their *Happy Trails* album in 1968).

'I Can Take You To The Sun' was neither rough nor ready: Campbell's fast, melodic acoustic picking, chock-a-block with cadenzas, echoed flamenco and seemed a world away from the long solos inspired by Hendrix and Clapton to which every guitarist aspired at the time.

Later in the 1960s Campbell came to London, where The Misunderstood promptly disbanded and he formed another band that included **Neil Hubbard** and saxophonist Chris Mercer and which by 1970 had become Juicy Lucy. But despite a brace of hits including a reworking of 'Who Do You Love', Campbell never surpassed the majesty of 'I Can Take You To The Sun'.

IAN CAMPBELL

Born: June 10th 1933, Aberdeen, Scotland.

The Ian Campbell Folk Group was formed in Birmingham in 1956, and became an important part of the revival of interest in traditional British folk music. Initially a skiffle group, they recorded *Ceilidh And The Crown* (1962), probably the first live folk album, and in 1965 they became the first non-US act to record a Bob Dylan song, 'The Times They Are A-Changin'. Campbell's solid guitar work was at the core of the group's sound, and over the years they have provided openings for debutants such as fiddler Dave Swarbrick, **Martin Carthy**, and bassist Dave Pegg. The group folded in 1978.

JOHN CAMPBELL

Born: 1952, Shreveport, Louisiana, US. Died: June 13th 1993.

Turning to the guitar after an almost fatal injury in a drag-racing crash in 1967, Campbell developed a rhythmically percussive style that owed much to **Lightnin' Hopkins**. At first he toured extensively, playing the club and bar circuit, making his debut with *A Man And His Blues* (1988) and teaming with fellow guitarist Alexander Kennedy.

This came to the attention of **Robert Cray**'s producer Dennis Walker, who encouraged the duo's writing and oversaw the production of *One Believer* (1991) and *Howlin' Mercy* (1993). Unfortunately in 1993, just as Campbell's following was increasing, he died.

MIKE CAMPBELL

Born: February 1st 1954, Panama City, Florida, US.

■ *Rickenbacker; Fender.*

Campbell is a fine all-round guitarist who has seldom been in the spotlight, primarily because the style of **Tom Petty** & The Heartbreakers militates against protracted solos. But his zinging guitar work, full of hooks and textures, as on 'American Girl' (1976), complements the sonorous jangling of Petty's Byrds-like playing. Moreover, Campbell's ability to pen a well-rounded tune (co-writing 'Boys Of Summer' with Don Henley, 'Aztec' with Brian Setzer and 'Refugee' with Petty, for example) indicates a musician of purpose and ability rather than one who prefers to indulge in flamboyance.

ROBIN CAMPBELL

Born: December 25th 1954, Birmingham, England.

Unashamedly populist in the execution of their infectious reggae-tinged style, UB40's distinguishing components are guitarist Robin Campbell, hornman Brian Travers and vocalist Ali Campbell. Ali's diffident vocals provide the group's clearest hallmark, and his brother Robin contributes the lilting guitar figures while Travers punctuates and complements with staccato horn bursts.

What this means is that they have been able to cover songs as diverse as Neil Diamond's 'Red Red Wine', Sonny & Cher's 'I Got You Babe' and Hugo & Luigi's 'I Can't Help Falling In Love With You' and make them their own. Although UB40's career started with the band defined as an overtly politically motivated outfit (*Signing Off* 1980, *Present Arms* 1981) this has gradually given way to a more user-friendly manifesto that embraces the mainstream without any apparent loss of face. They are one of the few bands to have set up their own label (Dep International) at the beginning of their career and made it work.

JERRY CANTRELL

Born: 1967, Seattle, Washington, US.

■ *G&L Rampage.*

One of the high-profile Seattle metal bands, Alice In Chains benefited considerably from an appearance in the Ben Fong-Torres movie *Singles*, but the group's all-round compositional and instrumental ability has ensured that they can vie confidently with Nirvana and similar outfits.

Their sound, dominated by Cantrell's guitar, combines strong melodies with rhythmic twists and acute lyrics, set off by a booming rhythm section. A good deal of the group's achievement can be traced back to their first album *Facelift* (1990) which showed a band not so much at the beginning of the learning curve but with their identity already set. The follow-up *Dirt* (1991) confirmed the promise of the debut, with tracks like 'Them Bones' showing Cantrell's guitar work to be improving by leaps and bounds.

LARRY CARLTON

Born: March 2nd 1948, Torrance, California, US.

■ *Gibson ES335; Valley Arts 'signature'.*

Larry Carlton is the doyen of Los Angeles session guitarists and has recorded with artists of the stature of Bill Withers, **Joni Mitchell**, Steely Dan, Bobby Bland, **BB King**, Randy Crawford and Quincy Jones. After years of session work Carlton joined the jazz-rock outfit The Crusaders in 1975 and started a parallel solo career in 1979 that generated a slew of virtuosic if bland solo albums.

If Carlton is ever to be illuminated by his own radiance, he has got to set himself up in a small combo and just play. In this regard, saxophonist David Sanborn should be the example for all session musicians who want to record on their own terms. Until Carlton decides to do that, forget about his solo albums and listen to this master of phrasing and economy on albums like The Crusaders' *Southern Comfort* (1974), Steely Dan's *Aja* (1977), Bobby Bland's *The Dreamer* (1974), and Joni Mitchell's *Hejira* (1976).

MARK CARO

Born: US.

Despite their short-lived career, Abattoir were one of the most distinctive heavy metal bands to emerge from Los Angeles in the early-1980s. While their career had finished by 1988, Caro's riffing on 'Screams From The Grave' deserves some sort of epitaph. Maybe this is it.

CLARENCE CARTER

Born: January 14th 1936, Montgomery, Alabama, US.

■ *Gibson L5.*

In common with **Bobby Womack**, Carter has had a career that has been divided into two parts: that of a session musician, and that of a solo performer. In the latter capacity he cut a string of magnificent records including '(Making Love At) The Dark End Of The Street', 'Slip Away', 'Too Weak To Fight', 'Snatching It Back' and 'Sixty Minute Man' during the mid-1960s. These leering, salacious sermonettes utilized the finest sessionmen that Muscle Shoals could offer, while Carter's mellow, understated guitar work dotted all the Is and crossed all the Ts... and left no doubt about his sexual agenda. Among Carter's other outstanding contributions was the guitar solo on his erstwhile wife Candi Staton's reworking of the Tammy Wynette classic 'Stand By Your Man'. A dearth of suitably lubricious material has curtailed his activities recently, but *Doctor C C* (1986) shows that his bluesy style remains intact.

FRED CARTER

Born: December 31st 1933, Winnsboro, Louisiana, US.

Although he never attained the dizzy heights achieved by **James Burton**, Carter's uncomplicated picking on a host of Nashville sessions contributed to the homogenization of the Nashville Sound during the late-1950s and 1960s. While that may appear a back-handed compliment, it was Carter's workmanship that helped to persuade young R&B sessionmen like keyboardist David Briggs, **Chips Moman**, bassist Norbert Putnam and a horde of other ambitious players to migrate to Nashville in search of fame, fortune or just work, proving that there was life after soul.

MAYBELLE CARTER

Born: Maybelle Addington, May 10th 1909, Nickelsville, Virginia, US. Died: October 23rd 1978, Madison, Tennessee, US.

■ *Gibson L5.*

Maybelle Addington joined the ground-breaking country group The Carter Family in 1926 through her marriage to founder AP Carter's brother, Ezra. Her addition to the lineup gave the group an instrumental depth and variety that complemented the wide-ranging sources of material that AP was collating: 'Wabash Cannonball', 'My Clinch Mountain Home', 'Keep On The Sunny Side', 'Foggy Mountain Top' and 'Great Speckled Bird'.

Maybelle's 'country lick' guitar style, which revolved around playing the melody with the thumb on the bass strings and the rhythm with the fingers on the treble, helped bring the guitar to the fore in country music and influenced generations of folk-oriented singers. While the extent of her influence is undisputed, her greatest achievement lay in her selfless promulgation of the music she loved, helping all sorts of artists to find their feet. Among those to benefit from her wisdom were her son-in-law Johnny Cash and her grand-daughter Carlene Carter, whom she taught to play the guitar, as well as pianist Floyd Cramer and **Chet Atkins**, among others. In 1971, she was the catalyst that helped the Nitty Gritty Dirt Band's genre-busting *Will The Circle Be Unbroken?* project become a reality.

MARTIN CARTHY

See also pages 115-117
Born: Martin Dominic Forbes Carthy, May 21st 1941, Hatfield, Hertfordshire, England.

■ *Martin 000-18.*

Arguably one of the most influential folk guitarists to emerge in Britain, Carthy was inspired by all manner of music, from the country blues of **Big Bill Broonzy** and **Lightnin' Hopkins** to traditional English and Irish folk songs. In the 1960s he helped to revitalize a British folk scene that had become dangerously parochial and myopic.

Carthy's elemental Englishness meant that his dalliance with the blues was short-lived, but his guitar style managed to combine into a wonderfully individual sound the heavy percussive leanings of the blues and the clawhammer style of picking that **Merle Travis** developed. Carthy's impact on the British folk scene has been massive, but he has also influenced Bob Dylan – and it was Carthy who introduced 'Parsley Sage Rosemary & Thyme' to **Paul Simon**.

During the 1970s Carthy was a member of two of the most distinguished British folk-rock bands of the era, Steeleye Span and The Albion Country Band. Throughout his career, Carthy has also been closely associated with Fairport Convention fiddler Dave Swarbrick, recently cutting *Skin And Bone* (1992) which shows two men at a peak.

AL CASEY

Born: Albert Aloysius Casey, September 15th 1915, Louisville, Kentucky, US.

■ *Gretsch.*

Casey first came to attention in Fats Waller's sextet, The Rhythm, where his economical licks were overshadowed by the larger than life flamboyance of his employer's piano playing and vocal style. In 1939 Casey joined jazz pianist Teddy Wilson's outfit, where once again by virtue of his unobtrusiveness his playing tended to be relegated to an auxiliary of the rhythm section. By 1943 Casey had branched out on his own, developing a solid reputation that gained him a steady stream of session work, increasing when he won the *Esquire* magazine jazz polls in successive years (1945/6).

It wasn't until the mid-1970s that Casey's understated playing came to be recognized for its eloquence, and it initiated a revival of interest in his work that resulted in a series of albums for JSP, including *Remembering King Curtis*. This was a fine, sparky set that contextualized Curtis as a jazz musician as well as a familiar, stellar sessionman. Casey remains a journeyman of the highest order and seems impervious to the vicissitudes of fashion.

PHILIP CATHERINE

Born: October 27th 1942, London, England.

A guitarist of considerable skill and expertise, Catherine in common with many fusion musicians still seems short on emotional intensity. While credentials such as his attendance at Boston's Berklee College and his work with violinist Jean-Luc Ponty and reedman Charlie Mariano are impressive, Catherine's decision to join the Dutch band Focus in the mid-1970s seems to these ears at least to have been an error of judgement.

After this sojourn Catherine teamed up with **Larry Coryell** for a trio of albums – *Twin House* (1978), *Splendid* (1978) and *Live* (1980) – that left no doubt about his technical prowess, but each album lacked personality and impressed only in its virtuosity: his interpretation of **Django Reinhardt**'s 'Nuages' on *Twin House*, for example, sounded strangely neutral and hollow. More recently *Chet's Choice* (1985), a trio album with trumpeter Chet Baker and a bassist, intimated a warmth that had hitherto been imperceptible in his output.

DANNY CEDRONE

Born: US.

Danny Cedrone's few minutes of fame hinged on his incisive, country-influenced guitar break on Bill Haley's 'Rock Around The Clock' (1954) which spun around itself delightfully, complementing drummer Billy Guesack's rimshots and proving to be a key ingredient in the success of the record. That success went to his head, however, and Cedrone left The Comets to form The Jodimars, who disappeared into oblivion faster than a falling star.

EUGENE CHADBOURNE

Born: January 4th 1954, Mount Vernon, New York, US.

■ *Ovation; Gibson; Hofner.*

Chadbourne took up the guitar through the influence of **Jimi Hendrix** but, unlike many who cop a style and thrash it to death, he used it as a starting point, assimilating different styles including bottleneck and the avant-garde. Richly inventive and totally incorrigible, Chadbourne has a lack of self-consciousness that enabled him to pursue a similar tack to that of **Derek Bailey**, with *Solo Acoustic Guitar*, volumes 1 and 2. During the 1980s, he teamed with Camper Van Beethoven, covering Tim Buckley songs as well as his own compositions. He has a commendable love of mixing styles (*Country Music In The World Of Islam* 1990) and a healthy disregard for the musical establishment.

Cha-Cip

JOE CHAMBERS

Born: August 22nd 1942, Lee County, Mississippi, US.

The Chambers Brothers started their career as a gospel outfit but, unlike many gospel groups, they accompanied themselves. During the early-1960s they began to draw elements of folk into their act which secured an invitation to appear at the Newport Folk Festival in 1965. A rough and ready reading of **Curtis Mayfield**'s 'People Get Ready', with both Joe and **Willie Chambers** stretching out, asserted their R&B roots. *Time Has Come Today* (1968) represented another change of emphasis, with Joe and Willie unleashing long, duelling solos that were reminiscent of **Elvin Bishop** and **Mike Bloomfield** in The Butterfield Blues Band. While they remained a popular act among rock audiences, playing venues like The Fillmore, the coming of disco in the 1970s made them obsolete.

WILLIE CHAMBERS

Born: March 2nd 1938, Lee County, Mississippi, US.

While **Joe Chambers** was the lead guitarist of The Chambers Brothers, Willie was the rhythmic counterpart. But as the 1960s progressed he became more assertive, particularly on *Love Peace And Happiness* (1969).

MICHAEL CHAPMAN

Born: January 24th 1941, Leeds, Yorkshire, England.

■ *Fylde.*

Chapman was something of an anachronism in that he was one of the few accomplished guitarists to emerge on the back of the British folk boom of the late-1960s. Having worked the folk club circuit for some years, he cut two fine albums for the Harvest label: *The Rainmaker* (1968) and *Fully Qualified Survivor* (1969) that included 'Postcards Of Scarborough', 'Naked Ladies & Electric Ragtime' and 'First Leaf Of Autumn'. Both albums evoked atmospheres of rural England at its most pastoral, while the arrangements utilized elements of jazz, blues and rock (**Mick Ronson** played on *Survivor*), and Chapman's nimble fingers left most of his contemporaries' three-chord tricks lagging some way behind.

In the years since then Chapman has recorded less regularly and his work has progressively intimated an approach similar to that of **John Martyn**. *Almost Alone* (1981) included a delicate, evocative reading of **Django Reinhardt**'s 'Nuages' that attempted to present the composition on its own terms instead of trying to imitate or surpass the original. To this day, Chapman remains an unobtrusive, obdurate champion of all that is intriguing about British music.

CRAIG CHAQUICO

Born: September 26th 1954, Los Angeles, California, US.

■ *Gibson Les Paul; BC Rich.*

Jorma Kaukonen would have been a tough act for anyone to follow, but in 1974 Chaquico had that unenviable task when Jefferson Starship superseded Jefferson Airplane, with Kaukonen side-stepping to Hot Tuna.

While the Jefferson machine revolved around Paul Kantner's impossibly dippy lyrics, former Airplane vocalist Marty Balin, one of the finest vocalists to emerge in the last 30 years, rejoined the band in 1975, adding more depth and scope.

Meanwhile Chaquico the ingénue gave the group a harder rock'n'roll sound and adopted more conventionally recognizable rock motifs, whereas Kaukonen had always been very bluesy. Balin's sense of melody gave ballads such as 'Miracles' (1975) a haunting lyricism that Chaquico was adept at complementing.

Although the band went through innumerable changes of personnel and any number of internal legal disputes, their popularity soared in the mid-1980s with a string of monsters: 'We Built This City' (1985), 'Sara' (1986) and 'Nothing's Gonna Stop Us Now' (1987), confirming them as purveyors of nothing more than rather standard AOR fare. Chaquico has throughout these changes become highly accomplished and is now less reliant on the good old rock'n'roll clichés, and has instead begun to assume something of the air of an elder statesman. Recently Chaquico followed the acoustic trend, recording *Acoustic Highway* (1993).

MANNY CHARLTON

Born: Dunfermline, Lothian, Scotland.

■ *Gibson Les Paul.*

Extraordinary to note that after all these years Nazareth, formed in 1969, are at the time of writing still going strong. Charlton's strident guitar work and Dan McCafferty's vocals have provided the continuity for a loyal, hardcore following in Europe and in the US. While they veer dangerously close to what can best be described as a middle of the road hard rock band (some contradiction, surely?) they are nonetheless effective, even on material as diverse and unexpected as **Joni Mitchell**'s 'This Flight Tonight', Felice and Boudleaux Bryant's 'Love Hurts', and Tomorrow's 'My White Bicycle'.

ALEX CHILTON

Born: December 28th 1950, Memphis, Tennessee, US.

After a career as lead vocalist in The Box Tops, recording such classics as 'The Letter', 'Cry Like A Baby' and 'Soul Deep' among others, Chilton joined a local Memphis band Ice Water, which was led by **Chris Bell**. Changing their name to Big Star, their debut *#1 Record* (1972) provided melodious songs full of neat guitar work.

However, Bell and Chilton quickly disagreed about the group's direction, and Bell left. Over the next 20 years Chilton's career was erratic but his mystique grew, and solo albums such as *High Priest* (1987) and *Black List* (1990) vindicated that reputation. His incisive melodies and his willingness to pay homage overtly to his many influences makes him one of the more significant documenters of a range of US styles.

CHARLIE CHRISTIAN

Born: July 29th 1916, Dallas, Texas, US. Died: March 2nd 1942, New York, New York, US.

■ *Gibson ES150.*

To some extent we have to blame Charlie Christian for the plethora of tedious jazz guitarists who have spent their lives bleating on about technique. Perhaps that's unfair to Christian, but it was he who, in a very brief career, provided a benchmark by which all others would be measured. His single-note runs on the electric guitar were thrust forward into bold solos of a kind that had previously been considered as the sole province of hornmen like Lester Young. Never again would the guitar be regarded purely as a rhythmic device.

Christian will go down in history as the guitarist chiefly responsible for the early popularization of the electric guitar, and his clean, articulated lines were only made possible with the clarity and volume that such an amplified instrument offered. Christian's first explorations with the electric guitar came in 1937 after he'd seen **Eddie Durham** use one in Jimmie Lunceford's band of 1935, and Christian quickly acquired an electric Gibson model of his own.

By 1939 he had joined Benny Goodman's band, cutting among other pieces 'Solo Flight' with the Orchestra, 'Wholly Cats' with Goodman and Count Basie, 'Rose Room' with Goodman's sextet, and a timeless transposition of Hoagy Carmichael's 'Stardust'. Many of Christian's fascinating, groundbreaking Goodman recordings are highlighted on a compilation *The Genius Of The Electric Guitar*.

Tirelessly experimenting, Christian also worked with trumpeter Dizzy Gillespie and drummer Kenny Clarke, often at late night sessions at Minton's club where the seeds of bebop were being sown. A few poor quality recordings remain of these 1941 jams, including 'Swing To Bop', and they shed some light on Christian's pioneering zeal.

JOHN CIPOLLINA

Born: August 24th 1943, Berkeley, California, US. Died: May 29th 1989, San Francisco, California, US.

■ *Gibson SG; Carvin custom.*

Back in the late-1960s the only real conduit between what was going on in San Francisco's Bay-area and what was happening in London was through DJ John Peel's *Perfumed Garden* show on Radio London (a 'pirate' station broadcasting from a ship) and his column in the underground newspaper *International Times*. One of the most celebrated West Coast bands of the period, and heavily featured in Peel's output, was Quicksilver Messenger Service.

QMS were spearheaded by two guitarists, **Gary Duncan** and John Cipollina, and were at their best live. Therefore, like fellow Bay-area habitués The Grateful Dead, they never quite made it on record until they recorded the obligatory live album. For The Grateful Dead this didn't happen until 1971, but Quicksilver recognized their limitations in the studio sooner, and their second album, *Happy Trails*, was recorded live at The Avalon ballroom and The

Fillmore auditorium at the end of 1968. Among the tracks was a 12-minute workout on Bo Diddley's 'Who Do You Love?' with Cipollina's distinctive vibrato punctuating the rhythmic chording of Duncan. That it still sounds fresh more than 25 years later underlines the extent to which Cipollina's guitar work was central to the band's style.

In common with many Bay-area bands Quicksilver went through several personnel changes, with each change bringing an alteration to their style. By the end of 1970 Cipollina had left to form Copperhead, but after one album he moved to Britain and toured with the Welsh band Man in the mid-1970s. For the rest of his life he returned to the Bay-area and played sessions and in the clubs and bars, but his magic was never effectively recaptured on record.

ERIC CLAPTON

Born: March 30th 1945, Ripley, Surrey, England.

■ *Fender Telecaster; Gibson SG Standard; Gibson Les Paul Standard; Gibson ES335; Gibson Explorer; Fender Stratocaster; Fender 'signature'.*

Musically, at least, Clapton is one of the fortunate ones. His reputation precedes him and, while that reputation has sometimes been tarnished by ill-advised comments and excessive adulation, his guitar work has been a major influence on goodness knows how many axe-wielding youths.

Given that Clapton's career spans three decades, isolating specific examples of achievement is tricky. During his early years, Clapton demonstrated a grasp of the guitar's capabilities that had been the preserve of bluesmen like **BB King** and **Freddie King** and jazz players like **Charlie Christian**. On The Yardbirds' *Five Live Yardbirds* (1964) Clapton contextualized the blues for British audiences with lyrical, inventive solos on tracks like 'Five Long Years' and 'Good Morning Little Schoolgirl'.

After The Yardbirds Clapton joined what was to become the unofficial academy for aspiring musicians in the mid-1960s, **John Mayall**'s Bluesbreakers. The one album on which Clapton appeared, *Blues Breakers* (1965), has become a manual for students of blues-rock guitar, from the slow, thoughtful drama of 'Have You Heard?' to the delicate, up-tempo, single-note solo on Freddie King's 'Steppin' Out'.

After leaving Mayall, Clapton helped the rock era to maturity (or excess, depending on your point of view) by forming the first genuine supergroup with drummer Ginger Baker and bassist Jack Bruce. At the time, Cream were hyped ridiculously, but their significance rested not so much on the strength of Clapton's solos but more on their integration into the bright, tuneful epics of Bruce and lyricist Pete Brown. *Disraeli Gears* (1967), featuring 'Sunshine Of Your Love' and 'Tales Of Brave Ulysses' among others, was, because of Bruce's background in jazz, sufficiently structured to enable Clapton the room to improvise. This ability to improvise was juxtaposed on the double album *Wheels Of Fire* (1968). One section was recorded live at the Fillmore West, San Francisco, and featured an extended version of **Robert Johnson**'s 'Crossroads', where Clapton's

improvisational mastery overshadowed any emotional statement. The other part of *Wheels* was cut in the studio and included Bruce/Brown compositions such as 'White Room', which featured Clapton's eloquent, pithy phrasing, foreshadowing the stylistic concision that would be fully harnessed as his solo career got under way.

Clapton's solo work started hesitantly in 1969, but germinated with Derek & The Dominoes, which included **Duane Allman** in a celebrated cameo role on 'Layla'. Since then Clapton has achieved an unprecedented level of commercial acceptance that culminated with the winning of a clutch of Grammy awards in 1993. As is often the case, commercial acceptance does not necessarily coincide with the peak of artistic achievement. Clapton's guitar playing has seen some distinct changes in style: clean-cut in The Yardbirds, effects-mad in Cream and Blind Faith, a back-seat rhythm player with up-front fills in Delaney & Bonnie and The Dominoes, and a mature eclecticism in his solo work. However, there are those who would maintain that Clapton reached his creative pitch while still assessing the technical limitations of the guitar.

GENE CLARK

Born: November 17th 1941, Tipton, Missouri, US. Died: May 24th 1991.

One of the highpoints of Clark's career was a pair of albums (*The Fantastic Expedition Of Dillard & Clark* and *Through The Morning, Through The Night*, both 1969) that he recorded with banjoist Doug Dillard and which emphasized the strong bond between traditional folk music and bluegrass. The partnership, though short-lived, was adventurous in style, virtuosity and quality of writing, and became a benchmark for others to approximate.

Initially a member of The New Christy Minstrels, Clark joined The Byrds in 1964 and remained with them until 1966, during which time his distinctive vocals, rhythm guitar playing and arranging skills were central to the group's sound, while his songwriting (for example 'It Won't Be Wrong') was a cornerstone. Leaving the group with the excuse that he hated touring, Clark embarked upon an independent career, cutting albums like *Gene Clark With The Gosdin Brothers* (1967), *White Light* (1971), *Roadmaster* (1972), *No Other* (1974) and *So Rebellious A Lover* (with vocalist Carla Olson, 1987). Although Clark participated in various Byrds reunions along the way, these paled into insignificance in comparison with his solo work. He died in 1991 after a heart attack.

NEIL CLARK

Born: July 3rd 1955, Glasgow, Scotland.

■ *Gibson ES335; Fender Stratocaster.*

A founder member of Lloyd Cole's group The Commotions, Clark contributed the distinctive, melodic phrases that set the band apart as one of the best guitar-based outfits to emerge in the early-1980s. While Cole's lyrics can be pretentious ('She looks like Eva Marie-Saint in *On The Waterfront*...', no less) the

group foreshadowed the intelligent introspection of American bands such as REM and American Music Club, with 'Forest Fire' and 'Are You Ready To Be Heartbroken?', for example (both from *Rattlesnakes*, 1984), great pop songs with virtually impeccable playing. When the band split in 1988 Clark disappeared from view and Cole took up residence in New York.

ROY CLARK

Born: April 15th 1933, Meaherrin, Virginia, US.

■ *Gretsch; Gibson ES335; Ovation; Heritage 'signature'.*

Clark is probably best known as an ambassador for country music. His genial air made country palatable to a vast number of viewers of the *Hee Haw* television show of the mid-1960s which he co-hosted with country singer Buck Owens. One of the show's high points was when the Hee Haw Gospel Quartet, comprising Clark, Owens, fiddler Grandpa Jones and comedian Kenny Price sang to the accompaniment of Clark's guitar. That this came about was due to Clark's prowess as a guitarist and banjo player, which had been acclaimed after his stint with Wanda Jackson during the early-1960s.

While with Jackson, Clark contributed some of the meanest, leanest guitar work heard west of the Appalachians – try 'Mean, Mean Man' and 'Let's Have A Party' (1960). Unfortunately his spell with Jackson was cut short by his success as a solo performer, which meant that Clark's guitar work was supplanted by the anonymity of the Nashville Sound. More recently Clark teamed up with **Clarence 'Gatemouth' Brown** for *Makin' Music* (1976) and showed that he could still strut his stuff when the mood suited him. Shame he doesn't do it more often.

STEVE CLARK

Born: April 23rd 1960, Sheffield, Yorkshire, England. Died: January 8th 1991, London, England.

■ *Gibson Les Paul.*

Def Leppard blazed a trail at the very start of the 1980s for a brand of heavy metal that combined advanced technology with eminently hummable tunes. While much of the credit for their success has been attributed to producer Robert 'Mutt' Lange, guitarist Clark's compositional talents gave the group a body of material that set them apart from most of their contemporaries. His melodic, economical phrasing on songs like 'Photograph' and 'Rock Of Ages' complemented **Phil Collen**'s vibrato-laden work, and the album from which they came, *Pyromania* (1983), was one of the biggest sellers of all time.

EDDIE CLARKE

Born: October 5th 1950, England.

■ *Fender Stratocaster; Gibson Les Paul.*

As a member of the power trio Motorhead, which left Cream looking as if they were having a tea party, ex-Curtis Knight guitarist 'Fast' Eddie Clarke's lack of sophistication and his total indifference to rock

Cle-Col

clichés was a vital fillip to the burgeoning heavy metal trend of the late-1970s and early-1980s. What he lacked in imagination was compensated for by a visceral enthusiasm: 'Bomber' and 'St Valentine's Day Massacre' are fine examples of the flying fingers of Fast Eddie... and of heavy metal at its most basic. Perhaps the band gave themselves away when they cut The Kingsmen's 'Louie, Louie', one of rock's great non-songs, rendering all the intellectual pontifications about rock music redundant. Fast Eddie is one of the old school and should be rated alongside **Mick Green** and **Fred Smith**.

ZEKE CLEMENTS

Born: September 9th 1911, Warrior, Alabama, US.

A good entertainer and a passable guitarist, Clements has sustained a long career on the fringes of country music. He made his debut on the *National Barn Dance* radio show in 1928, which was followed by a stint with vocalist Otto Gray's Oklahoma Cowboys. During the 1940s Clements made many radio broadcasts and in 1945 he co-wrote and recorded 'Smoke On The Water', which was covered by western swing mainman Bob Wills and country vocalist Red Foley. In later years Clements appeared on the *Louisiana Hayride* shows, before moving to Florida in the mid-1960s where he played banjo in a Dixieland jazz band. He still appears on the *Grand Ole Opry* country broadcasts in the US.

ZAL CLEMINSON

Born: May 4th 1949, Glasgow, Scotland.

■ *Gibson SG.*

Cleminson had been a member of a minor league Scottish band called Tear Gas when in the early-1970s he was appointed guitarist for the late Alex Harvey in his Sensational Alex Harvey Band. Cleminson became the foil for Harvey in much the same way as **Mick Ronson** was for David Bowie.

Harvey had built his career from the late-1950s throughout Britain and Europe, purveying a brash form of R&B interspersed with witty rejoinders. By the early-1970s Harvey's unfussy approach to live performances and his pithy, anecdotal narratives detailing the seamy side of life had started to pick up a substantial following on the burgeoning British college circuit. His ability to milk a crowd for all it was worth was artfully combined with Cleminson's knack for skilfully deploying a range of guitar styles, enabling the band to use an extensive palette of musical references from Jacques Brel to Leiber & Stoller (try *Framed* from 1972). After the group disbanded, Cleminson went on to join Nazareth in 1978, cutting *No Mean City*, which showed his affinity for heavy metal. Latterly he has played sessions.

DAVE CLEMPSON

Born: September 5th 1946, London, England.

■ *Fender Stratocaster; Fender Telecaster.*

'Clem' Clempson has for over 25 years been one of the stalwarts of the British R&B and sessions circuit.

Initially a member of Bakerloo, a small blues band which used to play the London club circuit towards the end of the 1960s, Clempson was enlisted to replace James Litherland in the pioneering jazz-rock band Colosseum in 1971.

With Colosseum, Clempson's abrasive, bluesy style antagonized some of the band's followers who found him too rock oriented, but on reflection Clempson's playing seemed to provide more of a complement to Dick Heckstall-Smith's earthy horn solos than had Litherland's understated noodlings.

Upon leaving Colosseum, Clempson joined Humble Pie as **Peter Frampton**'s replacement. In tandem with **Steve Marriott** Clempson's style went down a storm in the US where Pie became massively popular on the college circuit. Assisted in no small way by the contemporaneous trend for boogie bands like Lynyrd Skynyrd and The Marshall Tucker Band, albums such as *Smokin'* (1972) and *Eat It* (1973) were good examples of the hard rock style that would later inspire guitarists like **Eddie Van Halen** and **Mick Mars** to take up their axes. By 1976 Clempson had joined ex-Uriah Heep vocalist David Byron's Rough Diamond before hitting the session circuit.

KURT COBAIN

Born: February 20th 1967, Seattle, Washington, US.

■ *Fender Stratocaster; Fender Jaguar; Univox Hi-flier.*

Despite his snarling, mannered vocals, Cobain's guitar work has been pivotal in the development of what has been dubbed grunge. While his group Nirvana's output has been minimal, pieces like 'Smells Like Teen Spirit' and 'Come As You Are' (1991) have a visceral urgency that has underpinned the energy of grunge with a deceptively melodic quality that was seldom evident in punk. Cobain and the rest of the band have tried to become vocal champions of a rightfully disenchanted generation, and have encouraged other bands like Alice In Chains, PJ Harvey and Smashing Pumpkins.

JAMES R COBB

Born: February 5th 1944, Birmingham, Alabama, US.

■ *Gibson Les Paul; Fender Stratocaster.*

Formerly a member of Classics IV who contributed such epics as 'Spooky' and 'Stormy' in 1968, Cobb became the linchpin of The Atlanta Rhythm Section in 1972. In this new incarnation the group had metamorphosed into a southern boogie band, with hints of The Allman Brothers. Sadly, Cobb was no **Duane Allman** and it was all rather tame, lacking fire. However, songs like 'So Into You' and 'Imaginary Lover' had some charm, but so far as the plank-spanking department was concerned they should have recruited someone with a little more abandonment.

EDDIE COCHRAN

Born: October 3rd 1938, Albert Lea, Minnesota.
Died: April 17th 1960, Bristol, Avon, England.

■ *Gretsch 6120.*

One of the most accomplished guitarists of the rock'n'roll era, Cochran's early death terminated a career that would surely have made him even more influential as a guitar stylist.

Cochran started as a session musician until he was given a cameo spot in the Frank Tashlin film satire of the entertainment industry *The Girl Can't Help It*, during which Cochran played 'Twenty Flight Rock'. This generated a recording contract with Liberty, for whom he cut a string of fine singles including 'Summertime Blues' (1958), 'C'mon Everybody' (1959) and 'Somethin' Else' (1959). Cochran's ability to adapt to rockabilly, country and urban blues indicated a talent at odds with the contemporary trend among most pop stars to be complete ignoramuses once they got into the recording studio. His moody James Dean-like image caused many to overstress his looks and conveniently to overlook the fact that, like **Buddy Holly**, Cochran was not dependent on vast numbers of session musicians, writers or technicians to help him cut fine records.

DENNIS COFFEY

Born: November 11th 1940, Detroit, Michigan, US.

■ *Gibson Firebird; Gibson ES345.*

Coffey recorded regularly under his own name, accompanied by The Detroit Guitar Band, and scored hits with 'Scorpio' (1971) and 'Taurus'. But it's his muscular guitar work on a series of singles by The Temptations, including 'Cloud Nine' (1969), 'Runaway Child, Running Wild' (1969) and 'Papa Was A Rolling Stone' (1972), that proved an object lesson in how black music could assimilate rock influences without sacrificing any integrity.

Produced by Norman Whitfield, these elaborately arranged songs showed that rock had something to give back to black music... which was only fair, considering that it had pillaged black culture since the year dot.

DAVID COHEN

See DAVID BLUE

B J COLE

Born: England.

■ *Emmons.*

Cole seems to have been one of the few British musicians to master the steel guitar, and as a result has played sessions for any number of artists ranging from country funster Hank Wangford through to Procol Harum. In the late-1960s, as country-rock gained currency, Cole formed Cochise, who were signed by A&R man Andrew Lauder to United Artists. This group, like Clover and Brinsley Schwarz, sank without a trace, but they enabled Cole to establish himself as *the* pedal-steel guitarist. In recent years, after establishing his own Cow Pie label, he cut the excellent *Airmail* with multi-instrumentalist Wes McGhee, and has shown a keen interest in the musical possibilities of linking the pedal-steel guitar with the synthesizer.

CROPPER'S GUITARS Many country and R&B players have, like Steve Cropper, chosen Fender's Telecaster model. The Tele was launched in 1950 as the Broadcaster, the world's first commercially successful solidbody electric guitar, and is still made today. Its cutting treble and glassy tone have an ability to cut through surrounding instrumentation in most stage and studio situations.

JAMMED TOGETHER (Released 1969) *Tracks:* What'd I Say/Opus De Soul/Big Bird/Trashy Dog/Water/Tupelo/Baby What Do You Want Me To Do/Homer's Theme/Don't Turn Your Heater Down/Knock On Wood. An impressive collaboration between Cropper, Albert King and 'Pop' Staples of The Staple Singers, with Cropper's lean, crisp lines complementing the fiery chops of King and the bluesy languor of Staples. It is indicative of Cropper's low-key attitude, or perhaps of his incredible workload at the time, that collaborations such as this have been few and far between. In any case, both King and Staples were figures from a different era and it is debatable how much they had in common with Cropper.

WITH A LITTLE HELP FROM MY FRIENDS (Released 1971) *Tracks:* Crop Dustin'/The Land Of A Thousand Dances/99 And A Half (Won't Do)/Boogaloo Down Broadway/Funky Broadway/With A Little Help From My Friends/Oh Pretty Woman/I'd Rather Drink Muddy Water/The Way I Feel Tonight/In The Midnight Hour/Rattlesnake. Cropper's first solo album highlights the economy of his playing, and it's rare for a solo album by a guitarist to be so short on flamboyant flourishes. Indeed, this is so tasteful that on occasions a bit of vulgarity would come as a pleasant shock to the system.

NIGHT AFTER NIGHT (Released 1982) Cropper's second and third solo albums, despite including stellar session men such as Dan Ferguson, David Paitch, Jack Hale and Bill Payne (*Playin' My Thang*) and Barry Beckett, David Hood, Roger Hawkins, Burton Cummings and Jimmy Johnson (*Night After Night*), undeservedly sank without trace.

SESSIONS/PRODUCTIONS

Not including Cropper's early 1960s Stax work – see right.
- 1969 MITCH RYDER *The Detroit-Memphis Experiment* (guitar)
- 1972 JEFF BECK *The Jeff Beck Group* (producer)
- 1972 JOSE FELICIANO *Compartments* (producer)
- 1975 ROD STEWART *Atlantic Crossing* (guitar/co-producer)
  YVONNE ELLIMAN *Rising Sun* (producer)
  JOHN PRINE *Common Sense* (producer)
- 1976 STEPHEN BISHOP *Careless* (guitar)
  LYDIA PENSE & COLD BLOOD (producer)
- 1977 ROY BUCHANAN *Loading Zone* (guitar)

| 1961 | 1962 | 1963 | 1964 | 1965 | 1966 | 1967 | 1968 | 1969 | 1970 | 1971 | 1972 | 1973 | 1974 | 1975 | 1976 |

One afternoon in the summer of 1962, Booker T Jones (keyboards), Steve Cropper (guitar), Lewis Steinberg (bass) and Al Jackson Jr (drums) were in the studio of Stax Records, where they were the house band, waiting to record backing for a jingle. When the singer failed to turn up, they started jamming and ended by recording two instrumentals, 'Behave Yourself' and 'Green Onions'. Stax co-owner Jim Stewart liked what he heard and decided to put out a record, naming the band 'Booker T & The MGs'; and with 'Behave Yourself' as the A-side. Local radio stations immediately flipped the disc over and 'Green Onions' became a massive hit. This was the start of a

long recording career for Booker T & The MGs. An album, *Green Onions*, was quickly thrown together and released the same year. Like most of their recorded output it mixed original instrumentals with unlikely versions of some of the cheesier hits of the day, for instance Acker Bilk's clarinet tune 'Stranger On The Shore'.

BOOKER T: MO' ONIONS (Released 1963) The recording career of the MGs always had to take second place to their duties as a studio band turning out hit after hit for the vocal stars of the Stax label. A second album, with the imaginative title Mo' Onions, was released in 1963, bringing them modest

r'n'b interest in such tunes such as 'Jelly Bread' and 'Chinese Checkers' alongside the usual cover versions: the truth is that in the early 1960s soul and r'n'b (like pop generally) were all about singles. Albums were very much an afterthought.

BOOKER T: SOUL DRESSING (Released 1964)
In 1964, a major change took place when the black bassist Lewis Steinberg was replaced by Steve Cropper's high school friend and fellow Royal Spade Donald 'Duck' Dunn. Thus the perfect integrated image was created: two black, two white. The album spawned a modestly successful single of the same

name, but nothing more. Slightly more success attended 1965's efforts. The single 'Boot-Leg' was a hit on the r'n'b chart, scraping into the pop charts at number 58. 'My Sweet Potato', from the 1965 album of a similar name, reached only number 18 on the r'n'b chart, failing to make an impact on the general pop audience. A spate of further albums followed, until in 1967 the first signs of a revival of interest started to appear. 'Hip Hug-Her' pointed the way, and 'Groovin' stopped just short of the Billboard pop top 20.

BOOKER T: SOUL LIMBO (Released 1968) At last the necessity to record their own originals had started to

WHITE RABBIT (Released 1971) *Tracks:* White Rabbit/ Theme From The Summer Of '42/ Little Train/ California Dreamin'/ El Mar. *Line-up:* George Benson, Jay Berliner and Earl Klugh (guitars), Herbie Hancock (piano), Ron Carter (bass), Phil Krause (vibes/percussion), Airto Moreira (percussion), Billy Cobham. Benson mixes with the reigning giants of jazz-rock fusion.

BEYOND THE BLUE HORIZON (Released 1971) *Tracks:* So What/ The Gentle Rain/ All Clear/ Ode To A Kudu/ Somewhere In The East. *Line-up:* George Benson (guitar), Clarence Palmer (organ), Ron Carter (bass), Jack DeJohnette (drums) and Michael Cameron and Albert Nicholson (percussion).

THE OTHER SIDE OF ABBEY ROAD (Released 1970) *Tracks:* Come Together/ Something/ Maxwell's Silver Hammer/ Oh! Darling/ Octopus's Garden/ I Want You (She's So Heavy)/ Here Comes The Sun/ Because/ You Never Give Me Your Money/ Sun King/ Mean Mr Mustard/ Polythene Pam/ She Came In Through The Bathroom Window/ Golden Slumbers/ Carry That Weight/ The End/ Her Majesty. His Beatles tribute: compare that by Booker T & The MGs.

BODY TALK (Released 1972) *Tracks:* Dance/ When Love Has Grown/ Plum/ Body Talk/ Top Of The World. Line-up including: George Benson and Earl Klugh (guitars); Ron Carter and Gary King (bass); Harold Mabern (piano); Jack DeJohnette (drums); Mobutu (percussion).

BAD BENSON (Released 1974) *Tracks:* Take Five/ Summer Wishes, Winter Dreams/ My Latin Brother/ No Sooner Said Than Done/ Full Compass/ The Changing World. *Line-up:* George Benson (guitar); Phil Upchurch (guitar and bass); Kenny Barron (piano); Ron Carter (bass); Steve Gadd (drums). During Benson's tenure with the CTI label and producer Creed Taylor, he cranked out a steady stream of albums that maintained a level of consistency that accorded with CTI's status as the principal outlet for jazz funk. This is one of the best Benson albums of the early 1970s with another phenomenal cast of supporting players making sure he could do no wrong at this stage in his career.

BENSON & FARRELL (Released 1976) *Tracks:* Flute Song/ Beyond The Ozone/ Camel Hump/ Old Devil Moon. Duets between Benson and soprano saxophonist/flautist Joe Farrell make for one of the most striking collaborations of an era when jazz was being infiltrated by funk.

BLUE BENSON (Released 1976) *Tracks:* Billie's Bounce/ Low Down & Dirty/ That Lucky Old Sun/ Doobie, Doobie Blues/ What's New/ I Remember Wes. Featuring Clark Terry (trumpet), Herbie Hancock (keyboards), Ron Carter (bass) and Billy Cobham (drums), Blue Benson illustrates George's supposed debt to Wes Montgomery more accurately than anything else he has done.

BREEZIN' (Released 1976) *Tracks:* Breezin'/ This Masquerade/ Six To Four/ Affirmation/ So This Is Love/ Lady. Breezin' was a landmark album in more ways than one: not only did it place George Benson in view as an innovative and versatile performer, but it also re-affirmed the commercial potential of jazz, nabbing a fistful of Grammy awards and staying at the top of the US album charts for an age. Furthermore, it opened up fresh vistas for Benson as a vocalist; while this was to his detriment, ultimately, as most thought of him as a vocalist rather than a guitarist, it didn't stop him from getting backing for such projects as his Big Boss Band.

GOOD KING BAD (Released 1973) *Tracks:* Good King Bad/ One Rock Don't Make No Boulder/ 'Em/ Cast Your Fate To The Wind/ Siberian Workout/ Shell Of A Man. *Line-up:* George Benson and Eric Gale (guitars); Roland Hanna (piano); Don Grolnick (keyboards/clarinet); Bobby Lyle and Ronnie Foster (keyboards); Randy Brecker (trumpet); Michael Brecker (tenor sax); David Sanborn (alto sax); Ronnie Cuber (baritone sax); Fred Wesley (trombone); Joe Farrell (flute); Gary King (bass); Dennis Davis, Steve Gadd and Andy Newmark (drums); Sue Evans (percussion); David Friedman (vibes and percussion).

IN CONCERT AT CARNEGIE HALL (Released 1975) *Tracks:* Gone/ Take Five/ Octane/ Summertime. *Line-up:* George Benson (guitar); Hubert Laws (flute); Ronnie Foster (keyboards); Wayne Dockery and Will Lee (bass); Steve Gadd, Marvin Chappell and Andy Newmark (drums); Ray Armando and Johnny Griggs (percussion). Following hot on the heels of Benson's emergence into the mainstream with his first chart hit, 'Supership', this live album, featuring extended improvised work-outs, spanned the gap between his attempts to cross over and his role as a major jazz guitar stylist.

IN FLIGHT (Released 1977) *Tracks:* Nature Boy/ The Wind And I/ The World Is A Ghetto/ Gonna Love You More/ Valdez In The Country/ Everything Must Change. While any follow-up would have a job on its hands in matching the success of *Breezin'*, *In Flight* made a good attempt. Deceptively lightweight in character, Benson's lyrical guitar work and vocals made Nat 'King' Cole sound overwrought.

WEEKEND IN LA (Released 1978) *Tracks:* The Greatest Love Of All/ Down Here On The Ground/ Ode To A Kudu/ We As Love/ California P.M./ Lady Blue/ We All Remember Wes/ On Broadway/ It's All In The Game/ Weekend In L.A. Lithe and lissom, Benson romps through a sampling of choice material from all aspects of his career. This was the first time 'The Greatest Love Of All' had been performed on a George Benson album, as it was originally recorded for the soundtrack of *The Greatest*, the film biography of Muhammad Ali.

LIVIN' INSIDE YOUR LOVE (Released 1979) *Tracks:* Before You Go/ Welcome Into My World/ Love Is A Hurting Thing/ You're Never Too Far From Me/ Love Ballad/ A Change Is Gonna Come/ Prelude To Fall/ Soulful Strut/ Nassau Day/ Hey Girl. Asserting his individualism as a vocalist, with *Livin' Inside Your Love* Benson also showed his ability to play down his guitar work without any loss of quality. Although critics denigrated him for allowing his guitar work to play second fiddle to his vocals, the homogeneity of the project gave him a peerless position in contemporary US music.

George Benson

George Benson was a precocious talent who led his own rhythm and blues band in his mid-teens. He discovered jazz some years later, but from that point on he began the process of building a reputation as a jazz player, in bands and under his own name. But any discussion of George Benson's career is always going to have to deal with the apparent contradiction between his role as an acclaimed jazz guitarist and his other, more recent, life as a purveyor of smooth vocal ballads. In fact, each complements the other: the most obvious corollary is the career of Nat 'King' Cole, whose piano playing in the late 1940 was transmuted into a vocal style that was as genuine as it was approachable. So it is with Benson. He started out as a hard bop guitarist, playing with tremendous drive and a hard tone, but with a soulful approach and character. Since then, his approach to music hasn't changed: he hasn't sold out.

He may no longer be seen as an out-and-out jazz player, the natural heir of Wes Montgomery, but he has simply adapted his methods to a wider canvas, and with that adaptation different values have come into effect. More significantly, the change has enabled Benson to draw in a wider audience. But audiences are creatures of habit and tend to be set in their ways. Those who like his vocal work are not interested in his guitar playing, and vice versa. This, of course, is a matter of taste, but critical evaluation is inclined to be at least as partisan. Since Benson started his career as a vocalist, albums such as Collaboration (with Earl Klugh) and Big Boss Band (with the Count Basie Orchestra) have been given short shrift by those who should know better. Benson remains a major stylist, able to compete with the finest vocalists as well as the best guitarists.

LIVE WITH BROTHER JACK McDUFF (Released 1963)
George Benson joined McDuff's swing and blues band in 1962 when he was just 19 years old. It was his jazz debut: by that time he had already recorded 'It Shoulda Been Me' and 'She Makes Me Mad' in a rhythm & blues vein for RCA's Groove label. Today these mono recordings sound a little thin, thanks to unsympathetic repackaging as a poor version of "stereo"

THE NEW BOSS GUITAR OF GEORGE BENSON (Released 1964)
Tracks: The Shadow Dancers/ The Sweet Alice Blues/ I Don't Know/ Just Another Sunday/ Will You Still Be Mine/ Easy Living/ Rock A Bye.
One of George Benson's earliest solo offerings, in the company of Jack McDuff, who had spotted Benson's precocity and given him an opportunity as a sideman. George was never happy with his early recordings.

HOT BARBECUE (Released 1965)
Tracks: Hot Barbecue/ The Party's Over/ Briar Patch/ Hippy Dip/ 601 Poplar/ Cry Me A River/ The Three Day Thang.
Another session with Jack McDuff, which provided Benson with the opportunity to make that quantum leap from being a session man to a solo performer. In his days as a guitar specialist, Benson aimed at the type of harmonic awareness more associated with the piano.

1962 1963 1964 1965 1966 1967 1968 1969 1970 1971 1972

IT'S UPTOWN (Released 1966)
Tracks: Clockwise/ Summertime/ Ain't That Peculiar/ Jaguar/ Willow Weep For Me/ A Foggy Day In London Town/ Hello Birdie/ Bullfight/ Stormy Weather/ Eternally/ Myna Bird Blues.

BENSON BURNER (Released 1966)

GEORGE BENSON COOKBOOK (Released 1966)
Tracks: The Cooker/ Benny's Back/ Bossa Rocka/ All Of Me/ Big Fat Lady/ Benson's Rider/ Ready And Able/ The Borgia Stick/ The Return Of The Prodigal Son/ Jumpin' With Symphony Sid.

This trio of albums was recorded while Wes Montgomery, George Benson's role model, was still alive. Although they illustrate the extent of Montgomery's influence, they demonstrate Benson's prodigious grasp of technique: readings of standards like 'Stormy Weather' are executed with touching eloquence and style, while original material such as 'The Cooker' possesses an ebullient verve. Produced by John Hammond at Columbia, this has always been a notable album for Benson, although he complains that he was unprepared for its jazz direction, having been increasingly tending towards a rockier style of presentation.

GIBLET GRAVY (Released 1967)
Tracks: Billie's Bounce/ Low Down And Dirty/ Thunder Walk/ Doobie Doobie Blues/ What's New/ I Remember Wes/ Windmills Of Your Mind/ Song For My Father/ Carnival Joys/ Giblet Gravy/ Walk On By/ Sack O'Woe/ Groovin'.

The above tracks were formerly available on the albums listed here, but have since been compiled on to *The Silver Collection* (1985); more significantly, they were Benson's early sessions with producer Creed Taylor, who, after leaving the Verve label, took Benson with him to A&M.

THE SHAPE OF THINGS TO COME
(Released 1968) *Tracks:* Footin' It/ Face It Boy, It's Over/ The Shape Of Things That Are And Were/ Chattanooga Choo Choo/ Don't Let Me Lose This Dream/ Last Train To Clarksville.

TELL IT LIKE IT IS (Released 1968)
George Benson's two initial outings for A&M were unashamedly populist in their choice of material (The Monkees' 'Last Train To Clarksville', for instance, and Aaron Neville's 'Tell It Like It Is'), offering a glimpse of the path he would later pursue with *Breezin'* and subsequent albums.

Steve Cropper had his first hit, 'Last Night', in 1961, as a member of the Mar-Keys. An engineering student by day, he had taken his high school group, the Royal Spades, and transformed it into the best white r'n'b outfit in Memphis, adopting a more sensible name in the process. The Mar-Keys became the first house band of Stax Records. Then, while the Mar-Keys went touring with the first Stax artists, Cropper joined a trio of black musicians, led by 16-year-old organist Booker T Jones, to create a new studio band. In 1962, they filled a slack hour by creating the timeless instrumental hit 'Green Onions'. Attributed to Booker T & The MGs, it launched their own recording career, but for Cropper that would always have to take second place to writing and recording hits for the Stax artists. His contribution to the Stax sound cannot be overestimated. Not only did he play guitar on most of the Otis Redding sessions, he also produced and co-wrote many of Redding's finest records, including 'Dock Of The Bay', not to mention Wilson Pickett's 'In The Midnight Hour' and Eddie Floyd's 'Knock On Wood'. Cropper left Stax and the MGs in 1971, and set up his own studio and production company, with no great success. Later he moved to Los Angeles, playing sessions, and even reformed Booker T & The MGs for a tour and album in 1977. But he found his biggest new audience with the success of the film The Blues Brothers, in which he joined MGs bassist Duck Dunn in the band backing comedians John Belushi and Dan Aykroyd. A group was formed to capitalize on the success and enjoyed a hit with 'Everybody Needs Somebody To Love'. Subsequently, Booker T & The MGs have reformed for tours, most recently backing Neil Young in his 1993 concerts.

THE BLUES BROTHERS Original Soundtrack (Released 1980)
Tracks: Shake A Tail Feather/Think/ Minnie The Moocher/Rawhide/ Everybody Needs Somebody To Love/ Jailhouse Rock/She Caught Them Katy/ Gimme Some Lovin'/Old Landmark/ Sweet Home Chicago/Peter Gunn.

BLUES BROTHERS: MADE IN AMERICA (Released 1981)
Tracks: Soul Finger/Funky Broadway/ Who's Makin' Love/Do You Love Me/ Guilty/Perry Mason Theme/Riot In Cell Block 9/Green Onions/I Ain't Got You/ From The Bottom/Goin' To Miami.

BLUES BROTHERS: BRIEFCASE FULL OF BLUES (Released 1981)
Tracks: I Can't Turn You Loose/Hey Bartender/Messin' With The Kid/ I Got Everything I Need/Shotgun Blues/ Rubber Biscuit/Groove Me/Soul Man/ Flip, Flop & Fly/B-Movie Boxcar Blues.

| 77 | 1978 | 1979 | 1980 | 1981 | 1982 | 1983 | 1984 | 1985 | 1986 | 1987 | 1988 | 1989 | 1990 | 1991 | 1992 | 1993 |

become apparent. From this point, although the cover versions were still there, a higher proportion of the group's recorded output was devoted to new material. And it paid off. This album alone produced two hits which are still heard today, 'Soul Limbo' and 'Hang 'Em High', the latter the group's first top ten pop hit since 'Green Onions'.

BOOKER T: UPTIGHT (Released 1968) This album marked a departure, being Booker T & The MGs' first movie soundtrack recording. Indeed, the movie apparently featured Jones's singing voice for the first time, an experiment not often repeated. But the job gave the group the second-biggest hit of

their career, with 'Time Is Tight', a worthy successor at last to 'Green Onions'. Further albums followed, but success was elusive. They include *Time Is Tight*, their first Greatest Hits collection (released 1969) and *McClemore Avenue* (released 1970), a bizarre cover version of the Beatles' entire Abbey Road album. Booker T Jones himself left before 1971's *Melting Pot*, and Cropper left immediately thereafter.

BOOKER T: UNIVERSAL LANGUAGE (Released 1977)
Tracks: Sticky Stuff/Grab Bag/Space Nuts/Love Wheels/Moto Cross/Last Tango In Memphis/MGs' Salsa/Tie

Stick/Reincarnation. After Booker T and Cropper left, Dunn and Jackson tried to keep the group together, recruiting replacements. But in 1975 Jackson was murdered and that seemed to be that. Then, in 1977, Jones, Cropper and Dunn re-united, bringing in another long-term associate, Willie Hall, as drummer. They cut this album and appeared on the 25th anniversary of *American Bandstand*.

BOOKER T: I WANT YOU (Released 1981) After *Universal Language*, the Jones/Cropper/Hall/Dunn version of the MGs reverted to their solo careers. Then, in 1981, they tried a belated second album, but the magic was long gone.

BEST OF BOOKER T & THE MGs (Released 1984) *Tracks:* Green Onions/ Slim Jenkins' Place/Hip Hug-Her/Soul Dressing/Summertime/Boot-Leg/ Jellybread/Tic-Tac-Toe/Can't Be Still/ Groovin'/Mo' Onions/Red Beans And Rice. The second hits collection: you need both for completeness.

GIVE ME THE NIGHT (Released 1980) *Tracks:* Love X Love/ Off Broadway/ Moody's Mood/ Give Me The Night/ What's On Your Mind/ Dinorah, Dinorah/ Love Dance/ Star Of A Story/ Midnight Love Affair/ Turn Out The Lamplight. Confirming Benson's pre-eminence among vocalists, the title track 'Give Me The Night' became a monster hit thanks to Quincy Jones's lush production. While the album won him precious few fans among the jazz fraternity, it was a sleight-of-hand affair, with his guitar work achieving dazzling heights; it also picked up a slew of Grammy awards the following year. His vocal prowess reached new heights in a duet with Aretha Franklin on 'Love All The Hurt Away'.

BENSON'S GUITARS Having previously used Gibson, Guild and D'Angelico guitars, Benson settled on an Ibanez 'signature' model, based on the Gibson ES175.

COLLABORATION (Released 1987) *Tracks:* Mount Airy Road/ Mimosa/ Brazillian Stomp/ Dreamin'/ Since You're Gone/ Collaboration/ Romeo And Juliet Love Theme. Featuring the Spanish guitar jazzer Earl Klugh, this was the album that re-established Benson's credentials with jazz audiences and guitar enthusiasts alike.

TENDERLY (Released 1989) *Tracks:* You Don't Know What Love Is/ Stella By Starlight/ Stardust/ At The Mambo Inn/ Here, There And Everywhere/ This All I Ask/ Tenderly/ I Could Write A Book. Luscious arrangements of jazz standards and show-tunes, faultlessly played. A look back to the early days of his career as a big band jazz player.

BIG BOSS BAND (Released 1990) *Tracks:* Without A Song/ How Do You Keep The Music Playing?/ Baby Workout/ Portrait Of Jennie/ Skylark/ Ready Now That You Are/ On Green Dolphin Street/ I Only Have Eyes For You/ Walkin' My Baby Back Home/ Basie's Rag. Featuring the Count Basie Orchestra.

1984	1985	1986	1987	1988	1989	1990	1991	1992	1993

20/20 (Released 1985) *Tracks:* No One Emotion/ Please Don't Walk Away/ I Just Wanna Hang Around You/ Nothing's Gonna Change My Love For You/ Beyond The Sea (La Mer)/ New Day/ You Are The Love Of My Life/ Stand Up/ 20/20/ Shark Bite.

LOVE REMEMBERS (Released 1993) *Tracks:* I'll Be Good To You/ Got To Be There/ My Heart Is Dancing/ Love Of My Life/ Kiss And Makeup/ Come Into My World/ Love Remembers/ Willing To Fight/ Somewhere Island/ Lovin' On Borrowed Time/ Lost In Love/ Calling You. *Line-up:* George Benson and Wah Wah Watson (guitar); David Gamson and Richard Tee (keyboards); William Bryant (electric piano); Abraham Laboriel (bass); Leon 'Ndugu' Chancler (drums); Bill Summers (percussion); Randy Brecker (trumpet). Benson's most recent album at the time of going to press includes the usual excellent cast of musicians.

IN YOUR EYES (Released 1983) *Tracks:* Feel Like Makin' Love/ Inside Love (So Personal)/ Lady Love Me (One More Time/ Love Will Come Again/ In Your Eyes/ Never Too Far To Fall/ Being With You/ Use Me/ Late At Night/ In Search Of A Dream. Produced by Arif Mardin, the great Atlantic soul producer, who had worked with the Bee Gees, Aretha Franklin and Roberta Flack, among others. In other words, a fine example of slick arrangement and faultless production. As a consequence, the single 'Being With You' won a Grammy for Best Pop Instrumental Performance. This became one of George Benson's most successful albums in the UK.

WHILE THE CITY SLEEPS (Released 1986) *Tracks:* Shiver/ Love Is Here Tonight/ Teaser/ Secrets In The Night/ Too Many Times/ Did You Hear The Thunder/ While The City Sleeps/ Kisses In The Moonlight. Although these two albums did little to enhance Benson's reputation, they consolidated his fan-base among soul audiences, making him one of the most significant crossover artists of the 1980s. *While The City Sleeps* was produced by Narada Michael Walden, who started his career playing drums with John McLaughlin, Jeff Beck, Herbie Hancock and Weather Report before turning to production and working with Whitney Houston, Aretha Franklin, Natalie Cole and the Four Tops, to great commercial success.

TWICE THE LOVE (Released 1988) *Tracks:* Twice The Love/ Starting All Over/ Good Habit/ Everybody Does It/ Living On Borrowed Love/ Let's Do It Again/ Stephanie/ Tender Love/ You're Still My Baby/ Until You Believe. A bit of a curiosity this one, as Benson was in the middle of re-establishing his reputation as a serious jazz musician. This album was recorded to appease the insatiable appetite of the recently acquired crossover audience, who weren't interested in following Benson back into jazz. By comparison with earlier albums such as *Collaboration*, and its follow-up *Tenderly*, it is undeniably thin stuff.

Col-Coo

PHIL COLLEN

Born: December 8th 1957, London, England.

■ *Jackson 'signature'; Kramer; Ibanez; Fender Stratocaster.*

When **Pete Willis** was fired from Def Leppard in 1983, Collen was drafted in from the metal band Girl. During Collen's stay in that group, a lack of strong material had meant that he had never been pushed to his limits. In tandem with **Steve Clark** in Leppard, however, Collen brought a veneer of brash sophistication to the group's sound that producer 'Mutt' Lange was quick to exploit. While Collen played on some sessions that produced *Pyromania* (1983) it was not until they recorded *Hysteria* (1987) that, after several years of solid touring, he showed the extent of his abilities. Not only did Collen complement Clark's guitar work, but he also showed a compositional flair, nurtured by Lange.

ALBERT COLLINS

Born: October 1st 1932, Leona, Texas, US.
Died: November 24th 1993.

■ *Fender Telecaster; Fender 'signature'.*

Taught the guitar by his cousin **Lightnin' Hopkins**, Collins like many other Texans demonstrated an ability to synthesize many indigenous elements into his own style, made more unusual by use of an open minor tuning and high capo positions. His solos regularly sent shivers up the listener's spine, causing him to be described as the 'cold blues' player. One of his finest moments was *Showdown* (1985) with **Johnny Copeland** and **Robert Cray**, which showed both sides of his personality: the bluesman trading chops with a fellow Texan, the ghost of **T-Bone Walker** never far away; and the neo-traditionalist sparring with the flowing inventiveness of former sideman Cray. Collins' great strength was that he seemed closer to his roots than most, playing what he wanted rather than what he thought audiences wanted.

ALLEN COLLINS

Born: July 19th 1952, Jacksonville, Florida, US.
Died: January 23rd 1990, Jacksonville, Florida, US.

■ *Gibson Explorer.*

As founder member of one of the most successful southern boogie bands, Lynyrd Skynyrd, Collins in partnership with **Gary Rossington** and **Ed King** formed Skynyrd's triple-guitar attack. The group's material – including the breakneck guitar battling of 'Freebird', dedicated to **Duane Allman**, and the bluesy lyricism of 'Sweet Home Alabama' – exemplified the insular attitude prevalent in many Southern bands in the 1970s, such as The Allman Brothers, Marshall Tucker, Charlie Daniels and Wet Willie. Pride in the South's heritage was certainly a part, and the traditions were uniquely Southern in character, as typified by Skynyrd's 'Freebird', which echoed the duelling banjo/guitar duets of **Lester Flatt** and Earl Scruggs. Having survived the plane crash of 1977 which decimated the group, Collins and Rossington formed the successful Rossington-Collins

Band, but Collins' career ended in 1986 when he was paralyzed in a car accident.

EDWYN COLLINS

Born: Scotland.

■ *Fender Stratocaster; Fender Telecaster; Gretsch Blackhawk.*

Orange Juice were formed in the late-1970s, with Collins leading the way with his wistful vocals and acute guitar work. The group's pop sensibility, heard on songs like 'Blue Boy', 'Falling And Laughing', 'Rip It Up' and 'What Presence?' was counter-productive, as the group did not appear to be taken as seriously as they should have been. This was confirmed by albums such as *You Can't Hide Your Love Forever* and *Rip It Up* (1982), *Ostrich Churchyard* (1992) and *The Heather's On Fire* (1993). Accomplished and witty, like **Roddy Frame**'s Aztec Camera they are too good for their own good.

JOHN COLLINS

Born: John Elbert Collins, September 20th 1913, Montgomery, Alabama, US.

■ *D'Angelico; Gibson L5CES.*

Yet another underrated guitarist whose talents were constantly overshadowed by those whom he was backing, Collins' eloquent phrasing graced sessions with Art Tatum and Roy Eldridge in Chicago. Then in 1940 he moved to New York where he carried on the good work with Lester Young, Dizzy Gillespie, Benny Carter, Fletcher Henderson and Slam Stewart. In 1947 Collins won *Esquire* magazine's Newcomer Award and in 1951 he joined Nat King Cole. With Cole his reputation was bolstered by a constant round of touring that established him as one of the premier sidemen in the business. His unobtrusive lines would interweave with Cole's piano, and a discernible rhythmic counterpoint would emerge in the studio, especially on Cole's more elaborate Nelson Riddle-arranged albums of the late-1950s and early-1960s. Since Cole's death in 1965 Collins has continued to work sessions and has even embarked on a solo career, cutting *Interplay* with another stellar sideman, **Herb Ellis**.

CATFISH COLLINS

Born: Phelps Collins, US.

Apart from pioneering funk as we know it, James Brown has been sampled more than any other artist, alive or dead. And listening to Collins' guitar work on Brown's 'Get Up I Feel Like Being A Sex Machine' (1970) one begins to understand why. The most prominent feature of this particular song is the JBs' horn section... until one becomes aware of the repetitive guitar lick nagging away subcutaneously and providing insistent rhythmic interplay with the horns over Bootsy's bass and Jabo Starks' drums. 'Sex Machine' had a raw freshness that gave Brown the edge over other notable funksters of the day such as Marvin Gaye and The Temptations. Collins later resurfaced with brother Bootsy's Rubber Band, cutting *Aaahh.... The Name Is Bootsy* (1977), after a

stint with the other maestro of funk, George Clinton, in Parliament. Collins continues to work with Bootsy, but his guitar work has been overshadowed by his brother's flamboyant personality.

EDDIE CONDON

Born: Albert Edwin Condon, November 16th 1905, Goodland, Indiana, US. Died: August 4th 1973, New York, New York, US.

■ *Gibson tenor guitar.*

Throughout the ground-breaking bebop years of the early-1940s, Condon's larger than life personality was fundamental to the mainstream Chicago-Dixieland style that maintained the guitar – in his case a four-string tenor variety – as a rhythmic adjunct of the bass and drums. His skill as a musician tended to be overshadowed by his role as a mover and shaker, first on the Chicago club scene and then in New York.

In New York he organized his own club, Condon's, which became a regular venue for visiting Chicagoans, and in 1942 he promoted Fats Waller's first concert at the Carnegie Hall. His most enduring partnership was with tenor saxophonist Bud Freeman, a relationship that lasted until Condon's death. In the course of his career Condon worked with the biggest names of mainstream jazz: Louis Armstrong, Gene Krupa, Bix Beiderbecke and Jack Teagarden.

BILL CONNORS

Born: September 24th 1949, Los Angeles, California, US.

■ *Charvel Strat-style; Ovation.*

Formerly a member of keyboard player Chick Corea's jazz-rock group Return To Forever, which was established as a counterpart to **John McLaughlin**'s Mahavishnu Orchestra, Connors remained with the group for about a year, his deftly technical lines being featured on *Hymn Of The Seventh Galaxy* (1973). Thereafter he collaborated with jazzmen like Gary Burton, Paul Bley, Steve Swallow and Charlie Haden. Technically impeccable if sometimes rather dry, Connors has adopted the role of sideman too often.

RY COODER

See also pages 9-10
Born: Ryland Peter Cooder, March 15th 1947, Los Angeles, California, US.

■ *Fender Stratocaster (modified); Martin D-45.*

A session guitarist whose list of credits reads like a Who's Who, Cooder's versatility seems to know no bounds. At the heart of it lies an all-round knowledge of jazz, country, blues and rock which has enabled him to record strings of solo albums that have drawn on the myriad strands of contemporary US music.

The debut *Ry Cooder* (1970) featured a mix of blues and hillbilly, livened up by a smattering of obscure R&B songs. If this was eclectic, the follow-up *Into The Purple Valley* (1971), which featured a profusion of R&B obscurities and wry social comment, showed a masterful and original hybrid that transcended simple classification. Later albums would tend to examine each component of this hybrid: *Boomer's Story* (1972) dealt with rural blues, echoing his earlier involvement with Taj Mahal in Rising Sons; *Chicken Skin Music* (1976) and the live *Showtime* (1977) featured contributions from the arch exponent of Tex-Mex accordion, Flaco Jimenez, with much of the material being derived from traditional country writers; and *Jazz* (1977) was... self-explanatory.

Some of Cooder's most memorable work has been reserved for others, particularly on soundtracks like *Performance* (1970), where his slide guitar work on 'Memo From Turner' is gritty and grainy. An equally abrasive cameo occurs on the Rolling Stones cover of **Robert Johnson**'s 'Love In Vain' from *Let It Bleed* (1969), or his mournful slide on **Danny Whitten**'s 'I Don't Want To Talk About It' from *Crazy Horse* (1971).

In recent years Cooder has tended to concentrate on film soundtracks, but he also formed Little Village with **John Hiatt**, bassist Nick Lowe and drummer Jim Keltner, which had the potential to follow in the tracks left by Little Feat, but disbanded.

MIKE COOPER

Born: 1940, Reading, Berkshire, England.

A British country blues guitarist, Cooper flourished with **Jo Ann Kelly**, **Ian A Anderson** and drummer John Dummer at the end of the 1960s. His meticulous attention to detail, as demonstrated on *Oh Really* (1969), and his diligent promotion of the blues via his own club gave him an authority that was lacking in many of the contemporary British-based blues bands. In recent years Cooper recorded *The Continuous Preaching Blues* (1986) with Anderson, and continues to play both in Europe and the US.

COWBOY COPAS

Born: Lloyd Copas, July 15th 1913, Muskogee, Oklahoma, US. Died: March 5th 1963, Camden, Tennessee, US.

Copas' grandfather taught him the guitar and provided a range of songs for the keen youngster to follow. By the early-1930s Copas was traipsing across the country with a native American fiddler called Natchee, playing clubs, bars and radio stations. In 1940 the duo split up and Copas based himself in Cincinnati, commuting regularly to Nashville to buy songs which he duly recorded: 'Filipino Baby', 'Tragic Romance', 'Gone And Left Me Blues' and 'Signed, Sealed and Delivered'. In 1946 he joined Pee Wee King's Golden West Cowboys who scored a massive hit with 'Tennessee Waltz'. Copas then left for a solo career, cutting 'Hangman's Boogie' (1949) and 'Strange Little Girl' (1951), among others. During the 1950s his career slipped into the doldrums but was in the process of reviving when he was killed in the plane crash that also claimed the life of vocalist Patsy Cline.

JOHNNY COPELAND

Born: John Clyde Copeland, March 27th 1937, Homer, Arkansas, US.

■ **Peavey T60; Fender Telecaster; Fender Stratocaster.**

A fine but underrated guitarist, Copeland was one

of producer Huey Meaux's erstwhile protégés and achieved fleeting celebrity in Houston backing visiting blues artists like Big Mama Thornton and Sonny Boy Williamson. This gave him the grounding of an all rounder and the status of a local hero, not only in Houston but from 1975 in New York as well. Copeland's guitar work tended to reflect the influence of **T-Bone Walker**, **Albert Collins** and **Clarence 'Gatemouth' Brown**. Apart from the excellent pairing with Collins and **Robert Cray** on *Showdown* (1985), his melodic single-note solos on *Texas Twister* (1984) reflect a flamboyance often present in Texan music, with the country and Mexican influences never too far beneath the surface.

HUGH CORNWELL

Born: August 28th 1949, London, England.

■ **Fender Telecaster.**

Nominally associated with punk, The Stranglers' sound was dominated by an organ which echoed that of The Doors' Ray Manzarek. However, what set The Stranglers apart were Cornwell's vocals, compositional skills and understated guitar support. Unconcerned about addressing sensitive political or social issues, The Stranglers were tagged as racist, anti-feminist and myriad other transgressions, but at their heart lay a sense of dynamics and energy that enabled them to encapsulate themes: 'Get A Grip On Yourself', 'Peaches', 'Something Better Change', 'No More Heroes, 'Nice 'n' Sleazy', 'Golden Brown' and 'Strange Little Girl'. While they were brazenly populist with their hooks, they were clever at covering Burt Bacharach & Hal David's 'Walk On By' (while replicating the arrangement of The Doors' 'Light My Fire') and The Kinks' 'All Day And All Of The Night'. Cornwell remains a survivor of punk with perspective and musical acumen, and should be around for many years to come. His guitar work has that rare quality, usually only found in session guitarists, of tailoring the part to the arrangement and not the other way around.

LARRY CORYELL

Born: August 2nd 1943, Galveston, Texas, US.

■ **Gibson Super 400CES; Fender Stratocaster; Ovation; Gibson Les Paul Special.**

Coryell is a mostly self-taught guitarist who has always displayed a temperamental inability to stick with any one style. As a result, the spirit of invention is ever present, but emotional intensity can be at a premium.

Some of Coryell's most successful recordings have emerged as a sideman in established groups: in vibraphonist Gary Burton's group for *Lofty Fake Anagram* (1967) and on the **Chet Atkins**-produced *Tennessee Firebird*, Coryell displayed an ability to play jazz, rock and country with equal ease. Similarly, Herbie Mann's *Memphis Underground* featured instrumental versions of soul classics like Aretha's 'Chain Of Fools' and Sam & Dave's 'Hold On I'm Comin', as well as 'Battle Hymn Of The New Republic' with Coryell contributing steely, funky

lines that foreshadowed the explosion of jazz-rock in the 1970s.

While the skill of **Jimi Hendrix** has never been in any doubt, his influence on guitarists can be adverse: Hendrix was a genius, few others were. For a time Coryell fell into the trap of believing that he could emulate Hendrix. This meant that for much of the 1970s Coryell produced a string of albums that were high on prowess, zero on emotion, with just too many notes.

As the 1980s came and went Coryell partnered the prodigiously talented **Emily Remler** in concert and on *Together* (1985). This was one of the best partnerships to emerge in years, as Coryell's playing not only had the customary level of expertise, but also warmth ('How My Heart Sings') and a depth of understanding ('Gerri's Blues') that had been notably absent on previous outings. His transcriptions for classical guitar of Igor Stravinsky's *Le Sacre Du Printemps* (1987) and the *Firebird* and *Petrouchka* ballets (1984) illustrate his continuing reluctance to be pigeonholed and underline his I'll-play-what-I-like attitude. Quite right, too.

ELVIS COSTELLO

Born: Declan Patrick McManus, August 25th 1955, London, England.

■ **Fender Jazzmaster.**

Elvis Costello has spent his career vaulting through contemporary music. He became popular at the time of the British punk movement, and while manager, record company and indeed Costello were doubtless happy to be carried along as part of this blossoming of new talent, his estimable abilty as a songwriter and overlooked propensity for tight guitar parts were miles away from the aggression and nihilism which the press liked to think of as 'punk'. Standing up-front on stage with an unusual Fender, Costello helped popularize the notion that, during an era of increasing domination by synthesizers, good pop music was nonetheless always ready for the inclusion of electric guitar.

Costello's recorded guitar work is best heard on the more sparely arranged early records such as *This Year's Model* (1978) and *Armed Forces* (1979), working with The Attractions (Bruce Thomas bass, Steve Naive keyboards, Pete Thomas drums). Later, Costello's projects ranged more widely, such as in 1986 when he joined forces with producer/guitarist **T-Bone Burnett** to cut *King Of America*. This had Costello embracing styles like Tex-Mex and Cajun and using musicians such as **James Burton** and drummer Jim Keltner, featuring a classic version of 'Don't Let Me Be Misunderstood'. As if to emphasize his eclecticism, on *The Juliet Letters* (1993) Costello chose to work with a group of classical musicians, The Brodsky Quartet.

GERRY COTT

Born: England.

■ **Aria 'signature'.**

When The Boomtown Rats emerged during the punk era, many confused them with other bands of the genre. The difference was that the Rats' songs were witty and observant: 'Looking After No. 1', 'She's So Modern', 'Like Clockwork', 'Rat Trap', 'I Don't Like Mondays' and 'Someone's Looking At You'. They belonged, like Squeeze, to a tradition of groups which crafted their songs around neat, unfussy instrumentation, with snazzy hooks. In other words, pure pop for now people. Cott's guitar work, backed by rhythm player Gerry Roberts, was as effective as it was unpretentious. While vocalist Bob Geldof was frontman and main writer, no single member of the unit should be undervalued (which, of course, they have been). Cott left in 1981, and the group split in 1986.

ELIZABETH COTTEN

Born: Elizabeth 'Libba' Cotten, 1893, Chapel Hill, North Carolina, US. Died: June 29th 1987, New York, New York, US.

■ **Martin.**

Both **John Fahey** and Elizabeth Cotten had been quietly going about their business for years, making dazzling records that only got to be recorded because a handful of enthusiasts at record companies recognized their obligation to support and encourage important musicians. The left-handed Cotten, writer of 'Freight Train', combined elements of ragtime and gospel in her two-fingered picking style which became the standard for later folk singers.

Gradually her talent became more widely recognized and, in 1985, she won a Grammy for the sprightly *Elizabeth Cotten Live*. It was a majestic record by any standards, with deft evocations of traditional songs and fresh readings of self-composed material... but for a 92 year-old it is quite extraordinary.

JEFF COTTON

Born: US.

Better known as Antennae Jimmy Semmens, Cotton is often painted as the ignoramus who wouldn't know a guitar from a paddle. Captain Beefheart's take on the world may have been at odds with the contemporary view of reality, but it was not so proscribed that he would have to tell his musicians what to play. Directing **Ry Cooder** and **Bill Harkleroad**? No chance.

Cotton made his debut with the Captain's Magic Band on *Safe As Milk* (1967), but his real notoriety stemmed from his contributions to *Trout Mask Replica* (1969). Beefheart's stream-of-consciousness lyrics defied conventions, emphasizing the sound of a word rather than its meaning. While much of it was impressive as impromptu, random spillage, it was Cotton's riffing counterpoints to Harkleroad's soloing that provided the music with a firmer footing amid the unusual, atonal soundscape.

Later albums such as *Lick My Decals Off, Baby* (1970) and *The Spotlight Kid* (1972) used the same lineup, but lacked that element of immediacy (like being kicked in the solar plexus by a mule) prevalent on *Trout Mask Replica*. After leaving The Magic Band, Cotton was last heard of living in Hawaii.

SIMON COWE

Born: April 1st 1948, Jesmond Dene, Tyne & Wear, England.

Formed in the late-1960s by Alan Hull and Ray Jackson, Lindisfarne tried to combine elements of Geordie folk songs into a folk-rock hybrid. At first this worked well, such as on *Nicely Out Of Tune* (1970) and *Fog On The Tyne* (1971), but gradually they extended the group's music to incorporate a more worldly view, ignoring the fact that their parochialism was the source of their appeal. As a result, guitarist Cowe, drummer Ray Laidlaw and bassist Rod Clements formed Jack The Lad. Consequently, two mediocre groups emerged from one rather good one. Lindisfarne carried on until splitting in 1975, but three years later the original lineup reconvened. They still operate, and get together for successful seasonal tours around Christmas.

ANDY COX

Born: January 25th 1956, Birmingham, England.

Guitarist Cox and bassist David Steele formed in 1978 the nucleus of the Midlands-based ska revivalist band The Beat. While the outfit were prolific hitmakers, they lacked a distinctive voice to rank alongside Ali Campbell of UB40 and Jerry Dammers of The Specials. Fiercely critical of political matters, they issued a string of singles that included 'Mirror In The Bathroom' and 'Best Friend', but in 1982 Cox and Steele left to form Fine Young Cannibals.

Their debut *Fine Young Cannibals* (1985) included 'Johnny Come Home' and 'Suspicious Minds', before Cox and Steele cut 'Tired Of Getting Pushed Around' under the name of Two Men, A Drum Machine & A Trumpet. After Fine Young Cannibals reconvened, they cut a good version of Steve Diggle's 'Ever Fallen In Love'. This was followed by *The Raw And The Cooked* (1989) which featured 'She Drives Me Crazy', 'Good Thing' and 'Not The Man I Used To Be'. Cox and Steele, like The Pet Shop Boys, have a grasp of technology that doesn't dehumanize.

GRAHAM COXON

Born: March 12th 1969, Germany.

■ **Gibson Les Paul.**

Cute guitars and infectious harmonies are the watchword for Blur. Formed in south-east England, they started to hone their skills on the club circuit in the late-1980s. Within two years of their inception, their debut *Leisure* (1991) appeared, an immaculate set with such striking tunes as 'She's So High' and 'There's No Other Way'. Coxon's neat licks echoed those of **Jeff Lynne**, while vocalist Damon Albarn managed to avoid excessive posturing. *Modern Life Is Rubbish* (1993) was a fine sequel.

TONY CRANE

Born: Liverpool, Lancashire, England.

■ **Gibson ES335; Gibson Firebird.**

Crane presided over the various incarnations of

The Merseybeats, a rather dour Liverpudlian outfit formed in the 1960s. While their harmonies were appealing, they lacked distinctiveness, and Crane's guitar playing seemed perfunctory. Their EPs, such as *On Stage* (1964), showed the band at their best. Now active on the nostalgia circuit, it is debatable how closely their sound today reflects those early EPs.

ROBERT CRAY

Born: August 1st 1953, Columbus, Georgia, US.

■ **Fender Stratocaster; Fender 'signature'.**

Cray formed his first band, One Way Street, while still at school, but it wasn't until 1973 that he joined **Albert Collins**' touring band, after meeting Richard Cousins, Collins' bass player. In 1975 Cray and Cousins left to form The Robert Cray Band, bringing in Peter Boe on keyboards and David Olson on drums. They recorded their debut *Who's Been Talkin'* (1978) in between tours, although it wasn't released for two years.

In 1983, after almost a decade of touring, they recorded *Bad Influence*, which showed Collins' influence on Cray's use of the D-minor tuning. *False Accusations* (1985) won the Best Blues Album Award from the National Association of Independent Record Distributors. It nodded at the great soul albums of the 1960s and the lean, lyrical lines that had been used to such good effect by economic guitar players like **Steve Cropper**.

As if to emphasize his commitment to the blues, Cray collaborated with Collins and **Johnny Copeland** on *Showdown* for the Alligator label, winning a Grammy in the process. *Strong Persuader* (1987) was full of rustic charm; eschewing the desire to replicate the urban blues style of the late-1940s, it drew freely from recent memory. 'Right Next Door', for example, was more reminiscent of the playing of **Duane Allman** and **Eric Clapton** on Aretha Franklin's *Lady Soul* and *Soul '69* than anything **Muddy Waters** or **Hubert Sumlin** attempted.

The circle was completed by *Midnight Stroll* (1990), the pugnacious Memphis Horns trading chops with Cray in a way that only Cropper had previously managed on early Otis Redding songs; that it worked was due more to the way that perceptions of the blues had altered. Cray has steadfastly resisted the temptation to become hidebound by a putative role as **BB King**'s or **Muddy Waters**' successor, and his playing combines elements of the greatest traditions of black American music, which is constantly redefining itself.

JIM CREGAN

Born: Britain.

■ **Fender Telecaster; Zemaitis.**

Cregan, a perfect all-rounder, was originally a member of Blossom Toes, one of the best bands to emerge in the psychedelic era and responsible for the seriously collectable *We Are Ever So Clean* (1967) and *If Only For A Moment* (1969) on Giorgio Gomelsky's Marmalade label. Having played with everyone from Stud (Rory Gallagher's former rhythm section) to Linda Lewis (Cregan's erstwhile wife) and Rod Stewart, Cregan has proved that he can lead a band, co-write (or write alone) and happily provide the neat, all-pupose guitar break for any occasion. That he is not better known seems due to diffidence rather than lack of ability: his guitar work with Rod Stewart during the 1980s, for example, added sparkle to what were otherwise unimaginative affairs.

BRENDAN CROKER

Born: August 15th 1953, Bradford, Yorkshire, England.

■ *National resonator.*

Best known for his partnership with **Mark Knopfler** and **Steve Phillips** on *The Notting Hillbillies* (1989), Croker has spent most of his working life doing anything other than playing music, studying sculpture at art school before undertaking a variety of other occupations. While a theatrical designer, he met steel player Phillips and formed a duo, but Phillips reverted to his career as an artist and Croker formed The Five O'Clock Shadows, cutting the impressive *Close Shave* (1986) and *Brendan Croker & The Five O'Clock Shadows* (1989). Lyrical and inventive, Croker makes an excellent accompanist, primarily because he doesn't appear to be a show-off.

STEVE CROPPER

See also pages 31-32
Born: October 21st 1941, Willow Springs, Missouri, US.

■ *Fender Telecaster; Peavey Generation.*

Cropper was a founder member of Booker T & The MGs which during the 1960s was the house band at Stax Records. In 1962, as a result of an afternoon jam session, they recorded 'Green Onions', and Cropper's incisive phrasing characterized an era when soul was spawning more imitators than Otis Redding had mohair suits. Cropper continued to exert an influence on the Stax sound: not only did he play guitar on most of the Otis Redding sessions, he also produced and co-wrote many of Redding's finest records, including '(Sittin On The) Dock of the Bay', 'Fa-Fa-Fa-Fa-Fa (Sad Song)' and 'I Can't Turn You Loose', and collaborated with Wilson Pickett and Eddie Floyd in the writing of 'In the Midnight Hour' and 'Knock on Wood', respectively. Moreover, Cropper's elegant, spare guitar lines have proved to be a model for musicians keen to follow the less-is-more school of guitar playing.

RODNEY CROWELL

Born: August 7th 1950, Houston, Texas, US.

Crowell is one of a group of songwriter/performers who have bridged the gap between rock and country, creating a gutsy hybrid that draws in equal measure from both genres.

Crowell first came to the attention of **Jerry Reed**, and was recruited for Emmylou Harris' Hot Band in 1975 by producer Brian Ahern. His spirited rhythm playing provided a lively counterbalance to the delicate pickings of **James Burton** and **Albert Lee**. This led to a contract with Warner Brothers, and

the debut *Ain't Livin' Long Like This* (1978) illustrated his propensity for putting down pithy vignettes in a country-rock style. More significantly, his knack for arrangement was evidenced by his willingness to use the best players (Burton, **Ry Cooder** and so on) for specific jobs instead of adopting the lead guitarist's mantle for himself.

While commercial success was initially elusive, with a string of consistent albums such as *What Will The Neighbors Think* (1980) and *Rodney Crowell* (1981) failing to sell, he finally scored with *Diamonds And Dirt* (1988) which included 'It's Such A Small World', a duet with Rosanne Cash, and 'Above And Beyond'. More recently the breakdown of his marriage to 'new country' singer Rosanne Cash was documented on the understated *Life Is Messy* which was released in 1992.

DAVID CUMMINGS

Born: Britain.

A late arrival to Del Amitri, Cummings joined while they were making the transition from indie outfit to potential stadium filler. The band's adroit synthesis of folk, blues and country combined with bassist Justin Currie's subtle lyrics provided a fine springboard for Cummings' interplay with **Iain Harvie** on songs like 'Spit In The Rain' and 'Always The Last To Know'. Their album *Change Everything* (1992) was one of the most accomplished recent pop offerings.

SONNY CURTIS

Born: May 9th 1937, Meadow, Texas, US.

■ *Martin D28; Gibson Chet Atkins CE.*

The writer of such classic songs as 'More Than I Can Say', 'I Fought The Law' and 'Walk Right Back', Curtis began as a local session musician in Lubbock before moving to Nashville to join vocalist Slim Whitman's band.

In 1959, after Buddy Holly had moved to New York and left his backing group The Crickets behind, Sonny Curtis joined drummer Jerry Allison and bassist Joel Mauldin, and The Crickets continued as a pop group. Curtis' distinctive guitar work was not heard in as sympathetic a light after this change of tack, but following their break-up in 1965 his rockabilly inflections graced sessions by Waylon Jennings, **Willie Nelson**, Crystal Gayle, Bobby Bare, **Ricky Skaggs** and **Eric Clapton**, among others. In the early-1970s he reformed The Crickets with **Albert Lee**, cutting a brace of albums, *Remnants* (1973) and *Long Way From Lubbock* (1974), for Mercury.

TED DAFFAN

Born: Theron Eugene Daffan, September 21st 1912, Beauregard, Louisiana, US.

Daffan's keen interest in steel guitars and electronics enabled him to set up a repair workshop which became a mecca for visiting musicians. **Bob Dunn** and western swing innovator Milton Brown were some of his earliest clients, and it was through Brown's

influence that Daffan joined Floyd Tillman's Blue Ridge Playboys as steel guitarist. Crucially, Daffan's stints at Los Angeles's Venice Pier Ballroom assisted the popularization of the steel guitar on the West Coast and ultimately led to the inception of a country-based community in Bakersfield, spearheaded by vocalist Lefty Frizzell and Buck Owens' guitarist **Don Rich**. Daffan will also be remembered for a number of songs that have become country standards, including 'Worried Mind' (1940), 'Born To Lose' (1943), 'Headin' Down The Wrong Highway' (1945) and 'I've Got Five Dollars And It's Saturday Night' (1950). These numbers defined two separate characters common to country music: the honky-tonk hero, and the trucker.

DICK DALE

Born: Richard Monsour, c1937, Beirut, Lebanon.

■ *Fender Stratocaster.*

Dale grew up near Boston, Massachusetts, and was to surfing what The Ventures were to hot rodding. The Ventures turned hot rodding into their own definable sound (still big in Japan), while left-hander Dale simulated the rhythms of surfing with his heavily reverberated, furiously staccato guitar work – which was adapted by Beach Boy **Carl Wilson**. Other than his hit 'Let's Go Trippin' (1961) Dale was relegated to the footnotes of history while The Beach Boys became folkloric figures in the mythology of rock'n'roll. However, Dale did record a duet with **Stevie Ray Vaughan**, admittedly for a rather questionable movie *Back To The Beach* (starring Frankie Avalon, 1987), whereas The Beach Boys are pretty damn close to the oldies circuit. What did **John Lennon** say about karma?

EVAN DANDO

Born: Boston, Massachusetts, US.

Dando and The Lemonheads have already collated a startling body of material (*Lovey* 1990 and *It's A Shame About Ray* 1992). While the group were formed around the same time in the late-1980s as **Bill Janowitz**'s Buffalo Tom, they cut a series of affectionate covers – Suzanne Vega's 'Luka', **Michael Nesmith**'s 'Different Drum' and **Paul Simon**'s 'Mrs Robinson' – which had the effect of drawing them away from what might have become a predictable grungy Boston hardcore sound towards a more accessible, country-inflected output. Dando's gift for the pithy vignette reached a peak on *Come On Feel The Lemonheads* (1992), with 'The Great Big No' and 'Big Gay Heart' illustrating an understanding of the dynamics within a song's structure. Although Dando's guitar work is more intuitive than accomplished, he has the ability to moderate his indulgences for the sake of the song.

CHARLIE DANIELS

Born: October 28th 1937, Wilmington, North Carolina, US.

■ *Gibson Les Paul.*

In the early-1970s the deep south of the United States

Dar–Daw

was turning out boogie bands faster than Colonel Sanders could rustle up fried chicken. While most, like The Allman Brothers Band and Lynyrd Skynyrd, were blues based, The Charlie Daniels Band drew much of their inspiration from bluegrass. Daniels himself had long been regarded as a stellar sessionman, working with producer Bob Johnston for a variety of artists such as Leonard Cohen, Bob Dylan and Flatt & Scruggs.

With these credentials behind him, Daniels' band came into being with Tom Crain and Daniels providing the dual-pronged guitar attack. This paid dividends initially with 'Uneasy Rider' (1973), 'The South's Gonna Do It' and 'Long-Haired Country Boy' (1975). But when the group recorded the duelling guitar-and-fiddle breakdown 'The Devil Went Down To Georgia' (1979) their career caught fire.

Bluegrass at that time had a regional and semi-scholastic following on the folk and college circuits, but 'The Devil Went Down To Georgia' showed that traditional forms of country music could break out of narrow styles if presented in an appealing context – and subsequently **Ricky Skaggs** has achieved similar results. Daniels' guitar work has thus tended to take a back seat, and his band has the reputation for being one of the most entertaining live outfits on the circuit.

ERIK DARLING

Born: September 25th 1933, Baltimore, Maryland, US.

Along with Pete Seeger, The Kingston Trio, and Peter Paul & Mary, 12-string guitarist Darling made folk music palatable for the masses. While Seeger's songs had a sting in their tail, Darling's intimated the pristine, wholesome values of middle America from which John Denver would later make much capital.

Initially Darling was a member of The Tarriers with Alan Arkin (later to find fame as 'Yossarian' in the film version of *Catch-22*) who scored a massive hit with a reworking of Harry Belafonte's 'Banana Boat Song'. From 1958 until 1962 Darling was Seeger's replacement in The Weavers, after which he formed The Rooftop Singers.

This was very much Darling's project, and the prominent use of 12-string, combined with the sprightly, exuberant harmonies on Gus Cannon's 'Walk Right In' (1963), gave the introspective folk circuit a much needed shot in the arm. After the group's disintegration Darling recorded successively for the Vanguard and Elektra labels, emulating the repertoire of **Josh White** with a healthy mix of traditional folk songs, blues and spirituals. While his picking was fine, his voice lacked White's earthy authenticity, with the result that it all sounded rather dated.

DAVE DAVIES

Born: February 3rd 1947, London, England.

■ *Gibson Firebird; Fender Telecaster; Gibson Les Paul; Epiphone.*

Arguably the first British punk/garage band, The Kinks were defined by two specific elements: the writing of Ray Davies; and the guitar playing of his

brother Dave. While Ray's songwriting is best known for its wry observations of parochial English life delivered in an ironic world-weary voice, as on 'Sunny Afternoon' (1966), 'Waterloo Sunset' (1967), 'Autumn Almanac' (1967) and 'Lola' (1970), Dave's guitar work also set fresh standards. In some ways Dave's guitar playing has been undervalued, and yet it contributed significantly to the overall effect of The Kinks' witty and musical songs.

The repeated distorted guitar figure of 'You Really Got Me' (1964) has been incorporated into the stock of virtually every rock guitarist; the crashing riffs of 'All Day And All Of The Night' (1964), reminiscent of The Kingsmen's 'Louie, Louie', became as famous as Deep Purple's 'Smoke On The Water' did during the 1970s; while 'See My Friend' (1965) popularized the use of the drone/raga style.

Although Ray's writing has overshadowed Dave's instrumental abilities in the most general sense, it is Dave's guitar work that has discernibly left its mark on musicians as diverse as **Paul Weller**, The Pretenders, **Elvis Costello**, **Eddie Van Halen**, **Mick Ronson**, **Tom Verlaine**, **Fred Smith**, and **Mick Jones** of The Clash. It should be noted that during the punk era in Britain in the late-1970s The Kinks appeared to be the only established band not to be roundly derided or spat at.

REVEREND GARY DAVIS

Born: April 30th 1896, Laurens, South Carolina, US.
Died: May 5th 1972, Hammonton, New Jersey, US.

■ *Gibson flat-top.*

In much the same way as **Leadbelly** and **Josh White**, Reverend Gary Davis drew from all traditions of black American music, including marches, rags, airs, work songs and spirituals.

Following in the footsteps of the other great singing preacher, **Blind Willie Johnson**, Davis recorded initially for Art Satherley's ARC group of labels in 1935, where he influenced **Blind Boy Fuller**. He did not record again until after World War II; having moved to New York in 1940, he became widely known there on the club circuit and as a street singer. Through the 1950s and 1960s his deft playing graced dozens of records, many of which were religious but never sanctimonious. The dexterity of 'Candyman' is never flashy; with Davis nothing is played for effect, it is, simply, how it is. This simplicity of style is a welcome feature of virtually all his work.

It is perhaps for these reasons that Davis has been inspirational to players like **Stefan Grossman**, **David Bromberg**, **Ry Cooder** and **Taj Mahal**, all of whom have made a virtue of simplicity. However, attainment of such an ideal may not be that easy.

JESSE ED DAVIS

Born: US.

■ *Fender Telecaster; Fender Stratocaster; Gibson SG.*

Davis made his first tentative steps in The Rising Sons alongside **Taj Mahal** and **Ry Cooder**. While Cooder went off to play with Captain Beefheart, among others, Davis formed the nucleus of Taj Mahal's band.

Davis' slide guitar dominates the eponymous album of 1967, and 'Statesboro Blues' (belying its title) overflows with youthful éclat and provides the momentum for the rest of the album.

The follow-up, *The Natch'l Blues* (1968), was packed with the brittle shards of Davis' slide guitar work. After another album with Taj, *The Giant Step & De Ole Folks At Home* (1969), Davis left to cut his solo debut *Jesse Ed Davis* (1969) for Atco... and the consensus was that here was another Ry Cooder. Right. Wrong. Davis was even more self-effacing than Cooder. Result: one excellent album in the bargain bins within months. Over the next few years Davis' neat, unfussy playing adorned *The Concert For Bangla Desh* (1972) and **George Harrison**'s *Extra Texture* (1975), Ringo Starr's *Goodnight Vienna* (1974) and **Eric Clapton**'s *No Reason To Cry* (1976), among others. Then he disappeared from sight, and unconfirmed reports have it that he died a few years back.

JIMMY DAWKINS

Born: James Henry Dawkins, October 24th 1936, Tchula, Mississippi, US.

■ *Gibson ES335.*

Dawkins was was no mean guitarist, as his nickname 'Fast Fingers' implies. But he has adhered rigidly to the mainstream of Chicago urban blues, eschewing a tendency prevalent in some of his contemporaries to adopt the bluesy motifs of rock. After forming his own band and playing the club circuit in the late-1950s Dawkins worked sessions for Bob Koester's Delmark label, recording with **Otis Rush**, harp-man Junior Wells, **Magic Sam** and **Luther Allison**. This gave him the requisite impetus to start recording in his own name.

Among his best was *Fast Fingers* (1970), but despite his speed and technique Dawkins' most eloquent work comes on the slow blues tracks, where timing and phrasing is all, and his playing on **Guitar Slim**'s 'The Things That I Used To Do' from *Transatlantic 770* (released in 1978) shows what an apprenticeship in the clubs and on sessions can do for a guitarist.

JOHN DAWSON

Born: 1945, San Francisco, California, US.

The New Riders of the Purple Sage were initially a loose aggregation of musicians revolving around Grateful Dead guitarist **Jerry Garcia**, Dawson and **David Nelson**. By the early-1970s, with the spiralling interest in country-rock nearing its zenith, the band became a full-time operation and Garcia effectively ceased to be involved with the running of the group, steel guitarist **Buddy Cage** taking his place. Their debut *New Riders Of The Purple Sage* appeared in 1971 and was followed by *Powerglide* and *Gypsy Cowboy* (1972), with the former offering the most consistent indication of the group's abilities. By 1976 they had become established as a live outfit, often supporting the Grateful Dead, but thereafter their albums sounded increasingly strained. Dawson left in 1981.

MARK DAY

Born: December 29th 1961, Manchester, England.

■ *Schecter Strat-style; Fender Jaguar; Gibson Les Paul.*

The Happy Mondays might well fulfil their much-hyped potential, but their apparent belief in the power of the star-making machinery has often overshadowed their undoubted ability. Or just distracted them. While Day's guitar work has charm, it lacks fire, and the group's reliance on studio technology (*Pills 'N' Thrills And Bellyaches* 1990) presents a heartless if impeccable veneer.

JERRY DE BORG

Born: October 30th 1963, London, England.

Jesus Jones exploded on to the British scene in the late-1980s with *Liquidizer* (1989), which included 'Never Enough' and 'Bring It On Down'. Their propulsive blend of dance rhythms, samples and brash guitars, courtesy of De Borg, has provided songwriter Mike Edwards with the canvas for his material. Their next album *Doubt* (1991) catapulted them into the mainstream in the US.

OLIVER DE COQUE

Born: Oliver Sunday Akanite, Nigeria.

De Coque emerged in the 1970s as one of the most versatile and accomplished exponents of the African highlife style. He had a profound influence, and the guitar-led extravaganzas at the heart of his brand of highlife were dubbed the Ogene Sound. By the early-1980s he had established his own record label. While his records are plentiful in Nigeria, they are less so in Europe and the US, and to track them down requires perseverance. However, *Ogene Super Sounds* (1976), *I Salute Africa* (1979) and *Ogene King Of Africa* (1984) are well worth the effort.

CHRIS DEGARMO

Born: June 14th 1963, Seattle, Washington, US.

■ *ESP custom.*

Queensryche were formed in the early-1980s by Geoff Tate (vocals), Eddie Jackson (bass), **Michael Wilton** and DeGarmo (guitars) and Scott Rockenfield (drums). They made their debut with an EP, *Queen Of The Ryche* (1983), which prompted EMI to sign them immediately. Their debut *The Warning* (1984) failed to match the expectation, but *Rage For Order* (1986) showed the group to be one of the finest rock bands around, with Geoff Tate's immaculate vocals complementing Wilton and DeGarmo's expansive guitar work. *Empire* (1990) included 'Silent Lucidity', 'Best I Can' and 'Jet City Woman'; the former was uncharacteristically reminiscent of REM.

ALTON DELMORE

Born: December 25th 1908, Elkmont, Alabama, US.
Died: June 9th 1964, Huntsville, Alabama, US.

■ *Martin.*

Alton and his brother Rabon were brought up on a farm, both being taught to play the fiddle by their mother, and in 1930 they won a talent contest. After playing locally, Alton on guitar and Rabon on fiddle, they secured a recording contract with Columbia in 1931 and made their first broadcast on the *Grand Ole Opry* the following year. During the late-1930s they recorded 'Gonna Lay Down My Old Guitar' and 'Brown's Ferry Blues'. After the war they moved away from hillbilly music to a more blues-oriented style, cutting 'Freight Train Boogie', 'Hillbilly Boogie' and the magnificent self-penned 'Blues Stay Away From Me'. Rabon died in 1952, and Alton retired from music, but 'Blues Stay Away From Me' remains as one of the earliest recorded examples of what became known as country-rock.

PACO DE LUCIA

Born: Francisco Sanchez Pecino, December 21st 1947, Algeciras, Spain.

■ *Conde Hermanos.*

Although flamenco has been around in one form or another for years, its flashpoint of popularity occured in 1975 when a rumba, 'Entre Dos Aguas' by De Lucia, climbed to the top of the Spanish charts. Thereafter, flamenco was of the mainstream.

De Lucia's career has fallen into three areas: an accompanist to vocalist Camaron De La Isla; a soloist; and a virtuoso guitarist who transcends genre. A series of albums with Camaron cut in the 1970s rank as some of the finest flamenco ever recorded, and these include *Soy Caminante*; *Arte Y Majestad*; and *Castilo De Arena*.

Solo albums such as *Fabulosa Guitarra*, *Fantasia Flamenca*, *Duende Flamenco* and *Fuente Y Caudal* illustrate a vibrant technique with few parallels in contemporary guitar. De Lucia's willingness to stray from strict flamenco paths has enabled him to pull in other styles, especially jazz and Latin, and to collaborate with a range of musicians – notably **John McLaughlin** and **Al DiMeola** for *Passion, Grace & Fire* (1983), a landmark album that teams the three men at the peak of their powers, subordinating technique to emotion. And it works! It also has the advantage of being available everywhere, which cannot be said of De Lucia's other albums.

IAN DENCH

Born: c1963, Cheltenham, Gloucestershire, England.

■ *Gibson Les Paul; Gibson Les Paul Special.*

EMF represented the new wave of guitar-based dance bands where electronic samples underpinned the mood. But EMF departed from the norm in that their samples were phrases, not stonking great chunks of noise. This worked well enough for their debut *Shubert Dip* (1991), featuring the landmark 'Unbelievable' and 'Girl Of An Age' with Dench's robust deployment of the wah-wah, echoing the spirit of Cream. When *Stigma* (1992) materialized the samples had become part of the landscape in pretty much the same way as the drums and the guitars. Dench now plays the guitar with the savoir-faire of an old trouper, and it comes as little surprise that these days he puts the guitar parts together in single takes.

RICK DERRINGER

Born: Richard Zehringer, August 5th 1947, Fort Recovery, Ohio, US.

■ *Fender Stratocaster.*

Derringer has always given the impression of possessing a little too much vulgar flamboyance... and therein lies his appeal. Like **Eddie Van Halen** and **Leslie West**, Derringer has that supreme ability to trot out licks with a brash self-confidence that comes from caring little about the fact that it's all been done before. And such work is often more inventive than that of ardent students who strive for originality. 'Hang On Sloopy' is a case in point: cute harmonies with a neat little guitar break.

After a stint producing Edgar Winter and **Johnny Winter**, Derringer recorded his own solo album *All American Boy* (1973) and then replaced **Ronnie Montrose** as lead guitarist in The Edgar Winter Group, cutting *Shock Treatment* (1974). Both served to emphasize his knack for playing the most derivative solos imaginable, but all executed with considerable élan.

Nonetheless, Derringer did contribute the apposite slide guitar break to Steely Dan's 'Show Biz Kids' (*Countdown to Ecstasy*, 1973) proving that in such an elevated context he could deliver. After finishing with Winter, he concentrated on production and session work, contributing a few tasty solos to Donald Fagen's *Nightfly* (1982). As if to underline his commitment to the more banal side of rock'n'roll, he played on Weird Al Yankovitz's 'Eat It' (1984), contributing a pastiche of Eddie Van Halen's solo within a pastiche of Michael Jackson's 'Beat It'. In 1993 he issued *Back To The Blues*, which he described as a return to what he does best. It contains more clichés than your average romance novel.

WILLY DEVILLE

Born: William Borsay, August 27th 1953, New York, New York, US.

■ *Trussart.*

Founder of Mink DeVille, Willy DeVille has been something of an under-achiever, having come briefly to prominence on the back of punk during the 1970s with 'Spanish Stroll'. Thereafter the lineup of his band chopped and changed with DeVille drawing in new members whenever he had a fresh batch of material. While he is an accomplished guitarist, he comes across as a dilettante who operates without any apparent agenda. Consequently his albums, such as *Return To Magenta* (1978), *Savoir Faire* (1981) and *Miracle* (1988), lack cohesiveness.

HANK DEVITO

Born: US.

Steel guitarist DeVito has in recent years become a cornerstone in the bands of 'new country' singers Rodney Crowell and Rosanne Cash. But perhaps his best known work occurred as a member of Emmylou

Dia–Dis

Harris's Hot Band in its halcyon days, when the lineup featured **James Burton**, pianist Glen D Hardin, bassist Emory Gordy Jr and drummer John Ware. While the Hot Band has undergone myriad changes since then, this superb band backed Harris on albums such as *Pieces Of The Sky* (1975), *Elite Hotel* (1976), *Luxury Liner* (1977) and *Quarter Moon In A Ten Cent Town* (1978). Great band, crystal voice and, apart from the odd dog, material to die for.

DENNY DIAS

Born: Philadelphia, Pennsylvania, US.

■ *Fender Telecaster (modified).*
Although Steely Dan were essentially **Walter Becker** and Donald Fagen, it is impossible to undervalue the contribution of the guitarists in the original lineup of the group, Denny Dias and **Jeff Baxter**. Dias remained longer than Baxter and contributed a good deal of the lean, atmospheric rhythm guitar at the heart of the group's sound. He also managed the occasional taut, expressive solo, and his is the tumbling electric sitar that graces the band's early tour de force, 'Do It Again' (from *Can't Buy A Thrill*, 1972). Dias left the group in 1975 as it ceased touring and became Becker and Fagen plus session players in the studio.

BO DIDDLEY

Born: Elias Bates, December 30th 1928, McComb, Mississippi, US.

■ *Gretsch custom; Sherrin custom.*
From 1955 Bo Diddley recorded a string of records that were to prove inspirational to many groups of the early to mid-1960s, especially in Britain. Many of the tracks released as singles were his own compositions, including 'Who Do You Love', 'Say Man' – arguably the prototype rap record – 'Roadrunner' and 'Pretty Thing'. He toured constantly, developing a reputation with his band that variously comprised his half-sister The Duchess (guitar and vocals), Otis Spann (piano), Jerome Green (bass), Frank Kirkland (drums) and Billy 'Boy' Arnold (harmonica). Both Arnold and The Duchess remained the nucleus of the band well into the 1960s.

While Diddley could never have been accused of profundity, he wrote a number of songs that have become classics of the genre, and his guitar work, particularly the twangy breaks on 'Who Do You Love', exerted a massive influence upon **Keith Richards**, **Ron Wood**, **Duane Eddy**, **The Edge**, and many others. Although he seldom records now, Diddley continues to tour and is a much sought-after special guest at rock'n'roll revival shows.

CHRIS DIFFORD

Born: November 4th 1954, London, England.

■ *Fender Telecaster; Ferrington custom.*
Squeeze's songwriting team, Difford and **Glenn Tilbrook**, have made a virtue of their Englishness, along with other notables like Kinks writer Ray Davies, and **Paul Weller**. While the Squeeze

melodies are affecting, they are never glib, as on 'Take Me I'm Yours', 'Goodbye Girl', 'Cool For Cats', 'Up The Junction', 'Another Nail In My Heart', 'Is That Love' and 'Labelled With Love'. At first Squeeze were perceived as just a singles band, but both *Argy Bargy* (1980) and *East Side Story* (1981) showed they had developed their own identity. When they worked as a duo, oddly enough called Difford & Tilbrook, they lacked the punchiness of Squeeze, but this was redressed when they reformed the group for *Cosi Fan Tutti Frutti* (1985), *Frank* (1989) and *Play* (1991), on which Difford displays a penchant for some unusually over-the-top guitar solos.

STEVE DIGGLE

Born: England.

■ *Fender Telecaster; Rickenbacker.*
Often overshadowed by the more assertive **Pete Shelley**, Diggle demonstrated his abilities as a musician when he changed from bass to lead guitar in The Buzzcocks in 1977. The churning chords of 'Ever Fallen In Love' and 'Promises' (1979), delivered at breakneck pace, may have lacked the rough and ready rawness of their debut EP on Spiral Scratch and 'Orgasm Addict', but was compensated by a timeless quality that makes both songs still sound fresh.

RODNEY DILLARD

Born: May 18th 1942, East St Louis, Illinois, US.

During the mid-1960s The Dillards played the embryonic college circuit and thus brought bluegrass music out of the backwoods and into the open. While they failed to win mass appeal, like The Country Gentlemen they exerted a considerable influence on musicians such as **Chris Hillman**, guitarist Doyle Lawson, fiddler Sam Bush and singer/songwriter Gram Parsons.

After signing to the Elektra label The Dillards cut *Back Porch Bluegrass* (1963), *Live! Almost!* (1964) and the excellent *Pickin' And Fiddlin'* (1965). These albums combined the ethos of bluegrass, where the emphasis is indeed on hot pickin' and fiddlin', with material from contemporary folk singers and writers such as Bob Dylan, Gordon Lightfoot and Tom Paxton. But the group's appearance at the Newport Folk Festival in 1964 alienated them from the purists, who considered them too pop-oriented.

Rodney's picking has tended to be overshadowed by whoever happened to be playing the fiddle and banjo, but he came close to showing his mettle on *Silver Dollar City* (1984). The perfectly syncopated runs and his occasional adoption of the Appalachian three-finger banjo picking style, as popularized by Earl Scruggs, showed that perhaps it was time for Rodney to assume a greater role as a soloist.

This had been intimated on an earlier collaboration, *Dillard Hartford Dillard*, with fiddler John Hartford and banjo-playing brother Doug, where the combination of rags, reels and airs was offset by the odd ballad. While both brothers maintain solo careers and play on sessions, they are at their best when working together on traditional bluegrass material.

AL DIMEOLA

Born: July 22nd 1954, Jersey City, New Jersey, US.

■ *Ovation; PRS; Gibson ES175; Gibson Les Paul.*
Although DiMeola has been a prominent contributor to the jazz-rock school of music, he has avoided some of the dry academicism of the genre. This has been achieved by ignoring its specific conventions – lots of notes and technical brilliance to the fore – and allowing classical and Hispanic influences to creep in where appropriate. *Elegant Gypsy* (1977) has the sophistication of **Django Reinhardt** and the pungency of **Paco de Lucia** – in other words it combines technique with emotion.

When DiMeola turned to the electric guitar, then the mannerisms and the clichés of the rock guitarist did come to the fore. This was a shame, as he has no need to prove his virtuosity to anyone: the solo acoustic *Cielo E Terra* (1985) has more warmth, technique and suppleness than any of his outings with a fusion band. This remains an enduring problem for those who traverse the fusion path, and it leads one to wonder: if dexterity is all, why not just sample and stitch it all together? It is to be hoped that DiMeola never follows that route, and it would be interesting to hear him address more 'classical' material by contemporary composers such as Henze or Peter Maxwell Davies.

DIZ DISLEY

Born: England.

■ *Maccaferri; Gibson L5CES.*
For around 30 years Disley has been one of the staunchest members of the English folk club circuit, which peaked in the late-1960s before settling into a cosy but tight-knit fraternity of stylists and traditionalists. Disley, like **Davey Graham** and **Martin Carthy**, belongs to the former category, applying the styles of jazz and blues to a diverse repertoire, as demonstrated on *Rags, Reels & Airs* (1965) with fiddler Dave Swarbrick and Carthy.

Nowhere is Disley's versatility better described than on *Violinspiration*, his 1985 collaboration with Stéphane Grappelli, from tracks such as 'A Nightingale Sang In Berkeley Square' and 'Lover Come Back To Me' to Fats Waller's 'Ain't Misbehavin'. Grappelli plays like... Grappelli, but what makes the collaboration work is that Disley, rather than attempting to compete with the ubiquitous ghost of **Django Reinhardt**, plays in his own way, using three fingers and thumb clawhammer-style, with a metal thumbpick, and creates a plangent, ringing tone. And great stuff it is.

SACHA DISTEL

Born: January 29th 1933, Paris, France.

It's very difficult to understand why somebody as talented at jazz guitar playing as Sacha Distel should choose to spend his time recording easy-listening vocal versions of standards and pop songs. Jazz composer John Lewis's *Afternoon In Paris* (1956) shows Distel applying his deft, unfussy guitar style, reminiscent of **Kenny Burrell**, to a series of arrangements that would baffle most. Although Lewis was renowned for his ability to provide specific arrangements and direction for those with whom he worked, the players still required technical brilliance to execute his ideas. Distel proved himself to be more than game for the task. Since the late-1950s, however, Distel has been recording versions of songs like 'Raindrops Keep Falling On My Head' and scoring reasonably sized vocal hits. It just shows that the lure of lucre often exceeds the desire for intellectual or artistic probity.

DOCTOR JOHN

Born: Malcolm John (Mac) Rebennack, November 21st 1941, New Orleans, Louisiana, US.

■ *Fender Telecaster.*

A session musician playing guitar, piano and organ, Mac Rebennack worked with producers like Phil Spector, H B Barnum and Harold Battiste, the latter a former acquaintance from New Orleans. Rebennack had begun his career there in 1958, writing Jerry Byrne's 'Lights Out'.

Come the 1960s, Rebennack established a fresh identity as Dr John Creaux, The Night Tripper, and set about fusing the traditional sounds of country and New Orleans R&B with West Coast rock. In 1968 he released *Gris Gris* which, though it failed to sell in large quantities, attracted a substantial following among the cognoscenti. Over the next three years he released three more albums, *Babylon* (1969), *Remedies* (1970) and *Dr John The Night Tripper (The Sun Moon And Herbs)* (1971), the latter featuring an all-star cast of admirers, including **Eric Clapton**.

In 1972 Dr John returned to his roots with *Gumbo*, which consisted of R&B standards such as 'Iko Iko'. The follow-up, *In the Right Place*, included 'Right Place Wrong Time' and 'Such A Night'.

Since 1974, despite being plagued by ill health, he has continued to record, and although the sales of Dr John's records have been poor, their eclecticism has guaranteed interest from long term admirers. Throughout his career he has toured constantly, and his extensive knowledge of all styles of music make his live performances a treat. While he plays the guitar less than keyboards these days, he can strut his stuff when he chooses.

DOCTOR NICO

Born: Nicholas Kasanda Wa Mikalay, 1939, Kananga, Zaire. Died: 1985, Kinshasa, Zaire.

A seminal influence in the development of the guitar in Congolese music, Doctor Nico's career paralleled those of Mwenda Jean Bosco and **Franco**.

Inspired initially by his father who was an amateur accordionist, he applied tenets of the thumb piano to the guitar, such as riffs in sixths. From the late-1950s the bright, zinging sound of his guitar seemed to provide a metaphor for the independence celebrations, and he became one of the architects of the emergent soukous hybrid, which was essentially a synthesis of highlife and Cuban rhumba patterns tinged with indigenous styles.

The singles 'Independence Cha-Cha' and 'Kalle

Kato' (as collected on *Joseph Kabaselle et L'African Jazz*, 1963) illustrate African Jazz's unique combination of vocals, guitars and percussion. This opened the door for Doctor Nico and the group's vocalist Rochereau to form African Fiesta, with whom Dr Nico cut dozens of singles before Rochereau left to form his own version of the group, African Fiesta National, in 1965.

In later years Dr Nico recorded less, apparently because he thought he was being ripped off; only the self-consciously titled *Dieu De La Guitare* indicated the extent of his innovation and, as a result, both Rochereau and saxophonist Manu Dibango have overshadowed his influence, being more adept at coping with the demands of the African music industry.

CHRIS DOLLIMORE

Born: February 1st 1966, England.

An abrasive guitarist whose resounding riffs echo **Johnny Thunders** and **Wayne Kramer**, Dollimore has more finesse than either. He cut his teeth in The Godfathers (*Hit By Hit* 1986) and worked with Stiv Bators and The Damned before launching his current outfit, 69 Daze. Although they have loads of potential, they need stronger material to establish an identity.

JERRY DONAHUE

Born: September 24th 1946, New York, New York, US.

■ *Fender Telecaster; Fender 'signature' (see jacket); Fender Stratocaster.*

Donahue has become one of the most active session guitarists on the circuit. His precise, understated guitar work for the Fairport Convention/Sandy Denny axis during the early-1970s was a highpoint in a period more noted on the British scene for the bombastic overkill of groups like Emerson Lake & Palmer and the raucous high camp of Gary Glitter and Sweet. Playing on the sole *Fotheringay* (1970) album, a quartet of Sandy Denny solo albums and a trio of Fairport Convention albums, *Fairport 9* (1973), *Live* (1974) and *Rising For The Moon* (1975), Donahue's smooth, rhythmic lines give the impression of binding the sound together in much the same way as **Steve Cropper** did on the classic Stax sides of the 1960s.

Others to have benefited from Donahue's virtuosity have been **Joan Armatrading**, Gerry Rafferty (especially the excellent *North & South* 1988), **Ralph McTell**, **Albert Lee**'s Heads Hands & Feet, and one of **Roy Orbison**'s later road bands. Donahue's own solo album *Telecasting* (1986) was a fine testament to his skill, full of neat, melodic ideas, and it avoided most of the pitfalls endemic when session players move out front in their own name.

Now semi-resident in England, Donahue also turns up regularly at the annual Fairport convention in Oxfordshire, and put together in 1990 a fun touring band, The Backroom Boys, with vocalist Doug Morter, guitarist/harmonica-man Julian Dawson, bassist Rick Kemp and drummer Jerry Conway. He's also a member of the hell-raising trio

The Hellecasters, whose recording debut *The Return Of* (1993) drew whoops of delight from guitarists who could revel in the sounds of three top players – Donahue, **John Jorgensen** and Will Ray – all at once, and on top form.

LONNIE DONEGAN

Born: Anthony James Donegan, April 29th 1931, Glasgow, Scotland.

■ *Martin.*

That Elvis Presley and Little Richard had a considerable influence on British teenagers during the 1950s is undeniable, but Lonnie Donegan was one of the few homegrown artists to prove that anyone could be a musician. His adoption of the stand-up bass, the washboard and a cheap Spanish guitar proved to **John Lennon** and thousands like him that skiffle was music made easy.

Initially a member of the traditional jazz band led by Chris Barber, Donegan was instrumental in bringing the guitar to the foreground in British pop music of the 1950s, where its potential was more apparent, such as on 'Rock Island Line' (1956) with its primitive but driving rhythm guitar. Narrative folk/saga songs such as 'John Henry', 'Skewball', 'Cumberland Gap' and Woody Guthrie's 'Grand Coulee Dam' underscored the stark simplicity of the arrangements, while retaining surprise.

The other point to make about Donegan is that he was never tied to a specific genre. If he covered a song, whether by **Leadbelly** or **Lonnie Johnson**, it was because he could make something of it; as a result Donegan's covers of supposedly country material deviated wildly from the common perception of how that music should be treated. His version of the big Johnny Horton hit 'Battle Of New Orleans', for example, is never formulaic within the contemporary context of country, and has a good deal more life than Horton's original.

K K DOWNING

Born: Kenneth Downing, Birmingham, England.

■ *Gibson Flying V; Hamer; Fender Stratocaster.*

Although Judas Priest have contributed some memorable offerings to the heavy metal pantheon, their image has rendered them as comic book caricatures. Nowhere is this more noticeable than on anthems such as 'Beyond The Realms Of Death' (1978), 'Take On The World' (1979) and 'Living After Midnight' (1984) where the derivative dual-pronged guitar work of founder-member K K Downing and **Glen Tipton** vie for attention over the theatrical posturing of lead singer Rob Halford. That Downing and Tipton have proved themselves eloquent riffmasters in the past is undeniable, but their later work now was overshadowed by Halford and there seemed little need or inclination for them to develop.

NICK DRAKE

Born: June 19th 1948, Rangoon, Burma. Died: November 25th 1974, Tanworth, Warwickshire, England.

During the late-1960s producer Joe Boyd, allied to the

Dra-Eag

Island label, was one of the most active champions of the emergent folk-rock boom in Britain. Apart from quirky signings such as The Incredible String Band and more mainstream traditionalists such as Fairport Convention, he also signed Drake, at the suggestion of Fairport's bassist Ashley Hutchings.

Drake's gloomy evocations of a pastoral landscape revealed a brooding introspection, lightened only by the occasional string arrangement, such as Harry Robinson's work on 'River Man'. On Drake's final album *Pink Moon* (1972) the arrangements were minimal, with Drake accompanying himself: the melancholic, fractured images are quietly intoned, while the artful, bluesy guitar work augments the sense of impending doom. Drake died of an anti-depressant overdose aged just 26. Never properly acknowledged during his lifetime, he remains on a par with American writers such as Tim Buckley, another victim of his own muse. A good compilation exists, *Heaven In A Wild Flower* (1985).

PETE DRAKE

Born: October 8th 1932, Atlanta, Georgia, US. Died: July 29th 1988, Nashville, Tennessee, US.

■ *Sho-Bud.*

One of the busiest session steel guitarists of the 1960s and 1970s, Drake proved to other top country session players of the day that there was nothing intrinsically wrong in playing with rock musicians. Never what one could call a virtuoso soloist, Drake played in the style of the accompanist, unaccustomed to improvising to any great extent.

Drake was prevalent during Bob Dylan's Nashville sessions (such as *Nashville Skyline* 1969 and *Self Portrait* 1970), appeared on and produced Ringo Starr's *Beaucoups Of Blues* (1970), and then guested on **George Harrison**'s *All Things Must Pass* (1970).

LES DUDEK

Born: US.

■ *Gibson Les Paul.*

A session man par excellence who doesn't seem to know his limitations, Dudek has consequently launched a number of innocuous but hardly dynamic solo albums that are full of technique but short on commitment. Therefore to hear him at his best, listen to The Allman Brothers' 'Ramblin Man', where Dudek is controlled and melodic with a spring in his step and a zip in his stride. Similarly his session work with the Steve Miller Band on *Living In The 20th Century* (1986) illustrated the shortcomings of his own *Ghost Town Parade* (1978).

BILLY DUFFY

Born: May 12th 1961, Manchester, England.

■ *Gretsch White Falcon; Gibson Les Paul.*

The Cult are one of those curious bands which have managed partly to fill the void vacated by Led Zeppelin. Having said that, they have harnessed the energy and the zeal spawned by punk in a heavy metal context without any of the self-congratulatory posturing endemic in much of the metal fraternity.

Duffy's chops veer wildly from the derivative work-out to the imaginative pastiche. 'Love Removal Machine' and 'Li'l Devil' from *Electric* (1987), produced and remixed by Def Jam's Rick Rubin, contain deconstructed fragments of **Jimi Hendrix** and **Jimmy Page**. The later *Sanctuary* (1990) was much more a group effort, with Duffy's guitar work being less dependent on the wally-wally-wally-wee-wee-wee factor and more on the melodic, structured solo – brought about as much as anything by the change of emphasis in Duffy's and Ian Astbury's writing. The Cult remain one of the few outfits to rise above the depressingly familiar tag of 'just another metal band'.

GARY DUNCAN

Born: September 4th 1946, San Diego, California, US.

Forming the other half of the twin guitar attack of Quicksilver Messenger Service, Gary Duncan's rhythm complemented and offset the improvisatory, modal approach of **John Cipollina**. Although Duncan's style was effective, reflecting his folk and blues influences, it lacked Cipollina's incisiveness.

After Cipollina left the band, Duncan and flautist/vocalist Dino Valente (the author of 'Hey Joe' and 'Get Together') gave the group a more melodic base. This wouldn't have been such a disaster had it not been for the fact that both Duncan and Valente were locked into a time-warp of 1967. Consequently their lyrics sounded more and more dated as the 1970s wore on. Their best effort without Cipollina remains the album *Just For Love* (1970). Although the group is well past its sell-by date, Duncan has periodically reformed it.

BLIND WILLIE DUNN

See EDDIE LANG

BOB DUNN

Born: Braggs, Oklahoma, US. Died: 1970, Houston, Texas.

Dunn was the most impressive player to have learned the steel guitar through a correspondence course (offered by Hawaiian guitarist Walter Kolomoku). Dunn had started his career playing jazz and country, before joining the western swing outfit Milton Brown and the Musical Brownies in 1934, introducing the amplified steel guitar to the lineup. In tandem with fiddler Cliff Bruner he transformed tunes like 'Hesitation Blues', 'St Louis Blues' and 'Sweet Jenny Lee' from hokey hoedowns to hot instrumentals, comparable to those of the Reinhardt/Grappelli Hot Club Of France at their best. Charismatic bandleader Milton Brown died in a car crash in 1936, and the group fell apart a couple of years later (despite the efforts of **Durwood Brown**). Although Dunn formed other groups after the Brownies' demise, he never again sparkled with the same brilliance.

CORNELL DUPREE

Born: 1944, Fort Worth, Texas, US.

■ *Fender Telecaster; Yamaha custom.*

A master of the lean, concise and authoritative solo,

Dupree came to prominence in the late-1960s as a prime session player. Since those years of the late-1960s he has dignified thousands of sessions, but few illustrate the majesty of his playing so much as the two live sets he cut at the Fillmore West venue in California backing Aretha Franklin and King Curtis. (Both artists' albums are called *Live At The Fillmore West*, both released in 1971.) The spontaneity of playing live ensured that Dupree delivered top-flight solos with the minimum of fuss. While he has since branched out, cutting solo albums like *Teasin'* (1974), *Coast To Coast* (1988) and *Can't Get Through* (1992), Dupree remains a master session musician who lacks that vital ingredient to elevate his own records above the level of mood-music.

EDDIE DURHAM

Born: August 19th 1906, San Marcos, Texas, US.
Died: March 6th 1987, New York, New York, US.

■ *National resonator (+ pickup); Gibson; Epiphone.*

The man who, by example, pointed **Charlie Christian** in the direction of the electric guitar, Durham worked with jazz bandleader Jimmie Lunceford's outfit, and cut 'Hittin' The Bottle' (1935), a very early recorded appearance of electric guitar. Christian heard it, and it is reputed to have persuaded him to buy an electric guitar – with historic results.

Durham, however, was not a guitarist in the same pioneering style as Christian. He was first and foremost a composer who happened to play the guitar very well. With his writing and arranging skills to the fore, Durham assembled a bunch of compositions ('Topsy', 'Out The Window' and 'Time Out', among others) for the Count Basie Band between 1937 and 1938, pieces that helped make the band one of the best of the era.

As to Durham's greatest achievements, the 1938 Commodore recordings of The Kansas City Six take some beating. The lineup is: Lester Young, clarinet/tenor saxophone; Durham, guitar/trombone; Buck Clayton, trumpet; **Freddie Green**, guitar; Walter Page, bass; and Philly Joe Jones, drums. 'Them There Eyes' and 'Love Me Or Leave Me' are great examples of a small combo at the peak of its powers, the rhythm section swinging out with metronomic precision and each soloist contributing phrases of embellishment.

SNOOKS EAGLIN

Born: Fird Eaglin, January 21st 1936, New Orleans, Louisiana, US.

■ *Fender Telecaster.*

In the late-1950s folk-blues music was distinctly unfashionable. But Eaglin, blind from birth, made the genre appealing again, principally by virtue of his youth. (A similar thing was to happen when **Robert Cray** emerged in the 1970s.)

Eaglin came to the guitar through the church and gospel music, adopting a minstrelsy style comparable to that of **Big Bill Broonzy**. Drawing his repertoire from a variety of mostly local sources, his guitar work was ruminative and seemed to possess no stylistic reference points. In the early-1960s Eaglin recorded a slew of R&B singles for Imperial that saw him floundering, often seemingly lost in arrangements that were patently unsuited to his sparse style. A hiatus ensued and thereafter he resumed his role of a street singer, cutting solo material that included a version of Little Richard's 'Lucille'. (Eaglin has claimed authorship; Little Richard and Albert Collins are credited on Richard's version.) Eaglin's version has that enchanting quality often to be heard in a song that has become a part of the vernacular in a specific style; when heard in a totally different arrangement it causes a moment's confusion in trying to place it.

In 1971 Eaglin teamed up with pianist Professor Longhair for what was later issued as *House Party New Orleans Style* (1987) by Rounder. The set included Longhair classics such as 'Tipitina', and pitched two mavericks against one another to produce a surprisingly complementary mix that may well be the best of both men's recorded output. In recent years, with another lull in his recording career, Eaglin has reverted to the club and festival circuits.

STEVE EARLE

Born: January 17th 1955, Fort Monroe, Virginia, US.

In the vanguard of the 'new country' artists, Earle's blend of rock'n'roll and country provides the ideal backdrop for his tales of drifters, brawlers, bikers and no-hopers. The instrumental toughness of records like *Guitar Town* (1986) and the live *Copperhead Road* (1989) illustrates an affinity with **Keith Richards**, but the character of his guitar work recalls a debt to the Bakersfield king, Buck Owens' guitarist **Don Rich**. The similarities end, as the lyrical imagery of Earle's work draws extensively from the vernacular of blue-collar rock'n'rollers such as **Bruce Springsteen** and John Mellencamp and Texan writers like Guy Clark and Townes Van Zandt. Along with **John Anderson**, Earle is a prince among thieves.

ELLIOTT EASTON

Born: Elliott Shapiro, December 18th 1953, New York, New York, US.

■ *Fender; Gibson; Dean; Mosrite; Kramer 'signature'.*
The Cars pop-rock amalgam seemed something of an anachronism when they first emerged in the late-1970s, their melodic, immaculately crafted songs cutting a swathe through the prevalent trend of punk. Easton's best solos – 'My Best Friend's Girl' (1978), 'Touch And Go' (1980) and 'Tonight She Comes' (1985) – emphasized the bluesy bias of early influences such as **Mike Bloomfield, Roy Buchanan, Lonnie Mack, Johnny Winter** and **Jesse Ed Davis**, among others.

DUANE EDDY

Born: April 28th 1938, Corning, New York, US.

■ *Gretsch 6120; Guild 'signature'; Danelectro six-string bass.*
A vital ingredient in Eddy's success was producer Lee Hazelwood. Along with guitarist **Al Casey**, Hazelwood suggested that Eddy should employ a similar technique to that of Bill Justis's guitarist **Sid Manker**, and pick out the melody with bassy guitar parts – as Justis and Manker had done with the successful 'Raunchy' (1957). It proved a stroke of genius, and Eddy with his simple, unadorned style cranked out a string of hits, including 'Rebel Rouser' (1958), 'Because They're Young' and 'Peter Gunn' (1960). But that isn't the whole story. Hazelwood's production techniques, advanced for the time and including echo and tape delay, were crucial to the impact of Eddy's harsh, twangy sound that made much use of the basic Bigsby vibrato unit fitted to his Gretsch guitar.

For years after, Eddy languished in the unseemly obscurity of the oldies circuit until in 1986 he teamed up with electronic sample masters The Art Of Noise to cut a remake of 'Peter Gunn'. Given his track record with Hazelwood, this pairing was a spark of genius: The Art Of Noise emphasized Eddy's distinctive sound and concocted a modern version that pulled 'Peter Gunn' bang up to date.

EDGE

Born: David Evans, August 8th 1961, Dublin, Ireland.

■ *Gibson Explorer; Fender Stratocaster; Fender Telecaster; Gibson ES335.*
Edge's influence on contemporary guitarists is immense. If one looks through 'guitarists wanted' small ads, for instance, the number of musicians who refer to his style or U2's as an influence or a requirement is extraordinary. And Hothouse Flowers, Simple Minds and The Waterboys spring to mind as successful outfits who have trawled through their U2 record collection at least once for inspiration.

While vocalist Bono may also have his imitators, Edge is your key man: it's his use of the guitar to create an atmosphere that is second to none. He's achieved this by putting his limitations to work to his advantage, seldom indulging in the flamboyant solo but preferring instead to use techniques such as the drone ('I Will Follow'), feedback, and anthemic but simplistic power chords ('Sunday Bloody Sunday'). He also cleverly manipulates and exploits electronic effects to enhance specific atmospheres and embolden his basic guitar parts.

The sum of U2's individual parts can in no way approximate the whole. Curiously the more successful the group becomes, so individual contributions seem to stand out less – witness *Zooropa* (1993). Edge's understated guitar work is an object lesson in what it takes to be a successful band member, and eloquently illustrates the redundancy of 'the solo' in a certain segment of modern rock. These practical qualities place Edge in a category with supportive players such as **Al Casey** and **Steve Cropper**.

DAVE EDMUNDS

Born: April 15th 1944, Cardiff, Wales.

■ *Gibson ES335; Fender Telecaster.*
Edmunds is one of rock'n'roll's great enthusiasts,

seemingly unimpressed by the machinations of an industry where appearance is all.

While a member of Love Sculpture in the late-1960s Edmunds was ripping out as many notes as quickly as possible on their take of Khachaturian's 'Sabre Dance'... while his contemporaries were noodling away trying to be meaningful. This flirtation with popular classics was brief, and he set about applying his chunky chords to updated reworkings of Smiley Lewis's 'I Hear You Knocking' (1970), The Ronettes' 'Baby I Love You' (1973) and The Chordettes' 'Born To Be With You' (1973).

High on production technique but short on guitar solos, *Get It* (1977) was an encyclopaedia of the rock era's variegated styles. 'I Knew The Bride' was hardly a Proustian meditation on the nature of romantic love, but it showed how to bash out a few chords succinctly, while his jaunty version of Bob Seger's 'Get Out Of Denver' left the original standing. Edmunds' style leans heavily on the taut, crisp arpeggios of rockabilly, but when he does break out he tends to deploy a handful of notes with care and taste in a manner that aids the song.

With Rockpile, an occasional band that included bassist Nick Lowe, **Billy Bremner**, and drummer Terry Williams, Edmunds lovingly recreated moments from rock's golden era with covers of songs like The Everly Brothers' 'When Will I Be Loved' (1980). It should also be noted that Edmunds has carved out a parallel career as a producer, working with such undervalued artists as Del Shannon, **Brian Setzer**, The Flamin' Groovies, Graham Parker, **Jeff Beck** and **Carl Perkins**, to name but a few.

NOKIE EDWARDS

Born: May 9th 1939, Lahoma, Oklahoma, US.

■ *Fender Telecaster; Hunt; Mosrite 'signature'.*
Edwards started his career with The Ventures as bassist until swapping instruments with **Bob Bogle** in 1963. To celebrate this role reversal they cut 'Walk, Don't Run 64', an updated version of their biggest hit – but unfortunately, rather than being an interesting revival, it sounded dated. In 1969, they cut a version of the theme to the TV series *Hawaii Five-O*, which was characteristically jolly but lacked the incisive guitar work of the group's formative years. Edwards spearheaded their push into the Japanese market, where they sold over 30 million records during the 1960s and 1970s. To this day they still exert a considerable influence on the Japanese market to the extent that they are widely imitated by young Japanese bands.

MARK EITZEL

Born: US.

American Music Club have been kicking around in the US for over ten years during which time they have built up a solid reputation as purveyors of high quality country rock. Guitarist Vudi handles most of the lead guitar work while songwriter Mark Eitzel's distinctive acoustic guitar phrasing enhances the band's sound, particularly on albums like *Engine* (1987), *California* (1989) and *Everclear* (1991).

Ear-Eit

45

Eld-Fah

THOR ELDON

Born: Reykjavik, Iceland.

The Sugarcubes are all that is required in a pop band: wit, imagination and an instrumental talent which is not dictated by the technology of the studio. Eldon is no soloing magnate; rather, he has the ability to recognize what fits and to play accordingly. His guitar work is a small piece of the puzzle, with every phrase weighted accordingly. Consequently the 'cubes have been responsible for a series of albums that give pop music probity: *Life's Too Good* (1988), *Here Today Tomorrow Next Week* (1989) and *Stick Around For Joy* (1992).

RAMBLIN' JACK ELLIOTT

Born: Elliot Charles Adnopoz, August 1st 1931, New York, New York, US.

■ *Martin D-28.*

In developing a hybrid style that owes as much to folk as it does to country, the iconoclastic Elliott provided a model for many of the emergent younger artists of the 1960s such as Bob Dylan, John Sebastian, Jesse Colin Young and **Ry Cooder**.

After meeting **Woody Guthrie** in Greenwich Village, New York, in 1951 Elliott started to play the burgeoning local folk club circuit. While adopting the trappings of the troubadour his repertoire was diverse, including songs by Hank Williams, **Jimmie Rodgers** and the Carter Family, as well as Guthrie. He gathered more songs when touring in Europe, where he met leading folk musicians such as Ewan MacColl and Peggy Seeger. Like Guthrie, Elliott's style was unencumbered by superfluous flourishes, and he used the guitar as a vehicle for the more important matter of accompanying his songs. Latterly, partly through illness, partly as a result of unsatisfactory sales, he has recorded less, but the urgency of his style makes him one of the purest and least stylized contributors to the folk revival.

HERB ELLIS

Born: Mitchell Herbert Ellis, August 4th 1921, McKinley, Texas, US.

■ *Gibson ES175; Aria 'signature'.*

A magnificent jazz guitarist, Ellis can swing with the unfettered zeal of one who knows he is in total command of his trade.

His years with pianist Oscar Peterson (1953-58) as **Barney Kessel**'s replacement enabled Peterson to move with complete confidence through any repertoire he chose. While many purists dismissed Peterson as being a little too slick, his rapport with Ellis and bassist Ray Brown was fantastic, particularly when caught live. Albums like *My Fair Lady* (1958) showed master technicians at their peak on songs like 'I've Grown Accustomed To Her Face' and 'On The Street Where You Live'.

After finishing his stint with Peterson, Ellis worked with Ella Fitzgerald for a series of 'Jazz At The Philharmonic' dates (1958-61) that were recorded by the Verve label. While the relationship with Peterson had never been discordant, it was clear which man

was the soloist; with Fitzgerald, however, Ellis had the opportunity to branch out and extend himself. Fitzgerald's liquid larynx was the ideal complement to Ellis's supple but muscular phrasing.

Some years later Ellis teamed up with Joe Pass on *Two For The Road* (1982), two master craftsmen trading chops on classics like 'Lady Be Good', 'Try A Little Tenderness' and 'Am I Blue', faultlessly played.

BUDDY EMMONS

Born: January 27th 1937, Mishawaka, Indiana, US.

■ *Emmons.*

One of the doyens of the studio session, pedal-steel player Emmons has played with everyone from Henry Mancini to Ray Charles, gaining lengthy sojourns with Ernest Tubb and Ray Price's Cherokee Cowboys en route. While his reputation is based upon his prowess as a steel guitarist, he can turn his hand to almost any instrument.

With a resumé of such magnitude it's difficult to isolate individual examples of excellence, but his playing on Linda Ronstadt's 'Silver Threads And Golden Needles' (*Don't Cry Now* 1973) is as pithy and eloquent as the genre will allow. For sheer technical wizardry, his collaboration *Minors Aloud* (1979) with **Lenny Breau** showed two seriously inventive musicians at their inquisitive best.

In the 1950s Emmons set up the Sho-Bud guitar-making company to market pedal-steel guitars with his business partner and fellow steel man Shot Jackson and in the 1960s set up his own Emmons company. He has also issued several instructional records.

RORY ERICKSON

Born: Roger Erkynard Erickson, July 15th 1947, Dallas, Texas, US.

The Thirteenth Floor Elevators were a seminal psychedelic band who happened to be in the wrong state (Texas) at the wrong time (the mid-1960s), but still acquired a legendary tag. *The Psychedelic Sounds Of The Thirteenth Floor Elevators* (1966) included Erickson's finest moment (so far), 'You're Gonna Miss Me'. Crystal clear production and Erickson's teeming guitar work made it as compulsive as The Standells' 'Dirty Water' and The Seeds' 'Pushin' Too Hard'. Erickson was later committed to a mental institution for the criminally insane. After his release he started a solo career that promised much, but the clarity of his earlier outings was missing. In 1990 he was imprisoned once again but a tribute album, *Where The Pyramid Meets The Eye* (1990), featuring REM and ZZ Top among others, was assembled to alleviate his parlous state.

SLEEPY JOHN ESTES

Born: John Adam Estes, January 25th 1899, Ripley, Tennessee, US. Died: June 5th 1977, Brownsville, Tennessee, US.

Estes was one of the few bluesmen successfully to adapt the form of the blues to contemporary issues. Using his songs as a barometer for the times in which

he lived, his laconic observations had the feeling of the venerable sage, nodding his head sadly and muttering something to the effect of, 'I don't know what the world is coming to'. Combined with his moody, introspective guitar work, this style echoed other songsters such as **Skip James** and **Lightnin' Hopkins**, storytellers first and foremost who used their guitar work emphatically. Years of obscurity during the 1940s and 1950s led to a burst of activity from Estes following his rediscovery in the early-1960s.

JOHN ETHERIDGE

Born: January 12th 1948, London, England.

■ *Yamaha; Gibson.*

A stalwart of the British fusion circuit, Etheridge has achieved a commendable level of expertise working with others, including **Allan Holdsworth** in Soft Machine (*Softs* 1976), and violinist Daryl Way in Wolf. While that was all fine so far as it went, it took working with hornman Dick Heckstall-Smith to ignite the fire in his belly. With Heckstall-Smith Etheridge became more energetic and less contrived, recalling his formative years in Robert Greenfield's salsa band Cayenne in the early-1970s. In 1993 Etheridge cut an interesting duet album with ex-Police man **Andy Summers**, *Invisible Threads*.

KEVIN EUBANKS

Born: November 15th 1957, Philadelphia, Pennsylvania, US.

■ *Rivera custom.*

Eubanks exploded onto the scene with *Kevin Eubanks: Guitarist* (1983). It reflected his early influences such as Miles Davis and **Wes Montgomery** and the fusion style of **John McLaughlin**, but there were also suggestions of Eubanks' stints with drummer Art Blakey, trombonist Slide Hampton and drummer Roy Haynes. After cutting *Sundance* (1985) and *Opening Nights* (1986), the latter featuring hornman Branford Marsalis and pianist Kenny Kirkland, Eubanks seemed to get sidetracked, and the over-arranged *The Heat Of The Heat* (1987) featured playing that while technically fine was barely discernible amid the wash of synthesizers. For *Extensions* (1991) he teamed up with bassist Dave Holland, who encouraged him to use acoustic guitar, and he seemed back on course. The following year, having signed to Blue Note, he cut *The Turning Point* (1992) which included several more acoustic tunes, 'New World Order' and 'Colors Of One', and demonstrated his combination of Montgomery's thumb style and the clawhammer banjo-picking style, and Eubanks has at last developed his own trademark.

JOHN FAHEY

Born: February 28th 1939, Takoma Park, Maryland, US.

■ *Recording King; Yamaha FG180.*

Fahey's country-blues instrumentals on his steel-stringed acoustic were inspirational to many players on the US East Coast folk circuit during the 1960s and since. *The Transfiguration Of Blind Joe Death* (1959; revised version 1964) had an accessibility and easiness on the ear, not dissimilar to the much more self-conscious 'new age' music of more recent times, but 'I Am The Resurrection', for example, has an urgency that only **Elizabeth Cotten** approximates. Fahey recorded dozens more solo records: *The Yellow Princess* (1969) on Vanguard gives as good an indication of his playing as most, his style uncompromisingly melding country, blues, folk and even classical touches into a personal whole, often using adapted tunings and clearly enjoying dissonance.

ANDY FAIRWEATHER-LOW

Born: August 2nd 1950, Cardiff, Wales.

■ Fender Stratocaster.

One of the many surprises of the last few years is the emergence of Fairweather-Low as a guitarist of some distinction. In the 1960s he was a member of Amen Corner, and while his solo albums from the 1970s, such as *Spider Jiving* (1975) and *La Booga Rooga* (1976) were pleasant, his guitar work wasn't too much in evidence. Gradually this aspect of his career has blossomed, especially while touring with **George Harrison** and **Eric Clapton**, and he played to good effect on Clapton's acoustic *Unplugged* (1992). In 1993 Fairweather-Low was recruited by keyboardist Georgie Fame for Van Morrison's band.

TAL FARLOW

Born: Talmadge Holt Farlow, June 7th 1921, Greensboro, North Carolina, US.

■ Gibson 'signature'.

Jazz critic Leonard Feather once described Farlow as 'inventive and facile'. Quite what he meant is debatable, but Farlow has an astonishing facility for ultra-fast single-note runs and chording, best heard on albums such as a pair from 1956, *Tal* and *The Swinging Guitar Of Tal Farlow*. Earlier in the 1950s Farlow had been in a ground-breaking trio with vibesman Red Norvo and the great bassman/composer Charles Mingus. He collaborated with the Gibson company on a long-scale jazz guitar, the Tal Farlow model, introduced in 1962. Visiting a musical instrument convention in Germany in recent years, Farlow espied a character demonstrating a new 17-neck instrument that had sonic capabilities of which the NASA people would have been proud. Farlow took one look and shuffled on with the bemusement of one who has seen the future and doesn't like the look of it. But perhaps this was the pot calling the kettle black: Farlow's career has been dominated by technique and his playing is analytically chilly.

MARK FARNER

Born: September 28th 1948, Flint, Michigan, US.

■ Micro-Frets.

A very noisy and boring rock band of the early-1970s, Grand Funk Railroad were fronted by Farner and had

one redeeming feature: their album *We're An American Band* (1973) was produced by **Todd Rundgren**. Farner subsequently started a solo career, which as far as I am concerned has been pleasantly quiescent.

KARL FARR

Born: Karl Marx Farr, April 25th 1909, Rochelle, Texas, US. Died: September 20th 1961, West Springfield, Massachusetts, US.

The Sons Of The Pioneers have for almost 60 years been the leading western singing group, drawing their repertoire from traditional songs and group-composed material celebrating the 'old west'. Formed by **Roy Rogers** in 1934 as the Pioneer Trio, they became The Sons Of Pioneers when Rogers left to start his film career.

His replacement was fiddler Hugh Farr; Hugh's brother, guitarist Karl, joined a little later. Karl remained with the group right up to his death (he was replaced by **Roy Lanham**). Both Farrs were genuine Texan cowboys whose knowledge of traditional songs was first-hand and whose instrumental abilities had been passed down through the family. While not a particularly innovative picker, Karl was effective on a number of The Sons Of The Pioneers' songs like 'Cool Water', 'Tumbling Tumbleweeds' and 'Roomful Of Roses'.

ANDREW FARRISS

Born: March 27th 1959, Sydney, Australia.

■ Fender Thinline Telecaster; Gibson ES340.

Vocalist Michael Hutchence has been the most visible aspect of INXS, but the Farriss brothers – Andrew, Tim and Jon – have developed the musical structure of the group, cleverly fusing the disparate elements into a whole. Andrew, never the most flamboyant of soloists, has eschewed the traditional display of middle eight pyrotechnics, substituting lean, sinuous lines that duck and weave through the mix. *Kick* (1987) marked the group's ascent to the upper echelons of rock aristocracy with a series of nifty, well-played tunes such as 'Need You Tonight', 'Devil Inside' and 'Never Tear Us Apart'. The follow-up *Welcome To Wherever You Are* (1992) confirmed their status, with Andrew illustrating an eloquence and finesse rare in pop guitarists. Although he has the knack for ripping out solos to make the live audience squeal, he has this tendency firmly under control in the studio where he imparts a **Peter Buck**-like workmanship to his playing.

JOHN FEAN

Born: Ireland.

Joining the Irish group Horslips in 1977, Fean was able to embrace the strong Celtic influences from the band's earlier years as well as the more rock-oriented style (*The Man Who Built America* 1979) they addressed toward the end of their career. It was in the latter style that Fean seemed more comfortable, which resulted in some seemingly out-of-place contributions to the live *Belfast Gigs* (1980). After the

band split Fean formed the folk band Host with fellow Horslips drummer Eamonn Carr and fiddler Charles O'Connor.

CHARLIE FEATHERS

Born: June 12th 1932, Myrtle, Mississippi, US.

Feathers is one of the few surviving rockabillies – and by virtue of having survived he's acquired a nominal superstar status. A fine rocking guitarist and songsmith, he cut songs such as 'I Forgot To Remember To Forget', 'Send Me The Pillow That You Dream On' and 'Gone Gone Gone'. While he has endured many lean years with a variety of minor labels, *Charlie Feathers* (1991) showed he was still in complete control and could whip out those churning chops with the same alacrity as in years gone by.

DON FELDER

Born: September 21st 1947, Topanga, California, US.

■ Gibson Les Paul.

When The Eagles formed in 1971 as Linda Ronstadt's backing band they distilled many of the disparate influences implicit in West Coast rock. This synthesis was critical in establishing them as the most successful of the multitude of country-rock bands that emerged in the early-1970s.

By the time slide guitarist Felder joined for *On The Border* (1974), producer Glyn Johns had been replaced by Bill Szymczyk and the group's sound had hardened. Felder didn't really make his presence felt until *One Of These Nights* (1975) emerged: the opening bars of slide guitar and bass on the title track effectively severed any lingering connection with country music, establishing the group as a front-runner of emergent AOR.

The success of that album opened the door for the later domination of rock by bands like the revamped Fleetwood Mac and indeed The Eagles, encapsulating the move to accessible rock music with an emphasis on easy melodies and harmonies. While later songs such as 'Hotel California' highlighted the narcissism endemic in 1970s southern Californian rock, The Eagles' lyrical facility and individual instrumental prowess set them apart from their many imitators.

JOSE FELICIANO

Born: September 10th 1945, Larex, Puerto Rico.

■ Candelas; Gibson ES350.

Feliciano is best known for his latinate covers of pop and R&B material such as The Doors' 'Light My Fire' and Tommy Tucker's 'Hi Heel Sneakers'. His jazzy acoustic guitar accompaniment and mannered vocals gave the overall impression that he was striving a little too hard to win the appreciation of rock audiences. This was emphasized in the 1970s when **Steve Cropper** produced *Compartments* (1973) and Jerry Wexler and Barry Beckett produced *Sweet Soul Music* (1976). Not unreasonably, Feliciano's best work has been reserved for the South American market: *Una Voz Una Guitarra* is relaxed and fluid, a collection of tangos and cancioneros

Fen-For

that makes one wonder why he bothers to look elsewhere for material when it's all on his doorstep.

FREDDY FENDER

Born: Baldemar G Huerta, June 4th 1936, San Benito, Texas, US.

■ **Probably not Gibson.**

Naming himself after Leo Fender's musical equipment, Freddy found popularity as a country singer during the mid-1970s with lachrymose ditties such as 'Before The Next Teardrop Falls' and 'Walkin' Piece Of Heaven'. After drug and alcohol problems, Fender's career was revived after the guitarist teamed up with Tex-Mex accordionist Flaco Jimenez, vocalist Doug Sahm and organist Augie Meyers for *Texas Tornados* (1990). The individual and collective work of the group, mainly a performance outfit, has done much to increase the awareness of Tex-Mex, and Fender contributes a variant of the polka and the waltz known as conjunto to the group's repertoire.

RAY FENWICK

Born: England.

■ **Yamaha SG1000.**

Fenwick is a stalwart of the session circuit and has been a member of outfits like The Spencer Davis Group (1967) and The Ian Gillan Band (1975) among others. Unfortunately, his lack of charisma has ensured that all the bands he has joined have been either past their sell-by date or yet to peak. Thus his ability has seldom had the opportunity to shine, and he has remained a shadowy figure with a reputation for competence rather than heart-stopping originality.

NEIL FINN

Born: May 27th 1958, Te Awamutu, New Zealand.

■ **Fender Stratocaster; Fender Telecaster; Gibson Les Paul.**

Formed from the remnants of Split Enz in 1986, Crowded House have become one of the best pop bands in the world. Deft harmonies, clever melodies and Finn's insistent guitar lines dominate, with *Woodface* (1991) being among their best work, and the combination has led some to compare them to Squeeze or even The Beatles. Praise indeed.

ELIOT FISK

Born: August 10th 1954, Philadelphia, Pennsylvania, US.

■ **Humphrey.**

Classical guitarist Fisk has been active in transcribing works to the guitar that were originally written for other instruments, including pieces by Scarlatti and Paganini, thus widening the repertoire for himself and other players. In the late-1970s he helped set up the guitar department at Yale music school in the US and is an active performer, clearly out to impress. Fisk also undertakes guitar masterclasses, and has played duets with singer Victoria de Los Angeles. Fisk's recordings include familiar Spanish works as well as less familiar transcriptions, such as pieces by Scarlatti (on *Eliot*

Fisk, Guitar), while his *Latin American Guitar* album is a workmanlike introduction to that region's music.

LESTER FLATT

Born: Lester Raymond Flatt, June 19th 1914, Overton, Tennessee, US. Died: May 11th 1979.

■ **Martin D-18 (modified).**

As the first of Bill Monroe's many sidemen to leave and start up their own group, guitarist Lester Flatt and banjoist Earl Scruggs – Flatt & Scruggs – have become synonymous with bluegrass. They wrote or rearranged many of the standards of the genre, and much of what is now referred to as bluegrass was pioneered by the duo.

While with Monroe each was able to develop his own technique within the context of a larger group, with Flatt taking over principal vocal duties. Remaining with Monroe for only four years, the media coverage derived from regular radio broadcasts and records for Columbia made them stars. Flatt's guitar runs combined with his emotive vocals, alongside Scruggs' pioneering banjo style, made Monroe's Blue Grass Boys one of the best bluegrass outfits in the business.

In 1948 they left Monroe within a few months of one another and formed The Foggy Mountain Boys, an outfit that included fiddler Mac Wiseman and mandolinist Curly Seckler. Over the next five years, despite changing labels regularly, they cut a number of definitive sides: 'Foggy Mountain Breakdown' (1949), 'Roll In My Sweet Baby's Arms', 'Old Salty Dog Blues' (1950), 'Earl's Breakdown' and 'Flint Hill Special' (1952). Not content to be mere virtuosi, the duo were constantly finding new ways to develop the capabilities of their respective instruments. By 1969, after years of success, they went their separate ways. Scruggs adopted a more populist approach with his three sons in The Earl Scruggs Revue, while Flatt formed Nashville Grass with Curly Seckler, where he continued to explore acoustic bluegrass on traditional items like 'Some Old Day' and 'My Little Girl In Tennessee'.

Flatt's rigid adherence to the old ways and a refusal to go electric have probably had a greater impact on up-and-coming musicians than have contemporaries who made the break and tried to update the sound of bluegrass. Consequently, younger musicians such as guitarist/mandolinist Doyle Lawson, fiddler Sam Bush, and **Tony Rice** have adopted the traditional acoustic approach to bluegrass.

VIC FLICK

Born: England.

■ **Fender Stratocaster.**

The 'James Bond Theme' (1962) by John Barry is one of the most famous film themes in the world. The reason why? The distinctive melody picked out by Vic Flick on the guitar's bass strings, in true **Sid Manker** and **Duane Eddy** style. While it lacks the studied twanginess of Eddy, there is no mistaking the formula. Those first few bars conjure up images of

Sean Connery and a string of supporting characters and villains: very 1960s, and as camp as a row of tents. Mr Flick played guitar on hundreds more 1960s sessions, but what became of him is a complete mystery. One for 007 to solve.

JOHN FOGERTY

Born: John Cameron Fogerty, May 28th 1945, Berkeley, California, US.

■ **Rickenbacker 325; Gibson Les Paul.**

Inspired by rockabilly singers of the 1950s, Creedence Clearwater Revival's guitar-based, riff-laden songs made them the most popular singles band in the US in the late-1960s. Fogerty, the man behind the band, contributed songs like 'Proud Mary', 'Keep On Chooglin'', 'Bad Moon Rising', 'Green River', 'Down On The Corner', 'Travelin Band', 'Up Around The Bend', 'Lookin' Out My Back Door', 'Long As I Can See The Light', 'Have You Ever Seen The Rain', 'Sweet Hitch-hiker' and 'Someday Never Comes'.

The churning guitars led the band to be described as purveyors of swamp rock, along with **Tony Joe White**, but more significantly they were the catalyst in tandem with The Allman Brothers Band for a species known as southern boogie, a sub-genre that held sway throughout the early years of the 1970s.

After the disintegration of Creedence, Fogerty recorded as a solo artist, plundering his youth with the abandonment of a fox in a chicken coop and best heard on *Centerfield* (1985). Fogerty's choppy, churning riffs have informed the musical educations of countless youths hell bent on playing in rock'n'roll bands.

LITA FORD

Born: September 19th 1960, London, England.

■ **Hamer; BC Rich.**

Ford, along with the rest of her band The Runaways and countless other female musicians, have suffered from a perennial perceptual problem among audiences that girls can't rock with the same urgency and gusto as boys. For Ford it took 10 years as a solo artist before she cracked it with the platinum album *Lita* (1988) and the single 'Close My Eyes Forever' which she co-wrote with Ozzy Osbourne. It was a good example of metal, with Ford's guitar playing showing originality and sensitivity. While she remains locked into the rigorous touring schedule necessary for most US-based rock acts, Ford has resisted the temptation to become typecast as 'just another rock'n'roller', adding ballads like 'Lisa' (a tribute to her mother) and 'Bad Love' to her repertoire. These have given her the opportunity to show that she is not just a three-chord wonder.

ROBBEN FORD

Born: Robben Lee Ford, December 16th 1951, Woodlake, California, US.

■ **Fender Esprit; Fender 'signature'; Gibson Super 400CES.**

Despite the fact that Ford has played in jazz bands, including those of Miles Davis and hornman David Sanborn, this has not led to any apparent over-indulgence in technique. Since starting his solo career in 1988 with *Talk To Your Daughter*, full of exquisite guitar tones, he has balanced his output evenly between stints as an accompanist and recording with his trio.

Robben Ford & The Blue Line (1992) contains some of the best blues-based playing to emerge in recent years: 'Prison Of Love', which was cut live in the studio, has a warm, rough-edged spontaneity, while the wah-wah work on 'You Cut Me To The Bone' has a pleasant leaning toward organ phrasing and tonality – and it's this quest for the perfect tone that seems central to Ford's work.

As an accompanist on rhythm guitar he played with vocalist Jimmy Witherspoon at a Norwegian blues festival, which resulted in *Live* (1989). His neat riffs and chords complement Witherspoon and illustrate the sadly neglected potential of constructive rhythm guitar work. He has published a manual, *Rhythm Blues*, that goes much of the way towards demystifying the rhythm guitar.

BRINSLEY FORDE

Born: October 10th 1953, London, England.

■ *Steinberger; Aria.*

Aswad, led by guitarist Forde and formed in 1975, became one of the most successful British reggae outfits, touring constantly, particularly in Japan. While their lineup has undergone changes over the years, Forde has maintained the band's impetus and balance, penning titles like 'Warrior Charge', 'Chasing The Breeze', '54-46 (Was My Number)' and 'Don't Turn Around', while the album *Live And Direct* captures the motivating political thrust in much of their output.

CHRIS FOREMAN

Born: August 8th 1958, London, England.

■ *Fender Telecaster; Fender Stratocaster; Dobro resonator.*

Emerging in 1979 as a ska-influenced pop group, Madness chronicled the vicissitudes of life in London and beyond. While their on-stage antics and witty videos were beguiling, these didn't mask the group's musical integrity and lyrical acuity, with Foreman in particular blazing a trail with his snappy, chunky contributions. As a result the group issued a bunch of singles that were as good as anything to come out of the early-1980s, including 'One Step Beyond', 'My Girl', 'Baggy Trousers', 'Grey Day', 'It Must Be Love', 'House Of Fun', 'Driving In My Car' and 'Our House'. Madness broke up in the mid-1980s, reforming briefly in 1992.

RODDY FRAME

Born: January 29th 1964, East Kilbride, Scotland.

■ *Gretsch Country Gentleman; Gibson ES335; Schecter.*

A fine guitarist whose light, catchy tunes – 'Oblivious', 'Walk Out To Winter' and 'We Could Send Letters', among others – first got an airing on Aztec Camera's *High Land, Hard Rain* (1983). 'Oblivious' was a particular gem, boasting a glorious acoustic guitar solo that may have been notably out of tune by the

time it reached its conclusion, but was spot-on for feel and punch. In the years since that impressive debut album Frame has had difficulty in matching it, although *Knife* (1984), *Aztec Camera* (1985), *Love* (1987) and *Stray* (1990) would be excellent coming from anyone else. After taking a sabbatical, Frame returned with the magnificent *Dreamland* (1993) which fulfilled the strong promise of *High Land, Hard Rain*.

PETER FRAMPTON

Born: April 22nd 1950, Beckenham, Kent, England.

■ *Gibson Les Paul; Pensa-Suhr; Fender Stratocaster; Fender Telecaster.*

When he was a member of The Herd pop group, Frampton was dubbed The Face Of '68. A lot has happened since then, including a spell with **Steve Marriott** in Humble Pie. The group's debut *As Safe As Yesterday Is* (1969) remains their best outing, notable for its understatement and Frampton's deft guitar work on songs like 'Natural Born Boogie'.

Frampton is often noted for his use of a crude piece of music technology, the voice box, which allowed the performer's voice to 'play' and shape the sound of the guitar by use of a long tube from the guitar amp to the player's mouth. The gurgling, unusual sound was featured on 'Show Me The Way' and 'Baby I Love Your Way' from *Frampton Comes Alive!* (1976), but the album was hardly representative of his abilities. Frampton's natural affinities lay with the melodious lines of his boyhood hero, jazzman **Kenny Burrell**, and not with the bombast of stadium-rock. A series of unfortunate career moves thereafter tarred him as one of yesterday's men. Perhaps his worst moment was his appearance as Billy Shears in the film of *Sergeant Pepper's Lonely Hearts Club Band* (produced by Robert Stigwood, 1978). This was a donkey of such epic proportions that after all these years it has still failed to become 'a cult classic', the euphemism generally applied to appalling films that bomb at the box office.

In 1987 Frampton joined David Bowie's band for the *Glass Spider* tour, and this gave him the opportunity to step back from the spotlight and contribute concise phrases to Bowie's diverse repertoire, much of which had been popularized during **Mick Ronson**'s tenure as lead guitarist.

FRANCO

Born: L'Okanga La Ndju Pene Luambo Makiadi, July 6th 1938, Suna Bata, Zaire. Died: October 12th 1989, Brussels, Belgium.

Along with **Doctor Nico**, Franco was one of the best known of the Zairean guitarists. His style provided a template for modern soukous, being a mix of highlife and rhumba, based on indigenous Zairean styles.

In 1956 Franco formed OK Jazz, a ten-piece outfit that expanded to as many as 23 players and featured up to four guitarists, specializing in socio-political commentaries such as 'Lumumba Héros National'. By the end of the 1950s, Franco and Dr Nico were two of the finest guitarists in the genre. While nominally a

lead guitarist, Franco's function was much more that of a rhythm guitarist, providing the interface for the various parts of his band's sound.

Arguably the most striking indication of Franco's prodigious talents was *Live Recording* (1978) and *La Vie Des Hommes* (1986) which served notice to international audiences that Franco's music was at least as accessible as the funky fare of Cameroons hornman, Manu Dibango, and the Nigerian musician Fela Ransome-Kuti. Since Franco's death, **Souzy Kasseya** has become one of the key exponents of soukous.

PAUL FRANKLIN

Born: May 31st 1954, Detroit, Michigan, US.

■ *Franklin.*

Steel guitarist Franklin acquired a modicum of celebrity as a member of **Mark Knopfler**'s spin-off group, the Notting Hillbillies, which included **Brendan Croker** and Steve Phillips. While Franklin was added in for performances on TV's *Saturday Night Live* promoting *Missing... Presumed Having A Good Time* (1991), his real contribution was to provide a suitable context for the creation by Knopfler and Croker of seemingly authentic tinges of country for US audiences.

CHARLIE FREEMAN

Born: Memphis, Tennessee, US. Died: January 31st 1973, Austin, Texas, US.

In 1970 producer Jerry Wexler, having tired of spending his winters in New York, decided to purchase Criteria Studios so that he could spend the winter in Florida. His first move was to ask Jim Dickinson to assemble a house band. The band was dubbed The Dixie Flyers. Freeman, their guitarist, had been a founder member of the Memphis instrumental group The Mar-Keys, which had also included **Steve Cropper**.

The rest of The Dixie Flyers lineup was Jim Dickinson (keyboards), Mike Utley (keyboards), Tommy McClure (bass) and Sammy Creason (drums). Wexler's decision to move was instrumental in the establishment of Miami as a recording mecca in the early-1970s. A house band of the stature of The Dixie Flyers was one of the reasons for the exodus from Rick Hall's Muscle Shoals studios to Miami by artists like Joe Cocker and Rita Coolidge.

While the band always played well, the sessions with Aretha were special: 'The Thrill Is Gone', 'Eleanor Rigby' and 'Call Me' demonstrate a group of musicians at their peak, hitting a groove without the slightest concern for what tomorrow may bring. As for Freeman, he was, to quote Wexler, "High as a kite and playing like a bird."

ACE FREHLEY

Born: Paul Frehley, April 27th 1950, New York, New York, US.

■ *Gibson Les Paul.*

There are those who contend that Kiss have been an influential heavy metal band. To these ears, however, they put heavy metal back by a couple of decades. While Ace Frehley may be competent technically, his playing has been hackneyed and derivative throughout.

GLENN FREY

Born: November 6th 1948, Detroit, Illinois, US.

■ *Rickenbacker 'signature'.*

Guitarist Frey and drummer Don Henley formed one of the most successful songwriting partnerships of the 1970s in The Eagles, a band completed by guitarists **Don Felder** and **Bernie Leadon** and bassist Randy Meisner. While the group members were apparently constantly at loggerheads with one another, they created the soft country-rock template which was imitated by literally hundreds of bands.

Although Frey provided the hard edge to much of their material with his ringing chords, allowing Leadon to provide the nimble picking, his strong storylines provided light and shade in their mini-epics, particularly on the concept album *Desperado* (1973) in which the cowboy was compared with the contemporary rock star, on 'Tequila Sunrise' and 'Outlaw Man'.

After the departure of Leadon and the arrival of **Joe Walsh** most of the country influence disappeared, and Walsh complemented Frey far better than had Leadon. *Hotel California* (1976), where the group first unveiled the lineup, included 'New Kid In Town' and 'Hotel California' where Frey's melodic guitar was tinged with melancholy and evoked loss of innocence, while Walsh's spiky phrases inculcated a flashy optimism that served to emphasize the hollow lyrics. After The Eagles broke up, Frey started a successful solo career.

MARTY FRIEDMAN

Born: US.

■ *Jackson.*

Megadeth have brought a certain dignity to speed metal – if that's not a contradiction in terms. Melodic hooks are hardly the order of the day, but Megadeth founder/guitarist Dave Mustaine has formulated a perfect riposte to the swaggering flurries of Friedman with little jabs and tugs that hold the whole thing together.

Friedman was a relatively late addition to the ranks, having already recorded a loud and detailed solo album, *Dragon's Kiss* (1988), but he has since attended Megadeth's best work. *Rust In Peace* (1990), Friedman's debut with the band after Mustaine had undergone all sorts of very rock-star-like traumas, rekindled the energy that was fast disappearing from the band. *Countdown To Extinction* (1992) brought an awareness of melody and lyricism to a band that had thrived on riffs of thunderous density: 'Foreclosure Of A Dream', 'Countdown To Extinction' and 'Symphony Of Destruction' are held together by seemingly out of control unison phrases that still leave enough space for the rhythm section to underpin the vocal lines and strengthen the groove with a spare attentiveness.

ROBERT FRIPP

Born: May 9th 1946, Wimborne, Dorset, England.

■ *Gibson Les Paul; Tokai Les Paul-style; Ovation.*

With King Crimson, Fripp contributed some of the most musically arresting and considered guitar work to what was known as 'progressive' British rock.

The group's recording debut, *In The Court Of The Crimson King* (1969), was an astonishing piece of work, with the epic '21st Century Schizoid Man' pricking guitarists' ears with some breathtakingly rapid solo work from Fripp and his smooth, sustaining Les Paul. Later, with a modified lineup, Fripp cut the group's other great record, *Discipline* (1981), collaborating with **Adrian Belew** to create a swirling patchwork of interlocking guitar textures, especially on 'Frame By Frame'.

Such is Fripp's versatility and his pedagogic influence that some of the world's most disciplined and creative musicians have sought him out to play specific solos, including **David Byrne** (for Talking Heads' *Fear Of Music* 1979), David Bowie ('Ashes To Ashes' 1980), Brian Eno (*No Pussyfooting* 1973) and Peter Gabriel ('Games Without Frontiers' 1980).

Quite apart from these sessions and King Crimson, Fripp collaborated with ex-Policeman Andy Summers on *I Advance Masked* (1982) and *Bewitched* (1984). These, despite the common perception that they were no more than two expert noodlers noodling, illustrated Fripp's capacity for assembling guitar-based pieces that denied the solo's central position, concentrating instead upon form and structure. He also has a fascination for machines, resorting on occasion to his solo 'Frippertronics', an interface of guitar and tape-repeat effects.

Fripp has that rare facility of incorporating lyrical passages without pretending to play a solo. In more recent years he has taught guitar, encouraging his students to perform on *The League Of Crafty Guitarists* (1986), and has apparently abandoned 'traditional' EADGBE guitar tuning (what Ry Cooder calls flamenco tuning) to use a system of his own typically finger-twisting invention. What next?

BILL FRISELL

Born: March 18th 1951, Baltimore, Maryland, US.

■ *Klein.*

Another player who might have been a painter: his aural landscapes are full of notes and chords applied as light outlines or great textured chunks.

Frisell's mentor was **Jim Hall** who inculcated a thorough comprehension of harmonics and a sense of placement: 'Strange Meeting' and 'Wizard Of Odds' from *The Rambler* (1985), for example, use random intervals instead of specific chord forms to good effect. Despite being nominally regarded as an avant-garde player, Frisell's adherence to form and structure comes as quite a surprise, and the controlled 'airborne' styling on Marianne Faithfull's remake of 'As Tears Go By' on her *Strange Weather* (1987) album is a good example of this.

Intellectual curiosity, unhampered by the need for the self-regarding solo, has made Frisell one of the best sidemen in the business, playing with John Zorn,

Carla Bley and Paul Bley. His style has influenced many new age musicians, but unfortunately they have signally failed to get to grips with the aesthetic side of Frisell's abilities.

FRED FRITH

Born: 17th February 1949, Heathfield, East Sussex, England.

■ *Gibson ES345.*

Ever since Frith's emergence in 1968 in the British avant-garde rock group Henry Cow – best heard on their debut *Legend* (1973) – he has been a figure marked out for controversy and disparagement by the critics. For Frith, the guitar has been the medium for his musical expression in much the same way as paint and canvas are for artists, his style revolving around assimilation and reassimilation of fragments from disparate avant-garde influences.

While these lofty ideas have found little support with critics, Frith has influenced everyone from **Derek Bailey** and **Glenn Branca** to saxophonist John Zorn. On *Guitar Solos* (1974) Frith played a Gibson 345 with a pickup added at the nut, thus amplifying the vibrating string on either side of a held note. Furthermore, using a capo on the twelfth fret, he effectively managed to split the instrument in two, each with its own pickup, and by using the volume pedals and picking with both hands he was able to simulate a guitar quartet.

Although this wrestling with technique and electronics appears to be at the core of Frith's work, his willingness to experiment with fresh ideas and push back the boundaries of the guitar echoes the pioneering efforts of **Bob Dunn** with the steel guitar in the 1930s.

JOHN FRUSCIANTE

Born: 1971, New York, New York, US.

■ *Fender Jaguar.*

Despite the machismo of their pose The Red Hot Chili Peppers have been playing a brand of rock that gave Living Colour a few ideas and seems to owe more to James Brown than Led Zeppelin. Guitarist Frusciante has acquired sufficient technical sense to eschew technique for its own sake, and this becomes apparent with his playing on 'Funky Monks' and 'My Lovely Man' from *Blood Sugar Sex Magic* (1992), featuring sinuous, flowing lines juxtaposed with the odd choppy phrase and echoing **Leo Nocentelli** of The Meters. While they have always been a fine live band, the Peppers' aforementioned fifth album saw them functioning as a unit as opposed to four individuals, partly attributable to producer Rick Rubin whose forté is the marriage of seemingly conflicting styles – in this case, hip-hop and metal.

BLIND BOY FULLER

Born: Fulton Allen, 1908, Wadesboro, North Carolina, US. Died: February 13th 1941, Durham, North Carolina, US.

■ *National resonator.*

A sometime collaborator of the **Rev Gary Davis**,

and influenced by **Blind Blake**, Fuller exerted a massive influence upon musicians of the Carolinas and Georgia with a body of work that included 'I'm A Rattlesnakin Daddy' (1935), 'Step It Up And Go' (1936), 'Truckin My Blues Away' (1936), 'Mama Let Me Lay It On You' (1936) and 'Little Woman You're So Sweet' (1940). The steel-bodied National resonator guitar gave his songs a plangent percussiveness, and despite his early demise Fuller's style lived on in the work of bluesmen like Sonny Terry and **Brownie McGhee**, Alec Seward, and Curly Weaver.

CRAIG FULLER

Born: Cincinnati, Ohio, US.

Fuller formed Pure Prairie League in Cincinnati in 1971 with vocalist George Powell and steel player **John Call**. Their second album *Bustin' Out* (1972, with Powell and Fuller the only remaining original members) is an unsung country-rock masterpiece, but the group disbanded in 1973. Fuller formed the acoustic outfit American Flyer in 1976, with **Eric Kaz**, **Steve Katz** and Velvet Underground bassist Doug Yule, issuing *American Flyer* (1976) and *Spirit Of A Woman* (1977). Fuller then recorded *Craig Fuller/Eric Kaz* (1978) before joining the reformed lineup of Little Feat in 1986, after years of session work. Fuller was clearly unwilling to be hidebound by styles: his acoustic guitar work is as accomplished as his electric, his songwriting as impressive as his facility for arrangement.

JESSE FULLER

Born: March 12th 1896, Jonesboro, Georgia, US. Died: January 29th 1976, Oakland, California, US.

■ **Silvertone.**

Possessor of a rag-bag of styles, Fuller typified the troubadour. His repertoire comprised folk songs, blues and rags, and found its ideal expression in his quirky one-man band approach. Among the instruments he played were guitar, harmonica, kazoo, washboard and fotdella (a contraption of his own design that functioned as a footpedal-operated bass).

Due to the novelty value of his accompaniment, Fuller projected himself as an entertainer rather than as a bluesman. Having said that, the novelty value of 'San Francisco Bay Blues' did much to awaken interest in the blues in middle class audiences through his 1960s appearances on TV's *Steve Allen Show* and Johnny Carson's Tonight Show. His folksy style suited traditional songs such as 'Stag-O-Lee' and 'John Henry', and Fuller gave the impression that his interpretations were close in spirit to the songs' earliest performances.

JIM FULLER

Born: 1947, Glendale, California, US.

■ **Fender Stratocaster.**

'Wipe Out' by The Surfaris was the definitive surf anthem of the early-1960s. Fresh as a splash of cologne, Fuller's surging lead guitar lines make The Ventures sound lethargic. The group was still around

in the early-1990s, but only guitarist Jim Pash remained of the original lineup.

LOWELL FULSON

Born: March 31st, 1921, Tulsa, Oklahoma, US.

■ **Gibson ES355; Gretsch White Falcon.**

The writer of a fistful of R&B classics like 'Every Day I Have The Blues', 'Reconsider Baby', 'Three O'Clock Shadow', and 'Tramp', Fulson spanned the country blues and R&B eras with a basic guitar style that suited solo accompaniment as much as band work.

This adaptability was symptomatic of post-war blues musicians – say **John Lee Hooker** and **Muddy Waters** – who, before the blues became popular among white audiences, were having to depend for their livelihoods on the chitlin circuit, where wages were sometimes insufficient to sustain a regular band. Malleability was a prerequisite for survival. Fulson, perhaps less famously than either Hooker or Waters, was one of the first to adapt to soul and even rock with *In A Heavy Bag* (1968) for Stan Lewis's Shreveport-based Jewel label. Recorded at Muscle Shoals with session musicians **Jimmy Johnson** (guitar), Roger Hawkins (drums), David Hood (bass) and Barry Beckett (keyboards), it included an unusual version of **Paul McCartney**'s Beatles song 'Why Don't We Do It In The Road?'. Despite his limitations as a guitarist, Fulson's influence has contributed to the erosion of barriers between different types and styles of black music.

RICHIE FURAY

Born: May 9th 1944, Yellow Springs, Ohio, US.

Furay was the rhythm guitarist of Buffalo Springfield during the years when **Stephen Stills** and **Neil Young** still spoke to one another. Later, Young continued being Young. Stills got fat. And Furay ground his teeth because he wasn't either of them. It's very problematic being the third of a talented trio.

Furay's post-Springfield ventures, Poco and The Souther Hillman Furay Band, were overshadowed by Crosby Stills Nash & Young and The Eagles, respectively. In each instance, Furay must have known what the 18th century composer Salieri felt like when his best efforts were constantly overshadowed by Mozart. Songs like 'Child's Claim To Fame', 'Crazy Eyes' and 'Rose Of Cimarron' were fine pieces, but alongside 'Bluebird', 'Southern Man' or 'Take It To The Limit' they were a mite simplistic, and Furay's guitar work lacked the freewheeling inventiveness of Stills, Young or **Bernie Leadon**.

EDDIE FUREY

Born: December 23rd 1944, Dublin, Ireland.

Although The Fureys have been around for what seems like a long time, their pleasant middle-of-the-road approach to traditional Irish folk music has stimulated interest among those who would ordinarily never dream of listening to such fare. The group's versatility on a range of instruments (Eddie plays guitar, mandola, mandolin, harmonica, accordion, fiddle and bodhran) and their simple

arrangements imbues their sound with a direct authenticity. Best appreciated live, the band's *In Concert* (1984) album is a fair representation of them at their raggle-taggle best.

PETE GAGE

Born: August 31st 1947, Manchester, England.

With his erstwhile spouse, vocalist Elkie Brooks, Gage was a member of the jazz-rock band Dada which evolved into the R&B outfit Vinegar Joe in 1970. As lead guitarist, Gage was overshadowed by vocalists Brooks and Robert Palmer, and although their live shows had much to commend them, the trio of albums recorded for Island were unimaginative and ultimately derivative. Gage has since proved that he is best employed as an arranger or musical director.

SLIM GAILLARD

Born: Bulee Gaillard, January 1st 1916, Santa Clara, Cuba. Died: February 26th 1991, London, England.

After years of wandering, Gaillard eventually made his home in London in the 1980s and became a regular of the club circuit.

During the late-1930s as Slim and Slam, with bassman Slam Stewart, he recorded novelty items such as 'Flat Foot Floogie' and 'Tutti Frutti'. Both served notice that Slim's primary asset was his ability to extemporize: the guitar initially and then the piano were embellishments to his highly idiosyncratic use of language, culminating with 'vout' – a personalized argot, comprehensible only to Slim himself and using tenets of jive in his own free-form lingo.

ERIC GALE

Born: September 20th 1938, New York, New York, US.

■ **Gibson L5CES; Gibson Super 400CES.**

For much of the 1970s Gale occupied pole position on the session circuit. From the opening wah-wah bars of Isaac Hayes's 'Shaft' (with echoes of The Temptations' 'Cloud Nine') to the sinuous snake-like lines of Esther Phillips's 'What A Difference A Day Makes', Gale's economy has been his calling card. In 1973 he started to cut solo albums. While a session player's move into the limelight has never been an automatic cause for celebration, *Ginseng Woman* (1976) essayed **George Benson**'s preserve with finesse and style. Later efforts such as 'Wait Until The City Sleeps' from *Blue Horizon* (1982) were emblematic of a growing tendency among session musicians to cut albums of cocktail jazz, although Gale injected a subtle urgency through his muscular guitar work.

RORY GALLAGHER

Born: March 2nd 1949, Ballyshannon, Co Donegal, Ireland.

■ **Fender Stratocaster; Fender Telecaster; National resonator.**

First in a trio called Taste and then in his own band,

Gallagher carved a niche for himself in the late-1960s with a touring schedule so intense that band members were constantly leaving him – mainly, it seems, through exhaustion.

Along with other sterling British blues boomers of the 1960s such as **Tony McPhee**, **Stan Webb** and **John Mayall**, Gallagher promoted the blues so assiduously that many a British youth grew up believing that the Delta Blues originated in the Thames Valley and that the bottleneck referred to the North Circular Gyratory System in London – a permanent hindrance for any northbound itinerant.

Gallagher's main claim to fame was that he had memorized every note of the **Elmore James** songbook and could replicate it even faster than the late James had managed. A little short on originality, Gallagher's many live albums – *Live At The Isle Of Wight* (Taste; 1972) and *Irish Tour* (1974) – are the best examples of his work, as they convey at least an element of excitement.

CLIFF GALLUP

Died: October 10th 1988, Chesapeake, Virginia, US.

■ *Gretsch Duo Jet.*

In 1992 **Jeff Beck** recorded a reflective tribute to the legacy of Gallup, guitarist of Gene Vincent's group The Blue Caps. Some critics howled, 'What's the point?' while probably thinking, 'Who the hell's Cliff Gallup, anyway?'

The point, for the uninitiated, is that Gallup was a rockabilly guitarist in a similar style to **Scotty Moore** – but Gallup's hiccuping, picked phrases in 'Be-Bop-A-Lula' (1956) mirrored Gene Vincent's vocals, and the guitarist's brilliant cameos at the heart of Vincent's 45s remain perfect lessons in brevity and style. Gallup's lissom lines in 'Race With The Devil' (1956), drawn perhaps from the **Merle Travis** manual, opened the door for other stylists such as **James Burton** and later still **Robbie Robertson**. By the end of 1956, however, Gallup had left The Blue Caps and Vincent would never have such a good guitarist again.

JERRY GARCIA

Born: John Jerome Garcia, August 1st 1942, San Francisco, California, US.

■ *Irwin custom.*

There are a large number of people who firmly believe that God's earthly representative is not the Pope but a bearded, middle-aged man with long greying curly hair, steel-rimmed spectacles and a beatific smile that makes most saints appear choleric. For this is Jerry Garcia, founder of The Grateful Dead.

Since the 1960s, Garcia's unorthodox style has enabled him to stand on stage for up to five hours at a time and never play anything like the same solo twice. Garcia's soloing was as integral to the group's sound as the rhythm section, and thus his bluesy improvisations never really became abstract meanderings. Consequently the group's natural environment is the concert as opposed to the studio, and therefore the keenest representations of the

group's work are concert albums like *Live Dead* (1969) and *Grateful Dead* (1970) where the rich diversity of individual influences are much more apparent.

'Dark Star' from the former album is a 23-minute opus that eschewed all the accepted conventions of rock and made improvisation palatable. However *Workingman's Dead* (1970) with songs like 'Uncle John's Band' illustrated a cogency and, like The Band, an adeptness at recreating the bar-room blues and country form that constitutes the authentic sound of rural American music.

Garcia's affinity with rural styles has been fine-tuned with an occasional band, Old And In The Way. Having mastered the pedal-steel guitar in the early-1970s in another occasional band, New Riders Of The Purple Sage, Garcia is able to play bluegrass and western swing in an authentic context with traditional exponents like mandolinist David Grisman. The two also made an acoustic children's album in 1993, *Not For Kids Only*.

While detractors maintain that The Grateful Dead are a lumbering dinosaur, outmoded by the smooth, slimline, indie outfits of the 1990s, Garcia and his crew, with their ceaseless championing of local San Franciscan causes, represent an altruism and an independence recalling the better side of the spirit of the late-1960s.

HANK GARLAND

Born: November 11th 1930, Cowpens, South Carolina, US.

■ *Gibson L5CES; Gibson Byrdland; D'Angelico; Bigsby.*

Garland was initially a jazz guitarist - **George Benson** has named him as a prime influence – but made the transition to country in the 1950s. With this pedigree and the homogenization of a Nashville Sound, Garland slotted into the requirement for expert players who could work in specific styles, otherwise known as session musicians.

Under the direction of producers like **Chet Atkins**, Garland picked his way through hundreds of sides for artists as varied as Elvis Presley ('Little Sister', 'Are You Lonesome Tonight'), and country-pop singers such as Skeeter Davis, Don Gibson, Hank Locklin, Jim Reeves, Hank Snow and many more. Garland's own stab at immortality came with a fine jazz album *Jazz Winds From A New Direction* (1960) with vibes player Gary Burton. He helped design the Gibson Byrdland model with fellow guitarist **Billy Byrd**. Unfortunately Garland's career was brought to an abrupt end in 1963 when he was badly injured in a car crash.

AMOS GARRETT

Born: Canada.

■ *Epiphone Sheraton.*

Garrett is a slick picker who worked out of the Bearsville Studios in up-state New York with **Geoff Muldaur** and contributed deft stylings to a string of iconoclastic albums by singers like Paul Butterfield (*Better Days* 1973), **Bonnie Raitt** (*Give It Up* 1972) and Jesse Winchester (*3rd Down And 110 To Go* 1972). Garrett had little in common with fellow Bearsville

fretmeister **Robbie Robertson**, but the lean, atmospheric solos on Maria Muldaur's 'Midnight At The Oasis' (*Maria Muldaur* 1973) and Bobby Charles' 'Small Town Talk' (*Bobby Charles* 1972) were masterpieces of economy, much praised by other musicians.

DANNY GATTON

Born: September 4th 1945, Washington DC, US.

■ *Fender Telecaster; Fender 'signature'; Gibson ES295; Gibson ES350.*

An explosive mixture of rockabilly, bluegrass, jazz and blues is at the heart of Gatton's exciting Tele picking, which echoes much of the style and class of **Roy Buchanan**'s playing. Fellow guitar players tend to pass out if allowed too near this dazzling technician, and Gatton's two albums – *88 Elmira Street* (1991) and *New York Stories* (1992) – are required listening for anyone who wants to hear a talented player pulling out all the stops.

DICK GAUGHAN

See also pages 53-54
Born: Richard Peter Gaughan, May 17th 1948, Glasgow, Scotland.

Gaughan's tireless championing of Scottish traditional folk song has laid bare the rich heritage of Scottish music, giving it a much-deserved credibility abroad. Pointedly ignoring the thigh-slapping caterwauling beloved of Andy Stewart and Kenneth McKellar, Gaughan has chosen to celebrate the heritage through topically pertinent songs concerning the plight of the Scottish miners and the erosion of the shipbuilding industry. However, he should never be confused with the soapbox politics inherent in the work of many folk musicians, and his instrumental skills on traditional airs such as 'Erin-Go-Bragh' or contemporary pieces like Leon Rosselson's 'World Turned Upside Down' offer tantalizing glimpses of a man whose medium is the message. *A Different Kind Of Love Song* (1983), with Andy Irvine, has the touching refinement of one who cares and knows why. Oh yes, and he plays the guitar rather well, too.

MAC GAYDEN

Born: US.

A session man who worked out of Fred Foster's Monument Studios in Nashville for a spell during the 1960s, Gayden later became a member of the session group Area Code 615 (their 'Stone Fox Chase' was used as the theme for BBC TV's *Old Grey Whistle Test* show). Gayden was a great player, also surfacing in the interesting Barefoot Jerry group with **Wayne Moss**, but the proliferation of country-rock bands stymied that particular career move and Gayden returned to work as a session musician in Nashville. His fine solo album *Skyboat* (1975) includes his song 'Morning Glory', a hit in 1976 for James & Bobby Purify. But as The Lovin' Spoonful's John Sebastian once noted, 'There are fourteen hundred sixty-five guitar pickers in Nashville...' and Gayden is but one.

NO MORE FOREVER (Released 1972) *Tracks:* Rattlin' Roarin' Willie; The Friar's Britches; MacCrimmon's Lament; Mistress Jamieson's Favourite/ Jock O' Hazeldean/ Cam' Yer Ower Frae France/ The Bonnie Banks O' Fordie/ The Thatchers O' Glenrae/ The Fair Flower Of Northumberland/ The Teatotaller; Da Tushker; The Three Healths/ The John MacLean March/ The Green Linnet.

Featuring Dick Gaughan (guitar) and Aly Bain of Boys Of The Lough (fiddle), this was Gaughan's solo debut. Not unreasonably much of the material had been honed and refined to his own requirements during his years on the club circuit. The vocals display a visceral urgency, while the duets with Bain are filled with lingering nostalgia.

COPPERS & BRASS: Scots & Irish Dance Music On Guitar (Released 1977).
KIST O' GOLD Released 1977). *Tracks:* The Earl Of Errol/ The Granemore Hare/ Rigs O' Rye/ The Gypsy Laddies/ Lord Randal/ Maggie Lauder; Cathaoir An Iarla/ Banks Of Green Willow/ 51st Highland Division's Farewell To Sicily/ The City Of Savannah, Ril Gan Ainm/ Raglan Road/ Johnny Miner/ The Ballad Of Accounting.

Both *Coppers & Brass* and *Kist O'Gold* illustrate the extent to which Gaughan's repertoire has been shaped by the traditional folk tunes that have been handed down through families from one generation to the next.

DICK GAUGHAN

KIST O' GOLD

DAVE BURLAND, TONY CAPSTICK & DICK GAUGHAN: SONGS OF EWAN MacCOLL (Released 1978) *Tracks:* The Ballad Of Accounting/ The Moving On Song/ Jamie Foyers/ Freeborn Man/ The Manchester Rambler/ Schooldays End/ Thirty Foot Trailer/ The Big Hewer/ The First Time Ever I Saw Your Face/ Sweet Thames Flow Softly/ Shoals Of Herring. This collection of songs by Ewan MacColl is not just a bunch of tunes with strong lyrics. They reflect MacColl's humanitarian concerns, and through Burland, Capstick and Gaughan they take on the contemporary relevance essential in all folk music.

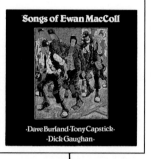

Songs of Ewan MacColl

·Dave Burland·Tony Capstick· ·Dick Gaughan·

HANDFUL OF EARTH (Released 1978) *Tracks:* Erin-Go-Bragh/ Now Westlin Winds/ Craigie Hill/ World Turned Upside Down/ The Snows They Melt The Soonest/ Lough Erne & First Kiss At Parting/ Scojun Waltz & Randers Hopsa/ Song For Ireland/ Worker's Song/ Both Sides The Tweed. *Line-up:* Dick Gaughan (vocals, guitars), Brian McNeil (fiddles, acoustic bass), Phil Cunningham (keyboards, whistle), Stewart Isbister (electric bass).

A landmark album in traditional folk music, *Handful Of Earth* established Gaughan as one of the most vital commentators and vibrant guitarists in Roots music, addressing contemporary concerns through a combination of traditional and regional material.

DICK GAUGHAN Handful of Earth

971   1972   1973   1974   1975   1976   1977   1978   1979   1980   1981   1982

BOYS OF THE LOUGH
The Boys Of The Lough were formed in 1967. The original line-up comprised Robin Morton (vocals, concertina, bodhran), Cathal McConnell (flute, whistle, vocals) and Tommy Gunn (fiddle, bones, vocals). After appearing at the *Aberdeen Folk Festival* in 1968, the group was augmented by Aly Bain and Mike Whelans, and that became the group's new line-up. In 1972, Whelans left to be replaced by Dick Gaughan. Although Gaughan remained with the band for a comparatively short period of time (he was replaced by Dave Richardson in 1973), his presence helped to consolidate the group's standing as one of the most authentic purveyors of Gaelic folk music. In the years since Gaughan's departure the group's standing has increased many times, particularly in the US: they celebrated their twenty first anniversary with a concert at New York's Carnegie Hall in 1988. After spending a few years as a solo performer, Gaughan co-founded another traditional folk group, Five Hand Reel.

DICK GAUGHAN
BOBBY EAGLESHAM
TOM HICKLAND
BARRY LYONS
DAVE TULLOCH

FIVE HAND REEL (Released 1976) *Tracks:* Both Sides Of The Forth/ The Death Of Argyll/ Kempy's Hat/ The Knight And The Shepherd's Daughter/ Slieve Gallion Braes/ Wee Wee German Lairdie/ The Maid Of Listowel/ When A Man's In Love/ Frankie's Dog. *Line-up:* Dick Gaughan (guitars, cittern, vocals), Bobby Eaglesham (guitars, mandolin, dulcimer, side drum, vocals), Barry Lyons (bass, keyboards), Tom Hickland (fiddle, keyboards, vocals), Dave Tulloch (percussion, side drum). The first album of three by Five Hand Reel, who were one of the most influential and authentic electric folk groups to emerge in the mid-1970s.

For A' That

DICK GAUGHAN
BOBBY EAGLESHAM
TOM HICKLAND
BARRY LYONS
DAVE TULLOCH

FIVE HAND REEL: FOR A' THAT (Released 1977) *Tracks:* Bratach Bana/ Pinch Of Snuff/ A Man's A Man For A' That/ Haugh's O' Cromdale/ Ae Fond Kiss/ P Stands For Paddy (including Paddy Fahey's Reel)/ The Cruel Brothers/ Carrickfergus/ Lochandside/ The Jig Of Slurs/ Linda Brechin's/ The Marquis Of Tullybardine.

THE BONNIE EARL O' MORAY (Released 1978) *Line-up:* Dick Gaughan (guitars, vocals), Bobby Eaglesham (guitars, dulcimer, side drum, vocals), Barry Lyons (bass), Tom Hickland (fiddle, keyboards, vocals), Dave Tulloch (drums).

GAUGHAN (Released 1978) *Tracks:* Bonnie Jeannie O' Bethelnie/ Bonnie Lass Among The Heather. 6/8 *Marches:* Alan MacPherson Of Mosspark & The Jig Of Slurs/ Crooked Jack/ The Recruited Collier/ The Augengeich Disaster/ Bonnie Woodha'/ The Pound A Week Rise. 12/8 *Jigs And Reels:* Ask My Father, Lads Of Laoise & The Connaught Heifers/ My Donald. *Jigs:* Strike The Gay Harp & Shores Of/ Lough Gowna/ Willie O' Winsbury/ Such A Parcel O' Rogues In A Nation. *Shetland Reels:* Jack Broke The Prison Door, Donald Blue & Wha'll Dance Wi' Wattie/ Gillie Mor. *Additional accompaniment:* Alistair Anderson (English concertina), Barry Lyons (bass guitar), Tom Hickland (piano).

BREAM'S GUITARS Having used a number of guitars during his long career, Bream has recently settled on a Hauser from Germany, similar to this 1930s example.

DISCOGRAPHY

- 1955 Anthology Of English Song
- 1956 Sor, Turina & Falla
  Villa-Lobos & Torroba
- 1957 A Bach Recital for the Guitar
  Julian Bream Plays Dowland
- 1958 A Recital of Lute Songs (with Peter Pears)
- 1959 The Art of Julian Bream
- 1960 Guitar Concertos: Arnold & Guiliani
- 1961 The Golden Age of English Lute Music
- 1962 An Evening of Elizabethan Music
  Popular Classics for Spanish Guitar
- 1963 Julian Bream In Concert (with Peter Pears)
- 1963 Music for Voice & Guitar (with Peter Pears)
- 1964 Julian Bream (Rodrigo & Britten)
  JS Bach: Suites for Lute
- 1965 Baroque Guitar
- 1966 Lute Music from the Royal Courts of Europe
  Twentieth Century Guitar
- 1967 Dances Of Dowland
- 1968 Julian Bream & His Friends
  Classic Guitar
- 1969 Sonatas for Lute & Harpsichord

- 1970 Elizabethan Lute Songs
  Romantic Guitar
  The Art Of The Spanish Guitar
- 1971 Julian Bream Plays Villa-Lobos
  Together (with John Williams)
- 1972 The Woods So Wild
- 1973 Julian Bream '70s
- 1974 Together Again (with John Williams)
  Julian Bream (Sor & Guiliani)
  Concertos & Sonatas for Lute
  Julian Bream (Rodrigo & Berkeley)
- 1976 Lute Music Of John Dowland
- 1978 Julian Bream: Villa-Lobos
  12 Etudes
  Live (with John Williams)
- 1979 Music of Spain, Volume I:
  Milan – Narvaez
- 1980 Music of Spain, Volume IV: Sor – Aguado
- 1981 Dedication
- 1982 Music of Spain, Volume V:
  Granados–Albeniz
- 1983 Twentieth Century Guitar II
  Music of Spain, Volume VII: Homage to Andres Segovia
- 1984 Music of Spain, Volume VIII:
  The Spanish Romantics Guitarra
- 1988 Fantasies, Ayres & Dances:
  The Julian Bream Consort
  Rodrigo & Brouwer
  Two Loves: Shakespeare & Dowland
  (with Dame Peggy Ashcroft)

- 1990 La Guitarra Romantica
- 1991 To The Edge Of Dream
- 1992 The Christmas Album
- 1993 The Ultimate Guitar Collection
  (28 CD Package)

| 1963 | 1964 | 1965 | 1966 | 1967 | 1968 | 1969 | 1970 | 1971 | 1972 | 1973 | 1974 | 1975 | 1976 | 1977 |

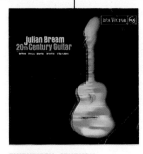

TWENTIETH CENTURY GUITAR (Released 1967)
Benjamin Britten: Nocturnal, Op.70.
Reginald Smith Brindle: El Polifemo De Oro 'Four Fragments For Guitar' (Ben Adagio/ Allegretto/ Largo/ Ritmico E Vivo).
Frank Martin: Quatre Pieces Breves (Prélude/ Air/ Plainte/ Comme Une Gigue).
Hans Werner Henze: Drei Tentos aus Kammermusik 1958 (Tranquilmente/ Allegro Rubato/ Lento).
Heitor Villa-Lobos: Etude No. 5 In C. Etude No. 7 In E.
The first album recorded at Bream's preferred venue, Wardour Chapel near his home in Wiltshire.

THE ART OF THE SPANISH GUITAR (Released 1970)
J.S. Bach: Prelude In D Minor; Fugue In A Minor/ Weiss: Tombeau Sur La Morte de M. Comte de Logy/ Scarlatti (arr. Bream): Sonata In E Minor/ Ravel (arr. Bream): Pavane Pour Une Infante Défunte/ Diabelli (ed. Bream): Sonata In A/ Boccherini (ed. Bream): Introduction & Fandango For Guitar & Harpsichord, with George Malcolm (harpsichord)/ Rodrigo: En Los Trigales/ Britten: Nocturnal, Op. 70/ Villa-Lobos: Choros No. 1/
Torroba: Madronos/ Albeniz (arr. Bream): Granada (No. 1 from Suite Espangnole)/ Falla: Homenaje/ Turina: Fandanguillo.

TOGETHER: JULIAN BREAM AND JOHN WILLIAMS (Released 1971)
Lawes: Suite For Two Guitars.
Carulli: Duo In G, Op. 34 (Largo; Rondo).
Sor: L' Encouragement, Op. 34 (Cantabile; Theme and Variations; Waltz).
Albeniz: Cordoba (Nocturne).
Granados: Goyescas (Intermezzo).
Falla: La Vida Breve (Spanish Dance No. 1).
Ravel: Pavan For A Dead Princess.
The pieces by Carulli and Sor were composed for two guitars. The balance are transcriptions from either the lute, piano or orchestra. The first album in a best-selling series.

JULIAN BREAM 70s (Released 1973) Richard Rodney Bennett: Concert For Guitar and Chamber Orchestra (with the Melos Ensemble, directed by David Atherton).
Alan Rawsthorne: Elegy.
William Walton: Five Bagatelles For Guitar.
Lennox Berkeley: Theme and Variations.
All these compositions were written specifically for, or commissioned by, Julian Bream. Elegy was Rawsthorne's final work; he died before it was completed and Bream added the final section from the composer's own notes. A challenging album for those new to contemporary music.

Julian Bream

In a multi-faceted career, Julian Bream has done a great deal to improve the perception of the classical guitar as an instrument for serious music-making. The Spanish master Andres Segovia, who made his debut in 1909, did the ground work. But Bream, a more versatile and adventurous musician, has taken the instrument a great deal further, in a career that has now entered its fifth decade. In particular, he has put his sensitive instrumental skills at the service of contemporary composers, and they, in return, have provided him with a challenging and serious repertoire. Richard Rodney Bennett, Hans Werner Henze, Lennox Berkeley and others have been encouraged to persevere with an instrument traditionally dismissed for its apparent inability to cope with anything but the most intimate of settings. Mozart, for instance, was highly impressed by Mauro Giuliani's compositions for the guitar, but never wrote for it. This resistance to the guitar persisted until Segovia's emergence: Spanish society had always seen the guitar as a vital accompaniment for informal gatherings. In the rest of Europe, however, the guitar was of minimal importance until Bream emerged.

Like Segovia, Bream initially set about finding a concert repertoire by transcribing pieces written for other instruments. Furthermore, his pursuit of a parallel career as a lutenist enhanced his reputation as a finder of lost masterpieces. The work of the Elizabethan composer John Dowland, for instance, owes its present exalted position to Bream's persistence at a time when it was very obscure indeed. Later, as his international reputation as a performer grew, thanks to relentless touring, he was able to build a repertoire of new compositions of quality. The three aspects, scholarship, the patronage of new composers, and his playing, have made Julian Bream's reputation as the leading classical guitarist of our day and a formidable musician.

DEBUT Julian Bream was taught the guitar by his father, a commercial artist and amateur musician, before taking his first lessons with Russian exile, Boris Perrot, then president of the Philharmonic Society of Guitarists in London. More of an influence were the records of Segovia, which convinced Bream that he wanted to become a professional classical guitarist. In 1947, Segovia made his debut in Britain and Bream was there to hear him and receive a couple of lessons. The same year, Bream made his own debut recital, for members of the Cheltenham Guitar Circle. Classical guitar was still a novelty.

FIRST TOURS In 1951, while still a student, Bream toured Britain, driving himself and sleeping in his van.

A BACH RECITAL FOR THE GUITAR (Released 1957) Works by J.S. Bach:
1. Chaconne (from Partita in D Minor, BWV 1004)
2. Little Prelude In C Minor, BWV 999
3/4. Sarabande/ Bourée (from Suite in E Minor, BWV 996)
5. Prelude & Fugue (from Partita in C Minor)
6. Prelude, Fugue & Allegro In E Flat Major

| 1948 | 1949 | 1950 | 1951 | 1952 | 1953 | 1954 | 1955 | 1956 | 1957 | 1958 | 1959 | 1960 | 1961 | 19 |

EARLY YEARS It is difficult to imagine the obstacles placed in Julian Bream's path as he began his career as a professional classical guitarist. At that stage, the only internationally-known player was Segovia, and Bream was faced with incredible scepticism. He already played piano and cello and had to study those instruments at the Royal College of Music, because he was banned from playing the guitar in the building: there was, of course, no-one to teach him the instrument. After college he was drafted into the British Army pay corps, but became a regular soldier so he could work as a musician in an army band. He took up electric guitar and played in the Royal Artillery's dance band. He was, he recalls, "the worst soldier the British Army had ever seen". The Royal Artillery were stationed at Woolwich, near enough central London for him to continue his classical concert career. On leaving the army, he went for an audition with the BBC, but failed it. He was, however, able to pick up work in radio and films, despite failing that initial audition. He had also, by now, taken up the lute, which provided a useful second source of income. He developed a useful relationship with Peter Burnett, a music producer at the BBC, who first recorded him in 1949. He made his London concert debut at the Wigmore Hall in 1951, and did his first real British tour the same year. A few recitals in Switzerland in 1954 led to his first European tours. His US debut came in a concert at Town Hall, New York, in 1958.

FIRST RECORD Julian Bream's first record was made in 1955, on the lute, accompanying the tenor Peter Pears in *An Anthology of English Song* works by Ford, Morley, Rosseter and Dowland. Many of these pieces were then completely unknown.

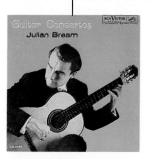

GUITAR CONCERTOS: ARNOLD AND GIULIANI (Released 1961) Malcolm Arnold: Guitar Concerto, Opus 67 (directed by the composer).
1. Allegro
2. Lento
3. Con Brio
Mauro Giuliani: Guitar Concerto In A, Opus 30.
1. Allegro Maestoso
2. Andantino Siciliano
3. Alla Polacca
Featuring The Melos Ensemble: Emanuel Hurwitz (violin), Ivor MacMahon (violin), Cecil Aronowitz (viola), Terence Weil (cello), Neil Saunders (horn), Richard Adeney (flute), Gervase de Peyer (clarinet).

RODRIGO & BRITTEN (Released 1964) Joaquin Rodrigo: Concierto De Aranjuez.
1. Allegro Con Spirito
2. Adagio
3. Allegro Gentile
Sir Colin Davis (conductor) and The Melos Chamber Orchestra.

Benjamin Britten: Gloriana – Courtly Dances (arr. Julian Bream).
Vivaldi: Concerto In D For Lute & Strings.
The Julian Bream Consort: Julian Bream (lute); Olive Zorian (violin); David Sandeman (alto flute, piccolo), Joy Hall & Desmond Dupré (bass viol); Robert Spencer (tabor, chittarone).

Dick Gaughan

Since his emergence in the late 1960s, Dick Gaughan has carved a niche for himself as one of the finest interpreters of traditional Irish and Scottish folk songs. Born into a working-class Glaswegian family well-versed in the rich heritage of Scottish folk song, he added Irish Republican songs and anthems and trade union songs to his repertoire and cultivated a following on the folk club circuit. With his reputation growing, he joined the Boys Of The Lough in 1972. His sonorous guitar work complemented Tommy Gunn's fiddle playing but he remained with them for less than a year. In 1972 he embarked on a solo career, cutting No More Forever. The choice of repertoire provided the template for later albums, combining traditional material with self-composed songs and covers of material by contemporary writers of a political bent, such as Ewan MacColl and Leon Rosselson. While his guitar work

was mellifluous, the passion of his vocals left no doubt about his convictions. Over the next few years, his solo work illustrated the rich diversity of his musical interests with Coppers & Brass being a collection of Scottish and Irish songs and dances, while Songs Of Ewan MacColl was a touching tribute to one of his muses. In the mid-1970s he joined the electric folk group Five Hand Reel for three albums and an extensive bout of touring in the US and Europe. Throughout this period he maintained his solo career. He left the group in 1978, although various members of the band later contributed to his solo albums. During the 1980s, he continued to expand his repertoire, adding material by younger writers such as Billy Bragg. He recorded the album Parallel Lines with Andy Irvine, a former member of Planxty and collaborator with Paul Brady. A restless spirit, Gaughan is one of the pillars of traditional folk music in the UK.

A DIFFERENT KIND OF LOVE SONG (Released 1983) *Tracks:* A Different King Of Love Song/ Revolution/ Prisoner 562/ Song Of Choice/ The Father's Song/ Think Again/ As I Walked On The Road/ Stand Up For Judas/ By The People/ Games People Play. *Line-up:* Dick Gaughan (guitars, vocal), Alan Tall (saxes), Bob Lenox (keyboards), Dave Pegg (bass), Dave Tulloch (percussion), Will Lindfors (drums).

TRUE AND BOLD: Songs Of The Scottish Miners (Released 1986) *Tracks:* Miner's Life Is Like A Sailor's/ Schoolday's End/ Farewell To 'Cotia/ Auchengeich Disaster/ Pound A Week Rise/ The Collier Laddie/ Which Side Are You On?/ The Drunken Rent Collector/ The Blantyre Explosion/ One Miner's Life/ The Ballad Of 1984. *Line-up:* Clarke Sorley (bass, keyboards), Alan Tall (sax), Jim Sutherland (percussion), Billy Jackson (pipes, whistles).

1983	1984	1985	1986	1987	1988	1989	1990	1991	1992	1993

DICK GAUGHAN & ANDY IRVINE: PARALLEL LINES (Released 1985) *Tracks:* The Creggan White Hare/ The Lads O' The Fair & Leith Docks/ At Twenty One/ My Back Pages & Afterthoughts/ The Dodgers Song/ Captain Thunderbolt/ Captain Colston/ Floo'ers O' The Forest. *Line-up:* Dick Gaughan (guitars, bass, vocals), Andy Irvine (bouzouki, mandola, mandolin, harmonica, vocals), Martin Buschmann (saxes), Nollaigh Ni Cathasaigh (fiddle), Judith Jaenicke (flute), Bob Lenox (Fender Rhodes piano). Recorded in partnership with Andy Irvine, who partnered Paul Brady during the 1970s.

LIVE IN EDINBURGH (Released 1985) *Tracks:* Revolution/ Now Westlin Winds/ Which Side Are You On?/ Victor Jara Of Chile/ Companeros/ Worker's Song/ Your Daughters And Your Sons/ Four Green Fields/ Ballad Of Accounting/ Jamie Foyers/ Glenlogie/ World Turned Upside Down.

This album represents a neat resumé of Gaughan's career. Recorded live, it comes from the heart of his political sensibility, while avoiding the hectoring rhetoric of so many politically-motivated performers.

ROD CLEMENTS, DICK GAUGHAN, RAY JACKSON, BERT JANSCH, RORY McLEOD, RAB NOAKES: WOODY LIVES! (Released 1988) *Tracks:* Hard Travellin'/ This Land Is Your Land/ Vigilante Man/ Pretty Boy Floyd/ Deportees (Plane Wreck At Los Gatos)/ Philadelphia Lawyer/ Do Re Mi/ Pastures Of Plenty/ Tom Joad/ Will You Miss Me. *Line-up:* Rod Clements (guitar, mandolin, bass), Ray Jackson (vocals, guitar, mandolin), Bert Jansch (vocals, guitar), Rory McLeod (vocals), Dick Gaughan (vocals, mandolin), Rab Noakes (vocals), Pat Rafferty (accordion).

CALL IT FREEDOM (Released 1985/89) *Tracks:* Bulmer's Fancy & The Silver Spire/ Shipwreck/ What You Do With What You've Got/ Ludlow Massacre/ That's The Way The River Runs/ Amandial/ Call It Freedom/ When I'm Gone/ Seven Good Soldiers/ Fifty Years From Now & Yardheads. Described by many as Scotland's greatest living troubadour, Gaughan showed with this compelling album the extent to which his muse is anchored firmly in the travails of the 20th century: every song is as relevant now as when it was first written. It scotches any notion that folk music is merely the dressing up of old songs for contemporary audiences.

SOR AND GIULIANI (Released 1974) Fernando Sor: Sonata In C, Opus 25 (Andante Largo/ Allegro Non Troppo/ Andantino Grazioso/ Minuetto & Trio/ Allegro).
Mauro Giuliani: Rossiniana No.1, Opus 119 (rev. Julian Bream).
Mauro Giuliani: Rossiniana No.3, Opus 121 (rev. Julian Bream).

Working at the end of the 18th century, Sor and Giuliani were among the first to write specifically for the guitar. While Sor's Sonata In C was a noble contribution to Spanish guitar music, Giuliani's Rossinianae were erratic. With Julian Bream's revisions, they have enhanced Giuliani's posthumous reputation as one of the most effective composers for the guitar.

VILLA-LOBOS: TWELVE ETUDES FOR THE GUITAR (Released 1978)
No.1: Allegro Non Troppo; Lento.
No.2: Allegro.
No.3: Allegro Moderato.
No.4: Poco Moderato; A Tempo; Grandioso.
No.5: Andantino.
No.6: Poco Allegro.
No.7: Tres Animé; Piu Mosso.
No.8: Moderato.
No.9: Tres Peu Animé.
No.10: Tres Animé; Vif; Un Peu Animé; Vif.
No.11: Lent; Animé.
No.12: Animé.
Heitor Villa-Lobos: Suite Populaire Brésilienne (Mazurka-Choro/ Schottisch-Choro/ Valse-Choro/ Gavotte-Choro).

GUITARRA (Released 1984)
Alonso Mudarra: Fantasia XIV.
Luis de Milan: Fantasia XXII.
Luys de Narvaez: La Cancion Del Emperador.
Narvaez: Conde Claros.
Mudarra: Fantasia X.
Santiago de Murcia: Prelude and Allegro.
Luigi Boccherini: Fandango (from Guitar Quintet In D, G.448).
Fernando Sor: Grand Solo. Op. 14.
Dioniso Aguado: Rondo In A Minor, Op. 2, No.3.
Sor: Variations On A Theme Of Mozart, Op.9 (Introduction: Andante Largo/ Theme: Andante Moderato/ Variations 1-5).
Francisco Tarrega: Etude In A/ Prelude In A Minor/ Recuerdos de la Alhambra.

RODRIGO & BROUWER (Released 1989) Joaquin Rodrigo: Fantasia Para Un Gentilhombre:
1. Villano
2. Ricercare
3. Espanoleta
4. Fanfare de la Caballeria de Napoles
5. Danza de la Hachas
6. Canario
Leo Brouwer: Concierto Elegiaco/ Guitar Concerto No. 3 (Tranquillo/ Interlude/ Finale: Toccata).
Julian Bream (guitar), Leo Brouwer (conductor), RCA Victor Chamber Orchestra.
Through Julian Bream's championing of his work, Leo Brouwer has become one of the 20th century's most respected composers for the guitar. While his own readings are interesting, he lacks Bream's zest as a performer.

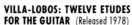

THE LUTE MUSIC OF JOHN DOWLAND (Released 1976)
1. Captain Digorie Piper's Galliard.
2. A Fancy.
3. My Lord Chamberlain, His Galliard.
4. Resolution.
5. Mr Langton's Galliard.
6. Forlorn Hope Fancy.
7. Sir John Souche's Galliard.
8. Piper's Pavan.
9. My Lord Willoughby's Welcome Home.
10. Galliard To Lachrimae.
11. A Fancy.
12. Farewell.
'My Lord Willoughby's Welcome Home' features two lutes in harmony, with Julian Bream using modern technology to overdub the second part.

MUSIC OF SPAIN, Volume I: MILAN & NARVAEZ (Released 1979)
Luis de Milan: From El Maestro.
Titles: Pavana1/ Pavana V/ Pavana V/ Fantasia X I I/ Fantasia VIII/ Fantasia IX/ Tento I/ Pavana IV/ Fantasia XVI.
Luys de Narvaez: From Los Seys Libros Del Delphin de Musica:
Book I: Fantasia V/ Book II: Fantasia V/ Book III: La Cancion Del Emperador/ Book II: Fantasia VI/ Book V: Arde Coracon Arde/ Book V: Ya Se Asiente El Rey Ramiro/ Book IV: O Gloriosa Domina/ Book VI: Conde Claros/ Book VI: Guardame Las Vacas/ Book VI: Tres Diferencias Por Otra Parte/ Book VI: Baxa De Contrapunto.

JULIAN BREAM AND DAME PEGGY ASHCROFT: TWO LOVES A Sequence Of Music & Poetry (Released 1988)
John Dowland: My Lady Hunsdon's Puffe/ The King Of Denmark's Galliard/ Envoi To The Phoenix & The Turtle/ Mignarda/ Queen Elizabeth's Galliard/ Loth To Depart/ The Earl Of Derby's Galliard/ Lachrimae Pavin/ Tarleton's Resurrection/ A Fancy/ Melancholy Galliard/ Semper Dowland, Semper Dolens/ Orlando Sleepeth.
Julian Bream's understated arrangements and Dame Peggy Ashcroft's untheatrical recitations bring warmth and affection to a project full of integrity.

THE COLLECTION (1993)
1. Golden Age of English Lute Music.
2. Lute Music from the Royal Courts of Europe.
3. Dances Of Dowland.
4. The Woods So Wild.
5. Concertos and Sonatas for Lute.
6. The Julian Bream Consort.
7. Fantasies, Ayres & Dances.
8. Popular Classics for Spanish Guitar.
9. Baroque Guitar.
10. Classic Guitar.
11. Romantic Guitar.
12. Twentieth Century Guitar 1.
13. Twentieth Century Guitar 2.
14. Dedication.
15. Guitar Concertos.
16. Julian Bream & Friends.
17. Two Loves.
18. Music for Voice and Guitar.
19. Elizabethan Lute Songs.
20. J.S. Bach: Lute Suites.
21. Villa-Lobos.
22. Guitar Concertos.
23. Milan-Narvaez.
24. Classical Heritage.
25. Granados-Albeniz.
26. La Guitarra Romantica.
27. Guitarra.
28. Rodrigo.

J GEILS

Born: Jerome Geils, February 20th 1946, New York, New York, US.

■ **Gibson Flying V (modified).**

Despite the fact that critically the J Geils Band could not put a foot wrong, they couldn't sell many records either. But their purism struck a chord with many old-timers who had become bored with modern rock. Prosaically, the J Geils Band cut titles like **Bobby Womack**'s 'I Found A Love', **John Lee Hooker**'s 'Serves You Right To Suffer' and Smokey Robinson's 'First I Look At The Purse', where Peter Wolf's vocals and Magic Dick's harmonica playing offset Geils's chunky chords.

After their debut, eponymous album of 1970, the band cut a string of albums – *Morning After* (1972), *Full House* (1972), *Bloodshot* (1973) and *Ladies Invited* (1973) among others – that increasingly featured group-composed material, culminating in songs like 'Centerfold' and 'Angel In Blue' (1982) which illustrated the more commercial path the band was taking. Detractors said they'd sold out; Wolf asserted they'd never described themselves as a blues band anyway. The only real drawback was that the group's principal writer, keyboardist Seth Justman, gradually assumed greater control over the group's output, and with this the synthesizer became the dominant instrument, relegating Geils's tasty licks to an auxiliary role. In 1983, Wolf left the group for a solo career. The band took some time before they formally split up, since when Geils has disappeared from sight.

LOWELL GEORGE

Born: April 13th 1945, Hollywood, California, US.
Died: June 29th 1979, Arlington, Virginia, US.

■ **Fender Stratocaster.**

One of the finest white slide guitarists, George combined a versatile knowledge of country and blues and contributed a body of material to his band Little Feat that went some way to defining the potential of the boogie band.

George's taste and sensitivity as a guitarist (and as a songwriter) were at odds with the prevailing knock-'em-dead attitude of most boogie bands. The tentatively picked opening bars of 'Willin' on *Little Feat* (1971) have a pathos belying the subject matter – nominally, it's a truckers' anthem. On 'Tripe Face Boogie' from *Sailin' Shoes* (1972) he gives full rein to his prodigious talents as a slide guitarist with some of the most scintillating playing since **Elmore James** kept his appointment with the reaper. *Dixie Chicken* (1973) showed a pronounced influence of New Orleans R&B, with George contributing punchy licks to Allen Toussaint's 'On Your Way Down' that would have made **Leo Nocentelli** of The Meters proud. Not content to make Little Feat one of the most evocative exponents of American music since The Band, George recorded a disappointingly uneven solo album, *Thanks I'll Eat It Here* (1979), and his grainy, textured slide playing graced sessions by Etta James, Robert Palmer, **Bonnie Raitt** and others.

BILLY GIBBONS

Born: December 16th 1949, Houston, Texas, US.

■ **Gibson Les Paul Standard; Gibson Flying V; Dean; St Blues.**

ZZ Top have become the most commercially successful boogie band of all. This has been achieved by extracting every last inch from a number of gimmicks, primarily videos that feature (a) women with stunning legs that must have been rented from a surgical appliance factory and (b) custom-built cars more authentic than those they seek to imitate.

The point about ZZ Top is that they have managed to assimilate cardinal cultural elements and pack them all into a recognizable, accessible format. As to whether Billy Gibbons is a good guitarist... who cares? Technical prowess does not figure in the ZZ Top manual. Each player contributes his part to the driving sound and the visual extravaganza, and that's all there is to it. *Eliminator* (1984) does for boogie bands what Arnold Schwarzenegger did for *Marvel* comics – but it's probably best heard as a soundtrack for the video collection. Gibbons is at his best when easing into longer guitar work-out sections, still in evidence on tracks like 'Pin Cushion' from *Antenna* (1994).

BRUCE GILBERT

Born: May 18th 1946, Watford, Hertfordshire, England.

Gilbert's manic, buzzsaw guitar characterized Wire's debut *Pink Flag* (1977) which included the bracingly aggressive 'Field Day For The Sundays' and 'Mr Suit'. The follow-up *Chairs Missing* (1978) showed the group tempering their aggression, with Gilbert applying delicate touches rather than the blistering runs of the first album.

154 (1979) contained some intriguing moments: 'A Touching Display' featured an extended blast of feedback, while 'A Mutual Friend' had a middle eight solo played on a cor anglais (a member of the oboe family). After these three early albums the group began to fall apart at the seams, disbanding in 1980. Gilbert started a solo career that was curious rather than interesting. Wire reformed in 1985, but the resulting *The Ideal Copy* (1987) and *A Bell Is A Cup (Until It's Struck)* (1989) lacked the imagination of those earlier outings.

ANDY GILL

Born: England.

■ **Jim Burns Magpie 2.**

Andy Gill spearheaded The Gang Of Four with a raw, unfussy style that led many to compare him with **Wilko Johnson** of Dr Feelgood. While the Gang's emergence coincided with punk, they possessed a political sense that far exceeded the posturings of their counterparts. The results were songs like 'Armalite Rifle' and 'Love Like Anthrax' that have a nervy twitchiness, nagging and grating effectively. Their debut album *Entertainment* (1979) was one of the least stylized and most plausible offerings to emerge, with Gill's loud, trebly rhythm guitar at its best when centrally placed. But the group changed lineups often, with later albums lacking consistency, and the Gang eventually went their separate ways in 1984.

VINCE GILL

Born: April 4th 1957, Norman, Oklahoma, US.

■ **Fender Telecaster.**

One of country music's better and brighter newcomers, Gill has been overshadowed by singers Garth Brooks and Clint Black. Gill's music reveals an understanding of the roots of country beyond that of the more flamboyantly successful artists, and he wields his Telecaster with such conviction that Mark Knopfler offered him a job in Dire Straits in 1990. After joining MCA with producer Tony Brown in 1989, Gill began to draw from a wide range of styles such as bluegrass, western swing and contemporary pop.

The first album from this stable, *When I Call Your Name* (1989), was orthodox but promising, and *I Still Believe In You* (1992) proved to be his most well-rounded album, with a willingness on Gill's part to break out and pick with confidence.

DAVID GILMOUR

Born: March 6th 1944, Cambridge, England.

■ **Fender Stratocaster; Squier Stratocaster.**

Gilmour would suddenly appear at the top of Pink Floyd's concert-built wall as the vocals spilled out, 'For I have become comfortably numb...' and would play a guitar solo of breathtaking simplicity and eloquence.

That was Gilmour's wonderful and dramatic contribution to the live 'Comfortably Numb' from *The Wall* (1979). He'd joined Pink Floyd in 1968 as replacement for the increasingly wayward **Syd Barrett**, and his guitar work has always contained similarities to that of **Frank Zappa**. Both reveal an ability to use spaces as much as notes that many would do well to emulate. Perhaps it may have something to do with both having operated as producers, and as a result knowing how to play within the context of an aural whole. Or perhaps they were both bone idle and wanted to get away with playing as little as possible?

Gilmour's succinct delivery and understanding of dynamics was invaluable to the highly charged atmosphere inherent in much of the best of bassist Roger Waters' writing for Pink Floyd. A couple of taut, stinging notes imbued the lyrics with greater weight than any number of Waters' snarled imprecations could achieve.

However, it must be said that since Gilmour and Waters ceased working together, neither has achieved individually what they managed together. In recent years Gilmour has increasingly been putting himself about on sessions with artists like Kate Bush, Bryan Ferry, Supertramp and Dream Academy. He makes regular guest appearances at charity concert bashes, made two decent solo albums, *David Gilmour* (1978) and *About Face* (1984), and has of course been part of the reformed Pink Floyd since 1987.

GORDON GILTRAP

Born: April 6th 1948, Tonbridge, Kent, England.

■ *Armstrong custom; Eggle; Hohner; Hofner.*

One of a clutch of guitarists who emerged at the end of the 1960s on the British folk club circuit, Giltrap seemed preoccupied with style and the development of a distinctive guitar sound. Being a technical wizard is no substitute for feel, and although Giltrap has contributed to a number of film scores, and his 'Heartsong' was used for a long time as the theme for a BBC TV holiday show, his best playing is heard when he's picking traditional material such as 'Magpie Rag' and 'O Jerusalem'.

GREG GINN

Born: US.

■ *Ampeg Dan Armstrong.*

A central figure on the Los Angeles hardcore scene, Ginn's weird cross of heavy metal and jazz in Black Flag was hefty, biting stuff, and has been an inspiration to other luminaries such as **Bob Mould**, **Thurston Moore**, **J Mascis** and **Mike Scaccia**. Although albums such as *Damaged* (1981), *Family Man* (1984) and *In My Head* (1985) have sold in small quantities, they are essential listening for any hardcore enthusiast. Black Flag split in 1989; Ginn helped to found the SST label which first recorded Hüsker Dü and Sonic Youth among others.

ANDREW GOLD

Born: August 2nd 1951, Burbank, California, US.

Gold is actually a better pianist and arranger than he is a guitarist, although he contributed some pleasant rhythm work to Linda Ronstadt's *Heart Like A Wheel* (1972) and Stephen Bishop's lovely *Careless* (1976). Since that time Gold has broadened his horizons and developed a successful solo career with a string of charming, refined albums which have about as much character as the interior of a McDonald's.

IAN GOMM

Born: March 17th 1947, London, England.

Joining **Brinsley Schwarz** in 1972, Gomm's country influenced guitar work gave *Silver Pistol* (1972) a cohesiveness that had been lacking in the group's previous outings. Central figures on the British pub circuit, Brinsley Schwarz were at their best live where the various qualities of blues, reggae, R&B and country were allowed to merge together, forming an easy-on-the-ear blend of knockabout pop. After the band split in 1975 Gomm started a solo career, cutting *Gomm With The Wind* (1978), *Summer Holiday* (1979) and *The Village Choice* (1982), full of cute tunes and crisp guitar work.

STEVE GOODMAN

Born: July 25th 1948, Chicago, Illinois, US.
Died: September 20th 1984, Seattle, Washington, US.

■ *Martin; Gibson flat-top.*

With his dry perceptive wit, Goodman promised to become one of the more acute documenters of American life until his demise at 36 from leukaemia. In 1971 he was signed to Buddah and cut *Steve Goodman in Nashville*, with Kris Kristofferson and Norbert Putnam producing, which included his best-known composition 'City Of New Orleans'. The follow-up, *Somebody Else's Troubles* (1973), took potshots at a variety of targets including the continued involvement of the US in Vietnam ('The Ballad Of Penny Evans'). Later albums such as *Jessie's Jigs And Other Favorites* (1975) and *Hot Spot* (1980) showed his versatility as a guitarist and featured contributions from mandolinist and banjo man Jethro Burns, formerly of the duo Homer & Jethro. Testimony to Goodman's fortitude and the affection in which he was held by his colleagues was eloquently amplified by those who participated in commemorative concerts: **Willie Nelson**, Emmylou Harris, Jackson Browne, Jimmy Buffett, Rosanne Cash, **Rodney Crowell**, The Nitty Gritty Dirt Band, **John Hartford**, **Richie Havens**, **Bonnie Raitt**, **David Bromberg** and John Prine.

JOHN GOODSALL

Born: February 15th 1953, London, England.

■ *Fender Stratocaster; Washburn Falcon; Shergold 6/12.*

For a brief period Brand X were one of the best jazz-rock bands in Britain. With appealing melodies and accomplished musicians – Goodsall plus Robin Lumley (keyboards), Phil Collins (drums), Morris Pert (percussion) and Percy Jones (bass) – they had every reason to believe they could endure where others had foundered. However, the group split in 1982, but during their years together Goodsall's guitar work, particularly on *Moroccan Roll* (1977) and *Do They Hurt* (1980), was as exciting as anything that **John Etheridge** or **Allan Holdsworth** managed.

SCOTT GORHAM

Born: March 17th 1951, Santa Monica, California, US.

■ *Gibson Les Paul; Hartung Strat-style.*

While Gorham didn't join Thin Lizzy until 1974, he did much to consolidate the group's gradual evolution from the directionless purveyors of the Irish folk tune 'Whisky In A Jar' to stadium-filling rock band. Many point to 'The Boys Are Back In Town' – a classic rock track from the same school as Van Halen's 'Jump' and Deep Purple's 'Smoke On The Water' – as the most important piece of Gorham's influence on Lizzy. Gorham had many fine hours on stage thereafter, but once he got in the studio it seemed that a tame playing-by-rote attitude took over. Gorham bounced back with a new band, 21 Guns, in 1992, their debut album called *Salute*.

STONE GOSSARD

Born: US.

■ *Gibson Les Paul.*

Gossard is Robin to **Mike McCready**'s Batman in Pearl Jam. While they have forged a formidable partnership, with Gossard's role primarily one of

rhythm guitarist, there is little about the band to inspire much confidence. Although *Vs.* (1993) sold by the truckload it lacked the gutbucket character of *Ten* (1992), and the group was already sounding tired.

BOON GOULD

Born: February 28th 1957, Hampshire, England.

■ *Gibson Les Paul.*

Smooth, glossy, jazzy, sophisticated and dull, Level 42 developed an innocuous blend of jazz and funk in the 1980s, and *World Machine* (1985) and *Running In The Family* (1987) are pleasant if bland. It all proved too much for Gould, who left the band in 1987 having suffered the indignity of being subordinated by bassist and bandleader Mark King. A solo career was threatened.

DAVEY GRAHAM

Born: November 22nd 1940, Leicester, England.

■ *Gibson flat-top.*

Graham has been one of the more notable casualties of contemporary music, his drug dependence destroying his style and dexterity. But at his peak he defined folk guitar picking for many British players.

Graham's emergence in the late-1950s heralded a new era in the appreciation of folk music, and he made connections between jazz, blues and folk as well as Eastern motifs. Graham arranged the Irish traditional song 'She Moved Through the Fair' as an Indian raga, while Charlie Mingus' 'Better Git It In Your Soul' illustrated his adeptness as an improviser. His lyrically fluent composition 'Angie' became the template for budding British folk pickers, including **John Renbourn** and **Bert Jansch**.

Folk Roots New Routes (1965) with Sussex-born singer Shirley Collins was an ambitious and successful attempt at combining jazz, blues and folk. Much play was made of Collins' regional inflections and as a result long established exponents of British folk music like The Copper Family began to assume a wider significance, and later had an impact on British folk-rock bands like Steeleye Span and The Albion Band.

Graham for his part remained aloof from the burgeoning rock fraternity, preferring instead to concentrate on the expansion of his repertory of instruments to include Eastern items such as bouzouki, sarod and oud. Then **Stefan Grossman** signed Graham to the Kicking Mule label, and Graham cut *The Complete Guitarist* (1978) which included pieces by British classical composer Ralph Vaughan Williams among others. But Graham's years of drug abuse have made him increasingly frail and hesitant: there are few things worse than hearing talent ravaged by physical incapacity.

BILLY GRAMMER

Born: August 28th 1925, Benton, Illinois, US.

■ *Grammer; Gibson Super 400.*

Grammer's playing career started in 1947, broadcasting over radio station WRAL, and this eventually led to a spot on *The Jimmy Dean Show* and a recording contract with Fred Foster at Monument in 1958. A fine picker and session musician, Grammer charted with The Weavers' 'Gotta Travel On' and 'Bonaparte's Retreat', and later cut *Country Guitar* (1965) which is a good all-round introduction to his range of styles. Grammer became involved with a guitar-making operation, producing flat-top steel-strung guitars. In the mid-1960s he had put over $18,000 into the development of the Grammer guitars, and his career as a performer had been brought to a standstill as he would appear to have been spending all his time working on rather than playing guitars.

EDDY GRANT

Born: Edmond Montague Grant, March 5th 1948, Plaisance, Guyana.

■ **Fender Stratocaster; Vantage.**

Grant belongs to a tradition similar to that of Jamaican producer Lee Perry, harnessing his skills as an arranger and producer to create a blend of rock, reggae and soul that has always managed to find the pulse of contemporary music. While his guitar work has never been above average his record making instincts are finely tuned. Grant had moved to England in 1960, and as a member of The Equals he first hit the mark with 'Baby Come Back' (1968). Later, in his own right, he had success with 'Living On The Front Line' (1979), 'Police On My Back' (1979), 'Electric Avenue' (1981) and 'Gimme Hope Joanna' (1986). A good writer, Grant has retained credibility by reflecting the concerns of the less privileged, and at his studio in Barbados he actively supports and encourages local talent.

BUCK GRAVES

Born: US.

■ **Dobro resonator.**

Also known as Uncle Josh, Graves was one of the first players to make the 'dobro' resonator guitar appealing to a younger generation of bluegrass players. Initially he played with bluegrass singer Mac Wisemaan and country duo Wilma Lee & Stoney Cooper until he joined **Lester Flatt** & Earl Scruggs' Foggy Mountain Boys in 1955 ('Foggy Mountain Breakdown', 'Cabin In The Hills'). There Graves perfected a rolling, syncopated style that could be adapted to ballads or breakdowns with equal ease. Had it not been for Graves' alter-ego Uncle Josh, **Mike Auldridge** would never have taken up the instrument. No sir. That would have been an awful shame.

JAY GRAYDON

Born: Los Angeles, California, US.

■ **Gibson ES335.**

A session man whose credibility was not impeded by being recruited for Steely Dan's *Aja* (1977) session by Messrs Fagen and Becker. His fluid groove on 'Peg' contributed many phrases to the laidback guitarist's manual. Sadly, Graydon has not bothered to amplify further, with the result that his work with singer/

songwriter Stephen Bishop and jazz-rock pianist Joe Sample, among others, is a tad repetitive.

COLIN GREEN

Born: England.

■ **Guild Starfire.**

While **Alexis Korner**'s Blues Incorporated group was the catalyst for the blues boom in Britain in the early-1960s, there were others experimenting with the style. Georgie Fame & The Blue Flames adapted the lean, Hammond-dominated sound of jazz organist Jimmy Smith to a repertoire that embraced Booker T & The MGs, Mose Allison and James Brown. Colin Green, Fame's main axeman in the Blue Flames, had been active on the British jazz scene since the mid-1950s, and contributed the silken threads that appeared to stitch together *R&B At The Flamingo* (1964). Recorded live at the London club, it came as close as anything to capturing the enthusiasm of such gigs, with versions of Nat Adderley's 'Work Song', Phil Upchurch's 'You Can't Sit Down' and Joe Williams's 'Baby Please Don't Go'. On later albums such as *Fame At Last* (1964) and *Sound Venture* (1965) Green's playing was little more than a rhythmic auxiliary, mixed well back to allow maximum prominence for Fame's vocals and Hammond organ. Still active, Green is the archetypal professional musician, seldom lauded but a vital component of the contemporary music scene in Europe.

FREDDIE GREEN

Born: Frederick William Green, March 31st 1911, Charleston, South Carolina, US. Died: March 1st 1987, Las Vegas, Nevada, US.

■ **Stromberg Master 400; Epiphone Emperor; Gretsch Eldorado.**

Never one to miss a fine musician, producer John Hammond Senior spotted Green in 1937 and recommended the guitarist to Count Basie. Green was recruited on the spot and became a linchpin of the Basie sound until the bandleader's death in 1984. Green's fine, accurate four-to-the-bar rhythm work supplemented drummer Jo Jones and bassist Walter Page, making them probably the finest big-band rhythm section of them all. Trumpeter Buck Clayton once said that Basie never played much with his left hand, and so Green did it for him. Pressed to choose just one record from the vast Basie output, it would be the classic 1959 album *April In Paris*.

GARY GREEN

Born: November 20th 1950, London, England.

Formed from the remnants of Simon Dupree & The Big Sound in 1969, Gentle Giant set aside the earthy R&B of their former incarnation and adopted a progressive art-rock approach. Green was added to the lineup to give the band's sound greater variation. While a string of albums including *Acquiring The Taste* (1971), *Octopus* (1972) and *In A Glass House* (1973) assiduously courted fans of **Robert Fripp**, they lacked real flair. Green seldom had the

opportunity to shine as his style was earthy and gritty, and not really compatible with the quasi-artistic noodlings of the rest of the group. They split in 1980.

GRANT GREEN

Born: June 6th 1931, St Louis, Missouri, US. Died: January 31st 1979, New York, New York, US.

■ **Gibson L7; Epiphone Emperor; D'Aquisto New Yorker Deluxe.**

Green was a post-bop guitarist of some stature who settled into the mainstream with a muscular, supple style that eschewed experimentation for its own sake. His playing with trombonist Grachan Moncur III and hornman Stanley Turrentine had an elliptical quality, foreshadowing the incisive, funk-style phrases of players like **Eric Gale** and **Mike Hampton** in the early-1970s. Arguably Green's best was reserved for his small-group albums of the 1960s where his interplay with organist Big John Patton has the sprightly verve more commonly associated with **Steve Cropper** and Booker T. A worthwhile compilation is *Best Of Grant Green: Street Funk & Jazz Grooves* on Blue Note.

LLOYD GREEN

Born: October 4th 1937, Mobile, Alabama, US.

■ **Sho-Bud.**

One of the busiest session steel guitarists on the Nashville circuit, Green contributed to the homogenization of the Nashville Sound with his accompaniment to a slew of records such as George Jones's 'She Still Thinks I Really Care', Faron Young's 'It's Four In The Morning', Lynn Anderson's 'Rose Garden', Crystal Gayle's 'Talking In Your Sleep', Don Williams' 'Gypsy Woman' and Tammy Wynette's 'Stand By Your Man'. He also played steel on The Byrds classic country-rock album, *Sweetheart Of The Rodeo* (1968).

While the Nashville Sound possessed a veneer of sophistication, it fell to individuals like Green to give recordings an earthy aura of authenticity. His solo albums – *Steel Rides* (1976), *Stainless Steel* (1978) and *Green Velvet* (1982) – had more character than is usual for sessionmen turned soloists, illustrating a willingness to extend and embroider upon a technique that had paid dividends over the years in the accompaniment of others.

MICK GREEN

Born: England.

■ **Fender Telecaster.**

In his heyday as guitarist in Johnny Kidd's Pirates, Green could crank out more volume from a simple Vox AC30 amp than most would manage later with several stacks. It was a technique that worked very well: he simply turned the volume controls up to ten and let rip. An early advocate of 'never mind art, let's dance', Mick Green had several licks – as on 'I'll Never Get Over You' and 'A Shot Of Rhythm & Blues' (both on a 1964 EP) – that were very close to his heart, and he didn't mind using them as regularly as possible. Later, Green's approach doubtless gave **Wilko**

Johnson of Dr Feelgood a few ideas about playing the guitar.

When The Pirates reformed and cut *Out Of Their Skulls* (1977), a decibel-cruncher if ever there was one, many budding metallurgists realized that cranking up the volume was probably a quicker way to a healthy bank balance than a diet of Michael Moorcock's science fiction books. The Pirates gradually disappeared, but their legacy remains in the shape of Iron Maiden. Thanks, Mick.

PETER GREEN

Born: Peter Greenbaum, October 20th 1946, London, England.

■ *Gibson Les Paul Standard; Gibson ES335; Fender Stratocaster.*

A member of the John Mayall academy, better known as The Bluesbreakers, Green appeared on *A Hard Road* (1966), the follow-up to the groundbreaking *Blues Breakers* album (1965) featuring Eric Clapton.

Clapton may have been God, but Green was a worthy Gabriel: the title track of *Hard Road* may have obliquely referred to the travails of negotiating the Watford Gap in a Ford Transit, but Green played as if hard luck and trouble had indeed been his only friend after lengthy sojourns avoiding the police at the bottom of Beale Street. And his version of Freddie King's 'The Stumble' was so economical, so incisive, that one could be forgiven for thinking its place of origin was the Thames Delta.

After leaving Mayall, Green formed Fleetwood Mac and made a better job of authenticating the source of his material ('Dust My Broom' was properly credited to Elmore James, for example). His guitar work blossomed, and the group revived songs such as Little Willie John's 'Need Your Love So Bad' (1968) alongside a liberal dose of self-composed material such as the languorous 'Man Of The World' (1969) and 'Albatross' (1969). Throughout, Green's guitar was considered and apposite, yet never lost its blues roots. On reflection, Green seems the most consistently inspired of the 1960s British blues-rock players.

But Green realized that all gods have feet of clay, and forsook stardom to become a grave-digger. Despite desultory attempts at comebacks, he has appeared content to stand or fall by what he did in the past. Poor old Eric has given up the booze and the one night stands and goes to fashion shows at Armani, interspersed by interminable stints at the Royal Albert Hall. Oh well...

MARLIN GREENE

Born: US.

When Quin Ivy set up Quinvy studios in 1965, Muscle Shoals studio owner Rick Hall recommended that he approach Marlin Greene as his factotum. Like Jimmy Johnson and songwriter Dan Penn, Greene could turn his hand to anything: playing guitar, arranging, designing, writing, producing or engineering. A vital person to have around, in fact.

With Percy Sledge, Greene contributed material in collaboration with Eddie Hinton like 'Cover Me' and 'You're all Around Me', but his real value crystallized with his co-production (with Ivy) of Sledge's 'When A Man Loves A Woman'. In 1969 he co-produced, with Jann Wenner (editor of *Rolling Stone* magazine) the Boz Scaggs' debut for Atlantic, featuring the mighty Duane Allman who wields his axe on 'Loan Me A Dime' as if he's auditioning for the role of Norman Bates. During the 1970s and 1980s Greene worked with the unsung Hinton and played on sessions at Muscle Shoals Sound, Atlantic South and Capricorn.

BRYAN GREGORY

Born: US.

During his brief tenure with The Cramps, Gregory contributed the torrid, frantic guitar work to the great garage-band trash single 'Drug Train', released after their debut album *Songs The Lord Taught Us* (1980, produced by Alex Chilton). Gregory left the group in 1981.

DAVE GREGORY

Born: England.

■ *Gibson Les Paul; Rickenbacker 330-12; Fender Stratocaster; Schecter Telecaster-style.*

In 1978 Gregory replaced Barry Andrews in the quirky and emphatically English band XTC, brainchild of Andy Partridge and based in that hotbed of teenage revolt, Swindon, Wiltshire. Gregory quickly provided a more reasoned and musical guitar foil to Partridge's wilder six-string ramblings, but has had to reserve his detailed work for XTC to the studio after Partridge gave up touring. Groups as clever and as witty as this lot seldom achieve commercial acceptability. However 'Making Plans For Nigel' was a hit, with Gregory's plangent chording offsetting Partridge's pithy lyrics, rounding out *Drums And Wires* (1979) to make one of the most arresting accomplishments of that year. The group's finest album to date is probably *Oranges And Lemons* (1989), just bursting with wonderful tunes and Gregory's perfectly measured guitar parts.

CLIVE GREGSON

Born: January 4th 1955, Manchester, England.

■ *Martin 000-18; Fender Telecaster; Fender Jazzmaster.*

Gregson might be forgiven for thinking that his 15 minutes of fame had eluded him when he was the subject of curious critical speculation back in 1980. It seems he might have been the new Bob Dylan, or Irving Berlin, or whoever else it may have been. Undaunted by these larger than life ghosts, Gregson and his group Any Trouble set about the business of penning quaint, quirky songs ('Trouble With Love' and 'To Be A King') in the Squeeze/Jules Shear mode. Didn't sell many records, though, and Any Trouble parted company.

A solo career followed, including a duo with the extravagantly talented vocalist Christine Collister. The two also worked in Richard Thompson's band, but years of abortive dogging around on the folk club circuit seemed likely until a production assignment came up for Gregson with English duo Pat Shaw and Julie Matthews. Country, folk, call it what you will, *Lies & Alibis* (1993) was a fine achievement. The quality of singing and writing was impeccable, and Gregson could bring to bear a perspective from his own honorable failures to tell what worked best, be it as producer or guitarist. Gregson also performed some memorable concerts in the 1990s with erstwhile Bible mainman Boo Hewerdine.

DAVID GRIER

Born: US.

Acoustic guitarist Grier's percussive picking on *Freewheeling* (1990) combines stylistic variations such as bluegrass, jazz and western swing to present a deft, accessible compendium that is as dynamic as it is virtuosic. He deserves to be better known.

SID GRIFFIN

Born: Kentucky, US.

The Long Ryders were formed in 1981 and, in tandem with others such as Rain Parade and Green On Red, contributed to the revival of interest in country-rock outfits. While many country-rock bands in the past had taken their reference points from Nashville, Griffin's stemmed from his enthusiasm for Buffalo Springfield, The Byrds and The Flying Burrito Brothers. However, after a fistful of consistently interesting albums, such as *Long Ryders* (1983), *Native Sons* (1984) and *State Of Our Union* (1985), they disbanded in 1987. Griffin lives in London and at the time of writing plays with The Coal Porters.

BRIAN GRIFFITHS

Born: England.

■ *Hofner Colorama; Guyatone LG50.*

In 1962 Griffiths replaced Adrian Barber in The Big Three. One of the most popular Liverpudlian bands of the early-1960s, they played the same circuit as The Beatles including The Cavern and the clubs of Hamburg. The Big Three were by all accounts a tough, rousing outfit, sowing seeds for later power trios, and were highly regarded by their fellow musicians in Liverpool. A great example of Griffiths' soloing can be heard on 'Some Other Guy' (1963), while the excitement of the group is captured on the *Live At The Cavern* EP (1963). Griffiths and bassist Johnny Gustafson left later in 1963.

MARK GRIFFITHS

Born: England.

■ *Squier Stratocaster; Hohner Revelation.*

Foil to steel-man Gordon Huntley in Matthews Southern Comfort, Griffiths attempted to take the departed Ian Matthews' place as vocalist on *Southern Comfort* (1971), *Frog City* (1971) and *Stir Don't Shake* (1972). It didn't work, and the group split. In the 1980s Griffiths was more often heard playing bass, but turned up playing six-string again in Matthews' revitalized Plainsong outfit in 1993.

STEVE GRIMES

Born: June 4th 1962, Liverpool, England.

Like Jesus Jones, The Farm had weighty expectations heaped upon their shoulders when they made a very good album at the very beginning of their recording career. Their debut *Spartacus* (1991) was assured and imaginative, lacking the artifice and cockiness prevalent in most bands who crack it so early. Although they maximize the potential of studio technology, it has not been allowed to take over, and Grimes' guitar work on, for example, 'Groovy Train' adds a pleasant shine to the overall group sound.

TINY GRIMES

Born: Lloyd Grimes, July 7th 1916, Newport News, Virginia, US. Died: March 4th 1989.

■ **Guild custom tenor guitar.**

Having started his career as a jazz pianist before gravitating to the electric guitar, Grimes was one of the premier stylists in the wake of **Charlie Christian** to absorb the soloing potential of the electric guitar. Grimes used a four-string 'tenor' guitar, popular with banjo players of the time who wanted an easier route into the guitar.

While Grimes' most impressive work was in the company of musicians like pianist Art Tatum and saxmen Coleman Hawkins and Charlie Parker – all stylists and innovators – his interplay with Parker on the legendary Savoy recordings (1944, notably 'Tiny's Tempo') offers a tantalizing glimpse of two virtuosi in the process of evolving their styles. Grimes in particular vacillates from four-to-the-bar rhythm work to the single-note picking style of Christian. A later outing with trumpeter Roy Eldridge, *One Is Never Too Old To Swing* (1978), lived up to its title and included a lyrical rendition of 'T Ain't What You Do'.

DAVID GRISSOM

Born: US.

■ **Fender; PRS; Collings.**

In 1987 country artist Joe Ely assembled a new band and brought in lead guitarist Grissom, whose R&B influences added a new power to Ely's albums. The result is that since Grissom joined just about everything Ely has done has been nigh on indispensable: *Lord Of The Highway* (1987), *Dig All Night* (1988), *Live At Liberty Lunch* (1990), *Love And Danger* (1992) and *Highways And Heartaches* (1993).

STEFAN GROSSMAN

Born: April 16th 1945, New York, New York, US.

■ **Martin OM-45; Maurer.**

One of the most diligent and industrious students of indigenous American musical styles, Grossman has been championing the cause of folk and blues ever since his arrival on the New York club circuit in the mid-1960s, when he brought **Rev Gary Davis**, **Son House**, **Mississippi Fred McDowell** and **Skip James** out of obscurity.

Grossman's solo records, such as *Aunt Molly's Murray Farm* (1968) and *Ragtime Cowboy Jew* (1970), while demonstrating his meticulous fingerpicking technique, suffer from a stiff correctness and give the impression that this is his day-job and should therefore be accorded due solemnity. If he attacked with a little more levity, his albums could be as accessible as that other scholar, **Ry Cooder**.

Having said that, Grossman's tuitional recordings and manuals on ragtime and blues guitar have guided many fledgling musicians through awkward learning curves. Grossman set up the Kicking Mule label to release his own albums and other guitar-based music, and has also issued tuitional albums through this outlet including guides by **Mickey Baker** (*Jazz Rock Guitar*), Charlie Musselwhite (*Harmonica According To...*) and Sam Mitchell (*Bottleneck & Slide Guitar*).

LUTHER GROSVENOR

Born: December 23rd 1949, Worcester, England.

As a member of the late lamented Spooky Tooth, Grosvenor's brisk playing and acute lyrics were like a breath of fresh air in 1968. The group had first assembled – minus keyboardist Gary Wright – as Art, and cut a curious album, *Supernatural Fairy Tales* (1967), and an even more curious cover of **Stephen Stills**' 'For What It's Worth'.

On changing their name, Spooky Tooth started to knock out a string of quietly impressive, noisy albums – *It's All About* (1968) and *Spooky Two* (1969) – with Traffic and later Rolling Stones producer Jimmy Miller. Titles like 'Better By You, Better Than Me' and neat versions of The Band's 'The Weight' and John D Loudermilk's 'Tobacco Road' were infused with a subtle wit and Grosvenor's ability to lift note-perfect solos at will.

In 1972, Grosvenor left the band to record an expansive but ultimately unsuccessful solo album, *Under Open Skies*, before changing his name to Ariel Bender and joining Mott The Hoople in 1973. Unfortunately Ian Hunter's Hoople had peaked, following their liaison with the mighty producer Guy Stevens and the less mighty David Bowie. A spell with Widowmaker in the mid-1970s followed, but obscurity beckoned and Bender bowed out. He was last heard of working behind the scenes in a grocer's shop in Wisconsin.

ISAAC GUILLORY

Born: February 27th 1947, Cuba.

■ **Martin D-35S; Gibson L5; Fender Telecaster; Fender Stratocaster.**

Born on a US Navy base, Guillory grew up in Florida and moved to England in the early-1970s where he began playing the folk circuit. Guillory's eponymous debut solo album appeared in 1974, since when he has become a respected and talented session player, appearing for example on two albums by singer-songwriter Al Stewart, *Past Present & Future* (1974), and *Modern Times* (1975) where he assists **Simon Nicol** and **Tim Renwick**. Guillory also indulged in

jazz-rock in the late-1970s as a member of Pacific Eardrum, who made two albums. Guillory issued more solo records in the late-1980s and, although best known for his acoustic work, is well able to adapt to most styles.

BONNIE GUITAR

Born: Bonnie Buckingham, March 25th 1934, Auburn, Washington, US.

Bonnie Guitar was from a musical household and started playing the clarinet before moving to the guitar. At school she played in various groups, after which she worked the clubs, playing in pop, country and R&B bands. Employed by producer Fabor Robison to work as a session guitarist at his studios, she played on recordings with early rock'n'roller Dorsey Burnette and Ned 'From A Jack To A King' Miller. Gradually her career picked up, she charted with Ned Miller's 'Dark Moon', and since the early-1960s she has run her own label, Dolton, and worked for the Dot label as head of A&R in the country department. After leaving Dot she cut 'I'm Living In Two Worlds' (1966), 'A Woman In Love' (1967), 'I Believe In Love' (1968), 'Happy Everything' (1972) and 'Honey On The Moon' (1980).

GUITAR SLIM

Born: Eddie Jones, December 10th 1926, Greenwood, Mississippi, US. Died: February 7th 1959, New York, New York, US.

■ **Gibson Les Paul.**

Arranged by pianist Ray Charles, 'The Things That I Used To Do' is a seminal chunk of gritty R&B that came out of nowhere, as did its purveyor Guitar Slim. He was a showman of dazzling proportions and, with an extended cord for his guitar, was the first modern guitarist to become fully mobile on stage, wandering around as he played. His only other song of note was 'Something To Remember You By' (1956), and his career was cut short by pneumonia.

JAMES GURLEY

Born: James Martin Gurley, 1942, Detroit, Michigan, US.

■ **Gibson SG; Fender Stratocaster; Fender Telecaster.**

As a member of Janis Joplin's first group, Big Brother & The Holding Company, guitarist Gurley was overshadowed by Joplin's histrionics to such an extent that the quality of the group's playing on songs like 'Ball & Chain' and Erma Franklin's 'Piece Of My Heart' was pretty much an irrelevance. When Joplin left the group, Gurley remained for albums like *Be A Brother*. While the group's other guitarist **Sam Andrew** went on to join Joplin's next outfit, The Full Tilt Boogie Band, Gurley disappeared into oblivion.

ROBIN GUTHRIE

Born: Falkirk, Scotland.

■ **Fender.**

One of the more creative guitarists to emerge in the 1980s, Guthrie eventually joined with bassist Simon Raymonde and vocalist Elizabeth Fraser early in that decade to form The Cocteau Twins, bastions of the indie circus who remained with British label 4AD until 1993 when they moved to Phonogram.

Throughout those years the distinctive stylings of Guthrie combined with Fraser's hauntingly evocative vocals gave the indie marketplace an intellectual probity that had previously been notably absent. Guthrie's guitar playing is often disguised, dressed up in the band's beloved studio effects, and as such typifies the approach of many modern players who use the instrument for its textural shadings rather than as a traditional soloing vehicle.

While the Cocteaus never attained the immense success of other indie bands such as The Stone Roses and The Shamen, their highly individual style, alternately melodic and ambient, proved sufficiently accessible for them to stitch together a number of modest hits – 'Pearly Dewdrops Drops', 'Tiny Dynamine' and 'Echoes In A Shallow Bay' – and an impressive sequence of albums that included *Head Over Heels* (1983) and *Heaven Or Las Vegas* (1990).

However, their most poignant outing was a collaboration as This Mortal Coil, the brainchild of 4AD head Ivo Watts-Russell, on a dramatic reworking of the Tim Buckley composition 'Song To The Siren'. The stark vocal lines and atmospheric guitar figures evoked memories of *The Marble Index* album by Nico, formerly chanteuse of the Velvet Underground.

WOODY GUTHRIE

Born: Woodrow Wilson Guthrie, July 14th 1912, Okemah, Oklahoma, US. Died: October 3rd 1967, New York, New York, US.

■ *Gibson L-00 (with 'This Guitar Kills Fascists' sticker); Gibson Southerner Jumbo.*

The music of Woody Guthrie occupies a very special place in the history of the United States. He became the voice of the people in the Depression of the 1930s when his simple guitar-and-vocal songs spoke graphically of the plight of the many migrant workers, and provided them with a message of hope.

Taught to play the guitar by an uncle whom he lived with in Pampa, Texas, Guthrie learned traditional tunes which he adapted with his own lyrics.

His spare guitar accompaniment to 'dust bowl ballads' and traditional songs such as 'Pretty Boy Floyd', 'Dust Bowl Refugees', 'I Ain't Got No Home', 'Gypsy Davy', 'Oklahoma Hills', 'This Land Is Your Land' and 'John Henry' wasn't designed to win plaudits for instrumental accomplishment, but simply to support and add weight to the lyrics. While the imagery of hymns, ballads, blues and dance tunes were pivotal to his message, increasingly Guthrie came to use chords emblematically, investing a word or a phrase with greater power through his command of the guitar. By the mid-1940s, his command of structure was such that the song cycle of 'Grand Coulee Dam' and 'Pastures Of Plenty', celebrating the building of hydro-electric dams in the Pacific Northwest, became deeply ironic thanks to his use of intonation and emphasis.

While Guthrie frequently raged at iniquity, it was never impotent: 'Plane Wreck At Los Gatos (Deportees)' is so strong that even later versions by

The Byrds, Dolly Parton and Emmylou Harris retain the essential indignation and outrage of the original. By 1950, he had started his long fight against illness that was to claim his life 17 years later. While he declined physically his reputation increased, with his songs being covered by **Ramblin' Jack Elliott**, Pete Seeger, Ewan MacColl, Bob Dylan and many others. Since Guthrie's death his influence shows no sign of letting up and to these ears his composition 'This Land Is Your Land' has become a more potent US national anthem than 'The Star-Spangled Banner'.

BUDDY GUY

**See also pages 91-92
Born: George Guy, July 30th 1936, Lettsworth, Louisiana, US.**

■ *Fender Stratocaster.*

One of the many benefits wrought by the wholesale popularization of the blues is that there are few survivors who are not being accorded the respect and financial reward that was always their due. Guy, like **John Lee Hooker**, has been one of the principal benefactors of this turnaround, with the result that a series of younger players wait in line to pay homage.

Guy and Hooker have been more successful than many at adjusting their music to facilitate the changing attitude towards the blues. The extent to which Guy's music has changed is reflected more by the production techniques in the studio than in any inherent alteration to his style: the volume of the amplification at gigs may have increased and his touring band may comprise young, white, middle-class rock'n'rollers, but the grittiness of his playing and his reluctance to be flashy for the sake of it remains intact.

During the mid-1960s Guy hit a peak of sorts, with the Chess label (collected on *The Complete Chess Studio Sessions* 1992) and with a series of collaborations with harmonica player Junior Wells, cutting *Hoodoo Man Blues* and *It's My Life, Baby* (1966). These albums reflected the rock era but showed little attempt to adopt the trappings of the period: when former Chess recording artist **Howlin' Wolf** cut *Electric Wolf* featuring white rock stars, the result was a sloppy mish-mash.

With Wells and in their natural habitat of the club circuit, Guy's tremolo-laden solos with plenty of sustain echoed the drama of **BB King**'s style, prompting rock stars like **Keith Richards** and **Jeff Beck** among others to beat a path to Guy's Chicago club. In the 1990s, with the British-based Silvertone label, Guy cut *Damn Right I Got The Blues* (1990) which came very close to recapturing the spontaneity and sparkle of the way the blues had always been played in Chicago.

FRED GUY

Born: Frederick Guy, May 23rd 1897, Burkesville, Georgia, US. Died: November 22nd 1971, Chicago, Illinois, US.

■ *Gibson L5; Stromberg.*

Initially a banjo man, Guy joined the Duke Ellington orchestra in 1926 and remained until the early-1950s.

Shortly after joining, Guy took up the guitar and became a vital adjunct of a rhythm section that was arguably the best Ellington ever had. It featured Guy, Ellington on piano, bassist Wellman Braud and drummer Sonny Greer, and remained unchanged for the best part of a decade. Guy was never a soloist, but like the best rhythm guitarists in any genre he had an innate ability to swing.

STEVE HACKETT

Born: February 12th 1950, London, England.

■ *Gibson Les Paul; Yairi; Schecter.*

Joining Genesis as replacement for Anthony Phillips in late-1970, Hackett's best moments occurred during his languid, sustained solos on tracks like 'Firth Of Fifth' from *Selling England By The Pound* (1973) or 'Robbery Assault And Battery' from *A Trick Of The Tail* (1976). Hackett left the band in 1978 before they had achieved the multi-platinum status of later years, and went on to work in GTR with **Steve Howe** (*GTR* 1986). While he has his admirers, Hackett seems prone to the technique-dominated noodlings of art rock. To me, reading the telephone book is only slightly less interesting. Great technically, though.

TERRY HAGGERTY

Born: 1947, California, US.

■ *Gibson L5S.*

Haggerty's Sons Of Champlin, a San Franciscan Bay-area band, distinguished itself by recording a double album *Loosen Up Naturally* for their debut in 1967. Nothing else about this outing was distinguished, and their record label Capitol promptly dropped the group, whereupon the Sons took up residency as opening act for more prestigious outfits like Jefferson Airplane or The Grateful Dead before splitting up in the early-1970s. Reports that Haggerty plays sessions in Nashville these days remain unconfirmed.

WILLIE HALE

Born: August 15th 1944, Forrest City, Arkansas, US.

Betty Wright's 'Clean Up Woman' (1971) with 'Beaver' Hale's crisp, economical guitar work was one of the records to come out of Henry Stone's Miami-based TK group of labels. While KC & The Sunshine Band's Harry Casey and Richard Finch gained most of the plaudits for their production work on their own and George McCrae's records, Hale defined the gospel-inflected urgency of the best soul output. As Little Beaver, Hale cut solo albums that were all right... but his intro to 'Clean Up Woman' is as impressive and important in its way as **Eric Gale**'s wah-wah work on Isaac Hayes' 'Theme From Shaft'.

JIM HALL

**See also pages 113-114
Born: James Stanley Hall, December 12th 1930, Buffalo, New York, US.**

■ *Gibson ES175; D'Aquisto.*

Waxing lyrical about the extent of jazz guitarist Hall's

influence does scant justice to his own approach to the guitar, which is versatile and understated. Hall shines in any size or shape of group, and is not confined to soloing for its own sake. For example, Hall's interplay with tenor player Sonny Rollins on *The Bridge* (1962) has an almost casual trading of chops, emphasized by the absence of a piano. This lies at the heart of his approach: he plays the guitar as if he's playing the saxophone or the piano, with solo improvisation contextualized through instinct and intuition. Even so, his work with pianist Bill Evans is superb, notably on *Intermodulation* (1966). Form and structure are prerequisites: *Concierto* (1975) with Paul Desmond (alto), Chet Baker (trumpet), Roland Hanna (piano), Ron Carter (bass) and Steve Gadd (drums) typifies a stylistic unity and concerted effort among the groups in which Hall has appeared that precludes individual achievement.

JOHN HALL

Born: 1948, Baltimore, Maryland, US.

■ *Fender Stratocaster; Fender Telecaster.*

A distinguished rhythm guitarist whose pedigree included stints with **Bonnie Raitt**, fusion bluesman Taj Mahal, singer/songwriter Loudon Wainwright III and **Al Kooper**, Hall formed Orleans in 1973. Following the line of least resistance, they settled into the easy groove of soft-rock harmony popularized by The Eagles. That they enjoyed modest success for a spell was symptomatic of the era. However Hall like many writers before him understood the value of brevity, and the debut *Orleans* (1973) and follow-up *Let There Be Music* (1975) delivered what was expected: tuneful and unchallenging songs such as 'Dance With Me' and 'Still The One', offering at least a perspective of blues and country stylings. A later contribution ('Power') to the *No Nukes* (1980) benefit concert album, fostering awareness of the anti-nuclear lobby, indicated that Hall's heart may well have been elsewhere.

NICOLA HALL

Born: March 3rd 1969, Ipswich, Suffolk, England.

■ *Smallman; Fleta.*

A classical guitarist with a promising technical ability, Hall's training included study with **John Williams**. *Virtuoso Guitar Transcriptions* (1993) was a collection of her own transcriptions for the guitar of music not originally written for the instrument, and included pieces well known in the guitar repertoire (by Albeniz) and others previously untried (a Rachmaninoff piano prelude, for example). *Guitar Concertos* (1994) also contained new transcriptions, including a Paganini violin concerto. The selection and execution of this work underlines Hall's precocious ability, and signals a talent worth watching in the future.

OLLIE HALSALL

Born: March 14th 1949, London, England.

A fine musician, Halsall incorporated the experimental aspects of the guitar into his style, as exemplified by **Robert Fripp** – although Halsall has greater versatility because he appears more able to play from the heart. He has made a string of albums with employers such as madcap songwriters Neil Innes and Kevin Ayers (*The Confessions Of Dr Dream* 1974, and *June 1 1974*, recorded live at London's Rainbow Theatre with John Cale, Nico and Brian Eno) as well as projects such as Boxer, Jon Hiseman's Tempest, and Patto, all of which have more than adequately demonstrated his knack for genrebusting. Perhaps it is this very versatility that has made Halsall less than a household name.

KIRK HAMMETT

Born: November 18th 1962, New York, New York, US.

■ *ESP 'signature'.*

Hammett joined Metallica in 1983 as replacement for Dave Mustaine, who later went on to form Megadeth. As arch-exponents of thrash/speed metal, Metallica have retained an unalloyed charm and an ability simply to go out and play. While they have avoided the high-gloss videos of many of their contemporaries, the gradual slide towards the mainstream has occurred with a string of albums including *Kill 'Em All* (1983), *Master Of Puppets* (1986) and *Metallica* (1991). This body of work, marked out by Hammett's plangent guitar work (as on 'Harvester Of Sorrow') and James Hetfield's hectoring vocals, has established them as the metal group least prone to self-parody and with the least ridiculous lyrics.

JOHN HAMMOND JR

Born: John Paul Hammond, November 13th 1942, New York, New York, US.

■ *Martin; National resonator.*

Despite having a distinguished father who signed Bob Dylan, Bruce Springsteen, Aretha Franklin and Billie Holiday, John Hammond Jr has been one of the most dedicated blues revivalists. His guitar style, informed by the playing of **Robert Johnson**, **Lonnie Johnson** and **Blind Lemon Jefferson**, has never been over-reverential or valedictory, but rather has sought to recapture the spirit of the past. While commercial success has been elusive, such is Hammond's dedication that he has contributed to the continued growth of interest in the blues. On balance, the early acoustic albums reflect the passion of his enthusiasm (compiled as *The Best Of John Hammond* on Vanguard) where his ability to differentiate between regional styles is a revelation.

MIKE HAMPTON

Born: 1957, US.

■ *Fender Stratocaster (modified).*

Hampton was one of a few guitarists used by funkmeister George Clinton, whose Parliament and Funkadelic co-operative in the late-1960s and early-1970s was at the cutting edge of the genre. Clinton, an eccentric figure with a lyrical propensity for idle speculation on subjects as far-flung as deportment at the local disco (*Free Your Mind And Your Ass Will Follow* 1970) to the arrival of extra-terrestrials (*Mothership Connection* 1975), was first and foremost a fine arranger. Where Clinton differed from James Brown was that he was better at employing studio technology to achieve effect, whereas Brown was happiest on stage with a battery of musicians to front his assault.

Clinton took leaves out of Sly Stone's and **Jimi Hendrix**'s books and used guitarists such as Hampton (who used a left-handed neck on his Strat), **Catfish Collins**, Gary Shider and Lucius Ross to provide slabs of psychedelically inspired riffs, supplementing a horn section that included Brown alumni such as Maceo Parker, Fred Wesley and Pee Wee Ellis. Hampton and the rest were bit players in the Clinton administration, but the number of times the guitar figures have been electronically sampled for use in modern dance music and elsewhere gives an indication of their influence.

BILL HARKLEROAD

Born: 1950, California, US.

Also known as Zoot Horn Rollo, Harkleroad was an important component of Captain Beefheart's Magic Band. He graced the uncompromising *Trout Mask Replica* (1969) contributing the memorable fractured glass-fingered guitar work, the counterpoint for **Jeff Cotton**'s riffing. Beefheart's use of language for its sound rather than meaning gave the whole affair a surreal quality, and while much of it impressed as impromptu and random, it was Harkleroad's soloing and arrangements that established the framework for the whole project.

Harkleroad remained with the Magic Band for *Lick My Decals Off, Baby* (1970), *The Spotlight Kid* (1972) and the remarkable *Clear Spot* (1973, with Beefheart intoning at one point: 'Mr Zoot Horn Rollo, hit that long, meaning note, and let it float...'). After those arresting records, Harkleroad left to form Mallard, dead in the water almost before it started. Harkleroad now lives in Oregon where he runs a record shop and gives guitar lessons.

ROY HARPER

Born: June 12th 1941, Manchester, England.

■ *Gibson Chet Atkins; Washburn Mirage.*

Harper's passionate songs and folk/blues guitar style first emerged on the London folk club circuit in the mid-1960s, drawn from an already eventful past that included psychiatric institutions and jail terms. Harper's notable debut album *Sophisticated Beggar* appeared in 1966. His subsequent concert appearances, alongside record releases such as *Stormcock* (1971) and *Valentine* (1974), saw him bolstering the sound of his flat-top acoustic guitar by amplification and the addition of electronic effects, although he never went so far in this direction as **John Martyn**. He is highly regarded by fellow musicians – **Jimmy Page** guests on some of Harper's records, such as the aforementioned *Stormcock* and the live compilation *Flashes From The Archives* (1974), and Led Zeppelin recorded a tribute piece called 'Hats Off To Harper'. The inspiration worked

Hal–Har

both ways, and in the mid-1970s Harper formed Trigger, an out-and-out rock band including **Chris Spedding**, well represented in the studio by *HQ* (1975). Harper continues his erratic and appealing career, most recently cutting *Once* (1990).

BILL HARRIS

Born: April 14th 1925, Nashville, Tennessee, US.

■ *Epiphone; various flat-top nylon.*

Harris began studying the guitar in 1945 in Washington DC, where he started to play jazz as well as some classical pieces. By 1950, he had joined the backing band of the R&B vocal group The Clovers, and appears on most of their biggest hits ('Don't You Know I Love You', 'One Mint Julep' and 'Your Cash Ain't Nothing But Trash'). At the suggestion of **Mickey Baker** he cut a number of jazz albums for EmArcy, including *Bill Harris* (1956), which showed an intuitive knack for jazz-style nylon-strung guitar playing. Harris also assembled a number of jazz guitar manuals.

PHIL HARRIS

Born: July 18th 1948, London, England.

Harris formed Ace Flash & The Dynamos with **Alan King** in 1972, the group soon becoming plain Ace and scoring a massive hit in 1974 with keyboardsman Paul Carrack's 'How Long'. Harris' lead work over King's rhythm backdrop employed bluesy phrasing with a spiky tone, and on the band's best album *Five-A-Side* (1974) he contributed fine, steely solos to 'Sniffing About' and 'Why', and a gritty, distorted interlude in 'How Long'. Ace split in 1977.

GEORGE HARRISON

Born: February 25th 1943, Liverpool, England.

■ *Gretsch Duo Jet; Gretsch Country Gentleman; Gibson Les Paul; Rickenbacker 12-string; Gibson SG; Fender Stratocaster; Fender Telecaster.*

While **John Lennon** and **Paul McCartney** both exhibited strong R&B influences, Harrison's most important influence was rockabilly. Throughout the early years Harrison's solos were informed by artists like **Buddy Holly**, **Carl Perkins**, **James Burton** and **Scotty Moore**: the opening bars of The Beatles' 'I Saw Her Standing There' (from *Please Please Me* 1963) are pure Perkins, and the group's covers of Perkins' compositions ('Honey Don't' and 'Everybody's Trying To Be My Baby' (*Beatles for Sale* 1964) seem almost more authentic than the originals.

Despite this subtext, Harrison was the more studious in his assimilation of other styles: 'Day Tripper' contained fragments of **Steve Cropper**; 'Paperback Writer' anticipated the crashing chords of heavy metal; 'I Feel Fine' featured feedback, arguably the first time such a technique was used on a record that hit the number one spot; fuzztone guitar was sprayed all over 'Revolution'; and, of course, there was Harrison's dabbling with the sitar, best absorbed into The Beatles' style on 'Norwegian Wood'.

Throughout, Harrison's contributions formed an integral part of the group's sound, which is why the flamboyant solo on 'While My Guitar Gently Weeps' was played by **Eric Clapton**. It's not that Harrison couldn't play it; but it was uncharacteristic for him to play the part of a screaming lead guitarist. Harrison seems more at home when delivering the carefully measured lines of the solo to 'Something' where he demonstrates for any non-believers just what a fine axeman he is.

For his solo debut *All Things Must Pass* (1970), neat licks and smooth chops are integrated into an all-encompassing sound by producer Phil Spector, and *Cloud Nine* (1987) was at times inspired. Harrison's ensemble approach to the guitar reached its apogee with *The Traveling Wilburys* (1988), an occasional band comprising Bob Dylan, **Roy Orbison**, **Tom Petty** and **Jeff Lynne**. Here, as with earlier efforts when enlisted as a guest by Delaney & Bonnie, Bob Dylan, **Eric Clapton** and **Leon Russell**, Harrison contributed rich variation to the whole. But of course it's his work with The Beatles that will last longer than any of these projects.

JOHN HART

Born: 1961, Fort Belvoir, Virginia, US.

■ *Gibson ES175.*

A jazz player with an old head on young shoulders, Hart has sidestepped the flamboyant pyrotechnics of his contemporaries and settled on a style that pays a respectful homage to past masters such as **Tal Farlow** and **Jim Hall**. While his session work for alto player Lou Donaldson and organist Brother Jack McDuff was impressive, his 1990 debut *One Down* included unaccompanied standards such as 'Embraceable You' and 'All The Things You Are' executed with a precision and tenderness that belie his years.

JOHN HARTFORD

Born: John Harford, December 30th 1937, New York, New York, US.

■ *Noble.*

A songwriter, fiddler, banjoist and guitarist, Harford was raised in St Louis where he became besotted with bluegrass and steamboats. He had mastered the banjo and the fiddle by the time he was 13 and performed regularly at square dances, developing his talents by learning dobro and guitar. In 1965 Harford married and moved to Nashville, where he became a session musician and was signed to RCA (who added the 't' to his name), cutting the self-penned 'Gentle On My Mind' (later covered by Glen Campbell and Dean Martin). By 1970 he had moved to Warner Brothers and recorded *Aero-Plain* which had strong bluegrass undercurrents and included 'They're Gonna Tear Down The Grand Ole Opry'.

A four-year hiatus followed, until in 1976 Hartford returned and signed with the independent Flying Fish label, recording with The Dillards, **Tut Taylor**, Vassar Clements and **Norman Blake**. Despite Hartford's eccentricity – notably a penchant for square dancing – he remains firmly committed to traditional US music, appearing at folk festivals and

the like with his own string-band backing group. The recent *Annual Waltz* (1986) for MCA has an accessibility that cuts through much of the purist posturing in traditional folk music.

LES HARVEY

Born: 1947, Glasgow, Scotland. Died: May 3rd 1972, Swansea, Wales.

■ *Gibson Les Paul.*

A fine, economical guitarist, Harvey was the heart of Stone The Crows while vocalist Maggie Bell was the soul. Although their albums (*Teenage Licks* 1971 and *Ontinuous Performance* 1972) were a little too rough and ready, Harvey had the potential to rank alongside **Jimmy Page** and **Jeff Beck**. He died after being accidentally electrocuted on stage in 1972.

POLLY HARVEY

Born: 1970, Corscombe, Dorset, England.

PJ Harvey, led by guitarist and writer Polly Harvey, have been one of the most visible bands to emerge amid the hype of grunge. Harvey is an accomplished lyricist with a gift for penning memorable tunes, such as 'She-La-Na-Gig' (1991), 'Oh My Lover' (1992), 'O Stella' (1992) and 'Missed' (1993). Her guitar work indicates a healthy curiosity and a willingness to take musical and aesthetic chances: 'Missed', for instance, contains a repetitive guitar figure in a strange time signature, while her banshee wailing makes the hairs on the back of the neck prickle.

ROY HARVEY

Born: 1892, Beckley, West Virginia, US. Died: 1958.

Charlie Poole formed the nucleus of The North Carolina Ramblers with the crippled miner and fiddler Posey Rorer in 1917. Initially a duo, they added guitarist Norman Woodlieff, who was later replaced by Harvey, and in 1928 Rorer was replaced by Lonnie Austin. Among their finest recordings were 'Don't Let Your Deal Go Down' (later revived by The Grateful Dead) and 'Ramblin Blues' (for Columbia). While their music was pure hillbilly, Harvey's long, flowing, melodic runs had a bluesy edge that foreshadowed the style of **Les Paul**. The group disintegrated after Poole's death, following an epic drinking binge in 1931, while Harvey continued to ply his trade until his death.

IAIN HARVIE

Born: May 19th 1964, Glasgow, Scotland.

Del Amitri were formed in Glasgow in 1980 by Harvie and bassist Justin Currie. Embraced by the indie scene, Currie's subtle lyrics won envious glances from The Fall's Mark E Smith and The Smiths' Morrissey. Their debut *Del Amitri* (1985) confirmed their position as one of the country's most sparklingly promising bands. This promise has not been wasted as the strongly melodic 'Kiss This Thing Goodbye', 'Nothing Ever Happens', 'Spit In The Rain' and 'Always The Last To Know' attest. Although they have endured personnel changes with **David Cummings**

Has-Hel

replacing Brian Tolland, the combination of the guitars of Cummings and Harvie is one of rock's more felicitous partnerships, and *Change Everything* (1992) was a perfectly formed offering.

PYE HASTINGS

Born: Julian Hastings, January 21st 1947, Canterbury, Kent, England.

■ **Fender Electric XII.**

Caravan was one of the more idiosyncratic bands to emerge in the late-1960s. Evoking the pastoral grandeur of English classical composer Ralph Vaughan Williams rather more than the avant-garde with whom they were nominally associated, they possessed a quirkiness much in evidence on albums like *Caravan* (1968), *If I Could Do It All Over Again, I'd Do It All Over You* (1970), *In The Land Of Grey And Pink* (1971) and *Blind Dog At St Dunstan's* (1976). Their records avoided the stereotype that beset bands like Barclay James Harvest whose sound, awash with mellotron, was ultimately characterless. Hastings' sparse phrasing alongside the work of flautist/saxophonist Richard Hastings provided much of the tonal variation in the group's sound. But the advent of punk and the concomitant disenchantment with jazz-influenced rock bands led many to believe that the group was just another old hippy band that had outlived its usefulness, the net result being that the group split in the early-1980s. Caravan, like Blossom Toes, Family and Kevin Ayers, are drastically undervalued artists of the period, but the compilation *Canterbury Tales* (1977) gives a good overview.

RICHIE HAVENS

Born: Richard P Havens, January 21st 1941, New York, New York, US.

■ **Guild flat-top.**

Havens was a charismatic figure on the festival circuit during the late-1960s and early-1970s. It took his appearance in the pouring rain at Woodstock to win the hearts of thousands of zonked-out hippies: the open-tuned, fast-strummed guitar work under his intense vocals, and a series of contemporary songs like Lennon & McCartney's 'Eleanor Rigby', Dylan's 'Just Like A Woman' and the self-penned 'Freedom', were highpoints of the festival. His albums have been over-reliant on replicating the electricity of his concerts, which never quite works, but an early double album *Richard P Havens 1983* (1968) demonstrated the breadth of his repertoire. Throughout the 1980s and 1990s he was less active, concentrating on film work and benefits for the conservation lobby.

TED HAWKINS

Born: October 28th 1936, Biloxi, Mississippi, US.

Hawkins emerged during the 1980s after years of obscurity, and bears comparison with the great troubadours and songsters of the 1930s and 1940s such as **Jesse Fuller** and **Mance Lipscomb**. His uncompromisingly world-weary style vindicates this

analogy with a repertoire – including 'Watch Your Step', Bob Dylan's 'Blowin' In The Wind' and Porter Wagoner's 'Green Green Grass Of Home' – that is based on songs he likes rather than the implementation of some sort of categoric imperative.

ROY HAY

Born: August 12th 1961, Southend, Essex, England.

Culture Club, formed in 1981, was dominated by vocalist Boy George, but their success was partly due to the tight instrumentation of Hay, drummer Jon Moss and bassist Mikey Craig. Hay's insistent guitar lines over the rock solid rhythm section contrasted well with George's soulful vocals. While the Club were basically just a pop band, they had a gift for accessible, tuneful melodies, and it's likely that 'Do You Really Want To Hurt Me?', 'Karma Chameleon', 'Time', 'Church Of The Poison Mind' and 'Victims' will all endure.

PETE HAYCOCK

Born: April 4th 1952, Stafford, England.

■ **Veleno; Westbury; Hohner.**

The Climax Blues Band, originally formed in 1969 as The Climax Chicago Blues Band, caught the tail end of the blues boom just as outfits such as Fleetwood Mac and **John Mayall**'s Bluesbreakers were beginning to address a less formulaic approach to the blues. Through the 1970s Climax released good, solid but unremarkable albums such as *Tightly Knit* (1971) and *Stamp Album* (1975). While they have continued working into the 1990s there is a pervasive sense of déjà vu about the band, and Haycock's licks seem to have progressed little over the years.

WARREN HAYNES

Born: US.

■ **Gibson Les Paul; Fender Stratocaster; PRS.**

He might not be **Duane Allman**, but Haynes was part of the reformed 1989 version of The Allman Brothers that marked a welcome return to form for a band decimated by internal strife and poor driving. *Seven Turns* (1989) combined much of the passion and hunger that had been absent for some time, with Haynes attractively instrumental in the re-introduction of R&B elements that had been all but obscured by **Dicky Betts**' country influences on the other good post-Duane LP, *Brothers & Sisters* (1973).

JUSTIN HAYWARD

Born: David Justin Hayward, October 14th 1946, Swindon, Wiltshire, England.

■ **Gibson ES335; Fender Stratocaster; Squier Stratocaster.**

The quasi-poetic lyrics and elaborate orchestral arrangements of The Moody Blues obliterated any individual instrumental prowess the group members might possess. Hayward's tuneful melodies – 'Nights In White Satin' (1967), 'Question' (1970) and the rather coy 'I'm Just A Singer In A Rock'n'Roll Band' (1972) – may have been eminently hummable, but the recordings were seriously short on fevered

fretwork. As a footnote, Hayward was a member of Marty Wilde's Wildcats for two days in 1966.

EDDIE HAZEL

Born: April 10th 1950, New York, New York, US.
Died: December 23rd 1992.

A key component in George Clinton's Funkadelic, Eddie Hazel's lines snaked through some of the most authoritative funk of the 1970s: *Cosmic Slop* (1972), *Hardcore Jollies* (1976) and *One Nation Under A Groove* (1978). While his style had the rhythmic precision of James Brown's **Jimmy Nolen**, Hazel's was the flashier and the more rock oriented style.

JEFF HEALEY

Born: March 25th 1968, Toronto, Ontario, Canada.

■ **Squier Stratocaster.**

Healey acquired his first guitar when he was three – a couple of years after becoming blind through eye cancer. This was the start of a long haul, culminating with the development of a style that owes more to rock than blues, and using a standard electric played something like a lap-steel. His debut *See The Light* (1989) with producer Greg Ladanyi included 'Angel Eyes' and had a simplicity and coherence rare in debuts, despite the superficial gimmickry. The sequel *Hell To Pay* (1990) continued where the predecessor left off, with greater emphasis on tone and variation and quality of material. At present there is a derivativeness about much of Healey's playing and an absence of an identifiable style. But no doubt in time it will come... for better or worse.

MICHAEL HEDGES

Born: December 31st 1956, Los Angeles, California, US.

■ **Martin D-28.**

Nominally a 'new age' guitarist – his albums have appeared on the Windham Hill label – Hedges' acoustic ramblings are technically accomplished, even if he has rather oddly incorporated mannerisms more evocative of **John Lee Hooker**'s into his style. Although the context differs significantly, both have integrated a collection of rhythmic inflections into their playing. While Hooker seems to have come upon these devices by accident to enhance atmosphere, Hedges has employed them dynamically. His compositional skills, formally learned, embrace elements of folk and classical in a curious hybrid that uses different tunings and impressive counterpoint, an approach that has enabled him to push back the accepted boundaries of fingerpicking, making much of **Merle Travis**' achievements appear dated. For all Hedges' expertise and the accessibility of albums like *Aerial Boundaries* (1985, with an interesting interpretation of Neil Young's 'After The Gold Rush') and *Taproot* (1986), to these ears his music has little charm.

FRED HELLERMAN

Born: May 13th 1927, New York, New York, US.

In the late-1940s The Weavers focused the energies of

the folk movement upon the grave iniquities inherent in US society. While today the group's efforts seem out of time, the guitar work of Hellerman and Pete Seeger was sufficient to pave the way for other folk groups and singers such as The Kingston Trio, The New Lost City Ramblers, **Joan Baez** and Bob Dylan. These artists, like **Woody Guthrie** and **Leadbelly**, showed that the most potent form of protest was self-contained, self-perpetuating and self-motivating, irrespective of irritants like blacklists. Apart from proving in this way that all that glistens is not gold, The Weavers' buoyant harmonies on songs like 'On Top Of Old Smokey' were the blueprint for the rather grim Mitch Miller 'singalong' packages of the 1950s.

DON HELMS

Born: February 28th 1927, Shreveport, Louisiana, US.

■ *Sho-Bud; MSA.*

The Drifting Cowboys, originally formed by Hank Williams as his backing group, had at its nucleus steel guitarist Helms and guitarist **Bob McNett**. In 1949 the lineup was supplemented by fiddler Jerry Rivers and bassist Hillous Butram, and Helms and Rivers provided the backbone of the honky-tonk ensemble sound that was so important to the insouciant swagger of Williams' early records. Later on, sides such as 'Hey Good Lookin'' and 'Jambalaya' featured a pool of Nashville session players like **Jerry Byrd**. After Williams' death in 1953 The Drifting Cowboys became the core of Ray Price's band, The Cherokee Cowboys. Later, Helms sessioned for country artists such as Ferlin Husky, Carl Smith, Marty Robbins and Hank Snow. In 1977 the group started to tour (on the strength of their association with Williams) and also to record, cutting *A Tribute To Hank Williams* (1980) among others. This arrangement continued until 1984, when the musicians moved into retirement.

JAMES HENDERSON

Born: May 20th 1954, Jackson, Mississippi, US.

By the time Henderson joined in 1975, southern boogie outfit Black Oak Arkansas was effectively vocalist Jim Dandy's backing band. By then their well hewn style was commonplace, but Dandy's histrionics served as a template for many a budding star. Henderson replaced **Harvey Jett**, and displayed his chops on *Balls Of Fire* (1976) as eloquently as can be expected under the circumstances.

JIMI HENDRIX

Born: James Marshall Hendrix, November 27th 1942, Seattle, Washington, US. Died: September 18th 1970, London, England.

■ *Fender Stratocaster.*

Of all the performers to emerge during the 1960s Hendrix has surely proved to be one of the most influential, and his technical and emotional prowess as a guitarist far exceeded the flamboyant show-manship for which he was mostly known.

It all started in 1954 when he was given an electric guitar, which he learned to play by listening to

records by **Muddy Waters**, **BB King** and **Elmore James**. After a spell in the army he became a session guitarist, adopting the pseudonym Jimmy James and backing artists like King and singers such as Sam Cooke, Jackie Wilson and Little Richard. This was followed by stints with The Isley Brothers' touring band, and with Curtis Knight's Kingpins.

By 1965 Hendrix had launched out on his own and was beginning to pull together the disparate strands that would make his electric guitar style the most widely copied and revered since the emergence of **Charlie Christian** in the late-1930s. The formation of The Jimi Hendrix Experience with drummer Mitch Mitchell and bassist Noel Redding provided the framework for the vibrant singles 'Hey Joe' and 'Purple Haze', and the debut album *Are You Experienced?* (1967) that made other guitarists sound as if they were auditioning for the annual village fete. In June 1967 the group appeared at the Monterey Pop Festival in California on the same bill as soulman Otis Redding and blues wailer Janis Joplin. Hendrix's performance pretty much blew all the others off stage, and the crowd could not believe their eyes, especially when at the end of the set Hendrix drenched his Stratocaster in lighter-fluid and set fire to it.

Hendrix's grasp of technique and bluesy lyricism on titles like 'Little Wing', 'The Wind Cries Mary' and 'The Burning Of The Midnight Lamp' was a revelation to those who believed that technique was all about playing as many notes as could be produced as fast as possible. His use on stage of early electronic gadgetry such as wah-wah and distortion pedals was influential too, but it was in the studio that Hendrix's sonic explorations really began to take shape, especially on his last offical studio album, *Electric Ladyland* (1968). Among the tracks there were 'Rainy Day Dream Away', at the session for which Hendrix joked about impersonating **Kenny Burrell**, and 'Voodoo Chile', with assistance from **Steve Winwood** on organ. Its style anticipated jazz-rock, and the track still sounds fresh today.

Despite his premature death, Hendrix managed to cram enough into his short career to last most people a lifetime. He seems to have been a shy man who loved to play: anywhere, any time, with anyone. The body of work he left influences all who come within its compass.

JAMES HETFIELD

Born: August 3rd 1963, Los Angeles, California, US.

■ *ESP Explorer-style.*

Hetfield's rhythm guitar work and lyrics have provided a firm grounding for lead guitarist **Kirk Hammett**'s solos in Metallica. While the group has avoided many of the clichés endemic in heavy metal, they have never been averse to dipping into the metal manual to perform covers of material by groups they liked (Budgie, Killing Joke, Uriah Heep). To this extent they are the proud inheritors of a tradition that stretches back to the early-1960s when garage bands such as The Standells, Blue Cheer and The Seeds first started to make waves. Hetfield's work on tracks such as 'Harvester Of Sorrow' and 'Enter

Sandman' have been instrumental in establishing the group's identity, no mean achievement in a genre where most bands are anonymous to a fault.

JOHN HIATT

Born: 1952, Indianapolis, Indiana, US.

■ *Fender Telecaster.*

Ever since his emergence in the early-1970s, Hiatt has been refining an authentic hybrid that has its roots in rock, folk or country. While his own style is still evolving he has become highly sought after as a rhythm guitarist, with singer Buffy Sainte-Marie and **T-Bone Burnett**, and luminaries such as **Dave Edmunds**, Nick Lowe, **Ry Cooder** and Rick Nelson covering his material.

Apart from solo albums such as *Overcoats* (1975), *Slug Line* (1979), *Two Bit Monsters* (1980) and *Bring The Family* (1987), he joined forces with Cooder, bassist Lowe and drummer Jim Keltner as Little Village, whose eponymous debut emerged in 1991. Like most 'supergroup' efforts this was a patchy affair which failed to cohere. Better was Hiatt's solo *Perfectly Good Guitar* (1993) with a great couplet on the title track: 'It breaks my heart to see those stars/ Smashing a perfectly good guitar.' Apparently ace guitar smasher **Pete Townshend** was played the track on a San Francisco radio station, and replied that it was OK, because as quickly as he smashed them the Koreans would make more...

TONY HICKS

Born: December 16th 1943, Nelson, Lancashire, England.

■ *Gibson ES345; Vox Phantom XII; Rickenbacker; PRS.*

Pretty much the quiet one of The Hollies, Hicks along with vocalists Allan Clarke and Graham Nash was responsible for the distinctive sound of the band at their peak during the 1960s. Despite being overshadowed by The Beatles, The Hollies knocked out a number of impressive singles that included covers of R&B material like Doris Troy's 'Just One Look' and Betty Everett's 'You're No Good', as well as group-composed songs such as 'Bus Stop', 'On A Carousel', 'Stop Stop Stop', 'King Midas In Reverse', 'Carrie Anne' and 'Jennifer Eccles'.

After Nash's departure the group fell into a routine of recording standard pop material, enlivened only by the odd gem such as 'Long Cool Woman In A Black Dress' and Bruce Springsteen's 'Sandy'. None of this did much credit to Hicks, whose phrasing had set them apart from the run-of-the-mill. A recent reissue of the grim 'He Ain't Heavy, He's My Brother' emphasized how far the mighty had fallen. Nevertheless *Evolution* and *Butterfly* (both 1967) give strong indications of squandered potential, while their legacy of a handful of slick 45s attest to Hicks' precise guitar work.

DAVID HIDALGO

Born: 1954, Los Angeles, California, US.

■ *Fender Telecaster; Fender Stratocaster; Ferrington custom; Gibson L-00.*

Having assimilated most of the salient aspects of

1950s rockabilly and Tex-Mex, Los Lobos came into being in 1974 in Los Angeles under the auspices of guitarist/accordionist Hidalgo and guitarist/vocalist **Cesar Rosas**. An affable bunch, their dedication to fun is only exceeded by their instrumental virtuosity, borne out by their adaptation of Ritchie Valens' songs like 'C'mon Let's Go' and 'La Bamba'.

What sets them apart is their ability to get to the heart of material with zeal and affection, evidenced by the hordes of musicians who have flocked to their sessions: **Ry Cooder**, **Brian Setzer**, **T-Bone Burnett**, Tex-Mex accordionist Flaco Jimenez, zydeco king Clifton Chenier and **Elvis Costello**, to name but a few.

DAVE HIGGS

Born: Southend, Essex, England.

The unstinting enthusiasm of Higgs in Eddie & The Hot Rods made Dr Feelgood appear lugubrious. The group was formed in 1975 by vocalist Barrie Masters and Higgs, and their blend of rock and R&B quickly won them a devoted following on the club circuit. One of their first releases was an EP *Live At The Marquee* (1976) which included a spectacular version of ? & the Mysterians' '96 Tears'. Then guitarist Graeme Douglas from The Kursaal Flyers joined, penning such stormers as 'Do Anything You Wanna Do' which encapsulated the spirit of punk with more verve than most. Although the group's career has been fitful, they still have get-togethers on the British pub circuit.

DAVE HILL

Born: April 4th 1952, Fleet Castle, Devon, England.

■ *Gibson SG (modified)*.
While Slade may have cut great singles and Hill may have had an impressive coiffeur and a range of footwear seldom seen beyond London's Victoria & Albert museum, a virtuoso guitarist he was not, as can be witnessed on hits like 'Cum On Feel The Noize'. Efficient, though.

STEVE HILLAGE

Born: August 2nd 1951, London, England.

■ *Fender Stratocaster; Fender Telecaster; Steinberger*.
More widely known as a producer these days, Hillage first came to prominence with Daevid Allen's Gong. Guitarist/vocalist Allen, who had been in the earliest incarnation of Soft Machine, had a curious lyrical preoccupation with pixies and flying teapots. Hillage, to his credit, still managed to set about his task as lead guitarist with a creditable determination and commitment, contributing a jazzy line in solos to albums like *Radio Gnome Invisible Part 1 (Flying Teapot)* (1973) and *You* (1974). After leaving Gong, Hillage embarked on a solo career that continued to embrace some of the less plausible aspects of hippy ideology, all couched in quasi-mystical terms. However, his guitar work is less simple to pin down, containing everything from rock, jazz, and new age to the kitchen sink. *Live Herald* (1979) gives a reasonably clear idea of where he was coming from.

Planet Zog, perhaps? In the late-1970s he co-produced an early Simple Minds album.

CHRIS HILLMAN

Born: December 4th 1942, Los Angeles, California, US.

For over 25 years Hillman has been one of the most significant contributors to the country-rock movement, appearing with some of the genre's most prestigious exponents.

The roots of Hillman's career were laid in the early-1960s when, having mastered the guitar, mandolin and bass, he formed his first group, The Scottsville Squirrel Barkers, and then a bluegrass outfit called The Hillmen. While probably best known for his bass guitar work over the next 15 years with The Byrds, The Flying Burrito Brothers, Stephen Stills' Manassas and The Souther Hillman Furay Band, Hillman is an assured mandolin player (as on a traditional bluegrass album *The Hillmen with Rex and Vern Gosdin*), and his fine guitar picking, often underrated, is especially notable on his string of solo albums such as *Slippin' Away* (1976), *Clear Sailing* (1977), *Morning Sky* (1982) and *Desert Rose* (1984), despite the unevenness of the material.

In 1985 Hillman formed the Desert Rose Band and continued his fine guitar work, assisted by **Herb Pedersen** (guitar/vocal), multi-instrumentalist **John Jorgenson** and bassist Bill Bryson, later augmented by **Jay Dee Maness** (steel guitar) and Steve Duncan (drums). After playing the LA club circuit they were signed to the Curb label and cut *Desert Rose Band* (1988). With this outfit Hillman has put the country back into country-rock with a vengeance and, perhaps surprisingly, has had more commercial success than in the early days of The Byrds, with a string of hit singles – 'Love Reunited', 'One Step Forward', 'He's Black And I'm Blue', 'Summer Wind', 'I Still Believe In You' and 'She Don't Love Nobody' – where The Desert Rose Band draw from authentic styles such as bluegrass and honky-tonk.

HARVEY HINSLEY

Born: January 19th 1948, Northampton, England.

While few may associate Hot Chocolate with virtuoso axemanship, Hinsley offered the group well crafted guitar support. He had fine credentials for the group, having formerly been a member of Cliff Bennett's Rebel Rousers, one of the more convincing soul-influenced combos of the 1960s. Despite Hot Chocolate's commercial appeal, Hinsley's opening bars on 'You Sexy Thing' ably caught the balance between reggae and disco-funk, and his power rhythm playing on other hits like 'Every One's A Winner', 'Emma' and 'Brother Louie' added a more distinctive touch to the group's sound than was customary when synthesizers were involved.

EDDIE HINTON

Born: Tuscaloosa, Alabama, US.

One of the greatest unsung heroes of Muscle Shoals, probably the top southern country-soul studio, Hinton formed a songwriting partnership with

Marlin Greene, penning hits for Aretha Franklin, Percy Sledge and Dusty Springfield, among others. In addition he became a session musician before branching out to cut the excellent *Very Extremely Dangerous* (1977). His world-weary, journalistic style has similarities with that of **Lightnin' Hopkins** while his lean guitar work has little more than the occasional flourish for emphasis. After several years of obscurity during which he had serious drug and alcohol problems, Hinton started to write and perform once more and recorded *Letters From Mississippi* (1986), *Cry & Moan* (1991) and *Very Blue Highway* (1992).

DAVE HLUBECK

Born: 1952, Jacksonville, Florida, US.

■ *Hamer*.
Lead guitarist Hlubeck formed Molly Hatchet in 1971 with former Ice guitarist **Steve Holland** and bassist Banner Thomas. For some years they worked in the shadows of Lynyrd Skynyrd, but in 1977 when Skynyrd were decimated in an aircrash Molly Hatchet moved into position as the principal purveyors of southern rock. While the group have signally failed to come up with compositions as memorable as Skynyrd's 'Freebird' or 'Sweet Home Alabama', Hlubeck has proved on 'Satisfied Man', 'Beatin' The Odds' and 'Fall Of The Peacemakers' that he has a range of chops well suited to the band's cause. The fact that they are seldom off the road would seem to indicate that studio albums are a somewhat academic exercise; therefore Hatchet are best heard in their natural habitat, as on *Double Trouble Live* (1985).

MABON HODGES

Born: US.

'Teenie' Hodges contributed the languid figures to classic Hi studio tracks such as Al Green's 'Tired Of Being Alone', 'Call Me', 'I Can't Get Next To You' and 'Love & Happiness', and Ann Peebles' 'Part Time Love' and 'I Can't Stand The Rain'. Producer Willie Mitchell had built a roster of artists at Hi that included Otis Clay, Syl Johnson, OV Wright, as well as Peebles and Green. The house band sure could swing – they were Mabon Hodges plus Charles Hodges (organ), Leroy Hodges (bass), Howard Grimes (drums), Wayne Jackson (trumpet), James Mitchell (baritone sax), Andrew Love (tenor sax), Ed Logan (tenor sax) and Jack Hale (trombone) – and were of such stellar proportions that the boys at Muscle Shoals and in Nashville offered the only real competition in a world going mad for disco.

WARNER HODGES

Born: June 4th 1959, Nashville, Tennessee, US.

■ *ESP; Heritage*.
Jason Ringenberg formed Jason & The Scorchers in 1981 with guitarist Hodges, specializing in thunderous riffs and owing a debt to garage and punk bands such as The Clash. Their recording debut was the EP *Reckless Country Soul*, followed by *Fervor* (1983) which included a storming version of Bob Dylan's 'Absolutely Sweet Marie' and Ringenberg's

self-penned 'Pray For Me Mama (I'm A Gypsy Now)'. Despite other guitar-fests such as Hank Williams' 'Lost Highway' and the self-penned 'Shop It Around', they split in 1988. Ringenberg returned as a solo artist with *One Foot In The Honky Tonk* (1992).

SUSANNA HOFFS

Born: January 17th 1957, Newport Beach, California, US.

■ *Rickenbacker 'signature'.*

In The Bangles, Hoffs' and Vicki Peterson's neat little guitar hooks on titles like 'All Over The Place' and 'Goin Down To Liverpool' gave the group depth and variation. Later singles such as 'Manic Monday' (written by **Prince**), 'Walk Like An Egyptian' and 'Eternal Flame' were replete with smooth harmonies and slick licks. They saved their best for last with a full-blown, chunky version of **Paul Simon**'s 'Hazy Shade Of Winter', produced by Def Jam's Rick Rubin. Internal dissension within the ranks caused them to split, as each member thought the others were coasting on their talent. Shame.

CARL HOGAN

Born: US.

Louis Jordan did for R&B what Elvis Presley did for rock'n'roll, and the guitar player firing it all was Hogan. Jordan assembled one of the liveliest combos of the 1940s and 1950s, and enjoyed over 50 Top 10 R&B hits between 1942 and 1955. Dubbed 'jump' by the cognoscenti, Jordan's music depended on a cohesive effort rather than virtuoso displays of instrumental prowess. Hogan, cited by **Chuck Berry** as a prime influence, remained throughout the halcyon years of Jordan's success, and his guitar work swung like a pendulum, giving the Tympany Five a tight rhythmic pulse on classic pieces like 'Look Out', 'Choo Choo Ch' Boogie', 'Is You Is Or Is You Ain't (My Baby)', 'Beans & Cornbread', 'Caldonia' and 'Let The Good Times Roll'.

ALLAN HOLDSWORTH

Born: August 6th 1948, Leeds, Yorkshire, England.

■ *Synthaxe; Steinberger; Ibanez 'signature'; Delap custom.*

After some years in the 1970s contributing tough, muscular solos to bands like Jon Hiseman's Tempest, Gong, Soft Machine and Bill Bruford's UK ('In The Dead Of Night'), Holdsworth stepped out of the spotlight for a spell as an ensemble player in his own outfits. This attitude, reminiscent of other great ensemble players like **Jim Hall** and, of the more recent batch, **John Scofield**, resulted in *IOU* (1981). Drawing inspiration from hornmen like John Coltrane and Charlie Parker, Holdsworth seems to have got over that vital hurdle in any musical education: the belief that speed is the criterion by which one is judged. Not that he is averse to soloing and self-expression, as *Metal Fatigue* (1986) and *Sand* (1987) demonstrated. They also provided growing evidence of a perverse interest in guitar-synthesis. But as Ry Cooder was once moved to say, "If you learn something new every day, then you're going towards something that'll serve you

later on," and this seems to have underlined Holdsworth's constantly growing stature among his fellow guitarists, especially after the uncompromising *Wardenclyffe Tower* (1993).

STEVE HOLLAND

Born: 1954, Dothan, Alabama, US.

■ *Gibson Firebird; Fender Stratocaster.*

A key member of Molly Hatchet's rhythmic barrage, Holland's main function – along with guitarist **Duane Roland** – is to give lead guitarist **Dave Hlubeck** the space to knock out his solos. Lack of memorable material has made the band somewhat derivative, but *Double Trouble Live* (1985) gives a fair indication of why they are seldom off the road.

BUDDY HOLLY

Born: Charles Hardin Holley, September 7th 1936, Lubbock, Texas, US. Died: February 2nd 1959, Clear Lake, Iowa, US.

■ *Fender Stratocaster; Gibson J45.*

Since his death over 30 years ago Holly has become a role model for more groups than one could possibly mention. With The Crickets he fronted the first truly self-contained group who wrote, played all the instruments on their records, and performed live as a group. Holly's compositional powers were intuitive, the trademark hiccups were spontaneous, and the guitar breaks were informed by country as well as rockabilly players like **Scotty Moore**.

In 1956 he cut 'That'll Be The Day' with producer Owen Bradley in Nashville for Decca, but Bradley's orthodox approach to country was inappropriate for Holly and he was dropped by Decca. After this setback, Holly formed a new band with drummer Jerry Allison, guitarist Niki Sullivan and bassist Joe Mauldin, and went to Clovis, New Mexico, to cut some sides with producer Norman Petty. This was the classic Crickets lineup that cut some of the finest rockabilly songs of the era.

By October 1958 Holly and The Crickets had separated, with Holly having moved to New York to pursue a solo career with a new group that included guitarist **Tommy Allsup**, drummer Carl Bunch and bassist Waylon Jennings. Before this new group could gain momentum as a unit, Holly and rock'n'rollers The Big Bopper and Ritchie Valens were killed in a plane crash. Over the next five years, material culled from Holly's final recording sessions in New York and unreleased material from the Petty sessions began to see the light of day: 'It Doesn't Matter Anymore', 'Peggy Sue Got Married', 'True Love Ways', 'What To Do', 'Reminiscing', 'Brown-Eyed Handsome Man', 'Bo Diddley', 'Wishing' and 'Love's Made A Fool Of You'.

HOMER

Born: Henry D Haynes, July 29th 1917, Knoxville, Tennessee, US. Died: August 7th 1971, Chicago, Illinois, US.

■ *Fender Stratocaster; Gibson Super 400 (+ pickup).*

Comedy duo Homer & Jethro were Homer (Haynes) the guitar player and Jethro (Kenneth C Burns) the

mandolinist. They had a string of novelty hits after World War II including 'Baby It's Cold Outside', 'That Hound Dog In The Window', 'Hernando's Hideaway', 'The Battle Of Kookamonga' and 'I Want To Hold Your Hand'. Nonetheless, Haynes and Burns each had a supreme instrumental ability, and played in The Nashville String Band which teamed them with **Chet Atkins** and displayed the complementary virtuosity of each performer.

HOMESICK JAMES

Born: James Williamson, April 30th 1910, Somerville, Tennessee, US.

■ *Elite 335-style.*

After the death of **Elmore James** in 1963, Homesick James embarked on a crusade to launch himself as the natural inheritor of his cousin's bottleneck style. Although he had been playing since the 1930s he started to tour throughout Europe and recorded with greater regularity than in bygone years. *Ain't Sick No More* (1973) remains a good introduction to his abrasive style.

JAMES HONEYMAN-SCOTT

Born: November 4th 1956, Hereford, England. Died: June 16th 1982, London, England.

■ *Gibson ES335; Gibson Les Paul; Zemaitis.*

The Pretenders adopted the pose of a new wave band in the late-1970s, notably through lead vocalist Chrissie Hynde, but really they were a straight-down-the-line rock outfit. Hynde's hard-edged yet sensitive vocals and Honeyman-Scott's lyrical guitar work combined to make records such as 'Stop Your Sobbing', 'Kid', 'Brass In Pocket', 'I Go To Sleep', 'Private Life' and 'Talk Of The Town' some of the most lasting and touching of the era, with the debut eponymous album of 1980 the best collection. After Honeyman-Scott's death, Hynde wrote 'Back On The Chain Gang' as a tribute to him. Featuring guitarist **Billy Bremner**, it is one of the most moving tributes in rock: emotive and full of passion, it still brings a lump to the throat, but also gets to the heart of Hynde's anger at Honeyman-Scott for chucking his life away.

EARL HOOKER

Born: Earl Zebedee Hooker, January 15th 1930, Clarksdale, Mississippi, US. Died: April 21st 1971.

■ *Gibson double-neck.*

The cousin of **John Lee Hooker**, slide guitarist Earl Hooker died of TB before reaping the rewards of many long years of touring on the chitlin circuit. Best known for his slide guitar work, he influenced **Ike Turner**, **Jimi Hendrix**, **Bonnie Raitt** and **Elvin Bishop**, and wrote songs like 'Two Bugs And A Roach' and 'Hold On I'm Coming'. Shortly before his death he joined forces with **Jimmy Dawkins** for *There's A Fungus Among Us* (1970), a collection of instrumentals which included a version of **Elmore James**' 'Dust My Broom', and with **Steve Miller** for the patchy *Hooker'n'Steve* (1969).

HOFF-HOOK

JOHN LEE HOOKER

Born: August 22nd 1917, Clarksdale, Mississippi, US.

■ *Epiphone; Gibson ES335.*

The venerable and venerated Hooker has assumed the mantle of an elder statesman, with any number of young blues players paying homage at his court. This has resulted in a plethora of reissues and some impressive new recordings, such as *The Healer* (1990) and *Mr Lucky* (1992), attended by young hopefuls like **Bonnie Raitt**, **Eric Clapton**, **Pete Townshend** and **Robert Cray**.

If technique is all, Hooker doesn't have it. If weight of emotion is the key, he has it by the bucketful. There are few players around who have managed to achieve so much through an instinctive understanding of form and how a song should feel. 'Crawlin Kingsnake', with its rhythmic tapping on the guitar's top, a fractured chord here and there and some mesmerizing foot-tapping, creates an atmosphere of foreboding sufficient to make the flesh creep and the teeth tingle. Even hardy Hooker perennials like 'Boogie Chillun' and 'Boom Boom' are steeped in mystery, punctuated by the odd yelp or shout to break up the rhythmic pattern – and regular use on a TV commercial didn't assuage the impact of 'Boom Boom'.

Hooker's charisma and aloof detachment has given him an enigmatic aura, and his stylistic shorthand with its characteristic thumps, grunts and groans implies that there be monsters out there that will gobble you up and spit you out. He remains a man of the past locked into the present, and has the appearance of one who has seen the future and doesn't much like the look of it.

SOL HOOPII

Born: 1902, Honolulu, Hawaii, US. Died: November 16th 1953, Seattle, Washington, US.

■ *National resonator; Rickenbacker electric Hawaiian.*

During the 1920s and 1930s when the Hawaiian guitar moved into the mainstream of American popular music through the offices of steel guitarists like **Bob Dunn**, **Don Helms**, **Jerry Byrd** and **Leon McAuliffe**, Hoopii was one of the few practitioners of the original style.

At first Hoopii played acoustic before moving on to the new electric Rickenbacker 'frying pan' in the early-1930s, which he used on a number of film scores such as *Waikiki Wedding* (1937, starring Bing Crosby) and the Charlie Chan series of movies. In 1938 he became an evangelist, but still toured occasionally.

LIGHTNIN' HOPKINS

Born: Sam Hopkins, March 15th 1912, Centerville, Texas, US. Died: January 31st 1982, Houston, Texas, US.

■ *Gibson flat-top (+ pickup).*

Prolific by any standards (he recorded over 100 albums) Hopkins was one of the blues' most gifted natural poets, with the ability to compose songs in much the same ad hoc way that a gifted raconteur might tell a story. This approach to songwriting gave

his work an inspired vitality that was powerful, lucid and fluent. His economical guitar playing echoed that of his earliest influence, **Blind Lemon Jefferson**, underscoring his cryptic observations on the mundane realities of life.

While a master of the 12-bar blues, Hopkins cut many boogies with pianist Wilson 'Thunder' Smith among others and was never governed by constraints of style or form, extemporizing with a verve and aplomb that only **John Lee Hooker** has been able to match. Whether as a soloist or backed by a band Hopkins was an original, with *The Complete Aladdin Recordings* from the mid-1940s and *Texas Blues Man* (1965) showing his range and versatility as well as any of his many recordings.

HOTEI

Born: Hotei Tomoyasu, February 1st 1962, Takasaki, Japan.

Originally inspired to take up the guitar by hearing **Marc Bolan**, Hotei joined the band Boowy in 1981 and over the next seven years honed his act and developed his guitar style. In 1988 he embarked on a solo career which has thus far produced *Guitarhythm I* (1988), *Guitarhythm II* (1991) and *Guitarhythm III* (1992). These illustrate a mastery of the guitar translated into elaborately textured soundscapes that are never bogged down by technique but retain a distinctly emotive power. Although he has become one of Japan's hottest properties, Hotei has not succumbed to the pressures of celebrity and his records have been improving with each release.

SON HOUSE

Born: Eddie James House, March 21st 1902, Riverton, Mississippi, US. Died: October 19th 1988, Detroit, Michigan, US.

■ *National resonator.*

In common with other Mississippi bluesmen like **Robert Johnson**, **Charley Patton** and **John Lee Hooker**, House possessed an intensity that was born of knowing and living the blues rather than reflecting some abstract, generic concept. Despite spending many years in obscurity, having at one time influenced a young Robert Johnson, House returned in the mid-1960s and recorded *The Legendary Son House: Father Of Folk Blues* (1965). One of the finest blues albums to appear in the 1960s it made no concessions to changes in fashion but concentrated on the interpretation of classic blues with spare accompaniment. It ranks alongside Johnson's *King Of The Delta Blues Singers* as one of the most accurate records of unadulterated blues.

STEVE HOWE

Born: April 8th 1947, London, England.

■ *Gibson ES175; Gibson Les Paul; Fender Stratocaster; Fender Telecaster; Steinberger; Martin 00-18; Fender Dual Professional.*

Howe joined Yes, the most successful and adventurous of progressive rock groups, in 1970 and

played on all their classic albums, beginning with *The Yes Album* in 1971. He has a wide-ranging ability and nimble dexterity on classical and steel-strung acoustic guitar ('Clap', 'Mood For A Day') in addition to his better known and eclectic electric work, probably best heard on the earlier Yes albums and his four solo albums, *Beginnings* (1975), *The Steve Howe Album* (1979), *Turbulence* (1991) and *The Grand Scheme Of Things* (1993).

Before Yes, Howe played in The Syndicats and The In Crowd, the latter becoming Tomorrow who, with Howe's guitar in the middle of the picture, recorded in 1967 the classic psychedelic single 'My White Bicycle'.

By the time Yes disbanded in 1981 Howe had won various Top Guitarist awards in Britain and the United States, and continued his success by forming Asia, whose first album appeared in 1982. Another new band, GTR, surfaced in 1985, while Howe joined former members of Yes to form Anderson Bruford Wakeman Howe in 1989, and made successful solo guitar tours in 1993 and '94.

Howe has also been active as a session player, including work for Lou Reed, Queen, Frankie Goes To Hollywood and Stanley Clarke, and produced *Artistry* (1993), an album by the talented British jazz guitarist **Martin Taylor**.

HOWLIN' WOLF

Born: Chester Arthur Burnett, June 10th 1910, Aberdeen, Mississippi, US. Died: January 10th 1976, Hines, Illinois, US.

■ *Fender Stratocaster (later).*

Initially Burnett worked on a farm before joining the army, which he left in 1948 and formed The House Rockers, one of the earliest electric R&B groups. The following year, having adopted the name Howlin' Wolf, he acquired a slot on a west Memphis radio station and was spotted by **Ike Turner** who recommended him to the Modern label in Los Angeles.

After a number of releases on the Modern subsidiary RPM, including 'Moanin At Midnight', Wolf signed with Chess in Chicago. Backed by the house band comprising bassist Willie Dixon, drummer Earl Phillips, pianist Otis Spann and guitarists **Hubert Sumlin** and **Willie Lee Johnson** Wolf cut a fistful of his own compositions including 'Smokestack Lightnin', 'Evil', 'Sittin On Top Of The World', 'Killin Floor' and 'No Place To Go' (all the classic Chess recordings are collected on *The Chess Box* 1991).

These sides retained some of the brooding intensity characteristic of most Delta bluesmen, but the roistering house style of Chess and the influence of **Muddy Waters** gave Wolf's simple chordal technique a tough majesty. Throughout the 1960s he was lionized by groups like The Rolling Stones and The Yardbirds who tried to emulate the 'in your face' quality of his records, and in 1971 Wolf recorded *The London Howlin' Wolf Sessions* with a number of these followers, including **Eric Clapton**, Stones bassist Bill Wyman, and **Keith Richards**, among others.

NEIL HUBBARD

Born: England.

Hubbard is a session guitarist who has been in a number of groups such as the The Graham Bond Organization, Juicy Lucy and Kokomo who, while highly rated by critics, have not exactly excited the public. That's a shame because Hubbard's chunky chords on Kokomo's debut *Kokomo* (1975) were a welcome relief from the profusion of disco dogging the airwaves at the time. Along with Gonzalez, Kokomo were one of the most engaging outfits on the British club circuit of the time. In 1980 Hubbard became more visible when recruited for Roxy Music's *Flesh & Blood* album, and contributed fine work to covers of 'Eight Miles High' (The Byrds) and 'In The Midnight Hour' (Wilson Pickett) among other tracks.

DANN HUFF

Born: US.

■ *PRS; Fender Stratocaster; Tyler.*

Huff is at the time of writing in the enviable position of being fashionable, having been used by David Bowie (*Black Suit White Tie* 1993), Michael Jackson (*Dangerous* 1992) and Elton John (*Duets* 1993) on recent albums and tours. Huff's work is efficient rather than original, but with such egos to deal with and, doubtless, good session rates, who cares about originality? Some of that, at least, went into his *Last Of The Runaways* solo (1992, credited to Giant).

STEVE HUNTER

Born: US.

Hunter is a veteran of many David Bowie and Lou Reed sessions, as well as playing in Hall & Oates' road band, although especially notable is his contribution to Reed's *Rock And Roll Animal* (1974), to which he contributed some epic duelling solos in partnership with **Dick Wagner**. The intro which segues into that old Velvet Underground classic 'Sweet Jane' shows the contrasting styles of the two guitarists, with Hunter's fluid phrasing punctuated by Wagner's punchy vibrato. When 'Lady Day' first appeared on Reed's album *Berlin* it was stark and forbidding; here it is transformed by the opening chords into a defiant guitar feast. Still one of the best live albums around, *Animal* captures the latent aggression in Reed's material thanks to Hunter and Wagner.

GORDON HUNTLEY

Born: England.

Matthews Southern Comfort, best known for their cover of **Joni Mitchell**'s 'Woodstock' in 1970 which prominently featured steel guitarist Huntley, came close to authenticating an English equivalent of country-rock. Much of the material on the albums *Later The Same Year* and *Second Spring* (1970) had been written by Ken Howard and Alan Blaikeley, who had written previously for The Herd among others. After Ian Matthews left the group to form Plainsong with **Andy Roberts** in 1972 Southern Comfort continued, having signed with the Harvest label.

Their debut *Southern Comfort* (1972) showed a purist country tendency and, despite Huntley's evident agility on pedal-steel, the absence of a strong vocalist caused the group to split in 1973. Since that time Huntley has hovered on the session circuit.

MISSISSIPPI JOHN HURT

Born: July 3rd 1893, Teoc, Mississippi, US.
Died: November 2nd 1966, Grenada, Mississippi, US.

Although known as 'Mississippi', Hurt had a gentle, homespun style of guitar work that was at variance with that of the bulk of the Delta bluesmen. His songs like 'Avalon Blues', 'Candy Man Blues', 'Spike Driver Blues', 'Salty Dog' and 'Stagger Lee Blues' were performed as slices of local and social history. When the Depression took hold in the 1930s Hurt went back to herding cattle near Greenwood, Mississippi until his rediscovery in 1963, when he started to play folk festivals, such as the annual event at Newport, Rhode Island. Hurt's delightfully tricky wit and affecting fingerpicking style ensured that his final years were spent in the glare of the spotlight.

WAYNE HUSSEY

Born: May 26th 1959, Bristol, Avon, England.

■ *Fender Starcaster; Vox Mk XII.*

Formed from the seminal goth band Sisters Of Mercy, the nucleus of The Mission comprised Hussey and bassist Craig Adams. While the band has acquired a significant European following, there is the suspicion that they are preaching to a coterie of devoted fans. The lyrical imagery and the instrumental skill of Hussey and guitarist Simon Hinkler have yet to be blessed with material that goes beyond mere derivativeness, despite a tuneful quality to songs like 'Deliverance', 'Wasteland' and 'Butterfly On A Wheel'.

JB HUTTO

Born: Joseph Benjamin Hutto, April 26th 1926, Blackville, South Carolina, US. Died: June 12th 1983, Chicago, Illinois, US.

■ *Fender Telecaster.*

A lesser known but impressive bluesman, Hutto is in the tough, urban Chicago style. The violence of his solo style was caught on *Slidewinder* (1972) but he could work within a group context, often with players like pianist Sunnyland Slim, harpman Walter Horton and harmonica player James Cotton. While Hutto's style was emblematic of the renaissance in Chicago blues he never lost sight of its antecedents: *Slippin' And Slidin'* (1970s, credited to JB Hutto & the New Hawks) straddles the great divide between ancient and modern. **Rory Gallagher** has covered Hutto's 'Too Much Alcohol'.

SCOTT IAN

Born: New York, New York, US.

■ *Jackson; Charvel.*

Like Ministry, Anthrax have taken speed/thrash metal to new heights (or depths, depending on your view)

with an uncompromising rhythmic intensity. Rhythm guitarist Ian provides the sheet-like riffs that feed and sustain the rest of the band. While lead guitarist **Dan Spitz** attempts dazzling highwire acts with his solos, it is Ian, bassist Frankie Bello and drummer Charlie Benante who enable the band to switch into the odd semi-rap number ('I'm The Man') with the metronomic efficiency of an electronic sample. Reputedly, drummer Benante develops riffs, Ian personalizes them (with age-old skills like strumming behind the bridge) and the results are numbers like 'H8 Red' and 'Intro To Reality'. Of all the hardcore metal outfits Anthrax seem the most instinctive and atmospheric.

AZIZ IBRAHIM

Born: Britain

■ *Fender Stratocaster.*

For a brief moment when Simply Red was a group and not just a bunch of players backing vocalist Mick Hucknall, there seeemed a chance that Ibrahim might become lead guitarist in an important outfit. He lasted a little over two years and contributed to *A New Flame* (1989), an album roundly vilified at the time by the press, as the group had apparently 'sold out' and the arrangements were too similar to those of soulmen like Luther Vandross and Teddy Pendergrass. Ibrahim's playing on 'If You Don't Know Me By Now' is tender and reverential. A new flame, indeed.

JAMES IHA

Born: Chicago, Illinois, US.

When Smashing Pumpkins issued their debut *Gish* (1991) it was their misfortune that the world could only focus on one grunge band at a time – and that happened to be Nirvana. Two years later, while **Kurt Cobain** and the rest of Nirvana dithered, Smashing Pumpkins steamed into the studio with producer Butch Vig and knocked out *Siamese Dream* (1993). Characterized by Iha's demented sonic thrash ('Cherub Rock') and vocalist Billy Corgan's highly personal and bile-laden lyrics ('Geek USA') this was as close to the bone as you get without severing an artery. While the vagaries of fashion may consign many of their contemporaries to the crematorium, the Pumpkins, like Nirvana, seem built of sterner stuff. Iha is a guitarist who before too long will be making regular appearances as a guest artist on any number of colleagues' projects.

TONY IOMMI

Born: February 19th 1948, Birmingham, England.

■ *Gibson SG; Birch; Jaydee; Eggle 'signature'.*

When Black Sabbath formed in 1969, naming themselves after a 1963 horror film, little did anyone realize that they would be architects of a genre. Left-hander Iommi's crunching chords – not many, but enough – and a succession of vocalists such as Ozzy Osbourne, Ronnie Dio and Ian Gillan conspired to give the band the tag of heavy metal. 'Paranoid', 'War Pigs' and 'Sabbath Bloody Sabbath' (collected on

We Sold Our Soul For Rock'n'Roll 1986) have become prime study material for the budding metallurgist. Simplistic and crass they may be, but they have struck chords with so many of limited musical outlook who have fancied careers in the music business that the band has become a model of sorts. The film *This Is Spinal Tap* would appear to be not a million miles from portraying Their Life & (Possible) Times.

BUD ISAACS

Born: US.

■ *Rus-ler custom.*

Vocalist Webb Pierce's group wasn't too different from other honky-tonk outfits of the 1950s, but one major difference was the inclusion of pedal-steel guitarist Bud Isaacs in Pierce's lineup. The addition of this vital component gave Pierce's records a distinctive edge that caused every self-respecting country band to hire a pedal-steel guitarist, and Isaacs' pitch-shifting pedal work on 'Slowly' (1954) was among the first recorded appearances of the pedal-steel's now customary trademark sound. Other Pierce records bearing Isaacs' fine playing include 'More And More', **Jimmie Rodgers**' 'In The Jailhouse Now', 'Love Love Love', 'I Don't Care', Felice and Boudleaux Bryant's 'Bye Bye Love', 'Honky Tonk Song', 'Tupelo County Jail' and 'I Ain't Never'. Pierce and others of his ilk are undervalued today, but his band could knock corners off most contemporary outfits. *The Wondering Boy* is a four-CD collection on Bear Family that covers Pierce's recordings from 1951 to 1958.

IKE ISAACS

Born: Isaac Isaacs, December 1st 1919, Rangoon, Burma.

■ *Aria 'signature'; Gibson L7.*

Isaacs moved to England and became a session musician in the 1940s, including work as group leader on BBC radio's *Guitar Club*, and played with many artists who would now be considered middle-of-the-road, such as bandleader Ted Heath and trombonist George Chisholm. In 1975 he joined violinist Stéphane Grapelli's quartet, no doubt brushing up his **Django Reinhardt** impressions. Isaacs has further indulged his primary love for jazz by sessioning with stalwarts like **Barney Kessel** and bright new lights such as **Martin Taylor**.

SHARON ISBIN

Born: August 7th 1956, Minneapolis, Minnesota, US.

■ *Humphrey.*

With a master's degree in music from Yale University, Isbin has since the mid-1970s established herself as a fine and respected classical guitarist. More recently she was appointed as the first professor of guitar at the Juilliard School Of Music in New York, one of the most prestigious jobs available to a player of her stature. Particularly interesting is her performance of the transcription for guitar of the dance suite from Leonard Bernstein's *West Side Story*, performed as a duet with fellow classical guitarist Carlos Barbosa-Lima, recorded in 1988.

ERNIE ISLEY

Born: March 7th 1952, Cincinatti, Ohio, US.

■ *Fender Stratocaster.*

The Isley Brothers had been going for some years when in 1969 the younger members of the family were enlisted to bolster the flagging and somewhat dated efforts of the original trio. The three young bloods in question were Ernest Isley (guitar), Marvin Isley (bass/percussion) and cousin Chris Jasper (keyboards). Overnight the influences of James Brown, Sly Stone and **Jimi Hendrix** became immediately more emphatic (Hendrix had in fact been a member of the original trio's road band earlier in the 1960s). After four comparatively lean years the Isleys started to cut material penned by Chris Jasper and Ernie and Marvin Isley. One of their first compositions was the soulful 'That Lady', which was followed by a string of highly atmospheric, funky hits – 'Highways Of My Life', 'Summer Breeze', 'Fight The Power', 'For The Love Of You', 'Harvest For The World', 'Livin' In The Life' and 'Don't Say Goodnight (It's Time For Love)' – with Ernie's choppy, staccato chording and long, flowing melody lines standing out from the urgent rhythm and the wash of keyboards.

What set them apart from the average disco band were their harmonies, the quality of material, and their air of elder statesmen. Jasper, Ernie and Marvin left to form their own imaginatively titled group Isley Jasper Isley in 1984, after which both groups have consistently delivered turkeys, apart from Isley Jasper Isley's 'Caravan Of Love' which did have a certain charm.

BRIAN JAMES

Born: Brian Robertson, England.

■ *Gibson SG.*

Founder member of The Damned, James' power chords, performed with a slapdash passion, caught the mood of the moment, and suitably demystified the process of making music. He wrote two classic punk anthems, 'New Rose' and 'Neat Neat Neat'. While The Sex Pistols and The Clash were the visible, public profile of punk, groups like The Damned provided much of the galvanizing energy for the trend. After he left the group in 1978, giving way to Captain Sensible's guitar work, James kept the pioneering faith by joining Lords Of The New Chuch.

ELMORE JAMES

Born: January 27th 1918, Richland, Mississippi, US. Died: May 24th 1963, Chicago, Illinois, US.

■ *Kay (+ pickup).*

'Dust My Broom', 'Dust My Blues' and 'I Believe My Time Ain't Long': same chords, same song, same writer – Elmore James. They became the staple of many a 1960s blues band's repertoire, thanks to their distinctive opening phrases that were perfect fodder for any aspiring slide guitarist. James' career revolved around this seminal guitar figure and, as a result, it tended to dominate his repertoire – even the other

James standard, 'The Sky Is Crying', incorporates the familiar run. Despite all this, the abrasiveness of his style influenced many bluesmen like **Hound Dog Taylor**, **Johnny Winter**, **JB Hutto** and **Luther Allison**, to name but a few.

RICK JAMES

Born: James Johnson, February 1st 1948, Buffalo, New York, US.

James joined the navy but deserted to settle in Toronto, where he formed The Mynah Birds with **Neil Young** in 1965. After moving to Detroit James signed with Motown, but nothing was released and so he moved to London where he formed The Main Line. By 1977 he had returned to the US and formed The Stone City Band who were signed to the Motown subsidiary, Gordy.

James' debut, *Come Get It*, exhibited the influence of soulman James Brown and funk-master George Clinton, particularly in the guitar work which was strongly reminiscent of **Eddie Hazel**. James peaked with *Street Songs* (1981) which included the singles 'Give It To Me Baby' and 'Super Freak Part 1'. Since then he has continued recording, but albums like *Throwin' Down* and *Cold Blooded* have lacked the sheer inventiveness of *Street Songs*.

SKIP JAMES

Born: Nehemiah James, June 9th 1902, Bentonia, Mississippi, US. Died: October 3rd 1969, Philadelphia, Pennsylvania, US.

■ *Martin.*

While working as a sharecropper in Mississippi in 1964 James was 'rediscovered' by guitarists **John Fahey** and **Henry Vestine**. This enabled him to rerecord a bunch of songs that he had penned in the 1930s, including 'Devil Got My Woman', 'Hard Time Killin' Floor Blues', '20-20 Blues', 'I'd Rather Be The Devil' and 'I'm So Glad'. In addition he hit the festival circuit, appearing at the Newport, Rhode Island event with **Mississippi John Hurt** where his smokey vocals and intensely lyrical guitar style complemented the folksy urbanity of Hurt. James' influence on blues aficionados remains almost as high as that of **Robert Johnson**.

BILL JANOWITZ

Born: Boston, Massachusetts, US.

Inspired by Sonic Youth and Hüsker Dü, Buffalo Tom were formed by Janowitz, bassist Chris Colbourn and drummer Tom Maginnis in the late-1980s while students in Boston. Contemporaries of **Evan Dando** and **J Mascis**, their first two albums (*Buffalo Tom* and *Birdbrain*, both 1990) invited comparisons with Dinosaur Jr and Nirvana, but by the time *Let Me Come Over* (1992) emerged they had established a retro 1960s sound that owed much to The Byrds and Moby Grape. Janowitz's guitar work on *Big Red Letter Day* (1993) was full of crisp licks and chiming chords ('Sodajerk' and 'Dry Land') while his impassioned vocals and the group's harmonies were executed with a refreshing disinterest.

BERT JANSCH

Born: November 3rd 1943, Glasgow, Scotland.

■ *Yamaha L24; Armstrong.*

Although Davey Graham composed the fingerpicking classic 'Angie', it was Jansch's version that many budding British guitarists studied. Jansch, who had played the club circuit for many years, was a folk and blues guitarist out of a similar 'folk-baroque' school to that of **Martin Carthy**.

Jansch's solo career had started in 1965 with an eponymous album that included 'Needle Of Death', a veiled tribute to Graham, 'Do You Hear Me Now?' and 'Angie'. Notable for its lack of artifice, it placed Jansch firmly in the vanguard of the folk revivalists. Later solo albums such as *Jack Orion* (1966) continued the theme with a magnificent piece of bluesy picking on 'Black Water Side' (later interpreted by **Jimmy Page**) and a sparse, evocative reading of Ewan MacColl's 'First Time Ever I Saw Your Face'.

In 1967 Jansch and **John Renbourn** became the mainstays of Pentangle, formed by manager Jo Lustig as something of a supergroup with vocalist Jacqui McShee, drummer Terry Cox and the ubiquitous bassist Danny Thompson. While there was a folksy feyness about much of what they issued, the duets between Jansch and Renbourn with their contrasting styles – the former visceral and bluesy, the latter florid and jazzy – were fine expositions of acoustic picking. The group's best albums are *Sweet Child* (1968) and *Reflection* (1971).

Jansch undertook a series of international tours with the group, which split in 1972, and recorded the remarkable solo album *Rosemary Lane* (1969) for Transatlantic before signing a fresh deal with Charisma, recording a run of solo albums that were in general over-produced. The self-effacing Jansch has in recent years reverted to the sparse arrangements of his early albums, and is a regular on the international festival circuit.

BLIND LEMON JEFFERSON

Born: July 1897, Couchman, Texas, US. Died: December 1929, Chicago, Illinois, US.

There is scant information on the details of his life, but Jefferson was one of the major Texan stylists to emerge before the Depression. His high-pitched, expressive vocals on self-penned items like 'Black Snake Blues', 'Pneumonia Blues' and 'See That My Grave Is Kept Clean' were given greater emphasis by his guitar style, which often sounded improvised and ran in counterpoint to the vocal. *King Of The Country Blues* on Yazoo is a good place to hear Jefferson's unique music. Although Jefferson died early, he influenced Texan musicians such as **Leadbelly**, **Lightnin' Hopkins** and **T-Bone Walker**, as well as the Mississippi-based **BB King**.

HARVEY JETT

Born: Marion, Arkansas, US.

■ *Gibson Les Paul; Fender Stratocaster.*

Forming one third of Black Oak Arkansas' guitar assault, Jett was on board during the band's early years when the group blazed a trail with a somewhat derivative melding of country and blues. That **Duane Allman** and **Dickey Betts** did it better doesn't alter the fact that *Keep The Faith* (1972) and 'Jim Dandy' showed that a bunch of good ole boys with a background in country didn't have to view the Grand Ole Opry as the zenith of musical ambitions. Jett, like **Ricky Reynolds**, left the band in the mid-1970s.

JOAN JETT

Born: Joan Larkin, September 22nd 1960, Philadelphia, Pennsylvania, US.

■ *Gibson Melody Maker.*

As a member of The Runaways, Jett's suitably spiky guitar slotted in beside that of **Lita Ford** on the six albums that the all-female punk-ish group made between 1976 and 1980 under the auspices of Los Angeles producer Kim Fowley. Jett then went solo and had a massive hit with 'I Love Rock'n'Roll' (1982), the album of the same name featuring assistance from ex-Sex Pistols guitarist **Steve Jones**.

BLIND WILLIE JOHNSON

Born: 1902, Marlin, Texas, US. Died: 1949, Beaumont, Texas, US.

In common with **Rev Gary Davis**, Johnson belongs to that apparently obsolete tradition of the singing preacher, and his slide playing is superb. Johnson's powerful attestations were, like Davis, never didactic, but the veracity cannot be doubted. Johnson's recordings, which are few and far between, say more about the role of religion in the development of black music than anything else that comes to mind. The guitar work may lack the accomplished dexterity of later country blues pickers, but Johnson has few peers in the slide guitar department. As a footnote, **Ry Cooder** has described Johnson's 'Dark Was The Night' as the most transcendent piece in American music. Various collections on Yazoo are available.

BOB JOHNSON

Born: March 17th 1944, England.

■ *Schecter Strat-style.*

When Johnson took over from **Martin Carthy** the role of main guitarist in Steeleye Span in 1972, the group were a restrained, almost traditional, folk outfit. His arrival indicated significant changes in the group's approach and they started a commercial spiral that would make them the most successful of all British electric folk bands. While Johnson remained an ensemble player, the emphasis within the band gradually toughened up to the extent that by the time they recorded 'Thomas The Rhymer' and 'Seven Hundred Elves' on *Now We Are Six* (1974) the arrangements had almost a metal feel.

The only thing which stopped Steeleye from becoming an out-and-out rock band was the timbre of Maddy Prior's voice: full of rich vowels and hard consonants, it was totally incompatible with rock. In 1977 Johnson and fiddler Peter Knight left to record a concept album based on Lord Dunsany's fantasy novel, *The King Of The Elfland's Daughter*. In recent years Johnson has participated in occasional Steeleye reunions and is still a usefully eclectic rather than dazzling guitarist.

ERIC JOHNSON

Born: August 17th 1954, Austin, Texas, US.

■ *Fender Stratocaster.*

One of the most enduring accolades bestowed on Johnson came from the lips of ZZ Top's **Billy Gibbons**: "Damn! That guy can play." This pithy if not eloquent statement underlines the esteem in which Johnson is held by some of his more venerated colleagues. Indeed, should anyone fill the spot vacated by **Stevie Ray Vaughan**, it is probably Johnson. *Ah Via Musicom* (1990) contains inspiringly varied playing, with Johnson displaying a purity of tone and dexterity more frequently associated with the likes of **Jimi Hendrix**, **Jeff Beck** and **Jerry Reed** on tracks like 'East Wes', the signature instrumental 'Cliffs Of Dover', and the country-tinged 'Steve's Boogie'. While his electric guitar work has drawn many of the plaudits, Johnson has been voted Best Acoustic Guitarist six years running by the discerning and critical inhabitants of (his home town) Austin.

GEORGE JOHNSON

Born: May 17th 1953, Los Angeles, California, US.

■ *Fender Stratocaster; Fender Telecaster; Gibson Les Paul; Gibson ES335.*

George and his brother Louis started their career in the early-1970s when they hit the LA club circuit while still at school, working as session musicians from 1975 with soul artists like David Ruffin, The Supremes, Billy Preston and producer Quincy Jones. Their break came when Jones featured them on his *Mellow Madness* album (1975), enabling them to secure a recording contract with A&M.

The Brothers Johnson debut album *Look Out For #1* (1976), produced by Jones, included 'I'll Be Good To You' and 'Get The Funk Outta Ma Face' and illustrated their knack for hooks and George's ability to inject emphatic phrases at just the right point. To some extent they were the beneficiaries of Jones' years of production experience, as demonstrated by 'Strawberry Letter 23', 'Stomp' and 'Light Up The Night', but the records had a bright, vivid spring assisted by George's succinct and never overblown guitar work.

In later years, having dispensed with Jones' expertise, the Brothers lost their former sharpness and before long both were back on the session circuit, playing second fiddle to the likes of jazz-rockers The Crusaders, **Lee Ritenour**, vocalist Patti Austin, and **George Benson**.

JIMMY JOHNSON

Born: 1944, Muscle Shoals, Alabama, US.

■ *Fender Telecaster.*

From the late-1950s, Johnson was the rhythm guitarist in The Del-Rays, playing the club circuit

Jan-Joh

73

and high school balls in and around Muscle Shoals, Alabama, US. When Rick Hall set up Fame studios there, Johnson was one of the first of many to work as rhythm guitarist and engineer.

After keyboards player David Briggs and the rest of the first house band left, Johnson became the principal guitarist with Roger Hawkins (drums), Spooner Oldham (keyboards) and Junior Lowe (bass). Then in 1969 Johnson, with Hawkins, bassist David Hood and keyboardist Barry Beckett, left Hall to open the Muscle Shoals Sound studios where Johnson continued in his former capacity as guitarist. The studios were sold to Malaco in 1985, but Johnson remained and worked on sessions for vocalists Bobby Bland and Johnnie Taylor.

Throughout his long association with Muscle Shoals Johnson has played with everyone from Aretha Franklin and **Bobby Womack** to **Eric Clapton** and **Duane Allman**.

LONNIE JOHNSON

Born: Alonzo Johnson, February 8th 1889, New Orleans, Louisiana, US. Died: June 16th 1970, Toronto, Ontario, Canada.

■ *Grunewald 12-string; Gibson J100; Kay solidbody; Martin.*

In the early years of the record industry, Johnson's all-round proficiency as a guitarist won the attention of jazzmen such as Duke Ellington and Louis Armstrong. At the same time Johnson maintained a strong reputation on the vaudeville circuit and as a blues musician at the Okeh label. Playing six-string and 12-string guitar, Johnson's sophisticated musical vocabulary enabled him to play blues and jazz with equal dexterity, and he has influenced many players since, from **George Barnes** to **Charlie Christian**.

While his guitar blues were somewhat mournful (a good compilation is the recent *Steppin' On The Blues*), he had an inventive and technically adept approach. Johnson's duets with **Eddie Lang** in the late-1920s illustrated his full range and are still influential today, and Johnson's 12-string is the principal solo instrument (the duets are included on Lang's *Jazz Guitar Virtuoso* and other compilations). In 1928 Johnson also played a delightful solo on the Chocolate Dandies' version of Hoagy Carmichael's 'Stardust'. Thereafter his career was erratic, although his version of 'Tomorrow Night' (1947) is notable, and during the 1950s he worked as a hotel janitor. Johnson resumed his career in the 1960s, touring extensively on club and festival circuits.

ROBERT JOHNSON

Born: May 8th 1911, Hazelhurst, Mississippi, US. Died: August 16th 1938, Greenwood, Mississippi, US.

■ *Gibson L1; Stella; Kalamazoo.*

There are few musicians in the history of 20th century music who have aroused such interest and speculation as Johnson. Almost anyone who has aspired to playing the guitar has been informed by the remarkable intensity of Johnson's guitar style coupled to the astonishingly emotional commitment of his vocals.

Inspired by **Lonnie Johnson** and pianist/vocalist Leroy Carr, Johnson's slide guitar work – sometimes played with a glass bottleneck, other times with a knife – is some of the most sensitive and emotive in all the blues. He penned a string of haunting, poetic songs like 'Love In Vain', 'Drunken Hearted Man', 'Crossroads Blues', 'Hellhound On My Trail', 'Rambling On My Mind' and 'Come On In My Kitchen' that later became important to the repertoires of players such as **Eric Clapton**, **Stevie Ray Vaughan**, **Taj Mahal**, **Johnny Winter**, **Johnny Shines** and **Keith Richards**. The indispensable classic collection is *The King Of The Delta Blues Singers*, although in 1990 the complete recordings were released by Columbia.

TOMMY JOHNSON

Born: 1896, Terry, Mississippi, US. Died: November 1st 1956, Crystal Springs, Mississippi, US.

'Canned Heat Blues' (from which the Californian 1960s blues band took their name) and 'Cool Drink Of Water Blues' were among the most celebrated of the small number of records made by Johnson, and were notable for intense performances. But Johnson seldom worked within the music industry, preferring instead to play throughout the southern states at parties, clubs and bars, collaborating with lesser known musicians such as fellow guitarist/vocalists Ishmon Bracey and Charlie McCoy. In common with **Robert Johnson**, stories abound that Tommy sold his soul to the devil in order to hone his refined guitar style.

WILKO JOHNSON

Born: John Wilkinson, 1947, Southend, Essex, England.

■ *Fender Telecaster.*

The sprightly Johnson provided the thrust for the British R&B group Dr Feelgood in the 1970s. Arguably, it was groups such as Feelgood, emerging from the club and pub circuits in the early-1970s, that gave punk its impetus – and no one was better equipped to spearhead this boom than Johnson.

His bold, stabbing chords and extrovert stage manner – essentially rushing around with an amphetamine stare – gave life to the Feelgoods' covers of R&B standards by Sonny Boy Williamson, **John Lee Hooker**, **Elmore James** and **Robert Johnson**. Their stripped down, anti-fashion image quickly became fashionable, Johnson careering across the stage while vocalist Lee Brilleaux bawled out the lyrics like a forsaken banshee.

In 1977, as the group's popularity increased with the release of *Sneakin' Suspicion*, their repertoire became more sophisticated and Johnson left to form his own group, with the intention of reverting to the type of music that Dr Feelgood played in their early days. He's still doing that to this day.

WILLIE LEE JOHNSON

Born: US.

Formerly a member of **Howlin' Wolf**'s group The House Rockers, Johnson contributed the punchy

chords to early records such as 'Moanin' In The Moonlight'. While Wolf's later guitarist **Hubert Sumlin** was technically more varied, Johnson was a journeyman.

RANDY JOHNSTON

Born: 1956, Detroit, Michigan, US.

■ *Epiphone Riviera; Gibson ES175.*

Influenced initially by **Jimi Hendrix**, Johnston studied jazz at the University of Miami before moving to New York in 1981. Two years later, despite the influence of **Albert King** and **BB King**, Johnston's sound had acquired an almost primitive warmth, which encouraged producer Houston Person to hire him for R&B organist Brother Jack McDuff's *Another Real Good 'Un* and vocalist Etta Jones's *Sugar*. This exposure enabled Johnston to cut his debut *Walk On*, and gradually he seems to be acquiring the reputation of a bluesy jazzman with similarities to **Grant Green**.

TOM JOHNSTON

Born: Visalia, California, US.

■ *PRS (later).*

Johnston and **Pat Simmons** were the first two guitarists in the Doobie Brothers lineup in the early-1970s and were responsible for defining the band's sound, a combination of pristine harmonies and a dual-pronged guitar attack that fused elements of country, folk and blues in a bright, energetic hybrid.

The best songs from their early albums illustrate this well, including 'Listen To The Music' and 'Jesus Is Just Alright' (*Toulouse Street* 1973), 'Long Train Running' and 'China Grove' (*The Captain And Me* 1973) and 'Black Water' (*What Were Once Vices Are Now Habits* 1974).

After the break-up of Steely Dan as a live band **Jeff Baxter** joined the Doobies and appeared on *Stampede* in 1975, giving the band a funkier sound with his incisive, chunky phrases. Johnston left briefly through ill-health and his replacement was Michael McDonald, also a Steely Dan alumnus. McDonald's soulful, impassioned vocals, as on *Minute By Minute* (1979), tended to obscure the former country influences of the group, which rapidly became little more than McDonald's backing band. Johnston's return was short-lived and he finally left for an unsuccessful solo career in 1977.

DAVEY JOHNSTONE

Born: May 6th 1951, Edinburgh, Scotland.

■ *Gibson Les Paul; Fender Stratocaster.*

Johnstone started his career playing banjo in the folk band Magna Carta, which caused him to be nicknamed Shaggis (don't ask why). In 1972 he joined Elton John's band and contributed to the next six albums, from *Honky Chateau* (1972) to *Rock Of The Westies* (1975). While Johnstone's forte was adding the tonal qualities of an acoustic guitar, so vital to John's occasionally haunting melodies and Bernie Taupin's evocative lyrics, he proved himself a fine electric player in the studio and on numerous tours. After leaving John, he attempted a solo career.

BILLY JONES

Born: Tampa, Florida, US.

■ **Gibson Les Paul.**

The Outlaws were formed in 1974 in the cast of The Allman Brothers Band and Poco. Gentle harmonies and a frontline of three duelling guitarists – Jones, **Hugh Thomasson** and **Henry Paul** – made the band a notable feature of the US live circuit, and pieces like 'Green Grass And High Tides' were real showstoppers. However, the group scored a brace of hits with modestly tuneful ditties like 'There Goes Another Love Song' and 'Lady In Waiting'. Jones apparently tired of the touring and left in 1979.

BRIAN JONES

Born: Lewis Brian Hopkin-Jones, February 28th 1942, Cheltenham, Gloucestershire, England. Died: July 3rd 1969, Hartfield, Sussex, England.

■ **Vox Mk VI; Gibson Firebird; Gretsch Double Anniversary.**

As with **George Harrison** in The Beatles, Jones was the Rolling Stones man always on the lookout for fresh instruments with which to experiment. Despite Mick Jagger's high profile as the group's celebrity and Keith Richards' absorption in the development of the big riff, Jones contributed some of the more interesting tonal variations to the band's sound in the mid-1960s, while drawing on his firmly blues-based influences. *Between The Buttons* (1967), *Their Satanic Majesties Request* (1968) and *Beggar's Banquet* (1969) showed the extent of Jones' influence in adding different characters and textures to the group's sound, such as on 'Backstreet Girl', 'She's A Rainbow' and the slide guitar of 'No Expectations'.

MALCOLM JONES

Born: July 12th 1959, Inverness, Scotland.

Runrig have become one of Scotland's biggest musical phenomena since singer Andy Stewart's celebrated loss of Donald's trewsers. Distinct from the plethora of guitar-based bands of the 1980s such as The Waterboys, Simple Minds and Big Country, Runrig have embraced Scotland's cultural past with one eye firmly on the future. They developed a coherent identity and sound in the ceilidh dance halls of the west Highlands, investing their sound with a pastoral rather than urban feel. After some changes in earlier lineups, Jones' guitar and accordion work have recently been the dominant sound, with big chords contrasting against lyrical acoustic interludes, as heard on the live *Once In A Lifetime* (1989) and on *Amazing Things* (1993).

MICK JONES

Born: June 26th 1955, London, England.

■ **Bond.**

One of the finest talents to emerge from the punk generation of the late-1970s as a member of The Clash, Jones has with wit and wisdom combined the punk ethos with a lyrical, melodic post-modernism. Never one to hype himself unduly, Jones' knack for a hook and a succinct chord sequence has out-distanced fellow Clash man Joe Strummer's less focused ventures elsewhere. Jones' work on The Clash's 'White Man In Hammersmith Palais', 'London Calling' (written with Strummer, and produced by the majestic Guy Stevens), 'Rock The Casbah', plus the more recent 'Should I Stay Or Should I Go?' and 'E=MC²' with Big Audio Dynamite, indicate a man with profound pop sensibilities tinged by a dry wit.

MICK JONES

Born: December 27th 1944, London, England.

■ **Gibson Les Paul.**

One-time member of Spooky Tooth and **Leslie West**'s band, Jones formed Foreigner in 1976. In combination with ex-King Crimson reedman Ian McDonald, drummer Dennis Elliott, bassist Ed Gagliardi, keyboards wizard Al Greenwood and vocalist Lou Gramm, Jones assembled a unit in the image of Bad Company with the pop vision of Chicago. The result was a series of macho semi-rockers and ballads such as 'Cold As Ice', 'Feels Like The First Time', 'Urgent' (with a key sax solo by Junior Walker), 'Waiting For A Girl Like You', 'I Want To Know What Love Is' and 'That Was Yesterday'. Each and every one was a highly effective embodiment of AOR. Jones' guitar work, while efficient, has generally taken a back seat to Gramm's vocals and the band's overall arrangements.

MICKY JONES

Born: June 7th 1946, Merthyr Tydfil, Glamorgan, Wales.

■ **Gibson SG.**

Man embodied the freewheeling ethos of the hippies, and the group's fluctuating lineup mirrored their role model, Quicksilver Messenger Service. Throughout their seven-year career, Man's lead guitarist Jones was the unifying factor.

The group was formed out of The Bystanders, a Swansea-based pop band who charted briefly with a cover of Keith's '98.6'. Man were a totally different kettle of fish, with the main thrust coming from lengthy guitar duels between Jones and whoever else happened to be playing guitar in the band at the time (Deke Leonard and Clive John, among others).

As a result studio albums such as *Man* (1970), *Do You Like It Here, Are You Settling In?* (1971) and *Be Good To Yourself At Least Once A Day* (1972) were uneven, but contained the material that would undergo an extraordinary metamorphosis on stage (*Live At The Padgett Rooms Penarth* 1972). This patchiness permeated their career, although they have acquired a legendary status and various combinations of Man still join up for the odd reunion or European tour.

NIC JONES

Born: Nicholas Paul Jones, January 9th 1947, Orpington, Kent, England.

Jones was tragically injured in a car crash in 1982 from which he is yet to fully recover, and it seems unlikely that he will ever be able to play again. Jones was at the peak of his powers then, having completed *Penguin Eggs* (1980) which had elevated him to the upper tier of English folk revivalists. His assured picking on 'The Humpback Whale' and 'Farewell To The Gold' echoed the percussive style of **Martin Carthy**, while his vocal delivery lacked the mannered intonations prevalent in most traditional music. Among Jones' other achievements were his contributions to the Maddy Prior and June Tabor album *The Silly Sisters* (1976), which illustrated his ability to bridge the gap between the traditional and the contemporary.

STEVE JONES

Born: May 3rd 1955, London, England.

■ **Gibson Les Paul.**

Jones' crashing guitar work, especially the chiming intro to 'God Save The Queen' or the raw power of 'Bodies', was as important to the impact of The Sex Pistols as Johnny Rotten's disdainful vocal delivery. While Jones has never managed to repeat the power and urgency of 'Anarchy In The UK' (1976), 'God Save The Queen' and 'Pretty Vacant' (1977) and 'C'mon Everybody' (1979) his playing is not, unlike **Pete Townshend**'s rowdier contributions to The Who, convinced other disenchanted adolescents that they too could have a go on the guitar. This proved beneficial as it showed that a thorough grounding in composition from the Royal College was not essential to becoming a musician. Unfortunately Jones seems virtually to have retired as a musician, concentrating instead on overseeing The Sex Pistols' business interests, although in 1987 he did work on Iggy Pop's *Mercy*. The Pistols' *Never Mind The Bollocks* (1977) remains his best work.

CYRIL JORDAN

Born: 1948, San Francisco, California, US.

A superlative garage band, The Flamin' Groovies were never looked upon with much respect in the US as they were perceived as just another rock'n'roll revival band. But Jordan's and **Tim Lynch**'s steaming guitar workouts on *Supersnazz* (1969) were highly effective tributes to the spirit of rock'n'roll, echoing the great unsung heroes of the past like **Cliff Gallup** and **Tommy Allsup**. Later albums such as *Flamingo* (1970) and *Teenage Head* (1971) updated that perspective to encompass contemporary outfits like the MC5, and 1970s albums (*Shake Some Action* 1976, *Jumpin' In The Night* 1979) continued to impress for their sheer energy and affection. While the group has undergone frequent changes of personnel, Jordan has remained at the group's core throughout.

RONNY JORDAN

Born: London, England.

■ **Gibson ES175; Gibson ES335; Ibanez custom.**

Jordan is one of the first British-bred black jazz guitarists to emerge, and his debut *The Antidote*

JON-JOR

(1992) combined the groove of jazz with the immediacy of rap/hip-hop. The involvement of remixers Longsy D and Ig of Dodge City Productions gave the album an edge, while the cover of trumpeter Miles Davis' 'So What', accompanied by bassist Arnie Somejee and pianist Joe Bashorun, vindicated the dedication on the liner notes to **Wes Montgomery**. He went further on *The Quiet Revolution* (1993), covering Montgomery's 'Mr Walker', but the hip-hop element was intact, this time with rapper Guru on board.

STANLEY JORDAN

Born: July 31st 1959, Chicago, Illinois, US.

■ *Casio PG380; Travis Bean.*

Jordan plays the guitar as if it were a keyboard, with a two-handed tapping technique. While there is nothing intrinsically wrong with this approach, it has tended to obscure his musical inventiveness and expertise. A shame really, because some sections of his albums like the live *Stolen Moments* (1991) have great sensitivity. For instance Jordan's reworking of John Coltrane's 'Impressions' is power-driven by bassist Charnett Moffett and drummer Kenwood Dennard (who echo Jimmy Garrison and Elvin Jones), a richly textured tour de force with Jordan drawing from a wide palette of styles. However, the same album includes a version of Led Zeppelin's 'Stairway To Heaven' that wouldn't have been out of place on a dreadful MOR record, all of which gives credence to the notion that Jordan has yet to decide what he wants to play.

STEVE JORDAN

Born: Stephen Philip Jordan, January 15th 1919, New York, New York, US. Died: September 12th 1993.

The number of times that we have stressed in this book the necessity of the possession of swing could make the casual reader believe that this is all there is to playing the guitar.

That is not entirely true. Strong rhythm guitarists are few and far between: **Freddie Green** was one of the main men, and so was Jordan. Neither player would solo much, but their ability to underline a rhythm section solidly has often been misinterpreted as a simple job.

Jordan worked with some of the finest swing orchestras in the 1940s and 1950s, including those of Artie Shaw, Jimmy Dorsey, Gene Krupa, Stan Kenton and Benny Goodman. In 1959 he hung up his axe and took up needle and thread to become a tailor. By 1965 he was back in business in small groups such as Buck Clayton's All Stars and The Vic Dickenson Septet.

JOHN JORGENSON

Born: US.

■ *G&L ASAT; Rickenbacker 12-string; Gibson Les Paul Junior; Fender Telecaster.*

Formed by **Chris Hillman** in 1985, The Desert Rose Band featured a stellar lineup of country rockers including **Herb Pedersen** and pedal-steel man **Jay Dee Maness**. While Jorgenson was perhaps the least

well known at the outset, his stunning guitar and mandolin playing gave the band an impetus and cohesiveness lacking in most comparable outfits. While the members were all experienced session players, albums like *Desert Rose Band* (1987), *Running* (1988), *Pages Of Life* (1990) and *True Love* (1991) possess imagination as well as expertise. Jorgenson's outside work included playing for **Bonnie Raitt** on the deservedly successful *Nick Of Time* (1989), and shortly after he started a solo career in 1992 he became a member of the lively guitar trio The Hellecasters, alongside **Jerry Donahue** and Will Ray, whose *Return Of* (1993) was packed full of guitar delights.

RISE KAGONA

Born: Zimbabwe.

One of the most exciting Zimbabwean outfits to emerge, The Bhundu Boys' jit style of dance music has crossed over to become acceptable to European audiences as well as African. Scoffed at by critics for crossing over, *Shabini* (1985) was one of the most complete and accessible albums of the 1980s, with Kagona's percussive style creating a layered effect and their British tours giving the band an unprecedented following (for a so-called 'world music' band, at least). Despite the popularity of *Shabini* later albums have failed to win many fresh admirers. This doesn't alter the fact that *Absolute Jit* (1991) is quite as impressive as *Shabini*.

HENRY KAISER

Born: 1953, Oakland, California, US.

■ *Klein; Steinberger; Ransom Strat-style.*

On the cutting edge of the avant-garde, Kaiser's work with **Fred Frith**, drummer John French and **Richard Thompson** on *Live Love Larf and Loaf* (1987) is all technique. A more recent solo outing from Kaiser is *Hope You Like Our New Direction* (1991), a surprising mixture of influences from **Buddy Holly** to Captain Beefheart and The Grateful Dead.

DANNY KALB

Born: New York, New York, US.

Founder member of the influential Blues Project, Kalb had previously backed folk artists like Phil Ochs and Judy Collins. He guided the Project to become one of the earliest and most influential electric blues outfits. Their storming debut *Live At The Cafe Au Go-Go* (1966) was a melting pot of jazz, blues and country influences. Later albums such as *Projections* (1966) and the live *At Town Hall* (1967) consolidated the debut, but the lineup, which had included **Steve Katz** and **Al Kooper**, was in a state of flux. Kalb left the group, reforming it briefly in the early-1970s.

MICHAEL KAROLI

Born: April 29th 1948, Straubing, Germany.

Along with German bands Kraftwerk and Amon Duul, Can were one of the most successful creators of the fusion between rock and the classical avant-garde.

Karoli's treated and untreated guitars were subordinated to the more dominant keyboards of Irmin Schmidt, but he contributed undulating parts over the insistent rhythm section. *Monster Movie* (1969), *Tago Mago* (1971) and *Ege Bamyasi* (1972) were innovative and ground-breaking, but later offerings like *Saw Delight* (1977) seemed to mark time. Karoli later started a solo career, before contributing to *Rite Time* (1989) by a reformed Can.

SOUZY KASSEYA

Born: 1949, Shabunda, Zaire.

An inheritor of the traditions of soukous initiated by **Dr Nico** and **Franco**, Kasseya has been one of the most successful at adapting the style within a contemporary dance-floor setting. Ironically, he had to move to Paris to advance his career properly. It was there that he cut his first solo album *Le Retour De L'Als* (1984) which included the monster dance-floor hit 'Le Téléphone Sonne'. His follow-up *The Phenomenal Souzy Kasseya* (1985) provided another hit with 'La Vie Continue'. While concessions have been made to European audiences with a stylistic accessibility that was lacking in Franco's and Dr Nico's output, Kasseya is a giant of the genre.

TERRY KATH

Born: January 31st 1946, Chicago, Illinois, US.
Died: January 23rd 1978, Los Angeles, California, US.

■ *Gibson Les Paul; Fender Stratocaster.*

Kath was guitarist in the jazz-pop band Chicago who in the early-1970s had a rough, tough, funky feel on energetic songs like keyboardist Robert Lamm's '25 or 6 To 4' and the cover of **Steve Winwood**'s 'I'm A Man'. Unfortunately the group's output became anodyne. Kath's guitar work was fine when limited to brief cameo solos, but the group's horn section was more emblematic of their overall sound. He died in a shooting accident, cleaning a loaded gun.

STEVE KATZ

Born: May 9th 1945, New York, New York, US.

■ *Gibson ES335.*

Guitarists Katz and **Al Kooper** set up Blood Sweat & Tears in 1968 after playing together in the influential New York electric folk/blues band The Blues Project. While Blood Sweat & Tears' debut *The Child Is Father To The Man* (1968) was a vehicle for Kooper's songs, Katz's guitar playing on 'I Can't Quit Her' was fluid and lyrical, his solo on 'My Days Are Numbered' taut and bluesy.

After Kooper left, the band became formidably successful with *Blood Sweat & Tears* (1969) selling over two million copies. Unfortunately, and despite Katz, vocalist David Clayton-Thomas's crass compositions 'Spinning Wheel' and 'You Made Me So Very Happy' marginalized the creative side of the band. This was to remain a fundamental problem and by the time they recorded *Blood Sweat & Tears 3* (1970) they were purveying little more than cocktail jazz-pop. Katz left to form country-rock supergroup American Flyer with **Eric Kaz**, **Craig Fuller** and bassist Doug Yule, and now works as a producer.

JORMA KAUKONEN

**Born: December 23rd 1940,
Washington DC, US.**

■ **Gibson ES345; Gibson J50.**

Kaukonen was a folk-blues guitarist who managed to translate and adapt his style to rock with quite staggering results in Jefferson Airplane.

Vocalists Grace Slick and Paul Kantner indulged their socio-politico tendencies in the Airplane's lyrics. But it was Kaukonen's drawn-out, introspective solos, the dense, implacable rhythms of bassist Jack Casady and (initially) the fine drumming of Spencer Dryden that established the musical credentials of the band, and *Bless Its Pointed Little Head* (1969) represented the zenith of this triumvirate's achievement. Kaukonen, drawing his influences from a variety of sources, possessed an adroit dexterity on Fred Neil's 'The Other Side Of This Life' that fused with his raga-like lines while the rhythm section behind him rang the changes.

Although Kaukonen remained with the Airplane until 1974, the departure of vocalist Marty Balin (by far the group's most interesting composer) and drummer Dryden gave greater rein to the simplistic pomp-rock of Slick and Kantner, which resulted in Kaukonen and Casady establishing the spin-off group Hot Tuna with violinist Papa John Creach. Their objective was to play folk and blues material in a less contrived atmosphere. Much of the group's outpourings were patchy if immediate, as can be heard on *Hot Tuna* (1970), *First Pull Up, Then Pull Down* (1971) and *Burgers* (1972). In recent years Kaukonen has participated in various Airplane reunions – which to these ears was a serious error of judgment.

JOHN KAY

Born: Joachim F Krauledat, April 12th 1944, Tilsit, Germany.

■ **Rickenbacker 381; Rickenbacker 'signature'.**

At one point in 1968 Steppenwolf were viewed as a heavy rock band from the same school as Iron Butterfly, Blue Cheer and Vanilla Fudge. They weren't. Kay's macho posturing on 'Born To Be Wild' and Hoyt Axton's 'The Pusher' were as banal as they come. However, his bassy chord-riffing on the opening bars of 'Wild' were highly evocative, mainly as a result of the song's inclusion on the soundtrack of the film *Easy Rider*, causing it to be dubbed a biker's anthem. 'Magic Carpet Ride' had some redeeming features, but by the early-1970s the group had split and Kay had launched a solo career. Later he would periodically assemble a new lineup of the group and tour.

ERIC KAZ

Born: Eric Justin Kaz, 1947, New York, New York, US.

Songwriter and guitarist Kaz had spent many years on the New York folk club circuit before forming American Flyer in 1976 with **Craig Fuller**, **Steve**

Katz and bass player Doug Yule. Despite the appreciation of their albums *American Flyer* (1976) and *Spirit Of A Woman* (1977) by a discerning few, it was insufficient to stop the band from splintering. With Fuller, Kaz then recorded *Craig Fuller/Eric Kaz* (1978) but reverted to session work and songwriting – his 'Love Has No Pride' has been covered by **Bonnie Raitt**.

DAVE KELLY

Born: 1948, London, England.

A bastion of the British blues scene since the 1960s, Kelly's slide work has appeared on a daunting number of records. His sense of purism has occasionally militated against a healthy bank balance, with few of his records popular beyond the cognoscenti. But Kelly's frequent involvement with vocalist Paul Jones in The Blues Band has given him a longer shelflife than might have been anticipated 20 years ago. Regular visitors to the festival circuit in Europe, The Blues Band's repertoire has revolved around classics by **Muddy Waters**, bassist/composer Willie Dixon, **John Lee Hooker** and **Lightnin' Hopkins**, combined with a liberal dose of self-composed items, all performed with verve. They remain enthusiasts first and foremost, with *The Official Bootleg Album* (1980) illustrating their zeal.

JO ANN KELLY

Born: January 5th 1944, England. Died: October 20th 1990, England.

■ **Zemaitis.**

One of the first successful British female blues guitarists, Kelly, like her brother Dave (see previous entry) cut a swathe through the blues boom of the 1960s and early-1970s. Her slide guitar work probably caused **Bonnie Raitt** to put on her thinking cap, and her spare interpretations of classic blues by artists like **Lonnie Johnson**, **Mississippi John Hurt** and **Blind Lemon Jefferson** came close to touching the spirit of the originals. Kelly was little appreciated during her lifetime, and history, disgracefully, has not seen fit to reevaluate, with none of her records remaining in print at the time of writing.

BARNEY KESSEL

Born: October 17th 1923, Muskogee, Oklahoma, US.

■ **Gibson ES350; Gibson 'signature'.**

One of the most widely known jazz guitarists in the business, Kessel is noted for an especially fluent way with chords. He has played with jazz stars Ella Fitzgerald, Oscar Peterson and Artie Shaw, and on sessions for many other artists and film soundtracks.

Since the early-1950s he has recorded regularly in a solo capacity. Among the most important was the *Poll Winners* album (1956) as a trio with drummer Shelley Manne and bassist Ray Brown, which helped to define the sound of such a lineup. But the need to perform to order so regularly on sessions – he played on Beach Boys and Phil Spector dates as well as the more expected jazz takes – seems to have had a

debilitating effect on Kessel's muse, to the extent that his albums always contain a fair proportion of mood music and other stale fare.

Guitar Workshop (1967), a live recording from the Berlin Festival, has fine moments, while *Feeling Free* (1969), a quartet outing with vibraphonist Bobby Hutcherson, drummer Elvin Jones and bassist Chuck Domanico, is magical in places, the buoyant interplay between Hutcherson and Kessel reminiscent of the collaborations between vibesman Gary Burton and **Larry Coryell**. *Summertime In Montreux* (1973) demonstrated Kessel's versatility within any context, be it trio, quartet or quintet. He wrote an interesting guide to career development for aspiring players, *The Guitar*, in the late-1960s.

ALAN KING

Born: September 18th 1946, London, England.

A fine rhythm guitarist who has seldom achieved the recognition that is his due, 'Bam' King's first group was The Action where he played alongside lead guitarist Peter Watson, the band emerging at about the same time as The Who. Cutting a string of singles that encapsulated the essence of the mod era in the mid-1960s, 'I'll Keep Holding On', 'Never Ever' and 'Baby You Got It' would be crucial pointers for The Jam's **Paul Weller**. After the group disintegrated due to lack of interest, King joined Mighty Baby to play foil to the equally underrated **Martin Stone** (who had replaced Watson in The Action). After one eponymous album in 1969 for the Head label, Mighty Baby disintegrated and King formed Ace with vocalist Paul Carrack and **Phil Harris**. One great single 'How Long' from a good album *Five-A-Side* (1975)... then obscurity and the session circuit beckoned.

ALBERT KING

Born: Albert Nelson, April 25th 1923, Indianola, Mississippi, US. Died: December 21st 1992.

■ **Gibson Flying V; custom Flying V.**

King's guitar playing was always associated with the blues, even if his vocals and arrangements seemed to be influenced more by the R&B of Bobby Bland than by the blues of **BB King**.

After playing the club circuit in Chicago and St Louis throughout the early part of his career, left-hander King was signed by Stax and recorded the classic *Born Under A Bad Sign* (1967). Featuring Booker T & The MGs and produced by Stax owner Jim Stewart, it included sterling rhythm work by **Steve Cropper** and confirmed King's status as a fine, emotive vocalist and a stinging guitarist. Far funkier than BB, despite a strong competitive edge, Albert cut strings of albums for Stax backed by the Bar-Kays and the Memphis Horns, including *Live Wire/Blues Power* (1968), *King Does The King's Things* (1969, a tribute to Elvis Presley), *Lovejoy* (1971), *I'll Play The Blues For You* (1972) and *I Wanna Get Funky* (1974).

Throughout the 1970s and 1980s King was frequently accused by blues purists of being too pop oriented, but this cut little ice with festival and college audiences. This criticism lessened with *New*

Orleans Heat (1978), San Francisco '83 and I'm In A Phone Booth Baby (1986). His popularity in the US and Europe remained unchallenged and encouraged younger adherents like Larry McCray, **Robert Cray** and **Stevie Ray Vaughan** to take up the blues and follow in his size 13 footsteps.

BB KING

See also pages 137-139
Born: Riley King, September 16th 1925, near Itta Bena, Mississippi, US.

■ *Gibson ES355; Gibson 'signature'; Gibson ES335; Fender Telecaster.*

Of all the bluesmen to cross over into R&B and soul, few have managed to be as resilient and as impervious to passing fads as BB King. He developed and refined his taut, tense and vivid style that reshaped and reviewed perceptions of how the blues could be played on the electric guitar.

His big break came in 1948 when Sonny Boy Williamson gave him an opportunity to play on Williamson's show on radio station KWEM, resulting in club work and a slot on radio station WDIA where King acquired the nickname Blues Boy – hence 'BB'. After cutting singles for Bullet, King came to the attention of **Ike Turner** who recommended him to the Bihari Brothers, owners of the Modern label in Los Angeles, starting an association that lasted to 1962.

In 1962 he joined ABC, in 1965 releasing *Live At The Regal*. Live albums seldom get better than this, with scintillating performances of 'Every Day I Have The Blues', 'How Blue Can You Get' ('I bought you a ten dollar meal/You said thanks for the snack/I gave you seven children/And now you want to give them back') and 'It's My Own Fault'.

Championed by white musicians such as **John Mayall**, **Eric Clapton**, **Mike Bloomfield**, Paul Butterfield of the Butterfield Blues Band, Bob Hite of Canned Heat, and British R&B man **Alexis Korner**, King's reputation started to flourish among white audiences with the result that he began to record with artists such as **Leon Russell** and **Joe Walsh** on albums like *Indianola Mississippi Seeds* (1970).

While some may well contend that his later albums have been too rocky and less purist, this view fails to recognize that blues is 90 per cent form and 10 per cent content, and that with players of King's quality all who play with him are touched by his genius. Among the wide range of those who have played with him in recent years are R&B vocalist Bobby Bland and jazz-rock outfit The Crusaders, as well as megastars Stevie Wonder and U2. And he still can't sing and play at the same time.

EARL KING

Born: Earl Silas Johnson, February 7th 1934, New Orleans, Louisiana, US.

■ *Fender Stratocaster.*

Despite his eminence as a session guitarist and the consistently high standard of his material, King's guitar work has remained a well kept secret.

After a stint on the New Orleans club scene he was signed to Specialty by Johnny Vincent, where he recorded tracks like the self-composed 'Trick Bag' and 'Let The Good Times Roll'. In 1955 he was signed by Vincent to the newly established Ace label where he cut classics like 'Those Lonely Lonely Nights', 'It Must Have Been Love' and 'My Love Is Strong'. After parting company with Vincent in 1959, he was signed to Imperial by Fats Domino's producer Dave Bartholomew and made an immaculate version of the **Guitar Slim** composition 'The Things That I Used To Do'. In the 1960s King stopped recording under his own name to concentrate on writing and session work for artists like **Dr John**, R&B vocalist Lee Dorsey and New Orleans funksters The Meters. He returned to recording in 1986, backed by A Roomful Of Blues, and cut the excellent *Glazed* which was followed by *Sexual Telepathy* (1990) and *Earl King* (1992).

ED KING

Born: US.

While a member of The Strawberry Alarm Clock, King contributed the urgent psychedelic licks to their *Incense And Peppermints* (1967), one of the more memorable slices of flower-power pap.

The group disbanded in 1971 and King joined Lynyrd Skynyrd, forming a triple pronged guitar attack with **Gary Rossington** and **Allen Collins**. While King remained only for the group's first two albums, he was central in determining their sound, and rejoined for the Lynyrd Skynyrd reunion tour of 1987.

FREDDIE KING

Born: September 3rd 1934, Gilmer, Texas, US.
Died: December 18th 1976, Dallas, Texas, US.

■ *Gibson Les Paul; Gibson ES335; Gibson ES355.*

Following in a long line of Texan bluesmen, King's principal stylistic influence was **T-Bone Walker**, despite a move to Chicago in his adolescence where he fell under the spell of **Muddy Waters** and bassist/composer Willie Dixon, and his reputation is for fast, flamboyant guitar work.

Throughout the 1950s and early-1960s King recorded a handful of classic blues – 'The Stumble', 'Hideaway', **BB King**'s 'Have You Ever Loved A Woman' and 'Driving Sideways' – for the Federal label, and these were taken up and covered during the 1960s by British players such as **Stan Webb**, **Eric Clapton**, **Jimmy Page**, **Mick Taylor** and **Peter Green**. The lightning agility of his fingering gave the erroneous impression to many budding guitarists that for King speed was all.

In the late-1960s, after a lull in his career, he moved away from Federal and cut *Freddie King Is A Blues Master* (1969) with legendary hornman King Curtis producing.

During the 1970s, like Albert King Freddie moved more towards soul, cutting *Gettin' Ready* (1971) and *Texas Cannonball* (1972) for **Leon Russell**'s Shelter label and *Burglar* (1974) with British producer Mike Vernon. King's swansong was the vivacious *Larger Than Life* (1975).

JIMMY KING

Born: 1949, Memphis, Tennessee, US. Died: December 9th 1967, Madison, Wisconsin, US.

■ *Fender Telecaster.*

The Bar-Kays were the second-unit backing band at the Stax studios, with King, Ronnie Caldwell (organ), Ben Cauley (trumpet), Carl Cunningham (drums), James Alexander (bass) and Phalin Jones (sax), scoring on their own in 1967 with the instrumental 'Soul Finger'. Their success was short-lived: in December 1967 the plane in which they were flying with their current frontman Otis Redding crashed into Lake Monona in Wisconsin; the only survivor was Cauley, while lucky Alexander was not on board. The fact that the hopes for Stax's continued prosperity had revolved around Redding has often obscured the equally important fact that with the obliteration of King and the Bar-Kays a generation of Memphis musicians had perished.

MICKY KING

Born: England.

Briefly a member of Cliff Bennett's Rebel Rousers, King played on the group's first two singles, 'You Got What I Like' and 'That's What I Said' (both 1961) with producer Joe Meek twitching the controls. A contract to play in Hamburg followed, but King stayed at home, later joining an outfit called James Royal & The Hawks. Result: obscurity.

BEECHER PETE KIRBY

See BASHFUL BROTHER OSWALD

BILL KIRCHEN

Born: June 29th 1948, Ann Arbor, Michigan, US.

■ *Gibson SG; Fender Telecaster.*

A central figure in Commander Cody & His Lost Planet Airmen, Kirchen's ability to merge differing styles such as country, country-rock, R&B and western swing contributed to the band's eclecticism. After moving to the West Coast they cut albums like *Lost In The Ozone* (1971), *Hot Licks, Cold Steel And Truckers Favorites* (1972), *Country Casanova* (1973) and *Live From Deep In The Heart Of Texas* (1974). In 1976 Kirchen left for a solo career, rejoining Cody in 1980 as a member of The Moonlighters. Together they cut *Let's Rock* (1986) which included such epic tales as 'Truckstop At The End Of The World'. Kirchen's versatility is still well regarded on the club circuit.

DANNY KIRWAN

Born: May 13th 1950, London, England.

■ *Gibson Les Paul.*

Kirwan joined Fleetwood Mac in 1969 and his melodic phrases and rhythm work contrasted with **Peter Green**'s mercurial, diamond-hard licks on successful singles like 'Oh Well' and 'The Green Manalishi'. But after Green's departure Kirwan's

Kin-Kir

shoe-gazing stance was scant compensation, and after *Kiln House* (1970) Kirwan too was out of the group. Two or three indifferent solo albums for DJM followed, but the material was never of a very high standard.

SNEAKY PETE KLEINOW

Born: US.

■ **Fender (modified).**

Sneaky Pete has been one of the most recorded session musicians on pedal-steel guitar, playing for everyone from Jackson Browne and Sandy Denny to Stevie Wonder and The Bee Gees. But a good deal of his career seems to have been spent ministering to the tender needs of the various spin-off groups of The Byrds, most notably The Flying Burrito Brothers. Although he's been involved with virtually all incarnations of the Burritos, the most impressive remains the first album, *The Gilded Palace Of Sin* (1970). Of course Kleinow's playing was exemplary, but Gram Parsons' splendid vocals and impeccable choice of material were at the core of the album's charm, and later albums without Parsons certainly seem thinner. And Sneaky Pete, like all good craftsmen, needs good raw materials.

EARL KLUGH

Born: September 16th 1953, Detroit, Michigan, US.

■ **Gibson Chet Atkins.**

Influenced at first by **Chet Atkins**, Klugh has the potential to become a premier jazz guitarist, seemingly more suited to nylon-strung acoustic work. He joined up with flautist Yusef Lateef in 1969 before moving on to accompany **George Benson** on Benson's classic *White Rabbit* album (1971). In the early-1970s Klugh replaced **Bill Connors** in keyboardist Chick Corea's fusion band Return To Forever where he started to play the electric guitar, but his tenure was short-lived as he moved on to a solo career and back to nylon-strung acoustic. Klugh's solo work has been pleasant rather than challenging, and he does seem unreasonably drawn to the provision of background music. But *Crazy For You* (1979), *Two Of A Kind* (1982, with keyboardist Bob James) and *Collaboration* (1987, with George Benson again) are difficult to fault aesthetically.

STANLEY KNIGHT

Born: February 12th 1949, Little Rock, Arkansas, US.

■ **Gibson ES345; Gibson SG.**

Guitarist in Black Oak Arkansas, Knight like his fellow founder members **Harvey Jett** and **Ricky Reynolds** left the group in the mid-1970s after he realized that he was little more than a sideshow in vocalist Jim Dandy's backing group.

MARK KNOPFLER

Born: August 12th 1949, Glasgow, Scotland.

■ **Fender Stratocaster; Pensa-Suhr; Gibson Chet Atkins; Schecter; Fender Telecaster.**

Formed in the mid-1970s, Dire Straits have since become something of an institution, while Knopfler is one of the most influential guitarists to emerge since **Eric Clapton** – despite the fact that in Britain at least, knocking Knopfler has become almost as popular a pastime as criticizing the national cricket team or football manager.

Other guitarists are probably most envious of the apparent ease with which Knopfler plays so consistently and so seamlessly, on electric and acoustic, all based on a seemingly straightforward picking technique. Isolating individual examples of excellence from Knopfler is a thankless task because he is constantly trying new things – which of course those who knock him fail to hear – but some of his Dire Straits work is worth underlining: the meandering and effortlessly spiky Strat on 'Sultans Of Swing'; 'Tunnel Of Love' with its quietly masterful solos; a rare Les Paul for the beautifully controlled melodies of 'Brothers In Arms'; the metallic chop of a resonator guitar on 'Wild West End'; the sensitive nylon-strung work on 'Private Investigations'; 'Money For Nothing' with its untypically raucous Stones-like riff; or the elongated work-out on 'Telegraph Road'.

Some of Knopfler's most impressive work has been in the service of others, such as Steely Dan (*Gaucho* 1980) and Van Morrison (*Beautiful Vision* 1982), while he has developed a career parallel to Dire Straits as producer (Bob Dylan's *Infidels* 1983), soundtrack writer (*Local Hero* 1983) and songwriter for others ('Private Dancer' for Tina Turner, 1984). Extra-curricular projects include his fine duo record with **Chet Atkins**, *Neck And Neck* (1992), and his goodtime band with **Brendan Croker** and **Paul Franklin**, The Notting Hillbillies, who made an eponymous album in 1990, which was awash with resonator guitars.

KONIMO

Born: Daniel Amponsah, 1934, Fause, Asante, Ghana.

An important contributor to the highlife tradition (a fusion of indigenous dance rhythms and melodies with Western influences) Konimo's broad-based abilities as a guitarist manifested themselves during the early-1950s while he worked as a schoolmaster in the village school. Although he maintained a regular professional career teaching he played highlife and covers of pop songs before studying Spanish guitar. After winning a scholarship to England, Konimo returned to Ghana to cut an album of *Ashanti Ballads* (1968) which generated sufficient interest to qualify him as an expert on highlife, resulting in several broadcasts for the BBC. However, he peaked in the mid-1970s with *Odonson Nkao* which combined regional instruments such as the gyamadudu drum and talking drums with the Spanish guitar. The main problem facing Konimo is the circular argument that highlife tours outside Africa are prohibitively expensive, and so records don't get widely circulated.

AL KOOPER

Born: February 5th 1944, New York, New York, US.

Better known as a keyboardist, composer and bandleader, Kooper was a key figure on the East Coast

during the 1960s, setting up The Blues Project and Blood Sweat & Tears with **Steve Katz**, working with Bob Dylan on *Highway 61 Revisited* (1965) and *Blonde On Blonde* (1966), **Taj Mahal** on *The Natch'l Blues* (1968) and the Rolling Stones on *Let It Bleed* (1969). He also set up or produced the first recording sessions for Lynyrd Skynyrd, **Shuggie Otis** and The Tubes.

As a guitarist Kooper performed with **Mike Bloomfield** and **Stephen Stills** on *Super Session* (1968) which made every other musician think they could go into the studio, turn on the tape machine and play. Right? Wrong. *Super Session* was fine; *Jamming With Edward* by various members of the Stones et al, and all the other questionable out-takes that have been issued as desirable 'jams', were three-legged donkeys. Extraordinarily, after *Super Session* Kooper and Bloomfield cut *The Live Adventures Of Mike Bloomfield & Al Kooper* (1969). Impaired donkey? Yes.

Super Session was the result of three fine musicians who were either so inspired they felt they could jostle Zeus off Olympus, or so whacked out that Zeus felt sorry for them and gave them leeway. Whatever, 'Season Of The Witch' on *Super Session* contains some of the finest duelling since Errol Flynn hung up his épée and took sick leave. Kooper has also cut a number of patchy solo albums over the years, including *Possible Projection Of Future* (1972), *Act Like Nothing's Wrong* (1976) and *Championship Wrestling* (1982).

ALEXIS KORNER

Born: April 19th 1928, Paris, France. Died: January 1st 1984, London, England.

■ **Kay; Gibson.**

Like **Al Kooper** in New York, Korner enjoyed a sort of Mr Fixit role in England for much of the 1960s and 1970s. A far more avuncular figure than his later counterpart **John Mayall**, Korner was a genuine catalyst for the emergent British blues scene, with groups like The Rolling Stones, Manfred Mann, The Graham Bond Organization, Cream, Led Zeppelin and Free all being formed, more or less, in Korner's living room.

Although Korner's acoustic guitar work tended to lean more heavily in the direction of the country blues of **Lonnie Johnson** and **Big Bill Broonzy**, his most celebrated group Blues Incorporated (heard on *Alexis Korner's Blues Incorporated* 1964) drew from the repertoires of jazz bassist/composer Charlie Mingus and the soul-jazz saxman Cannonball Adderley, while his later group CCS were something of an MOR big-band. It is the bands that Korner encouraged which will remain as his prime musical legacy.

DANNY KORTCHMAR

Born: 1947, New York, New York, US.

■ **Fender Telecaster; Gibson Les Paul; Fender Stratocaster.**

After joining several groups in the 1960s, including briefly The Fugs, Kortchmar moved to California and eventually became part of singer/songwriter Carole

Kle-Kor

King's studio and stage band, contributing sterling six-string work to her classic *Tapestry* album (1972) and many of King's records since. For a time he seemed to be a first-call session guitarist for many producers, not least Peter Asher, and Kortchmar's classy rhythm playing has graced tracks from many superior records, including James Taylor's *Mud Slide Slim* (1971), Crosby & Nash's *Wind On The Water* (1975), Jackson Browne's *Running On Empty* (1977), and Don Henley's *Building The Perfect Beast* (1985) and *The End Of The Innocence* (1989).

PAUL KOSSOFF

Born: September 14th 1950, London, England.
Died: March 19th 1976, New York, New York, US.

■ **Gibson Les Paul; Fender Stratocaster.**

At the tail end of the 1960s Free were formed out of a bunch of **Alexis Korner**'s protégés: bassist Andy Fraser was in **John Mayall**'s Bluesbreakers, vocalist Paul Rodgers in Brown Sugar, and drummer Simon Kirke and guitarist Paul Kossoff in Black Cat Bones. Free stuck rigidly to a blues-based repertoire, and 'All Right Now' with Kossoff's wailing guitar has become a timeless classic, charting whenever it's reissued.

While the atmosphere within the band was apparently far from harmonious, each member was in his own way a virtuoso. There are still few better vocalists than Rodgers to this day and Kossoff, despite the brevity of his career, was one of the most spontaneously gifted guitarists of the era. What set him apart was his ability to use very few notes and place them well, relying on his Gibson Les Paul's rich tone and potential for sustain.

Although much of the group's studio output was uneven, *Free Live* (1971) encapsulated their freewheeling, instinctive feel. Later singles such as the lyrical 'My Brother Jake' and the anthemic 'Wishing Well' illustrated a commercial sense combined with an instrumental prowess (and on reflection it's a pity that Kossoff didn't listen harder to the sentiments of 'Wishing Well'). After the inevitable split, Kossoff formed Kossoff Kirke Tetsu & Rabbit and cut one uneven album. *Back Street Crawler* (1974) followed, but Kossoff had rather lost the plot and his playing lacked the charismatic intuition that had been his calling card.

LEO KOTTKE

Born: Athens, Georgia, US.

■ **Hoffman Series II; Taylor 555; Taylor 'signature' 12-string; Bozo 12-string.**

Kottke is a fine folk guitarist who came to prominence as a protégé of **John Fahey**, for whose label Kottke cut arguably his most influential album, *Six & Twelve String Guitar* (1970). Despite later contracts with Capitol and then Chrysalis, his records remained well kept secrets, with Kottke making few concessions to commercialism on his brilliant expositions of finger-picked steel-strung acoustic. Furthermore, this lack of commerciality manifested itself in an out-and-out eclecticism, such as a medley comprising 'Crow River Waltz', JS Bach's 'Jesu, Joy Of Man's Desiring' and 'Jack Fig'. In the early-1980s a

wrist problem caused a stylistic rethink, and Kottke pursued a more classical approach (*My Father's Face* 1989) and even played some electric on *That's What* (1990). Kottke remains a fine example of the guitarist's guitarist.

OUSMANE KOUYATE

Born: 1955, Bamako, Mali.

A highly respected guitarist in singer/composer Salif Keita's band and Les Ambassadeurs Internationaux, Kouyate's reputation spread like a bushfire. His stunning guitar work is featured to resounding effect on the latter's *Djougouya* and *Tounkan*, and he also worked with Guinea's Bembaya Jazz, cutting the immaculate *Kefimba* (1985).

WAYNE KRAMER

Born: April 30th 1948, Detroit, Michigan, US.

Kramer and **Fred Smith** provided the guitar-based thrust to the legendary MC5 in 1969. While the group were best known for their revolutionary zeal, their association with John Sinclair's White Panther Party meant that their debut album *Kick Out The Jams* suffered from a surfeit of sloganizing.

The superb follow-up *Back In The USA* (1970) featured such gems as 'Call Me An Animal', 'Teenage Lust' and 'Tutti Frutti'. This high energy speed-metal was played with finesse and zero charm, emphasizing Kramer's propensity for riffs that were so heavy they made Iron Butterfly sound like John Denver. Needless to say, it did not sell. Only when punk took a grip years later did its intrinsic beauty become popularly apparent, and today it is still a five-star classic. But Kramer, after spending time in jail, remains a seriously underrated player.

LENNY KRAVITZ

Born: May 26th 1964, New York, New York, US.

■ **Epiphone semi-acoustic; Gibson Les Paul; Gibson Flying V; Fender Stratocaster; Fender Telecaster.**

Influenced by **Jimi Hendrix** and proto-funkster Sly Stone, Kravitz has at the time of writing become the wunderkind of black American music, eschewing the putative advantages of high-tech studio technology and adopting a live feel to his albums. An enthusiastic guitarist and fine songwriter, Kravitz's albums like *Let Love Rule* (1989), *Mama Said* (1991) and *Are You Gonna Go My Way?* (1993) possess a zinging vitality, best heard on compositions like 'Justify My Love', 'It Ain't Over Til It's Over' and 'Are You Gonna Go My Way?'. While his fascination with 1970s rock is clearly retrogressive it has helped him develop a musical identity that is unlike many of his contemporaries.

CARL KRESS

Born: October 20th 1907, Newark, New Jersey, US.
Died: June 10th 1965, Reno, Nevada, US.

■ **Gibson L5.**

Kress came to prominence with The Paul Whiteman Orchestra in the late-1920s, and was a contemporary

of legendary trumpet player Bix Beiderbecke. By the 1930s Kress had graduated to occasional session work for New York radio stations, which led to a series of dates duetting with **Eddie Lang** and with **Dick McDonough**. Kress's chordal work with Lang was viewed by many as innovative, and it has proved enduring. While the lion's share of his work was for radio and TV, Kress's rhythmic soloing with cornet player Red Nichols, among others, proved durable in a volatile climate, and a later set of duets with **George Barnes** proved worthwhile. Sadly, evidence of Kress's skill on record is rare.

ROBBIE KRIEGER

Born: January 8th 1946, Los Angeles, California, US.

■ **Gibson SG; Gibson ES355.**

It was on The Doors' album *Waiting For The Sun* (1968) that Krieger came of age, leaping from Morrison's shadow and distinguishing himself over and above organist Ray Manzarek. On 'Spanish Caravan' Krieger's neat, evocative acoustic picking illustrated the breadth of his musical abilities, which were generally buried beneath Morrison's histrionics.

LA Woman (1970) featured another indication of his under-exploited potential on a version of John Lee Hooker's 'Crawlin King Snake'. Tensely atmospheric and displaying the extent of Morrison's charisma, it also demonstrated how much Krieger influenced the shape of the group's sound.

After Morrison's death and a couple of unimaginative albums, Krieger and Doors drummer John Densmore formed The Butts Band which cut one eponymous album for Blue Thumb in 1974 with vocalist Jess Roden and **Jeff Beck**'s one-time bassist Philip Chen. Released to an unwarranted tumult of apathy, it contained striking solos and general support work by Krieger.

ALEXANDRE LAGOYA

Born: June 21st 1929, Alexandria, Egypt.

■ **Bouchet; Friedrich; Hopf.**

Born to Italian and Greek parents, Lagoya made an early choice between boxing and guitar playing as potential careers, and has become one of the leading classical guitarists. In his teens he moved to Paris, France, shortly after studying with **Segovia**. In the early-1950s he married **Ida Presti**, and their innovative performances and recordings together established them throughout the world and defined the concept of the guitar duo (see Presti entry for more details). After the early death of Presti in 1967, Lagoya continued as a solo artist, although one of his more unusual and interesting collaborations since then was with Claude Bolling for Bolling's *Concerto For Classic Guitar And Jazz Piano*.

BIRELI LAGRENE

Born: September 4th 1966, Strasbourg, France.

■ **Yamaha 335-style; Ovation.**

There are those who demonstrate affinities with musical instruments from such a tender age that 'prodigy' is something of an understatement. By the

Kos-Lag

time Lagrene was seven he was playing **Django Reinhardt** material with the accomplished verve of one many times his age.

By the time Lagrene made his debut in 1980 with *Routes To Django* his flowing lines had become fully integrated into the context of a small combo. Lagrene's recorded recreations of Reinhardt's best-loved pieces, including 'Sweet Georgia Brown' and 'I Can't Give You Anything But Love', swing as well as Reinhardt's originals, but have a resounding character of their own.

Throughout the 1980s Lagrene cut one fine album after another, embracing fresh ideas as he went: the waltz-like 'Made In France' from *Acoustic Moments* (1991) had a South American feel, while *Standards* (1992), a collection that included 'Body & Soul' and Charlie Parker's 'Ornithology', was pure bebop.

His admirable lack of stylistic impedimenta had also been proved by *Foreign Affairs* (1988), a fusion outing illustrating Lagrene's ability to rock out with the best of them.

DENNY LAINE

Born: Brian Hines, October 29th 1944, Jersey, Channel Islands.

■ **Fender; Gibson; Gretsch; Ibanez double-neck.**

An efficient rather than outstanding fretmeister, Laine was in a string of groups from the mid-1960s onwards: Denny & The Diplomats (with later Move men **Roy Wood** and Bev Bevan), The Moody Blues (singing the epochal 'Go Now'), Balls (led by another Move man, **Trevor Burton**), and ex-Cream drummer Ginger Baker's Airforce. And in 1971 Laine landed in **Paul McCartney**'s Wings where he played rhythm guitar and keyboards, co-writing 'Mull Of Kintyre' (Laine sold his share of the song to McCartney when he was broke).

He left McCartney unceremoniously in the early 1980s and has since tended to languish in obscurity.

EDDIE LANG

Born: Salvatore Massaro, October 25th 1902, Philadelphia, Pennsylvania, US. Died: March 26th 1933, New York, New York, US.

■ **Gibson L5; Gibson L4; Martin D-42.**

Lang was the first guitarist to make an international reputation as a soloist, with his acute chord patterns and effective single-string picking technique, and he defined early jazz guitar playing.

While **Django Reinhardt** was rewriting the guitarists' manual in France with the Hot Club, Lang with violinist Joe Venuti was making similar inroads with orchestras like Paul Whiteman and the Dorsey Brothers, eventually in the 1930s becoming accompanist to crooner Bing Crosby.

Some of Lang's best work though can be heard under the pseudonym of Blind Willie Dunn duetting with **Lonnie Johnson**, the contrasting styles of both men turning these sessions into a tour de force. Useful 1980s compilations of these and other fine Lang recordings can be found on *A Handful Of Riffs* on Living Era and *Jazz Guitar Virtuoso* on Yazoo.

ROY LANHAM

Born: January 16th 1923, Corbin, Kentucky, US.

■ **Fender Stratocaster.**

After years as a radio session player, and having played on doo-wop group The Fleetwoods' number 1 US hit 'Mr Blue' and his own accomplished instrumental LP *The Most Exciting Guitar* (1959), Lanham joined The Sons Of The Pioneers in 1961 as replacement for **Karl Farr**. The Sons Of The Pioneers have for almost 60 years been the leading western singing group, drawing their repertoire from the traditional songs of the 'old west'. Formed by **Roy Rogers** in 1934 as The Pioneer Trio, they became The Sons Of The Pioneers when Rogers left to start his film career. Over the years the lineup has changed, with internal strife or death being the principal causes. By the time that Lanham joined, the group's style was so firmly established that his expertise as an all-round guitarist was academic.

ANDY LATIMER

Born: May 17th 1947, Guildford, Surrey, England.

Formerly songwriter Philip Goodhand-Tait's backing band, Camel formed in 1972 with Latimer and keyboardist Peter Bardens providing the inspirational impetus. Nominally progressive, Camel's musical adaptation of Paul Gallico's children's story *The Snow Goose* (1975) became their best known piece. They survived well into the 1980s by which time Latimer, whose style is melodic and expansive, was the only remaining original member.

LEADBELLY

Born: Huddie William Ledbetter, January 29th 1889, Mooringsport, Louisiana, US. Died: December 6th 1949, New York, New York, US.

■ **Stella 12-string.**

Although his life was an absolute disaster area, Leadbelly did more than any other country blues guitarist and composer to elevate the public perception of the blues during the 1940s.

Under the aegis of folk song archivist Alan Lomax, Leadbelly recorded songs for the Library Of Congress, accompanying himself on his trusty 12-string in a roistering, barrelhouse style more frequently associated with the piano. These included 'Alberta', 'The Boll Weevil', 'Cotton Fields', 'Midnight Special', 'Rock Island Line', 'Goodnight Irene', 'Pick A Bale Of Cotton' (a great version with The Golden Gate Quartet, which taught the importance of rhythm to later folk revivalist Pete Seeger), 'Good Mornin Blues' and 'Black Betty'. Those whom Leadbelly influenced included Seeger, **Woody Guthrie**, Bob Dylan, Sonny Terry & **Brownie McGhee**, **Alexis Korner**, **Lonnie Donegan** and **Josh White**.

BERNIE LEADON

Born: July 19th 1947, Minneapolis, Minnesota, US.

■ **Fender Telecaster.**

A relaxed country picker, Leadon's movements

before he became a member of The Eagles were complicated. After moving to the West Coast as an accomplished bluegrass guitarist, Leadon joined up with **Chris Hillman** in 1964, first in The Scottsville Squirrel Barkers and then in The Hillmen. When Hillman joined The Beefeaters, Leadon moved on to Hearts & Flowers, remaining with them until summer 1968 when he joined Dillard & Clark, which outfit split after two albums. Leadon then joined Linda Ronstadt's backing group, The Corvettes, lasting a few months before replacing keyboardist/bassist Chris Ethridge in The Flying Burrito Brothers in summer 1969.

His tenure with the Burritos was marred by personality clashes, and he left in 1971 and returned to the relatively harmonious atmosphere of Ronstadt's band.

Shortly after Leadon's return the band, minus Ronstadt, became The Eagles, and his deft acoustic picking guided the relaxed country-style band through their most successful years on tracks such as 'Lyin Eyes', 'Peaceful Easy Feeling' and 'Tequila Sunrise', until his departure in 1976 when he was replaced by **Joe Walsh**. Since then Leadon has worked principally as a session guitarist, with **David Bromberg**, country-pop vocalist Rita Coolidge, **Chris Hillman**, **Stephen Stills** and **Andy Fairweather-Low**, apart from a brief stint in 1977 when he fronted his own group with vocalist/guitarist Michael Georgiades.

PAUL LEARY

Born: Paul Leary Walthall, Austin, Texas, US.

■ **Gibson Les Paul; G&L ASAT.**

The boisterous Butthole Surfers have acquired a significant following through their alignment with the Los Angeles hardcore circuit, and Leary's thrashing trash guitar, as heard on *Locust Abortion* (1987) and *Hairway To Steven* (1988), has become a template for other hardcore outfits. Furthermore, his solo album *The History Of Dogs* (1991) showed that he has a life beyond the band.

ALBERT LEE

Born: December 21st 1943, Leominster, Herefordshire, England.

■ **Fender Telecaster; Music Man Silhouette; Music Man Axis; Music Man 'signature'.**

Since the early-1970s Lee has been widely regarded as the English equivalent of US session guitarists like **James Burton**.

Where Lee has triumphed over his US counterparts, however, has been in his ability to make excellent solo albums. His pithy, concise guitar style suits the country leaning of his most successful projects, both solo and with others.

In 1959 Lee joined the British R&B band Chris Farlowe & The Thunderbirds, remaining with them until 1967. Among his most significant contributions was a particularly rousing solo on 'Stormy Monday Blues', the **T-Bone Walker** song. After leaving that group Lee played sessions for vocalist Joe Cocker among others before taking to the club circuit with

Country Fever and recording with Black Claw. While the group never made any recordings, they were part of a growing body of English bands such as **Brinsley Schwartz** who were influenced as much by country as by R&B.

Lee's next venture was to team up with songwriter Tony Colton and bassist Chas Hodges (later in Chas & Dave) to form Poet & The One Man Band, cutting one album for Verve before changing their name to Heads Hands & Feet. Considerably more successful in the US, the group disbanded after cutting three albums, *Heads Hands & Feet* (1971), *Tracks* (1972) and *Old Soldiers Never Die* (1973), which did much to raise Lee's profile in the US. Settling there he joined **Sonny Curtis**'s Crickets, who had managed to revive their career with the growing popularity of all things Texan.

In 1976 Lee started a liaison with country vocalist Emmylou Harris as a member of her Hot Band, and this resulted in Lee cutting his first solo album *Hiding* (1979) produced by Harris's husband, Brian Ahern, and including 'Country Boy' which has become *the* piece for aspiring country pickers to learn. Such was his impact in the Hot Band that Lee became sought after for sessions in Nashville as well as in Los Angeles and Britain, and he contributed to albums by artists such as The Everly Brothers and **Eric Clapton**, with both of whom he also toured, as well as Jerry Lee Lewis, Jackson Browne and **Dave Edmunds**.

ALVIN LEE

Born: Graham Barnes, December 19th 1944, Nottingham, England.

■ *Gibson ES335; Heritage 'signature'.*

As a member of Ten Years After with bassist Leo Lyons, drummer Ric Lee and keyboardist Chick Churchill, Alvin Lee became one of the most revered axemen of the 1960s and achieved superstar status through his frantic 11-minute workout on 'I'm Going Home' at the Woodstock festival in 1969 (a song first aired on TYA's *Undead* the previous year).

Meretricious to a fault, Lee was both praised and criticized for the speed of his playing: those for were impressed at such fleet-fingered dexterity; those against said it was merely a blur of notes with no underlying spirit. Nonetheless, Lee attempted similar flights of fancy on *Cricklewood Green*'s 'Love Like A Man' and on *Watt* (both 1970) but quickly the novelty wore off (except in the US and Germany). Still reassembling for the odd tour – in 1978 as Ten Years Later – time would seem to have stood still for Lee for over 20 years.

ARTHUR LEE

Born: March 7th 1944, Memphis, Tennessee, US.

Lee was the mastermind of the influential 1960s art-rock band Love. Along with The Doors and Spirit, Love gave the Los Angeles music scene some sort of intellectual kudos. Their eponymous debut of 1966 featured curiously frenetic versions of Dino Valenti's 'Hey Joe' and Burt Bacharach's 'My Little Red Book', while the follow-up *Da Capo* (1967) contained 'Seven

And Seven Is' with Lee's Southern background speaking through his funky, bluesy guitar.

But it failed to prepare the ground for *Forever Changes* (1968), which combined elements of folk and blues with rock, Lee essaying a symphonic grandeur through use of (for the time) elaborate studio techniques. Much of it had a pastoral warmth, with arpeggiating acoustic guitars and swirling horn and string sections, as on 'Andmoreagain', 'Alone Again Or' and 'Old Man', with Lee assisted in the six-string department as before by guitarist John Echols.

Lee went on to cut records of varying quality, including *Out Here* (1969) where his self-indulgence was given full rein, and later efforts saw him wandering through the repertory of rock stylings with scant regard for coherence.

JOHN LEES

Born: January 13th 1947, Oldham, Lancashire, England.

■ *Fender Stratocaster.*

Irrespective of the fashionable status of art-rock, Barclay James Harvest stuck rigidly to their chosen musical path. Symphonic, opulent, improvisational and richly melodic, albums such as *Once Again* (1971), *Baby James Harvest* (1972), *Time Honoured Ghosts* (1975), *Gone To Earth* (1977) and *Victims Of Circumstance* (1984) illustrate the coherence of the band's musical vision. Lees was accomplished within the band's tightly orchestrated style, and his extended solos, such as on 'For No One' from *Everyone Is Everybody Else* (1974), showed his ability as an improviser. He cut a patchy solo album, *A Major Fancy*, in 1977.

ADRIAN LEGG

Born: May 16th 1948, London, England.

■ *Ovation/Adamas.*

A brilliant acoustic guitarist and composer, Legg has become a leading authority on all matters pertaining to the guitar, contributing articles and books as well as instructional videos. Bridging all genres and styles, albums such as *Technopicker* (1983), *Lost For Words* (1986), *Guitars And Other Cathedrals* (1990), *Guitar For Mortals* (1991), *Mrs Crowe's Blue Waltz* (1992) and *Wine Women & Waltz* (1993) are the last word in technical refinement and eloquence. Legg's unnerving blend of country string-bending techniques and folk melodies is absorbed into a highly individual and, at its best, emotive finger-picking style that saw his popularity swell in the US during the early-1990s in line with the contemporary trend for acoustic guitar playing.

GREG LEISZ

Born: US.

Leisz first cut a storm as the effective pedal-steel guitarist in k d lang's group The Reclines on her *Absolute Torch & Twang* (1989), and he also appeared on her excellent follow-up *Ingenue* (1992). Leisz's session work included takes for **Chuck Prophet** among others, playing on *Balinese Dancer* (1992) where his versatility as a mandolinist,

pedal-steel and acoustic guitarist complemented Prophet's more rock'n'roll outlook.

JOHN LENNON

Born: John Winston Lennon, October 9th 1940, Liverpool, England. Died: December 8th 1980, New York, New York, US.

■ *Rickenbacker 325; Epiphone Casino; Gibson J160E.*

Unlike his band counterparts, Lennon was always into rock'n'roll, and often displayed the spirit of a **Scotty Moore** or a Gene Vincent trapped in the wrong space in time. While **George Harrison** was the studious sponge and **Paul McCartney** the magpie, Lennon had an experimental, freewheeling sense and was always apparently open to trying something a new way – whether it was likely to work or not.

While Lennon is usually classified as 'the rhythm guitarist' in The Beatles, he was no mean lead player. Furthermore, his arrangements were stark and barren, and yet when taken alongside McCartney's constant desire to be tasteful and accepted as a proper musician, it was actually Lennon who was the more tasteful – as demonstrated on The Beatles' cover of Smokey Robinson's 'You Really Got A Hold On Me', as well as on 'Not a Second Time', 'Norwegian Wood', 'And Your Bird Can Sing' and 'I'm Only Sleeping'. Even the experimental side of Lennon on 'Lucy In The Sky With Diamonds', 'Tomorrow Never Knows', 'Strawberry Fields Forever' and 'Revolution' illustrated his interest in dabbling with studio technology rather than unduly complex arrangements. When Lennon's solo career got under way, lyricism and the ethos of rock'n'roll were the motivating factors, as on Ben E King's 'Stand By Me', 'Instant Karma', 'Imagine', 'Woman' and 'Watching The Wheels'. If being a musician means instinctively knowing how a song should sound and where it all fits together, then Lennon most certainly was. You should of course own at least *Revolver* (1966) and the *Shaved Fish* collection (1975).

J B LENOIR

Born: March 5th 1929, Monticello, Mississippi, US. Died: April 29th 1967, Champaign, Illinois, US.

Lenoir's death in a car crash cut short a brilliant career as a boogie oriented guitarist and notable songwriter. What separated him from other bluesmen was his capacity to focus upon contemporary issues and relate them to his own circumstances: 'The Mojo Boogie', 'Eisenhower Blues', 'Mama Talk To Your Daughter', 'We Can't Go On This Way', 'Laid Off Blues', 'Alabama Blues', 'Born Dead' and 'Down In Mississippi'. *Alabama Blues* (1965) and *Natural Man* (1968) are two excellent introductions to his work.

KEITH LEVENE

Born: England.

Formerly a member of The Clash, Levene teamed up with ex-Sex Pistols vocalist John Lydon in Public Image Limited (PIL) in 1978. While Lydon's hectoring

Lee-Lev

vocals generated the initial interest, it was Levene's dense rhythms which proved more intriguing, with *Public Image* (1978) and *Metal Box* (1979) two of the most uncompromising albums of the late-1970s. After cutting *Flowers Of Romance* (1981) Levene and Lydon separated.

FURRY LEWIS

Born: Walter Lewis, March 6th 1893, Greenwood, Mississippi, US. Died: September 14th 1981, Memphis, Tennessee, US.

■ Martin.

When **Joni Mitchell** penned 'Furry Sings The Blues', it smacked of sentiment and only later – probably after Furry's death – did it ring true. For Lewis was probably an anachronism before the outbreak of World War II. Like **Big Bill Broonzy** and **Leadbelly**, Lewis had no truck with new-fangled devices such as electric guitars.

After his rediscovery in 1963, Lewis' repertoire comprised of rags, ballads, work songs and minstrel tunes ('Casey Jones', 'John Henry', 'Jim Jackson's Kansas City Blues') combined with a bottleneck and finger-picking style, and offered a view of the way in which blues had been performed in the early part of the century when Lewis had been a protégé of 'father of the blues' W C Handy. Only **Mississippi John Hurt** retained a comparable authenticity, and he like Lewis spent many years in the wilderness. Throughout Lewis' years of obscurity (to all except the inhabitants of Memphis) he worked as a street sweeper, which he continued to do right up to his death, playing only occasionally at local bars.

PETER LEWIS

Born: July 15th 1945, Los Angeles, California, US.

In the rush to sign psychedelic groups in the 1960s Moby Grape were one of the first to strike gold with a recording contract with Columbia. The group included three guitarists, lead player **Jerry Miller**, rhythm man **Skip Spence** and finger-picker Lewis, and echoed the close harmony vocals and melodic guitar work of The Byrds. Their debut *Moby Grape* (1967), despite a curious marketing strategy that involved issuing five singles simultaneously, was one of the strongest of the year with Lewis's picking on 'Omaha' and 'Failed On You' quietly impressive.

Their follow-up *Wow* (1968) included in the US a bonus album *Grape Jam* with **Mike Bloomfield** and **Al Kooper**. After these two fine starts they became increasingly erratic, with *Grape 69* and *Truly Fine Citizen* (1970) lacking the input of Spence who had departed for a solo career. From the 1970s to the 1990s they have reformed periodically, but nothing to date has managed to capture the sprightly charm of their early years.

ALEX LIFESON

Born: August 27th 1953, Surnie, British Columbia, Canada.

■ PRS; Gibson ES335; Signature.

One of Canada's most successful exports, Rush have built up an enviable reputation over the last 20 years for their consistency. Despite their individual anonymity, guitarist Lifeson makes no bones about drawing most of his inspiration from the **Jimi Hendrix** and **Eric Clapton** manuals of heavy-rock clichés (as on 'Fly By Night' and 'Spirit Of The Radio'), and this has given the group something of a trademark.

In addition, Rush have moved beyond the traditional sword-and-sorcery lyrical imagery so beloved of heavy metal bands to a more unusual socially-aware content, as on 'Distant Early Warning' and 'The Big Money'.

While Rush lack the flamboyance of many bands of the genre, Lifeson's general efficiency and the emphatic rhythm section of bassist Geddy Lee and drummer Neil Peart seem set to allow the band to continue for as long as they see fit.

LIGHTNIN' SLIM

Born: Otis Hicks, March 13th 1913, St Louis, Missouri, US. Died: July 27th 1974, Detroit, Michigan, US.

Best known for his collaborations with harmonica player Slim Harpo for the Excello label in the mid-1950s, Slim's visceral and gritty guitar work embodied the sweaty night club atmosphere occasionally hinted at by the best R&B but seldom captured on record. Recordings such as 'Rooster Blues', a fine, spunky version of Guitar Slim's 'The Things That I Used To Do' and a rollicking 'My Babe' all testify to his heroic status.

LI'L ED

Born: Edward Williams, Chicago, Illinois, US.

■ Gibson 335S; Robin; Epiphone.

Taught the slide guitar by his uncle **J B Hutto**, Li'l Ed formed the Blues Imperials in 1975. Stalwarts of the Chicago club circuit, they produced a raunchy, unfussy blend of rock and R&B on *Roughhousin'* (1987) and *What You See Is What You Get* (1993), each title an accurate description of the group's live act.

DAVID LINDLEY

Born: 1944, Marino, California, US.

■ Teisco; Danelectro; you name it.

Singer-songwriter Jackson Browne's introspective lyrics and liquid arrangements were underlined by session musician David Lindley's fine guitar playing in the 1970s. Lindley had spent his early career with the psychedelic Kaleidoscope on LPs like *Side Trips* (1967) and *Beacon From Mars* (1968) where his playing was lyrical and educated: only **Sandy Bull** and **John Fahey** had comparable expertise (**Jerry Garcia** was still developing).

In the early-1970s Lindley joined Jackson Browne's band for 1973's *For Everyman*: the title track exhibited a world-weary tenderness, with Lindley's guitar work suitably supportive and drummer Russ Kunkel providing a taut counterbalance. As the song neared its end, Lindley's guitar solo, organic and perfectly modulated, revived images of the good guy (in the white hat) riding off into the sunset. Ever since, Lindley has knocked out solos of comparable majesty, often in tandem with **Ry Cooder**, but that one piece of work will take some beating.

NIALL LINEHAM

Born: September 19th 1972, Cork, Ireland.

The Frank & Walters emerged in 1990, immediately dubbed saviours of the indie circuit with their intelligent blend of simple, tuneful songs and bright, chiming guitars. Their debut *Trains Boats And Planes* (1990) did nothing to undermine that confidence, with Lineham suggesting that he had more than just a couple of nice licks up his sleeve.

MANCE LIPSCOMB

Born: April 9th 1895, Navasota, Texas, US. Died: January 30th 1976, Navasota, Texas, US.

■ Gibson J200.

Like **Furry Lewis** and **Mississippi John Hurt**, Lipscomb upheld the traditional values of the songster. While the blues were an intrinsic part of that tradition for Lipscomb, his songs tended to reflect the immediate concerns of the community in which he lived, and to some extent the journalistic, thumbnail sketch in which he specialized was more reminiscent of fellow Texan **Lightnin' Hopkins**.

But there the similarity ended as Lipscomb used a variety of styles – ballads, spirituals, rags and children's songs, as well as the blues. Also, he worked as a tenant farmer for most of his life, singing purely for the benefit of family and friends. He cut his first records in the early-1960s for Chris Strachwitz's Arhoolie label and continued to do so regularly right up to his death. These albums chronicled his life and times with acuity and aplomb, making them slices of autobiography rather than mere musical statements.

LITTLE BEAVER

See WILLIE HALE

LITTLE MILTON

Born: Milton Campbell, September 7th 1934, Inverness, Mississippi, US.

Milton's reputation has been built upon his ability to transcend fashion with an almost effortless ease, and his at times scorching guitar playing. While he has never been of the mainstream, he has performed and recorded as an experienced craftsman throughout his 35-year career. Raised on gospel at his local church, he worked with **Ike Turner**, and this led to a contract with Sun in 1953.

While the Sun sessions failed to deliver many hits, they did Milton's reputation no harm and, after meeting bandleader Oliver Sain and recording 'Lonely Man', he was signed by Leonard Chess to the Checker label. With Checker he cut a string of raunchy, down-home blues – 'If Walls Could Talk', 'Blind Man', 'We're Gonna Make It', 'Who's Cheating

Who' and 'Grits Ain't Groceries' – before signing to Stax and then Henry Stone's Glades.

While at Glades, soul influences began to predominate with titles like 'Friend Of Mine' and 'Loving You' pointing the way for his later tenure with Malaco. Since joining Malaco, Milton has settled into a comfortable groove, producing superior blues-oriented albums like *Annie Mae's Cafe* (1986).

JACK LLEWELYN

Born: Britain.

During World War II violinist Stéphane Grappelli was based in London. At the end of hostilities, he and **Django Reinhardt** reformed their quintet with guitarists Alan Hodgkiss and Jack Llewelyn, along with bassist Coleridge Goode, as the short-lived Hot Club Of London.

RICHARD LLOYD

Born: New Jersey, US.

■ *Fender Stratocaster.*

Foil for the highly regarded **Tom Verlaine** in the seminal new wave band Television, Lloyd's post-TV career has been patchy. He cut a brace of solo records – *Alchemy* (1979) and *Field Of Fire* (1985) – that were light, twangy and effervescent, reminiscent of 1960s beatsmiths like The Hollies. In 1992 Verlaine and Lloyd reformed Television for a series of international dates.

ROBERT LOCKWOOD

Born: March 27th 1915, Marvell, Arkansas, US.

■ *Stella; Gibson ES335.*

Lockwood was for many years vocalist Sonny Boy Williamson's guitarist. After Williamson's death Lockwood took to the club circuit and started a famous alliance with **Johnny Shines** that resulted in a couple of albums, *Hangin' On* (1980) and *Mister Blues Is Back To Stay* (1981). The combination of Shines's explosive and emotive vocals with Lockwood's sinewy, punchy lines harked back to early traditions of the Delta bluesmen.

NILS LOFGREN

Born: June 21st 1951, Chicago, Illinois, US.

■ *Fender Stratocaster.*

Lofgren's distinctive guitar and piano work has graced albums by **Bruce Springsteen** and **Neil Young**, among others, while he has fronted his own solo projects and bands. He contributed sparkling guitar to his first group, Grin, whose finest album was *One Plus One* (1972).

On his debut solo, *Nils Lofgren* (1975), the incisive and abrasive guitaring, influenced by **Roy Buchanan** among others, on rockers like 'Back It Up' and 'Keith Don't Go (Ode To The Glimmer Twins)' cast Lofgren in the role of the thoughtful axe hero, while his piano on Goffin & King's 'Goin Back' gave the song a haunting nostalgia. This was followed by *Back It Up* (1976), a live recording of a radio broadcast on Californian station KSAN. Fiery and

gritty in equal parts, it demonstrated his ability to flip from one style to another. Later albums have failed to match the consistency of these opening efforts, but his appearances with Springsteen and Young – especially as part of the latter's Crazy Horse band, notably on their own *Crazy Horse* (1971) – have shown him to be a fine sideman with hidden depths.

MUNDELL LOWE

Born: April 21st 1922, Laurel, Mississippi, US.

■ *Gibson custom; Stromberg.*

Lowe was a versatile musician whose career started in New Orleans in the early-1930s in the bars of Bourbon Street, followed by a stint in western swing bandleader Pee Wee King's outfit in Nashville. Later, spells with jazzmen Charlie Ventura, Red Norvo and Benny Goodman resulted in the formation of Lowe's own quartet with bassist Trigger Alpert, saxophonist Al Klink and drummer Ed Shaughnessy. In the early-1960s, he cut a version of the Gershwin opera *Porgy & Bess* which showed that his skills as an arranger exceeded those as an individual soloist. Moving to the West Coast, Lowe started to compose and arrange for film and TV studios.

NICK LUCAS

Born: Dominic Nicholas Anthony Lucanese, August 22nd 1897, Newark, New Jersey, US. Died: July 28th 1982, Colorado Springs, Colorado, US.

■ *Gibson L1.*

Lucas was probably the first American to become a star as a result of making guitar-and-vocal records. In the 1920s crooner Lucas recorded big hits like 'Tiptoe Through The Tulips' and 'I'm Looking Over A Four-leafed Clover', as well as the guitar oriented pieces 'Pickin The Guitar' and 'Teasin The Frets'. He eventually sold over 80 million records, and such fame helped popularize the flat-top acoustic guitar at a time when the banjo and Hawaiian instruments were more in evidence in the US. The Gibson guitar company recognized his influence and in 1928 issued a Lucas model, the first 'signature' guitar.

STEVE LUKATHER

Born: October 21st 1957, Los Angeles, California, US.

■ *Music Man 'signature'; Ibanez 'signature'.*

Although much of Lukather's reputation revolves around membership of Toto, his biggest contribution has been as a session musician. **Boz Scaggs**'s *Silk Degrees* (1976) and *Down Two Then Left* (1977) contain some of the leanest, lithest lines heard outside a Steely Dan record. While Lukather's other clients have included Joe Cocker, Neil Diamond, Barbra Streisand, **Paul McCartney**, Elton John and Aretha Franklin, the Scaggs sides give a clear idea of what 'white soul' is and what it sounds like. These have depth and feeling; his work in Toto doesn't.

TIM LYNCH

Born: July 18th 1946, San Francisco, California, US.

A superlative garage band, The Flamin' Groovies were

never looked upon with much respect in the US as they were perceived as just another rock'n'roll revival band. However, the storming guitar work of **Cyril Jordan** and Lynch on *Supersnazz* (1969) effectively encapsulated the traditions of rock'n'roll. Later albums such as *Flamingo* (1970) and *Teenage Head* (1971) were more contemporary, echoing outfits like the MC5. Lynch left the group in 1972 after being arrested for draft evasion.

JEFF LYNNE

Born: December 30th 1947, Birmingham, England.

■ *Gibson Les Paul.*

Some years back David Bowie likened himself to a chameleon; a few years later to a sponge. Whenever he went into the studio, he wrung out the sponge. Jeff Lynne has never made public pronouncements about his muse, letting his audience draw their own conclusions. In the end, it is Bowie who reveals too much of how little there is. Lynne has contented himself with paying his obsequies in private. Imitator, certainly; fan, undoubtedly; and plagiarist? None of our business.

The important thing about Lynne is that, like **Tom Petty** and **Dave Edmunds**, he's a fan, and fans do odd things on occasions (they write books, for example). With **John Lennon** and **Paul McCartney** as his role models, Lynne vaulted through the repertoire of contemporary pop with little regard for anything other than replicating congruent chord sequences and felicitous harmonies.

In the process sacrifices were inevitable. Instrumentation was often the first to go, with synthesizers interpreting atmosphere or feeling. The Electric Light Orchestra, in its later guise without the experimental edge of **Roy Wood**, sold squillions of records (particularly *A New World Record* 1976) but was vulgar and derivative. Today Lynne has come to be acknowledged as a man in charge of the vocabulary of the studio, and The Traveling Wilburys' album (with Petty, **George Harrison**, **Roy Orbison** and Bob Dylan) worked because of these attributes. With all these things going for him, it doesn't much matter that Lynne is rather a rudimentary if effective guitarist.

BAABA MAAL

Born: November 12th 1960, Fouata, Senegal.

If Youssou N'Dour has any competition for the crown of Senegalese music it is from Maal. He has made a point of studying foreign music and in so doing has established a pan-cultural hybrid still rooted firmly in the traditions of Senegal but outward looking in its execution. A fine songwriter and guitarist, Maal's records *Nouvelle Generation* (1988), *Taara* (1990) and *Lam Toro* (1991) are good examples.

LONNIE MACK

Born: Lonnie McIntosh, 1941, Harrison, Indiana, US.

■ *Gibson Flying V.*

A rockabilly guitarist with a profound sense of pride in his own work, Mack has become best known for his

Lie-Mac

covers of the Chuck Berry evergreen 'Memphis', and 'Wham!'. Apart from that he cut albums like *The Wham Of That Memphis Man* (1963, reissued as *For Collectors Only* 1970), *Glad I'm In The Band* (1969), *The Hills Of Indiana* (1972) with Don Nix, and *Strike Like Lightning* (1985) with **Stevie Ray Vaughan**. Each is a classic, with Mack sounding like a cross between **Link Wray** and Robert Gordon.

DEREK MACKENZIE

Born: August 30th 1961, Aberdeen, Scotland.

As a member of The Shamen, Mackenzie contributed the surging, psychedelic guitars to the band's debut *Drop* (1987), but Mackenzie left as the group leaned more towards dancefloor electronics.

MAGIC SAM

Born: Samuel Maghett, February 14th 1937, Grenada, Mississippi, US. Died: December 1st 1969, Chicago, Illinois, US.

In common with the other premature fatality **Guitar Slim**, Magic Sam influenced a large number of Chicago-based guitarists through his willingness to adopt the abrasive electric blues of **Buddy Guy** and **Otis Rush**. His early singles for the Cobra label, 'All Your Love' and 'Easy Baby', bubbled with energy and enthusiasm and it was therefore surprising when he slipped out of the picture for some years. Signing with Delmark in 1968, he recorded the excellent *West Side Soul* (1968) and *Black Magic* (1969); both bore vital, accomplished vocal and guitar work, with Sam having assumed the dignity and confidence of an elder statesman. In 1969, he performed at the Ann Arbor Blues festival and blew many more celebrated performers off the stage. It didn't last, though, and by the end of that year he was dead.

TONY MAIDEN

Born: US.

Rufus were the premier funk band of the early-1970s, their main distinguishing feature being vocalist Chaka Khan, behind whom lurked Maiden and his choppy funk chords. Formed from the remnants of The American Breed who had a hit in 1968 with 'Bend Me Shape Me', their debut *Rufus* (1973) generated considerable interest, prompting Stevie Wonder to contribute 'Tell Me Something Good' to the follow-up, *Rags To Rufus* (1974), which also included 'You Got The Love'. This was followed by *Rufusized* (1975) and *Rufus Featuring Chaka Khan* (1976) which marked the emergence of Khan as the star of the group. *Ask Rufus* (1977) became their biggest selling album but also spelled their doom as Khan left for a solo career. The band couldn't survive and split up, although a reunion album *Live – Stompin' At the Savoy* was made in 1983.

YNGWIE MALMSTEEN

Born: June 30th 1963, Stockholm, Sweden.

■ *Fender Stratocaster; Fender 'signature'.*

Inspired to play the guitar by **Jimi Hendrix** whom he saw on TV in Sweden, Malmsteen has since taken the metal fraternity by storm. His career didn't kick-start into action until 1983 when he was invited to lay down some sides for the Shrapnel label in Los Angeles.

A deal with Polydor followed where he cut *Marching Out* (1985), a landmark record for all budding metalworkers as it proved the old adage that speed kills the creative impulses – underlined by the fact that Malmsteen's reference points have expanded to incorporate classical composers such as Bach, Paganini and Beethoven. We must hope that this will not prompt a rush of dreary classically-inspired records as happened in the early-1970s. Malmsteen's *Eclipse* (1990) abrogates technique for its own sake, which is very commendable.

HARVEY MANDEL

Born: March 11th 1945, Detroit, Chicago, US.

■ *Gibson Les Paul.*

For a time in the 1970s Mandel was widely touted as being a realistic successor to **Mick Taylor** in The Rolling Stones.

The reason for this was *Cristo Redentor* (1968), a bluesy instrumental album using Nashville sessionmen like **Pete Drake** and keyboardsman 'Pig' Robbins as well as blues harpist Charlie Musselwhite and organist Graham Bond. Cerebral but gutsy, it made few concessions to navel-searching and showcased Mandel's ability to construct lengthy solos with large chunks of feedback thrown in for good measure. Sales of this and Mandel's later solo albums were pitifully low, but its reputation enabled him to pick some plum jobs. He replaced **Henry Vestine** in Canned Heat for a year (1970) and then worked with British blues bandleader **John Mayall**. After Mayall, Mandel formed his own band Pure Food & Drug Act, and played sessions for blues vocalist Jimmy Witherspoon, Graham Bond, **Arthur Lee** and jazz bassist Ron Carter, among others.

JAY DEE MANESS

Born: US.

■ *Emmons.*

In 1985 **Chris Hillman** assembled The Desert Rose Band to open for singer-songwriter Dan Fogelberg on an upcoming tour. At first it comprised Hillman (guitar, mandolin and vocals), **Herb Pedersen**, **John Jorgenson** and Bill Bryson (bass), but such was the success of the group's slot on the tour that they turned into a full-time operation, with steel guitarist Maness (who had played with country singer Dwight Yoakam) and drummer Steve Duncan being brought in to bolster the sound. While they project themselves as being thoroughly modern in their approach, their records – such as 'Love Reunited', 'He's Black And I'm Blue' and 'She Don't Love Nobody' – pay more than lip-service to country music's rich heritage. Alongside the Rose Band, Maness continued to play sessions (including many of The Carpenters' records), and in 1991 he left to concentrate on studio work.

SID MANKER

Born: US.

With saxophonist and arranger Bill Justis, Manker co-wrote 'Raunchy' (1957), a twangy, bass-heavy guitar instrumental that proved the catalyst for **Duane Eddy**'s career. While Justis became the musical director for the Sun label, Manker played on sessions but never came up with such a good ruse again.

CLINT MANSELL

Born: Britain.

The controversial and eclectic Pop Will Eat Itself were formed in 1986 by Mansell. Initially they combined elements of contemporary pop through electronic samples, but this gradually gave way to a more conventional format with 'There Is No Love Between Us Any More', 'Def Con One', 'Wise Up Sucker', 'Can U Dig It', 'Touched By The Hand Of Ciccolina' and '92 Degrees', and their recruitment of a drummer indicated a desire to move away from the early-1990s ubiquity of mechanized music.

PHIL MANZANERA

Born: Philip Targett-Adams, January 31st 1951, London, England.

■ *Gibson Firebird VII; Fender Stratocaster; Gibson Les Paul.*

One of the best and most original guitarists to emerge in the 1970s, Manzanera's contributions to the success of Roxy Music were as distinctive as vocalist Bryan Ferry's.

Manzanera's rapier-like chords gave the material character and distinctiveness, forging a musical identity for the band that Ferry's mannered vocals could never hope to achieve.

Manzanera had an ability to plunder the past, as on the **Duane Eddy**-like twang of 'Remake/Remodel', combining with Andy Mackay's horn work and Bryan Ferry's avant-garde doodlings on the piano to create an arresting aural montage. While he can never be regarded as a purist, or as a cerebral guitarist in the way that **Robert Fripp** strives to be, Manzanera on *For Your Pleasure* and *Stranded* (1973) used effects like fuzz, distortion, feedback and reverb to enhance the mood rather than as ends in themselves.

This experimental aspect to his playing informed much of his solo work with The Explorers, 801 and Quiet Sun, but the absence of any memorable material militated against the durability of these projects. In 1992 Manzanera was instrumental in organizing the successful *Guitar Legends* events at Expo 92 in Seville, Spain.

JOE MAPHIS

Born: Otis W Maphis, May 12th 1921, Suffolk, Virginia, US. Died: June 27th 1986, Los Angeles, California, US.

■ *Mosrite custom double-neck; Gibson Super 400 (+ pickup).*

Maphis was one of the most influential figures in the

Mac–Map

development of the 'Bakersfield Sound', which spawned artists like country singers Merle Haggard and Buck Owens. Influenced initially by **Merle Travis**, Maphis' finger-picking technique allowed him to play runs on his guitar that had been written for the fiddle; applied to the electric guitar these became the key elements of the Bakersfield sound.

As a session musician Maphis appeared on early Rick Nelson records like 'Be Bop Baby' and 'Waiting In School', and his trademark picking technique was emulated by **James Burton** who succeeded him in Nelson's band. Maphis also contributed to Wanda Jackson's rock'n'roll records, such as 'Let's Have A Party' and 'Fujiyama Mama'. His best known solo work included the album *Joe & Rose Lee Maphis* (1961) and the composition 'Dim Lights, Thick Smoke (And Loud, Loud Music)'.

FRANK MARINO

Born: August 22nd 1954, Del Rio, Texas, US.

■ *Gibson SG Standard.*

Mahogany Rush were formed by Marino in Montreal, Canada in 1970 and were thoroughly derivative – although Marino's assertion that he was influenced by **Jimi Hendrix** who visited him while he was in a coma adds a piquancy to the overall crassness. Better live than in the studio, the group represents a type of heavy metal outfit that has currency for a spell, only to be replaced by another group of almost identical abilities with a slightly different gimmick. *What's Next* (1980) is a fair evaluation of their output.

JON MARK

Born: 1943.

■ *Gibson J45; Esteso.*

Formerly a member of **John Mayall**'s band, appearing on the jazzy *Turning Point* (1969) and *Empty Rooms* (1970), Mark later teamed up with English hornman Johnny Almond for *Mark-Almond* (1971).

Lush but delicate, Mark's acoustic guitar work complemented Almond's full-bodied soloing. Later collaborations failed to match the mellow debut and Mark reverted to session work.

BOB MARLEY

Born: Nesta Robert Marley, February 6th 1945, St Anns, Jamaica. Died: May 11th 1981, Miami, Florida, US.

■ *Gibson Les Paul Special.*

Although it was **Peter Tosh** who provided The Wailers' emblematic 'tchka-tchka-tchka', Marley came up with most of the songs and the sparse arrangements. Marley's guitar playing itself was even more sparse.

While instinct was Marley's watchword, his poetic literacy combined with a musical acumen comparable to producers such as Tom Dowd and Jerry Wexler enabled him to assemble some of the most powerful and evocative albums of the 1970s – *Catch A Fire* (1972), *Burnin'* (1973), *Natty Dread* (1974) and *Exodus* (1977) – that drew as much from R&B and soul as from African and Caribbean music. The live

version of 'No Woman, No Cry' remains a heartstring-tugger of epic proportions.

Such was Marley's impact that he was briefly lionized in the US, mostly because **Eric Clapton**, Barbra Streisand, **Taj Mahal** and Johnny Nash covered Marley originals such as 'I Shot The Sheriff', 'Guava Jelly', 'Slave Driver' and 'Stir It Up', respectively. Marley's death from cancer prompted prolonged legal battles over his rightful heirs which took over ten years to resolve.

JOHNNY MARR

Born: John Maher, October 31st 1963, Manchester, England.

■ *Fender Stratocaster; Gibson Les Paul; Gibson ES335; Rickenbacker 330; Giffin Tele-style; Gretsch.*

Of the many superlatives to fly around about the excellence of Marr, the one most keenly felt is the observation that no guitarist (in Britain) has had such a coherent grasp of melody and structure since the halcyon days of the 1960s. It was this facet of Marr's contributions to The Smiths' work that gave it a semblance of completeness.

Marr's grasp of the cardinal requirements of melody and structure enabled vocalist Morrissey to put together some of the most strikingly visual songs since Kink-man Ray Davies' heyday in the mid-1960s, especially 'Hand In Glove', 'This Charming Man', 'What Difference Does It Make?', 'Heaven Knows I'm Miserable Now', 'The Boy With The Thorn In His Side' and 'Panic'.

Marr left the group in 1987, since when Morrissey has still to find a replacement as lyrical and full of ideas.

Meanwhile, Marr took on the role of roving hand for hire, playing with **Paul McCartney**, Bryan Ferry, Talking Heads, The The and The Pretenders, among others, before joining forces with **Bernard Sumner** of New Order and Neil Tennant of The Pet Shop Boys to form Electronic. Once again Marr proved his value, contributing neat guitar parts that complemented Sumner's lyricism and Tennant's propensity for the grandiose.

STEVE MARRIOTT

Born: January 30th 1947, London, England. Died: April 20th 1991, Arkesden, Essex, England.

■ *Gretsch Tennessean; Gibson Les Paul; Fender Esquire.*

In The Small Faces, Marriott's energetic vocals and basic, rocking guitar style on songs like 'Whatcha Gonna Do About It' (based on Solomon Burke's 'Everybody Needs Somebody To Love'), 'All Or Nothing', 'My Mind's Eye' and 'I Can't Make It' had a tuneful simplicity that belied his musical ability, causing him and the rest of the group to be lumped together with travesties such as The Tremeloes. Only after signing with the Immediate label did the group begin to generate the critical plaudits that had always been due.

Ogden's Nut Gone Flake (1968) and *The Autumn Stone* (1969) are two of the best albums to emerge from that period, with Marriott illustrating the full range of his guitar styles on songs like 'Here Comes

The Nice', 'Itchycoo Park', 'Lazy Sunday', 'The Universal' and 'Afterglow (Of Your Love)'.

After the group's break-up Marriott formed Humble Pie with **Peter Frampton**. Their debut *As Safe As Yesterday Is* (1969) remains the group's best outing, notable for its understatement and Frampton's deft chording on songs like 'Natural Born Boogie', contrasting with Marriott's more abrasive style. After Frampton left the group in 1972, Humble Pie toured the US solidly, cornering the market in frenetic, good-time music, and disbanding in 1975. Although he played the London club circuit and toured Europe with a variety of bands, including a reformed lineup of The Small Faces, there was a hint of desperation in Marriott's work. He died in 1991.

MICK MARS

Born: Robert Deal, April 4th 1955, Terre Haute, Indiana, US.

■ *Gibson Flying V (modified); Kramer custom Tele-style.*

In Mötley Crüe, Mars seems to have a comprehensive grasp of rock's best loved chords ('Looks That Kill', 'Smokin In The Boys Room' and 'Girls Girls Girls') and the attendant attitudes to strike when playing them. One of the more curious aspects of heavy metal is that beneath the ostensible machismo of the pose there lurks a campness, often expressed in stage garb and the projection of the rock star persona. Mötley Crüe were very proficient at this, to the extent that, like Judas Priest, they became cartoon characters. While their music is efficient and sells formidably well, the chain of disasters that has befallen various members of the band and their followers gives credence to the notion that the movie *This Is Spinal Tap* (1983) was less fictional than the producers implied.

BERNIE MARSDEN

Born: 1942, Oxford, England.

■ *Gibson SG Standard; Gibson Les Paul; Gibson double-neck.*

Formerly with bands such as UFO, Wild Turkey and Babe Ruth, Marsden edged closer to the big league of heavy metal guitarists when he joined David Coverdale's Whitesnake in 1976. While Coverdale's bluesy, histrionic vocals often distracted attention from the quality of musicianship in the rest of the band, Marsden and **Micky Moody** were fine sparring partners. Marsden's capacity to riff endlessly complemented Moody's propensity for squeezing out large numbers of notes per second but with a keener ear for structure than most, as on 'Long Way From Home', 'Fool For Your Loving', Bobby Bland's 'Ain't No Love In The Heart Of The City' and 'Don't Break My Heart'. In 1983, Marsden left and formed Alaska. Most recently, Marsden has been playing again with Micky Moody in The Moody Marsden Band.

VINCE MARTELL

Born: November 11th 1945, New York, New York, US.

Martell was guitarist of Vanilla Fudge, who disbanded in 1970. The yawn-inducing tedium of their cover

Mar–Mar

versions of other artists' hits (there is a *Best Of* available if you really must) like The Supremes' 'You Keep Me Hangin On' and Cher's 'Bang Bang' were apparently arranged to simulate the effect of hallucinogenic drugs. Crass in the extreme, Vanilla Fudge might have lasted longer had they consumed something with a little bit more zip to it. The group's drummer Carmine Appice has made a full recovery and is one of the best session drummers around. Martell, however, left the music industry in 1970.

GRADY MARTIN

Born: January 17th 1929, near Chapel Hill, Tennessee, US.

■ *Gibson ES355 (later).*

A premier Nashville guitar picker, Martin has been one of the area's top session musicians for over 40 years. After making his debut as a fiddler on the Grand Ole Opry in 1946 he went on to record with singers Hank Williams and Marty Robbins. With Robbins he achieved the distinction of being among the first to use a distorted guitar, on the big hit 'Don't Worry' (1961). Although the effect was unintentional, produced by an error in the recording process, it now seems like a landmark.

Martin's early years as a fiddler encouraged him to adapt for the guitar many pieces that had been written for fiddle, enabling him to create long, scintillating runs that only The Delmore Brothers (see **Alton Delmore**), **Don Reno** and **Merle Travis** had previously attempted. While the detail of much of Martin's guitar work was buried in over-elaborate productions, in 1979 he joined **Willie Nelson**'s band where his fast picking was given greater prominence.

JIM MARTIN

Born: July 21st 1961, Oakland, California, US.

■ *Gibson Flying V.*

There is an intriguing definition of the term 'grunge' in the revised edition of *The Shorter Oxford English Dictionary*: "Raucous music performed by scruffy persons." This isn't entirely accurate. It implies that the music is purely raucous and lacks any degree of sophistication or, indeed, accomplishment. Martin of Faith No More isn't a technically minded guitarist but has the finesse, intuition and skill to deliver the right riff at the right time with all manner of neat connections into pithy solos. Although the power chords sometimes belie this notion, Martin's rough and ready approach on 'Zombie Eaters' and 'Surprise, You're Dead' indicates a sure understanding of rock'n'roll. On *Angel Dust* (1992) Martin, like **Bob Mould**, **J Mascis**, **Mike McCready**, **James Iha** and **Kurt Cobain**, delivered music with an energy to confound… and had the talent to get away with it.

PAT MARTINO

Born: Pat Azzara, August 25th 1944, Philadelphia, Pennsylvania, US.

■ *Gibson L5S.*

Martino started his professional career in the late-1960s with various organ-based jazz outfits, such as those of Brother Jack McDuff and Jimmy Smith. He soon began to develop an individual style on his own recordings, such as *East* (1967), *Consciousness* (1974) and *Footprints* (1981), where he mixes apparently disparate elements such as the smooth sound of **Johnny Smith**, the octave runs of **Wes Montgomery** and the raga-like qualities of some Eastern music into a fast, fluid style of his own.

JOHN MARTYN

Born: September 11th 1948, Glasgow, Scotland.

■ *Martin D-18 (+ pickup); Fender Stratocaster; Gibson SG; Gibson Les Paul.*

Since the late-1960s John Martyn has demonstrated a glorious unwillingness to be typecast by notions of category, and his style reflects the commitment of a guitarist who has spent much of his life investigating the possibilities of his instrument. Especially on-stage, Martyn has taken the acoustic folk guitar about as far away from its roots as possible through clever, atmospheric use of amplification and electronic effects (especially the multi-layering Echoplex machine).

The pastoral albums *The Stormbringer* (1970) and *Road To Ruin* (1971, with his wife at the time, Beverly) contained fine picking with elaborate arrangements and contributions from **Richard Thompson** among others.

Bless The Weather (1971) was sparsely arranged with principal accompaniment from bassist Danny Thompson, and featured the evocative 'Glistening Glyndebourne'. While 'May You Never' was touching and delicate, the bulk of *Solid Air* (1973) was the antithesis of his previous output, with Martyn using amplified guitar and employing chord structures redolent of bluesmen like **Skip James** and **Robert Johnson**.

This eclecticism has since permeated his career, with Martyn exhibiting an arrant disregard for those who try to categorize his work: he dabbled in Caribbean forms with veteran producer Lee 'Scratch' Perry on **One World** (1977), garnered contributions from **Eric Clapton** and Phil Collins (in his best role of drummer) on *Glorious Fool* (1981), and continued the successful partnership with Danny Thompson, supplemented by drummer John Stevens, on *Well Kept Secret* (1982). While many would have difficulty in ringing the changes with such panache, Martyn has flourished, giving all the signs of having undergone a spiritual metamorphosis. Long may he run. His work is, however, spread across numerous record labels.

HANK B MARVIN

Born: Brian Robson Rankin, October 28th 1941, Newcastle upon Tyne, England.

■ *Fender Stratocaster; Fender 'signature'; Burns Marvin; Burns Double 6.*

Arguably the first English-bred guitar hero, Marvin of The Shadows was and still is a technocrat. Very few British guitar fans around in the 1960s will ever forget the group's crisply recorded instrumentals such as 'Apache', 'FBI', 'The Man Of Mystery', 'Wonderful Land', 'Guitar Tango' and 'Dance On'. However, while they were all very jolly in their own way, ultimately they lacked spirit. Marvin undoubtedly influenced many generations of guitar players with his simple, tremolo-laden, melodic solos stacked with echo and reverb, but his association with pop singer Cliff Richard imbued them with a pristine image that seemed a little too good to be true.

Since the heyday of The Shadows, Marvin has come to embody the note-perfect professional, where expertise and prowess rather than emotional commitment have become the calling cards.

J MASCIS

Born: Amherst, Massachusetts, US.

■ *Fender Jazzmaster; Gibson SG Junior.*

With **Bob Mould**'s Hüsker Dü as a reference point, Dinosaur Jr have been one of the more visible exponents of what was dubbed grunge. Mascis' influential style injects a nervy, rhythmic warmth into apparently simple sequences.

Where You Been (1993) was not the guitar band stereotype: Dinosaur Jr use unexpected musical ingredients where appropriate, such as a string quartet and kettle drums, and Mascis' axe attack has a strong enough identity to enable him to absorb country-style material into songs like 'Get Me' and 'Drawerings'. As grunge became passé, Mascis and Dinosaur Jr seemed to have the potential to develop independently of fads and fixations.

DAVE MASON

Born: May 10th 1946, Worcester, England.

■ *Fender Stratocaster; Gibson Firebird.*

Mason's famous friends have often stolen his thunder, and seldom has the British guitarist reaped the rewards that lesser mortals have gathered up by the armful. After forming a number of bands including The Hellions (with drummer Jim Capaldi, keyboardist Poli Palmer and guitarist **Luther Grosvenor**) and Deep Feeling, he formed Traffic with **Steve Winwood**, ex-Locomotive reedsman Chris Wood, and Capaldi.

While Mason's relationship with Traffic was erratic, he penned some of their best known numbers such as 'Hole In My Shoe' and 'Feelin Alright'. His graceful, melodic guitar work eschewed the trend among guitarists at the time to ape **Jimi Hendrix** and **Eric Clapton**, instead showing a strong country influence reminiscent of pickers like **Jimmy Bryant**.

After leaving Traffic, Mason worked with Delaney & Bonnie and Clapton's Derek & The Dominoes before cutting his solo *Alone Together* (1970) which included contributions from all the aforementioned plus **Leon Russell** and vocalist Rita Coolidge. Despite Mason's propensity for startlingly fey lyrics, this was a tuneful outing that fared best in the US. Later albums such as *Headkeeper* (1972) were similarly melodious, with Mason's neat line in guitar licks taking pride of place.

MAR-MAS

CARMEN MASTREN

Born: Carmen Nicholas Mastrendrea, October 6th 1913, Cohoes, New York, US. Died: March 31st 1981, Valley Stream, Long Island, US.

■ *Epiphone Emperor; Gibson L4.*

Remaining with the Tommy Dorsey band through the peak years of swing in the 1930s, Mastren was a lucid and concise rhythm guitarist who also offered occasional solos. Trombonist Dorsey had split from the Dorsey Brothers Band (with sax-playing brother Jimmy) and took over the reins of Joe Haymes' Orchestra, which included such notables as trumpeter Bunny Berigan, drummer Buddy Rich and guitarist Mastren.

Leaving Dorsey in 1940, Mastren joined NBC and then served in the US Army until 1945, playing guitar with Glenn Miller's Air Force orchestra. After being demobilized he rejoined NBC, as well as contributing to film soundtracks and commercials. The increase of his commercial work precluded much creative activity, but that doesn't alter the fact that, while with Dorsey, Mastren was sufficiently rated to win the *Down Beat* magazine poll in 1937.

MIKE MAXFIELD

Born: February 23rd 1944, Manchester, England.

■ *Guild Starfire.*

Vocalist Billy J Kramer's backing band The Dakotas was a very efficient unit. Not as inspired as The Beatles, The Big Three or The Searchers, perhaps, but a cut above such average British outfits as Freddie & The Dreamers and Gerry & The Pacemakers. Maxfield's solo on the group's solo instrumental hit 'The Cruel Sea' had an intensity lacking in contemporary efforts from The Shadows and the studio-based wizardry of The Tornadoes. Maxfield left The Dakotas in 1965 to concentrate on songwriting.

BRIAN MAY

Born: July 19th 1947, Twickenham, Middlesex, England.

■ *Self-built custom; Guild 'signature'.*

Throughout the Queen years May was a rather unprepossessing guitar hero. Like **Hank Marvin**, May was a note-perfect soloist who was governed by technique and studio tricks rather than emotion. May was particularly talented at building up **Les Paul**-like guitar layers into an orchestrated whole. A profusion of fine solos on songs such as 'Seven Seas Of Rhye', 'Killer Queen', 'Somebody To Love', 'Bohemian Rhapsody', 'Another One Bites The Dust', 'I Want to Break Free', 'Radio Ga Ga' and 'A Kind Of Magic' were designed to satisfy a specific requirement and consequently lacked that vital spark of excitement.

With his own band May has contributed such stupendously dreary pieces as 'Driven By You', adopted by Ford for British TV commercials, and has contributed to the Armenia relief fund by appearing on the all-star remake of Deep Purple's 'Smoke On The Water'. Very worthy, and very dull.

JOHN MAYALL

Born: November 29th 1933, Macclesfield, Cheshire, England.

■ *Burns; Framus; Rickenbacker; Strat-style.*

Mayall was first encouraged to start playing and setting up groups in London by British R&B man **Alexis Korner** – and later Mayall found himself in a similar role to Korner, running bands that were virtual schools of excellence for white British blues musicians. The first lineups of Mayall's Bluesbreakers in 1963 and 1964 featured guitarists that virtually nobody remembers today. But that soon changed dramatically, and over the next few years the guitar slot in The Bluesbreakers was filled by **Eric Clapton** (1965-66, minus a short 'break'), **Peter Green** (1966-67), **Mick Taylor** (1967-69), and later **Jon Mark**, **Harvey Mandel** and **Jerry McGee** among quite a few others.

Mayall was instrumental in creating the blues-rock boom of the 1960s, and later moved to the West Coast of the US. Despite being an accomplished guitarist himself, with influences ranging from **Otis Rush** to **Django Reinhardt**, Mayall's own six-string work has tended to be marginalized in such exalted company. He continues to tour and record.

CURTIS MAYFIELD

Born: June 3rd 1942, Chicago, Illinois, US.

■ *Fender Stratocaster; Fender Telecaster.*

Jerry Butler and Mayfield were the successive leaders of The Impressions, one of the most influential R&B groups of the late-1950s and early-1960s. What set them apart from other groups of the era was that they were more or less artist-led rather than just being vehicles for producers' whims. Mayfield was the artist in this instant, and he contributed material like 'Keep On Pushing', 'People Get Ready' and 'We're A Winner', his lyrics reflecting growing racial tensions, while his guitar work anticipated funksters like **Jimmy Nolen**.

After leaving The Impressions in 1970 Mayfield started a solo career, having formed the Curtom label in 1968, and cut *Curtis* (1970). This included 'Move On Up', which was more funky than any of his previous work with The Impressions, the lyrical and emphatic guitar work punctuating the punchy horn arrangements. It was followed by *Curtis Live!* (1971), recorded at New York's Bitter End. Containing new material as well as reworkings of old Impressions material it featured a slimmed-down unit, comprising drummer, percussionist and bassist. Had there ever been doubt about Mayfield's ability as a guitarist, this confounded such critics, showing that he didn't need to hide behind studio technology. That didn't last: later albums such as *Roots* (1971), *Superfly* (1972) and *Back To The World* (1973) utilized all that the studio engineer could offer.

Throughout the 1970s and 1980s Mayfield continued recording his own material while producing Gladys Knight & The Pips, Donny Hathaway and Aretha Franklin. In August 1990 Mayfield was tragically paralyzed after an accident with a lighting rig at an outdoor festival in New York.

SYRAN MBENZA

Born: Zaire.

Cornerstone of Les Quatres Etoiles, Mbenza's reggae tinged guitar work has made the band one of the most influential Zairean outfits to emerge in recent years. While the group shows influences of **Dr Nico** they have absorbed Western styles, making them a genuine pan-cultural hybrid, as shown on *Mayi* (1983), *Enfant Bamileke* (1984) and *Quatre Grandes Vedettes De La Musique Africaine* (1989). In 1986 Mbenza launched his own band, Kiss Kass, but continued working with Les Quatres Etoiles.

PADDY MCALOON

Born: Patrick McAloon, June 7th 1957, Consett, Durham, England.

■ *Fender Stratocaster.*

The McAloon brothers, guitarist Paddy and bassist Martin, came into the spotlight in 1982 as the nucleus of one of Britain's more literate outfits of the era, Prefab Sprout. Tuneful to a fault, Paddy's clever lyrics and apposite picking, drawn from a variety of influences, caused many to liken him to Aztec Camera's **Roddy Frame**. Songs like 'When Love Breaks Down', 'When The Angels' (a tribute to Marvin Gaye) and 'Cars & Girls' (a poke at Bruce Springsteen) distilled the salient points of rock'n'roll into their own idiosyncratic hodgepodge, and *From Langley Park To Memphis* (1988) and *Jordan: The Comeback* (1990) were popular successes.

LEON MCAULIFFE

Born: January 3rd 1917, Houston, Texas, US. Died: 1988, Texas, US.

■ *Fender Stringmaster.*

Few performers have exerted as much influence on western swing as pedal-steel player McAuliffe. During McAuliffe's membership of The Texas Playboys, leader Bob Wills' admonition, 'Take it away, Leon!' was a hallmark of the group's performances of the 1930s. Along with **Bob Dunn**, McAuliffe (sometimes spelled McAuliff) laid down the parameters for future steel guitarists with titles like 'Steel Guitar Rag', 'Faded Love', 'Panhandle Rag' and 'Bluebonnet Rag'. Although his career was interrupted by World War II and the decline of interest in western swing, he reemerged in the late-1960s and with Wills reformed The Playboys. After Wills' death, McAuliffe led the group.

PAUL MCCARTNEY

Born: June 18th 1942, Liverpool, England.

■ *Epiphone Casino; Gibson Les Paul; Music Man Axis; Alvarez.*

While The Beatles have gone from strength to strength in the mythology of the 1960s, McCartney has been the sole survivor to devote his career to music in all its varying manifestations.

In The Beatles, the distillation of the many inherent differences between the four musicians created a vital, magical spark. Along with producer

George Martin, each complemented one another to the extent that they functioned as a single unit, with the join imperceptible: only with later releases, and especially *Let It Be* (1970), did individual contributions stand out, and that latter example could be ascribed to the influence of producer Phil Spector who remixed the tracks. Until then, it was of academic interest that bassman McCartney had for example played acoustic guitar on 'Yesterday', the excellent electric guitar solo on 'Eight Days A Week', or the distinctive six-string arpeggiating of 'Ticket To Ride'.

McCartney's desire to be the main man has dominated his solo material and that of his band Wings. But there have been some sublime moments from that body of work, including 'Maybe I'm Amazed', 'Helen Wheels', 'Jet', 'Listen To What The Man Said', 'Magneto & Titanium Man', 'Mull Of Kintyre', 'No More Lonely Nights' and 'My Brave Face'. Nonetheless, McCartney seems better off when he has other people around to complement his writing and to mitigate his propensity for idle slices of whimsy. 'Silly Love Songs'? Definitely.

THOMAS McCLARY

Born: October 6th 1950, Florida, US.

The Commodores came together in 1967 in Tuskegee, Alabama, when The Mighty Mystics and The Jays merged. By 1971, spearheaded by Lionel Richie (vocals and keyboards), the group had signed to Motown, touring for the next three years to hone their act. Although Richie's knack for big ballads quickly superseded the gritty funk of their early material – 'Machine Gun', 'The Zoo (Human Zoo)', 'Slippery When Wet' and 'Brick House' – McClary's choppy riffs complemented the dominant horn section, and his eccentric solo added some of the sparkle to the huge hit 'Easy' (1977, included on *Greatest Hits*). Tracks such as this gave the coffers at Motown a much needed cash injection – the company's fortunes had begun to wane in the 1970s. In 1983, after Richie's departure for a solo career, McClary followed suit. It proved to be a mistake: efficient guitarist McClary may be, but big-voiced soloist he ain't.

DELBERT McCLINTON

Born: November 4th 1940, Lubbock, Texas, US.

Singer and guitarist McClinton has been a key figure on the Texas club circuit since the early-1960s when he first achieved his reputation as the harmonica player on Bruce Channel's 'Hey Baby'. This was followed by years of dogging around in local groups like the Ron-Dels and recording local hits such as 'If You Really Want Me To, I'll Go'.

After a five-year sojourn on the West Coast McClinton returned to Texas and recorded a series of impressive country influenced R&B albums like *Victims Of Life's Circumstances* (1975), *Love Rustler* (1977), *Second Wind* (1978) and *Keeper Of The Flame* (1979). Minor celebrity beckoned briefly with 'Giving It Up For Your Love' from the Barry Beckett-produced album *The Jealous Kind* (1980), but

fame appeared to rest uncertainly on McClinton's shoulders and he was quickly back in the thick of the Texas club circuit, cutting *Live From Austin* (1989) among others and duetting with such luminaries as vocalist Tanya Tucker.

HUGH McCRACKEN

Born: US.

A session guitarist of some repute, McCracken has played with artists as varied as Aretha Franklin, **BB King**, Melanie and Donald Fagen. He formed an integral part of New York's session circuit, along with **Eric Gale** and **Cornell Dupree**, drummer Bernard Purdie, and hornmen Hank Crawford and Randy & Michael Brecker.

MIKE McCREADY

Born: 1967, Seattle, Washington, US.

∎ *Fender Stratocaster.*

While no man powers a group singlehandedly, the explosive punch of McCready's Strat on 'Why Go', the ingenuous noodlings on 'Deep' and the bluesy understatement of 'Release' made Pearl Jam's debut *Ten* (1992) one of the strongest, most uncompromising rock albums to emerge in a period that also saw the release of Smashing Pumpkins' *Gish* and Nirvana's *Nevermind*. While McCready's influences have been drawn from rock artists like Black Sabbath and **Jeff Beck**, these have been modulated by the purifying influence of R&B stylists **Muddy Waters** and **Howlin' Wolf**. So it's not all fretting: there's plenty of gutbucket in McCready's playing.

JIMMY McCULLOCH

Born: June 4th 1953, Glasgow, Scotland. Died: September 27th 1979, London, England.

∎ *Gibson ES335.*

The opening bars of Thunderclap Newman's 'Something In The Air' (1969) may have been a triumph for writer Speedy Keene, but the stark simplicity of McCulloch's chords evoke the mood of the era. Later, McCulloch went on to form Blue, as well as spending time with **John Mayall**, Stone The Crows (replacing the late **Les Harvey**) and Wings, but his playing remained unfocused and he never recaptured that moment.

HENRY McCULLOUGH

Born: 1943, England.

∎ *Guild Thunderbird; Gibson Les Paul.*

Some would contend that vocalist Joe Cocker's finest hour was when he fronted The Grease Band, a funky little combo comprising McCullough, keyboardist Chris Stainton, bassist Alan Spenner and drummer Bruce Rowlands, among others. At first they specialized in covers of soul material combined with Stainton/Cocker originals, a rough and ready repertoire that was ideally suited to Cocker's voice and which enabled McCullough to squeeze in tight, snake-like guitar lines.

Although McCullough played on Cocker's album *With A Little Help From My Friends* (1969), it was **Jimmy Page** who graced the big-hit title track. The follow-up album *Joe Cocker* (1970) featured the best ever version of the much-covered 'Delta Lady' and a fine take of 'The Letter'. After McCullough and Cocker parted ways, McCullough did sessions before joining **Paul McCartney** in the early-1970s for an apparently unharmonious 12 months, although he did contribute to 'Live & Let Die' (1973) and the rather nifty reggae-style guitar work to Wings' 'C Moon'. McCullough recorded a so-so solo album, *Mind Your Own Business*, in 1975.

DICK McDONOUGH

Born: 1904, New York, New York, US. Died: May 25th 1938, New York, New York, US.

∎ *Gibson L5.*

Most of McDonough's career was passed in the employ of big-band leader Benny Goodman, where he worked with vocalist Billie Holiday among others. In 1934 McDonough partnered **Carl Kress** and cut a number of fine acoustic duets of chord-style jazz guitar. His untimely death intervened just as his career was hitting its stride.

MISSISSIPPI FRED McDOWELL

Born: January 12th 1904, Rossville, Tennessee, US. Died: July 3rd 1972, Memphis, Tennessee, US.

∎ *National resonator; Hofner acoustic; Gibson Trini Lopez.*

A self-taught guitarist, McDowell spent most of his life working on a farm until in the early-1960s he was discovered by archivist Alan Lomax during one of Lomax's many field trips. This encouraged McDowell to hit the festival circuit where his slide guitar work combined with mesmeric runs on the bass strings gave him the stature of one who had been gigging throughout his life. McDowell's recording debut *Delta Blues* (1963) included standards as well as originals on acoustic guitar, while in the mid-1960s he switched over to electric. An inspiration to many, such as **Jo Ann Kelly**, **Dave Kelly** and **Bonnie Raitt**, McDowell's late development as a recording artist gave his records a harsh grittiness, particularly evident on the live *In London* (1969).

JOHN McFEE

Born: November 18th 1953, Santa Cruz, California, US.

∎ *Westwood Strat-style; Fender Telecaster; Gibson Les Paul.*

One of the earliest San Francisco-based country-rock outfits, Clover were formed in 1968 by guitarist and pedal-steel guitarist McFee, guitarist Alex Call, bassist John Ciambiotta and drummer Mitch Howie. After two albums – *Clover* (1970) and *Forty-Niner* (1971) – they were dropped by Fantasy and played local gigs in the Bay-area.

McFee also took to the session circuit, playing with Van Morrison, **Steve Miller** and **Boz Scaggs**.

In the mid-1970s Clover came to England to play the pub circuit where they hooked up with Dr Feelgood's manager Jake Riviera. Two or three good albums down the line the band split up, but not before they had backed Jake's protégé **Elvis Costello** on his fine debut, *My Aim Is True* (1977). McFee went on to join The Doobie Brothers in 1979, although the group were by this time in decline and dominated by vocalist Michael McDonald. McFee lasted the course until 1982 and then went back to sessioning.

JERRY McGEE

Born: 1938, Eunice, Louisiana, US.

■ **Fender Broadcaster; Fender Stratocaster; Gibson Les Paul.**

Playing an influential, bluesy, swamp-rock style, McGee was a noted session man in the 1960s and 1970s, appearing on records by The Monkees, Bobby Darin, Rita Coolidge and many others. In 1967 McGee brought some stability to the shifting lineup of instrumental pop group The Ventures, joining as main guitarist – a job he still holds at the time of writing. Today the band, into its 30th year, apparently hold a timeless fascination for concert-goers and record-buyers in Japan, which is where their work is chiefly based.

SAM McGEE

Born: May 1st 1894, Franklin, Tennessee, US.
Died: August 21st 1975, Franklin, Tennessee, US.

■ **Martin D-28; Martin 000-28; Martin D-18.**

In the early years when country music first began to achieve popular acclaim, singer/banjoist Uncle Dave Macon exerted a prodigious influence on the generation of young up-and-coming artists such as the brothers Sam (guitar and banjo) and Kirk McGee (guitar and fiddle). Sam was one of the first country musicians to use an electric guitar.

In 1924 the McGee brothers struck up a friendship with Macon, joining his group The Fruit Jar Drinkers, and in 1930 formed The Dixieliners with Fiddlin' Arthur Smith, cutting sides for Bluebird like 'Railroad Blues' and 'Buck Dancer's Choice'. After World War II both brothers slipped gradually into obscurity, but their careers were revitalized in the 1960s by invitations to play on the folk and country festival circuits. Consequently Sam's finger-picking style was imitated by young 'uns such as **Tony Rice** and **Herb Pedersen**, among others.

JOHN McGEOCH

Born: May 28th 1955, Greenock, Scotland.

■ **Yamaha SG1000; Carvin.**

There are few who cultivated the early-1980s British new wave guitar style with greater assiduousness than McGeoch. A founder member of Magazine, followed by stints with Steve Strange's Visage, Siouxsie & The Banshees, Billy Idol, Richard Jobson, and Public Image Limited, McGeoch brought an incisive mind to his playing, defining the new wave guitar ethos of texture and shade over soloing: witness Siouxsie's

Kaleidoscope (1980). McGeoch's sound has informed many lesser mortals who, poor souls, weren't old enough to know first hand the joys of **Scotty Moore** or **James Burton** but had to make do with the likes of **Tony Iommi** and **Ritchie Blackmore**. And in that sort of company McGeoch isn't such a bad role model.

BROWNIE McGHEE

Born: Walter Brown McGhee, November 30th 1915, Knoxville, Tennessee, US.

■ **Martin D-18.**

Having been in partnership with harmonica man Sonny Terry since 1939, McGhee became one of the most successful and authentic recreators of the Delta country blues when it was rediscovered in the mid-1960s. While he adhered rigidly to the old ways, his sense of adventure and purpose never left him. This enabled Terry and McGhee to pursue successful careers in movies such as *Buck & The Preacher* (1972) and *Leadbelly* (1976), while at festivals they represented genuine links to the past. Terry & McGhee's fund of songs, such as 'John Henry', 'Worried Life Blues', 'CC Rider', 'Trouble In Mind' and 'Goin Down Slow', were learned and played alongside those of folk heroes like **Big Bill Broonzy**, **Leadbelly** and **Woody Guthrie**, investing the duo with a majesty only matched by **John Lee Hooker**. Sonny Terry died in 1986, but at the time of writing Brownie McGhee still plays the occasional gig.

ROGER McGUINN

Born: James McGuinn, July 13th 1942, Chicago, Illinois, US.

■ **Rickenbacker 360-12; Rickenbacker 'signature'.**

McGuinn formed The Beefeaters in the early-1960s with vocalist David Crosby, **Gene Clark**, **Chris Hillman** and drummer Michael Clarke, before changing their name in 1965 to The Byrds. They scored immediately with a cover of Bob Dylan's 'Mr Tambourine Man', and while it featured session musicians like **Leon Russell** it also marked the first appearance of McGuinn's highly distinctive 12-string Rickenbacker, the sonorous jangling of which was to become the group's trademark in their early years. It was applied liberally to self-penned material as well as to Pete Seeger's adaptation of 'Turn! Turn! Turn!' and Jackie DeShannon's 'Don't Doubt Yourself'.

While the lineup of the group underwent constant changes, McGuinn's Rickenbacker set the group apart from any would-be imitators, with distinctive and evocative titles like 'Mr Spaceman', 'So You Wanna Be A Rock'n'Roll Star' and 'Eight Miles High', the latter notable for McGuinn's spluttering solo, apparently inspired by the phrasing of jazz trumpeter Miles Davis.

After Crosby was fired from the group they recorded *Notorious Byrd Brothers* (1968), superficially a glossy, high-tech album, but it showed the group in its best light, maximizing the potential of the recording studio without sacrificing any musical integrity. Although McGuinn remained nominally in control, the country influences from

Hillman, vocalist Gram Parsons and bluegrass guitarist **Clarence White** dominated *Sweetheart Of The Rodeo* (1969).

For the duration of the 1970s and 1980s McGuinn ran the group effectively as a solo vehicle, and much of what materialized was patchy at best. Solo albums or collaborative efforts emerged from time to time, but he had to wait until 1991 before starting to find his form again, with *Back From Rio*.

TOM McGUINNESS

Born: December 2nd 1941, London, England.

■ **Fender Telecaster.**

Initially McGuinness was bassist in Manfred Mann, one of the most underrated bands of the 1960s whose ability to combine the throwaway ethos of pure pop with a repertoire drawn from jazz and R&B makes them as important as The Rolling Stones. They were one of the first groups to raid the Bob Dylan archive and convert little-known songs into minor gems, such as 'With God On Our Side', 'If You Gotta Go, Go Now' and 'The Mighty Quinn'. The group was beset by internal rivalries which caused guitarist Mike Vickers and vocalist Paul Jones to leave and led McGuinness to take over lead guitar – and the jazz and R&B influences remained intact.

However, McGuinness's guitar playing didn't really shine until he took up duties with McGuinness Flint in 1970, which he formed with drummer Hughie Flint and songwriting team Benny Gallagher and Graham Lyle. Two notable singles were 'When I'm Dead And Gone' and 'Malt & Barley Blues', drawing from jug-band music and country, and with McGuinness illustrating a knack for straightforward picking. After the group splintered McGuinness moved into film production, later starting The Blues Band with **Dave Kelly** and old Manfred man Paul Jones. Despite their erratic course, their tours keep the spirit of the blues alive.

ROBBIE McINTOSH

Born: Britain.

■ **Fender Stratocaster; Fender Telecaster; Music Man Silhouette.**

Formerly a member of Night and Manfred Mann's Earth Band (*Chance* 1980), McIntosh joined The Pretenders after the death of **James Honeyman-Scott** in 1983. While Chrissie Hynde's charismatic vocals dominated proceedings, McIntosh's fluid playing on '2000 Miles' and 'Don't Get Me Wrong' had all the verve and lyricism of Honeyman-Scott at his peak.

However the band tended to operate erratically and McIntosh left to join **Paul McCartney** in 1989, and with **Hamish Stuart** formed the nucleus of one of the strongest lineups of Wings. 'My Brave Face' from *Flowers In The Dirt* (1989) was one of McCartney's most insidious compositions in years, with a hook strong enough to take a whale. *Tripping The Live Fantastic* (1991) exhibited a well-oiled machine able to lend weight to even the most risible of McCartney's solo compositions and to give an even better account of old Beatles material.

McG–McI

Buddy Guy is one of the few remaining blues guitarists who was active in Chicago at the peak of the post-war blues boom. He started out in the South, learning at the feet of Lightnin' Slim, who gave him the confidence to get up and play. But his career didn't take off until he moved north to Chicago and began cutting early sides with legendary figures such as Willie Dixon and Sonny Boy Williamson. It was in this era that Guy developed a style that was all his own, sparkling but still abrasive. He reached an early peak as a recording artist with A Man And The Blues, *produced by Sam Charters, which displayed his ability to express a distinctive musical identity while respecting the traditions of the music. However, as the blues became unfashionable, in the early 1970s, Guy took to running a bar, the "Checkerboard Lounge" in Chicago.*

A story went round that he was on the skids and had resorted to working behind a bar: nobody bothered to say that he owned it. The records he cut in this period were patchy in quality, but his reputation as a live performer continued to grow. By the end of the 1970s, he had started to cut albums regularly for specialist labels. Throughout the 1980s, he continued to record, but rather than attempting to satisfy record company demands for superstar-studded sessions, he cut albums that reflected the sets he played nightly in his club. At the end of the 1980s he had become fully established as one of the elder statesmen of the Chicago scene: this was reflected in albums such as Damn Right I Got The Blues *and the more recent* Feels Like Rain, *both of which are contemporary in approach while retaining the essential spirit of the blues.*

EARLY YEARS Although Buddy Guy's career started in his native Louisiana, playing with local bluesmen such as Slim Harpo and Lightnin' Slim, it was the move to Chicago in 1957 that gave his career the boost it needed. Playing initially with the Rufus Foreman Band, he met Otis Rush when he beat him in a 'Battle Of The Blues' contest. Impressed by the newcomer, Rush

A MAN AND THE BLUES (Released 1968) *Tracks:* A Man & The Blues/ I Can't Quit The Blues/ Money (That's What I Want)/ One Room Country Shack/ Mary Had A Little Lamb/ Just Playing My Axe/ Sweet Little Angel/ Worry, Worry/ Jam On A Monday Morning. *Line-up:* includes Buddy Guy (vocals, guitar), Wayne Bennett (guitar), Otis Spann (piano), Jack Myers (bass), Freddy Below (drums). Guy showcasing his gospel-influenced vocals.

| 1958 | 1959 | 1960 | 1961 | 1962 | 1963 | 1964 | 1965 | 1966 | 1967 | 1968 | 1969 | 1970 | 1971 | 1972 | 1973 | 1974 | 197 |

took him along to the Cobra label, and a deal was struck for Guy to cut such sides as 'Sit And Cry' and 'Try To Quit You Baby'. When Cobra collapsed, Guy moved on to the Chess label, where he became a member of the house band, accompanying the likes of Muddy Waters and Howlin' Wolf. At Muddy's instigation, he started to record in his own right. Songs from that period include the raw and scintillating 'First Time I Met The Blues' and the memorable 'Stone Crazy'. While continuing to play in the studio band for other artists' sessions, he established himself on the Chicago club circuit, honing a live act that would stand him in good stead in later years when blues on record was unfashionable.

JUNIOR WELLS In 1965, Buddy Guy forged a partnership with singer and harmonica player Junior Wells, a former child prodigy, whom he had met at an earlier 'Battle Of The Blues' contest. Together, they cut a series of albums for Sam Charters' Vanguard label: *Hoodoo Man Blues* (1965), *On Tap* (1966), *It's My Life Baby* (1966) and *Southside Blues Jam* (1967). While these albums generally show Wells in the better light, they did pave the way for a brace of albums under Buddy Guy's name for the same label: *A Man And The Blues* and *This Is Buddy Guy* (1968). The latter, incidentally, featured Wells, though this time Guy is firmly in the driving seat. Later collaborations included the amusingly-titled *Buddy And The Juniors* (1970), which also featured pianist Junior Mance, and *Buddy Guy And Junior Wells Play The Blues* (1972). By the early 1980s, the partnership had dissolved as Wells's role had increasingly become no more than that of an accompanist. However, despite that, *Alone And Acoustic*, recorded in 1981, shows the partnership at its most potent.

IN THE BEGINNING (Released 1971) *Tracks:* Sit And Cry/ Try To Quit You Baby/ You Sure Can't Do/ This Is The End/ Slop Around/ Broken Hearted Blues/ I Got My Eyes On You/ First Time/ Stone Crazy/ Skippin'/ When My Left Eye Jumps/ The Treasure Untold/ I Dig Your Wig/ My Time After While. *Line-up:* includes Buddy Guy (vocals, guitar), Otis Rush (guitar), Bob Neely, Gerry Gibson & Donald Hankins (tenor sax), Otis Spann (piano), Mack Easter & Willie Dixon (bass), Odie Payne & Freddy Below (drums). With this album Guy moved further into the heart of the Chicago scene represented by the likes of Willie Dixon and Otis Rush.

BUDDY GUY AND JUNIOR WELLS PLAY THE BLUES (Released 1972) *Tracks:* A Man Of Many Words/ My Baby Left Me (She Left Me A Mule To Ride)/ Come On In This House/ Have Mercy Baby/ T-Bone Shuffle/ A Poor Man's Plea/ Messin' With The Kid/ This Old Fool/ I Don't Know/ Bad Bad Whiskey/ Honeydripper. *Line-up:* Junior Wells (vocals, harmonica), Buddy Guy (vocals, guitar), Eric Clapton (guitar), A.C. Reed (tenor sax), Mike Utley (piano), Dr John (piano, organ), Leroy Stewart (bass), Roosevelt Shaw (drums).

JAZZ (Released 1978) *Tracks:* Big Bad Bill Is Sweet William Now/Face To Face That I Shall Meet Him/The Pearls/Tia Juana/The Dream/Happy Meeting In Glory/In A Mist/Flashes/Davenport Blues/Shine/Nobody/We Shall Be Happy. This provides ample proof of Cooder's ability to translate any style and includes a string of distinguished jazz musicians such as Red Callender (bass and tuba), Oscar Brashear (cornet) and Earl Hines (piano), with arrangements by Joseph Byrd who cut the excellent *United States Of America* (1968). Despite its charms, now totally disowned by Cooder, who calls it 'a wretched mistake'.

SHOWTIME (Released 1977) *Tracks:* School Is Out/Alimony/Jesus On The Mainline/The Dark End Of The Street/Viva Sequin/Do Re Mi/Volver, Volver/How Can A Poor Man Stand Such Times And Live?/Smack Dab In The Middle. Recorded live over three days at San Francisco's Great American Music Hall, *Showtime* featured The Chicken Skin Revue, which included Flaco Jimenez (accordion), Isaac Garcia (drums), Henry Ojeda (bass), Jesse Ponce (bajo sexto), Frank Villarreal (alto sax) and vocalists Bobby King, Terry Evans & Eldridge King. A 'warts and all' record of a typically vibrant Cooder live show.

THE LONG RIDERS (Released 1980) *Tracks:* The Long Riders/I'm A Good Old Rebel/Seneca Square Dance/Archie's Funeral (Hold To God's Unchanging Hand)/I Always Knew That You Were The One/Rally 'Round The Flag/Wildwood Boys/Better Things To Think About/My Grandfather/Cole Younger Polka/Escape From Northfield/Leaving Missouri/Jesse James. Cooder's first soundtrack, a collaboration with film director Walter Hill, included help from Jim Dickinson and Jim Keltner, as well as David Lindley (fiddle, electric guitar, banjo and mandolin) and Milt Holland (drums and percussion).

PARIS, TEXAS (Released 1985) *Tracks:* Paris, Texas/Brothers/Nothing Out There/Canción Mixteca/No Safety Zone/Houston In Two Seconds/She's Leaving The Bank/On The Couch/I Knew These People/Dark Was The Night And Cold Was The Ground. One of the best films of that year, *Paris, Texas* was directed by Wim Wenders. The theme was based on Blind Willie Johnson's 'Dark Was The Night And Cold Was The Ground', while 'Canción Mixteca' featured an atmospheric vocal by the film's male lead Harry Dean Stanton, who has occasionally reprised the performance in concert. The doom-laden slide guitar opening of the score has been widely imitated and parodied.

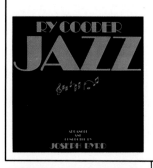

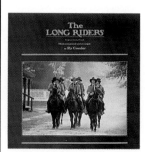

BOP TILL YOU DROP (Released 1979) *Tracks:* Little Sister/Go Home, Girl/The Very Thing That Makes You Rich/I Think It's Going To Work Out Fine/Down In Hollywood/Look At Granny Run Run/Trouble, You Can't Fool Me/Don't You Mess Up A Good Thing/I Can't Win. After The Chicken Skin Revue and *Jazz*, *Bop Till You Drop* was a return to a more traditional R&B, featuring the rhythm section of Jim Keltner and Tim Drummond with additional contributions from Chaka Khan (vocals), David Lindley (guitar) and Milt Holland (percussion). The first widely-available digital recording, incidentally.

BORDERLINE (Released 1980) *Tracks:* 634-5789/Speedo/Why Don't You Try Me/Down In The Boondocks/Johnny Porter/The Way We Make A Broken Heart/(Every Woman I Know Is) Crazy 'Bout An Automobile/The Girls From Texas/Borderline/Never Make A Move Too Soon. Sidemen included vocalist and guitarist John Hiatt, bassists Reggie McBride and Tim Drummond, drummer Jim Keltner and backing vocalists Bobby King and Willie Green. Hiatt's song, 'The Way We Make A Broken Heart' is transformed into a Cooder classic.

THE SLIDE AREA (Released 1982) *Tracks:* UFO Has Landed In The Ghetto/I Need A Woman/Gypsy Woman/Blue Suede Shoes/Mama, Don't Treat Your Daughter Mean/I'm Drinking Again/Which Came First/That's The Way Love Turned Out For Me. Featuring the same line-up as *Borderline*, *The Slide Area* was rather poor in comparison with Cooder's other outings, falling well short of the high standards he had set himself. Unfortunately, it was also the first non-soundtrack album on which he had written the bulk of the material.

COODER'S GUITARS In the 1970s Cooder mostly used a white Strat and a Martin D.45, but gradually he has become associated with a bewildering assortment of unusual guitars, either modified versions of instruments from well known makers, or guitars of lesser known brands such as National and Teisco. Cooder's current Strat, for example, has a Japanese plastic leopard skin pickguard with various pickups fitted from other guitars, including one from a lap-steel electric. Cooder often borrows guitars from his friend, session guitarist David Lindley, who has a formidable collection of oddities, including Weissenborn hollow-necked Hawaiian instruments.

Ry Cooder

Although there have been many session guitarists before and since Ry Cooder's emergence, few have managed to establish themselves in their own right with such effect He is recognized particularly as one of the best slide players working today. Cooder was raised in Los Angeles and taught the rudiments of the guitar by Rev Gary Davis – no mean picker himself – who imbued Cooder with an awareness of the rich heritage of American music. This was followed by a stint in Jackie De Shannon's band, De Shannon being the writer of such classics as 'When You Walk In The Room', recorded by The Searchers and De Shannon herself. Her own version features a truly stunning guitar break, which could well be a precocious Cooder. Since the late 1960s he has become one of the key figures on the Los Angeles session circuit.

In the early 1970s Cooder launched a solo career with the Ry Cooder album which marked the beginning of a series of albums and film soundtracks that examined the many facets of traditional American music. These records demonstrated his ability to transmute archaic styles into a new sound where authenticity is as important as instrumental accomplishment. Nowhere is this more noticeable than in the soundtracks. While fulfilling their primary role of complementing the images, they stand on their own as fine pieces of music. To this day Cooder remains one of America's finest interpreters and most individual guitar stylists. Now well into his third decade as a session man and performer, he has always stood for good taste, technical excellence and the joy of musical collaboration, even when these were unfashionable virtues.

RY COODER (Released 1970) *Tracks:* Alimony/France Chance/One Meat Ball/Do Re Mi/Old Kentucky Home/How Can A Poor Man Stand Such Times And Live?/Available Space/Pig Meat/Police Dog Blues/Goin' To Brownsville/Dark Is The Night. Produced by Van Dyke Parks and Lenny Waronker, this announced Cooder's ability to find a distinctive repertoire and to hold the stage on his own account.

INTO THE PURPLE VALLEY
(Released 1972) *Tracks:* How Can You Keep On Moving/Billy The Kid/Money Honey/FDR In Trinidad/Teardrops Will Fall/Denomination Blues/On A Monday/Hey Porter/Great Dreams From Heaven/Taxes On The Farmer Feeds Us All/Vigilante Man. Produced by Jim Dickinson and Lenny Waronker. Cooder's exploration of the Depression era.

Timeline: 1969 1970 1971 1972 1973 1974 1975 1976

EARLY YEARS After leaving Jackie De Shannon's band, Cooder formed The Rising Sons with drummer Ed Cassidy (later a mainstay of Spirit) and Taj Mahal. The resulting Rising Sons sessions were shelved until 1993, although one single, 'Candy Man', was released. When they disbanded, Cooder played on sessions with Paul Revere & The Raiders after having met Byrds' producer Terry Melcher.
In 1967 Cooder joined Captain Beefheart's band for the landmark *Safe As Milk*, contributing superb slide, before returning to the session circuit and working with Van Dyke Parks, Randy Newman, Jack Nitzsche (the soundtrack of the film *Performance:* note 'Memo From Turner'), The Rolling Stones and Little Feat. While sessions provided Cooder with regular work, it was his solo output that gave him his reputation as a knowledgable devotee of traditional styles.

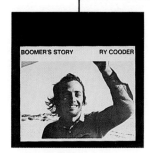

BOOMER'S STORY (Released 1973) *Tracks:* Boomer's Story/Cherry Ball Blues/Crow Black Chicken/Ax Sweet Mama/Maria Elena/Dark End Of The Street/Rally 'Round The Flag/Comin' In On A Wing And A Prayer/President Kennedy/Good Morning Mr Railroad Man. A bleak and desolate set that evoked a rural America populated by itinerants. It provided a model that would be used extensively in Cooder's soundtracks, particularly on Tony Richardson's *The Border* (1980) and Walter Hill's *The Long Riders* (1980). Ry assembled an amazing band, as usual.

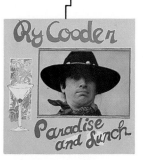

PARADISE AND LUNCH
(Released 1974) *Tracks:* Tamp 'Em Up Solid/I'm A Fool For A Cigarette/Feelin' Good/Married Man's A Fool/Mexican Divorce/It's All Over Now/Tattler/Ditty Wa Ditty/If Walls Could Talk/Jesus On The Mainline. Produced by Russ Titelman and Lenny Waronker, and featuring Oscar Brashear (cornet), Chris Etheridge and Red Callender (bass), Milt Holland and Jim Keltner (drums), Plas Johnson (alto sax), Earl 'Fatha' Hines (piano), Ronnie Barron (keyboards) and vocalist Bobby King, among others. The element of 'Ry' humor comes to the fore.

CHICKEN SKIN MUSIC
(Released 1976) *Tracks:* The Bourgeois Blues/I Got Mine/Always Lift Him Up/He'll Have To Go/Smack Dab In The Middle/Stand By Me/Yellow Roses/Chloe/Goodnight Irene. Influenced by the Bahamian guitarist Joseph Spence, this included Hawaiian steel guitarist Gabby Pahinui and accordionist Flaco Jimenez. The latter became a central figure in Cooder's Chicken Skin Revue, a project that sought to bring Tex-Mex to a wider audience with an extensive round of touring. Here the emphasis is shared with the 'slack-key' music of Hawaii.

LIVE AT THE CHECKERBOARD LOUNGE CHICAGO (Recorded 1979, Released 1988) *Tracks:* Buddy's Blues (Part 1)/ I've Got A Right To Love My Woman/ Tell Me What's Inside Of You/ Done Got Over You/ The Things I Used To Do/ You Don't Know How I Feel/ The Dollar Done Fell/ Buddy's Blues (Part 2)/ Don't Answer The Door/ Tell Me What's Inside Of You (Version 2). *Line-up:* Buddy Guy (guitar, vocals)/ Phil Guy (guitar), Little Phil Smith (guitar), J.W. Williams (bass), Ray Allison (drums), L.C. Thurston (vocals). Buddy relaxed and at his best, among friends and in his natural habitat. In this case he is playing in the intimate surroundings of his own Chicago club. This release ranks as one of the most authentic of all live blues albums and bears comparison with B.B. King's classic *Blues Is King*.

STONE CRAZY (Released 1981) *Tracks:* I Smell A Rat, Are You Losing Your Mind, You've Been Gone Too Long, She's Out There Somewhere, Outskirts Of Town, When I Left Home. *Line-up:* Buddy Guy (guitar, vocals), Phil Guy (guitar), J.W. Williams (bass), Ray Allison (drums). Recorded in the unlikely setting of Toulouse in southern France, and produced by Didier Tricard, this record marks Buddy's return to the unembellished style that had won him his reputation in the first place. Since 1968's *A Man And The Blues*, his recording career had been somewhat erratic, but *Breaking Out* and *Stone Crazy* heralded a new phase of his career. From now on he would be relatively free of the management and agency problems that traditionally afflict blues artists.

THE COMPLETE DJ PLAY MY BLUES (Released 1981) *Tracks:* Girl You're Nice And Clean/ Dedication To The Late T-Bone Walker/ Good News/ Blues At My Baby's House/ She Suits Me To A T/ D.J. Play My Blues/ Just Teasin'/ All Your Love/ Garbage Man Blues/ Mellow Down. *Line-up:* Buddy Guy (guitar, vocals), Phil Guy (guitar, vocals), Doug Williams (guitar), Mike Morrison (bass), Ray Allison (drums). Produced by Buddy himself, this is an excellent example of what happens when a finely-tuned band starts working out in the studio. Here Guy's regular band cut a straightforward set that differs little from the stuff they would have performed on the club circuit at the time. Buddy's brother, Phil, a recording stalwart, took the vocals on 'Garbage Man Blues' and 'Mellow Down'.

DAMN RIGHT, I'VE GOT THE BLUES (Released 1991) *Tracks:* Damn Right, I've Got The Blues/ Where Is The Next One Coming From/ Five Long Years/ Mustang Sally/ There Is Something On Your Mind/ Early In The Morning/ Too Broke To Spend The Night/ Black Night/ Let Me Love You Baby/ Rememberin' Stevie. *Line-up:* Buddy Guy (guitar, vocals), Jeff Beck, Eric Clapton, Neil Hubbard, Mark Knopfler & John Porter (guitar), Greg Rzab (bass), Richie Hayward (drums), Mick Weaver (keyboards), Pete Wingfield (piano), Andrew Love & Wayne Jackson (horns). Producer: John Porter. In which Buddy Guy plays host to a party of white, predominantly British, blues wannabees and produces the kind of star-studded album that record companies love.

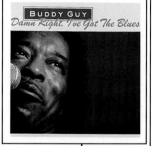

0 7 6 | 1 9 7 7 | 1 9 7 8 | 1 9 7 9 | 1 9 8 0 | 1 9 8 1 | 1 9 8 2 | 1 9 8 3 | 1 9 8 4 | 1 9 8 5 | 1 9 8 6 | 1 9 8 7 | 1 9 8 8 | 1 9 8 9 | 1 9 9 0 | 1 9 9 1 | 1 9 9 2 | 1 9 9 3

BREAKING OUT (Released 1980) *Tracks:* I Didn't Know My Mother Had A Son Like Me/ Have You Ever Been Lonesome/ She Winked Her Eye/ Boogie Family Style/ Break Out All Over You/ You Called Me In My Dreams/ Me And My Guitar/ You Can Make It If You Try/ Feeling Sexy. *Line-up:* Buddy Guy (guitar, vocals), Phil Guy & William McDonald (guitar), Jene Pickett (keyboards), Nick Charles (bass), Merle Perkiss (drums). Recorded in Chicago, in September 1980, this album represents a return to form in the studio, where Guy's confidence had been severely dented by a string of over-produced albums in the 1970s.

TEN BLUE FINGERS (Released 1985) *Tracks:* Girl You're Nice And Clean/ Garbage Man Blues/ Tell Me What's Inside Of You/ You Can Make It If You Try/ Have You Ever Been Lonesome/ She Winked Her Eye. *Line-up:* Buddy Guy (guitar, vocals), Phil Guy, Doug Williams, Little Phil Smith & William McDonald (guitar), Jene Pickett (keyboards), Mike Morrison, Nick Charles & J.W. Williams (bass), Merle Perkiss & Ray Allison (drums). No superstars on this album, just an honest reflection of one of the most flamboyant and emotional of recent blues artists in confident form. The kind of music you would have expected to hear in a club at the time.

BUDDY GUY & JUNIOR WELLS: ALONE & ACOUSTIC (Released 1991) *Tracks:* Give Me My Coat And Shoes/ Big Boat (Buddy And Junior's Thing)/ Sweet Black Girl/ Diggin' My Potatoes/ Don't Leave Me/ Rollin' And Tumblin'/ I'm In The Mood/ High Heel Sneakers/ Wrong Doin' Woman/ Cut You Loose/ Sally Mae/ Catfish Blues/ My Home's In The Delta/ Boogie Chillen/ Medley: Baby What You Want Me To Do and That's All Right. Recorded in Paris, France, in 1981, this revived a partnership that had started in the 1960s with some sides for the Vanguard label. With maturity the two men produce a sound that is more low-key, but at least as affecting.

FEELS LIKE RAIN (Released 1993) *Tracks:* She's A Superstar/ I Go Crazy/ Feels Like Rain/ She's Nineteen Years Old/ Some Kind Of Wonderful/ Sufferin' Mind/ Change In The Weather/ I Could Cry/ Mary Ann/ Trouble Man/ Country Man. *Line-up:* includes Buddy Guy (guitar, vocals), Bonnie Raitt (slide guitar), John Porter & Johnny Lee Schell (guitar), Greg Rzab (bass), Richie Hayward (drums), Mick Weaver (keyboards), Ian McLagan (piano), John Mayall (vocals, piano), Bill Payne (piano), Travis Tritt & Paul Rodgers (vocals). Producers: John Porter, with R.S. Field & Dave McNair. More stars, including John Mayall, the British guitarist who started the blues revival.

BLUE CITY (Released 1986) *Tracks:* Blue City Down/Elevation 13 Ft./Marianne/Nice Bike/Greenhouse/Billy And Annie/Pops & Timer/Tell Me Something Slick/Blue City/Don't Take Your Guns To Town/A Leader Of Men/Not Even Key West. Directed by Michelle Manning, *Blue City* demonstrated Cooder's ability to provide soundtracks for movies with contemporary themes. It followed contributions to another soundtrack *Alamo Bay* (1985), directed by Louis Malle, which also featured work by John Hiatt, Van Dyke Parks and Los Lobos. Unfortunately *Blue City* (the movie) sank without trace.

CROSSROADS (Released 1986) *Tracks:* Crossroads/Down In Mississippi/Cotton Needs Pickin'/Viola Lee Blues/See You In Hell, Blind Boy/Nitty Gritty Mississippi/He Made A Woman Out Of Me/Feelin' Bad Blues/Somebody's Callin' My Name/Willie Brown Blues/Walkin' Away Blues. Another soundtrack in the series Cooder provided for the movies of Walter Hill: apart from those featured here, he also wrote the *Southern Comfort* and *Streets of Fire* scores. As moody as ever, the score for *Crossroads* brought Cooder together with Sonny Terry, a living legend of blues harmonica, as well as his usual band of high-class session men.

WHY DON'T YOU TRY ME TONIGHT? (Released 1986) *Tracks:* How Can A Poor Man Stand Such Times And Live?/Available Space/Money Honey/Tattler/He'll Have To Go/Smack Dab In The Middle/Dark End Of The Street/Down In Hollywood/Little Sister/I Think It's Gonna Work Out Fine/(Every Woman I Know Is) Crazy 'Bout An Automobile/634-5789/Why Don't You Try Me Tonight? A 'Greatest Hits' compilation for a man who hasn't had one, it gives a very sketchy idea of Cooder's prodigious range. While few such albums get to grips with the basic details of an artist's career, this is notable for its omissions.

TRESPASS (Released 1993) Another Ry Cooder soundtrack for a Walter Hill movie. This one came four years after his *Johnny Handsome* score of 1989. Unfortunately, despite the habitual excellence of Cooder's music, this movie was at least as unsuccessful as that doomed Mickey Rourke/Ellen Barkin crime picture. Hill's particular forte, desperate people engaging in frenzied violence over a tasteful guitar-driven score, has fallen well out of fashion in Hollywood. The time may well have arrived for both parties to make a clean break if either is to remain within striking distance of a return to the (comparative) success they once enjoyed.

| 1986 | 1987 | 1988 | 1989 | 1990 | 1991 | 1992 | 1993 |

GET RHYTHM (Released 1987) *Tracks:* Get Rhythm/Low-Commotion/Going Back To Okinawa/13 Question Method/Women Will Rule The World/All Shook Up/I Can Tell By The Way You Smell/Across The Borderline/Let's Have A Ball. This had a strong backing band, including Flaco Jimenez (accordion), Steve Douglas (saxophone), Van Dyke Parks (keyboards), Jorge Calderon (bass), Buell Niedlinger (acoustic bass), Jim Keltner (drums), Miguel Cruz (percussion) and vocal contributions from Larry Blackmon of Cameo and Harry Dean Stanton. Possibly too trendy for Cooder purists, it didn't entirely convince.

SELECTED SESSIONS
- 1965 RISING SONS
- 1967 CAPTAIN BEEFHEART *Safe As Milk*
- 1968 CANDY *Original Soundtrack* VAN DYKE PARKS *Song Cycle*
- 1969 PHIL OCHS *Greatest Hits* PERFORMANCE *Original Soundtrack* ROLLING STONES *Let It Bleed*
- 1970 RANDY NEWMAN *12 Songs*
- 1971 ROLLING STONES *Sticky Fingers* LITTLE FEAT *Little Feat*
- 1972 NICKY HOPKINS *Jamming With Edward* RANDY NEWMAN *Sail Away*
- 1973 MARIA MULDAUR *Maria Muldaur*
- 1978 RODNEY CROWELL *Ain't Living Long Like This*
- 1981 ERIC CLAPTON *Another Ticket*
- 1983 T-BONE BURNETT *Proof Through The Night* ERIC CLAPTON *Money And Cigarettes*
- 1987 DUANE EDDY *Duane Eddy*
- 1991 JOHN LEE HOOKER *Mr Lucky*

LITTLE VILLAGE (Released 1992) *Tracks:* Solar Sex Panel/The Action/Inside Job/Big Love/Take Another Look/Do You Want My Job/Don't Go Away Mad/Fool Who Knows/She Runs Hot/Don't Think About Her When You're Trying To Drive/Don't Bug Me When I'm Working. A supergroup that never quite cohered, given the individuals concerned: Cooder (guitars), John Hiatt (rhythm guitar), Nick Lowe (bass) and Jim Keltner (drums). That the project failed to gel was partly due to the fact that each contributor – apart from ace sessioneer Keltner – was accustomed to running the show himself.

A MEETING BY THE RIVER (Released 1993) One of the most intriguing collaborations in recent years, between Cooder, who plays his customary bottleneck style, and Indian slide player VM Bhatt (playing 'mohan vina', a guitar which was built to his own specifications). The resulting sessions were unplanned and unrehearsed and make for one of the most breathtaking recorded events in Cooder's long career. Cooder's interest in all kinds of ethnic music remains unparalleled. He claims to be able to play any fretted instrument, whatever its cultural provenance.

ONNIE MCINTYRE

*Born: Owen McIntyre, September 25th 1945,
Lennoxtown, Strathclyde, Scotland.*

The Average White Band was formed in 1972 by bassist Alan Gorrie, who recruited Robbie McIntosh (drums), Mike Rosen (guitar/trumpet), Roger Ball (alto/baritone saxes), Malcolm Duncan (tenor/ soprano saxes) and guitarist McIntyre. Rosen didn't last long and his replacement was **Hamish Stuart**. First at the Lincoln Festival and then at The Rainbow in London, supporting **Eric Clapton**, the band generated sufficient interest to cut *Show Your Hand* (1973) for MCA, which included a tasty version of jazz-rock outfit The Crusaders' 'Put It Where You Want It'.

The death of McIntosh from a heroin overdose didn't do much for their confidence, but a trip to the US and a fresh contract with Atlantic saw them hitting their stride. *Average White Band* (1975), produced by Arif Mardin, was full of jagged, choppy riffs and proved that Scotsmen could be funky, as on 'Pick Up The Pieces', 'Work To Do' and 'You Got The Love'. *Cut The Cake* (1975) was equally incisive, with 'If I Ever Lose This Heaven' being another cool classic.

While later albums, including a collaboration with vocalist Ben E King on *Benny & Us* (1977), were better than most artists dream about, the band had set themselves such high standards that repetition was inevitable. Bit by bit the group disintegrated, and each member became a keenly sought-after session musician. They reformed in 1989, minus Stuart, for one further outing, *Aftershock*.

AL MCKAY

Born: February 2nd 1948, Louisiana, US.

One of the best funk bands of the 1970s, Earth Wind & Fire was the brainchild of former Chess session drummer Maurice White, and in 1972 McKay was brought into the group to replace Roland Battista. McKay's jazz influences were critical to the development of the group's sound: his staccato, choppy phrasing on songs like 'Serpentine Fire', 'After The Love Is Gone', 'Fantasy' and 'Let's Groove' counterbalanced the horn section that ducked and weaved through the percussive, rhythmic overlay provided by White and his bassist brother Verdine. While the band fitted the disco mood of the era, by the turn of the 1980s their pretentious lyrics and theatrical stage performances had become dated. In 1981 McKay left the group to play with jazzmen like Herbie Hancock and Deodato, and to work as a producer. The gap in EW&F was filled by the return of Battista, but White broke up the band in 1984.

JOHN MCLAUGHLIN

Born: January 4th 1942, Kirk Sandall, Yorkshire, England.

■ *Bogue double-neck; Gibson double-neck; Gibson Les Paul; Gibson ES345; Wechter acoustic; Gibson J200 custom.*

In the field of jazz-rock guitar playing, only **Larry Coryell**'s work with vibesman Gary Burton rivals the innovation of McLaughlin, whose influence has been much wider among fellow musicians. McLaughlin was the first to play tricky altered scales, stinging bent notes, and odd meters, all with the distorted tone of a solid electric guitar played at rock-music volume.

While McLaughlin's *Extrapolation* (1969) revealed an early interest in bebop and free jazz, his work with trumpeter Miles Davis on *In A Silent Way* (1969) and *Bitches Brew* (1970) and then with drummer Tony Williams on *Emergency* (1970) defined and paved the way for much of the jazz-rock fusion movement of the 1970s, established primarily through bands such as McLaughlin's own Mahavishnu Orchestra and keyboardist Chick Corea's Return To Forever.

That this movement encouraged a swathe of lesser guitarists to crank up the volume and let rip in 7/8, and that McLaughlin's *The Inner Mounting Flame* (1972) was high on technique but short on charm, does not ultimately detract from his considerable expertise.

His acoustic work on *Devotion* (1972) and *Shakti With John McLaughlin* (1976) enabled McLaughlin to combine the viciously rhythmic patterns of Eastern music with the more subtle and lyrical inflections of jazz. *Passion Grace & Fire* (1983) featuring McLaughlin, **Al Di Meola** and **Paco de Lucia** was further confirmation of his ability in absorbing styles and influences that did not naturally fall within his own immediate sphere, and he remains one of the most influential guitarists in contemporary music.

IAN MCNABB

Born: November 3rd 1962, Liverpool, England.

■ *Fender Telecaster; Gretsch White Falcon; Rickenbacker 12-string.*

Icicle Works have enjoyed a cult following ever since their formation in 1981 by McNabb, a highly underrated guitarist and songwriter whose sardonic wit and ironic detachment have made him a keen commentator. A string of singles down the years have seen the emphasis shift from the gentle subtlety of the group's early years – as on 'Birds Fly (Whisper To A Scream)' and 'Love Is A Wonderful Colour' – to the harder sound heard on 'Hollow Horse' and 'Understanding Jane'. In 1989 McNabb disbanded the original lineup and formed a new band, a temporary move as he embarked on a solo career in 1992.

JOHN MCNALLY

Born: August 30th 1941, Liverpool, England.

■ *Hofner Club; Fender Telecaster; Aria.*

With an almost identical pedigree to The Beatles, The Searchers were one of the more original Merseybeat bands of the early-1960s. While both groups shared an early affinity for obscure R&B material, the Beatles quickly developed the necessary songwriting skills that guaranteed longevity, whereas The Searchers could only extend their net to encompass work by lesser known contemporary American writers such as PF Sloan, Jack Nitzsche and Jackie De Shannon. Be that as it may, tight harmonies, McNally's driving lead and **Mike Pender**'s jangling rhythm guitar on 'Needles & Pins', 'Ain't Gonna Kiss Ya', 'Don't Throw Your Love Away', 'What Have They Done To The Rain?', 'When You Walk In The Room' and 'Take Me For What I'm Worth' had a notable influence on **Roger McGuinn** and others of his ilk. By 1967 The Searchers had become fixtures on the British cabaret circuit and, despite cutting the excellent *The Searchers* (1979) for the Sire label, they have remained there ever since.

BOB MCNETT

*Born: October 16th 1925,
Philadelphia, Pennsylvania, US.*

Originally formed by country singer Hank Williams as his backing group, The Drifting Cowboys had at their core steel guitarist **Don Helms** and guitarist McNett, and in 1949 the lineup was supplemented by fiddler Jerry Rivers and bassist Hillous Butram. These personnel remained with Williams until his death in 1953, after which the group joined singer Ray Price as The Cherokee Cowboys and played sessions for country artists such as Ferlin Husky, Carl Smith, Marty Robbins and **Hank Snow**. In 1977 the group started to tour on the strength of their previous association with Williams, and recorded *A Tribute To Hank Williams* (1980) among others, retiring in 1984.

TONY MCPHEE

*Born: Anthony S McPhee, March 22nd 1944,
Humberstone, Leicestershire, England.*

■ *Gibson SG Standard.*

Had it not been for diehard blues purists like McPhee, the British blues boom wouldn't have lasted the best part of 15 years. Most of the practitioners were limited to a few bars of **Elmore James**, but McPhee in The Groundhogs along with **Stan Webb** in Chicken Shack ensured that the blues was carried to all four corners of the British Isles. No venue was too small or too distant and they set about their task with the zeal of missionaries to leper colonies.

As a guitarist McPhee seemed to have a better technical grounding than most, ably demonstrated on The Groundhogs' *Split* (1971), and probably understood the finer points of the slide guitar better than many Delta bluesmen. But McPhee could never transmit the real feeling of the blues (*Blues Obituary* 1969) and his brief spell addressing topical issues (*Thank Christ For The Bomb* 1970) had little conviction. McPhee's work seems well meaning but a tad dull: a shame because he is a very good guitarist, as his collaborations with **Jo Ann Kelly** indicate, for example *Same Thing On Their Minds* 1971.

BLIND WILLIE MCTELL

*Born: May 5th 1901, Thomson, Georgia, US. Died: August
19th 1959, Milledgeville, Georgia, US.*

■ *Stella 12-string.*

The author of such gems as 'Statesboro Blues', later covered by **Taj Mahal** and The Allman Brothers, McTell shares few similarities with any other bluesman. Whether that's because he didn't come from Mississippi, Chicago or Texas is impossible to tell, but his distinct, almost pedantic, enunciation and the lyrical yet dense 12-string guitar work rendered him one of the most individual stylists of the 1930s. Like **Blind Willie Johnson** whom he worked with briefly, McTell's ability to sanctify secular material and infuse it with an other-worldliness seemed at odds with the wit and delicacy of his delivery. This facility remained intact until his final recordings (*Last Session* 1956) when the only indication of failing health was a lassitude in the vocal delivery.

RALPH MCTELL

Born: Ralph May, December 3rd 1944, Farnborough, Kent, England.

■ *Gibson J45.*

A leading folk singer in Britain in the late-1960s. McTell adopted his new surname from **Blind Willie McTell**. At first he was a purist who combined elements of blues and ragtime into his picking... but his second album *Spiral Staircase* (1969) included his song 'Streets Of London'. At the time it seemed sentimental and glib, but despite its formidable popularity with every MOR entertainer with a bleeding heart and every busker with an appalling grasp of chord structures, it has acquired a poignancy through the inability of successive British governments to combat or even apparently care about the rise of homelessness. In later years McTell became a staunch supporter of many causes, espousing liberal views with acerbic brevity, but his guitar playing retained its essential sophistication, despite his tendency to over-produce the most simple pieces. After years of primetime popularity on TV shows and on concert tours, he returned to his roots with a collection of blues and rags, *Blue Skies Black Heroes* (1988), that left no doubt about his prowess as a picker.

JOHNNY MEEKS

Born: US.

■ *Fender Stratocaster.*

Moving into the lineup of rock'n'roller Gene Vincent's group The Blue Caps as replacement for **Cliff Gallup** in 1957, Meeks proved himself an able contender. Unfortunately Vincent's erratic career was in the process of hitting one of its many troughs, and Meeks' recordings with the group were confined to songs such as 'Lotta Lovin' and 'Dance To The Bop'. He added chunky arpeggios, but made little attempt to emulate the flair of his predecessor. England beckoned and Vincent complied, breaking up the band in the process. Meeks' last known assignment was as an unexpected bassist in **Mike Nesmith**'s Second National Band in 1971.

BARRY MELTON

Born: 1947, New York, New York, US.

The fortunes of Country Joe & The Fish were indissolubly linked to the psychedelic era in which they operated – and as a result the perception of the group has through that association dated them irrevocably. This is unfortunate because Melton's lyrical, potent guitar work stands on its own merits, for example on 'Not So Sweet Martha Lorraine', 'Porpoise Mouth' and 'Bass Strings'. What proved to be the albatross for the group was the 'Fish Cheer': "Give me an F, give me a U... what's that spell?".

This rousing chorus became synonymous with disenchantment over the American view of global politics and the country's continued involvement in Viet-nam. Melton still plays with Country Joe occasionally, but has become part of Bay-area sub-culture, still working local clubs and bars, and he's best heard on the *Collected* Country Joe & The Fish compilation of recent years.

WENDY MELVOIN

Born: US.

■ *Rickenbacker 360.*

Lisa Coleman, daughter of session musician Gary Coleman, joined **Prince**'s group The Revolution as a keyboards player and vocalist in 1980. Wendy Melvoin, daughter of session musician Mike Melvoin, joined in 1983 as the replacement for guitarist Dez Dickerson (who'd played the fine solos on Prince's 'Little Red Corvette').

At first Coleman and Melvoin wrote together, contributing 'Mountains' to Prince's *Parade* (1986), but in 1986 they embarked upon a career as the duo Wendy & Lisa. Their eponymous debut of 1987 illustrated their growing confidence as instrumentalists, with Melvoin showing a knack (not surprisingly) for Prince-inspired figures, such as the solo on 'Waterfall'. *Side Show* (1988), *Fruit At The Bottom* (1989) and *Eroica* (1990) indicated their emergent identity as a unit apart from Prince. While still given to wild fluctuations, they lack the sparky spontaneity that would make them truly memorable.

MEMPHIS MINNIE

Born: Elizabeth Douglas, June 3rd 1897, Algiers, Louisiana, US. Died: August 6th 1973, Memphis, Tennessee, US.

Memphis Minnie's spare style echoes that of **Big Bill Broonzy**, and her neat, plain, virtuosic picking on 'Bumble Bee' with her husband Kansas Joe McCoy is as exciting as anything to emerge in the early-1930s. With her next husband Little Son Joe Lawlars she cut 'Boy Friend Blues', 'Nothing In Rambling' and 'Me & My Chauffeur Blues', chunky slices of urban blues that anticipated the Chicago style of **Muddy Waters** and **JB Lenoir**.

JOE MESSINA

Born: US.

■ *Fender Telecaster.*

The Motown house band of the 1960s shifted lineups, but the classic team comprised the supreme bassist James Jamerson, drummer Benny 'Papa Zita' Benjamin, keyboardist Earl Van Dyke and guitarists **Robert White** and Messina, each and every one a jazzman at heart who earned a living playing sessions. This band provided the real sound of Motown; shove any vocalist in front, be it The Supremes, Martha & the Vandellas, Marvin Gaye, The Temptations, whoever... and the sound would vary little. Great formulas will always bear repetition: these boys knew how to execute that formula, melding into a chugging, liquid backbeat that fell inch perfect.

PAT METHENY

Born: August 12th 1954, Lees Summit, Missouri, US.

■ *Gibson ES175; Roland GR300; Ibanez custom.*

Since his emergence in the mid-1970s Metheny has become the archetypal guitar hero of new age, fusion and jazz. Though there is a rare delicacy to his acoustic and electric improvisations, influenced mainly by **Wes Montgomery** and **Jim Hall**, his dalliances with avant-garde musicians such as hornman Ornette Coleman (*Song X* 1986) and keyboardist Paul Bley have a brutal ferocity. He has attracted a cult following among part of the rock audience, struck by his accessibility and thoughtful, introspective soloing.

At the heart of Metheny's own albums, such as *As Falls Wichita So Falls Wichita Falls* (1981), the live *Travels* (1983) and *Secret Story* (1992), is an essentially acoustic feel wrapped in the dynamics of the electric guitar. Metheny has taken the instrument even further in his experiments with guitar synthesizers, primarily the digital Synclavier.

But his experimentation has never appeared to become an end in itself, and Metheny is one of the few jazz musicians to play comfortably with those more often associated with rock: witness his superb contribution along with bassist Jaco Pastorius to **Joni Mitchell**'s live *Shadows & Light* (1980), and his work on David Bowie's 'This Is Not America' (1985).

VLADIMIR MIKULKA

Born: December 11th 1950, Praha, Czech Republic.

■ *Fleta.*

A talented classical guitarist, Mikulka came to prominince in the late-1960s while still a teenager, winning a prestigious French international guitar competition, and has since toured and recorded widely. While he has recorded the apparently obligatory Bach and Rodrigo pieces, he is best known for popularizing eastern European composers of guitar music, including the demanding output of the Ukrainian player/composer Stepan Rak, heard on Mikulka albums such as *European Guitar Premieres* and *Music Of Stepan Rak*.

JOHN MILES

Born: April 23rd 1949, Jarrow, Tyne & Wear, England.

■ *Gibson Les Paul; Pack Leader; Gibson SG; Fender Stratocaster.*

After local success in north-east England, Miles moved to London in the mid-1970s and hit the charts with the epic 'Music' (included on *Rebel* 1976), featuring Miles' strident guitar work and a clever, dynamic arrangement. Miles has continued to make records but has never recaptured the power and scope of that one piece. More recently he has been a regular member of singer Tina Turner's band.

DOMINIC MILLER

Born: 1961, Buenos Aires, Argentina.

■ **Fernandes Strat-style; Gibson Les Paul; Ovation; Rodriguez.**

An accomplished player who grew up in Wisconsin, US, and is now based in Britain, Miller came to prominence as a member of World Party in 1986, since when as a session player he has contributed thoughtful electric and acoustic guitar work to records by Julia Fordham (*Porcelain* 1989) and Phil Collins (*But Seriously* 1989) among others. More recently he joined Sting's touring band after recording the ex-Police vocalist's *Soul Cages* (1991).

JERRY MILLER

Born: July 10th 1943, Tacoma, Washington, US.

Psychedelic group Moby Grape included three guitarists, lead player Miller, rhythm guitarist **Skip Spence** and finger-picker **Peter Lewis**, and echoed the close harmony vocals and melodic guitar work of The Byrds. Their debut *Moby Grape* (1967) was one of the strongest of the year, with Miller's lead on 'Omaha' and '8.05' standing out. Their follow-up *Wow* (1968) included (only in the US) a bonus album, *Grape Jam*, with **Mike Bloomfield** and **Al Kooper**. After such a fine start the group became increasingly erratic, with *Grape 69* and *Truly Fine Citizen* (1970) lacking the input of Spence who had departed for a solo career. Throughout the 1970s and 1980s they reformed periodically, but nothing to date has managed to match their fine early offerings.

STEVE MILLER

Born: October 5th 1943, Milwaukee, Wisconsin, US.

■ **Ibanez Artist; Fender Stratocaster; Gibson Les Paul; Steinberger.**

The Steve Miller Band's durability is testimony to Miller's autocratic definition of his band's style – meaning that there has been little appreciable difference in the group's style since the early-1970s when it played host to hordes of musicians of different persuasions.

The Miller Band's debut *Children Of The Future* (1968), including the bluesy 'Sittin In Circles', had Glyn Johns producing and made sterling use of studio technology, but signally failed to recapture the spirit of *At The Fillmore* (1967) where they backed Chuck Berry. It was one of those great retro albums, warts and all, where a bunch of star-struck ingenues – in this case the Steve Miller Blues Band – flexed their muscles with a veteran. What it lacked in muscle it made up for with heart.

The smooth productions of *Sailor* (1969), *Brave New World* (1969) and *Your Saving Grace* (1970) detracted from their immediacy, although highpoints were many. Later albums confirmed the initial prognosis that Miller's destiny was FM radio: the

results were anonymous and tuneful, if ultimately dull, although he created enjoyably memorable guitar moments in his best known pieces 'Fly Like An Eagle' (1976) and 'The Joker' (1973). Miller still issues albums and tours regularly, most recently cutting *Wide River* (1993), so he must be doing something right.

JUNE MILLINGTON

Born: 1949, Manila, Luzon, Philippines.

■ **Gibson Les Paul.**

Fanny were one of the first all-female rock bands. Richard Perry's accessible productions tried in vain to cover up the absence of strong material, but albums like *Charity Ball* (1971) and *Fanny Hill* (1972) were the best of an uneven career which ground to a halt in 1975. June cut *Millington* (1977) with her bassist sister Jean, and still plays on sessions.

JONI MITCHELL

Born: Roberta Joan Anderson, November 7th 1943, Fort McLeod, Alberta, Canada.

■ **Martin; Ibanez George Benson; Klein.**

The singer-songwriter era of the late-1960s brought forth some crepuscular creatures who had half an idea, and then bored everyone rigid for the next ten years as they extended the same idea. Mitchell, however, emerged simultaneously and was singular in her inspired use of language, her direct, supportive guitar style, and her keen ability in arranging her songs. It could be said that she was unerringly tasteful, but that smacks of a backhanded compliment. Her music is, like her paintings, expressionistic and seldom governed by arcane precepts such as 'correct' or 'incorrect', enabling her to delve into a range of styles with conviction.

While her albums often developed thematically, she always managed to avoid pastiche by treating the recording studio or the concert hall as a confessional of sorts. Drawing from a coterie of musicians such as drummers Jim Keltner and Russ Kunkel, guitarists **Stephen Stills** and **Sneaky Pete Kleinow**, and singer James Taylor, her best early albums, *Songs For A Seagull* (1968) and *Blue* (1971) were largely acoustic, with Mitchell accompanying herself primarily on piano or open-tuned guitar.

By 1974 she had started to use jazz musicians like hornman Tom Scott, bassist Wilton Felder, drummer John Guerin, pianist Joe Sample, and guitarists **Robben Ford** and **Larry Carlton**, who gave the superb *Court & Spark* (1974), the live *Miles Of Aisles* (1974) and *Hejira* (1976) a light and airy quality, despite the introspective lyrics.

As the 1970s closed Mitchell composed lyrics for pieces written by jazz bassist/composer Charles Mingus, who was dying from Gehrig's disease, but unfortunately Mingus didn't survive to hear the fruits of her efforts. *Mingus* (1979) had support from the electrifying bassist Jaco Pastorius, after which she teamed with **Pat Metheny** for the live *Shadows & Light* (1980). Throughout the 1980s albums such as *Dog Eat Dog* (1985), *Chalk Mark In A Rainstorm*

(1988) and *Night Ride Home* (1991) reflected Mitchell's concerns with global issues.

MIKE MITCHELL

Born: US.

Mitchell was the axeman in the middle of one of rock's great non-anthems, 'Louie, Louie'. Was this the riff that launched a thousand bands? Could be. Doesn't matter: this trashy, relentless original version by The Kingsmen is the one to go for.

GARY MOFFETT

Born: June 22nd 1949, Montreal, Quebec, Canada.

April Wine were formed in Montreal in 1969. While Moffett is efficient, he cannot disguise the ultimate drawback that his band sounds like any number of other hard-rock outfits. However, *Live At El Macambo* (1977) possesses a certain raw enthusiasm.

CHIPS MOMAN

Born: Lincoln Moman, 1936, La Grange, Georgia, US.

A producer of impeccable credentials, Moman has worked with Elvis Presley, Waylon Jennings, **Willie Nelson**, Aretha Franklin and **Bobby Womack**, among others. Although his principal impact has been as a producer, it is well worth noting his fine guitar work for Aretha Franklin on 'I Never Loved A Man (The Way I Love You)' and 'Do Right Woman, Do Right Man', and for Wilson Pickett on 'Funky Broadway', 'Land Of A Thousand Dances', 'Mustang Sally', 'Everybody Needs Somebody to Love' and the revival of The Falcons' hit 'I Found A Love'.

CHARLIE MONROE

Born: July 4th 1903, Rosine, Kentucky, US. Died: September 27th 1975, Reidsville, North Carolina, US.

While not exerting so great an influence on the development of bluegrass as his younger brother, mandolinist Bill Monroe, Charlie and his group The Kentucky Pardners were a capable and entertaining hillbilly outfit.

Charlie's career started when he joined the *National Barn Dance* radio show in Chicago, forming The Kentucky Pardners in 1938. While he spent most of the time trying to find a mandolinist of his brother's quality – and there were a string of players including Curly Seckler, Ira Louvin and Red Rector who passed through the group's ranks – they remained essentially a hillbilly outfit whose best known songs were 'Rose Conley' and 'Bringing In The Georgia Mail'. Monroe retired in the mid-1950s.

WES MONTGOMERY

Born: John Leslie Montgomery, March 6th 1925, Indianapolis, Indiana, US. Died: June 15th 1968, Indianapolis, Indiana, US.

■ **Gibson L5CES.**

Montgomery had a phenomenal ability to create lucid, melodic single-string runs with his distinctive thumb-picking style, wrapped in a sound and timbre of such startling clarity and presence that, through his recordings, he continues to be one of the most accessible and popular players for rock guitarists keen to investigate jazz for the first time.

Montgomery was self-taught and played in groups with his brothers Buddy and Monk before joining the Lionel Hampton band. In 1959 Wes was signed by producer Orrin Keepnews to the Riverside label. Albums like *The Wes Montgomery Trio* (1959), *The Incredible Jazz Guitar Of* (1960), which really does live up to its title, and the live *Full House* (1962) illustrate Montgomery at his most inspired.

Later, Montgomery moved to Verve, signed by Creed Taylor, where he cut the memorable *Jimmy & Wes* (1966) with organist Jimmy Smith. While these albums for Verve were larded with strings and choruses, it didn't affect the impact of his style on virtually every jazz guitarist of note, including **George Benson**, **BB King**, **Ronny Jordan**, **John Scofield** and **Herb Ellis**.

After leaving Verve, Montgomery joined A&M and cut albums consisting largely of covers of standard pop material, such as Beatles tunes, anticipating George Benson's comparable excursions in the 1970s and 1980s. Although Montgomery died early, his legacy, like that of **Charlie Christian**'s, lies as much in the careers of those who took up the guitar as a result of hearing his records as it does in the surviving recordings, many of which are timeless.

CARLOS MONTOYA

Born: December 13th 1903, Madrid, Spain. Died: March 3rd 1993, Wainscott, New York, US.

■ *Arcangel Fernandez; Barbero.*

Montoya seldom played in Spain after the 1940s, but he remained one of the most spirited exponents of flamenco until his death.

In the 1950s he made significant changes to the way in which flamenco was presented by dispensing with the singers and dancers, elevating the guitar to the role of sole protagonist. After that the transition from bar or restaurant – the traditional preserve of flamenco – to the concert platform was relatively simple. This enabled Montoya to make drastic changes to the performance of flamenco, for example recording *Suite Flamenco* (1966) with St Louis symphony orchestra.

Into the 1970s, Montoya assimilated indigenous US forms such as folk, blues, jazz and country into his style. This anticipated the rise of 'new flamenco' where young bands such as Ketama and Pata Negra adopted some of the characteristics of salsa and other non-flamenco music. In his later years Montoya never played in Spain: he reasoned that all concerts had to be arranged through the Ministry of Culture and he had no time for bureaucracy.

RONNIE MONTROSE

Born: November 29th 1947, Colorado, US.

■ *Strat-style custom.*

There must be few putative heavy metal guitarists who came to prominence sessioning for Van

Morrison, but such is Montrose – although admittedly, it was the input of producer Ted Templeman that caused him to be used on the *Tupelo Honey* (1971) sessions.

Be that as it may, it gave Montrose sufficient credentials to join The Edgar Winter Group and play on the influential *They Only Come Out At Night* (1973).

Produced by **Rick Derringer**, it isolated the kitsch factor in heavy metal. With the band on the cover in full make-up, *Night* featured 'Frankenstein' and 'Free Ride' with Montrose cranking out riffs of quite remarkable density, while Derringer's production was both crass and sophisticated (and Jim Steinman must surely have taken a few hints for Meatloaf's later *Bat Out Of Hell*). Montrose, believing he had invented heavy metal, started his own band Montrose, with vocalist Sammy Hagar, cutting their eponymous debut in 1973 that is still viewed as a landmark metal album.

But when Hagar left in 1975, the band foundered and Ronnie went solo in 1976, with *Mean* (1986) his best effort so far.

MICKY MOODY

Born: August 30th 1950, Middlesbrough, Cleveland, England.

■ *Gibson Les Paul.*

Formerly with bands such as Zoot Money's, Juicy Lucy (he played lead guitar on their version of Bo Diddley's 'Who Do You Love') and Snafu, Moody edged closer to the big league of heavy metal guitarists when he co-founded Whitesnake with David Coverdale in 1976. While Coverdale's bluesy, histrionic vocals often distracted attention from the quality of musicianship in the rest of the band, Moody and **Bernie Marsden** were able partners both for Coverdale and one another.

Complementing Marsden's capacity to riff endlessly, Moody's propensity for squeezing out as many notes per second was coupled with a keener ear for structure than most, as on 'Long Way From Home', 'Fool For Your Loving', Bobby Bland's 'Ain't No Love In The Heart Of The City' and 'Don't Break My Heart'. After leaving Whitesnake, Moody co-wrote with songwriter Bob Young a pithy glossary of rock'n'roll terms, and recently has been playing again with Marsden in The Moody Marsden Band.

RALPH MOONEY

Born: US.

■ *Fender 1000.*

At first Mooney was pedal-steel guitarist in the band of country singer-songwriter Wynn Stewart, an early exponent of the Bakersfield sound, before moving on to contribute wonderfully strident steel to Buck Owens' Buckaroos. Mooney's style owed much to old-timers like **Joe Maphis** but was also informed by rock'n'roll, and his picking and sparring with **Don Rich** on Owens titles like 'Under Your Spell Again', 'Foolin Around' and 'Under The Influence Of Love' provided the template for Owens' refinement of the Bakersfield style. After leaving Owens in 1963

(replaced by **Tom Brumley**) Mooney played on many of country singer Merle Haggard's hits (including 'Swinging Doors'), and then played sessions before joining singer **Waylon Jennings'** outfit The Waylors.

Mooney's association contributed to Jennings' general preeminence as one of the most enduring of all country artists.

GARY MOORE

Born: April 4th 1954, Belfast, Northern Ireland.

■ *Gibson Les Paul Standard; Fender Stratocaster.*

Despite having started his career as a heavy blues-rock guitarist, Moore's style has become progressively more authentic in its attempt to get to grips with the essence of Chicago-style blues.

Initially influenced by **Eric Clapton** on **John Mayall**'s *Blues Breakers* album, Moore joined Skid Row in 1970 where he first met bassist/vocalist Phil Lynott. After leaving Skid Row, Moore briefly joined Lynott's group Thin Lizzy, showing his mettle on 'Still In Love With You' on *Nightlife* (1974). But Moore didn't stay long as he was encouraged to join Jon Hiseman's Colosseum for a spell in the mid-1970s.

In 1978 Moore cut *Back On The Streets* with Lynott helping out on vocals, and the album included 'Parisienne Walkways' which featured a tough, lyrical solo that set Moore apart from the profusion of metal heads: the style and panache were more reminiscent of **Carlos Santana** than **Ritchie Blackmore**.

Throughout the 1980s Moore chopped and changed from solo career to sideman and back again, until in 1990 he cut *Still Got The Blues* which illustrated his ability to adapt to a variety of styles, and seemed to mark a welcome end to his dalliance with note-splitting pyrotechnics.

OSCAR MOORE

Born: Oscar Frederic Moore, December 15th 1912, Austin, Texas, US. Died: October 8th 1981, Las Vegas, Nevada, US.

■ *Stromberg; Gibson.*

From 1937 Moore earned wide acclaim for his relaxed, against-the-beat solos and rich, imaginative chord work in the Nat 'King' Cole Trio, making him the first electric guitar player in a contemporary piano/bass/guitar combo. The trio signed to Capitol in 1942 and the success that followed did much to popularize the newly emerging electric instrument, with Moore a trailblazer: from 1945 until 1948 he was rated as the country's leading guitarist by the readers of *Down Beat* magazine. Highlights of his work with Cole include 'Sweet Lorraine', 'Straighten Up And Fly Right', 'Honeysuckle Rose', 'Early Morning Blues', 'This Will Make You Laugh', 'Route 66', 'It's Only A Paper Moon', and 'This Side Up'. Moore is heard on the bulk of Capitol's excellent *Best Of The Nat King Cole Trio* (1992).

After leaving Cole in 1949 Moore worked with his brother, singer Johnny Moore (soon to join The Drifters), in The Three Blazers with pianist/vocalist Charles Brown, before cutting a number of instrumental pop albums in the late-1950s. Moore went on to play sessions in Los Angeles and played support in Las Vegas on the all too familiar gravy train.

SCOTTY MOORE

Born: Winfield Scott Moore, December 27th 1931, Gadsden, Tennessee, US.

■ **Gibson Super 400CES; Gibson ES295.**

When producer Sam Phillips teamed Elvis Presley with bassist Bill Black and guitarist Moore in the mid-1950s he must have had little conception of the impact upon popular music that would occur as a result of this apparently innocuous decision. Quite apart from the effect that Presley had on youth culture, Moore's cracking rockabilly guitar work has influenced generations of rock'n'roll guitarists.

Initially a member of Doug Poindexter's Starlite Wranglers with Bill Black, Moore was lured to the Sun label by Phillips in 1954. After working on the first Presley sessions, Moore became Presley's first manager and organized all his club bookings until Memphis DJ Bob Neal took over in early-1955. The same year, drummer DJ Fontana was brought in to the group and, with Moore and Black (who both stopped touring with Presley in 1957 because of the atrocious wages), backed Presley on his records until 1958. Some of the best rock'n'roll records of all time were cut during those years, including 'Good Rockin' Tonight', 'That's Alright Mama', 'Baby Let's Play House', 'Mystery Train', 'Don't Be Cruel', 'Heartbreak Hotel' and 'Jailhouse Rock', and Moore's guitar plays a central role. Essential listening is Presley's *The Sun Sessions CD* (1987).

Moore played again on occasions with Presley – the last time was on the famous comeback TV special in 1968 when Elvis commandeered Scotty's Gibson Super 400. Moore has also played a few sessions, but more recently has become concerned with production and other studio-related areas of the business.

THURSTON MOORE

Born: US.

■ **Fender Jazzmaster.**

Moore was a founder member of the highly influential New York-based new wave band Sonic Youth, formed in 1981 after Moore and fellow guitarist Lee Ranaldo had been recruited to perform and record **Glenn Branca**'s second and third symphonies for massed guitars.

Throughout the 1980s the group built their reputation with a series of polished and inventive albums that echoed a more refined version of The Jesus & Mary Chain and of The Velvet Underground in their 'Sister Ray' guise. While Sonic Youth had a propensity for such unpromising themes as the Charles Manson murders, Moore and Ranaldo's playing was based on altered tunings, 'prepared' guitars, and noise-for-its-own-sake. Enormous riffs, such as 'Cotton Crown' (*Sister* 1987), underpin their ability to build strong tunes into a discordant setting, like 'Shadow Of A Doubt'.

Daydream Nation (1988), a double album, was altogether more expansive, user friendly and ultimately danceable. In 1990 Sonic Youth signed with Geffen, cutting *Goo*, which was followed by *Dirty* (1992). Produced by Butch Vig, who's also worked with Nirvana, it included a vitriolic attack on ex-president George Bush, 'Youth Against Fascism', and a trenchant epic on sexual harassment by bassist Kim Gordon, 'Swimsuit Issue'. They remain one of the few power outfits with a healthy attitude to guitar experimentation.

JORGE MOREL

Born: Jorge Scibona, May 9th 1931, Buenos Aires, Argentina.

■ **Hopf.**

Morel studied at the University of Buenos Aires under Argentinian guitarist/composer Pablo Escobar, and soon began to develop his own style and his own compositions that reflect the music of South America. Morel also transcribed to guitar the work of popular composers like Leonard Bernstein and Lennon & McCartney, and in the early-1960s Morel began to absorb jazz influences into his playing when he settled in New York, where he continues to live. This has led to a fascinating blend of classical, Latin and jazz that add up to Morel's individual style, best heard on recodings like *Virtuoso South American Guitar*, *Latin Impressions*, and *The Art Of*.

STERLING MORRISON

Born: August 29th 1941, Long Island, New York, US.

■ **Fender Jaguar; Fender Electric XII; Gibson ES335; Gibson SG; Vox.**

When The Velvet Underground regrouped in 1993 for a series of gigs and concerts, **Lou Reed** and late lamented vocalist Nico were the two icons from the original lineup that every fan could immediately remember from the past. The names of the other members of the group were less familiar to the uninitiated: John Cale, drummer Maureen Tucker and guitarist Morrison.

Morrison had spent his years out of the music industry pursuing various occupations, including teaching and sailing. During The Velvet Underground's time (effectively 1966-1972) Reed was good at feedback, while Morrison was the principal axeman, providing the rhythmic pulse that gave songs like 'All Tomorrow's Parties', 'Waiting For The Man', 'White Light, White Heat', 'Sweet Jane' and 'Rock'n'Roll' their vicarious appeal. While Morrison was quite able to adopt some of Reed's more obtuse practices, such as the atonal jangling on 'Venus In Furs', he was informed by the R&B of **Chuck Berry**, **Muddy Waters** and **Jimmy Reed**. In the 1990s, after years of cult worship from every British or American indie band worth their salt, the Velvets resolved their differences and regrouped.

STEVE MORSE

Born: July 28th 1954, Hamilton, Ohio, US.

■ **Music Man 'signature'; Fender Telecaster; Nova.**

Little known beyond the US, Morse has developed a reputation among fellow guitarists for his seamless technique and his versatile, melodic feel.

Morse started his career in The Dixie Dregs in the early-1970s, playing a brand of southern boogie in the style of The Allman Brothers Band and The Marshall Tucker Band. In common with **Toy Caldwell** of Marshall Tucker, Morse was influenced by country and jazz, as well as R&B, and this led to him learning the banjo and pedal-steel guitar.

In 1982 the band renamed themselves The Dregs and released *Industry Standard*, with Morse fusing elements of metal, jazz-rock, country and blues. Despite the emphasis on technique, the addition of Santana's vocalist Alex Ligertwood, **Pat Simmons** and **Steve Howe** on a few tracks imbued it with a spirit of immediacy.

Although Morse is so highly rated, and despite solo records like *High Tension Wires* (1989), he has never appeared to harness his talents and, as a result, has had to rely on session work with groups like Kansas.

WAYNE MOSS

Born: Charleston, West Virginia, US.

After joining a variety of R&B groups in the early-1960s, Moss spent two years playing in pop singer Brenda Lee's backing group before joining The Escorts, which included Charlie McCoy (harmonica) and Kenny Buttrey (drums). When that group disbanded Moss became one of Nashville's top session men and joined the house band at the Monument label which came to be known as The Music City Five.

In 1969 Moss co-founded Area Code 615 (615 is the Nashville telephone code) with McCoy, Buttrey and other session musicians such as **Mac Gayden**, keyboardist Bobby Thompson, **Weldon Myrick**, bassist Norbert Putnam, pianist Ken Lauber and fiddler Buddy Spicher, most of whom had played on Bob Dylan's *Nashville Skyline* (1969) and had consequently given country music a veneer of topicality.

Area Code 615 (1969) featured a fine selection of country instrumentals, all executed with consummate skill, as did the follow-up *Trip In The Country* (1970) which featured 'Stone Fox Chase', used for some time as the theme from BBC TV's music magazine show *The Old Grey Whistle Test*. The group broke up in 1971, with Moss forming Barefoot Jerry with keyboardist John Harris, pedal-steel man Russ Hicks and drummer Kenny Malone. Throughout the 1970s Barefoot Jerry recorded efficient rather than earth-shattering records for a string of labels, but with little commercial success.

Moss remains a top session guitarist/bassist working in Nashville and runs his own studio, Cinderella.

BOB MOULD

Born: US.

■ **Fender Stratocaster; Ibanez Flying V-style.**

The hardcore thrash of Hüsker Dü on albums like *New Day Rising* (1985) was driven by Mould's guitar, and gave him the unsought role of mentor to a generation of Seattle bands like Smashing Pumpkins, Nirvana and Pearl Jam, among others.

After the break-up of Hüsker Dü and Mould's subsequent solo albums *Black Sheets Of Rain* (1990) and *Workbook* (1991), he formed Sugar. The debut *Copper Blue* (1992) was a departure from the bleakness of the two solos, using a combination of effects to create a brisk, buoyant collection of songs: 'A Good Idea' echoed the early years of Talking Heads, with staccato, jagged chords, while the psychedelic 'Hoover Dam' used elaborate layers of overdubs from treated guitars. But the glossy sheen doesn't disguise the heart of gold.

GEOFF MULDAUR

Born: 1945, New York, New York, US.

In the early-1960s the folk revival boom initiated by **Woody Guthrie** and furthered by The New Lost City Ramblers, The Weavers and Pete Seeger caused a spate of revival groups such as The Jim Kweskin Jug Band, this last including guitarists Muldaur and **Amos Garrett**. Rather than presenting folk as an anodyne singalong, they used authentic instrumentation and hung as close as possible to the original vocal inflections. Employing elements of blues and ragtime, Muldaur and Garrett brought a freshness and vitality to traditional folk music that had been in danger of disappearing from an increasingly lifeless scene.

After leaving Kweskin, Muldaur became a regular on the New York folk club circuit and married Maria d'Amato. His best work appeared in duet form with Maria on a brace of albums, *Pottery Pie* (1969) and *Sweet Potatoes* (1972). Sophisticated and charming, both musicians shone and complemented one another, Maria's voice taking on a variety of hues, and Geoff's flat-top picking running the gamut of stylistic variations from blues through to rock and back again.

After a stint with Paul Butterfield's group Better Days, Muldaur and Garrett started to record albums of acoustic duets for Flying Fish, including *Blues Boy* (1979) among others. Like Garrett, Muldaur impresses most because he gives the impression that he isn't playing the guitar as if he's working from a text-book and has just remembered an impressive solo that he thinks he can replicate.

JIM MULLEN

Born: November 26th 1945, Glasgow, Scotland.

■ *Fender Telecaster.*

The Morrissey-Mullen band was formed in the late-1970s by hornman Dick Morrissey and Mullen, proving to all the wayward punks and musos that jazz wasn't just for duffle-coated art-school lecturers in search of their lost youth. Mullen picks mainly with his right thumb – reminiscent of **Wes Montgomery** – in a fine jazz/blues style.

Both Mullen and Morrissey had been through a variety of bands, finding little success other than on the session circuit where both were constantly in demand. With the growing awareness of jazz and an expanding club circuit, Morrissey-Mullen were

signed to EMI where they cut a couple of albums that would today probably be dubbed acid-jazz. Back then, however, they couldn't give them away.

By the early-1980s, their brand of post-bop had given them a reputation with hep-cats everywhere, and a string of singles ('Badness', 'One Step', 'Stay Awhile' and 'Bladerunner') and albums (*Life On The Wire* 1982 and *It's About Time* 1983) gave them an unexpected bankability – which among purists was A Bad Thing because the band had the nerve to assume mass market potential. The immediacy and vitality of their style was light years away from the academicism of the avant-garde or the old-school preoccupation with traditional jazz that had always plagued the British jazz scene. Morrisey-Mullen were neither, and the interplay between the two principals showed that years of listening to Lester Young and **Charlie Christian** had not been wasted.

ALAN MUNDE

Born: US.

A distinguished bluegrass guitarist and banjoist, Munde started playing with Jimmy Martin's Sunny Mountain Boys in the late-1950s. During the 1970s, he was a central figure on the West Coast bluegrass circuit, playing with The Flying Burrito Brothers, fiddler Byron Berline, and Country Gazette. Still active on the session circuit, Munde's varied style is best demonstrated on the Burritos' *Live In Amsterdam* (1972).

ALAN MURPHY

Born: 1954, London, England. Died: October 19th 1989, London, England.

■ *Fender Stratocaster; Aria Esprit; Gibson ES335; Giffin Strat-style.*

Murphy was a talented session player whose best known work was with Go West and Kate Bush. The mid-1980s records of jazzy pop outfit Go West – albums like *Bangs And Crashes* (1985) and hit singles such as 'We Close Our Eyes' – were awash with Murphy's melodic, singing guitars, while his work with Bush included 'Violin' from *Never for Ever* (1980) and 'Waking The Witch' on *Hounds Of Love* (1985).

In 1988 Murphy joined the funk/jazz/pop group Level 42 alongside bassist Mark King, playing international tours and helping to 'lift' the recordings already down for *Staring At The Sun* (1988). But after 18 months with the group, Murphy died after complications related to the AIDS virus, aged just 35. **Mike Rutherford**, who had used Murphy for his Mike & The Mechanics project, said at the time, "All the musicians knew about Alan, but I think the saddest thing about his death was that the public were just beginning to recognize him."

JOAQUIN MURPHY

Born: Earl Murphy.

While Bob Wills is widely regarded as being the most significant contributor to the evolution of western swing, Spade Cooley did much to popularize – and

emasculate – the style, by adding lush string arrangements in place of the more feisty horn sections. His band, sometimes containing as many as 20 members, proved to be a useful training ground for young and ambitious musicians such as steel guitarists Murphy and **Speedy West**.

Murphy had started his career as a jazz guitarist before linking up with Andy Parker in The Plainsmen. After leaving Parker, Murphy joined Cooley's western swing orchestra, appearing spectacularly on his own showpiece, 'Oklahoma Stomp', and, among others, 'Shame On You' with vocalist Tex Williams. When Williams formed his own outfit, Western Caravan, Murphy went along for the ride, playing on Williams' biggest hits such as 'Smoke! Smoke! Smoke (That Cigarette)!', 'Don't Telephone, Don't Telegraph, Tell A Woman' and 'Bluebird On Your Windowsill'. Although Williams' records were over-arranged, as usual Murphy's incisive lines cut through everything with piercing clarity.

DAVE MURRAY

Born: December 23rd 1958, London, England.

■ *Fender Stratocaster; ESP.*

It has always seemed somewhat peculiar that heavy metal bands associate themselves, by name, with either satanic rites or the blacker side of human nature. Whether this is to seek some sort of identification in the minds of their audience with **Jimmy Page**, whose alleged interest in the occult was the subject of many extraordinary stories, is difficult to establish. Iron Maiden are a case in point – their name derives from a medieval instrument of torture. So while Maiden formed an integral part of what was given the unwieldy title of 'new wave of British heavy metal', there remains an anachronistic image of hordes of youths involved in arcane rituals. Not very salubrious.

Murray for his part has the felicitous knack of being able to wring out squillions of notes at an alarmingly fast rate ('The Number Of The Beast' and 'Flight Of Icarus') and to string together appropriate power riffs ('Run For The Hills', 'Running Free' and 'Bring Your Daughter To The Slaughter'), which is, after all, exactly what he's supposed to do. Maiden are very entertaining live, if only for all the posturing.

WELDON MYRICK

Born: 1938, Jayton, Texas, US.

■ *Emmons.*

There are few things that can be stated with absolute certainty, but those who attempt to become session musicians in Nashville had better be several notches above the average player, otherwise they won't work. Myrick became steel guitarist with fellow sessioneers Area Code 615 in 1969. The lineup included some of Nashville's finest, including **Wayne Moss** and **Mac Gayden**. Myrick, along with most of 615, had played on Bob Dylan's *Nashville Skyline* (1969), and when the 615ers broke up in 1971 Myrick continued to notch up Nashville sessions.

KING BENNY NAWAHI

Born: Hawaii, US.

■ National resonator.

Hawaiian guitarist Nawahi was a formative influence during the 1920s on steel guitarists. Unlike **Sol Hoopii** who was inclined to use his skill as a novelty, Nawahi played traditional Hawaiian hulas as well as jazz and blues, which encouraged **Jimmie Rodgers** to use a steel guitarist (Joe Kaipo) in his group.

BILL NELSON

Born: December 18th 1948, Wakefield, Yorkshire, England.

■ Yamaha SG2000; Veillette-Citron; Gibson ES345.

Influenced by **Jimi Hendrix**, Nelson in Be Bop De-Luxe became one of the most technically accomplished guitarists of the early-1970s. While his material sometimes lacked the spark of originality that separates the wheat from the chaff, he cut a number of impressive titles including 'Maid In Heaven' and 'Ships In The Night'.

By the time the punk era had arrived, Be-Bop's brand of futuristic heavy metal sounded dangerously out of sync. After disbanding the group Nelson formed Red Noise, before starting a solo career which eventually yielded *Quit Dreaming And Get On The Beam* (1981). Pleasant though it was, his vocals lacked authority and his guitar work had little emotional commitment, despite its effectiveness. *Das Kabinett* (1981) was inspired by the silent movie *The Cabinet Of Dr Caligari*. This suggested that Nelson might be better off cutting ambient music or soundtracks, and indeed his more recent largely homegrown output has moved in this direction, tending to push the guitar into a supportive and unremarkable role.

DAVID NELSON

Born: San Francisco, California, US.

Nelson was a founder member of The New Riders Of The Purple Sage with Grateful Dead guitarist **Jerry Garcia** and **John Dawson**. Their debut *New Riders Of The Purple Sage* (1971) featured 'Dirty Business', country-rock at its finest. As Garcia participated less and less in the group, Nelson and Dawson's guitar work moved up-front, supplemented by steel guitarist **Buddy Cage**, and later albums such as *Powerglide* (1972) and *Gypsy Cowboy* (1972) illustrated both guitarists' growing confidence as writers. However, the group's live work dominated and their albums became increasingly unsatisfactory, although *The Adventures Of Panama Red* (1973) was a substantial commercial success. By the early-1980s the group had disbanded, with Nelson joining Jerry Garcia's acoustic band.

WILLIE NELSON

Born: April 30th 1933, Abbott, Texas, US.

■ Baldwin flat-top (+ pickup).

One of the guiding lights of modern country music, Nelson's original nylon-strung guitar style has been a common thread running through the dozens of albums he's made as a solo artist and with others, and has strong elements of western swing and honky tonk. Finding his first success in Nashville, Nelson returned to Texas in the early-1970s and helped to establish Austin as the number two country music town in the US. The best places to start appreciating Nelson's music are probably the Columbia or Capitol *Greatest Hits* packages, although *Red Headed Stranger* (1975) is his most celebrated work.

MICHAEL NESMITH

Born: December 30th 1942, Houston, Texas, US.

■ Gretsch.

A founder member of TV pop group The Monkees, Nesmith left them in 1969 to pursue his first love, country music. The Monkees were much maligned because their huge commercial success was contrived by television producers, but they notched up a string of tuneful hits, mostly featuring session musicians. By the time Nesmith left the group he had composed songs like 'Different Drum', which was recorded by Linda Ronstadt, and had cut *The Wichita Train Whistle Sings* (1968).

On his departure Nesmith formed The First National Band, which included steel guitarist **Red Rhodes**. Their debut *Magnetic South* (1970) featured the affecting ballad 'Joanne', and two other albums followed, *Loose Salute* (1971) and *Nevada Fighter* (1972), the latter featuring contributions from **James Burton** and keyboardist Glen D Hardin. Although the First National Band split, with Rhodes and Nesmith remaining, other albums such as *Tantamount To Treason* (1972), featuring **Johnny Meeks** on bass (!), the ironically titled *And The Hits Just Keep On Coming* (1972), and *Pretty Much Your Standard Ranch Stash* (1973) ensured that Nesmith remained discreetly in the vanguard of country-rock artists.

In later years, Nesmith continued recording, but that part of his career played second fiddle to his other ventures, including a multi-media operation. He remains a fine, unobtrusive guitarist who has penned some memorable songs, including 'Silver Moon' and 'Some Of Shelley's Blues'.

HAYDEN NICHOLAS

Born: US.

Country singer-songwriter Clint Black has been fortunate in having a long-term sparring partner in guitarist/fiddler Nicholas. Much of the melodic impetus and stylistic consistency of Black's records has emanated from Nicholas, and although he doesn't let rip with the bravura of old-time pickers, he always acquits himself efficiently, as on Black's US country hits 'A Better Man', 'Loving Blind' and 'Killin' Time'.

ROY NICHOLS

Born: US.

■ Fender Telecaster.

One of the earliest country pickers to wield a Telecaster with authority, Nichols started his career as a sideman in The Maddox Brothers And Rose in the early-1950s. Nichols' hot picking on songs like 'Step It Up And Go' and 'Hangover Blues' foreshadowed the emergence of rockabilly by some years, and the whole ensemble gaudily attired in their ever-so tasteful Nudie suits whooped it up on stage with an exuberance rarely seen in country acts.

After leaving the group, Nichols joined forces with country singer Merle Haggard in The Strangers, often alongside ace pedal-steel man **Ralph Mooney**, thereby contributing to the growing Bakersfield monopoly on the West Coast. Nichols' lightning-fast staccato single-string runs with the volume cranked way up became known as 'chicken-picking', the other chief popularizer of which was **James Burton**.

As Haggard's popularity increased through the 1960s the contribution of Nichols, while still distinctive and distinguished, was diluted by the addition of horn sections to the original lineup of The Strangers. As the 1970s arrived, strings were also being added, but Haggard's earlier records like 'Branded Man', 'Sing Me Back Home' (1967) and 'Mama Tried' (1968) stand up to the test of time.

SIMON NICOL

Born: October 13th 1950, London, England.

The roll-call of Fairport Convention reads like a Who's Who of folk-rock in Britain, and no single member has remained as close to the heart of the group as Simon Nicol. His rhythm guitar work has over the years complemented guitarists **Richard Thompson**, **Jerry Donahue**, Trevor Lucas and Martin Allcock, and violinists Dave Swarbrick and Rick Sanders.

Furthermore, Nicol has managed to keep a firm hand on the reins of the repertoire of the group through the myriad changes of lineup. Albums like *Unhalfbricking* and *Liege & Lief* (1969) with vocalist Sandy Denny provided the agenda for a generation of folk-rock bands such as Steeleye Span and Lindisfarne, while *Bonny Bunch Of Roses* (1977) kept the flag flying through the emergence of punk and the all-instrumental *Expletive Delighted* (1986) proved that their imaginative musicianship was just as potent a force as it had been at their inception. Nicol has also maintained a working relationship with ex-Fairport bassist Ashley Hutchings' Albion Band in its many forms and guises.

RICK NIELSEN

Born: December 22nd 1946, Rockford, Illinois, US.

■ Hamer; Gibson; Fender.

Cheap Trick, like REO Speedwagon and Aerosmith, were one of the many bands to emerge in the 1970s who achieved their breaks through constant touring. Nielsen provided the core of the group with his pithy, effervescent songs and a flamboyant stage act that involved bouncing around the stage like some sort of whirling-dervish on acid, often with unusual custom-built guitars in tow. Consequently, it was the live *Cheap Trick At Budokan* (1979) that offered the best recorded view of the band: 'I Want You To Want

Me', 'Look Out' and 'Surrender' were all indicative of Nielsen's pop sensibility and his ability to knock out chunky power-chords.

ROBERT NIGHTHAWK

Born: US.

Influenced most noticeably by **Tampa Red**, Nighthawk has been a fixture on the Chicago club circuit for over 40 years. During that time he has worked with R&B singer Big Joe Turner and **Earl Hooker**. While Nighthawk's recording career has been sporadic, *Live On Maxwell Street* (1989) illustrates the cutting resonance of his style.

LEO NOCENTELLI

Born: June 15th 1946, New Orleans, Louisiana, US.

■ *Fender Starcaster; Fender Telecaster; Gibson ES175.*

No single member was more influential than guitarist Nocentelli in establishing the instrumental sound of the highly rated proto-funk New Orleans band, The Meters.

At first, Nocentelli's distinctive licks graced a spate of records where producer Allen Toussaint used The Meters as a house band, such as on Lee Dorsey's hit 'Ride Your Pony' (1965) and his follow-ups 'Working In The Coalmine' and 'Holy Cow'.

Toussaint decided to record the group in their own right as an instrumental group in an attempt to emulate the success of Booker T & The MGs. It proved to be a wise move as they had a succession of hit singles: 'Sophisticated Lady', 'Cissy Strut', 'Ease Back', 'Look-Ka Py Py' (all 1969) and 'Chicken Strut' (1970). In 1972 they signed to Reprise and recorded the fine quartet of *Cabbage Alley* (1972), *Rejuvenation* (1974), *Fire On The Bayou* (1975) and *Trick Bag* (1976).

Although their recording career as a group began to wane, they were still in demand as session musicians, backing artists like **Dr John**, vocalists Labelle and Robert Palmer, and Toussaint himself. After parting company with Toussaint they teamed up with producer David Rubinson for *New Directions* (1977), but legal problems with Toussaint ensued and the group split.

Nocentelli opted for studio work, turning up recently on Peter Gabriel's *Us* (1992), while vocalist Art Neville joined his brothers Aaron and Charles to form The Neville Brothers.

JIMMY NOLEN

Born: April 3rd 1934, Oklahoma City, Oklahoma, US. Died: December 18th 1983, Atlanta, Georgia, US.

■ *Gibson; Acoustic Black Widow; Fresher Straighter.*

Anyone who has ever thought of playing the guitar could do a lot worse than listen to James Brown's output from 1965 until 1983, for those were the years of Jimmy Nolen. Never a household name, Nolen was indisputably the funkateer extraordinaire. When Brown was electronically sampled by all and sundry in the dance music game of the 1980s and 1990s, James' grunts sounded great... but the clipped, syncopated grooves were the thing. And right at the

heart of those grooves was Nolen's tight, concise chording.

Nolen settled in Los Angeles in his twenties and worked with pop sax-man Chuck Higgins (playing on his 1952 instrumental hit 'Pachuko Hop') and vocalist Johnny Otis (playing on his 1958 hit 'Willie And The Hand Jive'). Nolen joined Brown in 1965, first appearing on the 'Papa's Got A Brand New Bag' single recorded around February 1965 in Arthur Smith Studios in Charlotte, North Carolina. With the exception of a break around 1972 when Brown's entire band defected, Nolen has appeared on virtually every classic Brown recording and concert, sometimes credited, often not.

Thus the Jimmy Nolen guide to funk rhythm guitar includes great moments like 'I Got You (I Feel Good)', 'It's A Man's, Man's, Man's World', 'Cold Sweat', 'I Got The Feelin', 'Say It Loud – I'm Black And I'm Proud', 'Mother Popcorn', 'Super Bad' and 'Get On The Good Foot'.

As well as the electronic theft of Nolen's work already discussed, his style and sound have had great influence on every funk and R&B guitarist, not least **Catfish Collins**, **Nile Rodgers** and **Prince**.

JOHN NUESE

Born: US.

Whatever happened to John Nuese? His fleeting appearance as the guitarist in country singer-songwriter Gram Parsons' International Submarine Band was sufficient for some to think that a career of fame and fortune was spreading out before him. They were wrong. Nuese's legacy is his peerless picking on the band's few singles and solitary album, *Safe At Home* (1968), with titles like 'The Russians Are Coming, The Russians Are Coming', 'Luxury Liner' (later covered by vocalist Emmylou Harris), 'A Satisfied Mind' and 'Folsom Prison Blues' proving that Parsons could justifiably lay claim to having helped to originate country-rock.

TED NUGENT

Born: December 13th 1948, Detroit, Michigan, US.

■ *Gibson Byrdland; Gibson Howard Roberts Fusion; PRS.*

One of the founding fathers of heavy metal, Nugent started musical life in The Amboy Dukes (not to be confused with a British white soul band of the 1960s). Although of course the term hadn't been coined then, The Dukes recorded a fine garage/speed metal version of 'Baby Please Don't Go' (1967).

But the group didn't last and Nugent started a solo career, and his high energy guitar style, played at deafening volume, was based not so much on a compositional whim but rather the ability to fling out notes as rapidly as possible. This caused the self-possessed Nugent to stage contests with **Wayne Kramer** (MC5) and **Mike Pinera** (Iron Butterfly), presumably to see who could deafen whom first. Lyrically, Nugent espoused a doctrine slightly to the right of Attila The Hun. At heart, though, he's a nice lad who just wants to have fun and play his axe, and this humble desire is realized for all to hear on *Cat Scratch Fever* (1977).

E K NYAME

Born: 1927, Kwahu, Ghana. Died: 1977.

Nyame is in his home country a very influential exponent of highlife (the fusion of indigenous dance rhythms and tunes with Western influences), at first adhering strictly to the original instrumentation of guitars, brass section, string bass and drums, although electric guitars tended to dominate from the 1960s.

This effectively modernized highlife to the extent that, despite the concurrent rise of juju, Nyame retained his iconic status. *Sankofa* was a collection that emerged in the 1970s of rerecorded versions of his most famous tunes. It was Nyame who made it possible for the Nigerian musician King Sunny Ade to make his presence felt throughout the West in the 1970s and 1980s.

JOHN OATES

Born: April 7th 1949, New York, New York, US.

■ *Fender Stratocaster; Fender Telecaster; Pensa-Suhr.*

Daryl Hall and John Oates were together the most convincing exponents of blue-eyed soul to emerge in the 1970s, both having had extensive apprenticeships with a variety of bands up and down the East Coast. While it was the soulful timbre of Hall's voice that made David Bowie's efforts in the genre appear forced and fake, Oates' knack for picking out rhythmic guitar lines and figures echoed the work of Motown guitarists like **Marv Tarplin** and **Joe Messina**, giving the arrangements a lift that the mere addition of a horn section would never achieve.

Inevitably, the more successful Hall & Oates became, the more blurred was the dividing line between rock and soul, but they still appeared to function within the parameters of a soul band, cutting one sublime single after another: 'She's Gone', 'Sara Smile', 'Do What You Want, Be What You Are', 'Rich Girl', 'Kiss On My List', 'Private Eyes', 'I Can't Go For That (No Can Do)', 'Did It In A Minute', 'Maneater', 'One On One', 'Family Man', 'Say It Isn't So', 'Adult Education', 'Out Of Touch' and 'Method Of Modern Love'. Although Oates tended to play many of the guitar parts on record, their road band variously included Caleb Quaye, G E Smith and **Steve Hunter**.

LUCKY OCEANS

Born: Reuben Gosfield, April 22nd 1951, Philadelphia, Pennsylvania, US.

■ *Sho-Bud.*

Asleep At The Wheel have proved to be one of the more durable country-rock outfits due to their ability to synthesize some of the more diverse elements of country music such as western swing, Tex-Mex and bluegrass into a readily accessible and identifiable style of their own. Where this adaptability has led many of their contemporaries into AOR, Asleep At The Wheel have won admirers among the traditionally minded country fraternity.

Formed by vocalist/guitarist **Ray Benson** and

steel guitarist Lucky Oceans in California in the late-1960s, the band was supplemented by a floating pool of session or local musicians. Oceans' steel work complemented a succession of fiddlers such as Bill Mabry and Johnny Gimble, giving the group's sound a vitality with which few country-rock outfits could compete. Albums such as *Comin' Right At Ya* (1973), *Texas Gold* (1975) and *Ten* (1987) exhibit an infectious enthusiasm that has contributed to a revaluation of the vintage bands of western swing king Bob Wills and other similar outfits.

ODETTA

Born: Odetta Holmes Felious Gorden, December 31st 1930, Birmingham, Alabama, US.

A fine and influential gospel vocalist, Odetta moved later in her career further towards folk and the blues, enabling her to develop a powerful acoustic guitar style that echoed that of **Josh White** and **Big Bill Broonzy**. The range of her repertoire is most accurately captured on *Odetta In Japan* (1965) and *Odetta At Carnegie Hall* (1967).

MICHAEL O'DOMHNAILL

Born: Ireland.

O'Domhnaill was a founder member of The Bothy Band, who became one of the leading Irish folk-rock bands of the 1970s. While they played traditional Irish folk songs like their compatriots Planxty, their arrangements were more rock-oriented. Surprisingly, albums like *The Bothy Band* (1976) and *After Hours: Live In Paris* (1978) have endured remarkably well, retaining their zip and vitality. After the group disbanded in the late-1970s O'Domhnaill moved to Portland, Oregon, US where he teamed up with fiddler Kevin Burke.

MIKE OLDFIELD

Born: May 15th 1953, Reading, Berkshire, England.

■ **Gibson Les Paul Junior; Fender Stratocaster; Fender Telecaster; Ovation; PRS.**

Better known as a multi-instrumentalist and for his solo works *Tubular Bells* (1974) and *Tubular Bells 2* (1993), Oldfield had been a guitarist of some distinction with madcap songwriter Kevin Ayers and his band The Whole World.

Appearing on *Shooting At The Moon* (1971), *Whatevershebringswesing* (1972) and *Bananamour* (1973), Oldfield's apparent ease with style-jumping complemented Ayers' quirky and quasi-philosophical lyrics. 'May I' from *Shooting At The Moon* contained the elements of the pastoral lyricism that characterized *Tubular Bells*, but when performed live it offered much scope for improvisation, while 'Stranger In Blue Suede Shoes' from *Whatevershebringswesing* had a sinister ambiguity that Oldfield's phrases enhanced.

Oldfield seems to have had a great time chucking guitars into the *Tubular Bells* melée, using them for textural nuance as well as theme-stating – slightly distorted or not. Oldfield's work after the *Bells* had charm, but lacked the impromptu qualities of the Ayers sessions. It would be good to hear him relying less on overdubs and treated guitars and more on general instinct.

DAVID O'LIST

Born: December 13th 1948, London, England.

O'List seems to have a knack for leaving groups just before they peak. Whether he's difficult or just gets bored, who knows? Formerly a member of the R&B band The Attack, he formed The Nice who backed R&B singer P P Arnold before they branched out on their own. O'List stayed long enough to appear on the debut *The Thoughts Of Emerlist Davjack* (1968), a distinguished piece of work that predated Nice keyboardist Keith Emerson's embarrassing flirtations with sword-swallowing and pyromania, but nonetheless indicated Emerson's growing preoccupation with classical music. Nothing wrong with the original works, but Emerson jazzed them up: most unpleasant.

As for O'List, he high-tailed it out of the band and joined Roxy Music, briefly, leaving before they recorded their first album. Then he formed Jet, another short-lived exercise, and hit the session circuit where his bluesy style (he had been considered as a replacement for **Peter Green** in **John Mayall**'s Bluesbreakers) graced sessions with vocalist Bryan Ferry and pianist Tony Ashton.

GRAHAM OLIVER

Born: July 6th 1952, Yorkshire, England.

■ **Gibson SG; Fernandes.**

Saxon came out of the smoke in 1977 in the wake of metal bands like Def Leppard and Iron Maiden. Unlike many of their ilk, Saxon eschewed the tired imagery of the occult and paganism, concentrating instead upon good, honest, wholesome fare – like steam trains ('Princess Of The Night') and the assassination of President Kennedy ('Dallas 1pm'). As for Oliver and **Paul Quinn**, both wield their axes with as much purpose as **Dave Murray** or **Tony Iommi**.

The Eagle Has Landed (1983) remains the most accurate reflection of their stage performance, which is the cornerstone of their appeal.

JOHN O'NEILL

Born: August 26th 1957, Londonderry, Northern Ireland.

While vocalist Fergal Sharkey was the most visible member of The Undertones, it was the guitar-playing brothers John and Damian O'Neill who gave the band their resonance. Although the group failed to achieve the success due to them during their time together, in hindsight the punkish stridency of 'Teenage Kicks', 'Jimmy, Jimmy' and the pithy 'You've Got My Number (Why Don't You Use It?)' mark them out as one of the most imaginative groups of the punk era. After Sharkey left for a solo career, the brothers O'Neill started That Petrol Emotion, who stick firmly to the traditions of the guitar-based band, with big chords and chiming riffs on tracks such as 'Big Decision', 'Genius Move' and 'Abandon'.

ROY ORBISON

Born: Roy Kelton Orbison, April 23rd 1936, Vernon, Texas, US. Died: December 6th 1988, Hendersonville, Tennessee, US.

■ **Gretsch (modified).**

The distinctive timbre of Roy Orbison's voice and the quality of his songwriting would probably have made him a star under any circumstances. But while in the studio the main guitar parts would be handed to session players of the stature of **Grady Martin** and **Hank Garland**, it was often Orbison who filled the guitarist's role on stage when playing his classic early-1960s songs such as 'Only The Lonely', 'Cryin', 'In Dreams', 'Blue Bayou', 'It's Over', and 'Oh, Pretty Woman'.

Even in later years, on the revival tours and as a member of The Traveling Wilburys with **George Harrison**, **Tom Petty** and **Jeff Lynne**, Orbison was a charismatic figure.

MARY OSBORNE

Born: July 17th 1921, Minot, North Dakota, US. Died: March 4th 1992, California, US.

■ **Gibson; Barker (later).**

One of the first female electric jazz guitarists, Osborne progressed to guitar from banjo and ukulele at an early age, and was inspired to go electric after seeing **Charlie Christian** on stage with his ES150 in the late-1930s. She collaborated with jazz players such as pianist Mary Lou Williams, saxman Coleman Hawkins, and violinist Joe Venuti, known for his work with **Eddie Lang**. She made solo records too, where her versatility and ability to swing were paramount, and from the late-1940s settled in New York and worked primarily as a sessionwoman, moving to the West Coast in the 1960s.

SHUGGIE OTIS

Born: John Otis Jr, November 30th 1953, Los Angeles, California, US.

■ **Gibson ES335.**

Throughout the 1950s R&B singer Johnny Otis, through The Johnny Otis Show, provided a springboard for a crop of artists to further and develop their careers. History repeated itself when his son Shuggie made his debut for the show at the tender age of 12. In 1969 Shuggie appeared on his dad's *Cold Shot*, featuring 'Country Girl', heralding his emergence as one of the most promising young guitarists of his generation.

But it was a promise that never fulfilled itself, as Otis's solo work tended to concentrate on rib-tickling solos of epic proportions, rather than the development of a body of material in which to integrate his prodigious talents. Apart from *Cold Shot*, his appearance at the Monterey Jazz Festival in 1970 with R&B veterans like Ivory Joe Hunter, Esther Phillips and Eddie 'Cleanhead' Vinson showed that his true skill was as an accompanist. By the mid-1970s his career had stalled and at the time of writing he tends only to play on sessions for his father's Blues Spectrum label.

Ode-Oti

JOHN OTWAY

Born: October 2nd 1952, Aylesbury, Buckinghamshire, England.

■ *Gibson SG.*

Otway has made a virtue of his basic guitar work, but it hasn't stopped him from acquiring a celebrity status on the British club circuit where his whacky antics and eclectic repertoire ensure a steady stream of bookings (over 2000 gigs and counting). Although he has recorded regularly over the years (*Where Did I Go Right* 1979, *All Balls And No Willy* 1981), sometimes with fiddler Wild Willy Barrett, Otway's zaniness becomes wearing and doesn't really stand up to repeated listenings.

RANDY OWEN

Born: December 13th 1949, Fort Payne, Alabama, US.

One of the most successful country groups of the 1980s, Alabama were spearheaded by guitarist Owen and supplemented by Jeff Cook (guitar/fiddle), Ted Gentry (bass) and Mark Herndon (drums). Despite their success, they seem to these ears one of the more plodding country outfits, lacking bite in their delivery. But they must be doing something right as they've got more record sales to their credit than any other comparable country band. Songs like 'Tennessee River', 'Old Flame', 'Feels So Right', 'Mountain Music', 'Take Me Down', 'The Closer You Get', 'If You're Gonna Play In Texas (You Gotta Have A Fiddle In The Band)', 'Song Of The South', 'Jukebox In My Mind', 'Down Home' and 'I'm In A Hurry (And I Don't Know Why)' say little about Owen's proficiency as a guitarist as all that appears to be required in that department is competence.

JIMMY PAGE

Born: James Patrick Page, January 9th 1944, Heston, Middlesex, England.

■ *Gibson Les Paul Standard; Gibson double-neck; Fender Telecaster; Danelectro.*

Page, **Eric Clapton** and **Jeff Beck** all came to the public's attention as members of the British white-blues group The Yardbirds. But Page had been busy beforehand. Aged 16, he'd joined his first group, Neil Christian And The Crusaders, and went on to gain a reputation as one of the hardest working and most efficient session musicians on the early-1960s London studio circuit. (Reputedly, he used to hang around the reception areas of studios and when musicians failed to show, Page slotted in.) He worked with everyone from Van Morrison to Burt Bacharach (and much of his 1960s studio work is collected on *Session Man Vol 1* 1989 and *Vol II* 1991).

Page joined The Yardbirds in summer 1966, initially on bass guitar (Page on bass, then guitar; Keith Relf vocals; Beck guitar; Chris Dreja guitar, then bass; Jim McCarty drums). Although The Yardbirds with Page failed to make as significant a recording contribution as they had with his predecessors, on stage Page had begun to develop a strong soloing technique, and for the few months

until Beck left the group had engaged in some wild twin-guitar battles.

The Yardbirds ground to a halt and split in summer 1968, when Page formed the 'New Yardbirds' which became Led Zeppelin. Despite Zeppelin being regarded as the template for heavy metal bands thanks to titles like 'Communication Breakdown', 'Whole Lotta Love' and 'Black Dog', Page's instrumental virtuosity extended through all styles of guitar work. His prowess on acoustic guitar was apparent on 'Black Mountain Side' (an adaptation of **Bert Jansch**'s work) and the **Leadbelly**-style 'Gallows Pole', and on 'That's The Way' and 'Tangerine' his steel-strung acoustic provided a conduit from the rock fraternity to folk artists such as **Roy Harper** and **Michael Chapman**. Page also got to grips with pedal-steel parts on 'Babe I'm Gonna Leave You' and 'Your Time Is Gonna Come'.

His six-string electric work wasn't bad, either, the anthemic Telecaster solo on 'Stairway To Heaven' and the Eastern influences of 'Kashmir', among many others, causing a swathe of lesser players to attempt to imitate his style – be it the more introspective playing that often surfaced in the studio, or the wilder, violin-bow-assisted stage work.

After the disintegration of Zeppelin following drummer John Bonham's death in September 1980, Page teamed up with ex-Free singer Paul Rodgers in The Firm (*The Firm* 1985, *Mean Business* 1986), and in 1988 released his debut solo album, *Outrider*, with plenty of guitar treats and a contribution from former Zeppelin vocalist Robert Plant.

In summer 1990 with engineer George Marino, Page remixed the classic Zeppelin tracks for a series of CD reissues, *Remasters*. Later, Page got together with former Whitesnake vocalist David Coverdale for *Coverdale Page* (1993) but the material he had at his disposal seemed inferior to that of Led Zeppelin.

PHIL PALMER

Born: Philip John Palmer, September 9th 1952, London, England.

■ *Fender 'Nocaster'; Fender Stratocaster; Fender Telecaster.*

Palmer has been active on the British session circuit for some years, having started out at the suggestion of his uncles Ray and Dave Davies of The Kinks. Among those whom he's played with are singers Iggy Pop, The Sutherland Brothers and David Essex, as well as **Frank Zappa**, **Joan Armatrading** and **Michael Chapman**.

RICK PARFITT

Born: October 12th 1948, London, England.

■ *Fender Telecaster.*

Status Quo have for over 25 years been close to the top of their profession, having pioneered (very loosely) a blues-based boogie that owes more to having a good time than any meditation on the fecklessness of women or the frequent visitations of misfortune. Parfitt and **Francis Rossi** as boogie-meisters extraordinaire have turned base metal into gold with a steady string of 12-bar blues, using the

bare minimum number of chords: 'Paper Plane', 'Caroline', 'Down, Down', 'Wild Side Of Life', 'Rockin' All Over The World', 'Whatever You Want', 'What You're Proposing', 'Something 'Bout You Baby I Like', 'Marguerita Time', 'In The Army Now' and 'The Anniversary Waltz'. That it is unpretentious, wholesome fare speaks volumes for their lack of guile, and there seems little reason why they shouldn't go on for the next 25 years.

CHRISTOPHER PARKENING

Born: December 14th 1947, Brentwood, California, US.

■ *Ramirez.*

A classical guitarist who came to prominence in the late-1960s and hasn't looked back, Parkening has been taught by **Segovia** and **Pepe Romero**. His studio output has seen the predictable interpretations of Rodrigo's 'Concierto De Aranjuez' and 'Fantasia Para Un Gentilhombre', which he addressed with gusto and panache, and very popular recordings of Bach, while less predictable has been the inclusion of William Walton's 'Five Bagatelles'.

While he is an accomplished soloist, Parkening's recitals with vocalist Kathleen Battle on a range of English songs from Dowland and Purcell through to Britten illustrate his instinctive feel, and the duo recorded *The Pleasures Of Their Company*. Although he has been recording for over 25 years, his workload shows little sign of relief, and at the time of writing a CD set of earlier recordings, *Collection*, was about to be released.

ALAN PARKER

Born: England.

One-time co-owner of Morgan Studios in north London with drummer Barry Morgan, Parker achieved distinction as a member of Blue Mink, a group of session musicians fronted by writer Roger Greenaway and vocalist Madeleine Bell. Parker's ability to handle most styles proficiently gave the group an MOR credibility ('Melting Pot' 1969, 'Banner Man' 1971). When the group split in 1975 Parker continued as a session player.

RAY PARKER JR

Born: May 1st 1954, Detroit, Michigan, US.

■ *Gibson ES335; Gibson Les Paul; Valdez custom.*

Parker started his career in the most auspicious surroundings of the Motown studios when he was 16, and this resulted in a position as guitarist in Stevie Wonder's touring band.

While never likely to unfurl solos of much imagination, Parker slotted into the contemporay requirement for guitarists with a few funky chops that could be deployed where appropriate – or, as film writer Andrew Sarris once dubbed up, "Less than meets the eye." This has informed Parker's solo career: neat licks and lissom lines that bear an extraordinary familiarity to much that has gone before ('Jack and Jill', 'Ghostbusters' and 'I Don't Think A Man Should Sleep Alone', all on *Chartbusters* 1984). One of these days Parker will

Otw-Par

make a stupendous record – but it won't be while cutting film themes on the Universal back lot.

ANDY PARTRIDGE

Born: December 11th 1953, Swindon, Wiltshire, England.

■ *Ibanez Artist; Squier Telecaster.*

A founder member of XTC, one of the more interesting British new wave bands of the late-1970s, Partridge and his observant, literate songs ('Life Begins At The Hop', 'Making Plans For Nigel', 'Generals and Majors', 'Senses Working Overtime' and 'Love On A Farmboy's Wages') drew more acutely from the experiences of being English than anything since Kinks writer Ray Davies' work. After keyboards player Barry Andrews was replaced by **Dave Gregory** in 1979, the wilder chording of Partridge was tempered by Gregory's more considered licks. Partridge stopped touring years ago, and while never prolific has been less active of late, but *Oranges And Lemons* (1989) is the group's most successful outing, proving that all Partridges mature with age.

JOE PASS

Born: Joseph Anthony Passalaqua, January 13th 1929, New Brunswick, New Jersey, US.

■ *Gibson ES175; Ibanez 'signature'; D'Aquisto.*

Since the death of **Wes Montgomery**, Pass has become the most influential jazz guitarist of his generation with an ability to adapt to any style and an unerring ability to swing.

His career started in the early-1960s when he was formally acknowledged by being named best new instrumentalist in the 1963 *Down Beat* magazine poll. From the latter half of the 1960s to the present day Pass has recorded for Norman Granz's Pablo label, teaming up with singer Ella Fitzgerald (*Fitzgerald & Pass...Again* 1975 and *Take Love Easy* 1973), violinist Stéphane Grappelli (*Tivoli Gardens* 1979) and pianist Oscar Peterson (*Porgy & Bess* 1976).

Furthermore, an album of duets with **Herb Ellis** on *Two For The Road* (1974), particularly 'Love For Sale' and 'Lady Be Good', has a vibrant fluidity that illustrates total confidence in one another – seldom heard when two players lock horns. A series of solo albums entitled *Virtuoso* (from 1973) were for once not record company hyperbole but fine demonstrations of a range of styles. Never obsessively technical, Pass is an accomplished sideman whose solo work incorporates the speed and excitement of bop with the discipline of session work and the craftmanship of a soloist.

CHARLEY PATTON

Born: 1887, Edwards, Mississippi, US. Died: April 28th 1934, Indianola, Mississippi, US.

While his guitar style lacked the resonance of **Tommy Johnson** or **Blind Willie Johnson**, Patton was a key man in the development of Delta blues presentation. Patton's vocal style caused many to adopt his mannerisms, with the result that his barking inflections became a model for **Son House**,

---

Robert Johnson and **Howlin' Wolf**. Patton's gutsy, rhythmic guitar work weaved in and out of his vocals, which in later years would be echoed by white blues-influenced singers such as Jack Bruce in Cream, Captain Beefheart, and Bob Hite in Canned Heat.

Moreover, Patton came up in the late-1920s/early-1930s when racism, while endemic, was not as virulent as it was to become in later years, and it was feasible for bluesmen to develop reputations in their own right. Patton succeeded famously, adapting spirituals, work songs and his own compositions to an identifiable style, for example 'Frankie & Albert', 'Pony Blues', 'Screamin & Hollerin The Blues' and 'Some Of These Days I'll Be Gone'.

HENRY PAUL

Born: US.

The Outlaws were formed in 1974 in the style of The Allman Brothers Band and The Eagles. Gentle harmonies and a frontline of three duelling guitarists – **Billy Jones**, **Hugh Thomasson** and Paul – made the band a feature on the US live circuit, where titles like 'Green Grass And High Tides' echoed Lynyrd Skynyrd in their prime. Although The Outlaws scored with 'There Goes Another Love Song' and 'Lady In Waiting', Paul left to form The Henry Paul Band, cutting the crunchy *Grey Ghost* (1979) and *Feel The Heat* (1980). However, Thomasson and Paul reformed the band for *Soldiers Of Fortune* (1986) before touring and going their separate ways.

LES PAUL

Born: Lester William Polfus, June 9th 1915, Waukesha, Wisconsin, US.

■ *Gibson L5; Epiphone (modified); Gibson 'signature' (modified).*

One of the most innovative guitarists of his day, Paul left a legacy in his melodic, humorous playing and in the overdubbing techniques that he developed, best combined in the early-1950s hits of Les Paul & Mary Ford.

Initially Paul played with country outfits until being bitten by the jazz bug, starting to play in small groups and orchestras. While his jazz work was strongly influenced by **Django Reinhardt** and **Eddie Lang**, the fluid style of his country playing was light years away from the traditional country pickers. In 1936 he formed the Les Paul Trio with bassist Ernie Newton and drummer Jim Atkins (the older half-brother of **Chet Atkins**).

After moving to Los Angeles in 1941 he started playing sessions for artists like Bing Crosby, and also recorded under his own name, scoring hits with 'It's Been A Long Long Time', 'Lover' and 'Nola'. In 1947 he teamed up with vocalist and accomplished guitarist Mary Ford, who'd played with singing cowboys Gene Autry and Jimmy Wakely. Paul and Ford married, and the combination of Ford's vocals and Paul's lyrical guitar work provided him with a perfect opportunity to exploit the potential of overdubbing. It was called the New Sound by his record company Capitol and used on hits like 'Tennessee Waltz' (1950), 'How High The Moon' (1951), 'The World Is Waiting For The

---

Sunrise' (1951), 'Tiger Rag' (1952), 'Vaya Con Dios' (1953) and 'I'm A Fool To Care' (1954). The CD set *Les Paul: The Legend & The Legacy* (1991) admirably documents this period.

Paul eagerly experimented with modified electric guitars in the 1940s, and in 1952 the Gibson guitar company launched their first solidbody electric, the Les Paul model. With minimal changes over the years, it is still in production in the 1990s.

With the emergence of rock'n'roll in the mid-1950s the duo's style became terribly dated. In 1963 the couple divorced and a few years later Paul, who was suffering from hearing difficulties, retired to his electronics workshop (Ford died in 1977). Paul made a limited comeback in 1968 with instrumental rerecordings of the hits on *Les Paul Now*, and made *Chester & Lester* (1976) and *Guitar Monsters* (1978) with Chet Atkins, revealing two tireless technicians at their relaxed best. At the time of writing Paul, in his seventies, continues to play every week at a small New York club.

LOWMAN PAULING

Born: Winston-Salem, North Carolina, US. Died: 1975.

In 1952 Pauling, leader of the gospel group The Royal Sons, changed its musical direction and renamed it The 5 Royales. The group had been formed in 1942 in Winston-Salem and six years later started to record for Apollo, cutting 'Baby Don't Do It', 'Too Much Lovin', 'Help Me Somebody', 'Crazy, Crazy, Crazy' and 'Laundromat Blues'.

In 1954 they signed with the King label and, in an occasional partnership with Ralph Bass, A&R supremo at King, Pauling wrote some of the most potent R&B compositions of the 1950s including 'Dedicated To The One I Love', 'Think', 'Tell The Truth' and 'The Slummer The Slum', in all of which his guitar work was inspirational.

By the time they stopped recording in 1966 the influence of their records had percolated through into all idioms of contemporary music: to girl groups of the early-1960s like The Shirelles, to harmony groups of the mid-1960s such as The Mamas & The Papas, to guitarists like **Eric Clapton** and **Steve Cropper** and, of course, to architects of soul Ray Charles, James Brown and Aretha Franklin.

HERB PEDERSEN

Born: April 27th 1944, Berkeley, California, US.

Stalwart of the country music session circuit, banjoist/guitarist Pedersen made his debut in 1968 as a member of The Dillards before leaving to form Country Gazette in 1971. He remained with them until 1973, when he left, returning to studio work and playing with artists including Dan Fogelberg, Emmylou Harris, Linda Ronstadt and John Denver. In 1982 Pedersen teamed up with **Chris Hillman** for some of Hillman's solo projects, and ended up forming The Desert Rose Band, which, as the 1980s gave way to the 1990s, remained one of the few country-rock bands prepared to draw effectively from country music's rich heritage. While he has often been involved with the more populist side of country

Par-Ped

music, Pedersen has also remained at the cutting edge of bluegrass in its most unadulterated form, and as such is a guitarist closely watched by his fellow players.

TONY PELUSO

Born: US.

■ **Gibson.**

The Carpenters' 'Goodbye To Love' features one of the best guitar solos of the 1970s. Sweeping statement that may be, but the controlled lyricism of Peluso's distorted work-out has an eloquence that few others have managed. He never hit such dizzy heights again – although his brief country-style solo on their 'Jambalaya' is superb – but 'Goodbye To Love' has stood the test of time.

PACO PEÑA

Born: June 1st 1942, Córdoba, Spain.

■ **Gerundino Fernandez.**

Brazenly and blatantly populist in his approach to marketing flamenco, Peña first achieved fame outside Spain. While he has been flamenco's greatest ambassador, he has avoided outright commercialization, preferring instead to emphasize the richness of the flamenco tradition. As a consequence his career has not been marred by troughs of inconsistency.

Although Peña's albums are generally more easily available than those of some of his compadres, patience and diligence are still required in looking out these records. It is worth searching out titles such as *Fabulous Flamenco*, *The Music of Ramon Montoya And Nino Ricardo*, *Azahara*, and in particular *Misa Flamenca*, a recent recording featuring three other guitarists, a chorus and percussion, destined to confound flamenco purists but delight those who enjoy music without boundaries.

MIKE PENDER

Born: Michael Prendergast, March 3rd 1942, Liverpool, England.

■ **Burns Vibra-Artiste; Burns Double Six.**

The Searchers were one of the most original bands to emerge in England at the same time as The Beatles in the early-1960s. The big – and crucial – difference between the two was that The Beatles developed an incomparable writing partnership in Lennon and McCartney, while the Searchers remained dependent on obscure R&B material or contemporary writers such as Jack Nitzsche and Jackie De Shannon.

Tight harmonies, Pender's jangling rhythm and **John McNally**'s driving lead guitar on 'Needles & Pins', 'Ain't Gonna Kiss Ya', 'Don't Throw Your Love Away', 'What Have They Done To The Rain?', 'When You Walk In The Room' and 'Take Me For What I'm Worth' played a big part in the inspiration of players such as **Roger McGuinn** and The Byrds. Although The Searchers subsequently spent years plying their trade on the 'soup in a basket' cabaret circuit, they returned with *The Searchers* (1979) which drew from

the repertoires of contemporary writers such as **Tom Petty**. Pender started a solo career in 1985.

AL PERKINS

Born: US.

■ **Fender 1000.**

Throughout the 1970s Perkins was second only to **Sneaky Pete Kleinow** as the busiest steel guitarist on the West Coast session scene. With The Flying Burrito Brothers he took over where Kleinow left off, appearing on *The Last Of The Red Hot Burritos* (1971), which included sparky improvisations by Perkins on 'Hot Burrito #1', for example, that were more characteristic of the bluegrass of Bill Monroe than the up-dated, inferior counterpart played in contemporary country-rock bands.

Perkins then joined up with **Stephen Stills** in Manassas, one of the great under-acknowledged bands of the 1970s. Lacking any discernible star quality in their lineup (Stills might have the kudos of a superstar, but has never had the charisma) the group's self-titled debut (1972) was very much a group effort, Stills contributing a range of songs that allowed each member of the band to shine.

After Manassas, Perkins joined the much vaunted Souther Hillman Furay Band in the mid-1970s, but the sum of the various parts never approximated the potential. Perkins still plays sessions.

CARL PERKINS

Born: April 9th 1932, Tiptonville, Tennessee, US.

■ **Gibson ES5 Switchmaster; Gibson Les Paul; Fender; Guild; Peavey; G&L Broadcaster.**

A formative figure in the early days of rock'n'roll, Perkins' career was put on the skids by a serious car crash in 1956, ending his contention for the crown that for so long rested uneasily on Elvis Presley's head. But Perkins' bright rockabilly guitar playing, influenced by the choppy, staccato guitar riffs of **T-Bone Walker**, inspired in turn a plethora of later artists such as **George Harrison**, **Dave Edmunds**, **Ry Cooder** and **John Fogerty**.

Perkins was at first a country artist, an area of his work that he never totally left behind. His first three singles were 'Turn Around', 'Let The Jukebox Keep On Playing' and 'Gone, Gone, Gone', but his fourth was the self-penned hit 'Blue Suede Shoes' (1956), the lyrics dealing explicitly with rock'n'roll while the arrangement and guitar style were pure rockabilly. Over the next few years Perkins never garnered the plaudits accorded to many lesser artists, despite the consistently high standard of his Sun material: 'Boppin The Blues' (1956), 'Matchbox' (1957), 'Honey Don't' (1956), 'Everybody's Trying To Be My Baby' (1956) and 'Lend Me Your Comb' (1958). He remains, along with Johnny Cash, one of the few survivors of rock'n'roll's golden age still able to strut his stuff with any authority.

LUTHER PERKINS

Died: 1968.

Perkins' muted bass runs were at the heart of

country/rock'n'roller Johnny Cash's recorded and stage sound in the 1950s and 1960s. Cash's first Sun single, 'Cry Cry Cry' (1955), was credited to Johnny Cash and The Tennessee Two, the latter being bassist Marshall Grant and guitarist Perkins. After the arrival of drummer W S Holland in 1958 the group became The Tennessee Three, and Perkins remained a valuable part of the Cash sound until Perkins' death. Perkins was the perfect foil for Cash's sanguine world-weariness, with a lyrical facility that owed more to rural blues than to hillbilly. The best known songs such as 'I Walk The Line' (1956) and 'Ring Of Fire' (1963) are on *The Sun Years* 1955-58 compilation and *The Columbia Years 1958-86*.

JOE PERRY

Born: September 10th 1950, Boston, Massachusetts, US.

■ **Gibson Les Paul.**

Without wishing to dwell upon the group's past, I think Perry and the rest of Aerosmith are better known for partying. That was then. Now they've become old-timers of the US stadium circuit, with Perry a role model for many budding guitarists. This has been achieved through a combination of strong material that caught the mood of the mid-1970s and a penchant for catchy riffs and incisive solos.

At the turn of the 1980s Perry left the band temporarily and formed The Joe Perry Project, cutting *Let The Music Do The Talking* (1980) which established Perry in a bracket of heavy metal guitarists who pursued technique as if it were some kind of holy grail. During the 1980s, when the group had arguably passed their sell-by date, Perry, having returned to the fold, and vocalist Steven Tyler teamed up with rap band Run-DMC for 'Walk This Way'. This did much to bring rap into the mainstream, exploiting the brash rhythm of Perry's guitar work and, despite the latent sexism of the lyrics, made the band appear to have their fingers on the fashionable pulse.

Pump (1989) saw the band essaying fresh heights with a glossy metal that made their earlier efforts – the best of which is *Toys In The Attic* (1975) – appear unimaginative.

TOM PETTY

Born: October 20th 1953, Gainesville, Florida, US.

■ **Rickenbacker; Rickenbacker 'signature'; Gibson J200.**

Petty has gradually emerged as an astute tunesmith and assured rhythm guitarist with his band The Heartbreakers (including **Mike Campbell**), each successive record densely packed with rich morsels. The recent *Greatest Hits* compilation (1993) is a good place to start. Petty, like **Dave Edmunds**, **Jeff Lynne** and **Dave Stewart**, appears always on the look-out for fresh ways to enliven the spirit of rock'n'roll but, unlike so many, seems to be constantly maturing.

DAVE PEVERETT

Born: April 10th 1950, London, England.

In 1966 **Kim Simmonds** formed The Savoy Brown

Pel-Pev

Blues Band, and shortly after added Peverett. In Britain they were confined to slogging around minor-sized venues, but in the US were considered quite a draw with albums such as *A Step Further* (1969) and *Raw Sienna* (1970) all selling better than in Britain. In 1971 Peverett and drummer Roger Earl left to form Foghat with the specific objective of touring the US exclusively. Although the group's style was more boogie- than blues-based, Peverett's speed licks and dexterous picking gave them a reputation for on-stage entertainment, and *Live* (1977) features a great version of Willie Dixon's 'I Just Want To Make Love To You' with Peverett's wah-wah guitar solo a high spot. By the end of the 1970s as heavy metal took hold the band recorded less but continued to tour, albeit on a smaller scale than at their peak, and they finally split in 1984.

EDDIE PHILLIPS

Born: England.

■ *Gibson ES335.*

It is inconceivable to think that Phillips of The Creation gave **Jimmy Page** a tip on playing the guitar: "Use a bow, son." Page later popularized this occasional effect, dragging a violin bow across the strings to help sustain. But Phillips had also managed to use guitar feedback well before most people had discovered their volume controls, and cut two excellent singles with The Creation, 'Makin Time' (1966) and 'Painter Man' (1967), but the group split in 1968 and Phillips disappeared into the mist.

STEVE PHILLIPS

Born: February 18th 1948, London, England.

■ *National resonator; self-built acoustics.*

Phillips is typical of a fast disappearing breed that plays for the love of it. His picking with **Brendan Croker**'s band The Five O'Clock Shadows on songs like Frankie Miller's 'Darlin', a simple tune at best, echoes the unobtrusive stylishness of **Blind Blake** while retaining a magical, contemplative quality. However, with **Mark Knopfler** and Croker on The Notting Hillbillies' *Missing Presumed Having A Good Time* (1990), especially on titles like **Alton Delmore**'s 'Blues Stay Away From Me' and **Lonnie Johnson**'s 'Bewildered', Phillips emphasized the wide ranging sphere of his influences.

RAY PHIRI

Born: Chikapa Phiri, July 17th 1950, Natal, South Africa.

■ *Sadowsky Strat-style.*

Phiri, already well known in South Africa, contributed wonderful African-rockabilly support throughout **Paul Simon**'s 'Graceland' (1986), lent a sure hand to other tracks on the album, and featured prominently in Simon's touring bands of the period. While Simon was roundly berated at the time of the release of *Graceland* for breaking the cultural boycott of South Africa, his collaboration with Phiri and Ladysmith Black Mambazo isolated much of the common musical ground between the two nations. Phiri's fine guitar work was also featured on the sublime 'She Moves On' from Simon's *The Rhythm Of The Saints* (1990), while Phiri has also been recruited by others, like **Joan Baez** for *Speaking Of Dreams* (1990).

HOWARD PICKUP

Born: England.

Is this the perfect surname for an electric guitarist? Briefly a member of The Adverts, Pickup contributed to the group's early success, appearing on 'One Chord Wonders', the bracingly anthemic 'Gary Gilmore's Eyes' and 'No Time To Be 21'. Their first album *Crossing The Red Sea With The Adverts* (1978) lacked coherence, and by the time the second one came around Pickup had been removed. However, those early singles still bring a twinkle to the eye.

MIKE PINERA

Born: September 29th 1948, Tampa, Florida, US.

■ *Mosrite.*

Iron Butterfly were one of the pioneering heavy rock bands that emerged in the late-1960s. Pinera joined the group in 1970 after the band had recorded their side-long epic 'In-A-Gadda-Da-Vida' (the album of the same name remained on the US charts for approximately three years, accruing sales of around three million units). By the time Pinera joined, the group had been eclipsed by rather more accomplished metal bands such as Led Zeppelin, with the result that *Metamorphosis* (1970) seemed undistinguished. When they disbanded Pinera joined ex-Vanilla Fudge drummer Carmine Appice and bassist Tim Bogert in Cactus. This band failed to raise the collective pulse of the record-buying public, despite a decibel level that would have made them audible on Mars.

JOHN PISANO

Born: February 6th 1931, New York, New York, US.

■ *Fender Telecaster; Gibson ES335.*

Pisano was the guitarist with Herb Alpert's Tijuana Brass, a mighty force on the MOR record market in the 1960s, playing well organized 'south of the border' music with absolutely no sharp edges.

After playing in the Crew Chiefs' Air Force Band between 1952 and 1955, Pisano had toured with jazz drummer Chico Hamilton's Quintet before playing sessions on the West Coast with clarinet man Buddy DeFranco, big-band composer Jimmy Giuffre and flautist Paul Horn, among others.

In the early-1960s Pisano joined Alpert, appearing on all the biggest hits such as 'The Lonely Bull' (1962), 'Spanish Flea' (1965), 'Tijuana Taxi' (1966) and 'Casino Royale' (1967), to name but a few.

After Alpert established with producer Jerry Moss the A&M label, signing acts like Sergio Mendes & Brasil '66, The Sandpipers and songwriter Burt Bacharach, Pisano and other members of the Tijuana Brass formed the nucleus of a nominal A&M house band. While Pisano seldom soloed during these years, his ability to maintain a metronomic groove made him one of the West Coast's most reliable studio players.

ANDY POWELL

Born: February 8th 1950, England.

■ *Gibson Flying V; Music Man Silhouette; PRS.*

Powell and **Ted Turner** were the duelling guitarists of Wishbone Ash during the halcyon days of the group, when they were based very loosely on the style of The Allman Brothers Band. Both Powell and Turner were later recruits to the group's lineup, which had been in existence since the late-1960s as, among others, The Empty Vessels.

Once Powell and Turner joined the group, through continuous touring they established a solid following on the British college circuit with pieces such as 'Phoenix' from *Pilgrimage* (1971) and 'Warrior' and 'The King Will Come' from *Argus* (1972). It was fiery stuff, with album sleeves adorned by helmeted warriors, UFOs and Roger Dean graphics, conspiring to give the group the taint of progressiveness when in fact they were just another blues-based band with more grandiose visions than most. Through the late-1970s the group's popularity declined in Britain and the lineup underwent a variety of changes, with **Laurie Wisefield** replacing Ted Turner, and by the late-1980s they had metamorphosed into a new age outfit, recording *Nouveau Calls* (1987).

BADEN POWELL

Born: August 6th 1937, Rio De Janeiro, Brazil.

One of the foremost Brazilian guitarists and composers, Powell plays on his nylon-strung flat-top a dazzling synthesis of his native samba and bossa nova rhythms with jazz and flamenco undertones. He has recorded widely, and something like *Estudos* (1975) is a good introduction to his work.

GEORGE POWELL

Born: US.

After **Craig Fuller** left Pure Prairie League in 1973, rhythm guitarist Powell became the common denominator in later lineups. While they missed Fuller's songwriting ability, the group was given variety when Powell recruited lead guitarist Larry Goshorn, and the addition of **Vince Gill** in the early-1980s enabled the band to last successfully without undue reliance on the retreading of well beaten paths.

IDA PRESTI

Born: Yvette Ida Montagnon, May 31st 1924, Suresnes, France. Died: April 24th 1967, Rochester, New York, US.

■ *Bouchet.*

Born to French and Italian parents, Presti studied in the early-1930s with Mario Maccaferri, a guitarist famous for his designs for guitars, one of which was used by **Django Reinhardt**. Presti made her Parisian concert debut at the age of ten, and became a renowned concert guitarist in the 1940s and 1950s. In 1953 she married **Alexandre Lagoya** and their performances and recordings together established them throughout the world and defined the idea of the guitar duo. The brilliant work of the Lagoya/

Presti duo is well captured on the series of *...Pour Deux Guitares* albums and on *Music For The Classic Guitar*. Presti's death at the age of just 43 was a great loss to the world of classical guitar.

PRINCE

Born: Prince Rogers Nelson, June 7th 1958, Minneapolis, Minnesota, US.

■ *Morris/Hohner Tele-style; Knut Koupée Cloud; Sadowsky Tele-style.*

Prince, one of the most prodigiously talented artists to emerge in the 1980s, was set apart by his tremendous all-round ability, seemingly equally gifted in writing, producing, playing and performing. There are few areas in which he has not dabbled, and his combination of the influences of soul and funk stars Sly Stone, Stevie Wonder and James Brown, as well as **Jimi Hendrix**, has produced a style that is both distinctive and unpredictable.

Prince has never been one to underline the contributions of other musicians (though see also **Wendy Melvoin** and **Levi Seacer**), but then the majority of the slinky rhythm work, clever textural stuff and powerful, melodic leads are all his own work anyway. Dig around on Prince's finest studio recordings – *1999* (1983), *Purple Rain* (1984, with The Revolution), *Sign Of The Times* (1987) and *Diamonds & Pearls* (1991, with The New Power Generation) – and you'll find some treasure worthy of closer examination.

JOHN PRINE

Born: October 10th 1946, Maywood, Illinois, US.

A superior songwriter with impeccable credentials, Prine suffered the setback of being compared to Bob Dylan. While they share folk influences, there the similarity ends: Prine has a much harder sound than Dylan, and unlike Dylan his lyrical imagery evokes the urban landscape. Prine's seemingly simple, supportive guitar work is a model for the singer-songwriter, always underlining and interweaving with the thrust of the subject matter, using fine sessioneers like **Grady Martin**, **Reggie Young** and **Steve Goodman** to embellish where necessary. His eponymous debut (1971) was a stunner, including 'Hello In There', 'Angel From Montgomery' and 'Six O'Clock News', while *Bruised Orange* (1978) was also a fine collection. In 1981 he formed his own Oh Boy label, issuing *Aimless Love* (1985), a sparsely arranged and bluesy set, and *Live* (1988) which included a duet with **Bonnie Raitt**. In 1992 he returned with the aptly titled and excellent *The Missing Years*.

CHUCK PROPHET

Born: 1963, San Francisco, California, US.

■ *Squier Telecaster.*

Since joining its ranks in 1984, Prophet has co-fronted the idiosyncratic country-rock band Green On Red, contributing to a variety of moderately successful albums that have somehow failed to lift

them into the major league. In 1990 Prophet launched a parallel solo career with *Brother Aldo*, following it up in 1992 with *Balinese Dancer*. The latter announced his growth to maturity, demonstrating an impressive prowess on guitar and a vocal confidence that had hitherto been overshadowed by Green On Red's main singer Dan Stuart. The deft, economical solos on songs like '110° In The Shade', 'Starcrossed Misbegotten Love' and 'Heartbreaks Like The Dawn' illustrated his willingness to adapt traditional country styles to his own requirements – and also the extent to which he has been influenced by guitarists such as **Roger McGuinn**, **Tom Petty** and **Peter Buck**.

ALAN PROSSER

Born: April 17th 1951, Wolverhampton, England.

Currently the best folk outfit in Britain, The Oyster Band have since their formation in 1980 combined traditional English folk songs with pristine contemporary arrangements. Prosser's incisive, lyrical solos have invited comparisons with **Richard Thompson**, while **Clive Gregson**'s sensitive productions of *Liberty Hall* (1985) and *Wide Blue Yonder* (1987) suggested Fairport Convention in their prime.

RILEY PUCKETT

Born: George Riley Puckett, May 7th 1894, Alpharetta, Georgia, US. Died: July 13th 1946, US.

Along with Fiddling John Carson, Riley Puckett was one of the first country musicians to record on a regular basis. He was educated at the School for the Blind in Macon, Georgia, where he learned to play banjo and guitar, after which he became a full-time professional musician. His first sides for Columbia in 1924 included 'Little Log Cabin In The Lane' and 'Rock All Our Babies To Sleep' – the latter was the first recorded country song to feature yodeling. Later that year he joined The Skillet Lickers as principal vocalist and guitarist, his resonant baritone contributing significantly to the group's popularity with audiences on Atlanta's WSB. After the Skillet Lickers disbanded in 1934 he resumed his solo career, cutting sides for Decca and Bluebird. He continued playing and singing until his death from blood poisoning.

MATTHEW PUICCI

Born: Los Angeles, California, US.

Shortlived and underrated, Rain Parade had in Puicci a versatile, imaginative guitarist who contributed sitar as well as guitar to admirable effect on the group's fine debut *Emergency Third Rail Power Trip* (1983). But then some bands never make one decent record in careers five times as long.

ROBERT QUINE

Born: December 30th 1942, Akron, Ohio, US.

■ *Fender Stratocaster.*

As a member of The Voidoids, vocalist Richard Hell's group, Quine (alongside guitarist Ivan Julian) was on

the cutting edge of New York's new wave of the late-1970s, along with other such charismatic figures as **David Byrne**, **Johnny Thunders** and **Tom Verlaine**.

Quine's technical ability was head and shoulders above many new wave guitarists, however, and he didn't find his true place until he joined Lou Reed for *Blue Mask* (1982), *Legendary Hearts* (1983), *New Sensation* (1984) and *Mistrial* (1986). These albums not only established Quine as a superior guitarist, they also assisted the rehabilitation of Reed in the minds of the public as one of the supreme chroniclers of American life. Quine has played sessions elsewhere, notably on singer/songwriter Matthew Sweet's recreation of the 1960s, *Girlfriend* (1992).

PAUL QUINN

Born: Paul Anthony Quinn, December 26th 1951, Yorkshire, England.

■ *Fernandes.*

Saxon came out of the smoke in 1977 in the wake of Def Leppard and Black Sabbath, but unlike many of their ilk they eschewed the tired old imagery of sex and the occult, concentrating instead upon such wholesome fare as steam trains ('Princess Of The Night') and the assassination of President Kennedy ('Dallas 1pm').

The group is spearheaded by the accomplished Quinn and **Graham Oliver** who seem perhaps unwittingly to sidestep the bravura posturing of most 'cock-rockers'. Among their best recorded examples is the live *The Eagle Has Landed* (1983).

MARTIN QUITTENTON

Born: England.

Doubtless there are some who would argue that any musician who gave Rod Stewart the time of day got everything he deserved. But at various points in his long career Stewart has surrounded himself with session musicians or band members of such quality that even the most trite lyric or banal arrangement is going to come rattling out of the woods smelling as fresh as a daisy and as bonny and blithe as a new-born baby. Stewart's solo career started with *An Old Raincoat Won't Ever Let You Down* (1969) on which he was joined by guitarist and mandolinist Quittenton (as well as guitarist Martin Pugh; Quittenton and Pugh had previously worked together in Steamhammer). On this album and the follow-ups *Gasoline Alley* (1970) and *Every Picture Tells A Story* (1971) Quittenton's acoustic guitar work embellished songs such as the traditional 'Man Of Constant Sorrow', Ewan MacColl's 'Dirty Old Town', Tim Hardin's 'Reason To Believe', Bob Dylan's 'Only A Hobo' and 'Maggie May' (written by Stewart and Quittenton), giving Stewart's voice a weight and delicacy unimaginable from his days with The **Jeff Beck** Group.

While Stewart's career went into overdrive, Quittenton disappeared into studio work, working on such delights as **Ron Wood** of The Faces' *I've Got My Own Album To Do* (1974).

BONNIE RAITT

Born: Bonnie Lynn Raitt, November 8th 1949, Burbank, California, US.

■ *Fender Stratocaster; National resonator; Gibson ES175; Guild F50.*

Ever since she was eight Raitt has played the guitar, and at first she played folk songs and was influenced by blues singer Sippie Wallace and **Odetta**. After moving from the West Coast to Boston, Massachusetts, she enrolled at Radcliffe College and majored in African Studies before leaving in 1969 to play the club and coffee bar circuit.

Raitt's boyfriend Dick Waterman (later to become her manager) introduced her to the work of bluesmen such as **Mississippi Fred McDowell**, **Son House**, **Muddy Waters** and **Otis Rush** among others. Playing a mixture of blues and traditional folk material, she gained a contract with Warner Brothers, cutting *Bonnie Raitt* (1971), and over the next 15 years she made nine albums. While her guitar work, particularly on slide, improved steadily and her repertoire broadened, she gradually took on the mantle of the musicians' musician, with guitarists **Lowell George** and **John Hall** and vocalists Linda Ronstadt, JD Souther, Jackson Browne and Tom Waits all guesting on her albums. But the public at large steadfastly resisted the temptation to buy her records.

In 1989 Raitt, having moved to Capitol, finally scored a commercial success with *Nick Of Time*. Produced by Don Was, it included **John Hiatt**'s 'Thing Called Love', graced by her edge-of-the-seat slide work, and self-composed titles such as 'The Road's My Middle Name'. In fact it varied little from her previous outings, but Was helped a glistening sound issue forth, and there was a serious dearth at the time of such well-crafted albums with strong material. Also in '89 Raitt cut the playful 'I'm In The Mood' as a duet with **John Lee Hooker** illustrating once again her innate tastefulness. *Luck Of The Draw* (1991) followed, featuring a magnificent duet with **Delbert McClinton** on 'Good Man, Good Woman' and self-penned compositions such as 'One Part Be My Lover'.

Although her career has peaked commercially, little else has changed. She remains one of the few to uphold her political convictions by playing as many benefits as possible, and is indeed one of the finest slide guitarists in the business.

MICK RALPHS

Born: March 31st 1948, Hereford, England.

■ *Gibson Les Paul Junior; Gibson Thunderbird; Fender Stratocaster.*

Although Ralphs achieved fame and fortune with Bad Company it was in Mott The Hoople, with producer Guy Stevens, that he assembled one of the best and earliest British hard rock bands. With a repertoire that was blues-based in character, Ralphs was very good at memorable riffs ('Midnight Lady' and 'Rock & Roll Queen' 1972) while Ian Hunter's vocals were reminiscent of Bob Dylan.

Despite the presence of Stevens the group couldn't replicate their live act on record and Hunter gradually wrested control of the band from Ralphs and Stevens, bringing in David Bowie as producer – who had been impressed by guitarist **Mick Ronson** and such idiosyncratic Mott songs as 'The Wheel Of The Quivering Meat Conception'.

Ralphs left to form Bad Company with vocalist Paul Rodgers, drummer Simon Kirke (formerly of Free) and bassist Boz Burrell (formerly of King Crimson). Although they became one of the quintessential hard-rock supergroups of the 1970s, Ralphs' strong-arm guitar driving songs like 'Can't Get Enough', 'Good Lovin Gone Bad' and 'Feel Like Makin Love', they quickly became a strutting self-parody, and their inspiration dissipated.

By the early-1980s the group had all but broken up, and Rodgers had assembled The Firm with **Jimmy Page**. In recent years, Ralphs has reformed Bad Company with a new vocalist and they have resumed touring in the US.

JOHNNY RAMONE

Born: John Cummings, October 8th 1948, Long Island, New York, US.

■ *Mosrite (modified).*

Archetypal punk band The Ramones, while real enough, were larger than life cartoon characters who would have been invented if the group hadn't come into existence by itself.

Johnny was the embodiment of the punk guitarist; many tried to imitate him, but his pared down riffs rattled out like a supercharged gatling-gun on late-1970s fare such as 'Now I Wanna Sniff Some Glue', 'Blitzkrieg Bop', 'You're Gonna Kill That Girl', 'Oh Oh I Love Her So' and 'Sheena Was A Punk Rocker'. Inevitably once the commotion surrounding punk had died down the group's albums became more orthodox – although 'orthodoxy' when Phil Spector is the producer (*End Of The Century* 1980) is an over-simplification.

But the group remain as icons of punk – they still have the leather jackets, pudding-basin haircuts and sneakers – and any band that tries to adopt the motifs of punk today usually ends up, consciously or otherwise, aping The Ramones.

ELLIOTT RANDALL

Born: 1947, New York, New York, US.

■ *Fender Stratocaster.*

Randall briefly played with the rock'n'roll revival band Sha-Na-Na – but that shouldn't be held against him, because he became one of the most underrated session musicians on the East Coast during the early-1970s.

Although he recorded occasionally under his own name – his band Randall's Island cut an acclaimed if unsuccessful eponymous album for Polydor in 1970 – Randall was at his best when somebody stuck some charts under his nose and told him to get on with it. Steely Dan's **Walter Becker** and Donald Fagen had charts a-plenty, and enlisted Randall for some of his best known work on *Katy Lied* (1975) and *The Royal Scam* (1976).

JIMMY RANEY

Born: James Elbert Raney, August 20th 1927, Louisville, Kentucky, US.

■ *Gibson L7; Gibson ES150.*

Jazz writer Leonard Feather in a flight of fancy once said that Raney was to the electric guitar what Lee Konitz was to the alto sax. Without detracting from Konitz in any way, this is misleading, as in recent years Konitz has embraced the avant-garde and dissonance with a vengeance, while Raney has stuck firmly to the mainstream. Be that as it may, Raney is more than just another **Charlie Christian** imitator, as *Two Guitars* (1957) with **Kenny Burrell** illustrates: the chordal interplay between the two has a bold assertiveness that doesn't come from mere imitation.

However, Raney had hit his peak during a two-year tenure with saxophonist Stan Getz in the early-1950s. Getz had the reputation for being the most exacting of taskmasters, even in his younger days, and Raney came into his own within the quintet, trading licks and strapping down the rhythm with a majestic ease (*At Storyville* 1951). That it worked so well was due to Getz not dominating quite so forcefully as he was to do in later years. After finishing with Getz, Raney joined vibraharpist Red Norvo's trio, replacing **Tal Farlow**, before embarking on a lengthy solo and sessions career.

ERNEST RANGLIN

Born: 1933, Kingston, Jamaica.

■ *Gibson; Guild.*

Better known by reputation than by his exploits, Ranglin was a founder of the ska group Clue Jay & The Blues Blasters, which included later Skatalites saxman Roland Alphonso in its lineup. Duke Reid, owner of the Treasure Isle Studios, appointed Ranglin musical director of the studios in 1965, and over the next five years Ranglin's choppy rhythms heralded the transition from ska to rock steady and thence reggae.

While *From Kingston JA To Miami USA* (1983) is one of the few albums Ranglin has recorded in his own name, his album of duets with Jamaican jazz pianist Monty Alexander gives a clear indication of the brilliance and versatility of his style (*Monty Alexander & Ernest Ranglin* 1980).

MOSES RASCOE

Born: July 27th 1917, Windsor, North Carolina, US.

One could easily describe Rascoe as a late developer. Despite learning to play the guitar when he was 13, most of his working life was spent driving a truck, picking the odd tune at truck stops to alleviate the tedium or, literally, to sing for his supper. By the time he retired from the wheel in 1983, Rascoe had graduated to playing in local clubs, and made his recording debut in 1987 (aged 70) for the Flying Fish label. His self-accompanied work on six- and 12-string guitars combined rural blues and folk with an eloquent dignity that evoked a time when musicians played for pleasure.

CHRIS REA

Born: March 4th 1951, Middlesbrough, Cleveland, England.

■ **Fender Stratocaster.**

Rea's taut, atmospheric guitar work stands out in stark relief against the freneticism of many of the guitar heroes of the 1990s. While some find his propensity for big ballads irksome, Rea's ability to skip around the fretboard has few peers and his compositional skills mean that he has established a good, wide ranging repertoire.

Influenced initially by **Joe Walsh** and **Ry Cooder**, Rea played with Magdalene (featuring Whitesnake vocalist David Coverdale) and Beautiful Losers before gaining a solo contract. His debut *Whatever Happened To Benny Santini?* (1978) was polished, replete with the un-bluesy slide guitar that is Rea's distinctive speciality, although it included ballads such as 'Fool If You Think It's Over'. More hits of a similar tempo followed, and while his popularity in Britain was growing, in Germany and northern Europe he had been popular from the outset.

Dancing With Strangers (1987) changed all that, featuring 'Loving You Again' and 'Let's Dance', and established his credentials in Britain and the US. His guitar work was becoming more personal and was growing in confidence, paving the way for *The Road To Hell* (1989). The title track, a meditation on the horrendous M25 (London's principal ring road) contained a moving, reflective guitar solo of epic proportions, illustrating his ability to construct lyrical cameos that add weight to the imagery rather than merely embellishing. *Auberge* (1991) continued the meditative theme in an attempt to evoke the landscape of rural France.

JERRY REED

Born: Jerry Reed Hubbard, March 20th 1937, Atlanta, Georgia, US.

■ **Baldwin electric-acoustic; Barbero-Marcellina; Fender Telecaster; Gibson Super 400CES.**

One of Nashville's most versatile performers, Reed has appeared in movies, written songs and been one of the finest, fastest guitar-pickers on the Nashville session circuit. Reed deploys an unusual 'clawhammer' picking style – sort of classical-country-bluegrass – with skill and flair, sometimes on amplified nylon-strung guitar (like Atkins) or on the more expected Telecaster.

He was taught the guitar by his father, and in 1955 Capitol signed him as a writer (Gene Vincent covered his composition 'Crazy Legs'). After a stint in the army, Reed was signed by Columbia, cutting instrumentals such as **Leadbelly**'s 'Goodnight Irene' and 'Hully Gully Guitars'.

In 1965 Reed was signed by RCA for whom he cut a string of hits that continued right up to the early-1970s, such as 'Guitar Man' (covered by Elvis Presley, as was another Reed composition 'US Male'), 'Tupelo Mississippi Flash', 'Amos Moses', 'When You're Hot You're Hot' and 'She Got The Goldmine (I Got The Shaft)'. His albums were patchy and are rarely seen today, although *The Unbelievable Guitar And*

Voice Of from the late-1960s is well worth seeking. Also good are two sets of duets with **Chet Atkins**, *Me And Jerry Reed* (1970) and *Me And Chet* (1970), fine examples of two men having fun and turning in some attractive interplay.

JIMMY REED

Born: Mathis James Reed Leland, September 6th 1925, Dunleith, Mississippi, US. Died: August 29th 1976, Oakland, California, US.

■ **Kay.**

The long, lean, sinuous boogie lines of Jimmy Reed exerted as much influence on the impressionable youth of Britain during the late-1950s and 1960s as **Muddy Waters**. This was evident by the profusion of covers of Reed songs by bands such as The Rolling Stones ('Honest I Do'), The Animals ('Big Boss Man') and Them ('Bright Lights Big City').

Reed's career had started in Chicago in the late-1940s, leading to a lengthy partnership with guitarist **Eddie Taylor**. With Taylor playing bass guitar and Reed playing guitar and harmonica, he had a string of hits from the mid-1950s that avoided the implicit menace of bluesmen like **Howlin' Wolf** and **John Lee Hooker**, including 'Bright Lights Big City', 'Ain't That Loving You Baby', 'Shame Shame Shame' and 'Honest I Do' among others. Towards the end of the 1960s Reed signed with ABC Bluesway, but ill health and poor production militated against him.

LOU REED

Born: Louis Firbank, March 2nd 1942, New York, New York, US.

■ **Klein; Gretsch; Gibson ES355.**

During Reed's years in The Velvet Underground, **Sterling Morrison** was the principal axeman, but Reed was good at employing the ambient potential of the guitar, having been influenced by avant-garde musicians such as saxmen Ornette Coleman and Archie Shepp, and by doo-wop groups like The Clovers. So Reed used under-exploited areas of the guitar, previously the preserve of jazz musicians, such as atonality and feedback to create the atmosphere behind his lyrics on pieces like 'Heroin', 'Venus In Furs', 'All Tomorrow's Parties', 'Waiting For The Man' and 'White Light, White Heat'. Meanwhile John Cale on viola, Morrison on guitar and Maureen Tucker on drums provided the specifics.

The group split in the early-1970s and Reed started a solo career, his serious claims to being a guitarist of note evaporating as he became, effectively, a three-chord wonder. Not that this mattered much as he enlisted musicians like **Mick Ronson**, **Robert Quine**, **Steve Hunter**, **Steve Howe** and **Dick Wagner** to embroider his string of highly literate albums, including *Berlin* (1973), *Coney Island Baby* (1976), *The Blue Mask* (1982), *New York* (1989) and *Magic & Loss* (1992). Reed became the godfather of the new wave, influencing groups as diverse as Blondie, 10,000 Maniacs, Talking Heads, The Jesus & Mary Chain, U2, Radiohead, Manic Street Preachers, New Order and The Fall.

VERNON REID

Born: London, England.

■ **Hamer custom.**

Living Colour have adopted a similar approach to recording as the most inventive rappers: it doesn't matter about the provenance; if it sounds good then use it. As a consequence, Reid's wonderful combination of funk, metal, jazz and hip-hop has made him one of the most creative guitarists to emerge since **Jimi Hendrix**.

What has made the difference is that Reid swings, and is more concerned with phrasing and timing than cramming in as many notes as possible. The literate ferocity of 'Cult Of Personality' (*Vivid* 1988) and 'Go Away' (*Stain* 1993) owe as much to the fractured metal of groups like Anthrax and the power-riffing of Led Zeppelin as to the jazz funk of the 1980s.

WILLIAM REID

Born: 1958, East Kilbride, Scotland.

■ **Gibson ES330.**

The Jesus & Mary Chain were natural forerunners to the grunge trend of the early-1990s. They cut a string of albums – *Psychocandy* (1985), *Darklands* (1987), *Automatic* (1989) and *Honey's Dead* (1992) – that owed allegiances to The Velvet Underground and The Stooges as well as to punk. Reid pushed feedback and distortion to its practical limits on songs like 'Almost Gold' and 'Teenage Lust', underpinned by brother Jamie's subtle changes of rhythm. This was not a case of noise for its own sake, as the group insisted that if a song didn't work on acoustic guitar it was dumped.

DJANGO REINHARDT

Born: Jean Baptiste Reinhardt, January 23rd 1910, near Liverchies, Belgium. Died: May 16th 1953, Fontainebleau, France.

■ **Selmer Maccaferri.**

The Quintet Of The Hot Club Of France has assumed almost mythical status over the years, with Reinhardt and violinist Stéphane Grappelli contributing in no small part to the intellectual probity of the jazz idiom. Reinhardt, a gypsy, had picked up the rudiments of the guitar, violin and banjo while travelling through France and Belgium. In 1928 he damaged two fingers of his left hand in a fire, and had to adopt a modified technique to play the guitar. He joined Grappelli in 1934, the remainder of the famous Quintet comprising guitarists Joseph Reinhardt and Roger Chaput, and bassist Louis Vola, and recorded widely until 1939, as well as during a number of later reunions.

Influenced by **Eddie Lang**, Louis Armstrong and Duke Ellington, Reinhardt's incredibly bright and assertive single-string improvisations and arresting chordal punctuations leap from pieces like 'Ain't Misbehavin', 'I'll See You In My Dreams', 'Stardust', 'Sweet Georgia Brown' and self-penned titles such as 'Nuages' and 'Djangology'. These, as well as some of the recordings the itinerant Reinhardt made before

Rea-Rei

and after the Quintet's classic 1934-39 period, made a significant impact on contemporary guitarists and, despite his early death, Reinhardt's fluid, melodic style has influenced **Bireli Lagrene**, **Al DiMeola** and **Diz Disley** among many others.

HERB REMINGTON

Born: June 9th 1926, Mishawaka, Indiana, US.

■ *BMI.*

Legendary steel guitarists Remington and **Noel Boggs** were members of Bob Wills' Texas Playboys at the time of the *Tiffany Transcriptions* in the 1940s. These sides illustrate the excellence of Wills as a bandleader, his knack for surrounding himself with stellar sidemen, and the role the band played in popularizing electric guitars (steel and Spanish).

While some steel men got bogged down in technicalities, Remington had a light, fluid touch that imbued standards like 'Sweet Georgia Brown' and 'The Woodchoppers Ball' with a jaunty inventiveness. As western swing declined in popularity Remington moved on and joined Hank Penny's Radio Cowboys in the early-1950s. Although Penny was a fine showman he was no Bob Wills and, despite players of the quality of Remington in the ranks, the arrangements lacked the inventiveness of the Playboys. While Remington played many sessions, one of his finest more recent contributions was to the excellent *Merle Travis Story* (1980), with veteran fiddler Johnny Gimble.

EMILY REMLER

Born: September 18th 1957, New York, New York, US. Died: May 4th 1990, Australia.

■ *Gibson ES330.*

Remler established herself as a notable jazz guitarist, primarily through her series of solo albums, including *Firefly* (1981), *Transitions* (1984) and *Catwalk* (1985), leading her own quartet. In 1985 she cut an album of duets, *Together*, with **Larry Coryell** where she seemed to temper Coryell's flamboyance, bringing out a softer, more lyrical side to his playing as a complement to her own tasteful melodies on titles like 'Arabian Nights' and 'Gerri's Blues'. Her early death was a shocking loss to the world of jazz guitar. *Retrospective* (1991) is a useful compilation.

JOHN RENBOURN

Born: 1944, London, England.

■ *Guild D55; Gibson ES335.*

Prior to joining Pentangle, Renbourn had an illustrious solo career on the British folk club circuit. In 1967 he teamed up with **Bert Jansch** for an album of duets entitled *Bert & John*, demonstrating their wildly contrasting styles: the former visceral and bluesy, the latter florid and jazzy.

Renbourn managed to mix not only jazz, but blues, ragtime and folk into his style, as well as medieval music from Elizabethan composers such as John Dowland – and while a member of Pentangle (1967-72, see Bert Jansch entry) he recorded *Sir John*

Alot Of Merrie Englandes Musyk Thyng & Ye Greene Knyghte (1968) and *The Lady & The Unicorn* (1969). Doffing his hat to **Julian Bream**, Renbourn rearranged and transcribed to the guitar many of the tunes on these albums from original lute pieces, playing them with a light, deft touch.

After Pentangle went their separate ways Renbourn made some fine solo albums, and also teamed occasionally with **Stefan Grossman**, such as on *John Renbourn & Stefan Grossman* (1978) and *Live In Concert* (1985). While testifying to the skill of each player, these did seem more studied and less fluid than Renbourn's own solo records, among the best of which is *The Hermit* (1973).

DON RENO

Born: Spartanburg, South Carolina, US. Died: 1984.

Reno was one of the most versatile performers of his generation, mastering guitar, steel guitar, banjo and mandolin, possessor of an excellent voice... and was even able to turn a step as a comedian. Working initially with The Morris Brothers in the early-1940s, Reno moved on to play with country mandolinist Bill Monroe in 1948. A year later Reno formed The Tennessee Cutups, which included guitarist **Red Smiley**. Playing banjo and mandolin at first, Reno started to broaden his appeal by playing the guitar on titles such as 'Freight Train Boogie' and 'You Never Mentioned Him To Me' in 1954. In 1955 Reno and **Arthur Smith** cut 'Feuding Banjos', later adapted for the movie *Deliverance* as 'Dueling Banjos'. He toured regularly with Smiley until 1964, and then teamed up with vocalist Bill Harrell, playing club dates, concerts and the festival circuit until his death.

TIM RENWICK

Born: August 7th 1949, England.

■ *Fender Stratocaster.*

Renwick and **Cal Batchelor** in Quiver used to play some of the finest country-influenced guitar to be heard in Britain in the early-1970s. Quiver never amounted to much commercially, but they garnered plaudits as musicians' musicians, making them extraordinarily popular as session men. Renwick always seemed to have the edge over Batchelor when it came to holding down the prestigious gigs (Elton John, Cliff Richard, Gary Brooker, Pink Floyd, among others), and indeed for a time it was supremely difficult to pick up an album on which Renwick didn't feature. Had it not been for Renwick, goodness knows what Al Stewart would have done: Renwick's playing on *The Year Of The Cat* (1975) gave Stewart's pretentious lyrics an unwarranted weight and credibility.

Furthermore, when Quiver linked up with The Sutherland Brothers, Renwick and Batchelor gave the brothers' cutesy songs like 'Arms Of Mary' and 'Sailing' a touch of steel. In fact Renwick seems to have spent most of his career making silk purses out of sows' ears. Generally this is not a very rewarding occupation, but Renwick has turned it into a going and growing concern.

ALVINO REY

Born: Alvin McBurney, July 1st 1911, Oakland, California, US.

■ *Gibson Super 400; Fender.*

Best known as a bandleader who came to prominence during the 1930s leading an all-female orchestra, Rey is also notable for his early use of electric guitars, both steel and Spanish. During the 1940s he toured extensively, using arrangements by such luminaries as Neal Hefti, Billy May and Ray Conniff, while his orchestra featured hornmen like Zoot Sims and Al Cohn. In the 1950s Rey and a smaller group appeared regularly on television. When his star as a bandleader faded, he took up classical guitar.

JIM REYNOLDS

Born: James McReynolds, February 13th 1927, Coeburn, Virginia, US.

Brothers Jim (guitar) and Jesse (mandolin and fiddle) were encouraged by their grandfather, an old-time fiddler, to take up music professionally. Inspired by the work of country outfits like The Blue Sky Boys, The Delmore Brothers and The Louvin Brothers, they made their radio debut in 1947 as The Virginia Trio (with Larry Roll), their repertoire gospel oriented and featuring songs like 'God Put A Rainbow In The Clouds'. After cutting sides for the Kentucky label they moved to Capitol and recorded bluegrass items like the Louvins' 'Are You Missing Me' and 'My Little Honeysuckle Rose'.

In 1954, after Jesse had done his bit in Korea, they performed throughout the southern US, landing regular radio slots, and later formed The Virginia Boys (including fiddler Vassar Clements). The revival of interest in folk music and a recording contract with Epic provided them with a string of sizable hits, such as 'Cotton Mill Man', 'Diesel On My Trail', 'Ballad Of Thunder Road' and 'Golden Rocket'.

While their popularity dipped towards the end of the 1960s as the folk boom tailed off, their immaculate harmonies and virtuosic picking made them popular choices among followers of country and folk, and gave them status with the emerging generation of bluegrass musicians like David Grisman, Sam Bush and **Peter Rowan**.

RICKY REYNOLDS

Born: October 28th 1948, Manilan, Arkansas, US.

With Black Oak Arkansas, vocalist Jim Dandy became one of the first posturing, heavy metal heroes, and as such Reynolds and the subsequent guitarists in the band seemed to be Dandy's puppets. Nominally a blues-based boogie band, any musical strengths were subordinated by Dandy's antics, and Reynolds left in 1975 for fresh, unspecified pastures.

RANDY RHOADS

Born: 1957, Los Angeles, California, US. Died: March 19th 1982, Orlando, Florida, US.

■ *Gibson Les Paul; Sandoval Flying V-style; Jackson.*

Formerly a member of Quiet Riot, Rhoads left the

EARLY YEARS In 1956, a year after first arriving in Los Angeles, the 25-year-old Jim Hall was invited to join an unusual quintet being put together by drummer Chico Hamilton. He joined a line-up that benefited from the new textures of cello and flute as well as the traditional bass and drums. Alto saxophonist Buddy Collette was the featured player in a band that mixed all-out blowing and delicate arrangements. Then Hall moved to Jimmy Giuffre's trio before taking an accompanist's role with the incomparable Ella Fitzgerald. Hall reported that his work on such albums as *The Intimate Ella* (1960) and *The Harold Arlen Songbook* (1961) forced him to explore areas that he had previously ignored. "It gave me a sense of space, a way of placing notes in relation to the lyrics, which is quite different from accompanying another instrument," he said in a 1968 interview. Hall's playing has always been intimate in character, his tone round and warm. Both of these make him an ideal accompanist for voices.

THE JIMMY GIUFFRE THREE

(Released 1958) *Tracks:* Gotta Dance/ Two Kinds Of Blues/ The Song Is You/ Crazy She Calls Me/ Voodoo/ My All/ That's The Way It Is/ Crawdad Suite/ The Train And The River. *Line-up:* Jimmy Giuffre (clarinet, tenor & baritone sax), Jim Hall (guitar), Ralph Pena (bass). The idea behind the Jimmy Giuffre trio was that improvisation would take place on all three instruments simultaneously, rather than one leading while the other two filled in behind. Hall found it a very demanding but ultimately rewarding experience. Without drums the instrumentalists had to find their own tempo, then a new and difficult skill. Recorded between Hall's stints with the Chico Hamilton Quintet and Ella Fitzgerald.

THE ART FARMER QUARTET, FEATURING JIM HALL: INTERACTION (Released 1963)

Tracks: The Days Of Wine And Roses/ By Myself/ My Little Suede Shoes/ Embraceable You/ My Kinda Love/ Sometime Ago. *Line-up:* Art Farmer (flugelhorn), Jim Hall (guitar), Steve Swallow (bass), Walter Perkins (drums). In the late summer of 1962, Art Farmer set aside his trumpet, took up the flugelhorn and formed this quartet, which is unusual in having no piano. Hall's excellence as an accompanist makes up the deficit. Recorded when the quartet was a year old, Interaction shows that the group had definitely found its groove. Nonetheless, this was still a demanding new direction for each of the musicians involved.

IT'S NICE TO BE WITH YOU: LIVE IN BERLIN (Released 1974)

Tracks: Up Up And Away/ My Funny Valentine/ Young One, For Debra/ Blue Joe/ It's Nice To Be With You/ In A Sentimental Mood/ Body And Soul/ Romaine. *Line-up:* Jim Hall (guitar), Jimmy Woode (bass), Daniel Humair (drums). This album was recorded in 1969. The producer was jazz writer Joachim Berendt, who asked Hall why he hadn't recorded more pop tunes such as Jim Webb's 'Up Up And Away': "If you try to use pop techniques or pop songs to sell jazz, there's a danger you'll end up selling pop, not jazz . . . and if it catches on you'll be stuck with it," he replied. True enough, although it wasn't a danger that worried the likes of Miles Davis.

| 1956 | 1957 | 1958 | 1959 | 1960 | 1961 | 1962 | 1963 | 1964 | 1965 | 1966 | 1967 | 1968 | 1969 | 1970 | 1971 | 1972 | 1973 | 1974 |

SONNY ROLLINS In 1959, the virtuoso saxophonist and band-leader Sonny Rollins announced his retirement from public performance and recording. This came as a blow to the jazz world, as Rollins was one of the most expressive and imaginative tenor players to have emerged since Lester Young and Coleman Hawkins. As it turned out, the retirement was purely temporary. In late 1961, Rollins pushed a note into Hall's letterbox (he didn't have a telephone) and asked him if he wanted to join forces. Rollins had spent the hiatus away from the hurly-burly of gigging and recording, considering the direction he wanted his music to take, and the band that created *The Bridge* was the result. The title was both symbolic, representing a passing from one phase of his life to the next, and literal, in that the Williamsburg Bridge was where he sought solace during his retirement. The partnership with Hall endured long enough to create a second album,

What's New (1962). Both albums demonstrated the improvisatory flair of the participants within the context of an ensemble.

SONNY ROLLINS & CO.: THE BRIDGE (Released 1962) *Tracks:*

Without A Song/ Where Are You/ John S./ The Bridge/ God Bless The Child/ You Do Something To Me. *Line-up:* Sonny Rollins (tenor saxophone), Jim Hall (guitar), Bob Cranshaw (bass), Ben Riley and H.T. Saunders (drums). Recorded after Sonny Rollins's return from retirement in 1961, this album emphasised the contrast between Hall's delicacy and

Rollins's fire. There was a tremendous mutual respect between the two men. Hall says Rollins inspired him more than any other musician he had played with, even though he was scared of the sax player's formidable musical intelligence: "My year with Sonny was extremely enriching. He navigated with such disconcerting facility in and out of different keys and at the fastest tempos. He and Bill Evans are the only virtuosi that I've ever played with."

SONNY ROLLINS & CO.: WHAT'S NEW (Released 1962) *Tracks:* If Ever I

Would Leave You/ Brownskin Girl/ Don't Stop The Carnival/ The Night Has A Thousand Eyes/ My Ship/ Love Letters/ Long Ago (And Far Away). *Line-up:* Sonny Rollins (tenor saxophone), Jim Hall (guitar), Bob Cranshaw (bass), Ben Riley and H.T. Saunders (drums). This album was recorded immediately after *The Bridge*. The bossa nova feel of titles such as 'Don't Stop The Carnival' came from Hall, who had picked up the new sound in Brazil in 1960. "I sometimes feel I'm only a mediocre musician when I listen to guys like Sonny Rollins," said Hall, later.

BILL EVANS One of the most influential modern jazz pianists of the post war era, Bill Evans first came to prominence on Miles Davis's *Kind Of Blue* (1959) before starting a solo career. With a discursive and hectoring style, Evans was indebted to boppers such as Bud Powell, as well as to hard boppers Horace Silver and Lennie Tristano. This background lay behind his collaborations with Jim Hall on *Undercurrent* (1962) and *Intermodulation* (1966). In both instances Hall approached soloing in much the same way as Sonny Rollins, improvising lines and phrases on a melodic basis, although the sounds they made could hardly be more different. Hall's guitar helps make these two of the most accessible albums of Evans's career. For Hall they were a key element in his musical life in a period that saw him teaching at Lennox School Of Jazz by day and testing his theories by night with some of the most intelligent players of the era.

As a boy soprano, Martin Carthy was groomed for a career in the spotlight. After a spell in the theatre he worked as a musician – dressed as an Elizabethan minstrel – in a London restaurant, until he fell under the influence of Lonnie Donegan in 1959 and started a skiffle group, The Thameside Four. The group's repertoire illustrated Martin's wide range of influences including Rev Gary Davis, Big Bill Broonzy and Josh White, although his guitar work echoed the technique of Uilleann-piper Seamus Ennis. Skiffle gradually gave way to folk as Carthy started to perform solo at London's Troubadour club. In 1963, he made his solo debut on a Decca compilation entitled Hootenanny In London; Martin's

contribution was 'Your Baby 'As Gone Down The Plughole' (later revived by Cream). This was followed two years later by another Decca album The Three City Four with songwriter Leo Rosselson which led to a solo recording contract with the Fontana label. Carthy remained with them until 1971, during which time he recorded six albums and established himself beyond any reasonable doubt as the leading singer/guitarist of traditional English folk song, influencing US performers such as Bob Dylan and Paul Simon in the process. While the traditional folk music revival, and the electric folk-rock that followed, have long passed out of the commercial limelight, Car has flourished in a career built on musical integrity and authentic

Martin Carthy

SWEET WIVELSFIELD (Released 1974) *Tracks:* Shepherd O Shepherd/Bill Boy/Three Joy Sneaksman/Trimdon Grange/All Of A Row/Skewbald/Mary Neal/King Henry/John Barleycorn/The Cottage In The Wood. Produced by Ashley Hutchings who was taking a sabbatical from The Albion Country Band, the outfit he'd formed after leaving Steeleye Span shortly before Carthy himself.

CROWN OF HORN (Released 1976) *Tracks:* The Bedmaking/Locks And Bolts/King Knapperty/Geordie/Willie's Hall/Virginny/The Worcestershire Wedding/Bonny Lass Of Anglesey/William Taylor The Poacher/Old Tom O' Oxford/Palaces Of Gold. Produced once again by Ashley Hutchings, with Tony Cox providing additional accompaniment on synthesizer, an unusual presence among folk revivalists.

973 | 1974 | 1975 | 1976 | 1977 | 1978 | 1979 | 1980 | 1981 | 1982

LANDFALL (Released 1971) *Tracks:* Here's Adieu To All Judges And Juries/Brown Adam/O'er The Hills/The Cruel Mother/Cold, Haily, Windy Night/His Name is Andrew/The Bold Poachers/Dust To Dust (The Gravediggers' Song)/The Broomfield Hill/The January Man. Included in *Landfall* are three contemporary songs, 'His Name is Andrew', 'The January Man' and 'Dust To Dust (The Gravediggers' Song)', composed by David Ackles, Dave Goulder and John Kirkpatrick. Ackles is an American singer who found celebrity with *American Gothic* (1972) while Kirkpatrick has become a fixture on the scene, performing with Richard Thompson among others.

THE WATERSONS: FOR PENCE AND SPICY ALE (Released 1975) *Line-up:* Mike Waterson, Lal Waterson, Norma Waterson, Martin Carthy. *Tracks:* Country Life/Swarthfell Rocks/Barney/Swinton May Song/Bellman/Adieu, Adieu (The Flash Lad)/Apple-Tree Wassailing Song/Sheepshearing/Three Day Millionaire/King Pharim/T Stands For Thomas/Malpas Wassail Song/Chickens In The Garden/The Good Old Way. Carthy had married Norma Waterson in 1972.

CARTHY'S GUITARS Like many players from the world of folk and roots music, Carthy uses a Martin flat-top acoustic guitar. Martin remains the pre-eminent producer of such instruments. The company was established in the US in 1833 by Christian Frederick Martin, an immigrant German-born guitar maker, and today is still based in Nazareth, Pennsylvania. The Martin company's designs for the shape of the flat-top guitar's body, its internal system of bracing and its subtle decorative inlays have influenced virtually every maker of acoustic guitars during the past 160 years or more. Carthy chooses to play a Martin 000-18 model: the '000' refers to the body size and shape, in this case of medium size, while the '18' indicates the style of body decoration. The '18' style is one of Martin's more austere; extravagant pearl abalone inlays are reserved for instruments such as their expensive style-45 models.

OUT OF THE CUT (Released 1982) *Tracks:* The Devil And The Feathery Wife/Reynard The Fox/The Song Of The Lower Classes/Rufford Park Poachers/Molly Oxford/Rigs Of The Time/I Sowed Some Seeds/The Friar In The Well/Jac Rowland/Old Horse. Produced by Martin Carthy, with engineer Jerry Boys, it featured contributions from John Kirkpatrick, who played accordion on 'The Devil And The Feathery Wife' and concertina on 'I Sowed Some Seeds', 'The Friar In The Well' and 'Old Horse', Howard Evans, who played trumpet on 'I Sowed Some Seeds' and 'The Friar I The Well' and flugelhorn on 'Old Horse' and Richard Thompson, who played guitar on 'Old Horse'.

MARTIN CARTHY (Released 1965) *Tracks:* High Germany/The Trees They Do Grow High/Sovay Sovay/Ye Mariners All/The Queen Of Hearts/Broomfield Hill/Springhill Mine Disaster/Scarborough Fair/Lovely Joan/The Barley And The Rye/The Wind That Shakes The Barley/The Two Magicians/The Handsome Cabin Boy/And A Begging I Will Go. With guest appearances from fiddler Dave Swarbrick, at that time a member of The Ian Campbell Folk Group, Carthy's debut created the template for the rest of his career: sparse arrangements illustrating a rich percussive style, and material emphasising a keen commitment to the traditions of English Folk song.

BUT TWO CAME BY (Released 1968) *Tracks:* The Ship In Distress/The Banks Of Sweet Primroses/Jack Orion/Matt Hyland/The White Hare/Lord Of The Dance/The Poor Murdered Woman Laid On The Cold Ground/Creeping Jane/The Streets Of Forbes/Long Lankin/Brass Band Music. Credited to Martin Carthy & Dave Swarbrick, *But Two Came By* is the felicitous result of two accomplished musicians acknowledging the traditions of their repertoire, adding a unique spark of vitality: Martin attributes the arrangement of 'Jack Orion' to A L Lloyd for making it singable. The guitar work is peerless, the precursor to a general folk revival.

PRINCE HEATHEN (Released 1969) *Tracks:* Arthur McBride And The Sergeant/Salisbury Plain/Polly On The Shore/The Rainbow/Died For Love/Staines Morris/Reynardine/Seven Yellow Gypsies/Little Richard And Lady Bernard/Prince Heathen/The Wren (The King). Another collaboration with Swarbrick, *Prince Heathen* is a distillation of Martin's interest in English folk song, with particular emphasis on the rogue elements implicit in its mythology: 'Reynardine', the fox, courses through mythology with its predatory instincts offsetting its latent powers. These powers show the fox as the aggressor, with its guile and cunning, and as the victim.

PLAIN CAPERS Morris Dance Tunes From The Cotswolds (Released 1972) *Line-up:* John Kirkpatrick (anglo concertina, melodeon, button accordion, jaw's harp), Sue Harris (oboe, hammered dulcimer), Martin Carthy (guitar), Martin Brinsford (mouth organ, tambourine), Fi Fraser (fiddle). *Tracks:* Glorishears/Hammersmith Flyover/Old Molly Oxford/Black Jack & Old Black Joe/Blue-Eyed Stranger & Willow Tree/Brighton Camp & The March Past/Bobby And Joan & Bobbing-A-Joe/Monk's March & The Fieldtown Processional/Sweet Jenny Jones & The Sherborne Jig/Lumps Of Plum Pudding/Highland Mary/Wheatley Processional and others.

1963 1964 1965 1966 1967 1968 1969 1970 1971 1972

MARTIN CARTHY'S SECOND ALBUM (Released 1966) *Tracks:* Two Butchers/Ball O' Yarn/Farewell Nancy/Lord Franklin/Ramblin' Sailor/Lowlands O' Holland/Fair Maid On The Shore/Bruton Town/Box On Her Head/Newlyn Town/Brave Wolfe/Peggy And The Sailor/Sailor's Wife. Featuring the violin of Dave Swarbrick once again, this album saw the consolidation of a partnership that had commenced with Martin's debut the previous year. It was consolidated over the next two years with a constant round of touring that made the duo the most accurate interpreters of traditional English song, then on the brink of a revival.

BYKER HILL (Released 1967) *Tracks:* The Man Of Burnham Town/The Fowler/Gentleman Soldier/Brigg Fair/The Bloody Gardener/The Barley Straw/Byker Hill/Davy Lowston/Our Captain Cried All Hands/Domeama/The Wife Of The Soldier/John Barleycorn/Lucy Wan/The Bonny Black Hare. Credited to Martin Carthy & Dave Swarbrick, *Byker Hill* included songs such as the title track which have become staples in the duo's repertoire, but like all great interpreters their performances of a song are never the same: a live version of 'Byker Hill' is included on 1990's *Life And Limb*, but the original here was as spare as the later version was expansive.

STEELEYE SPAN: TEN MAN MOP OR MR RESERVOIR BUTLER RIDES AGAIN
(Released 1971) *Line-up:* Maddy Prior (vocals, tambourine, tabor, bells), Martin Carthy (vocals, guitar, banjo), Tim Hart (vocals, guitar, dulcimer), Ashley Hutchings (vocals, bass guitar), Peter Knight (vocals, fiddle, mandolin, organ, bass guitar). *Tracks:* Gower Wassail/Paddy Claney's Jig/Willie Clancy's Fancy/Four Nights Drunk/When I Was On Horseback/Marrowbones/Captain Coulston/Reels: Wee Weaver/Skewball. The final outing for this line-up of Steeleye Span before Martin departed for pastures new, hanging up his Telecaster.

STEELEYE SPAN: PLEASE TO SEE THE KING (Released 1971) *Line-up:* Maddy Prior (vocals, tambourine, tabor, bells), Martin Carthy (vocals, guitar, banjo, organ, bells), Tim Hart (vocals, guitar, dulcimer, bells), Ashley Hutchings (vocals, bass guitar, bells), Peter Knight (vocals, fiddle, mandolin, organ, bass guitar, bells). *Tracks:* The Blacksmith/Cold, Haily, Windy Night/Jigs – Bryan O'Lynn The Hag With The Money/Prince Charlie Stuart/Boys Of Bedlam/False Knight On The Road/The Lark In The Morning/Female Drummer/The King/Lovely On The Water. The first Steeleye Span album with Carthy followed Fairport Convention's *Liege & Lief*.

Jim Hall

Jim Hall has never quite reached the heights of acclaim afforded to other contemporary jazz guitarists. But he has built a reputation among the cognoscenti, both as a prolific soloist and as an ensemble player. His solo outings illustrate his formidable understanding of form and technique, but everywhere his music his sparse, lyrical and passionate runs indicate his adherence to an approach more generally associated with horn players, for instance Sonny Rollins. Although this individual style is well-suited to solo excursions, he is at least as successful in his ensemble work, which shows an ability to work within closely defined parameters. Hall studied the guitar privately while still at school, forming his first bands as a teenager. He was influenced initially by Charlie Christian and Django Reinhardt, and by saxophonists such as Zoot Sims. After school he attended the Cleveland Institute of Music, earning a Batchelor of Music degree. His first big break came in 1955, after he had moved to Los Angeles. After playing with the Bob Hardaway Quartet, the Ken Hanna Band and the Dave Pell Octet, he was recruited to join the Chico Hamilton Quintet. This was followed by a spell with pianist and arranger John Lewis, cutting Two Degrees East, Three Degrees West (1956). In late 1956, Hall joined the experimental trio of saxophonist/clarinetist Jimmy Giuffre, but also moonlighted on sessions with Bob Brookmeyer and Paul Desmond, among others. After leaving Giuffre, he backed Ella Fitzgerald, his first experience with a singer, and played with pianist Bill Evans, before joining Sonny Rollins for the epochal albums The Bridge (1962) and What's New (1963). Since the mid-1960s, Hall has been his own man and pursued a solo career with a variety of sidemen, but he never attempts to dominate. Anybody sounds good in his company.

THE JIM HALL TRIO: CIRCLES (Released 1981) *Tracks:* (All Of A Sudden) My Heart Sings/ Love Letters/ Down From Antigua/ I Can't Get Started/ T.C. Blues/ Circles/ Aruba. *Line-up:* Jim Hall (guitar), Don Thompson (piano & bass), Rufus Reid (bass), Terry Clarke (drums). This was Hall's most enduring trio, featuring on a number of other Hall albums including Live! (1975) and Live In Tokyo (1976).

JIM HALL QUARTET: ALL ACROSS THE CITY (Released 1989) *Tracks:* Beija-Flor/ Young One (For Debra)/ All Across The City/ Something Tells Me/ Prelude To A Kiss/ How Deep Is The Ocean/ Bemsha Swing/ R.E.M. State/ Drop Shot/ Big Blues/ Jane. *Line-up:* Jim Hall (guitar), Gil Goldstein (keyboards), Steve La Spina (bass), Terry Clarke (drums). Hall says he chose the members of this band because "they listen well"

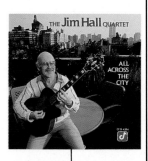

| 1976 | 1977 | 1978 | 1979 | 1980 | 1981 | 1982 | 1983 | 1984 | 1985 | 1986 | 1987 | 1988 | 1989 | 1990 | 1991 | 1992 | 1993 |

BILL EVANS & JIM HALL: UNDERCURRENT (Released 1962) *Tracks:* My Funny Valentine/ I Hear A Rhapsody/ Dream Gypsy/ Romain/ Skating In Central Park/ Darn That Dream. Richard Rodgers and Lorenz Hart's 'My Funny Valentine' has been dignified with classic status ever since its first appearance in the 1937 show Babes In Arms. Others – for instance, Miles Davis, Gerry Mulligan and Elvis Costello – have recorded more famous versions, but Bill Evans and Jim Hall find the melancholy and resignation that lies at the heart of the song.

JIM HALL – RON CARTER DUO: ALONE TOGETHER (Released 1972) *Tracks:* St. Thomas/ Alone Together/ Receipt, Please/ I'll Remember April/ Softly As In A Morning Sunrise/ Whose Blues/ Prelude To A Kiss/ Autumn Leaves. *Line-up:* Ron Carter (bass), Jim Hall (guitar). Recorded live at the 'Jazz Adventures' concert at the Playboy Club, New York City, on August 4, 1972. This is the first album Hall made with Carter, one of the great bass players. Any duo depends upon perfect musical and extra-musical communication, but their understanding verges on the supernatural. Also recorded with Ron Carter **TELEPHONE** (1985)

JIM HALL'S THREE (Released 1986) *Tracks:* Hide And Seek/ Skylark/ Bottlenose Blues/ And I Do/ All The Things You Are/ Poor Butterfly/ Three. *Line-up:* Jim Hall (guitar), Steve La Spina (bass), Akira Tana (drums). One of the reasons Jim Hall has stayed at the top of his profession is his economy. There is nothing superfluous in his playing. He goes beyond the notes to speak from his heart, through his chosen instrument. This quality is clear in his ballad playing, particularly in such standards as the Jerome Kern & Oscar Hammerstein 'All The Things You Are' or the Johnny Mercer & Hoagie Carmichael 'Skylark'.

HALL'S GUITARS Long known as a player of the Gibson ES175 electric guitar, Hall has occasionally used other Gibson guitars such as an L5, and has had guitars made for him by specialist luthiers like Jimmy D'Aquisto. But it's with the 175 that Hall's reputation has been built. The rich chordal tone of Gibson's hollow-bodied single-cutaway ES175 has become the preferred guitar of many jazz guitarists as well as Hall, including Joe Pass and Pat Metheny. When Gibson launched the ES175 in 1949 it was the first serious electric guitar from that respected company, and it made players and guitar makers sit up to the possibilities of such an instrument. Later Gibson added a second pickup to the original design, but Hall's most-used ES175 – which once belonged to jazz guitarist Howard Roberts, and has been modified over the years to include a new fingerboard and sturdier tuners – is of the earlier single-pickup type.

BRASS MONKEY (Released 1983)
Tracks: The Waterman's Hornpipe/Fable Of The Wings/The Miller's Three Sons/ The Maid And The Palmer/Bad News/ Sovay/Tip Top Hornpipe Primrose Polka/ The Jolly Bold Robber/The Old Grenadier. *Line-up:* John Kirkpatrick (anglo concertina, melodeon, button accordian & vocals), Howard Evans (trumpet, flugelhorn & vocals), Martin Carthy (guitar, mandolin & vocals), Martin Brinsford (mouth organ, tambourine, drum & saxophone) and Roger Williams (trombone & vocals). Produced by Jerry Boys, *Brass Monkey* was the formalization of an occasional outfit that had gigged together on and off.

RIGHT OF PASSAGE (Released 1989) *Tracks:* The Ant And The Grasshopper/Eggs In Her Basket/ A Stitch In Time/McVeagh/All In Green/Company Policy/The Banks Of The Nile/La Cardeuse/Bill Norrie/ The Sleepwalker/The Dominion Of The Sword. Produced by Martin Carthy and Dave Kenny, Right Of Passage was Martin's first solo album in seven years. However, it featured additional support from John Kirkpatrick on one row melodeon and button accordion and Chris Wood on fiddle. Fiddler Dave Swarbrick appeared on 'All In Green', which was the first time Carthy and he had recorded together since 1969's *Prince Heathen*.

LIFE AND LIMB (Released 1990) *Tracks:* Sovay/The Begging Song/The Bows Of London/The Pepperpot, Sailing Into Walpole's March & Bunker Hill/A Question Of Sport/Oh Dear Oh/Carthy's March & The Lemon Tree/Lochmaben Harper/Byker Hill. Credited to Martin Carthy & Dave Swarbrick, Life & Limb was recorded live at Folcal Point, St Louis, Missouri, USA, with the exception of 'Byker Hill', which was recorded live at McCabe's Guitar Shop, Santa Monica, California, USA. The tour was the direct result of Dave's appearance on the previous year's Right Of Passage; it re-affirmed their position as two of the most powerful instrumentalists in traditional folk music.

SKIN AND BONE (Released 1992) *Tracks:* The Sheepstealer/The Poacher/ I Courted A Damsel/Lucy Wan/The Trip We Took Over The Mountain/The Skewbald/The Ride In The Creel/The Brown Girl/Such A War Has Never Been/ Perfumes Of Arabia/Carthy's Reel/The Return To Camden Town/The New Mown Hay/Clyde's Water/Mrs Bermingham/No 178/Blind Mary. Another Carthy/ Swarbrick collection of mainly traditional songs, performed with the usual love and astringency. Most of the songs are taken from collections made at the beginning of the century by the likes of Vaughan Williams and Percy Grainger. In these readings their emotional power is undimmed.

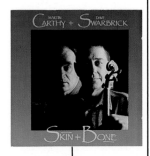

| 1984 | 1985 | 1986 | 1987 | 1988 | 1989 | 1990 | 1991 | 1992 | 1993 |

BRASS MONKEY: SEE HOW IT RUNS (Released 1986).
Tracks: George's Son/Da Floo'er O' Taft & The Lass O' Paties Mill/The Handweaver And The Factory Maid/The Rose Lawn Quadrille/Willie The Waterboy/Doctor Fauster's Tumblers, The Night Of Trafalgar & Prince William/ Riding Down To Portsmouth/Trowie Burn/The Foxhunt. *Line-up:* John Kirkpatrick (anglo concertina, melodeon, button accordian & vocals), Howard Evans (trumpet & flugelhorn), Martin Carthy (guitar, mandolin & vocals), Martin Brinsford (mouth organ, percussion & C melody saxophone) and Roger Cheetham (trombone). Produced by Tony Engle & John Kirkpatrick.

Carthy's early years saw the development of a unique acoustic guitar style and a partnership with fiddler Dave Swarbrick, with Carthy guesting on Swarbrick's albums such as *Rags, Reels & Airs* (1967). But the 1970s and 1980s were notable for Carthy's ensemble work with the electric folk-rock band Steeleye Span, then The Watersons and Brass Monkey. Despite the brevity of his tenure with Steeleye Span (just two albums, *Please To See The King* and *Ten Man Mop*), Carthy's lean, concise electric guitar work on Fender Telecaster echoed that of Richard Thompson of Fairport Convention, lending weight and substance to the embryonic English folk-rock movement.
After Ashley Hutchings left Steeleye Span to form The Albion Band, Carthy left shortly thereafter as Steeleye Span were moving more towards rock, although he returned briefly to record *Storm Force Ten* (1977). After leaving Steeleye Span,

Carthy re-applied himself to his solo career, as well as joining The Watersons who had become during the 1960s the most authentic interpreters of traditional English folk song, popularising hymnals and unaccompanied singing. Carthy's arrival added an extra dimension to the group's sound.
While working with the Watersons, Carthy embarked on a number of

● The partnership of Martin Carthy and fiddler Dave Swarbrick remains the lynchpin of contemporary English folk song.

side projects, such as a collaboration with Ashley Hutchings and The Albion Band on *Battle Of The Field* (1973; released 1976), on the music for London's National Theatre production of Flora Thompson's pastoral memoir *Lark Rise To Candelford: A Country Tapestry* (1979), and on *The Transports* (1977), a folk opera penned by Peter Bellamy, formerly of The Young Tradition. In addition Carthy cemented a relationship with accordionist John Kirkpatrick in Brass Monkey which had begun during the recording of Steeleye Span's *Storm Force Ten*. Although Brass Monkey only recorded two albums, *Brass Monkey* and *See How It Runs*, they reconvene for the odd performance and play as if they've never been apart.
More recently, tours and two albums with Dave Swarbrick have perpetuated Carthy's standing as Britain's most vital interpreter of traditional music.

band in 1979 to join vocalist Ozzy Osbourne in his newly formed Blizzard Of Oz. While Rhoads was an efficient guitarist, it wasn't his expertise that was the issue.

Like the rest of the band he was a bit player in the Ozzy Osbourne Experience, which was high on effect and showmanship and short on everything else. Nonetheless, the sheets of notes that Rhoads unleashed on *Diary Of A Madman* (1981) became highly rated components of the metal guitar manual of the early-1980s, but Rhoads' career was cut short in 1982 when he was killed in an air-crash at the age of just 25. (The Jackson company issued Rhoads 'signature' guitars in 1986 and 1992.)

DAVID RHODES

Born: England.

■ *Steinberger; Ovation; Fender Jazzmaster.*

Influenced by **Chris Spedding**, **John McLaughlin** and **Jimi Hendrix**, Rhodes has been ex-Genesis vocalist Peter Gabriel's principal guitarist since 1979. Although Rhodes at the time was a member of a little-known new wave band, Random Hold (1979-82), he has grown in stature and his presence has lent some continuity to the groove of Gabriel's albums.

'Big Time' and 'Sledgehammer' from *So* (1986) were sinuous and sexy, with Rhodes forswearing improvisation and instead offering melodic support. The later *Us* (1992) was described by some as being Gabriel's guitar album, but naturally this was a simplification of Gabriel's and Rhodes' apparently intuitive approach to playing. *Us* was in fact more layered and Rhodes, complemented once more by producer Daniel Lanois, plus (on two tracks) **Leo Nocentelli**, was able to apply a tapestry-like weave of sounds over the album's structure, such as the distorted feedback on 'Come Talk To Me'.

While his diffidence as an axeman is somewhat anachronistic in an ego-heavy vocation, Rhodes' reluctance to spit out as many notes per bar as possible should be an inspiration for any novice. He has also played with **Joan Armatrading** and **T-Bone Burnett**, and contributed to a number of tracks on Talk Talk's excellent *The Colour Of Spring* (1986).

LEON RHODES

Born: 1933, Dallas, Texas, US.

■ *Gibson ES345; Gibson L5.*

Rhodes spent much of his career as principal guitarist in Ernest Tubb's Texas Troubadours. Today Tubb's honky-tonk style is regarded as a bit passé, emblematic of the rampant conservatism that country seems to predicate. However, Tubb and his band were true pioneers in breaking down Nashville's resistance to the electric guitar, first by guitarist Fay 'Smitty' Smith in the 1940s, as well as by later Tubb guitar sidemen such as Rhodes, Jimmie Short and **Billy Byrd** whose hard-edged sounds would later be emulated by **Don Rich** and the rest of the Bakersfield denizens. Tubb's rigorous recording and touring schedule helped popularize the electric

guitar (documented on the *Country Hall Of Fame* retrospective), as did western swing pioneer Bob Wills' various guitarists, and the instrument soon became an accepted part of the country arsenal.

RED RHODES

Born: Orville J Rhodes, December 30th 1930, East Alston, Illinois, US.

Rhodes was taught to play a resonator guitar as a young child, and by the time he was 15 had become an expert steel guitarist, playing the clubs and bars with his stepfather. In 1960 he moved to Los Angeles and as a pedal-steel player tapped into the lucrative studio session world, issuing some solo records in 1962 and 1963. By the end of the decade he was employed regularly by **Michael Nesmith** in the First (and Second) National Bands, a position Rhodes held until 1973, although he also contributed to some of Nesmith's later albums. Rhodes cut a pleasant solo album *Velvet Hammer In A Cowboy Band* (1973) for Nesmith's Countryside label, and during the 1970s and 1980s he returned to the session circuit and established his own guitar workshop, where he builds guitars and runs instructional masterclasses.

TONY RICE

Born: 1951, Danville, Virginia, US.

■ *Martin D-28 (ex-Clarence White); Santa Cruz 'signature'.*

One of the most prolific of the new wave of bluegrass artists, guitarist and vocalist Rice started his career in 1960 when, obsessed with the work of guitarist **Clarence White**, he joined The Rice Brothers (with his brothers mandolinist Larry and bassist Ronnie, later adding guitarist Wyatt). Tony remained with them until the early-1970s when he joined JD Crowe's New South, followed by stints with Ricky Skaggs and Emmylou Harris.

With Skaggs he cut *Skaggs & Rice* (1980) which featured fine mandolin/guitar duets on a range of traditional tunes like 'Bury Me Beneath The Weeping Willow' and 'There's More Pretty Girls Than One' as well as Bill Monroe titles such as 'Mansions For Me' and 'Tennessee Blues'. In the 1970s Rice was a member of a couple of bands formed by mandolinists: Quicksilver, with Doyle Lawson, and The David Grisman Quartet. Rice had his own band The Outfit for a while, as well as collaborating with **Norman Blake**. Rice's solo work ranges from the traditional **Doc Watson** approach (*Manzanita*) to a more experimental style (*Mar West*), and he is without doubt one of the finest modern bluegrass flat-pickers around.

DON RICH

Born: August 15th 1941, Olympia, Washington, US. Died: July 17th 1974, near Morro Bay, California, US.

■ *Fender Telecaster.*

An influential member of Buck Owens' Buckaroos during their halcyon years, Rich had learned to play guitar by 1946. Five years later, having mastered the fiddle, he appeared in a talent contest and won a trip

to Hollywood, which eventually resulted in meeting Owens in 1958 and joining The Buckaroos.

He was a very important contributor to the embryonic Bakersfield sound, with a clean, cutting sound and highly individual performances, heard on tracks like the instrumental hit 'Buckaroo', 'Faded Love', 'Act Naturally' (covered later by The Beatles, more evidence of **George Harrison**'s rockabilly roots), 'Turnwater Breakdown', 'Love's Gonna Live Here' and 'Orange Blossom Special'. Rich also penned songs for Owens, such as 'Waiting In The Welfare Line', where he appears on acoustic. Capitol's *Best Of* sets have everything you need. Owens himself was no mean player, and the two of them would occasionally duel Telecasters to dazzling effect.

Rich left the group briefly in the 1960s to qualify as a music teacher, and was killed in 1974 aged just 32 when his motorcycle crashed, a terrible loss to country guitar playing.

KEITH RICHARDS

Born: Keith Richard, December 18th 1943, Dartford, Kent, England.

■ *Fender Telecaster; Music Man Silhouette; Gibson Les Paul; Harmony; Guild Bluesbird; Zemaitis.*

There are few rhythm guitarists who can accurately lay claim to having changed the face of rock'n'roll as comprehensively as Richards, and his **Chuck Berry**-styled riffing has caused him to be dubbed the human riff. So many Rolling Stones songs are instantly memorable through the opening chords, more emblematic of the Stones than Mick Jagger's lips will ever be.

Stretching over 30 years, Richards' style has constantly evolved to encompass fresh influences, often using a five-string guitar minus the low E and open-tuned. What remains today is a no less distinctive blend of R&B, country, reggae, jazz and soukous. Isolating excellence in the Richards canon is a bit like asking which of JS Bach's fugues is best, but riffs that have etched themselves indelibly into successive generations include those on 'Satisfaction', 'Jumpin Jack Flash', 'Midnight Rambler', 'Street Fighting Man', 'Brown Sugar', 'Tumbling Dice', 'Miss You' and 'Start Me Up'.

Remarkably, after all these years, Richards' enthusiasm for music seems undimmed and his championing of lesser-known players or styles sets him in relief against the social aspirations of many of his contemporaries. Since the arrival of **Ron Wood** in the Stones camp in 1976, Richards seems to have developed a valuable partnership, governed by gut and feel rather than intellect.

SYLVAN RICHARDSON

Born: Britain.

■ *Fender Stratocaster.*

Despite his rather attractive name, Sylvan Richardson failed to withstand the bloodletting that followed in the rise to iconic status of Simply Red's vocalist Mick Hucknall. The first two albums, *Picture Book* (1985) and *Men & Women* (1987), had a cohesiveness and energy that only comes from group efforts.

RHO-RIC

Richardson's slinky chops gave added weight to Hucknall's muscular phrasing on songs like 'Holding Back The Years', 'Jericho', 'Money's Too Tight To Mention' and 'The Right Thing'. By the time Hucknall had hit the big time, Richardson had hit the road; his replacement was **Aziz Ibrahim** who failed to last much longer.

WENDELL RICHARDSON

Born: Antigua.

When 'world music' was still a prepubescent concept with little idea of its own identity, Osibisa emerged as a front-runner in Afro-rock. The group got its name from the Fanti term for highlife, and comprised a mix of African and West Indian musicians living in London. Richardson informed much of the stylistic content of the group's repertoire, being well versed in Caribbean and African rhythms. The group's first outing was unexceptional, but the follow-up *Woyaya* (1972) had a sparky, churning inventiveness that utilized Richardson's hard, trebly sound to the maximum, and the title track had an anthemic nostalgia that predicated the increasing volubility among African musicians for basic human rights. While the group failed to last much beyond the mid-1970s, they heralded a new age for many African musicians who had hitherto believed that there was little or no commercial scope among Western audiences, although few African musicians have since managed to capitalize on that aspect of Osibisa's achievement.

GARY RICHRATH

Born: October 10th 1949, Peoria, Illinois, US.

■ *Gibson Les Paul.*

REO Speedwagon, named after a type of fire engine, were formed in 1967 by keyboardist Alan Gratzer and drummer Neal Doughty at the University of Illinois; the lineup was supplemented by Richrath, vocalist Terry Luttrell and bassist Gregg Philbin. Throughout the 1970s they joined an increasing army of faceless bands like Styx, Kansas and Mahogany Rush which toured ceaselessly and built up formidably large followings – wherever they toured, their records were promoted with intensive radio airplay. Richrath provided much of the material and demonstrated a well developed grasp of rock's salient clichés ('Keep On Lovin' You' and 'Take It On The Run') but REO's popularity remains something of an enigma as we have yet to find anyone who has actually heard one of their many albums (for example *You Can Tune A Piano But You Can't Tuna Fish* 1978, *Hi Infidelity* 1980, or *Life As We Know It* 1987).

LEE RITENOUR

Born: November 1st 1952, Hollywood, California, US.

■ *Gibson ES335; Fender Stratocaster; Ibanez 'signature'; Valley Arts; Roland.*

Nicknamed Captain Fingers, Ritenour is one of the most technically accomplished session players to have emerged in the last 20 years. Those with whom he has recorded include Sergio Mendes, Herbie Hancock, Peggy Lee, Gato Barbieri, Grover Washington, Bob James, Oliver Nelson, Dave Grusin and Carly Simon. While many of his own earlier recordings such as *The Captain's Journey* (1978) and *Rit* (1981) are suffused with a bland user-friendliness best suited for airports or shopping malls, Ritenour's biggest problem seems to be in finding material and arrangements that test his undoubted expertise. With that in mind, the all-acoustic *Rio* (1982) and *Harlequin* (1985) are amongst his best work.

ANDY ROBERTS

Born: June 12th 1946, Harrow, Middlesex, England.

From the late-1960s Roberts was a familiar figure on the flourishing British folk club circuit. His earliest ventures included a stint with The Liverpool Sound, which comprised Merseyside poets Adrian Henri and Roger McGough, with Roberts providing acoustic accompaniment to readings. He was also involved in later offshoots such as Scaffold, The Liverpool Scene, and Grimms.

While Roberts' solo albums such as *Home Grown* (1971) were pleasant, with his guitar work reminiscent of the fluid style of **John Fahey**, his material lacked the impact of the more voluble and imaginative **Roy Harper** and **John Martyn**, and his guitar work was without the studied seriousness of **John Renbourn**.

In 1972 Roberts teamed up with ex-Fairport Convention singer Ian Matthews in the short-lived Plainsong, recording the concept album *In Search Of Amelia Earhart*, based on the life of the American aviator. Since then Roberts has recorded intermittently, cutting *Loose Connections* (1984) and *From Time To Time* (1985), among others, as well as touring occasionally in Hank Wangford's British country/goodtime band, where Roberts' pseudonym was Brad Breath. More recently Roberts has concentrated on session work and TV theme composition.

HOWARD ROBERTS

Born: Howard Mancel Roberts, October 2nd 1929, Phoenix, Arizona, US. Died: June 28th 1992, Seattle, Washington, US.

■ *Gibson 'signature'; Epiphone 'signature'.*

Principally self-taught, Roberts was one of a legion of jazz musicians who spent most of their time working in Hollywood film or TV studio orchestras (for example *The Twilight Zone* theme), as well as playing on countless record sessions (from Chubby Checker to Frank Sinatra). Consequently Roberts' success with his own albums and groups was limited, but *Good Picking* (1957) featured a string of standards such as 'Lover Man', 'The More I See You' and 'All The Things You Are', indicating a style reminiscent of **Barney Kessel**. As a sideman, Roberts worked with trumpeter Shorty Rogers (his original mentor), clarinettist Buddy DeFranco and drummer Chico Hamilton, among others. He helped set up the Guitar Institute of Technology (GIT), a school for musicians in Los Angeles.

BRIAN ROBERTSON

Born: September 12th 1956, Glasgow, Scotland.

■ *Gibson Les Paul.*

While Robertson didn't join Thin Lizzy until 1974, he did much to consolidate the group's gradual evolution from the directionless purveyors of the Irish folk tune 'Whiskey In The Jar' to a stadium-filling rock band. This was achieved notably through 'The Boys Are Back In Town', which some point to as being a classic rock track from the same school as Van Halen's 'Jump' and Deep Purple's 'Smoke On The Water'. Robertson and **Scott Gorham** had many fine hours on stage, but Robertson left in 1977 after suffering an injured hand, and much of his thunder was stolen by successive replacements such as **Gary Moore**, **Snowy White** and **Midge Ure**.

ROBBIE ROBERTSON

Born: Jaime Robertson, July 5th 1943, Toronto, Ontario, Canada.

■ *Fender Telecaster; Fender Stratocaster.*

Along with **John Fogerty**'s Creedence Clearwater Revival, The Band represented the swing in the late-1960s toward the appreciation of indigenous American music styles, and their guitarist Robertson had the ability to create evocative images with his concise, melodic contributions – what he has described as "sweet little cries between the lines".

Robertson had been hired by rockabilly vocalist Ronnie Hawkins in 1959 as guitarist for his backing band, The Hawks, and Robertson demonstrated his flair with a wailing solo on the group's reworking of Bo Diddley's 'Who Do You Love' (1963), by far the best thing about the recording. Consequently they were enlisted by Bob Dylan to back him on his infamous 'folkie goes electric' British/Irish tour, and Robertson's superbly spiky support can be heard on the widely circulated *Albert Hall* bootleg (1966, actually mostly from the Manchester show).

Afterwards, Dylan hid himself away with the group, now known simply as The Band, and over the next 18 months they backed him on a series of tracks that emerged on bootlegs and the official *Basement Tapes* (1975), while also recording their own debut for Capitol, *Music From Big Pink* (1968). Robertson's solo on 'To Kingdom Come' and his interjections throughout 'This Wheel's On Fire' were particularly notable. *The Band* (1969) was a classic, a loving representation of a disappearing America, again with fine guitar work from Robertson, especially on 'Look Out Cleveland' and at the close of 'King Harvest'.

Later albums saw the group's collective edge dissipated by the trials of life on the road, although they perform superbly on the live albums *Rock Of Ages* (1972) and *Before The Flood* (with Bob Dylan; 1974). Complete with magnificent horn arrangements by Allen Toussaint, *Rock Of Ages* featured a reworking of 'Unfaithful Servant' from *The Band*, and it's interesting to compare the acoustic solo at the end of the studio recording with Robertson's harmonic-infested electric work on *Rock*. The Band split in 1976, since when Robertson has cut

RIC-ROB

a brace of solo albums, *Robbie Robertson* (1987) and *Storyville* (1991), and scored film soundtracks.

DUKE ROBILLARD

Born: 1950, Providence, Rhode Island, US.

■ *Fender Stratocaster.*

Robillard's guitar style is a pot-pourri of disparate influences, from the blues of **BB King**, **T-Bone Walker** and **Guitar Slim** to the jazz of **Charlie Christian** and **Tiny Grimes**.

Inspired initially by **Buddy Holly**, **Duane Eddy** and **Chuck Berry**, Robillard built his first guitar while at high school, formed Roomful Of Blues in 1967, and the group's reputation quickly took hold as they accompanied artists like Professor Longhair, Helen Humes, Red Prysock and **Earl King**. In 1977 Roomful Of Blues cut their debut, and on pieces like 'Duke's Jazz', 'Still In Love With You' and 'Stormy Monday' Robillard indicated his debt to Walker by recreating the nuances of his jazzy style, with passing nods to hornmen like Johnny Hodges and Lester Young. The follow-up *Let's Have A Party* (1979) had a harder, more metallic sound, showing allegiance to **Albert Collins** and **Johnny Guitar Watson**.

In 1980 Robillard left Roomful Of Blues and played stints with bluesman Robert Gordon and ex-**Muddy Waters** sidemen The Legendary Blues Band. After cutting solo albums such as *Swing* (1987) with Scott Hamilton, which evokes the jazzy roadhouse style of the 1930s and 1940s, and *Too Hot To Handle* (1989), Robillard was recruited to replace **Jimmy Vaughan** in The Fabulous Thunderbirds for the excellent *Walk That Walk, Talk That Talk* (1991).

While the Thunderbirds album was fine, with Robillard's searing solos matching those of Kid Bangham chop for chop, it couldn't pave the way for Robillard's solo *Turn It Around* (1991). Never merely a demonstration in guitar virtuosity, this album's energy level is unfaltering, with the rollicking shuffle of 'I Think You Know', the Tex-Mex cha-cha of Buddy Holly's 'Tell Me How' and the rousing 'Don't Look At My Girl Like That' conspiring to give the record a wonderful depth and sense of purpose. Along with **Eric Johnson**, Robillard remains one of the brightest and most inventive blues-rock guitarists around today.

RICH ROBINSON

Born: May 24th 1969, Atlanta, Georgia, US.

■ *Gibson Les Paul.*

Since their emergence in 1989 The Black Crowes have lent a touch of rural rough'n'tumble to the plethora of noisy navel-searchers currently clogging the airwaves. Formed by brothers Chris (vocals) and Rich Robinson (guitar), they made their debut with *Shake Your Money Maker* (1989), which managed to echo both The Allman Brothers Band and Metallica. The follow-up *The Southern Harmony And Musical Companion* (1992) was more accomplished, with epic riffing on 'Sometimes Salvation', the goodtime rock-a-boogie of 'Hotel Illness' and the deep, wailing blues of 'Black Moon Creeping' lending the album an aura of spontaneity. Much of this was attributable to

Robinson's propensity for experimentation with different styles. While he doesn't always bring it off he is at least interesting, which is more than can be said for many contemporary players.

JIMMIE RODGERS

Born: James Charles Rodgers, September 8th 1897, Meridian, Mississippi, US. Died: May 26th 1933, New York, New York, US.

■ *Weymann; Martin; Gibson.*

Rodgers established the singing cowboy tradition in American country music, drawing on blues influences to accompany himself on guitar with instrumental solos. In the years since his death, Rodgers' influence has permeated every facet of American music, with performers including **Woody Guthrie**, Elvis Presley, **Ry Cooder**, Merle Haggard, Hank Williams, The Allman Brothers Band, Gene Autry and **Big Bill Broonzy** paying tribute to his legacy.

Rodgers started to perform professionally in 1925, after moving to Asheville, North Carolina where he assembled The Jimmie Rodgers Entertainers and began to broadcast on the local radio station. Two years later Rodgers was about to record some sessions with producer Ralph Peer, but a disagreement led to his band walking out. Rodgers cut the sides with just his guitar in support – making the best of the situation, and in the process creating a sound with alternating bass and chords and spacious solos that provided a model for many other country singer/ guitarists in the 1930s and later. These songs, such as 'The Soldier's Sweetheart', 'Sleep Baby Sleep', 'T For Texas' (also known as 'Blue Yodel'), 'Ben Dewberry's Run' and 'Mother Was A Lady' are collected on compilations such as *First Sessions* and *Early Years*.

Rodgers became progressively more popular, with records selling by the truckload, and he toured constantly throughout the southern and south-western states, broadcasting his own twice-weekly radio show from San Antonio, Texas. But he was gradually wasting away with tuberculosis, and died aged just 35.

NILE RODGERS

Born: September 19th 1952, New York, New York, US.

■ *Fender Stratocaster; Fender Telecaster; Guitarman Strat-style.*

As Chic, Rodgers and bassist Bernard Edwards were arguably the most creative team to emerge in the wake of disco. Edwards' distinctively melodic basslines and Rodgers' steely rhythm licks informed a generation of samplers and remixers, to the extent that Sister Sledge's 'We Are Family', underpinned by Chic's insistent groove, has been issued at least three times, with a different mix on each occasion.

Rodgers met Edwards in 1970, and they formed The Big Apple Band in 1972. Five years later they changed the group's name to Chic, and their debut, 'Dance, Dance, Dance (Yowsah, Yowsah, Yowsah)' emerged in 1976. The parenthetic 'Yowsah, Yowsah, Yowsah' was latched on to by DJs throughout the world and became a sort of disco war-cry.

Their debut album *Chic* (1978) followed shortly after and included 'Everybody Dance', proving – if it were necessary – that they were not just one-hit wonders capitalizing upon the disco-boom. 'Good Times' was their finest moment, a blueprint for good dance music. Rodgers throughout maintained a **Steve Cropper**-like scantiness, contributing mean licks where appropriate but never launching into 'guitar solo' territory.

Inevitably, Chic went their separate ways, each into production. Rodgers produced Madonna, David Bowie and Debbie Harry, among others, and cut the odd solo album, but it's his work with Chic, widely available in decent compilations, that redefined the underrated art of the rhythm guitar player.

DONALD ROESER

Born: November 12th 1947, New York, New York, US.

Nicknamed Buck Dharma, Roeser's flamboyant guitar pyrotechnics were as important to Blue Oyster Cult's style as the quasi-mystical occult influences of their lyrics. Formed in 1967 under the auspices of rock critics Richard Meltzer and Sandy Pearlman, they evolved into an art-rock metal band in 1971. In this incarnation Roeser was able to indulge his propensity for protracted solos on titles like the anthemic 'Cities On Flame With Rock'n'Roll' and the live *On Your Feet Or On Your Knees* (1975). Their best known song, albeit an atypical example, remains the quaintly menacing 'Don't Fear The Reaper' which bears greater resemblance to the 12-string janglings of The Byrds than the occult-metal of Black Sabbath. While BOC remained a popular live attraction throughout the 1970s and 1980s their material was inconsistent and their albums lacked coherence, with Roeser's abilities seemingly under-used.

JIMMY ROGERS

Born: June 3rd 1924, Ruleville, Mississippi, US.

■ *Gibson ES335.*

When it comes to sidemen, there are few that come close to rhythm guitarist Jimmy Rogers. He held down a position, along with **Hubert Sumlin** and Pat Hare, as one of the principal session guitarists at the famous post-war Chicago blues label, Chess, accompanying Sunnyland Slim, Sonny Boy Williamson, **Howlin' Wolf** and **Muddy Waters**. But you have to remember that at the peak of Rogers' session playing days, musicians didn't have the luxury of multiple takes: they went into the studio and cut it while it was hot. If the outcome was bad, there might be a retake, but there were few chances. Anyone who kept on getting it wrong was quickly shown the door.

The Muddy Waters band was definitive, including a host of musicians who went on to individual glory (Sunnyland Slim, Otis Spann, Little Walter, **Robert Lockwood**, James Cotton) but in Rogers, Waters had an invaluable ally: both an accomplished vocalist and an unfussy rhythm guitarist. This was session work of the highest order that few have matched, and among the titles Rogers participated on with Waters were 'Screamin & Cryin', 'She Moves Me', 'Country Boy', 'Please Have Mercy', 'Iodine In My Coffee', 'Baby Please Don't Go', 'Hoochie Coochie Man' and many others.

Rogers' solo work, however, lacked confidence – mainly because it was so rare.

ROY ROGERS

Born: San Francisco, California, US.

■ **Chappell custom double-neck; Martin; Gibson ES125TD3/4; Fender Telecaster.**

John Lee Hooker's *The Healer* (1990) brought the ageing bluesman out of the wilderness, and while it was an undoubted commercial triumph, with a superb combination of ancient and modern, the man in the control booth turning the knobs was Roy Rogers. He'd been a member of Hooker's band for some four years before launching out on his own account with a string of solo albums: *Chops Not Chaps* (1986), *Sidewinder* (1987), *Blues On The Range* (1990) and *Slide Of Hand* (1993). While slide guitar is Rogers' forté, he seldom resorts to the standard 12-bar format, but rather uses the blues as a catalyst for his own style liberally dosed with New Orleans-derived rhythms, and the few covers are genuine reworkings.

DUANE ROLAND

Born: December 3rd 1952, Jeffersonville, Indiana, US.

■ **Gibson Flying V.**

Molly Hatchet assumed the role of kings of southern rock after Lynyrd Skynyrd's fatal plane crash in 1977. **Steve Holland** and Roland form the vital rhythmic assault with **Dave Hlubeck** providing the wilder bits. Nothing particularly virtuosic here, but mildly entertaining live after seventeen pints of electric soup. For domestic use, *Double Trouble Live!* (1985) is nearly as effective.

PEPE ROMERO

Born: March 8th 1944, Malaga, Spain.

■ **Rodriguez.**

Angel Romero is one member of the remarkable Romero family: father Celedonio (born 1918, Malaga) is a fine player whose three sons – Pepe, Angel (born 1946, Malaga) and Celin (born 1936, Malaga) – have all grown into more or less talented classical guitarists. The family moved to the US in 1958, and their group, Los Romeros, has become the most distinguished ensemble of classical guitarists to emerge recently.

While their individual repertoires adhere firmly to the great Spanish composers such as Rodrigo, Falla, Castelnuovo-Tedesco and Villa-Lobos, Los Romeros are more unusual in their choice of ensemble material.

The intuitive interaction between the brothers, especially on Rodrigo's 'Concierto Andaluz' for four guitars, specially commissioned by the Romeros in 1967, is as thrilling as it is unusual, often echoing the spirit of flamenco rather than the sometimes stolid traditions of classical music.

MICK RONSON

Born: May 26th 1947, Kingston Upon Hull, Humberside, England. Died: April 29th 1993, London, England.

■ **Gibson Les Paul; Fender Telecaster.**

Ronson will always be best known for his role as David Bowie's sidekick and principal collaborator in The Spiders From Mars.

As a child Ronson had learned to read music and to play piano and guitar, which gave him a solid grounding in composition and arrangement. After forming The Cresters and The Rats he worked with **Michael Chapman** before meeting and joining up with David Bowie. Ronson was partially responsible for the coherence of Bowie's music, providing arrangements and much of the impetus, from the melodramatic 'The Man Who Sold The World' (1970), through the fey artiness of 'Life On Mars' (1971), to the semi-metal of 'Suffragette City' (1972) and the fiery 'Panic In Detroit' (1973), echoing Ronson's work with **Lou Reed** on the David Bowie-produced *Transformer* (1972).

With these achievements under his belt Ronson left Bowie and started a solo career with *Slaughter On Tenth Avenue* (1974), but his self-effacing attitude made him uncomfortable as a frontman, and after *Play Don't Worry* (1975) he returned to the role of henchman, this time with Mott The Hoople's Ian Hunter. Ronson sporadically collaborated with Hunter right up until his death.

Indeed, Ronson seemed to have a knack for being able to work with some of the most reputedly temperamental performers: Bob Dylan, Van Morrison, **Roger McGuinn**, David Johansen (ex-New York Dolls), Morrissey and, of course, Bowie. In 1991 Ronson was diagnosed as having cancer of the liver, but he continued to assemble a new solo album right up to his death, and performed Hoople's 'All The Young Dudes' with Hunter and Bowie at the Freddie Mercury memorial concert.

CESAR ROSAS

Born: 1954, Los Angeles, California, US.

■ **Fender Stratocaster; Gibson Les Paul.**

Having assimilated most of the salient aspects of 1950s rockabilly and Tex-Mex, Los Lobos came into being in 1974 in Los Angeles under the auspices of guitarist/accordionist **David Hidalgo** and guitarist/vocalist Rosas. By 1980 they were adapting the traditionally acoustic songs to more varied electric arrangements while retaining essential ingredients of Tex-Mex in the instrumentation. Although they have become best known for their reworkings of Ritchie Valens' songs like 'C'mon Let's Go' and 'La Bamba', *La Pistola Y El Corazon* (1988) was a collection of traditional Mexican and American folk songs, with both Rosas and Hidalgo demonstrating an instrumental prowess that belied the rowdy, good-natured style of the Valens covers.

Respect for the group was indicated by the award of a Grammy to *Pistola* and the quality of the artists guesting on their albums: **Ry Cooder**, **Brian Setzer**, **T-Bone Burnett**, Tex-Mex accordionist Flaco Jimenez, zydeco king Clifton Chenier, and

Elvis Costello, to name but a few. Rosas, a left-hander, has helped to incorporate Hispanic guitar-related instruments into the Los Lobos repertoire, including the small four-course requinto, the five-course jarana and the larger five-course huapanguera.

FRANCIS ROSSI

Born: April 29th 1949, London, England.

■ **Fender Telecaster; G&L ASAT.**

Rick Parfitt and Rossi, the dual-pronged guitar attack of Status Quo, have for over 25 years been very close to the top of their profession, having loosely pioneered a blues-based good-time boogie, using as few chords as possible but in appetizing mouthfuls that even the most punch-drunk numbskull can swallow, as on 'Caroline', 'Down Down', 'Rockin All Over The World', 'Whatever You Want', 'In The Army Now' and many more almost identical and commendably unpretentious work-outs.

GARY ROSSINGTON

Born: December 4th 1951, Jacksonville, Florida, US.

■ **Gibson Les Paul.**

At the heart of Lynyrd Skynyrd, one of the most successful southern boogie bands, was the triple-pronged guitar assault of Rossington, **Allen Collins** and **Ed King** (replaced by Steve Gaines). The group's material included the breakneck guitar duelling of 'Freebird' (dedicated to **Duane Allman**) and the bluesy lyricism of 'Sweet Home Alabama', and had a uniquely Southern character that could also be felt in the work of The Allman Brothers, Marshall Tucker, Charlie Daniels and Molly Hatchet. Ten years after the terrible plane crash of 1977 that killed two members of the group and two of their entourage, Rossington reformed the band, bringing in Johnny Van Zant, brother of one of those killed, as vocalist. Although their formula has changed little over the years, they still exert a grip on the imagination of the US record buying public to the extent that a medley of **Peter Frampton**'s 'Baby I Love Your Way' and 'Freebird' (entitled 'Will To Power') found its way to the top of the US charts in 1988.

ARLEN ROTH

Born: October 30th 1952, New York, New York, US.

■ **Fender Telecaster; Fender Stratocaster; ESP; Steinberger; Guild F40; Martin 000-18.**

Although Roth has recorded a number of solo records (including *Hot Pickups* 1980 and *Lonely Street* 1985) and has worked as a stage and studio session player with Simon & Garfunkel, Phoebe Snow and Janis Ian among others, he is best known to guitarists as the founder of Hot Licks, a company producing guitar instruction video tapes. Roth established Hot Licks in the early-1980s, and his own series of tapes and books covering rock, blues, metal, country and other styles has become very popular and must have encouraged hundreds of fledgling players. Also, artists as diverse as **Adrian Legg**, **Duke Robillard**, **Eric Johnson** and **Brian Setzer** have

Rog-Rot

all contributed lessons in front of the Hot Licks video cameras to add to the company's growing list of teaching tapes. Other producers of similar videos have come along in the wake of Roth's Hot Licks, including DCI (**Albert Lee, John Scofield**), REH (**Paul Gilbert, Allan Holdsworth**) and Starnite (**Martin Taylor, Steve Howe**).

STEVE ROTHERY

Born: November 25th 1959, Brompton, Yorkshire, England.

■ *Fender Stratocaster; Squier Stratocaster; Yamaha SG2000.*

Marillion (originally called Silmarillion after a book by fantasy author J R R Tolkien) attempted to cast themselves as 1980s recreations of progressive rock bands of the 1970s such as Yes, Gentle Giant and Genesis. That anyone should consciously attempt such a task is curious, and that they should be successful and achieve commercial acceptance indicates a strain of masochism unprecedented since the abolition of the corset during pregnancy.

Lead vocalist Fish, the group's principal writer, was responsible for the group's overt theatricality, meaning that guitarist Rothery and his fellow musicians took something of a back seat until *Misplaced Childhood* (1985) appeared and Fish shed his layer of stage make-up. While this album spawned a trio of hits in 'Kayleigh', 'Lavender' and 'Heart Of Lothian', the group had become so immersed in its own mythology that individual performances were lost in the amorphous swell.

Even after Fish left for a solo career in 1988, bombast lurked close to the surface. Rothery has technical ability, for sure, but if Fish's replacement Steve Hogarth and the rest of the group are to salvage anything from the wreckage, Rothery will have to be more imaginative and assertive.

MARTIN ROTSEY

Born: Sydney, Australia.

■ *Fender Stratocaster; Fender Jazzmaster; Gibson Les Paul.*

Midnight Oil were formed by drummer Rob Hirst in 1971, with guitarists Jim Moginie and Rotsey arriving shortly after. By 1977, lead singer Peter Garrett, having received his law degree, joined the band full-time, and since then Rotsey and Moginie have shown an interesting allegiance to the work of Grateful Dead's **Bob Weir** and **Jerry Garcia**. Sometimes uneasy listening, the group's recorded work such as *Red Sails In The Sunset* (1985) and *Diesel And Dust* (1987) often deals with political issues like aboriginal land rights, oil companies fouling the environment, Australian nationalism and nuclear disarmament.

PETER ROWAN

Born: 1942, Wayland, Massachusetts, US.

■ *Martin D-28; Thompson; Henderson; Bown.*

Rowan has been one of the key guitarists in the popularization of bluegrass over the past 30 years, contributing to a number of varied projects. He started his career as lead singer, guitarist and mandolinist in The String Band Project, cutting one album for Elektra in 1963, followed by a stint with Bill Monroe's Blue Grass Boys. In 1967 he formed Earth Opera with mandolinist David Grisman, and they cut a brace of albums for Elektra: *Earth Opera* (1967) and *The Great American Eagle Tragedy* (1968).

When Earth Opera split up Rowan started session work and reunited with fiddler Richard Greene whom he had first met during his days with The Blue Grass Boys. Rowan joined Greene's group Seatrain, recording an eponymous Capitol album in 1970, produced by fifth Beatle George Martin, as well as *Marbleheaded Messenger* (1971). Rowan then worked with **Jerry Garcia** and Robert Hunter (lyricist with the Grateful Dead), cutting *Old And In The Way* (1973) before forming the purer bluegrass outfit Muleskinner with **Clarence White**, banjoist Bill Keith, Greene and Grisman.

They cut *Muleskinner* (1974), but the group broke up and Rowan formed The Rowans with brothers Chris and Lorin, who made three albums: *The Rowans* (1974), *Sibling Rivalry* (1976) and *Jubilation* (1978). While these sold indifferently, the group built up a significant following on the college circuit, with Peter introducing bluegrass-style soloing to a generation brought up on The Eagles.

By the late-1970s Rowan had gone back to recording traditional bluegrass albums such as *Medicine Trail* (1979), *Walls Of Time* (1981) and *The First Whippoorwill* (1986). In 1988 he contributed to zydeco king Flaco Jimenez's *Flaco's Friends* along with **Ry Cooder**, which garnered a Grammy nomination. Rowan followed with *Dust Bowl Children* (1989), a collection of self-composed and self-accompanied songs that reflected his concerns with ecological and humanitarian issues. More recently he issued *All On A Rising Day* (1991) which featured contributions from resonator guitarist Jerry Douglas and vocalist Alison Krauss, continuing Rowan's welcome combination of traditional values and experimentation, where nothing is gratuitous.

TODD RUNDGREN

Born: June 22nd 1948, Upper Darby, Pennsylvania, US.

■ *Gibson SG; Fender Mustang; Veleno.*

A prodigiously talented and multi-faceted performer, Rundgren is quite content to play a variety of roles including that of guitar wizard, studio expert and producer. Simultaneously, if necessary.

He entered music in the mid-1960s with Nazz, a smart little pop group that aped the studied seriousness of British groups like The Hollies, and while the three albums the group cut were roundly dismissed at the time they have subsequently been dignified with 'classic' status. Rundgren started picking up tricks in the studio, causing The Band's manager Albert Grossman to recruit Rundgren as engineer and producer at Bearsville studios. This gave Rundgren the clout to pull together his own recording deal with the parent Bearsville label.

Runt (1970), *The Ballad Of Todd Rundgren* (1971) and *Something/Anything?* (1972) followed in swift succession. All demonstrated his knack for a cute tune but also highlighted his tongue-in-cheek attitude to the whole recording industry machinery. A skilful imitator, Rundgren incorporated references to pop, soul, heavy metal and progressive rock; indeed such was his range that his records ran the risk of being too densely packed with ideas for public consumption. *A Wizard, A True Star* (1973) with its neat medley comprising 'I'm So Proud', Smokey Robinson's 'Ooh Baby', The Delfonics' 'La La Means I Love You' and The Capitols' 'Cool Jerk' was kitsch but elegiac.

Rundgren's guitar playing is a model of efficiency, always apposite and invariably bristling with melodic invention. In other words, he thinks about what he does: one need look no further than the majestically soaring melody of the cameo solo in 'I Saw The Light' (*Something/Anything?*) for considered guitar playing at its finest.

There followed over the next dozen or so years a sequence of albums made under the auspices of Utopia and replete with studio wizardry; the group's live shows starred Rundgren as the man of a thousand heavy metal licks and were visual feasts, with lasers, pyramids and, no doubt, kitchen sinks as well.

Throughout his career Rundgren has regularly produced outside projects, including Meatloaf's *Bat Out Of Hell*, plus Jules Shear, Patti Smith, The Psychedelic Furs, Cheap Trick, Tom Robinson, The New York Dolls, Badfinger, XTC and Sparks. His most recent album is reputed to be the first to be issued as an interactive CD.

OTIS RUSH

Born: April 29th 1934, Philadelphia, Mississippi, US.

■ *Fender Stratocaster; Gibson ES335.*

One of the great blues guitarists in the Chicago pantheon, Rush's 1950s recordings for the Cobra label rank alongside the best of **Muddy Waters**, **Buddy Guy** and **Howlin' Wolf**. Among the sides he cut were 'Double Trouble', 'I Can't Quit You Baby', 'Groaning The Blues', 'All Your Love' and 'Keep On Loving You Baby', characterized by his moaning and groaning vocals to the accompaniment of ferocious flurries of stinging (left-handed) solos. Indeed such was the excellence of these early sides that later records were hard pressed to compete.

During the 1960s Rush was briefly contracted to the Chess label, and despite the intensity of the competition at that label his 'So Many Roads, So Many Trains' came close to the pick of the Cobra sides. After Chess, he was contracted to Don Robey's Duke label, but for various complicated reasons Rush didn't record again until 1965 when he took part in Sam Charters' overview of the Chicago blues scene for the Vanguard label.

Thereafter Rush recorded occasionally, often with white bluesmen like **Mike Bloomfield** and guitarist Nick Gravenites, but albums such as *Mourning In The Morning* (1969) lacked the visceral attack of his earlier recordings. Throughout the 1970s Rush toured regularly, appearing in Europe with **Jimmy Dawkins**. A number of live albums appeared at this time as a result of a San Francisco

Rot-Rus

blues festival and visits to France, Sweden and Japan. Critically rated by **John Mayall**, **Eric Clapton**, **Mick Taylor**, **Stevie Ray Vaughn** and many others, Rush remains curiously undervalued.

LEON RUSSELL

Born: Hank Wilson, April 2nd 1941, Lawton, Oklahoma, US.

Better known for his keyboard work, Russell could turn his hand to almost any instrument, and as a guitarist he was first rate. While he had been one of the bricks in Phil Spector's Wall Of Sound, his guitar playing ability didn't become appreciated until he cut his own records in the early-1970s. The succinct songs of his debut *Leon Russell* (1970) were masterpieces of economy, informed by years of listening to the self indulgences of others, and his guitar work echoed **Steve Cropper** on the classic Booker T & the MGs sessions, with melodic, arpeggiated phrases filling those awkward middle eights and a neat line in tasteful fills that take most a lifetime to perfect. Later albums such as *Leon Russell & The Shelter People* (1971) and *Carny* (1972) showed the debut to be no fluke, and the latter's self-penned 'This Masquerade' helped **George Benson** make the transition from jazz guitarist to pop star. In 1981 Russell revealed some deeper roots by cutting a bluegrass album with New Grass Revival, *Commonwealth*, a record progressive in feel but sticking closely to the original notion of what a bluegrass band should be about.

RAY RUSSELL

Born: England.

■ *St Clair Strat-style.*

During the 1960s Russell was a frequent contributor to the British jazz scene, playing with drummer Tony Oxley, composer Mike Westbrook and bassist Graham Collier.

In recent years, while he still plays jazz, Russell has become a prolific composer of incidental and soundtrack music for television, and contributed some fine playing to jazz arranger Gil Evans' version of **Jimi Hendrix**'s 'Little Wing' (1978).

MIKE RUTHERFORD

Born: October 2nd 1950, Guildford, Surrey, England.

■ *Steinberger; Fender Stratocaster; Shergold double-neck.*

Despite his position as bassist and number two guitarist in Genesis in the late-1960s and 1970s – behind Anthony Phillips until 1970, **Steve Hackett** from 1970 to 1977, and then Daryl Stuermer – Rutherford is an able guitar player whose abilities have been more evident since the group slimmed down to the trio of Phil Collins, Tony Banks and Rutherford, best heard on *Abacab* (1981) and *We Can't Dance* (1992). Rutherford also had success with Mike & The Mechanics (notably *Living Years* 1988), formed in 1985 during a lull in Genesis' workload and employing guitar work from other players such as Adrian Lee and **Alan Murphy** alongside that of Rutherford.

SABICAS

Born: Agustin Castellon Campos, March 15th 1912, Pamplona, Spain. Died: April 14th 1990, New York, New York, US.

■ *De Voe (later).*

How odd that in an age when so much emphasis is placed upon indigenous music from all around the world, such scant regard is paid to flamenco. Sabicas, in a recording career of over 50 albums, has long been regarded as one of the purest exponents of flamenco.

Superlative as an accompanist, he worked with the great Camaron, whose cante jondos (deep songs) are as evocative and passionate as a soul singer in full flight. Sabicas' solo work included *Flamenco Puro* which is a fine introduction to the art of flamenco. Possessed of an extraordinary dexterity and an unswerving passion, Sabicas brings these qualities to bear on traditional Spanish folk tunes as well as on his own compositions. There is also an album of duets – *The Fantastic Guitars Of Sabicas and Escudero* – which is acknowledged by many as being the finest collection around, but this has been unavailable for many years.

Although there are more flamboyant guitarists emerging all the time, embracing the skills that former Spanish dictator Franco tried hard to suppress, Sabicas and the more populist **Carlos Montoya** laid out the ground rules and gave flamenco its reputation.

DAVE SABO

Born: US.

■ *Spector Les Paul Junior-style.*

They're noisy, they're arrogant and they don't give a damn, which is probably just as well as Skid Row present a serious case of déjà vu. Sabo, aka The Snake, punches out his licks on *Slave To The Grind* (1991) with the abandonment of a guileless cobra in an enclosure of small furry mammals. Even so, Skid Row's grunt-and-grind vision of rock'n'roll has many admirers. There are those who say that Sabo is an accomplished guitarist... but then Elvis was last spotted doing his mother's laundry in Wisconsin.

SAL SALVADOR

Born: November 21st 1925, Monson, Massachusetts, US.

■ *Gretsch 'signature'; Gibson ES300.*

Salvador never knew what jazz was until the early-1940s when he first heard some **Charlie Christian** sides. He was sold immediately and started to play professionally in and around Springfield in 1945. In 1949 he moved to New York City and started to play at Radio City Music Hall, before joining Stan Kenton's Orchestra. White jazz big-band leader Kenton provided a university of sorts for players like Salvador, and enabled him to experiment with dissonance and atonality. While his tenure with Kenton was brief (June 1952 to December 1953) it provided Salvador with the intellectual sustenance to address the guitar on his own terms.

In 1958 Salvador appeared in what is arguably the most influential jazz film of them all, *Jazz On A Summer's Day*, and assembled his own big band for touring purposes. Throughout the 1960s and 1970s he recorded little but began teaching – one of his pupils was **Joshua Breakstone**. In 1983 Salvador cut *In Our Own Sweet Way* with **Carl Kress** and **George Barnes**, among others. It was as the title implies a highly idiosyncratic collection ('Blue Monk', 'In Your Own Sweet Way' and 'Somewhere Over The Rainbow'), demonstrating again how Kenton's unorthodoxy has rubbed off: Salvador is very much his own man, performing and recording when he chooses.

RICHIE SAMBORA

Born: July 11th 1959, New Jersey, US.

■ *Fender Stratocaster; Fender 'signature'; Gibson Les Paul; Kramer; Taylor custom.*

At the height of Beatlemania in the US a well-known toy manufacturer launched models of those four lovable mop-tops. Each was recognizable, despite the scale rendering facial features irrelevant, be it through stance or how the guitar was held – Ringo behind the drum kit wasn't a problem. Now all these years later, with the advent of virtual reality, there is the possibility of implanting facsimiles of musicians into environments where they never were or into situations that never occurred.

Enter Richie Sambora of Bon Jovi. For if someone wanted a 'virtual' heavy metal guitarist, he'd be the role model. During the 1980s Bon Jovi became one of the biggest selling metal bands in the world. It wasn't that they were better than anyone else: they were identifiable. They had a pitch and an attitude that fitted into the known parameters of what a heavy metal band should be. The fact that the multi-platinum *Slippery When Wet* (1986) and *Keep The Faith* (1993) had little or no evidence of soul and the chutzpah of a pair of concrete boots is hardly germane. No, Sambora's versatile guitar work is the backbone of the group – although lead vocalist Jon Bon Jovi may disagree. Sambora has the ability to out-riff some of the best, and on stage the group has few peers.

PAUL SAMSON

Born: England.

■ *Gibson SG.*

Samson (the band) were dignified with the questionable accolade of being protagonists in the new wave of British heavy metal. While they are effective, they do take themselves a mite seriously. I wonder why vocalists in British heavy metal bands have about three words in their vocabulary and speak them with American accents of indeterminate origin? Guitarist Samson formed his band in 1979 and set about developing a bluesy, hard rock sound that nodded at Black Sabbath and **Eddie Van Halen**. Early albums such as *Before The Storm* (1982) and *Don't Get Mad Get Even* (1984) denoted an ability to transcend the normal. By 1988, after the group had splintered, Paul cut the solo *Joint Forces* (1984)

Rus-Sam

123

before reforming the band for *Refugee* (1990) and *Joint Forces* (1993), both very ho-hum affairs.

CARLOS SANTANA

Born: July 20th 1947, Autlán de Navaro, Mexico.

■ *PRS; Yamaha SG2000; Gibson L6S; Gibson Les Paul; Gibson SG.*

Since the late-1960s Carlos Santana has been at the apex of the San Francisco music scene. His guitar style has been informed by two fundamental influences – the blues, and Afro-Cuban rhythms – later laced with jazz. Santana has always been distinctive for the purity of his guitar tone.

Santana's father was a mariachi (Mexican street-band) violinist and encouraged Carlos to take up the guitar, and he developed his style in the clubs and bars of Tijuana. After moving to San Francisco Santana formed the first lineup of the Santana Blues Band with Greg Rolie (keyboards). Fillmore owner Bill Graham became the band's manager.

With Carlos' reputation spiralling upwards, he was enlisted to appear on *The Adventures Of Mike Bloomfield & Al Kooper* (1969); meanwhile the group, now known simply as Santana, were signed to Columbia. Their debut *Santana* (1969) included 'Evil Ways' and created the template for the group's sound and style: a relaxed fluidity in Carlos' guitar work and flexible arrangements which made Afro-Cuban rhythms accessible to white audiences. The group's appearance at Woodstock was critical in establishing their reputation beyond San Francisco, underlined by *Abraxas* (1970, with **Peter Green**'s 'Black Magic Woman' and Tito Puente's 'Oye Como Va').

Throughout the 1970s Carlos' stature expanded through his work with **John McLaughlin** (*Love Devotion Surrender* 1973) and jazz pianist Alice Coltrane (*Illuminations* 1974) while the group albums continued to incorporate Afro-Cuban rhythms. Carlos' association with McLaughlin inevitably led him in the direction of fusion, which should not be held against him. The advent of disco gave the South American influences a contemporaneity, but the group's style was governed by the timbre of Carlos' guitar work.

Through the 1980s Carlos' solo and group albums have continued to reflect the two principal influences but his playing has never been mechanical, with waves of different styles ebbing and flowing. In 1986, he produced the soundtrack for the biopic based on the life of rock'n'roller Ritchie Valens, which saw him working with Los Lobos. In 1989 he was one of the prime movers in **John Lee Hooker**'s *The Healer* project.

Over the years the lineup of Santana has fluctuated, effectively providing a school for a host of young musicians, many of whom have gone on to different (if not necessarily better) surroundings, most notably **Neal Schon** who formed Journey.

JOEY SANTIAGO

Born: US.

■ *Gibson Les Paul.*

Santiago and Black Francis (Charles Michael Kittridge Thompson IV) were students at the University Of Massachusetts in Boston when they decided to form The Pixies. Signed to British indie label 4AD, their debut *Come On Pilgrim* (1987) defined the band's sound, Santiago's powerhouse riffing combining with Black Francis's wry lyrics to make the group instantly appealing on the college circuit.

Later albums such as *Surfer Rosa* (1988) were instrumentally tougher, Santiago's guitar work dominating courtesy of producer Steve Albini. However The Pixies' albums never appeared to be rites of passage: *Come On Pilgrim* was as accomplished as *Trompe Le Monde* (1991), for example. By 1993 the group had effectively broken up, with bassist Kim Deal having formed The Breeders in 1990 with (Throwing Muse) Tanya Donnelly, and Black Francis launching a solo career. It shows considerable integrity to nip a money-making machine in the bud. It's a shame more don't follow their example.

JOE SATRIANI

Born: 1956, Long Island, New York, US.

■ *Ibanez JS.*

There is a consensus that Satriani is one of the most accomplished rock guitarists around, a fact that wasn't wasted on **Kirk Hammett** and **Steve Vai**, both of whom sought his expert guidance in earlier days. However, Satriani's peerless technique has failed to win him the commercial success accorded many lesser lights. His ability to switch through the spectrum of rock styles, often with spectacular results that leave fellow players slack jawed, was never better evidenced than on Greg Kihn's *Love & Rock'n'Roll* (1986), while work with Alice Cooper and Mick Jagger predicated an awareness of his own pedigree.

Satriani's successive solo albums suffer from an over-zealous need to illustrate his technical prowess, often paying less attention to the quality of the material and emotional commitment. The instrumental *Surfing With The Alien* (1987) remains his tour de force as it possesses a muscular warmth that is not totally obliterated by the quest for technical perfection, while *Flying In A Blue Dream* (1990) indicates the need to assemble a unit that is commensurate with his own prodigious talents.

JAN SAVAGE

Born: US.

The Seeds, featuring the peerless talents of vocalist Sky Saxon, enjoyed a moment of celebrity with the seminal 'Pushin Too Hard' (1967). While initially they bridged the gap between garage/punk and psychedelia (as on *The Seeds* and *A Web Of Sound*, both 1966) Saxon was moving with agility into another map square, and the group cut the peculiar *Future* (1967) which featured enough variations of instrumentation to mollify the most demanding of conductors. Savage was too nimble, and departed for the Los Angeles police, leaving Saxon to ponder upon the imminent arrival of spacemen and aliens.

MIKE SCACCIA

Born: 1965, Texas, US.

■ *Gibson Explorer EX2; Washburn; Ibanez Iceman.*

The seven-piece Ministry are distinct from most other combos in that they comprise a four-pronged front line of axemen. The group was assembled by guitarist Al Jourgensen, and the remainder of that front line consists of Sam Ladwig, Michel Bassin and lead guitarist Scaccia. While the group's industrial barrage is somewhat daunting, Scaccia's frenetic soloing on 'Jesus Built His Hotrod', 'Scarecrow' and 'TV 11' (*Psalm 69* 1992) represents a departure from the fleet-fingered forays of his years with Rigor Mortis.

Ministry depend on Scaccia's chunky, structured solos to adorn the rhythmic assault of Bassin and Ladwig. While Scaccia gives the impression of a gratuitous noise merchant, his acoustic instrumental 'Rigor Mortis Versus The Earth' from the last Rigor Mortis album has a charm and sophistication that is slightly incongruous when set within the context of Ministry's current output. Despite being an acquired taste, the band have the virtue of being totally uncompromising.

BOZ SCAGGS

Born: William Royce Scaggs, June 8th 1944, Ohio City, Ohio, US.

■ *Gibson Les Paul.*

Originally vocalist and second guitarist in The **Steve Miller** Band (*Children Of The Future* 1968 and *Sailor* 1969), Scaggs left the band for a solo career in 1969. Although an able and often inventive guitar player in his own right, Scaggs has on a number of occasions been overshadowed by his guests, such as **Duane Allman** (in fine form on 'Loan Me A Dime' from *Boz Scaggs* 1969), **Les Dudek** (*Silk Degrees* 1976), **Carlos Santana** and **Steve Lukather** (*Middle Man* 1980).

MICHAEL SCHENKER

Born: January 10th 1955, Savstedt, Germany.

■ *Gibson Flying V; Gibson Les Paul.*

Although Schenker has propped up both The Scorpions and UFO at various times, his most impressive work has been reserved for his own outfit, The Michael Schenker Group. *One Night In Budokan* (1982) has acquired over the years the reputation for being not only one of the best live heavy metal albums around, but also the exemplar of Schenker's guitar work, from the lyricism of his playing on 'Never Trust A Stranger' and 'Cry For The Nations' to the power riffing of 'Armed And Ready' and the infinitely subtle 'Are You Ready To Rock?'. Above all, it has a lot of heart, and doesn't feel like another cynical exercise to part the fans from their cash, which is how many live albums come across. In recent years Schenker has returned to The Scorpions: quite why is a something of a mystery. Perhaps he just needs the money. There can't be any other reason, particularly if he is still able to make records like *One Night In Budokan*.

San–Sch

ERIC SCHENKMAN

Born: 1964, Canada.

■ *Koerner Strat-style custom; Pensa-Suhr; Fender Stratocaster.*

Raised on a heady mixture of influences such as jazzmen Duke Ellington, **Wes Montgomery**, Miles Davis, modern classic composers like Bartok, and **Jimi Hendrix**, Schenkman and The Spin Doctors have managed to include the raw edge of groups like Pearl Jam and Nirvana without succumbing to the posturing nihilism that seems a prerequisite for international acceptance. Much of the success of *Pocketful Of Kryptonite* (1991) can be ascribed to the band's relentless touring schedule – to such an extent that when the album failed to break at first, they just kept right on touring instead of going into the studio to cut a new one. However, songs like 'Two Princes', 'What Time Is It?' and 'Little Miss Can't Be Wrong' nod at the spiky lyricism of **Duane Allman** while retaining a pop sensibility. Although Schenkman's sound has an unpolished roughness to it, his approach to the guitar can be traced back to his father who was a cellist and his grandfather who was a conductor and viola player. Perhaps *Pocketful Of Kryptonite* will turn out to be a flash in the pan – or maybe they'll just continue to tour, like The Grateful Dead.

TOM SCHOLZ

Born: March 10th 1947, Toledo, Ohio, US.

■ *Gibson Les Paul.*

Boston were one of the awful, faceless bands that emerged in the US in the 1970s and struck home immediately with their debut, the imaginatively titled *Boston* (1978). A single from the album, 'More Than A Feeling', went on to sell in zillions. It would have been all right if the group's mastermind Tom Scholz had let it rest there. Unfortunately he didn't. What is more unfortunate is the fact that Scholz seemed to believe that because he'd mastered certain aspects of recording, he had become an interesting musician and songwriter. Consequently and every so often Scholz issues another album that is the result of many painstaking hours in the studio. Somebody should be kind and tell him to join The Moody Blues who would probably appreciate his technical ability and his knack for a cliché. Otherwise he's great.

NEAL SCHON

Born: February 27th 1954, San Mateo, California, US.

■ *Gibson Les Paul; Guild; Schon.*

There are many reasons why good guitarists leave successful bands and start up their own outfits. There is of course the great Musical Differences, a phrase that has resonated through the annals of pop history, and which is often a euphemism for something far deeper and more emotionally consuming, such as the need for more cash, more power, or perhaps both.

Schon started Journey after leaving Santana in 1971. Musical differences might have arisen from **Carlos Santana** playing all the main solos, or even

from Schon thinking that his talents weren't being properly recognized. If the latter was in Schon's mind, it was a shame, because a preference to lead Journey indicates greed of quite mind-numbing dimensions – or just an absence of talent.

Schon's work with Santana confirms that he has an abundance of ability: his single-note solos, echoing both **George Benson** and **Wes Montgomery**, on *Santana III* (1971) complemented the timbre and clarity of Carlos Santana's bluesy runs. Therefore, it has to be said that Journey were formed for one reason only. And they have fulfilled that objective quite fulsomely since their formation in February 1973, as they have sold piles of records in the US.

BRINSLEY SCHWARZ

Born: Hove, Sussex, England.

■ *Fender Jazzmaster.*

Not unreasonably, most have forgotten how Brinsley Schwarz's first self-named group was launched: a plane load of journalists was flown to New York to witness the band's debut. When the journalists returned they set about dismembering with relish any reputation the band might previously have had.

Schwarz and his band never overcame the mortification, despite issuing one album after another that established country-rock in Britain as plausibly as its US counterpart. *Despite It All* (1970), *Nervous On The Road* and *Silver Pistol* (1972) made albums by groups like Poco sound like cynical exercises in genre placement, with material such as 'Country Girl', 'Don't Lose Your Grip On Love' and '(What's So Funny About) Peace, Love And Understanding' showing an acerbic wit (courtesy of principal writer/bassist Nick Lowe) and an instrumental aplomb that made the 'progressive' groups of the day sound as if they were wearing boxing gloves.

Needless to say the group couldn't last, despite helping to pioneer 'pub-rock', and Schwarz joined the definitive pub-rock band Ducks Deluxe before teaming up with singer/songwriter Graham Parker and the excellent Rumour, with rhythm guitarist **Martin Belmont** and bassist Andrew Bodnar.

Throughout his career Schwarz's guitar work has been pithy and eloquent, and his ability to play any style has made him a dream session musician. Two examples from his guitar work with The Rumour sans Parker underline his abilities: 'This Town' (*Max* 1977) and 'One Good Night' (*Frogs Sprouts Clogs & Krauts* 1979). If some bright spark were to assemble a compilation of Schwarz's work it would provide a very instructive overview of much that was good about the 1970s. During the 1980s Schwarz continued working with Graham Parker (eg *Mona Lisa's Sister* 1988) and as a guitar-maker/repairer.

JOHN SCOFIELD

Born: December 26th 1951, Wilton, Connecticut, US.

■ *Gibson ES335; Ibanez Artist AS200.*

Initially dubbed a fusion artist, Scofield, a Berklee music school graduate, has described his work as

"instrumental music with a firm base in jazz traditions, shaded by samplings of rock, R&B, and even country". He's played with jazzmen Miles Davis (co-composing on *Decoy* 1984), Gerry Mulligan, Chet Baker, Billy Cobham and George Duke, and while his guitar work shows signs of these formative influences, Scofield has created a style that is uniquely his own, eschewing the temptation to play 'too many notes' and demonstrating an airy vitality that is lacking in the dry academicism that so often dogs contemporary jazz guitarists. *Grace Under Pressure* (1992) on which Scofield was partnered by **Bill Frisell**, with bassist Charlie Haden and drummer Joey Baron, exhibited a sure touch on compositions such as 'Unique New York' and 'Scenes From A Marriage' which stand out for their evocative, lyrical phrasing.

Furthermore, Scofield seems to have jettisoned synthesizer and keyboards from the instrumentation, giving his group a pleasing clarity that helps to focus on his own abilities.

ANDY SCOTT

Born: June 30th 1951, Wrexham, Wales.

■ *Gibson ES335; Gibson Les Paul; Fender Stratocaster.*

Brian Connolly was the fair-haired lead vocalist and Andy Scott the dark-haired guitarist with the fixed grin. Sweet were one of the finest proponents of the early-1970s Chinnichap sound (by songwriters Nicky Chinn and Mike Chapman) and 'Blockbuster', 'Hellraiser' and 'Ballroom Blitz', written by Chinnichap and produced by Phil Wainman, were the best examples of British bubblegum. It was disposable pop music at its trashiest and most commercial.

Producers such as Mickie Most and Jonathan King tried hard to emulate it, and later Stock Aitken & Waterman had to import it from Australia. After Sweet parted company with Chinnichap, only 'Fox On The Run' made any impression and albums like *Desolation Boulevard* (1974) were a case of too little, too late.

Today, various incarnations of the band ply their trade on the oldies and cabaret circuit; in their heyday, Sweet were driven along brilliantly by Scott's muscular guitar work.

HOWARD SCOTT

Born: March 15th 1946, San Pedro, California, US.

War managed to brave the disco years of the 1970s and emerge with not a stain upon their character, creating a fine blend of jazz, funk, salsa, rock and soul.

The group underwent a variety of lineup changes before settling in 1969 with Eric Burdon, former lead singer of The Animals. *Eric Burdon Declares War* (1970) included the superb 'Spill The Wine' with Scott in fine form, and the following year the group released *The Black Man's Burdon*. Midway through a European tour Burdon left the group, pleading acute exhaustion.

The group's solo debut *War* attracted some benevolent notices but caused few ripples, but the

Sch-Sco

follow-up *All Day Music* set their style with Scott's incisive lines snaking through a rich hybrid of funky Afro-Cuban rhythms, as on 'Slippin Into Darkness'. *The World Is A Ghetto* and *Deliver The Word* (1973) were as good as anything to emerge from the funk era, combining a dense rhythm section with subtle overlays of horns, keyboards and guitars, and their live performances, as captured on *War Live!* (1974), enabled and encouraged each member of the group to harness his own specific influences.

By the mid-1970s, despite *Why Can't We Be Friends?* (1975) and *Platinum Jazz* (1977), the group had misplaced their compositional thrust. Throughout the 1980s and 1990s the songs remained the same but the groove had lost its urgency.

KEITH SCOTT

Born: US.

■ Fender Stratocaster.

Co-writer and guitarist in **Bryan Adams**' band, Scott provides much of the instrumental muscle upon which Adams bases his live shows. Arguably one of the best working partnerships of the early-1990s, ranking alongside the rather older duo of **Keith Richards** and **Ron Wood**, Scott and Adams never appear to play shows by rote, always adapting and modifying even the oldest material.

RANDY SCRUGGS

Born: US.

■ Gallagher.

The eldest son of the innovative bluegrass banjo player Earl Scruggs, Randy has become one of Nashville's best guitarists and producers. His career started in 1969 when his father formed The Earl Scruggs Revue, severing a long working relationship with **Lester Flatt**. The revue was based on Earl's sons, Gary, Steve and Randy, but by 1980 the three brothers had broken away to form their own band and Randy had become co-owner of Scruggs Sound, the family studio in Nashville. While Randy's guitar work is a model of taste and excellence, his songwriting partnership with Earl Thomas Conley has also earned him praise. He produced the latter's *The Heart Of It All* (1988) and contributed to The Nitty Gritty Dirt Band's *Will The Circle Be Unbroken? Volume 2* (1989).

LEVI SEACER

Born: US.

■ Epiphone; Gibson.

In common with many others whose misfortune it is to get tied up with supreme egocentrics, Seacer's opportunity to shine has been seriously hampered by his employer, **Prince**.

Guitarist Miko, a number of other session players and Prince himself handled most of the six-string duties on earlier albums, but Seacer, previously Prince's bassist, dealt the luscious rhythm grooves for *Diamonds And Pearls* (1991), on the liner note to which Prince referred to Seacer, calling him 'fonkiest guitar on the planet'.

SON SEALS

Born: Frank Seals, August 13th 1942, Osceola, Arkansas, US.

■ Guild Starfire.

An inventive second division blues guitarist, Seals learnt the guitar from his father Jim, a drummer who owned a club in Osceola and had been a member of The Rabbit Foot Minstrels. By the time he was 11, Son Seals was sitting in with a variety of visiting musicians such as **Earl Hooker**, **Johnny Shines** and **Robert Lockwood**. In the early-1970s he settled in Chicago and started a lengthy association with the blues label Alligator. Seals has never penetrated the inner sanctum of the bluesman's confederation, but albums like *Chicago Fire* (1988) possess a depth of passion and a plain simplicity often lacking in some of his more celebrated colleagues.

TROY SEALS

Born: November 16th 1938, Big Hill, Kentucky, US.

Despite a couple of attempts to get his recording career moving with *Now Presenting Troy Seals* (1973) and *Troy Seals* (1976), Seals' success has come from his work as a guitarist and songwriter. At first Seals played with **Lonnie Mack**, but after marrying vocalist Jo Ann Campbell they recorded briefly as a duo. Seals left music for a while, but upon moving to Nashville he met producer David Briggs and took on regular session work at Monument studios alongside guitarists **Mac Gayden** and **Wayne Moss**, drummer Kenny Buttrey and bassist Tim Drummond. Although Seals' reputation as a session musician flourished, he has also become one of the most sought after songwriters in Nashville.

MIKE SEEGER

Born: August 15th 1933, New York, New York, US.

Seeger formed The New Lost City Ramblers with fiddler John Cohen and banjo player Tom Paley during the late-1950s on the back of the explosion of interest in traditional American music. Before forming the group, Seeger had been encouraged by his father, musicologist Charles Seeger, to rediscover and record American folk artists such as **Elizabeth Cotten**, Dock Boggs and Eck Robertson.

While Mike was a virtuoso instrumentalist, proficient on guitar, autoharp, dulcimer and dobro, there was an air of superficial dabbling about the Ramblers group, and their most effective records were live concerts such as *Second Annual Farewell Reunion* (1973). Today Seeger tends to confine himself to the collection of traditional songs, having done as much as anyone to promote and sustain interest in rural Southern styles.

SEGOVIA

Born: Andrés Torres Segovia, February 21st 1893, Linares, Spain. Died: June 2nd 1987, Madrid, Spain.

■ Ramirez; Hauser; Fleta.

The foremost influence on the development of the classical guitar as a solo instrument, Segovia made his first public appearance when he was 14 and his concert debut in Paris in 1924. Since that time he has exercised as strong a grasp on the imagination of young classical guitarists as has **Charlie Christian** on jazz guitarists.

While today Segovia's recordings tend to sound studied, his grasp of technique was formidable. Such was his inspirational presence that contemporary composers like Villa-Lobos, Castelnuovo-Tedesco, Falla and Casella all wrote pieces especially for him. Segovia also transcribed and rearranged for the guitar a large number of pieces written for other instruments, and as a result of these efforts greatly increased the repertoire available to the modern classical guitarist.

WILL SERGEANT

Born: April 12th 1958, Liverpool, England.

■ Fender Telecaster.

New wave noodlers Ian McCulloch, Pete Wylie and Julian Cope formed The Crucial Three in 1977, a nascent supergroup if ever there was one, but the rehearsals came to nothing and each went off to pursue other projects. Vocalist McCulloch formed Echo & The Bunnymen in 1978 with former restaurant chef Sergeant, plus Les Pattinson (bass) and Pete DeFreitas (drums).

McCulloch's songs, in the style of Jim Morrison meeting Jacques Brel, were a perfect setting for Sergeant's elliptical solos which were high on atmosphere and short on notes. A string of impressive albums followed, such as *Ocean Rain* (1984), *Songs To Learn & Sing* (1985) and *Echo & the Bunnymen* (1987).

Sergeant's guitar work was becoming progressively more adventurous ('The Back Of Love', 'The Porcupine', 'The Killing Moon', 'Bring On The Dancing Horses' and 'The Game').

After McCulloch left for a solo career in 1988, Sergeant and the remainder of the group issued *Reverberation* (1990). The paucity of any memorable material illustrated the extent of McCulloch's influence.

BRIAN SETZER

Born: April 10th 1960, New York, New York, US.

■ Gretsch 6120; Guild; Gretsch 'signature'.

Setzer's rockabilly revival trio The Stray Cats emerged in the wake of new wave at the end of the 1970s, and his elaborate hairdo created an erroneous impression that he was all looks and no substance. Beneath the attitude, however, lurked a guitarist of consummate skill; for example, his acoustic guitar runs on a **Carl Perkins** TV special (1985) with **Eric Clapton**, **Dave Edmunds**, Ringo Starr and George Harrison illustrated a genuine feeling for traditional country picking.

The following year Setzer co-wrote with **Mike Campbell** and **Steve Van Zandt** the material for his *The Knife Feels Like Justice* (1986) and this went some way toward establishing him in his own right, underlined by the release of *Live Nude Guitars*

Sco-Set

(1988) produced by **Dave Stewart** on which Setzer ran through a variety of picking styles that continued his rehabilitation as a highly individual stylist. Despite a lack of commercial acceptance for his solo work, Setzer has generated considerable respect among his peers, and The Stray Cats reunited for two albums with producers **Dave Edmunds** and **Nile Rodgers**.

CHARLIE SEXTON

Born: 1968, San Antonio, Texas, US.

■ *ESP; Rickenbacker 12-string; Fender Stratocaster.*

Sexton made his first bid for stardom when he was 13, sitting in with country singer Joe Ely's band. His reputation spread rapidly and he was recruited by Bob Dylan to contribute to *Empire Burlesque* (1985) and by ex-Eagles singer Don Henley to appear on *Building The Perfect Beast* (1984). Signed to MCA, Sexton cut *Pictures For Pleasure* (1985), but it smacked too much of the blue-collar rock of **Bruce Springsteen** and John Mellencamp. Having established himself as a guitar prodigy, all that remains is for Sexton to develop his own style and avoid the clichés.

ELDON SHAMBLIN

Born: Weatherford, Oklahoma, US.

■ *Rickenbacker Model B; Fender Stratocaster.*

From 1937 Shamblin, formerly of The Alabama Boys, was a key member of top western swing band Bob Wills & His Texas Playboys, supplementing a lineup that included steel guitarist **Leon McAuliffe**, pianist Al Stricklin and vocalist Tommy Duncan. Shamblin's single-note jazz style probably derived from **Charlie Christian** and **T-Bone Walker**, but it was primarily his assured rhythm playing that complemented McAuliffe on a range of titles such as 'Cotton-Eyed Joe', 'Ida Red', 'That's What I Like About The South' and 'Take Me Back To Tulsa'. Shamblin remained with Wills throughout the war years, and was an early user of electric guitars.

DAVE SHARP

Born: January 28th 1959, Salford, Lancashire, England.

■ *Fender Stratocaster; Pilgrim; Zemaitis; Epiphone.*

During the 1980s The Alarm were to Wales what Simple Minds were to Scotland, even employing a comparable nationalistic passion. While Sharp and fellow guitarist Mike Peters showed that they were as accomplished as the Minds' **Charlie Burchill** on titles like '68 Guns', 'Where Were You When The Storm Broke', 'Rain In The Summertime' and 'Sold Me Down The River', they lacked a vocalist of Jim Kerr's charisma, a component that enabled Simple Minds to acquit themselves so memorably on the stadium circuit. Still working regularly in the US, The Alarm have never managed to assemble a strong enough portfolio of evergreens sufficient to elevate them to the major league. Sharp cut the solo *Hard Travellin'* (1991) which showed that he was not just restricted to cranking out riffs but appeared to have something of a flair for acoustic picking too.

SONNY SHARROCK

Born: Warren Sharrock, August 27th 1940, Ossining, New York, US.

■ *Gibson Les Paul.*

Sharrock once dispensed a few thoughts on the nature of improvisers. One such player he describes as a fool who claims that he is bored with music, and that noise is an alternative. In Sharrock's words, noise in the hands of a fool equals bullshit.

For over 25 years Sharrock has played music that might be bundled together with the avant-garde abstractions of saxmen Ornette Coleman, John Coltrane and Albert Ayler, and pianist Cecil Taylor. Within that area Sharrock has essayed a height of passion and commitment that will always require a commensurate commitment from the audience, and Sharrock is without doubt an acquired taste.

From his earliest albums with flautist Herbie Mann and through his stints with sax player Wayne Shorter (*Super Nova* 1969) and trumpeter Miles Davis, Sharrock's chord work has possessed an awesome power while his solos employ huge slabs of electric clatter. But his most enduring association has been with saxophonist Pharoah Sanders whom he worked with on *Izipho Zam* (1969) and Sharrock's own astonishing *Ask The Ages* (1991), the latter with some towering interplay between two men who continually spark off one another. That it works, despite its unsettling nature, is testimony to both players' command of their instruments.

TOMMY SHAW

Born: September 11th 1954, Montgomery, Alabama, US.

■ *Gibson Les Paul; Gibson Explorer; Silver St 'signature'.*

Despite the success of Styx albums such as *Equinox*, *Crystal Ball* (1976), *The Grand Illusion* (1978) and *Cornerstone* (1979), none has managed to alleviate the gloomy monotony of their style nor become anything but lightweight. Shaw, who had replaced John Curulewski in the group in 1975, illustrated a hitherto dormant propensity for extended solos of matchless vulgarity on his solo debut *Girls With Guns* (1984), although its cartoon cut'n'paste quality did at least provide some relief after the Stygian vacuousness of *Paradise Theater* (1981), *Kilroy Was Here* (1983) and the rest. Shaw had made his solo debut while the band were taking a sabbatical, and decided against rejoining the band when they reformed in 1990. Instead he teamed up with **Ted Nugent** to form Damn Yankees. More vulgarity ensued, but at least they sounded like they were having fun.

PETE SHELLEY

Born: Peter McNeish, April 17th 1955, Manchester, England.

■ *Gordon Smith; Gibson Les Paul.*

At the back end of the 1970s when the new wave was beginning to find its style, there was a bunch of writers who used punk as a means to make songs in the traditional format (a single lasts three minutes maximum, right?). This represented a departure

from the 'progressive' norm of the 1970s. Shelley of The Buzzcocks, like **Elvis Costello** and **David Byrne**, was one of the best writers of the period. With his knack for a tune came an equal gift for the snappy solo and crisp rhythm part that concentrated on supporting and communicating the song's melody with the minimum of fuss. Among Shelley's finest moments were 'Orgasm Addict', 'What Do I Get', 'Love You More', 'Ever Fallen In Love (With Someone You Shouldn't Have)' and 'Everybody's Happy Nowadays'. In 1981 Shelley left the group for a solo career, cutting *Homosapien* which did big business in Australia, but his own projects lacked the spontaneous simplicity of The Buzzcocks. Shelley revived the group for a series of reunion gigs in 1989 and 1990.

TONY SHERIDAN

Born: Anthony Esmond Sheridan McGinnity, May 21st 1940, Liverpool, England.

Better known through his association with The Beatles who backed him on a pretty ghastly version of 'My Bonnie', Sheridan's career had started in the late-1950s as the guitarist in a group who backed visiting rock'n'roll luminaries such as Conway Twitty and Gene Vincent. While this established him in the eyes of many fellow Liverpudlians as a local celebrity, he was never more than competent as a guitarist. After his stint with The Beatles he settled in Germany and continued to work as a session musician.

KEVIN SHIELDS

Born: Dublin, Ireland.

■ *Fender Jazzmaster; Fender Jaguar.*

My Bloody Valentine proved to be one of the most inventive (and enigmatic) groups to emerge from the late-1980s indie scene. Formed by guitarist Shields and drummer Colm O'Ciosoig in 1984 the group have emulated The Jesus & Mary Chain's use of a barrage of guitars, but set them against meticulously crafted songs. After recording for a brace of small labels they joined Creation where they used rather more sophisticated recording techniques. This was immediately apparent with the EP *You Made Me Realise* (1988). The alluring tunes combined with the nerve-wracking collage of guitar sound gave them a reputation for being one of the most coherent of all indie bands. *Loveless* (1991) would have been influential under any circumstances, but compared to the plethora of emerging outfits it became one of the year's most durable affairs, with Shields showing every indication of leaving **William Reid** behind in the under-achievers' class.

JOHNNY SHINES

Born: April 26th 1915, Frayser, Tennessee, US. Died: April 20th 1992, Tuscaloosa, Alabama, US.

■ *Gibson flat-top.*

Much has been written about **Robert Johnson**, and most is steeped in myth, but one thing seems certain: Johnny Shines played frequently with him and even

Sim-Sko

made some radio broadcasts with Johnson in Detroit during the mid-1930s. Shines was an immaculate slide guitarist with a vivid tenor voice, and after Johnson's death in 1938 did as much as anyone to perpetuate his legend by performing striking recreations and settings of Johnson's compositions.

After settling in Chicago in 1941, Shines stuck to the club circuit and cut his first sides for Columbia in 1946. These stuck closely to the country blues that he had grown up with, out of step with the popular urban blues of **Muddy Waters** and **Elmore James**. Shines' lack of success caused him to quit playing music altogether, and during this time he compiled a portfolio of photographs taken at various Chicago clubs. In 1965 Shines was rediscovered and encouraged to hit the festival trail, and among his best albums from this period was *Last Night's Dream* (1968) for Mike Vernon's Blue Horizon label. Other albums included a fine later collaboration with **Robert Lockwood**, *Hangin' On* (1981).

KIM SIMMONDS

Born: December 6th 1947, London, England.

■ *Fender Stratocaster; Gibson Flying V; Gibson ES345.*
In 1966 Simmonds formed the Savoy Brown Blues Band; over the next 15 years or so over 50 musicians passed through the ranks of Savoy Brown, as they came to be known, with Simmonds operating on a similar principle to that of the 'trainers' of the British blues-rock scene, **Tony McPhee**, **Stan Webb** and **John Mayall**.

Simmons and Savoy Brown knocked out one album after another, none remarkable but all more competent than most, such as *A Step Further* (1969), *Raw Sienna* (1970), *Hellbound Train* (1972), *Boogie Brothers* (1974), *Savage Return* (1978), and *Rock'n'Roll Warrior* (1981), with Simmonds demonstrating an admirable grasp of harmonica as well as slide guitar.

While in Britain the group was confined to slogging around minor sized venues, in the US they were considered quite a draw (and indeed in 1971 former Savoy Brown members **Dave Peverett** and drummer Roger Earl formed Foghat with the specific objective of touring the US exclusively).

Still touring into the 1980s, Simmonds has adhered to the same blues-based boogie format and shows little inclination to hang up his Strat and climb into his carpet slippers. It is to his credit that he has never compromised himself by embracing the dark satanic forces of heavy metal.

PAT SIMMONS

Born: January 23rd 1950, Aberdeen, Washington, US.

■ *Gibson ES335; Fender Stratocaster; Brown Strat-style.*
Tom Johnston and bluegrass/folk musician Simmons were the first two guitarists in The Doobie Brothers' lineup of the early-1970s and were responsible for defining the band's sound. With songs like 'Listen To The Music', 'Jesus Is Just Alright', 'Long Train Running', 'China Grove' and 'Black Water', their high, light harmonies and the rhythmic guitar-led attack fused elements of country, folk and blues in a

bright, energetic hybrid. Ex-Steely Dan guitarist **Jeff Baxter** joined the Doobies in 1975, adding deeper, chunkier phrases to the band's sound. Johnston left and was replaced by Michael McDonald, also of Steely Dan. In the Doobies' late-1970s work McDonald's soulful, impassioned vocals tend to obscure the country influences of the group, which sounds more like McDonald's backing band. Simmons soon left for a solo career and session work, notably with **Steve Morse**'s The Dregs on *Industry Standard* (1982).

PAUL SIMON

Born: October 13th 1941, Newark, New Jersey, US.

■ *Yamaha custom; Gurian; Martin; Guild; Velazquez; Fender Telecaster; Sadowsky Strat-style.*
Paul Simon has become one of the elder statesmen of contemporary music through a combination of diligence and perspicacity. He has steadily become one of the most accomplished acoustic guitarists of the post-war singer-songwriter school, while his recognition of the potential applications of English folk guitar styles as practiced by **Martin Carthy** and then his adoption of African and South American rhythms for a brace of highly influential albums – *Graceland* (1986) and *Rhythm Of The Saints* (1990) respectively – have given him a respectability among even the most conservative audiences.

Underpinning all this has been his ability as a composer. First with childhood friend Art Garfunkel his often sugary lyrics were bathed in arrangements that distracted the ear from their inherent glibness and resulted in timeless classics such as 'Sounds Of Silence', 'I Am A Rock', 'Bridge Over Troubled Water' and 'The Boxer'. Once Simon's solo career got underway he started to surround himself with musicians appropriate to the arrangement: the jazzy style of 'Hobo's Blues' was predicated by Stéphane Grappelli's violin; 'Take Me To The Mardi Gras' was recorded in Muscle Shoals; the reggae rhythms of 'Mother And Child Reunion' were captured in Jamaica; and the gospel-styled 'Loves Me Like A Rock' featured The Dixie Hummingbirds. However, throughout this careful pillaging of the musical heritages of others Simon has intimated an awareness of his own frailty and the ephemeral nature of fame, as noted on 'American Tune', 'Still Crazy After All These Years', 'Fifty Ways To Leave Your Lover', 'My Little Town' and 'The Late Great Johnny Ace'.

While his albums have always featured the best musicians on the block, *Live Rhymin'* (1974) is a fine example of his own dexterity. Despite all the criticisms that have been laid at his door, Simon's gift for melody is undeniable, while the effect on other musicians of Simon's combination of fine songs supported by good guitar playing has been immeasurable.

MARTIN SIMPSON

Born: May 5th 1953, Scunthorpe, Humberside, England.

■ *Sobell.*
Seriously undervalued, Simpson's lyrical and effusive style has given him a reputation as one of the finest folk guitarists currently working in Britain. Whether

this is as solo performer or accompanist, his playing has wit and finesse: June Tabor's *A Cut Above* (1980) emphasized his turn of phrase, while his own *Grinning In Your Face* (1983) contained an eclectic range of covers, from **Buddy Holly**'s 'It Doesn't Matter Any More' and Hank Williams' 'Your Cheatin' Heart' to traditional staples like 'Reuben's Train'. Despite the fact that he records infrequently, Simpson – like **Martin Carthy** – is one of the few accomplished acoustic guitarists who doesn't rely on flashiness for effect. He now works in the US, and a good recent compilation of Simpson's work is *Collection*.

RICKY SKAGGS

Born: July 18th 1954, Cordell, Kentucky, US.

■ *Martin D-28; Gibson L5; Fender Telecaster; Glaser Tele-style; G&L ASAT.*
A prodigiously talented multi-instrumentalist, Skaggs achieved the seemingly impossible feat of adapting traditional features of country music to contemporary demands without any concomitant loss of authenticity.

He mastered the mandolin, guitar and fiddle by the age of five and made his debut in 1961 on **Lester Flatt**'s TV show, later joining Ralph Stanley's Clinch Mountain Boys where he met and joined forces with **Keith Whitley**. In 1971 they cut *Tribute To The Stanley Brothers* and followed it with *Second Generation* (1972). Skaggs then went on to play with The Country Gentlemen and JD Crowe before forming his bluegrass outfit, Boone Creek, breaking up in 1978.

The following year Skaggs made his solo debut for Sugar Hill with *Sweet Temptation*, which was followed by a collaboration with singer Emmylou Harris on *Roses In The Snow* (1980) and then with guitarist **Tony Rice** on *Skaggs & Rice*. From 1981 he cut a string of hits that included 'Crying My Heart Out Over You', 'Highway 40 Blues' and 'Uncle Pen'.

In 1985 Skaggs toured Britain and went on to release *Live In London*, but between 1986 and 1989 Skaggs fell victim to a series of personal tragedies – including the shooting of his eight-year-old son, Andrew, by a trigger-happy trucker. He nonetheless produced singer Dolly Parton's *White Limozeen* and cut 'Lovin' Only Me' and the *Kentucky Thunder* (1989) album with producer Steve Buckingham.

NICKY SKOPELITIS

Born: US.

The Golden Palominos enjoy the prestigious position of having plenty of celebrated friends who queue up whenever the band is about to cut a record, partly attributable to bassist Bill Laswell's reputation as a producer. As a result the most memorable contributions to *Drunk With Passion* (1991) come from vocalist Michael Stipe of REM, **Bob Mould** of Sugar and **Richard Thompson**, thereby subordinating the nonetheless able Skopelitis to that of a useful auxiliary. However, Skopelitis' association with Laswell has landed him in exalted company on occasions, playing with German saxophonist Peter

Brotzmann and Laswell's Curlew. Just how good he is seems destined to remain a closely guarded secret.

SLASH

Born: Saul Hudson, July 23rd 1965, Stoke-on-Trent, Staffordshire, England.

■ *Gibson Les Paul; Gibson double-neck; custom Les Paul-style; Gibson Melody Maker.*

Slash is one of the most technically effective guitarists to have emerged in the 1980s. While much press speculation has surrounded non-musical aspects of Guns N'Roses, when the group does its job they are one of the most exciting around. And that's the point. Slash has an ear for a well-turned lick and a supportive riff in much the same way that **Keith Richards** has: governed by gut, Slash has the intuition to adapt his solos instinctively. But while 'Sweet Child Of Mine' was one of the most influential songs of the 1980s, and *Appetite For Destruction* (1987) spawned a generation of imitators, both *Use Your Illusion 1* and *2* (1991) seem complacent. It is all very well for, say, **Muddy Waters** to have out-takes packaged and issued, as they have an intrinsic historical value. But neither Slash nor Guns N'Roses possess that cachet, and their reputation was not enhanced by *The Spaghetti Incident* (1993) which largely consisted of covers of punk classics recorded at the same sessions as the *Illusion* records, but with since-departed second guitarist **Izzy Stradlin**'s playing wiped and replaced.

EARL SLICK

Born: October 1st 1951, New York, New York, US.

■ *DiMarzio; Phantom.*

Slick landed the plum job of guitarist alongside **Carlos Alomar** in David Bowie's band in the mid-1970s (*Young Americans* 1975, *Station To Station* 1976), played on **John Lennon**'s *Double Fantasy* (1980), and later in the 1980s was recruited by **Dave Edmunds** to participate in a televised concert celebrating the career of **Carl Perkins**. In between these stints Slick worked with British vocalist Jim Diamond, Fanny (he's married to **Jean Millington**), and bassist/drummer Lee Rocker and Jim Phantom from the Stray Cats, forming his own band for a couple of indifferent offerings.

HILLEL SLOVAK

Born: 1963, Israel. Died: June 1988, US.

Before **John Frusciante** joined The Red Hot Chili Peppers, Slovak, one of the group's founders, occupied the guitarist's slot. Due to various contractual problems, Slovak didn't make an appearance until the group's second album. Produced by funkmeister extraordinaire George Clinton and featuring the molten riffs of hornmen Maceo Parker and Fred Wesley, *Mother's Milk* (1989) featured Slovak's funky guitar, eliciting memories of **Jimmy Nolen**, **Leo Nocentelli** and **Jimmy Page**, all rolled into one. Slovak's drug-related death in 1988, before the album's release, led to the appointment of Frusciante.

ROY SMECK

Born: February 6th 1900, Reading, Pennsylvania, US.

■ *Harmony 'signature'; Gibson 'signature' flat-top.*

During the early years of the record industry Smeck was one of the most influential performers and session musicians. His Hawaiian guitar playing was influenced by **Sol Hoopii**, his Spanish style by **Eddie Lang**. At first Smeck earned his living by playing the vaudeville circuit as The Wizard Of The Strings, but he gravitated to the lucrative New York session circuit where his expertise on a variety of stringed instruments found him endless employment with songsters such as Frank Luther, Carson Robison and Vernon Dalhart, producers like Ralph Peer and Art Satherley, and jazz musicians like Louis Armstrong and Kid Ory. Smeck was an early dabbler in studio overdubbing techniques, and while today his playing sounds curiously antiquated, his instructional manuals are good insights into how little technology has affected basic styles.

RED SMILEY

Born: Arthur Lee Smiley, Asheville, North Carolina, US. Died: January 1972.

In 1949 Smiley formed the Tennessee Cutups with multi-string-instrumentalist **Don Reno**. Initially they broadcast on the local radio station in Roanoke, Virginia, before moving into a regular spot on radio's *Wheeling Jamboree*. Their recording career picked up momentum in 1952 when they moved from Federal to its parent label, King, cutting titles like 'I'm Going To Use My Bible For A Roadmap' and 'Let's Live For Tonight'. Developing a style characterized by Reno's three-finger banjo technique and Smiley's distinctive guitar runs and close vocal harmonies, they secured a regular spot on the TV show *Old Dominion Barn Dance*, and Reno began playing guitar more on titles like 'Freight Train Boogie' and 'You Never Mentioned Him To Me' in 1954. Because of illness Smiley's full-time collaboration with Reno had finished by 1964, but they continued to record and perform occasionally until Smiley's death.

ARTHUR SMITH

Born: April 1st 1921, Clinton, South Carolina, US.

■ *Gibson ES335; Martin.*

The scene everyone remembers from the film *Deliverance* (1972) featured two guys playing banjo and guitar on the front porch. The piece they played was called 'Dueling Banjos' and on the film soundtrack it was performed by **Eric Weissberg** and banjoist Steve Mandel, but it was only later that it was recognized as having been based on the **Don Reno** and Arthur Smith composition 'Feuding Banjos' (1955).

Smith had come to prominence after achieving a substantial hit with 'Guitar Boogie' (1948) which opened many ears to the pop potential of electric guitars. The piece was so successful that he became known as Arthur 'Guitar Boogie' Smith.

While there is no doubting Smith's expertise, later records for Starday, Dot and Monument failed to

match the superiority of 'Guitar Boogie', and he opened his own studio in North Carolina in the 1950s. 'Guitar Boogie' was later covered successfully by the 1950s British session ace **Bert Weedon**.

CLAYDES SMITH

Born: Charles Smith, September 6th 1948, Jersey City, New Jersey, US.

Kool & The Gang was formed by bassist Robert 'Kool' Bell in 1964 in New Jersey while he was still at school. At first it was known as the Jazziacs, through the influence of Bell's father who had played with jazz pianist Thelonious Monk. By 1969 Kool & The Gang's lineup had settled, and the combination of a strutting horn section with Smith's rhythmic, textured guitar work and a rock solid rhythm section made them palatable for jazz audiences as well as soul and funk fans. They broadened their scope when vocalist James Taylor was added in 1979 and enjoyed hits aplenty through the 1970s and 1980s with soft-soul ballads such as 'Cherish', as on the compilation *Greatest Hits & More* (1988). But their best work occurred in their early years, with albums like *Kool And The Gang* (1969), *Music Is The Message* (1972) and *Wild And Peaceful* (1973).

EARL CHINNA SMITH

Born: 1955, Kingston, Jamaica.

■ *Gibson Les Paul; Yamaha SG2000.*

Smith was a session guitarist, used principally by producer Bunny Lee in the pool of musicians known as the Aggrovators. Lee struck out in the face of fashion by ignoring the disco beat of the 1970s that was beginning to saturate reggae, and adopted the 'flying cymbals sound'. Among the artists Smith and the Aggrovators backed were Dennis Alcapone, Horace Andy, Cornell Campbell, Rupie Edwards, John Holt, I Roy and U Roy. In 1976, when **Peter Tosh** left the Wailers, Lee was joined by guitarist Al Anderson while Smith was hired by **Bob Marley** to play on the *Rastaman Vibration* sessions (1976) among others. Smith still works on sessions, sometimes with Sly & Robbie, and has his own band The Soul Syndicate.

FLOYD SMITH

Born: January 25th 1917, St Louis, Missouri, US. Died: March 29th 1982.

■ *Gibson; Epiphone Electar lap-steel.*

Smith became proficient on the ukulele and banjo before graduating to the guitar, having gained an interest in music from his father, a drummer. In 1939 Smith joined saxophonist Andy Kirk's 12 Clouds Of Joy and cut 'Floyd's Guitar Blues', one of the first appearances of an electric (steel) guitar solo on a jazz record. The inspiration may have come from **Eddie Durham**'s pioneering use of the electric... and the two might have partly inspired **Charlie Christian** to take up amplified guitar. Today the track sounds stilted and rather wooden, where Durham and particularly Christian sound remarkably modern. But it swings – and it was a first. After World War II Smith worked with keyboardist Wild Bill Davis in an R&B style trio and with drummer Christopher Columbus.

FRED SMITH

Born: West Virginia, US.

The mighty MC5 have a lot to answer for. There are few that would call them to mind as being a source of inspiration, but Fred 'Sonic' Smith and **Wayne Kramer** subliminally informed a later generation of punksters and metallurgists. *Back In The USA* (1970) is more heavy, more fun loving and more accomplished than the entire output of the new wave (and old wave, come to that) of British heavy metal. The MC5 were loud and anarchic, and 'Sonic' Smith could make a guitar go into therapy. If Iron Maiden and others of their ilk had bothered to listen to the MC5 they wouldn't have had a career. Shame, really. Fred now resides in matrimonial bliss with poetess Patti Smith.

JEROME SMITH

Born: June 18th 1953, Hialeah, Florida, US.

In 1973 Harold Wayne Casey met Richard Finch, bassist and engineer at TK Records, and they decided to pool resources and form KC & The Sunshine Band with guitarist Smith and drummer Robert Johnson. While this lineup increased for gigs, these four were the nucleus of the house band at TK, working with artists like George and Gwen McCrae and Betty Wright. Furthermore they strung together a succession of disco-funk hits, all written by Casey and Finch, that were the apotheosis of disco. These included 'That's the Way (I Like it)', '(Shake Shake Shake) Shake Your Booty', 'I'm Your Boogie Man' and 'Give it Up', with Smith's spare, rhythmic guitar at the heart of each. When disco disappeared, however, so did KC. Historians should consult their 1990 *Best Of*.

JOHNNY SMITH

Born: John Henry Smith, June 25th 1922, Birmingham, Alabama, US.

■ Guild 'signature'; Gibson 'signature'; D'Angelico.

Smith taught himself to play guitar and made his debut performing hillbilly music. During the war years he played trumpet in an Air Force band, violin and viola in an ensemble at local venues, and guitar with the Philadelphia Orchestra under conductor Eugene Ormandy. After the war Smith joined the NBC staff in New York City, playing on sessions. While at NBC he formed a quintet and cut the memorable *Moonlight In Vermont* (1952) with saxophonist Stan Getz. This was a vibrant collection of standards such as 'Where Or When', 'Autumn Leaves' and 'When I Fall In Love', both players seeming to strike a chord with one another and Smith employing a beautifully cool, floating chordal sound and a clever precision with harmonics. The record turned out to be a flash of brilliance never to be repeated, and Smith virtually retired after 1960. Although he recorded a number of other albums, they are hard to find today. Smith's

tune 'Walk Don't Run', in an arrangement by **Chet Atkins**, was a hit in 1960 for The Ventures.

ROBERT SMITH

Born: April 21st 1957, Crawley, Sussex, England.

■ Fender Jazzmaster (modified); Gibson Chet Atkins; Fender Bass VI; Ovation.

The Cure have breasted the new wave and entered the mainstream of monster bands who cut an album every couple of years and then tour for a year promoting it. Smith is hardly an axeman extraordinaire, but his cleverly textured work epitomizes the modern pop approach that uses the guitar to decorate rather than dominate songs, demonstrated on the drone-laden *17 Seconds* (1980) or the occasionally acoustic *The Top* (1984); *Standing On The Beach* collects the group's best singles up to 1985 – the year in which guitarist Porl Thompson joined the group to complement Smith's six-string work. After a period of more dance-oriented sound, *Wish* (1992) was the group's most guitaristic record for some time, combining the efforts of Smith, Thompson and Perry Bamonte.

PAUL SNEEF

See PAUL LEARY

HANK SNOW

Born: Clarence Eugene Snow, May 9th 1914, Liverpool, Nova Scotia, Canada.

■ Martin; Gibson Super 400.

Snow is one of the longest established country artists in the music business and a fine, underrated guitarist. While his recent disenchantment with the commercialism of country music sounds rather hollow given his popularization of gaudy 'western' outfits in the 1930s, he remains an original. Snow has managed to straddle the fine line between out-and-out commercialism and authentic traditional styles with a raw, unembellished acoustic picking style (influenced in part by **Karl Farr** of Sons Of The Pioneers) that has changed little in his long career.

After leaving home in 1926 to enter the merchant navy he returned to Nova Scotia in 1930 to play the club circuit, resulting in his own radio show in Halifax. Signed to Bluebird in 1936, where he was known as Hank the Yodeling Ranger, he moved to US in 1944 where he was signed by RCA and known as the Singing Ranger.

In spite of the approval of artists like Ernest Tubb and broadcasts on *The Grand Ole Opry*, Snow initially failed to penetrate the cliquey country scene. Success came at last with 'Marriage Vow' (1949) and set in train a career that lasted well into the 1970s. Among his best known songs are 'I'm Moving On', 'A Fool Such As I', 'Let Me Go, Lover', 'I've Been Everywhere' and 'Hello Love'. Snow has cut over 100 albums, including all-instrumental work-outs and duets with **Chet Atkins**, and has worked hard to keep alive the memory of his hero **Jimmie Rodgers** by recording innumerable tributes to him. At the time

of writing he still makes intermittent appearances at The Grand Ole Opry.

GORAN SOLLSCHER

Born: December 31st 1955, Växjö, Sweden.

■ Six-string & 11-string customs.

Throughout Söllscher's career he has made a point of avoiding the staples of guitar repertoire by periodically recording a composer's lesser known pieces, such as Rodrigo's 'Passacaglia', 'Zapateado' and 'Por Los Campos De Espana'. He is also known for his interpretations of baroque works, for which he tends to use an 11-string guitar. This has broadened his canvas, and Söllscher has sought to establish the antecedents of the classical guitar by rearranging for guitar JS Bach's lute works, Vivaldi's lute and mandolin concertos and the music of Elizabethan composer John Dowland. Versatile and energetic, Söllscher's style has the warmth and character more readily associated with Spanish players.

ANDY SOMERS

See ANDY SUMMERS

CHRIS SPEDDING

Born: June 17th 1944, Sheffield, England.

■ Gibson Flying V; Gretsch 6120.

One of Britain's most prolific session musicians, Spedding has performed in so many different set-ups that he can play in virtually any style. At school he had violin lessons and formed The Vultures on leaving, moving to London in 1960 and joining Bill Jordan's Country Boys, followed by a stint entertaining tourists on board a P&O liner and summer seasons with the Nat Temple and Monty Frank Orchestras in Torquay and Jersey.

Around the same time Spedding started to play sessions for jazz composers like Mike Gibbs, Mike Westbrook and Graham Collier, until in 1967 he formed The Battered Ornaments to back lyricist and poet Pete Brown. While this precipitated more session work, Spedding met Cream bassist Jack Bruce who was just about to start work on his debut solo album *Songs For A Tailor* (1969). Spedding's guitar work on the fine material written by Bruce and Brown was considered so evocative, adding to the elegiac atmosphere of most of the album.

A spell followed with jazz-rock group Nucleus, fronted by trumpeter Ian Carr, and the formation of Sharks with former Free bassist Andy Fraser and vocalist Snips. Sharks never found success, principally because of a glut of supergroups at the time; Sharks were simply overlooked. More session work followed, including an inglorious spell with composer/arranger Mike Batt as one of the lovable, furry, guitar-toting TV characters The Wombles.

After The Wombles, Spedding started a solo career under the auspices of producer Mickie Most; the single 'Motorbikin' was great, but the album *Chris Spedding* (1976) and the follow-ups *Hurt* (1977), *Guitar Graffiti* (1979) and *I'm Not Like Everybody*

Else (1980) were marred by indifferent material. In recent years Spedding has toured with the rockabilly revivalist Robert Gordon and played sessions with **Paul McCartney** and **Hotei** among others. Despite his efforts to the contrary, Spedding seems destined to remain best man, but never the groom.

JOSEPH SPENCE

Born: August 3rd 1910, Andros, Bahamas.

A profound influence on **Ry Cooder** and **Taj Mahal**, Spence is one of the most accurate documenters of indigenous Bahamian music. While his style calls to mind **Eddie Lang**, Spence's repertoire comprised hymns, anthems, folk songs and work songs, many of which had been passed on from one geeneration to the next, and never written down or otherwise recorded until Spence started his work. Therefore, while his guitar work was innovative, Spence's role as a collector was comparable to that of A L Lloyd in Britain and Alan Lomax in the US. *The Complete Folkways Recordings* (1958) contains Spence's best work and offers a rare insight into how colonialism was perceived by an indigenous population. Also worthwhile is *The Bahamian Guitarist* (1981).

SKIP SPENCE

Born: Alexander Spence, April 18th 1943, Windsor, Ontario, Canada.

After drumming with the first lineup of Jefferson Airplane, rhythm guitarist and songwriter Spence formed Moby Grape with lead guitarist **Jerry Miller** and finger-picker **Peter Lewis**, recording *Moby Grape* (1967), *Wow* (1967) and *Grape Jam* (1967). In 1969 Spence departed for a solo career, cutting *Oar*, and this proved beyond reasonable doubt the extent to which Spence had shaped the musical policy of Moby Grape. Underrated and a genuine curio, it remains one of the great lost albums of the epoch. Spence has been present at some of the Grape reunions, notably for *Grape Live* (1979).

JEREMY SPENCER

Born: July 4th 1948, Hartlepool, Cleveland, England.

Before stepping out one bright California morning to buy a pack of cigarettes but finding God instead, Spencer was the man best equipped to keep alive the memory of **Elmore James**. Indeed, so accurate were his recreations that, on that bright California morning, Spencer might actually have believed for a moment that he was Elmore James. Divine revelation? Who can say. All that aside, the opening bars of Fleetwood Mac's 'I Believe My Time Ain't Long' (on *Pious Bird Of Good Omen* 1969), with Spencer's wonderful slide guitar, seem in hindsight to have been the soundtrack to the British blues boom of the late-1960s. Spencer played slide and rhythm in the original Fleetwood Mac, formed in summer 1967, alongside **Peter Green**, bassist Bob Brunning (soon replaced by John McVie) and drummer Mick Fleetwood, and later augmented by **Danny Kirwan**. Spencer remained with the group until 1971,

featuring notably on *Then Play On* (1969) and *Greatest Hits* (1971).

DAN SPITZ

Born: US.

■ **Jackson.**

Like Ministry (see **Mike Scaccia**) Anthrax have taken thrash metal to new heights thanks to their commanding rhythmic onslaught. While rhythm guitarist **Scott Ian** provides the all-encompassing riffs that feed and sustain the rest of the band, lead guitarist Spitz performs the dazzling highwire acts with his surprisingly structured solos. However, the group remain a unit with no member subordinating another, each contributing in equal part to the feel of each song, as on the definitive *Among The Living* (1987). Spitz employs a variety of instruments and styles to create the desired effect, on *Persistence Of Time* (1990) for example featuring acoustic guitars on the intro to 'Blood' and 12-string slide on 'Keep It In The Family'. While Anthrax remain most true to the notion of hardcore metal, they are notably lacking in cynicism.

BRUCE SPRINGSTEEN

Born: September 23rd 1949, Freehold, New Jersey, US.

■ **Fender Telecaster; Ovation; Gibson J200.**

Springsteen's albums generally boast session players of the highest quality, but on stage his considerable talent as a guitarist comes into its own. Springsteen first played in groups in the early-1960s, mainly influenced by British pop and rock outfits, and in 1971 assembled Dr Zoom & His Sonic Boom which evolved into the nucleus of the E Street Band. John Hammond signed Springsteen to Columbia and – sensing the emergence of another Bob Dylan – encouraged him to accompany himself on acoustic guitar and play a series of dates with a minimal backing band.

After half a dozen proper studio albums and myriad problems with bootleggers Springsteen finally issued *Live 1975-1985* (1986), a collection of five records giving the clearest indication of how his guitar work and confidence had developed. Still couched in the rock'n'roll vernacular, as the years fall away solos become more refined, more elegiac, with licks copped from his formative influences – and Springsteen is among a handful of players, **Robbie Robertson** included, to recognize that **Lowman Pauling** was one of the best R&B guitarists ever.

JOHN SQUIRE

Born: November 24th 1962, Sale, Greater Manchester, England.

The Stone Roses were one of the most critically rated bands to emerge at the end of the 1980s as part of the explosion of interest in all things Mancunian. Their debut *Stone Roses* (1989) had two things going for it: (1) The music industry needed someone to lionize, and (2) the band had been touring regularly to knock the material into shape. 'Fool's Gold', 'What The

World Is Waiting For' and 'Made Of Stone', among others, showed the extent to which guitarist Squire had absorbed the benefits of understatement, while 'One Love' showed that he could be florid too. While much of their career has been overshadowed by legal tussles with record companies, they resisted the temptation to rush into the studio to record that difficult second album.

CARTER STANLEY

Born: Carter Glen Stanley, August 27th 1925, McClure, Virginia, US. Died: December 1st 1966, Bristol, Virginia, US.

Carter and Ralph Stanley, better known as The Stanley Brothers, occupy a special place in the development of bluegrass that ranks them alongside other great originals like mandolinist Bill Monroe, and **Lester Flatt** & Earl Scruggs. They were taught the rudiments of the guitar (Carter) and banjo (Ralph), and were raised against the austere backdrop of the Baptist church.

In 1946 they became professional musicians, with Roy Sykes & The Blue Ridge Mountain Boys, but left shortly after, taking mandolinist Pee Wee Lambert with them to form The Clinch Mountain Boys. After recording 'Man Of Constant Sorrow', 'Little Glass Of Wine' and 'Molly And Tenbrooks' they were signed to Columbia where they recorded 'The Fields Have Turned To Brown' and 'The White Dove'.

They were never as inventive as Flatt & Scruggs, but Carter's vocal talents and guitar work emphasized his maturity as a songwriter, and George Shuffler often contributed fine lead guitar work to the Brothers' recordings. Throughout the 1950s and 1960s they established themselves on the emergent festival circuit, but Carter succumbed to a heart attack after constant touring. Ralph, however, kept the group going with a succession of younger players like **Ricky Skaggs** and **Keith Whitley**.

PAUL STANLEY

Born: Paul Eisen, January 20th 1950, New York, New York, US.

■ **Ibanez Iceman; Ibanez 'signature'; Gibson SG; Gibson Les Paul.**

Up until the arrival of Kiss, cosmetics and make-up had played an insignificant part in most guitarists' set-ups. With Kiss the question wasn't, "Will it be the Strat or the Les Paul tonight?" but "Is it Revlon or Elizabeth Arden sponsoring this part of the tour?" Cartoon characters throughout their career, Kiss had the charm of a fox in a chicken coop: the clichés Stanley and his pals meted out were utterly devoid of feeling. Licks gnawed at the back of the brain because they'd all been heard before. They were massive on the US stadium circuit (*Alive!* 1975, if you must).

POPS STAPLES

Born: Roebuck Staples, December 28th 1915, Winoma, Mississippi, US.

■ **Fender Stratocaster; Gibson Les Paul.**

A couple of years back, Pops Staples issued a blues

131

album that proved once and for all that he has been one of the most underrated guitarists around.

Pops' career had started as a blues guitarist while still a teenager, until in 1935 he joined the first of a succession of gospel groups. He formed The Staple Singers as a family gospel quartet in 1951 in Chicago with his son Pervis and two daughters Mavis and Cleotha, and they recorded for independent labels, scoring a monster gospel hit with 'Uncloudy Day'. Their style began to veer more towards R&B and country-soul due to the influence of producers like Larry Williams and Billy Sherrill, and in 1968 they signed to Stax where they were teamed with producers **Steve Cropper** and then Al Bell, resulting in a string of country-soul titles such as 'Respect Yourself', 'I'll Take You There', 'This World', 'Oh La De Da', 'If You're Ready (Come Go With Me)' and 'Touch A Hand, Make A Friend'.

The warmth of Pops' voice complemented the more soulful, strident tones of Mavis, while the sound was beefed up with Pops' lean, understated guitar lines. After Stax stopped business, the Singers' music became more dance oriented and the result was a succession of distinctly patchy outings – including a version of **David Byrne**'s 'Slippery People'. While the group still toured, there was little direction and in 1988 Mavis relaunched her solo career by signing with **Prince**'s Paisley Park label. In 1992 Pops cut his guitar album, *Peace To The Neighborhood*, which turned out to be one of the year's biggest and most pleasant surprises.

DAVID STAROBIN

Born: September 27th 1949, New York, New York, US.

■ *Southwell; Humphrey.*

In the late-1960s Starobin studied classical guitar at the Peabody Institute in Baltimore, Maryland, US, and in the early-1970s took charge of the institute's guitar ensemble. Since then he has become known principally for his determination to play in concerts and studios the works of 20th century composers for the 'classical' guitar, rather than take the more common route of reworking and/or transcribing older composers' pieces. He has also played in a good number of guitar ensembles, building on his early work at the Peabody Institute. In the early-1980s Starobin set up his own record label, Bridge, and released many interesting recordings, such as the *New Music With Guitar* series, *Lukas Foss: Night Music For John Lennon*, and *The Great Regondi*.

CHRIS STEIN

Born: January 5th 1950, New York, New York, US.

■ *Fender Stratocaster; Burns.*

Blondie became one of the most successful groups of the late-1970s and early-1980s, as much through vocalist Debbie Harry's estimable charms as the group's knack for a tune. Some may assert that apart from Debbie Harry's contribution, individual efforts were subordinated to the group's sound, but Stein was responsible for the group's visual image and the style of the group's sound. His guitar work, like **David Byrne**'s, was functional and he never projected

himself as the soloing axeman, but his capacity to supply a pithy and appropriate phrase at the right spot was integral to the group's reputation for cogency, as demonstrated on 'Picture This', 'Hanging On The Telephone', 'Sunday Girl', 'The Tide Is High' and 'Call Me'. Through much of the 1980s Stein was grievously ill, but towards the end of the decade Harry, having launched a solo career, used Stein in her new band.

LEIGH STEPHENS

Born: Bruce Stephens, Boston, Massachusetts, US.

Blue Cheer were one of the first heavy metal bands – although the term had yet to be coined – and their debut *Vincebus Eruptum* (1967) included a priceless version of **Eddie Cochran**'s 'Summertime Blues'. This and other pieces were delivered at a furious speed, making bands like Vanilla Fudge and Iron Butterfly sound as if they were auditioning for *The Sound Of Music*. Stephens left after the debut for a solo career and issued a string of rather dull records.

STEVE STEVENS

Born: 1959, New York, New York, US.

■ *Hamer 'signature'; Washburn 'signature'.*

One of 'punk' singer Billy Idol's cutest moves was to collaborate with Stevens, a player who didn't rely on effect to make a point and gave body to Idol's music. In tandem with producer Keith Forsey, Stevens set about building a repertoire for Idol that was in keeping with his image: arrogant and posturing. A cartoon cut-out, sure, but eminently more likeable than other caricatures such as Judas Priest and Kiss – although Idol's manic posturing is so hilarious he deserves approbation for audacity. 'White Wedding' (1983) and 'Rebel Yell' (1984) are amok with every rock cliché, while his cover of 'Mony Mony' (1987) is so crass and obvious that it's likeable. Stevens added the necessary guitar bombast, joining the mid-1980s penchant for screaming, dive-bombing sounds, and also played with Michael Jackson, on 'Dirty Diana' (*Bad* 1987), and left Idol to form his own short-lived Atomic Playboys in 1988.

DAVE STEWART

Born: David Allan Stewart, September 9th 1952, Sunderland, Tyne & Wear, England.

■ *Gretsch; Robin; Fender Stratocaster.*

In some ways The Eurythmics were the quintessential band of the 1980s, representing the more positive aspects of the drive for assertiveness and independence that gripped Britain in a decade whose music was for the most part creatively bankrupt. Both vocalist Annie Lennox and guitarist Stewart were fine writers with gifts for evoking atmosphere, best demonstrated by songs like 'Love Is A Stranger', 'Here Comes The Rain Again', 'Sexcrime (1984)', 'There Must Be An Angel (Playing With My Heart)' and 'You Have Placed A Chill In My Heart'.

Stewart assimilated music of all types into his guitar style, always supporting the song and the mood with his reflective playing, and his studio

wizardry ensured that technology was deployed to enhance, never being allowed to take over.

Although in recent years Stewart and Lennox have gone their separate ways (Lennox cut *Diva* in 1992), Stewart has produced and worked with a variety of artists such as Bob Dylan, **Tom Petty**, **Roy Orbison**, Daryl Hall and Mick Jagger, and formed his own band The Spiritual Cowboys. The object of this group is to enable Stewart to play more frequently in less formal circumstances, indicating his continuing love affair with the spirit of rock'n'roll.

ERIC STEWART

Born: January 1st 1945, Manchester, England.

■ *Gibson Les Paul; Gibson ES345.*

Stewart joined Wayne Fontana's backing group The Mindbenders in 1964, and after a number of hits such as 'Um Um Um Um Um', 'The Game Of Love' and 'Just A Little Bit Too Late', Fontana left for a solo career and The Mindbenders went it alone with 'A Groovy Kind Of Love' (1966). While in the group Stewart was joined by bassist Graham Gouldman, a prolific songwriter, and after The Mindbenders split the two put together Strawberry Studios to work on projects for the New York-based Kasenatz-Katz operation, the main producers of bubblegum music.

In 1969 Stewart and Gouldman brought in guitarist Lol Creme and drummer Kevin Godley to work on sessions, and their first collaboration was 'Neanderthal Man' under the name of Hot Legs. This provided the impetus for the quartet's more lasting contributions, under the name 10cc. Throughout the 1970s the group were responsible for some of the pithiest lyrics and cleverest pop arrangements to grace the charts, as on 'Donna', 'Rubber Bullets', 'The Dean And I' and 'Wall Street Shuffle'.

As the group became more established, 'I'm Not In Love' and 'I'm Mandy Fly Me' exemplified Godley and Creme's increasing preoccupation with studio technology, which – in addition to their hatred of touring – caused them to leave the group in 1976. Stewart and Gouldman continued, reverting to the less elaborately arranged styles of their earlier records: 'The Things We Do For Love' and 'Dreadlock Holiday'. It has never been a part of Stewart's job to unfurl rib-tickling or, indeed, spine-tingling solos with much regularity. He is more adept at and indeed has great experience in playing for the song, and is sufficiently accomplished to have been enlisted by **Paul McCartney** to play on *Tug Of War* (1982).

FREDDIE STEWART

Born: June 5th 1946, Dallas, Texas, US.

In 1966 vocalist/keyboardist Sylvester Stewart (known hereafter as Sly Stone) formed Sly & The Family Stone with Cynthia Robinson (trumpet), Sly's brother Freddie (guitar), sister Rosemary (piano and vocals), cousin Larry Graham (bass), Greg Errico (drums), and Jerry Martini (horns).

What set the group apart was Sly's willingness to experiment. He absorbed the influences of the fledgling psychedelic movement of San Francisco

Std-Ste

and combined it with his native flair for programming music (he was formerly a DJ at KSOL), forming a hybrid that owed as much to soul and R&B as white rock'n'roll. 'Dance To The Music' (1968) heralded the arrival of a sparkling new group, with Freddie's guitar occasionally wailing out from amongst the horn and rhythm sections that wouldn't have been out of place on a James Brown record.

In general Freddie's guitar work tended to merge effectively into the mass of the Family Stone's sound, but his wah-wah stands out on 'Don't Call Me Nigger Whitey' (Stand 1969) and his glassy funk chords provide the hook on 'Running Away' (There's A Riot Going On 1971). By the mid-1970s the group had effectively disbanded, but they remain a potent influence upon disparate artists like **Prince**, George Clinton, Run-DMC and Public Enemy.

STEPHEN STILLS

Born: January 3rd 1945, Dallas, Texas, US.

■ *Gibson Les Paul Special; Gretsch White Falcon; Gretsch Country Gentleman; Martin D-45; Gibson Firebird; National resonator; Fender Stratocaster.*

In retrospect Stills' career has been marred by under-achievement, and it was only when in partnership with players such as **Neil Young** or **Mike Bloomfield** whom he considers his (almost) equals that his true talent has shone. Elsewhere, his guitar work has been largely complacent.

After majoring in politics at the University of Florida Stills played in various New York folk groups before moving to the West Coast. In Los Angeles he formed Buffalo Springfield, which included in its lineup **Neil Young** and **Richie Furay**, both excellent songwriters and guitarists who provided the inspiration that Stills needed. As a result *Buffalo Springfield* (1966) and *Buffalo Springfield Again!* (1967) are faultless, with Stills' contributions including 'For What It's Worth', 'Rock'n'Roll Woman', 'Bluebird' and 'Everyday'.

With three such dominant personalities the band didn't last, and Stills teamed up with **Al Kooper** and **Mike Bloomfield** for *Super Session* (1968), which included a majestic reading of Donovan's 'Season Of The Witch'. This album became the template for a spate of supergroups – including Crosby Stills & Nash, featuring former Byrds man David Crosby and ex-Hollie Graham Nash.

The group's debut *Crosby Stills & Nash* (1969) featured some of the finest acoustic picking from Stills heard outside of Nashville, but when Neil Young joined the following year battle commenced, and Stills and Young locked into some of the fiercest guitar duels imaginable. These were restricted to their live shows, but the Crosby Stills Nash & Young album *Déjà Vu* (1970) took an age to record as neither Stills nor Young could agree on anything, losing much spontaneity in the process.

Inevitably each member of the group undertook solo projects, with Stills releasing several solo albums, including the fine *Stephen Stills* (1970), and formed the big group Manassas. Pleasant though Manassas' albums were, they lacked edge, despite the involvement of **Chris Hillman** and **Al Perkins**

among others. Throughout the 1980s and 1990s Stills has become one of the grandees of contemporary US music, but his records have become very bland, as have the periodic reunions with Crosby, Nash and Young.

MARTIN STONE

Born: December 11th 1946, Woking, Surrey, England.

Whatever happened to Martin Stone? For a spell at the end of the 1960s he was rated as one of the most accomplished players in Britain. As a member of Savoy Brown his reputation kicked off with *Shake Down* (1967), but he left to join the remnants of The Action that eventually metamorphosed into Mighty Baby. On *Mighty Baby* (1968) Stone's inspired raga-style solos seemed set to help the band to wider success, but after a string of club dates up and down the country they disbanded. In 1972 Stone and guitarist Phil Lithman, who had been members of Junior's Blues Band back in 1963, joined up to form the country rock outfit Chilli Willi & The Red Hot Peppers. Over the next three years they were stalwarts of the club circuit, but their exquisite *Bongos Over Balham* (1974) failed to make a commercial impression and the group split, with Stone joining The Pink Fairies. Since then he seems to have gone into retirement.

IZZY STRADLIN

Born: Jeffrey Isbell, 1967, Lafayette, Indiana, US.

■ *Gibson ES175; Gibson Les Paul; Gibson Byrdland; Gibson ES335; Fender Telecaster.*

Stradlin was a significant figure in the Guns N'Roses scheme as he seemed to hold the band together on stage. **Slash** may have been churning out one solo after another, but Stradlin's rhythm work provided the necessary link with the rhythm section, as on 'You Could Be Mine' or 'Don't Cry'. To use The Rolling Stones analogy: Stradlin was to Slash what **Ron Wood** is to **Keith Richards**. Stradlin left after *Use Your Illusion* (1991) to organize his own outfit.

DAVE STRYKER

Born: 1957, Omaha, Nebraska, US.

■ *Gibson ES347.*

A bluesy player who was influenced initially by **Duane Allman**, Stryker was caused to redefine his approach when recruited by jazz organist Brother Jack McDuff and then saxophonist Stanley Turrentine. By 1990 Stryker had branched out to form his own group and, after two hesitant outings, he cut *Guitar On Top* which showed how both McDuff and Turrentine had instilled in him the need to swing. The hip-hop arrangement of Thelonious Monk's 'Evidence' illustrates a lesson well taken.

HAMISH STUART

Born: October 8th 1949, Glasgow, Scotland.

■ *Fender Stratocaster; Epiphone Casino.*

Formed in 1972 by bassist Alan Gorrie, The Average White Band were Robbie McIntosh (drums), Mike

Rosen (guitar/trumpet), Roger Ball (alto/baritone saxes), Malcolm Duncan (tenor/soprano saxes) and **Onnie McIntyre** (guitar). Rosen didn't last long and his replacement was Stuart.

They cut *Show Your Hand* (1973) which included a tasty version of jazz-rock outfit The Crusaders' 'Put It Where You Want It', but they didn't hit their stride until *Average White Band* (1975), produced by Arif Mardin, which was full of jagged, choppy riffs that proved Scotsmen could be funky too, as on 'Pick Up The Pieces', 'Work To Do' and 'You Got The Love'. *Cut The Cake* (1975) was equally incisive, but gradually the group disintegrated, and each member was keenly sought after on the session scene. In 1989 Stuart became an integral part of **Paul McCartney**'s band, appearing on *Flowers In The Dirt*, one of McCartney's best efforts in years.

RORY STUART

Born: January 9th 1956, New York, New York, US.

■ *Monteleone Eclipse.*

Stuart is one of the new breed of jazz guitarists who look to formal composition as a means of widening the musical palette, rather than flirting with rock. After studying under pianist/arranger Jaki Byard, Stuart studied classical guitar until he heard **Wes Montgomery** and **George Benson**. His first break came when he was recruited by organist Brother Jack McDuff for a tour, and this gave him the confidence to assemble his own quartet. His playing on *Nightwork* (1983) and *Hurricane* (1986) has a richness of tone and a developed structure seldom evident in one so relatively young, while the solo *A Reverie* (1984) demonstrates immaculate fretwork and a pleasing reluctance to flatter or dazzle the listener.

BIG JIM SULLIVAN

Born: February 14th 1941, London, England.

■ *Gibson; Fender; Ovation; Eggle.*

Sullivan was the first British session man to regularly use a solid electric guitar in the studio, and the first to use a 12-string acoustic. He was also the first session man to turn up regularly for sessions with more than one guitar.

Sullivan's career started in the late-1950s when he was co-opted to join rock'n'roller Marty Wilde's backing group, The Wild Cats, taking time off to record instrumentals in their own right as The Krew Kats. His reputation flourished and he was recruited to back visiting US rockers such as **Eddie Cochran** and Gene Vincent. Since that time he has read the charts for everyone from Frank Sinatra to Tom Jones, The Kinks to The Walker Brothers, and Stevie Wonder to **Stefan Grossman**.

Along the way Sullivan has encouraged other fledgling session players like **Jimmy Page** and **Ritchie Blackmore** (with whom he teamed up alongside **Albert Lee** for *Green Bullfrog* 1972), and was the catalyst for session groups such as Blue Mink and The Brotherhood Of Man. His solo recordings have demonstrated his eclecticism and an expansive range of influences, such as *Sitar Beat* (1968, with

Ustad Vilayat Khan), *Big Jim's Back* (1974) and *Test Of Time* (1983), produced by Mike Vernon. A journeyman of breathtaking experience, Sullivan's professionalism would get him a job in any orchestra or band on any day of the week.

JUSTIN SULLIVAN

Born: 1956, Bradford, Yorkshire, England.

Formed in Bradford in 1982, New Model Army were a by-product of the punk era and a growing disaffection with British politics. After scoring an independent hit 'The Price' they signed to EMI and, while many would have viewed this as compromising their radicalism, it served to get their music to a wider audience, with songs like 'No Rest', 'Stupid Question', 'Vagabonds' and 'Get Me Out'. Sullivan, known as Slade The Leveller, combines power with subtlety, and retains a pop sensibility sufficient to win new admirers without alienating long-term fans. After ten years, *Love Of Hopeless Causes* (1993) is if anything more trenchant than their previous outings.

HUBERT SUMLIN

Born: November 16th 1931, Greenwood, Mississippi, US.

■ **Gibson Les Paul; Gibson ES335; Rickenbacker.**

In 1948 **Howlin' Wolf** founded The House Rockers, one of the earliest electric R&B groups, and included in the lineup was guitarist Sumlin. He became a key element in the sound of Wolf, contributing incisive, pungent licks to classic takes from the 1950s and early-1960s like 'Moanin At Midnight', 'Smokestack Lightnin', 'Evil', 'Sitting On Top Of The World', 'Killin Floor' and 'No Place To Go'.

Through his association with Wolf, Sumlin participated in sessions at Chess with **Muddy Waters**, playing on titles like 'Forty Days And Forty Nights', 'I Live The Life I Love (I Love The Life I Live)' and 'Rock Me'. On these sides Sumlin's guitar work was more structured than it had been with Wolf, while his interplay with harp man Little Walter provides counterpoint to Waters' vocals.

Although much of the early part of Sumlin's career was spent accompanying others, the 1980s brought some acceptance in his own right, and albums like *Hubert Sumlin's Blues Party* (1987) and *Healin' Feeling* (1989) showed he possessed a rich, expressive voice.

ANDY SUMMERS

Born: Andrew James Somers, December 31st 1942, Blackpool, Lancashire, England.

■ **Fender Telecaster; Fender Stratocaster; Hamer.**

Andy Summers (he changed his surname in 1974) spent years on the session circuit achieving a reputation as a great player, and his career started with Zoot Money's Big Roll Band, a British R&B combo who traded stints with Georgie Fame & the Blue Flames at London's Flamingo club.

But Zoot (real name George) made an error of judgement in 1967 when he tried to embrace psychedelia, changing the group's name to Dantalian's Chariot, no less. The sight of portly George in a kaftan proved too much for most booking agents and the band split, with Summers joining Eric Burdon & The New Animals, appearing on *Love Is...* (1969).

Based on the West Coast until 1974 Summers studied classical guitar and listened to jazz guitarists such as **Django Reinhardt**, **Joe Pass**, **Herb Ellis** and **Larry Coryell**. On returning to Britain he rejoined the session community, playing with Mike Oldfield and Kevin Ayers, David Essex, Neil Sedaka, Soft Machine and Kevin Coyne until he was recruited to join The Police in 1976, replacing Henry Padovani.

What has characterized Summers' Police work has been his ability to play concisely, never indulging in ornate fripperies but rather providing character and atmosphere from minimal, treated arpeggios. Combined with his wide grasp of styles, this enabled Summers to complement Sting's knack for melody and make some of the most exhilarating and musical pop of the late-1970s/early-1980s (as collected on *The Singles* 1986).

Since The Police got divorced, Summers has taken a more experimental route, working solo (*Charming Snakes* 1990), with **Robert Fripp** (*I Advance Masked* 1982) and **John Etheridge** (*Invisible Threads* 1993), searching further into the land of tone and texture to create elaborate, minimalist structures that are absorbing and technically exacting.

BERNARD SUMNER

Born: Bernard Dicken, January 4th 1956, Manchester, England.

The seeds of the explosion of interest in all things Mancunian were sown in 1977 when Joy Division were formed by vocalist Ian Curtis and Sumner (then known as Bernard Albrecht). The band and the sparse, minimalist production of Martin Hannett inspired many others, such as Durutti Column. While Curtis' songs like 'Love Will Tear Us Apart', 'Atmosphere' and 'Dead Souls' intimated a brooding menace, Albrecht's basic, tentative phrasing mitigated the bleakness.

In 1980 Curtis committed suicide, Albrecht changed his name to Sumner, and the group was renamed New Order. The prestige garnered by Joy Division gave them an instant reputation that belied their experience, but with the assistance of Hannett and US producer Arthur Baker they began to assemble material that once again inspired others, such as The Stone Roses and Happy Mondays.

Sumner, who had taken on the vocalist's chores, echoed Curtis' sense of foreboding, but his minimalist riffs were set increasingly against spacious, mechanized rhythm tracks.

Toward the end of 1989 Sumner teamed up with The Pet Shop Boys' Neil Tenant and Chris Lowe, plus **Johnny Marr**, for Electronic. In 1993 New Order reconvened, having signed to London, making the fine *Republic*. Sumner and the rest of the gang seem to have achieved the impossible: a British cult band who have hit the mainstream and yet still have their credibility unimpaired.

GABOR SZABO

Born: March 8th 1936, Budapest, Hungary. Died: February 26th 1982, Boston, Massachusetts, US.

■ **Ovation (later).**

A fine self-taught jazz stylist, Szabo learned the rudiments of guitar through listening in Hungary to the radio station Voice Of America, adopting a technique that combined jazz and gypsy idioms. In 1956 he left Hungary weeks after the October uprising was suppressed by the Russians, and became a refugee in the US, settling in Boston and studying at Berklee School Of Music.

Throughout the 1960s Szabo played with a host of jazz musicians, notably with the Chico Hamilton Quintet but also with Gary McFarland and the Charles Lloyd Quartet, before embarking on a solo career. Signed initially to Impulse, he cut albums like *The Sorcerer* (1968) that were technically refined but lacked true inspiration.

Later partnerships with vocalist Lena Horne among others showed Szabo's appetite for trying fresh ideas, with *Lena And Gabor* (1970) a great duet album. *Nightflight* (1976) was one of his most successful solo outings as it paid little heed to contemporary trends and demonstrated his refined picking technique. His death in 1982 interceded before he had really peaked.

TAJ MAHAL

Born: Henry St Clair Fredericks, May 17th 1942, New York, New York, US.

■ **National resonator.**

Taj Mahal has become respected for the breadth of his knowledge and technical expertise, although his commercial impact has been minimal. For once the term ethno-musicologist is close enough to describing the extent of his influences: like **Ry Cooder**, he is galvanized by curiosity and enthusiasm.

Taj's bluesy, absorbing guitar style is complemented by an aptitude for harmonica, piano, banjo, vibes, mandolin, dulcimer... and, no doubt, anything else he tries.

The son of an arranger, Taj's opening shots were the initially shelved but now much lauded Rising Sons' sessions, which featured Jesse Ed Davis and Spirit drummer Ed Cassidy. Hearing these sessions today (they were finally released in 1993) it's clear that they must have struck as much fear into the hearts of record company executives as Gram Parsons' International Submarine Band album did – both shared the common characteristic of precociousness. While very loosely it could be described as folk-rock, it was a far cry from the preppy, collegiate style of most folk bands of the time and had a more abrasive edge than folk-rock bands such as The Byrds.

After the group disbanded Taj settled on a solo career that initially took root on the West Coast club circuit, and he cut *Taj Mahal* (1967) for Columbia. His band included the mighty **Jesse Ed Davis**, bassist Gary Gilmore and drummer Chuck Blackwell. The result was a rich but meditative introduction to

Sul-Taj

Steve Vai

In an era when heavy metal guitarists are everywhere, Steve Vai has managed to stand out from the crowd by assembling a dazzling body of work that embraces both the commercial and the idiosyncratic. Initially a pupil of Joe Satriani, he learned at least as much in the six years he spent in Frank Zappa's band, both from the man himself, whose demands upon musicians are the stuff of legend, and from his fellow players. Since then, Vai's instrumental skills, his compositional abilities and his command of musical technology have continued to evolve. Never a purist, he has nonetheless always had a deep understanding of the necessity for form and structure. He has always appreciated something that lesser musicians often miss. In guitar playing, as in other areas of life, rules are made to be bent or broken: but it helps to know the rules first. This musical awareness enabled Vai to compose note-perfect solos for the likes of Zappa while giving vent to more spontaneous, improvisatory leanings in his work with Alcatrazz, in David Lee Roth's band, and with Whitesnake. The two disciplines meet on Vai's two solo albums, Passion And Warfare and Sex And Religion, which also provide formidable evidence of Vai's skills as an instrumentalist. When guitarists get the chance to cut loose after years as sidemen, always operating under someone else's musical direction, they risk becoming either self-indulgent or unbearably wooden. Vai has managed to avoid these pitfalls, but it remains to be seen whether he is capable of coming up with a range of material broad enough to be worthy of his obvious instrumental expertise.

VAI'S GUITARS With Zappa, Vai used a 1976 Fender Stratocaster with heavily modified pickups and circuitry. The Japanese company Ibanez took note of Vai's rising popularity and invited him to collaborate in the design of some new models, resulting in the highly decorated JEM six-string series (1988) with body 'monkey grip', and the 1990 Universe seven-string design (shown right) which had an extra low-tuned string to extend the guitar's range.

976 1977 1978 1979 1980 1981 1982 1983 1984

ZAPPA: TINSELTOWN REBELLION (Released 1981) *Line-up:* Frank Zappa, Ike Willis, Steve Vai, Ray White, Warren Cucurullo (guitar, vocals), Denny Walley (slide guitar, vocals), Tommy Mars (keyboards, vocals), Peter Wolf (keyboards), Bob Harris (keyboards, trumpet, boy soprano), Arthur Barrow (bass, vocals), Patrick O'Hearn (bass), Ed Mann (percussion), Vinnie Colaiuta, David Logemann (drums).

ZAPPA: YOU ARE WHAT YOU IS (Released 1981) *Line-up:* Frank Zappa (guitar, vocals), Steve Vai (guitar, vocals), Ray White, Ike Willis (guitar, vocals), Denny Walley (slide guitar, vocals), Tommy Mars (keyboards), Bob Harris (trumpet, boy soprano), Arthur Barrow/Scott Thunes (bass), David Ocker (clarinet), Motorhead Sherwood (tenor sax, vocals), Ed Mann (percussion), David Logemann (drums), Craig Stewart (harmonica), Jimmy Carl Black, Ahmet Zappa, Moon Zappa, Mark Pinske (vocals).

ZAPPA: SHIP ARRIVING TOO LATE TO SAVE A DROWNING WITCH (Released 1982) *Line-up:* Frank Zappa, Ike Willis, Ray White (guitar, vocals), Steve Vai (guitar), Bob Harris, Tommy Mars (keyboards), Lisa Popeil, Moon Zappa (vocals), Bobby Martin (keyboards, sax, vocals), Arthur Barrow (bass), Roy Estrada, Scott Thunes, Patrick O'Hearn (bass), Ed Mann (percussion), Chad Wackerman (drums).

Vai appeared on three further Zappa albums in the mid-1980s: *The Man From Utopia*, *Thing-Fish* and *Jazz From Hell*. Zappa was, of course, no mean guitarist himself. In his later career he went for elaborate orchestrations, though he increasingly preferred the Synclavier synthesizer to working with musicians. On *Jazz From Hell*, for example, Vai is a key member of a tiny ensemble of trusted players.

FLEX-ABLE (Released 1984) *Tracks:* Little Green Men/Viv Women/Lovers Are Crazy/Salamanders In The Sun/The Boy/Girl Song/Attitude Song/Call It Sleep/Junkie/Bill's Private Parts/Next Stop Earth/There's Something Dead In Here. In the gap between leaving the hothouse atmosphere of the Zappa studio band and starting a new career as a peripatetic guitar hero, Vai found time to pay homage to Uncle Frank with this promising solo set. The titles speak volumes about Vai's musical lineage, as do the tricksy arrangements and the pervasive sense of things being just that little bit too clever for their own good. Valuing brain and flying fingers above heart and soul,

COMPLETELY WELL (Released 1969) *Tracks:* So Excited/ No Good/ You're Losin' Me/ What Happened/ Confessin' The Blues/ Key To My Kingdom/ Cryin' Won't Help You Now/ You're Mean/ The Thrill Is Gone. From 1969 BB recorded in the studio with white musicians such as Leon Russell and Carole King (piano), Bryan Garofalo (bass), Russ Kunkel (drums) and Joe Walsh (guitar).

LIVE IN COOK COUNTY JAIL (Released 1971) *Tracks:* Introduction/ Every Day I Have The Blues/ How Blue Can You Get/ Worry, Worry, Worry/ That Evil Child/ Medley: Three O' Clock Blues; Darlin', You Know I Love You; Sweet Sixteen; The Thrill Is Gone; and

Please Accept My Love. While King's popularity in concert continued to grow, his records proved patchy: *In London* (1971) teamed him to liitle effect with sidemen like Ringo Starr, Peter Green, Steve Winwood and Alexis Korner.

LA MIDNIGHT (Released 1972) *Tracks:* I Got Some Help I Don't Need/ Help The Poor/ Can't You Hear Me Talking To You?/ Midnight/ Sweet Sixteen/ (I Believe) I've Been Blue Too Long/ Lucille's Granny.

GUESS WHO (Released 1972) *Tracks:* Summer In The City/ Just Can't Please You/ Any Other Way/ You Don't Know Nothin' About Love/ Found What I

Need/ Neighbourhood Affair/ It Takes A Young Girl/ Better Lovin' Man/ Guess Who/ Shouldn't Have Left Me/ Five Long Years. Neither this nor *LA* matched the earlier *Indianola Mississippi Seeds* (1970) as they lacked fire and thrust, principally due to unimaginative and bland production that ironed out all the rough edges and inserted slickness.

TO KNOW YOU IS TO LOVE TO LOVE YOU (Released 1973) *Tracks:* I Like To Live The Love/ Respect Yourself/ Who Are You/ Love/ To Know You Is To Love You/ Oh To Me/ Thank You For Loving The Blues. Featuring a contribution from Stevie Wonder, who co-wrote the title track with his erstwhile wife Syreeta Wright, this

marked King's initial efforts to woo an audience more accustomed to the smooth, soulful funk of Wonder and T Crusaders. While purists were not impressed, it illustrated King's awareness of the need to keep movin on. It was followed by a collaboration with R&B vocalist Bobby Bland, *Togeth For The First Time... Live!* (1974). The repeated the exercise with *Together Again... Live!* in 1976.

LUCILLE TALKS BACK (Released 1975) *Tracks:* Lucille Talks Back/ Breaking Up Somebody's Home/ Reconsider Baby/ Don't Make Me Pay For Mistakes/ When I'm Wrong/ I Know The Price/ Have Faith/ Everybody Lies A Little.

| 1973 | 1974 | 1975 | 1976 | 1977 | 1978 | 1979 | 1980 | 1981 | 1982 |

THE STORY In 1951 King scored a Number One R&B hit with 'Three O'Clock Blues', the first of a series. Throughout the 1950s he toured continually, building his reputation with a live act that would remain essentially unchanged for the rest of his career, although *My Kind Of Blues* (1960) is a landmark of these early years, providing the seldom bettered groundwork for later studio albums. In 1962 King was given an advance of $25,000 to join ABC. His first records for that company were

over-produced, but in 1965 they released the epochal *Live At The Regal*, the first time that the raw excitement of his concerts had been successfully captured on record. Its success was part of a process that would culminate in King's decision in 1969 to aim at white rock-oriented audiences instead of continuing to play the chitlin' circuit.
King's attraction for rock audiences was based upon the large number of white musicians such as Eric Clapton, Mike Bloomfield, Paul

Butterfield and Alexis Korner who consistently championed his work by recording their own versions of his material. This development had an unfortunate side effect, when some listeners got the feeling that King was merely along for the ride. But it wasn't until the 1980s that the full measure of King's abilities became apparent.

KING SIZE (Released 1977) *Track:* Don't You Lie To Me/ I Wonder Why/ Medley: I Just Want To Make Love To You; Your Lovin' Turned Me On/ Slow And Easy/ Got My Mojo Workin'/ Walkin' In The Sun/ Mother For Ya/ T Same Love That Made Me Laugh/ It's Just A Matter Of Time.

MIDNIGHT BELIEVER (Released 1978) *Tracks:* When It All Comes Dow Midnight Believer/ I Just Can't Leave Your Love Alone/ Hold On/ Never Mak Your Move Too Soon/ A World Full Of Strangers/ Let Me Make You Cry A Little Longer.

KING'S GUITARS Using a Telecaster in the early 1950s, King moved to his beloved Gibson thinline electric ES355 soon after it appeared in 1958 (a similar ES355 is shown below). Gibson marketed a BB King model from 1981.

TAKE IT HOME (Released 1979) *Tracks:* Better Not Look Down/ Same Old Story/ Happy Birthday Blues/ I've Always Been Lonely/ Secondhand Woman/ Tonight I'm Gonna Make You Star/ Story Everybody Knows/ Take It Home. Recorded with the cream of Los Angeles session men, this has King's voice better than ever, with the materi sounding as if it were tailor made.

Of all the bluesmen to cross over into the mainstream, few have had such consistency and resilience as BB King. Born on a plantation in Mississippi in 1925, he knew almost nothing of the blues until he joined the US Army during World War II, having heard only church music at that point. Thereafter he began to sing and play in gospel groups and on street corners, making a break from the privations of Mississippi existence to join a cousin, Bukka White, in Memphis, Tennessee. There he found a job singing commercials on WDIA, the first black radio station, before becoming a disc jockey and instrumentalist. He billed himself first in his real name, Riley King, before dubbing himself the Blues Boy from Beale Street. This was shortened to BB King in time. He was first recorded by Sam Phillips, the man who discovered Elvis Presley some time later, and began his career on the Bihari brothers' Modern Records label, staying there, or on its subsidiaries, until

1962. At the same time he developed a successful live act, though his greatest fame only came after he had been discovered by the new white blues artists of the early and mid-1960s, many of them British. From that point on, he never looked back, recording an astonishing series of albums (of which only a fraction are listed here) in a variety of styles. Starting in a crude instrumental manner, redolent of Blind Lemon Jefferson or T-Bone Walker, he moved on to much more mellow sounds, offending purists by his collaborations with such slick instrumentalists as the Crusaders. Several of his middle period albums were produced by Bill Szymczyk, celebrated for his work with The Eagles, amongst others, which enhanced their pop chart appeal. In the 1990s he is still singing and playing with conviction and strength, even after nearly 45 years in one of the toughest areas of the music business.

LIVE AT THE REGAL (Released 1965) Tracks: Every Day I Have The Blues/ Sweet Little Angel/ It's My Own Fault/ How Blue Can You Get/ Please Love Me/ You Upset Me Baby/ Worry, Worry/ Woke Up This Morning/ You Done Lost Your Good Thing Now/ Help The Poor. A classic King album, caught live in concert in Chicago on November 21st 1964. This was his second for ABC; the debut was Mr Blues (1962).

BLUES IS KING (Released 1967) Tracks: Introduction/Waitin' On You/ Introduction/Gamblers' Blues/Tired Of Your Jive/Night Life/Buzz Me/Don't Answer The Door/Blind Love/I Know What You're Puttin' Down/Baby Get Lost/Gonna Keep On Loving You. Line-up includes: Kenneth Sands (trumpet), Bobby Forte (sax), Duke Jethro (organ), Louis Satterfield (bass), Sonny Freeman (drums). Recorded live.

1962 1963 1964 1965 1966 1967 1968 1969 1970 1971

LUCILLE (Released 1968) Tracks: Lucille/ You Move Me So/ Country Girl/ No Money, No Luck/ I Need Your Love/ Rainin' All The Time/ I'm With You/ Stop Puttin' The Hurt/ Watch Yourself. Named after of King's guitar, a Gibson ES355, Lucille followed Confessin' The Blues (1966), the excellent Blues Is King and Blues On Top Of Blues (1968).

EARLY YEARS BB King's recording career began at the studios of WDIA, the Memphis black music station on which he sometimes appeared. The four songs he recorded were released on the Nashville-based Bullet label and had some local success. But his career proper didn't begin until, in 1950, the Los Angeles-based brothers Jules, Joe and Saul Bihari were hunting for talent for their Modern Records label. They heard King and were impressed enough to let him head the roster on their new subsidiary, RPM. Over the next 11 years, he recorded hundreds of songs

for Modern, RPM and two further subsidiaries, Kent and Crown. He had his first rhythm & blues number one in 1951, with 'Three O'Clock Blues', and a further 30 or so hits followed in his time with the Biharis. The British record company Ace has made it a mission to reissue all of those early records and, indeed, many more tracks that were recorded but never released. They are available on a variety of CDs, repackaged from the original master tapes. Particularly notable are the CD which combines the first two original albums, Singing The Blues

and The Blues. There are also two excellent Best Of volumes, plus The Fabulous BB King and Do The Boogie, which includes much rare material from the early-1950s. Joe Bihari did his first recordings on portable equipment at the Memphis YMCA. Later, King was recorded at a real studio in Houston, Texas, and then, finally, from 1954, he moved to Los Angeles for recording purposes. At that stage Maxwell Davis was a dominant figure in the West Coast recording scene, and he would bring the pick of session men to King's recordings.

LIVE AND WELL (Released 1969) Tracks: I Want You So Bad/ Friends/ Get Off My Back, Woman/ Let's Get Down To Business/ Why I Sing The Blues/ Don't Answer The Door/ Just A Little Love/ My Mood/ Sweet Little Angel/ Please Accept My Love.

ALCATRAZZ: DISTURBING THE PEACE (Released 1985) *Line-up:* Graham Bonnet (vocals), Steve Vai (guitar), Jimmy Waldo (keyboards), Gary Shea (bass), Jan Uvena (drums). *Tracks:* God Bless Video/Mercy/Will You Be Home Tonight/Wire And Wood/Desert Diamond/Stripper/Painted Lover/Lighter Shade Of Green/Sons And Lovers/Sky Fire/Breaking The Heart Of The City. After leaving Frank Zappa's Band, Vai joined Alcatrazz, replacing Scandinavian Yngwie Malmsteen. Although *Disturbing The Peace* was disjointed and slipshod, it consolidated Vai's reputation as he made the best of what was available, and displayed his virtuosity despite the musicial environment.

DAVID LEE ROTH: SKYSCRAPER (Released 1988) *Line-up:* David Lee Roth (vocals), Steve Vai (guitar), Brett Tuggle (keyboards), Billy Sheehan (bass), Greg Bissonnette (drums). *Tracks:* Knucklebones/Just Like Paradise/The Bottomline/Skyscraper/Damn Good/Hot Dog And A Shake/Stand Up/Hena/Perfect Timin'/Two Fools A Minute. Not quite as impressive as its predecessor, but nevertheless it holds up remarkably well, despite the fact that Vai could just as easily be playing in his sleep, such is the facile nature of the repertoire. No great challenges here, certainly. Roth is not alone among the hard rock fraternity in coming up with crass lyrics and hackneyed sentiments: he is, however, one of the few who is able to get away with it.

PASSION AND WARFARE (Released 1990) *Tracks:* Liberty/Erotic Nightmares/Animal/Answers/The Riddle/Ballerina 12/24/For The Love Of God/Audience Is Listening/I Would Love To/Blue Powder/Greasy Kids Stuff/Alien Water Kiss/Sisters/Love Secrets. *Passion And Warfare* was the record that brought Steve Vai international recognition as a stupendous guitarist capable of assimilating a variety of disparate influences and welding them all into a fascinating hybrid. While it sold well, it made few concessions to the contemporary perception of Vai that had been shaped by his tenure with Whitesnake, David Lee Roth and Alcatrazz. He is, in fact, a much more interesting player than those names might suggest.

1986 1987 1988 1989 1990 1991 1992 1993

ex-able is the kind of solo album made by young men with something to prove. Later, playing with the likes of Whitesnake, Vai would have to unlearn a lot of this ingenuity in favour of high volume and low cunning. After this album, that must have seemed like a walk in the park. The sessions gave birth in the same year to an album of out-takes – a fashion item now rendered redundant by the greater playing time of CD – bearing the unappetizing name *Flex-able Leftovers* and all the virtues (and flaws) of its parent.

DAVID LEE ROTH: EAT 'EM AND SMILE (Released 1986) *Tracks:* Yankee Rose/Shyboy/I'm Easy/Ladies Nite In Buffalo?/Goin' Crazy/Tobacco Road/Elephant Gun/Big Trouble /Bump And Grind/That's Life. For this little beast, vocalist Roth confounded the critics by proving that he had as much chutzpah as his erstwhile collaborator, Eddie Van Halen, assembling a band that included Steve Vai (guitar), Billy Sheehan (bass) and Greg Bissonnette (drums). *Eat 'Em And Smile* was the result – loud and lairy, immaculately produced, and a durability seldom encountered in metal or heavy rock.

WHITESNAKE: SLIP OF THE TONGUE (Released 1989) *Line-up:* David Coverdale (vocals), Steve Vai (guitar), Adrian Vandenberg (guitar), Rudy Sarzo (bass) and Tommy Aldridge (drums). *Tracks:* Slip Of The Tongue/Cheap An' Nasty/Fool For Your Lovin'/Now You're Gone/Kittens Got Claws/Wings Of A Storm/The Deeper The Love/Judgement Day/Slow Poke Music/Sailin' Ships. While Vai's solo albums have shown him to be a man of some expertise and versatility, a swift browse through his CV proves that he has a finely tuned sense of humour, underlined by this flirtation of his with Whitesnake.

SEX AND RELIGION (Released 1993) *Tracks:* Earth Dweller's Return/Here And Now/In My Dreams With You/Still My Bleeding Heart/Sex And Religion/Dirty Black Hole/Touching Tongues/State Of Grace/Survive/Pig/The Road To Mount Calvary/Deep Down Into The Pain/Rescue Me Or Bury Me. Confirming the promise of the earlier *Passion And Warfare*, this album spawned a single that included two versions of 'Deep Down Into The Pain', as well as 'Just Cartilage'. Although peer pressure from Joe Satriani still exerts a hold, Steve Vai continues to prove himself one of the most inventive guitarists of the era.

NOW APPEARING AT OLE MISS

(Released 1980) *Tracks:* Intro- BB King Blues Theme/ Caldonia/ Blues Medley: Don't Answer The Door; You Done Lost Your Good Thing Now; I Need Love So Bad; Nobody Loves Me But My Mother/ Hold On/ I Got Some Outside Help (I Don't Really Need)/ Darlin' You Know I Love You/ When I'm Wrong/ The Thrill Is Gone/ Never Make Your Move Too Soon/ Three O'Clock In The Morning/ Rock Me Baby/ Guess Who/ I Just Can't Leave Your Love Alone. King returns to basics in his native Mississippi, and gives the impression of a great guitarist playing with the vitality and enthusiasm reserved for old friends.

THERE MUST BE A BETTER WORLD SOMEWHERE (Released 1981) *Tracks:* Life Ain't Nothing But A Party/ Born Again Human/ There Must Be A Better World Somewhere/ The Victim/ More, More, More/ You're Going With Me. Featuring David 'Fathead' Newman on tenor sax and Hank Crawford on alto, *There Must Be A Better World Somewhere* won a Grammy the following year for best traditional album, vindicating the popular belief, which had not always been shared by the record industry, that King was one of America's national treasures.

SPOTLIGHT ON LUCILLE (Released 1986) *Tracks:* Slidin' And Glidin'/Blues With BB/King Of Guitar/Jump With BB/38th Street Blues/Feedin' The Rock/ Goin' South/Step It Up/Calypso Jazz/ Easy Listening (Blues)/Shoutin' The Blues/Swinging With Sonny. A newly repackaged album of a series of guitar showcases made in 1960 and 1961. Uniquely, he doesn't sing a note: Lucille gets to say it all. The mood varies between thoughtful and aggressive, and BB's guitar is backed by a variety of instrumental arrangements. This is BB King and Lucille when they were at their early peak: man and instrument in perfect harmony.

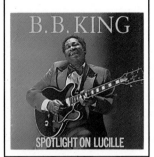

KING OF THE BLUES: 1989

(Released 1989) *Tracks:* You've Become A Habit To Me/Drowning In The Sea Of Love/Can't Get Enough/Standing On The Edge/Go On/Let's Straighten It Out/ Change In Your Lovin'/Undercover Man/ Lay Another Log On The Fire/Business With My Baby Tonight. *Line-up:* Mick Fleetwood (drums), Steve Cropper (rhythm guitar), Jerry Williams (rhythm guitar), Tom Scott (saxophone), Stevie Nicks (backing vocals) and many others. Another case of BB King bringing in the aristocracy of Adult Orientated Rock to guest on some excellent songs.

THERE IS ALWAYS ONE MORE TIME (Released 1992) *Tracks:* I'm Movin' On/ Back In LA/ The Blues Come Over Me/ Fool Me Once More/ The Lowdown/ Mean And Evil/ Something Up My Sleeve/ Roll, Roll, Roll/ There Is Always One More Time. Recorded in Los Angeles with a bunch of session men like Joe Sample (formerly of The Crusaders), Neil Larsen and Jim Keltner. Much of the material was penned by Sample and Will Jennings, which may account for its lack of fire. King is, of course, well past normal retirement age by now.

LOVE ME TENDER (Released 1982) *Tracks:* One Of Those Nights/ Love Me Tender/ Don't Change On Me/ (I'd Be) A Legend In My Time/ You've Always Got The Blues/ Nightlife/ Please Send Me Someone To Love/ You And Me, Me And You/ Since I Met You Baby/ Time Is A Thief/ A World I Never Made.

BLUES'N'JAZZ (Released 1983) *Tracks:* Inflation Blues/ Broken Heart/ Sell My Monkey/ Heed My Warning/ Teardrops From My Eyes/ Rainbow Riot/ Darlin', You Know I Love You/ I Can't Let You Go. As King's 'country' album, *Love Me Tender* proved the point that great players are going to sound good whatever they play. *Blues'n'Jazz* nabbed a Grammy for best traditional blues recording the following year.

SIX SILVER STRINGS (Released 1985) *Tracks:* Six Silver Strings/ Big Boss Man/ In The Midnight Hour/ Into The Night/ My Lucille/ Memory Blues/ My Guitar Sings The Blues/ Double Trouble. 'My Guitar Sings The Blues'

picked up a Grammy for best traditional blues recording in 1986, and this immediately led to invitations to attend record industry functions and award ceremonies. Consequently King hosted the 7th National Blues Awards with Carl Perkins and was inducted into The Rock'n'Roll Hall Of Fame in 1987. He also made a cameo appearance – playing himself, with his guitar Lucille – in the John Landis film *Into The Night*.

LIVE AT THE APOLLO (Released 1991) *Tracks:* When Love Comes To Town/ Sweet Sixteen/ The Thrill Is Gone/ Ain't Nobody's Bizness/ All Over Again/ Night Life/ Since I Met You Baby/ Guess Who/ Peace To The World. There is a rule of thumb in the record industry that whenever an artist is either out of contract or taking too long to cut a studio album, the company knocks out a live album (it can act as a handy greatest hits). King seems to be an exception: the stages of his development as a blues icon have been chronicled by his live work, and all the live recordings he's made are worthwhile, although *Live At The Regal* remains the must-have classic.

LIVE AT SAN QUENTIN

(Released 1990) *Tracks:* Introduction/ Let The Good Times Roll/ Everyday I Have The Blues/ A Whole Lot Of Lovin'/ Sweet Little Angel/ Never Make A Move Too Soon/ Into The Night/ Ain't Nobody's Bizness/ The Thrill Is Gone/ Peace To The World/ Nobody Loves Me But My Mother/ Sweet Sixteen/ Rock Me Baby. *Live At San Quentin* won a Grammy in 1991 for best traditional blues recording. King also partnered country singer Randy Travis in a duet, 'Waiting On The Light To Change', on Travis's *Heroes And Friends* (1990).

BLUES SUMMIT (Released 1993) *Tracks:* Playin' With My Friends (with Robert Cray)/ Since I Met You Baby (with Katie Webster)/ I Pity The Fool (with Buddy Guy)/ You Shook Me (with John Lee Hooker)/ There's Something You Got (with Koko Taylor)/ There's Something On Your Mind (with Etta James)/ Little By Little (with Lowell Fulson)/ Call It Stormy Monday (with Albert Collins)/ You're The Boss (with Ruth Brown)/ We're Gonna Make It (with Irma Thomas)/ Medley: Gotta Move Out Of This Neighborhood; Nobody Loves Me But My Mother/ Everybody's Had The Blues (with Joe Louis Walker).

country blues. The follow-up *The Natch'l Blues* (1968) was similarly affectionate, but broadened the terms of reference to include blues in its upbeat, uptown, urban configuration.

Thereafter Taj rang the changes, incorporating Latin, African and Caribbean rhythms into self-penned titles as well as traditional blues, folk songs and spirituals. Although Taj has the instincts of a magpie he has the form of a chameleon, and this enables him to get to the heart of any style he chooses.

A bit like Robert De Niro, perhaps – but Taj has more heart than method.

TAMPA RED

Born: Hudson Whittaker/Woodbridge, December 25th 1900, Atlanta, Georgia, US. Died: March 19th 1981, Chicago, Illinois, US.

■ National resonator.

Nicknamed The Guitar Wizard, Tampa Red's supreme bottleneck work has somehow been undervalued, mainly because his diffident nature was at odds with the trappings and aspirations of success. Touchingly, in the 1950s, when there was every chance that he would be able to reap some long overdue dividends with the resurgence of interest in the blues, his wife died, shifting him into a downward spiral of depression and disinterest which lasted for the best part of five years. Of his output, there are some sides he cut with the great gospel vocalist and composer Thomas A Dorsey in The Hokum Jug Band that possess a warmth and muscularity that are quite unlike anything else to emerge during the 1930s. In the early-1960s he returned to recording and occasional live performance but his heart didn't appear to be in it. However his legacy is a bunch of songs ('Sweet Black Angel', 'Love Her With A Feeling', 'Don't You Lie To Me' and 'It Hurts Me Too') while the best recordings are on a compilation of his work from the late-1920s to the late-1930s, *Bottleneck Guitar* (1974).

JIMMIE TARLTON

Born: 1892, Chesterfield County, South Carolina, US. Died: 1973.

During the 1920s, Tarlton and Tom Darby exemplified the influence of the blues on country artists. Predating the arrival of the steel guitar by some years, Tarlton adopted the bottleneck technique preferred by bluesmen like **Charley Patton**.

After leaving home Tarlton moved around the US and ended up in Texas where he got work in the oilfields, before returning to Carolina and the cotton mills. In 1926, having taken to the road once again, he met Tom Darby, a native of Columbus, Georgia, and they started performing together as a duo. The following year they recorded 'Birmingham Jail' and 'Columbus Stockade Blues' and over the next three years cut songs like 'Where The River Shannon Flows', 'Lowe Bonnie' and 'Slow Wicked Blues'. By 1933 Darby had returned to farming while Tarlton continued to play in bars and at dances. After years of obscurity, he was rediscovered in the late-1950s by **Mike Seeger**

and encouraged to come out of retirement to play the college and festival circuit.

MARV TARPLIN

Born: US.

One of the enduring curiosities of Motown was that for years they had a crack team of session musicians of whom they must have been immensely proud... but whose identities were shrouded in anonymity. Tarplin was a case in point. For most of his time at Motown he worked with vocalist Smokey Robinson and, by the mid-1960s, he was officially regarded as an unofficial Miracle and became one of Robinson's most frequent collaborators. Tarplin's real forté was as a guitarist: his bittersweet, stinging licks graced any number of records by The Miracles ('You've Really Got A Hold On Me', 'Tracks Of My Tears' and 'I Second That Emotion'), The Temptations ('The Way You Do The Things You Do'), Smokey Robinson ('Cruisin') and Marvin Gaye ('One More Heartache', 'Ain't That Peculiar' and 'I'll Be Doggone'). And that's just the tip of the iceberg: soulful, and miracles of economy.

DICK TAYLOR

Born: January 23rd 1943, Dartford, Kent, England.

An early member of The Rolling Stones, Taylor moved on to found The Pretty Things with singer Phil May. Their brash and abrasive brand of R&B, with Taylor at first playing guitar alongside Brian Pendleton, was captured on singles such as 'Rosalyn', 'Don't Bring Me Down', 'Honey I Need', 'Midnight Top Six Man', 'Come See Me' and 'Cry To Me' with an uninhibited power that often made the Stones sound tame. But by 1967 the Pretties had become assimilated into the emergent underground scene, with Taylor and May penning a brace of singles ('Defecting Grey' and 'Talking About The Good Times') that combined deft harmonies with an acute pop sensibility.

Later that year they recorded the concept album *SF Sorrow* (1967), reputedly the inspiration for **Pete Townshend** to compose *Tommy*. Written by May and Taylor it illustrated the group's increasing confidence, with Taylor's guitar work possessing a range of tonal variations that gave texture and character to the thematic development of the project. Highly rated by critics in the US, it failed to win many admirers in Britain, and Taylor left the group.

May kept the group going until 1971, but Taylor's distinctive guitar work was hard to replace. Throughout the 1970s May presided over different lineups with scant success, until in 1978 Taylor, having produced Hawkwind among others in the interim, rejoined, and they issued *Cross Talk* (1978). Throughout the 1980s the group reformed and split with considerable regularity, Taylor joining former punksters The Mekons to cut *Fear & Whisky* (1985) and *Honky Tonkin'* (1987). In 1989, May and Taylor reformed The Pretty Things for a revival of Barry McGuire's 'Eve Of Destruction'. Taylor remains undervalued, but his ability to treat the whole thing as a bit of a joke enables him to slip in and out of the music business at whim.

EDDIE TAYLOR

Born: January 29th 1923, Benoit, Mississippi, US. Died: December 25th 1985, Chicago, Illinois, US.

Taylor was an influential Chicago-based session guitarist who was pivotal to the success of R&B man **Jimmy Reed**. While Reed's guitar style was basic, Taylor provided much of the cut and thrust to a string of Reed hits such as 'Big Boss Man', 'Bright Lights, Big City', 'Ain't That Lovin You Baby' and 'Honest I Do'. Taylor recorded regularly with **John Lee Hooker** and **Elmore James** as a sideman in the early-1950s, cutting *Street Talkin'* with James. Although his own records have been few (*I Feel So Bad* 1979, and *Ready For Eddie* 1982) his guitar style is discernible in the work of **Freddie King** and **Robert Lockwood**, among others.

HOUND DOG TAYLOR

Born: Theodore Roosevelt Taylor, April 12th 1917, Natchez, Mississippi, US. Died: December 17th 1975, Chicago, Illinois, US.

■ Kingston solidbody.

Taylor played an intense bottleneck style that he picked up from **Elmore James** after running away from home in the 1920s. By 1942 he'd ended up in Chicago, having worked his way there playing clubs and juke joints en route. Working the club circuit until the early-1960s, Taylor's raucous, unsophisticated blend of R&B and rock'n'roll eventually landed him a contract with the minor Firma label.

However Taylor's reputation ignited when he formed The House Rockers with rhythm guitarist Brewer Phillips and drummer Ted Harvey. They cut their first album *Hound Dog Taylor & His House Rockers* (1971) when their manager Bruce Iglauer set up the Alligator label. This and successive albums combined with an intensive international touring schedule gave Taylor an unrivalled renown for no-nonsense, powerhouse R&B, with his bottleneck playing (on a cheap Japanese guitar) at the heart of the affair.

Unfortunately he died before he could reap his just rewards.

MARTIN TAYLOR

Born: 1956, Harlow, Essex, England.

■ Barker; Yamaha custom; Benedetto.

Taylor has taken a central position between the twin camps of folk and jazz with an evocative, percussive picking style that has enabled him to duet with artists as diverse as violinist Stéphane Grappelli and **Gordon Giltrap**. With the latter, *One To One* (1989) has an enthusiasm and deftness that only occurs when two supreme technicians come together to exchange ideas. Similarly, Taylor's earlier *Tribute To Art Tatum* (1986) has a jazzy lightness of touch and a delicacy that accurately evokes the spirit of the great pianist, while the aptly titled *Artistry* (1992) was produced by **Steve Howe**. Taylor is one of the most creatively ambitious guitarists working today, and he shows little enthusiasm for the negative aspects of becoming commercial.

MICK TAYLOR

Born: January 17th 1948, Welwyn Garden City, Hertfordshire, England.

■ **Gibson Les Paul; Fender Stratocaster.**

One of a long line of British guitarists whose technical expertise has been a hindrance to his earning potential, Taylor's grasp of style has on occasion – and ironically – caused him to be under-used.

He first came to prominence as a member of **John Mayall**'s Bluesbreakers on *Crusade* (1967), having earlier deputized for **Eric Clapton** in that group. He remained with Mayall for another two years before being recruited as the replacement for **Brian Jones** in The Rolling Stones.

Few guitarists can have had such a daunting debut thrust upon them: a free concert in London's Hyde Park in front of 250,000 people. But Taylor's work with the Stones was characteristically understated and his contemplative solos sometimes seemed at odds with **Keith Richards**' propensity for big riffs.

By 1975 he had left the Stones to collaborate with bassist Jack Bruce and jazz keyboardist Carla Bley, and eventually released a solo album, *Mick Taylor* (1979). While it bombed commercially, it was far better than this would indicate, with Taylor's controlled, melodic solos sounding much happier than in their former Rolling Stones' context.

During the 1980s Taylor spent time recording and touring with Bob Dylan (*Infidels* 1983) before cutting another solo album *Stranger In This Town* (1990), and he recently guested on **John Mayall**'s *Wake Up Call* (1993). As time has passed Taylor has gradually acquired the status of journeyman par excellence. His playing is never contrived and his solos always lend grace and dignity to the proceedings.

TUT TAYLOR

Born: Robert Taylor, November 20th 1923, Milledgeville, Georgia, US.

■ **Dobro resonator.**

A virtuoso dobroist, Taylor showed his precocity by learning the mandolin, autoharp, dulcimer, fiddle and banjo before he was 12. Starting off as a guitar and stringed-instrument maker, he went on to establish his own guitar shop in Nashville. In the early-1960s he began to play the club circuit and record with various groups like The Folkswingers and The Dixie Gentlemen. Together with fiddler Vassar Clements, Taylor established himself on the session circuit and contributed to the growth of interest in bluegrass. In 1972 he linked up with **John Hartford** and **Norman Blake** to form the nucleus of The Dobrolic Plectral Society, a loose aggregation of musicians who played the festival circuit. By the late-1970s Taylor was cutting solo albums like *Friar Tut* for Rounder and *The Old Post Office* for Flying Fish. In recent years his public performances and recording commitments have given way to running his guitar shop.

TOMMY TEDESCO

Born: Niagara Falls, New York, US.

■ **Yamaha SA2000; Fender Telecaster; Gibson ES175; Ovation.**

After moving to LA in the early-1950s, Tedesco first made his mark as a session guitarist later that decade and especially in the early-1960s, playing on dates for The Beach Boys, Jan & Dean, for producer Phil Spector at the Gold Star studios in Los Angeles in the 1960s, and later at Motown's LA studio. Since that auspicious start, Tedesco has played on countless other West Coast sessions, and is generally referred to as session call Number One in that competitive city. Tedesco has played on TV music from *Charlie's Angels* to *MASH*, film dates from *Love Story* to *The Godfather*, and record sessions from Dean Martin to **Frank Zappa**. What you might call versatile.

PETER TEREL

Born: England.

A Certain Ratio are one of the few bands successfully to have combined the ethos of punk in funky settings. Formed in 1979 and signed to Factory they cut *The Graveyard And The Ballroom* (one studio side, one live), Terel's chunky chords complementing Simon Topping's and Martin Moscrop's trumpet blasts. After *To Each...* (1981) they issued *Sextet* (1982) which was mostly instrumental, featuring Terel's muscular guitar work snaking through a dense rhythm section. This was followed by *I'd Like To See You Again* (1982), Terel's final album with the band; he left the following year.

SISTER ROSETTA THARPE

Born: Rosetta Nubin, March 20th 1915, Cotton Plant, Arkansas, US. Died: October 9th 1973, Philadelphia, Pennsylvania, US.

■ **Gibson SG Custom.**

Tharpe brought a zing to the stride of bandleader Cab Calloway's music in the late-1930s: her earthy, uninhibited approach to both the guitar and singing was informed by the gospel traditions of her upbringing. After her spell with Calloway she moved on to Lucky Millinder's band where she recorded a string of shouters such as 'Trouble In Mind', 'Rock Me', 'Shout Sister Shout' and 'That's All'. Her strident, punchy licks on electric guitar foreshadowed rock'n'roll by many years, and it was only **Chuck Berry** who managed to essay a comparable potency. During the 1950s Tharpe performed regularly, but left R&B behind and moved to gospel (heard on the *Gospel Train* compilation). Gradually she was lost in the plethora of emergent R&B and blues guitarists from Chicago's west-side, but whenever she made a major appearance she was always a show-stopper – her appearance at the 1967 Newport Jazz Festival being, by all accounts, a case in point. In 1970 she suffered a stroke from which she never fully recovered and which resulted in the amputation of a leg, but that failed to stop her from appearing on crutches in 1972. In her later years her reputation

was revitalized by a string of albums for Savoy, with the compilation *The Best Of...* offering a brisk introduction to her style.

HUGH THOMASSON

Born: Tampa, Florida, US.

■ **Fender Stratocaster.**

The Outlaws were formed in 1974 in the style of The Allman Brothers Band and Poco. Gentle harmonies and a frontline of three duelling guitarists – Thomasson, **Billy Jones** and **Henry Paul** – gave the band a presence on the US live circuit where titles like 'Green Grass And High Tides' were real show-stoppers. But the group's lineup fluctuated and by the time *Les Hombres Malo* (1982) was recorded Thomasson was the sole survivor of the original group. Thomasson and Paul reformed the band for *Soldiers Of Fortune* (1986) before parting.

RICHARD THOMPSON

Born: April 3rd 1949, London, England.

■ **Fender Stratocaster; Ferrington custom; Lowden.**

In 1967, through the miasma of incense and other assorted combustibles, the form of Fairport Convention made itself known. Despite early influences from the West Coast rock of America, they did not indulge in long paeans to the pleasures of altered states of consciousness. Instead they became the prototype British folk-rock band, with a lineup that now reads like a Who's Who of British folk.

Thompson's eloquent guitar work formed the core of the group's sound, and their debut *Fairport Convention* (1967) introduced a hitherto unknown Canadian writer called **Joni Mitchell** to British audiences through their cover of 'Chelsea Morning'. By the time their second album *What We Did On Our Holidays* (1968) was released the lineup had undergone the first of many changes, with Sandy Denny replacing vocalist Judy Dyble. While this album showed the individual compositional skills of each member, nothing was quite as evocative as Thompson's 'Meet On The Ledge' with its ringing harmonies and strongly melodic guitar lines.

On later albums such as *Unhalfbricking* and *Liege & Lief* (1969) the group combined traditional English folk songs with material by contemporary writers such as Bob Dylan and self-penned compositions. Thompson, whose style drew from sources as diverse as **Charlie Christian**, **Django Reinhardt**, **Scotty Moore**, **BB King** and **Jorma Kaukonen**, left the group in 1971 for a solo career, the first result of which was the seriously underrated *Henry The Human Fly* (1972). Later he teamed up with his vocalist wife Linda for a string of albums that included *I Want To See The Bright Lights Tonight* (1974) and *Hokey Pokey* (1975). While Thompson's guitar work in the studio was usually a model of concision and style, it's on stage that he tended to stretch out and take chances, as documented on 'Night Comes In' and 'Calvary Cross' from *guitar, vocal* (1976). After his separation from Linda he issued *Strict Tempo* (1981), a wonderful instrumental collection of jigs, reels, airs and ballads.

Tho-Tay

Throughout the 1980s Thompson's reputation continued to flourish, even if wider commercial success remained elusive (as it still does). His later solo albums – the best of which are *Hand Of Kindness* (1984), *Across A Crowded Room* (1985, acoustic live), *Rumour & Sigh* (1990), *Sweet Talker* (1992) and *Mirror Blue* (1994) – are of such transparent quality that they confirmed the suspicion that most record buyers must have cloth ears. Thompson has played many sessions with other musicians, and is best employed when allowed to let his imagination run wild over the frets, as on his devastating cameo appearance on Crowded House's 'Sister Madly' (*Temple Of Low Men* 1988).

A wide-ranging compilation of his work appeared in 1993, *Watching The Dark*. Thompson has refused to remain still, performing with **Fred Frith** and **Henry Kaiser**, and also appearing with **David Byrne** and The Golden Palominos. The impression that remains of Thompson's output is its extraordinary consistency, and his growth to maturity as a highly individual guitar stylist and a talented, versatile songwriter.

GEORGE THOROGOOD

Born: December 31st 1952, Wilmington, Delaware, US.

■ *Gibson ES125.*

In the early-1970s when the blues boom had died down George Thorogood & The Destroyers emerged from Delaware playing a rough'n'ready form of R&B that was as tough and authentic in its execution as anything that **John Mayall**'s Bluesbreakers managed in their heyday. While Thorogood was less purist in his approach, he created an earthy, spontaneously energetic hybrid that reeked of Chicago's west-side.

Initially playing the New England club circuit, they failed to win a recording contract until 1975 when they were signed to Rounder and their debut, *George Thorogood & the Destroyers*, was finally released in 1978. Since then they have concentrated on playing live, opening for The Rolling Stones and issuing albums such as *Move It On Over* (1978), *Bad To The Bone* (1982) and *Born To Be Bad* (1988). Although their style has changed little they remain committed to the idea of the bar-band, rather than seeking a wider audience by playing a more glossy, homogenized version of their act.

JOHNNY THUNDERS

Born: John Anthony Genzale Jr, July 15th 1952, New York, New York, US. Died: April 23rd 1991, New Orleans, Louisiana, US.

■ *Gibson Les Paul Junior.*

The late, lamented Johnny Thunders had his day as a member of The New York Dolls. While the Dolls fell between two eras in contemporary music – psychedelia and punk – they combined the energy of garage metallurgists such as the MC5 with the untutored freneticism of The Sex Pistols, making them in hindsight one of the most important bands to appear in the early-1970s. Much of that was due to Thunders and the band's total indifference

to the mechanics of the record business.

Their debut *New York Dolls* (1973) was one of those rare records that occasionally emerge for no apparent reason: it didn't really constitute a backlash against the 'progressive' groups of the time, but was more typically a product of an era when everything was going to seed – which The New York Dolls' overtly sleazy and decadent image mirrored. Thunders' brazen, strutting chords provided a manual for a host of aspiring axemen who would find their voices with the arrival of punk.

The group's follow-up *Too Much Too Soon* (1974) proved to have an apposite title, and Thunders and drummer Jerry Nolan left the band in 1975, both pursuing a variety of projects in the developing New York new wave scene. For Thunders, his work with The Heartbreakers is a pale shadow of that which he had shown himself capable. His remaining years were spent shrouded in the myths spawned by the Dolls, and his death in 1991 was suitably enigmatic.

GLENN TILBROOK

Born: August 31st 1957, London, England.

■ *Fender Telecaster; Taylor 12-string.*

One half of the Squeeze songwriting team with **Chris Difford**, Tilbrook's lyrical and underrated guitar solos were as pithy and incisive as the group's observant and sometimes acerbic lyrics. Along with Ray Davies and Paul Weller, Difford and Tilbrook have made a virtue of their Englishness, never adopting stock Americanisms to sound more 'rock 'n'roll'. Initially they were accused of being a singles band, but both *Argy Bargy* (1980) and *East Side Story* (1981) showed that they had assimilated their influences and developed their own identity.

JOHN TILL

Born: US.

When vocalist Janis Joplin died, despite the myriad personal problems that had always been a feature of her professional life, she had begun to put in place a band that was commensurate with her standing, the Full Tilt Boogie Band. Her first outfit, Big Brother & The Holding Company, had been merely effective, while The Janis Joplin Revue and The Kozmic Blues Band intimated ability but never fully delivered the goods. With guitarist John Till and bassist Brad Campbell from the latter band, The Full Tilt Boogie Band, suppplemented by Richard Bell (piano), Ken Pearson (organ) and Clark Pierson (drums), was the most supple unit with which she had worked. Each musician had a job to do and each played like a professional, none more so than Till whose delicate lines and knowing licks underscore every phrase that Joplin utters on *Pearl* (1971), on which 'A Woman Left Lonely' and 'Me And Bobby McGee' indicate the scale of Joplin's talent – part of which was knowing her musical limitations.

MICHAEL TIMMINS

Born: April 21st 1959, Montreal, Quebec, Canada.

With a repertoire that juxtaposes Lou Reed's 'Sweet

Jane' with country classics such as 'I'm So Lonesome I Could Cry', The Cowboy Junkies have become one of the more eclectic outfits to emerge. Formed by Michael Timmins out of the remnants of Germinal with his brother Peter and sister Margo, the Junkies bear comparison with other new-wave country rock groups like Green On Red where ironic affection is just as much a reason for performing a song as the chance to demonstrate instrumental brilliance. Their 'live' approach to the recording process has given albums like *The Trinity Session* (1988) an immediacy and spontaneity. Despite their growing reputation (they contributed to a Grateful Dead tribute album in 1990) they remain unfussed by conventions, and Timmins' stature as a guitarist continues to grow with some stunning slide playing on **J Mascis**'s 'The Post' (from *Pale Sun Crescent Moon* 1993).

GLENN TIPTON

Born: October 25th 1948, Birmingham, England.

■ *Gibson SG; Fender Stratocaster.*

Joining Judas Priest in 1974, Tipton has been jointly responsible for forging the double-barrelled guitar frontline of the band. Their lack of finesse underlined what was described as the new wave of British heavy metal, a 'movement' that had its basis in the work of Black Sabbath. With a succession of albums that have included *British Steel* (1980), *Screaming For Vengeance* (1982), *Defenders Of The Faith* (1984) and *Ram It Down* (1988), **KK Downing** and Tipton do their raucous thing professionally and competently. The fact that they only seem to know a few chords between them is more a by-product of market forces: the group's followers seem to lap up those chords with scant regard for the possible existence of others.

PETER TOSH

Born: Winston Hubert McIntosh, October 9th 1944, Westmoreland, Jamaica. Died: September 12th 1987, Kingston, Jamaica.

Although the writing skills of **Bob Marley** were in themselves impressive, The Wailers were not just his backing band, but contained a number of other highly talented writers and musicians, none more so than Tosh. By all accounts Marley and Tosh enjoyed a turbulent relationship, but Tosh's distinctive 'tchka-tchka-tchka-tchka' guitar figures were as central to the group's overall sound as Marley's songs. The main argument seems to have been Marley's and record label Island's reluctance to let Tosh contribute many songs to each album. Those of Tosh's that did pass the acid test included the anthemic call to arms 'Get Up, Stand Up' and the trenchant attack on slavery '400 Years'.

Tosh left the group in 1973 and, although it would be patently untrue to say that The Wailers work deteriorated thereafter, they certainly lacked the aggressive edge of Tosh's guitar work. The converse was also true: Tosh's solo albums lacked the polish and lyricism that Marley brought to bear on the subsequent Wailers recordings. But Tosh's guitar

THO-TOS

playing remained a treat, particularly when he launched into his breakneck version of Chuck Berry's 'Johnny B Goode'. Despite regularly issuing albums – *Legalize It* (1976), *Bush Doctor* (1978), *Mama Africa* (1983) and *No Nuclear War* (1987) among others – Tosh was by nature erratic and was totally unprepared to deal with the machinations of the music business on terms other than his own.

RALPH TOWNER

Born: March 1st 1940, Chehalis, Washington, US.

■ *Guild; Elliott/Burton classical.*

Towner, a technically able and inventive acoustic player, studied classical guitar but spent some time as a jazz pianist in New York. After switching back to guitar, Towner first came to attention in 1971 when his 12-string work was heard at the heart of jazz group Weather Report's early album *I Sing The Body Electric*.

In the same year Towner helped form Oregon, a cross-cultural group that blended various styles, including jazz, classical and Eastern music in an occasionally acoustic framework, as on *Music Of Another Present Era* (1972), with superb results. At that time the 'new age' label didn't exist, but Oregon virtually invented the style, while managing on their best work to avoid the fey directionlessness that marked the later excesses of the genre.

Towner has also made some absorbing solo records, for example *Trios/Solos* (1972) and *City Of Eyes* (1989), and has recorded with the likes of vibesman Gary Burton (*Matchbook* 1975) and **John Abercrombie** (*Sargasso Sea* 1977).

PETE TOWNSHEND

Born: Peter Denis Blandford Townshend, May 19th 1944, London, England.

■ *Rickenbacker 330; Rickenbacker 'signature'; Gibson Les Paul; Gibson SG; Fender Stratocaster; Fender Telecaster; Schecter.*

It is distressing to say this, but Townshend has taken the role of rock's elder statesman a tad too seriously. But of course his body of work over the years has the breadth to quell any doubt about his musical contributions.

I would point to the pungent assertiveness of 'The Kids Are Alright' with its brash, cascading chords; the lyrical inventiveness and melodic verve of 'Substitute' and 'Happy Jack'; the anthemic stride of 'My Generation' and 'Won't Get Fooled Again'; and the sheer naked ambition of projects such as *Tommy* (1969) and *Quadrophenia* (1973). Always more of a rhythm guitarist and supporter than a wild soloist, Townshend's stage acrobatics and his pioneering use of effects, feedback and even synthesizers influenced legions of aspiring rock guitarists.

However, since the disintegration of The Who, Townshend's solo work has been marred by a belief that he has to make big statements. He is still one of the most instinctively powerful guitarists around, but disenchantment and, perhaps, the imminence of middle-age have rent this asunder, and have been replaced by earnest jargon.

PAT TRAVERS

Born: April 12th 1954, Toronto, Ontario, Canada.

■ *Gibson Les Paul; Gibson Melody Maker.*

The Pat Travers Band made a storming debut at the 1976 Reading Festival which gave their debut *Pat Travers* (1976) an unexpected boost. While the band projected themselves as medium range rockers, Travers was more contemplative than his counterparts and indulged in fits of experimentation with **Scott Gorham**, among others. Despite the power of albums such as *Heat In The Streets* (1978) and *School Of Hard Knocks* (1990), he released *Blues Tracks* in 1992 which showed him to be not just another grimacing rocker, but rather an accomplished and stylish bluesman with hidden depths.

MERLE TRAVIS

Born: November 29th 1917, Muhlenberg, Kentucky, US.
Died: October 20th 1983, Tahlequah, Oklahoma, US.

■ *Gibson Super 400CES; Mosrite; Bigsby.*

A prodigiously talented musician, Travis' innovative finger-picking technique revolutionized country guitar playing, and is generally referred to as 'Travis picking'.

Travis picked up the rudiments of guitar from two local musicians, Mose Rager and Arnold Schultz. After finishing school he played in bars all over the country, developed his unique style using thumb for bass and index finger (and sometimes second finger) for melody, and ended up with Clayton McMichen's band, The Georgia Wildcats, in 1937. Later he moved to Cincinnati to broadcast on radio station WLW and began recording with The Delmore Brothers. After World War II Travis moved out to the West Coast where he worked with country singers Cliffie Stone, Ray Whitley and Jimmy Wakely before signing with King and then Capitol.

At Capitol Travis' compositional skills flourished with songs like 'Sixteen Tons' and 'Smoke! Smoke! Smoke (That Cigarette)!' and artists such as Tennessee Ernie Ford and Rose Maddox covered his material. Meanwhile his guitar work was emulated by the likes of **Les Paul**, **Doc Watson** and, most notably, **Chet Atkins**. During the late-1940s Travis co-designed a solidbody electric guitar with engineer Paul Bigsby, apparently predating Leo Fender's popularization of the style. In the 1950s and 1960s Travis was an inspiration to many emerging young players, including **Jerry Reed** and **Scotty Moore**.

Among Travis' later records were *The Atkins-Travis Traveling Show* (with **Chet Atkins**, and produced by Reed), *Country Guitar Giants* (with **Joe Maphis**) and *Walkin' The Strings*. In 1971 he went full-circle with *The Merle Travis Story* which teamed him with veteran session men like fiddler Johnny Gimble and steel guitarist **Herb Remington**.

ROBIN TROWER

Born: March 9th 1947, London, England.

■ *Fender Stratocaster.*

Often criticized for basing some of his style too closely on that of **Jimi Hendrix**, Trower cut his teeth with R&B outfit The Paramounts, whose members – including Trower – went on to form the nucleus of Procol Harum. Trower's departure from Procol Harum in 1971 to start his own band did little for either party as Trower's guitar work had tended to lend a harder edge to the group which, despite their stylishness, veered dangerously close to a pompous grandeur. The best recordings with Trower are *Procol Harum* (1967) and *A Salty Dog* (1969).

The Robin Trower Band, with bassist Jimmy Dewar providing the vocals and co-writing much of the material, issued a string of albums – *Twice Removed From Yesterday* (1973) and *Bridge Of Sighs* (1974) among others, with Trower's guitar redolent of the Hendrix school of feedback and wah-wah but showing signs of moving toward a purer form of R&B. This led to a partnership with Stax producer Don Davis, and while *In City Dreams* (1977) did little to encourage record-buyers it stands up today remarkably well.

In 1981 Trower teamed up with bassist Jack Bruce and drummer Bill Lordan (former Sly Stone and Robin Trower Band) for BLT, who didn't quite manage to make the grade. By 1983 he had reformed the Robin Trower Band, based on the 1973 version, and the result was consequently derivative. The 1991 compilation *Essential* is not quite that, but interesting nonetheless.

IKE TURNER

Born: November 5th 1931, Clarksdale, Mississippi, US.

■ *Fender Stratocaster; Danelectro.*

Of all the R&B bandleaders of the 1950s few were more autocratic than guitarist and pianist Turner, and his guitar playing has the spare confidence you would expect from such a character. He formed his first band, The Kings of Rhythm, while he was still at school and acted as a talent scout for the Modern label. He participated in one of the first big hits of the rock'n'roll era, 'Rocket 88' (1951, with Willie Kizart on early fuzz guitar) by saxophonist Jackie Brenston, which was recorded at Sun studios in Memphis and stormed up the R&B charts.

Turner's role as Modern's talent scout enabled him to secure session work, backing artists like **BB King**, **Howlin' Wolf**, Johnny Ace and others whom he had signed. In 1956 he met Annie Mae Bullock (later Tina Turner) while performing with his band at a club in East St Louis, Illinois. She became the band's vocalist, and in 1958 they were married. Their first record 'A Fool In Love' (1960) came about by mistake when the session singer booked to sing Ike's song failed to show up, and so Tina stepped into the breach. The following year they notched up their first Top 20 hit with 'It's Gonna Work Out Fine'.

During the next five years they established a reputation for being one of the most exciting and entertaining live R&B acts in the US: billed as The Ike & Tina Turner Revue the act featured not only Tina but also a trio of female backing vocalists, The Ikettes. Their first major international success came in 1966 when they were enlisted by producer Phil Spector to record some songs by Brill Building writers

Tow-Tur

Jeff Barry and Ellie Greenwich. The single from the sessions, 'River Deep, Mountain High' (1966), was a big hit all over the world, yet failed to register in the US. However, they were chosen to support The Rolling Stones on their US tour, which affirmed their gradual movement away from R&B to rock – albums such as *Outta Season* (1969), *Come Together* (1970) and *Workin' Together* (1970) included rowdy versions of songs like Sly Stone's 'I Wanna Take You Higher' and **John Fogerty**'s 'Proud Mary'. Their final hit as a duo was 'Nutbush City Limits' (1973).

In 1976 Tina walked out on Ike and divorced him, claiming that he had persistently beaten her up throughout their years of marriage. Her precipitate departure spelled the effective end of Ike's career. Despite periodic attempts to relaunch it, he has spent most of his time entangled with the law for a variety of transgressions.

TED TURNER

Born: David Alan Turner, August 2nd 1950, Birmingham, England.

■ *Fender Stratocaster; Gibson Les Paul; Tokai Strat-style.*
Turner and **Andy Powell** were the duelling guitarists of Wishbone Ash during the group's heyday. Based very loosely on the style of **Duane Allman** and **Dicky Betts** in The Allman Brothers Band, both Powell and Turner were later recruits to the group's lineup which had been in existence since the late-1960s as (among others) The Empty Vessels.

Once Powell and Turner joined the group they established a solid following on the British college circuit through continuous touring, duelling on pieces like 'Phoenix' from *Pilgrimage* (1971) and 'Warrior' and 'The King Will Come' from *Argus* (1972), but really they were just another blues-based band with more grandiose visions than most. At the peak of their fame Turner got religion, and he left the group in 1973. His replacement was **Laurie Wisefield**, but in 1987 Turner and the original lineup reformed for *Nouveau Calls* (1987).

JAMES BLOOD ULMER

Born: James Ulmer, February 2nd 1942, St Matthews, South Carolina, US.

■ *Gibson Byrdland.*
Always an individual player, Ulmer has more in common in **Sonny Sharrock** than anyone else, although Ulmer's guitar playing is informed by traditions of R&B and gospel. During his childhood, he sang gospel in church and learned to play the guitar before moving first to Philadelphia in the early-1960s and then to Detroit. Through these early years he developed a style that was influenced by **Jimi Hendrix** and **Johnny Guitar Watson**. In 1971, he moved to New York and started to work with jazzmen such as Ornette Coleman, Paul Bley, Rashied Ali and Art Blakey, and with Coleman he was given the room to expand a free-form soloing style into what the pair called 'harmolodics': interweaving soloists without conventional harmonic structure.

Ulmer cut his own album *Are You Glad To Be In America?* (1980) on which he amalgamated rocking

southern R&B and jazz, cut with the dynamics of rock. *Freelancing* (1981) and *Black Rock* (1982) were about as commercial as Ulmer gets, including a cover of Sly Stone's 'Family Affair'. *America – Do You Remember Love?* (1987) extended the themes he had embraced on *Are You Glad To Be In America?*, examining the moral and intellectual climate in the US. There are few as passionate and intense as Ulmer, but he remains criminally underrated.

LEE UNDERWOOD

Born: Los Angeles, California, US.

Tim Buckley made his debut in 1966 when folk-rock, inspired by Bob Dylan and The Byrds, was beginning to attract column inches in thinking people's papers. Folkies like Tom Paxton, Tom Rush and Phil Ochs were developing their desire to incorporate strains of jazz and R&B, but Buckley, the ingénue, was even more successful at harmonizing the strains of jazz with folk. This was primarily due to Buckley's airy compositions, but also to Lee Underwood's fine guitar work, a memorable feature of Buckley records that was melodiously textured to fill the gaps as Buckley's voice swooped and glided.

Remember, this was at a time when jazz-rock was thought to be the preserve of other musicians altogether. But Underwood's supple, dulcet lines underscored Buckley's voice, amplifying his range and creating the landscape, as on Buckley's sublime *Blue Afternoon* (1969) or the overtly funky *Greetings From LA* (1974). After Buckley's death in 1975 Underwood took up a variety of assignments including that of *Down Beat* magazine's West Coast editor, and in 1991 he cut the acoustic *California Sigh*. An excellent Buckley concert from London in 1968, with Underwood in good form, turned up on *Dream Letter* (1990). There is a saying to the effect that we all deserve those with whom we end up, and nowhere does this have greater resonance than in the case of Buckley and Underwood's work together.

PHIL UPCHURCH

Born: July 19th 1941, Chicago, Illinois, US.

■ *Guild; Polytone Improv II.*
Although in recent years Upchurch has been primarily a session guitarist with artists like **George Benson**, Grover Washington, The Crusaders, Ben Sidran and **Bo Diddley**, he achieved some eminence with a dancefloor hit 'You Can't Sit Down' in the early-1960s. He learned to play guitar while at school, and after playing in various local groups worked at the Chess studios as a bassist. Throughout the late-1950s and early-1960s, in partnership with drummer Maurice White, he backed artists such as **Howlin' Wolf**, The Dells, Jerry Butler and **Muddy Waters**. Consequently he got the opportunity to record the instrumental 'You Can't Sit Down' and its success encouraged him to make further such records, but they failed to register. Through the late-1960s and early-1970s Upchurch recorded a number of funky jazz albums, culminating with the excellent *Darkness Darkness* (1972). He was signed by Creed Taylor to the Kudu label, where he cut

Upchurch Tennyson (1975) with pianist and vocalist Tennyson Stephens, and then *Companions* (1985). His fluid style is reminiscent of **Eric Gale** and Benson, but his albums attract less attention.

MIDGE URE

Born: James Ure, October 10th 1953, Cambuslang, Strathclyde, Scotland.

■ *Ibanez Roadstar; Gordon Smith; Yamaha AE2000.*
Along with his joint composition of the Band Aid/Live Aid charity single 'Do They Know It's Christmas?', Ure has penned many a tuneful ditty that often comes to mind while one is waiting at the bus stop or putting the laundry into the machine. Ure has never been strong on big statements but his gift for melody and arrangement has enabled him to assemble a broad-based portfolio, and his well-rounded guitar style has supported him in these efforts. In short, Ure is adept at turning any limitations he might have into advantages, and this he has done in Slik (1974-77), The Rich Kids (1977), Thin Lizzy (1978), Visage (1980), Ultravox (1981-86) and, since the mid-1980s, under his own name.

STEVE VAI

See also pages 135-136
Born: June 6th 1960, Long Island, New York, US.

■ *Ibanez 'signature' seven-string; Ibanez JEM 'signature'.*
Along with Joe Satriani, Vai is one of the most gifted guitarists to emerge in recent years, combining metallic bombast with a keen melodic and structural sense. He formed his first band Rayge when he was 13, while being taught guitar by Satriani. Thereafter he attended Berklee School of Music in Boston, but moved to Los Angeles in 1979 where he was recruited by **Frank Zappa**.

His years with Zappa gave Vai the confidence to expand, dragging in nuances of rock, jazz and classical to what was predominantly a heavy metal style. This was followed more prosaically by stints with Alcatrazz (as **Yngwie Malmsteen**'s replacement) for *Disturbing The Peace* (1985), with David Lee Roth for the excellent *Eat 'Em And Smile* (1986) and for *Skyscraper* (1988), and with Whitesnake for *Slip Of The Tongue* (1989), before his solo career kicked into life with the magnificent *Passion And Warfare* (1990).

This album proved to be a fine example of a flashy guitarist not being flashy, but playing well within himself and unleashing the odd salvo across the bow just to remind us that there was plenty in reserve. The wild use of studio dynamics had many listeners calling it an *Electric Ladyland* of the 1990s, but my own view is that Vai's great ability is to make the mundane sound remarkable, which he has done time after time for most of his former employers and on sessions for such as Public Image Limited and Alice Cooper. Vai also helped to develop a seven-string guitar for Japanese manufacturer Ibanez. *Sex And Religion* (1993), his second solo work, was less spectacular than *Passion*, but Vai's next moves will be followed closely by everyone with an interest in modern rock guitar styles.

HILTON VALENTINE

Born: May 2nd 1943, North Shields, Tyne & Wear, England.

■ *Gretsch Tennessean; Fender Telecaster; Gibson SG Custom.*

Valentine's spiky, bluesy contributions to the sound of The Animals were always dwarfed by the throaty roar of vocalist Eric Burdon and the silky organ lines of Alan Price. Valentine eventually discovered God and left the music business, but the group's legacy was a bunch of singles including 'The House Of The Rising Sun', 'Don't Let Me Be Misunderstood', 'We Gotta Get Out Of This Place' and 'Bring It On Home To Me' and a much maligned album (*Animal Tracks* 1965) that were as good as anything that came out of the 1960s British blues boom.

TONY VALENTINO

Born: US.

■ *Gretsch 6120.*

Valentino was guitarist of The Standells who were responsible for such early garage/punk classics as 'Dirty Water' and 'Why Pick On Me'. Although they recorded several albums, including *Live And Out Of Sight*, they are best appreciated in three minute bursts (as on the recent *Best Of*). They had an ever changing lineup – **Lowell George** and Walker Brothers' drummer Gary Leeds all did time with them – but it's Valentino's chunky chords on 'Dirty Water' that loom large in the memory.

ADRIAN VANDENBERG

Born: January 31st 1954, Netherlands.

■ *Peavey 'signature'; Fernandes.*

An erstwhile member of Whitesnake from 1987, Vandenberg's injury to his wrist while playing the piano (quite an achievement) was responsible for **Steve Vai**'s arrival in the band. When Vandenberg's injury had healed he returned to the fold, proving himself to be an admirable foil for Vai. Furthermore, Vandenberg's compositional talents gave *Slip Of The Tongue* (1989) a continuity lacking in their previous outings. After the group disbanded in 1991 Vandenberg played on sessions. He's also made two albums under his own name with Dutch musicians, *Vandenberg* (1982) and *Alibi* (1985).

GEORGE VAN EPS

Born: August 7th 1913, Plainfield, New Jersey, US.

■ *Epiphone seven-string; Gretsch 'signature' seven-string.*

Van Eps came from a highly musical family, presided over by father Fred who played the banjo rather well. During the 1930s George played with the Freddy Martin and Ray Noble orchestras, but his main claim to fame at this time was his sojourn with Benny Goodman in 1934, where his fluent chording gave much of the zing to the Goodman swing. After World War II Van Eps based himself on the West Coast, primarily working on film soundtracks. Not only is he a fine guitarist, but he is also an accomplished engineer, having built a fully operational steam

locomotive in 1954 which is believed to be the smallest of its kind in the world. Furthermore, in the 1940s he came up with and played a seven-string guitar with an extra bass string (see also **Steve Vai**), made for Van Eps by Epiphone, and a production version was later put on the market by the Gretsch guitar company.

EDWARD VAN HALEN

Born: January 26th 1957, Nijmegen, Netherlands.

■ *Music Man 'signature'; Kramer; Ripley.*

Van Halen is a flashy guitarist with a superb grasp of dynamics, and has contributed some magnificent solos to the heavy metal canon. He was among the most influential guitarists in the 1980s, popularizing 'tapping' (playing with both hands hitting the fingerboard), 'dive bombing' (extreme use of the guitar's pitch-bending vibrato system) and a wide deployment of screaming harmonics.

When his band, Van Halen, released their eponymous debut in 1978, *Guitar Player* magazine dubbed Eddie the best new guitarist of the year, and the acclaim led to Eddie's injection of steely shards of brilliance into Michael Jackson's 'Beat It' (*Thriller* 1982) which catapulted the guitar player into the big time. Van Halen's *1984* was released on New Year's Day of that year, and featured 'Jump', an audacious meeting of synthesizer and guitar, built around an exploding riff that echoed The Who's 'Won't Get Fooled Again', the only difference being that 'Jump' was leaner and more agile... and boasted a splendid solo.

In 1985, David Lee Roth, the group's leather-lunged, posturing frontman, departed for a solo career and his replacement was Sammy Hagar from **Ronnie Montrose**'s band. For a time, the future of Van Halen seemed to be in doubt, but *5150* (1986) and 'Why Can't This Be Love' allayed any fears.

After a disappointing *OU812* (1988), Van Halen released *For Unlawful Carnal Knowledge* (1991) which contained supreme flash and thunder from Eddie on a batch of gritty, arresting ditties; and *Live: Right Here, Right Now* (1993) caught the band in peak form, with Eddie soloing like a crazed demon. The only real problem with Eddie is that he is so close to embodying Nigel Tufnel in *This Is Spinal Tap* that it is difficult not to burst out laughing.

DAVE VAN RONK

Born: June 30th 1936, New York, New York, US.

The folk revival boom in New York in the early-1960s threw up a legion of guitarists such as Eric Von Schmidt and **Eric Andersen**, drawing their inspiration from The Carter Family, **Leadbelly**, **Woody Guthrie**, **Josh White** and **Big Bill Broonzy**. Van Ronk was at first enthused by New Orleans jazz, but a meeting with **Odetta** in 1957 drew him into folk and the blues. Through the early-1960s his style was best described as jug band music – despite playing prestigious gigs at New York's Carnegie Hall, among others, and being allied to the politically motivated and disenchanted left along with Phil Ochs, **Joan Baez**, Tom Paxton and Bob

Dylan. During the 1970s and 1980s Van Ronk recorded little, but *Sings Earthy Ballads & Blues* (1976) was a fitting testimony to his undiminished power and stark, evocative guitar style, while *Statesboro Blues* (1992) was arguably the raunchiest piece of work he ever committed to tape.

MIAMI STEVE VAN ZANDT

Born: November 22nd 1950, Boston, Massachusetts, US.

■ *Guild X79; Fender Stratocaster.*

Van Zandt has become one of rock's more charismatic backroom boys with an enviable list of guest slots and production credits to his name. After a spell backing The Dovells (they featured Len '1-2-3' Barry in their lineup) he became immersed in the New Jersey bar-band scene that spawned Southside Johnny & The Asbury Jukes and **Bruce Springsteen**. In common with singers Peter Wolf, Southside Johnny and Springsteen, Van Zandt had an abiding passion for R&B, and this led to a production job with Gary US Bonds and his joining Bruce Springsteen's famed E Street Band.

Van Zandt's guitar sound, with its propensity for big riffs and meaty chords, hallmarks everything on which he plays. On stage Van Zandt attacks the guitar with a flair and zeal similar to that of **Keith Richards**, attesting to the genuine enjoyment he seems to derive from playing live. Strangely, his own recorded efforts, such as *Men Without Women* (1982), lack discipline and sound as if he has become bored half way through.

JIMMY VAUGHAN

Born: March 20th 1951, Dallas, Texas, US.

■ *Fender Stratocaster; Robin.*

When The Fabulous Thunderbirds were formed in 1977 by Vaughan they filled a gap in the US market for a white-blues band that put across authentic sounding versions of the Chicago west-side style of R&B. Vaughan's playing seldom dazzled but, while often eclipsed by his more celebrated brother **Stevie Ray Vaughan**, he had a supreme gift for playing within himself, infusing studio recordings (*T-Bird Rhythm* 1982, *Tuff Enough* 1986) with a spontaneity comparable to the live concerts. His decision to quit the group and make way for **Duke Robillard** in 1991 has to be viewed as a sensible option: 14 years on the road is probably enough for anyone who isn't a masochist.

STEVIE RAY VAUGHAN

Born: October 3rd 1954, Dallas, Texas, US. Died: August 27th 1990, East Troy, Wisconsin, US.

■ *Fender Stratocaster.*

One of the most talented guitarists of his generation, Vaughan learned to play guitar from his brother **Jimmy Vaughan** and a bunch of records by artists like BB King, **Lonnie Mack** and **T-Bone Walker**. He moved to Austin and joined a procession of groups until forming Triple Threat Revue with vocalist Lou Ann Barton (who would later join Vaughan in Double Trouble). His big break came in 1982 when producer

Val-Vau

Jerry Wexler added Vaughan to the lineup for the Montreux Jazz Festival, where he was spotted and hired by David Bowie for the forthcoming *Let's Dance* (1983) sessions.

This was followed by Vaughan's debut album, *Texas Flood* (1983), which with veteran producer John Hammond combining elements of rock and blues – and 'Rude Mood', a bouncy, abrasive instrumental – grabbed a Grammy. Curiously, later albums such as *Couldn't Stand The Weather* (1984) seemed to indicate a slight lack of confidence in his own style – principally blues-based with the distinctive phrasing and character of R&B and jazz creeping in – and a greater reliance on outside inspirations, especially from the work of **Jimi Hendrix**.

Personal problems and a plethora of sessions (for artists such as James Brown, Lonnie Mack, **Dick Dale** and Jennifer Warnes) sidelined Vaughan until *In Step* (1989) and *Family Style* (1990), the latter with brother Jimmy. Stevie Ray's untimely death intervened at a time when he seemed set to taste real success. Since his death, Vaughan has entered the gallery of guitar greats, and his records have become manuals for future generations of aspiring guitarists. (The Fender company issued a Vaughan 'signature' Stratocaster in 1992.)

LARRY VEEDER

Born: US.

A member of the Motown house band, Larry Veeder's guitar work was featured on many of the Holland-Dozier-Holland productions. While it has often been said that The Miracles and The Temptations were the most charismatic of the Motown artists, The Four Tops and The Supremes were wonderfully consistent, and for me it is their records that personify the sound of Motor City. Veeder moved to Los Angeles when Motown relocated in 1971, but the disintegration of the house band system that had existed in Detroit and its subsequent replacement by freelancers encouraged him to return to the Midwest.

TOM VERLAINE

Born: Thomas Miller, December 13th 1949, Mount Morris, New Jersey, US.

■ *Fender Jazzmaster.*

Verlaine, bassist Richard Hell and drummer Billy Ficca formed The Neon Boys in the early-1970s. Verlaine had trained as a pianist, but hearing The Rolling Stones' '19th Nervous Breakdown' caused him to change tack and embrace rock'n'roll. The Neon Boys were short-lived but proved to be the catalyst for Television, with the addition of **Richard Lloyd**. The group's debut, the superb *Marquee Moon* (1978), was one of the critical successes of New York new wave, with 'Marquee Moon', 'Torn Curtain' and 'Prove It' all gilt-edged classics, with Verlaine's fractured lead breaks and textural shapes underpinned by Lloyd's implacable rhythm work.

The group wound down after the difficult sequel, *Adventure* (1978), and Verlaine embarked on a solo career with a string of impressive albums – *Tom*

Verlaine (1979), *Dreamtime* (1981) and *Cover* (1985) among others – with his hesitantly melodic guitar style happily intact. But comparisons with **David Byrne** and the fact that Verlaine constructed thoughtful music militated against wider acceptance, and a reformed band issued *Television* (1992) to little acclaim. Extraordinary. His day will come.

HENRY VESTINE

Born: December 25th 1944, Washington DC, US.

Vestine started his career with **Frank Zappa**'s Mothers and toured with **John Fahey**. In the course of his collaboration with Fahey he discovered **Skip James** who was languishing in a Memphis hospital, and Vestine helped him back to his feet by securing him a recording contract.

When Vestine formed blues band Canned Heat with slide guitarist **Al Wilson** the group's sound bore comparison to **Peter Green**'s Fleetwood Mac. Initially, they were diligent rather than inspired, but *Boogie With Canned Heat* (1968), featuring Jim Oden's 'On The Road Again' and 'Fried Hookey Boogie', gave Vestine's rapier-like solos an opportunity to sparkle against Wilson's hypnotic slide work.

By the early-1970s, having played the festival circuit and achieved some commercial success with 'Goin Up The Country', they were recording with **John Lee Hooker** (*Hooker'n'Heat* 1971). A series of personnel changes brought about by Wilson's death and a gradual change in attitude towards blues bands marginalized their appeal, despite a string of good albums such as *Historical Figures & Ancient Heads* (1972). Vestine moved in and out of the band, leaving vocalist Bob Hite to sustain continuity and interest. Since Hite's death in 1981 Vestine has severed all connection with the band, which now frequents the oldies circuit.

WADDY WACHTEL

Born: Robert Wachtel, May 24th 1947, New York, New York, US.

■ *Fender Stratocaster; Gibson Les Paul.*

A key player on the Los Angeles session circuit, Wachtel has been credited almost as much as **James Burton**. He played with Linda Ronstadt throughout the late-1970s and early-1980s, before which he'd been in The Everly Brothers' road band. Others with whom he's played include **Keith Richards**, Warren Zevon, Jackson Browne, Carly Simon, **Joni Mitchell** and Bob Seger. Wachtel is a great all-purpose guitarist who can be flashy if necessary, although such is the taste of most of his clients that this is seldom required.

DICK WAGNER

Born: US.

■ *Gibson Les Paul.*

A veteran of many Alice Cooper and Lou Reed sessions, Wagner and **Steve Hunter** contributed the epic duelling solos to Lou Reed's live *Rock And Roll*

Animal (1974). The intro which segues into the Velvet Underground's 'Sweet Jane' indicates the contrasting styles of the two guitarists, Hunter's fluid phrasing punctuated by Wagner's punchy vibrato. When 'Lady Day' first appeared on Reed's *Berlin* (1973) it was stark and forbidding, but on *Animal* it is transformed by the opening chords into a defiant guitar work-out. Wagner seems to work frequently in touring bands, and has also played sessions with Peter Gabriel, Daryl Hall & **John Oates**, and **Mark Farner**, among others.

JERRY JEFF WALKER

Born: Paul Crosby, March 16th 1942, Oneonta, New York, US.

Walker is best known for his composition 'Mr Bojangles', a tribute to the legendary tap- and street-dancer Bill 'Bojangles' Robinson, but in the early-1970s he relocated to Austin, Texas and became one of the key figures in its flourishing music community alongside **Willie Nelson**, Guy Clark, Townes Van Zandt and Doug Sahm.

Walker became a folk singer in 1959, performing in clubs and bars all over the US prior to forming the folk-rock group Circus Maximus with singer Bobby Bruno in 1966. They cut two albums, *Circus Maximus* and *Neverland Revisited*, before splitting in 1968. Walker's solo debut was *Driftin' Way Of Life* (1969), after which he cut 'Mr Bojangles', covered by The Nitty Gritty Dirt Band among others.

After settling in Austin, Walker issued a string of high quality albums like *Jerry Jeff Walker* (1972) and *It's A Good Night For Singing* (1976). Backed by The Lost Gonzo Band he toured incessantly, appearing at festivals and on the college circuit, until in 1978 he reverted to solo performances. He belongs to a diminishing band of troubadours, and his efficient guitar style and laconic wit enables Walker to play to country, folk or rock audiences with equal ease.

T-BONE WALKER

Born: Aaron Thibeaux Walker, May 28th 1910, Linden, Texas, US. Died: March 16th 1975, Los Angeles, California, US.

■ *Gibson ES5; Gibson ES335.*

Walker belongs to an elite of guitarists, having exerted a staggering influence on the development of the electric guitar as one of the most emotive and evocative instruments for musical expression, and it is not unreasonable to place him in a similar context to **Charlie Christian** and BB King. Walker was one of the first players to see the potential of the electric guitar, and used it from the late-1930s onward. Through his influence, blues guitarists – who in turn influenced later rock guitarists – started not only to move away from the 12-bar format but began to adopt single-note soloing techniques, derived from applying the soloing techniques of the saxophone, and chording of increasing sophistication. In fact Walker's influence can be heard in just about every blues-rock guitar solo.

While his recorded output, which included such classics as 'I'm Gonna Find My Baby', 'T-Bone Shuffle',

'Mean Old World', 'I Got A Break Baby' and 'They Call It Stormy Monday', was poorly represented for many years, recently entire inventories are beginning to see the light of day, as on *The Complete 1940-1954 Recordings* (1990), and they making fascinating musical and historical listening.

CHARLIE WALLER

Born: January 19th 1935, Joinerville, Texas, US.

■ **Dobro resonator.**

The Country Gentlemen were formed by Waller in Washington DC in 1957, comprising John Duffey (mandolin and vocals), Bill Emerson (banjo, replaced by Eddie Adcock on mandolin in 1959) and Jim Cox (string bass and banjo). This lineup remained unchanged until the retirement of Duffey in 1969. Waller's scintillating runs on the guitar, executed at a gallop, along with Duffey's jazz-tinged mandolin solos brought a challenging new direction to bluegrass, with the emphasis on instrumental prowess and versatility. Their repertoire was drawn from a variety of sources – folk, traditional country, rock and R&B, and they covered material by Bob Dylan, Charlie Poole, Molly O'Day, Lefty Frizzell and Lennon & McCartney. Despite the considerable influence they exerted in the US (try *Country Songs Old & New* 1960), they remained largely unknown elsewhere. By the 1970s Waller was the only member of the original lineup to remain (Duffey went on to form Seldom Scene with **Mike Auldridge**) while Doyle Lawson (mandolin) and **Ricky Skaggs** were notable additions, and during the late-1970s they recorded regularly for the Rebel label.

LARRY WALLIS

Born: England.

In 1976 Wallis, erstwhile member of The Pink Fairies (*Kings Of Oblivion* 1973), Blodwyn Pig and Motorhead, issued a solo single, 'Police Car'. This suited a musical climate that eschewed the grandiose intentions of 'progressive' music, replacing these with a more visceral form of entertainment. 'Police Car' foreshadowed the anarchic attitude of The Sex Pistols and The Clash and intimated the emergence of heavy metal. Wallis, for his part, never showed much interest in a recording career and consequently has spent time languishing on the club circuit.

JOE WALSH

Born: November 20th 1947, Wichita, Kansas, US.

■ **Gibson Les Paul; Fender Stratocaster.**

During his days in The James Gang, Walsh was described by **Pete Townshend** as the guitarist the Who man most admired – and hearing 'Take A Look Around' from *Yer Album* (1969) one can sympathize. Walsh has since pursued two separate careers: as **Bernie Leadon**'s replacement in The Eagles and as leader of his own group (at first called Barnstorm and then just plain old 'Joe Walsh').

In The Eagles, Walsh's role was that of a hired hand, little different from that of session man, and

his contributions to *Hotel California* (1975) toughened up the sound of the band, giving it more steel. However, his work there lacked the carefully structured, atmospheric feel of his solos on *Barnstorm* (1972) and, especially, *The Smoker You Drink The Player You Get* (1975), the latter including 'Rocky Mountain Way' which featured Walsh on a voice box, which allows the musician's voice to 'play' and shape the sound of the guitar by use of a long tube from the guitar amp to the player's mouth.

Later in the 1970s Walsh issued 'Life's Been Good' (on *But Seriously Folks* 1978), a pleasantly ironic meditation on the trappings of celebrity. Since then his solo career has prospered little and his principal occupation has been that of session musician, touring recently as a member of Ringo Starr's band.

TRAVIS WAMMACK

Born: 1946, Walnut, Mississippi, US.

In common with **Eddie Hinton**, Wammack was one of the key session players around the turn of the 1970s at Muscle Shoals. Working out of Rick Hall's Fame studios he contributed to albums by The Osmonds, Aretha Franklin, Clarence Carter, Wilson Pickett and Mac Davis. In 1975 Wammack started his solo career in earnest and scored a hit with 'Easy Evil'. Much session work followed, with **Tony Joe White**, The Allman Brothers Band, Percy Sledge and Hinton, but Wammack remains drastically underrated.

MUDDY WATERS

Born: McKinley Morganfield, April 4th 1915, Rolling Fork, Mississippi, US. Died: April 30th 1983, Chicago, Illinois, US.

■ **Fender Telecaster; Gibson Les Paul.**

Waters occupies a hallowed position as one of the most important architects of rock'n'roll. His brisk, business-like style and lively slide work gave the Chicago blues an identity in the post-war period that would serve as a template for an entire generation of bluesmen and rock musicians.

Like jazzmen Duke Ellington, Art Blakey and Miles Davis, Waters was a master at surrounding himself with young musicians who were keen to learn – these have included Little Walter, James Cotton, Otis Spann, Hubert Sumlin, Jimmy Rogers and Luther Johnson. His compositional talents were awesome: 'I Got My Mojo Working', 'I'm Ready', 'I Can't Be Satisfied', 'Rolling Stone', 'Rollin' & Tumblin', 'Hoochie Coochie Man', 'Just Make Love To Me' and 'Just To Be With You'. These titles, recorded for Chess in the early-1960s, have formed the repertoire of countless musicians, black and white, who have hit upon Waters as the man who comes closest to embodying the spirit of the blues. Listen to one of the Chess collections on record, from single compilations to boxed complete sessions.

While the shimmering slide guitar playing of his early records is most often remembered, it is sometimes forgotten just how impressive was his acoustic work, with *Muddy Waters, Folk Singer* (1964) emerging at a time when the acoustic blues was being subordinated by the electric blues band – a

trend that he had helped to pioneer some years earlier.

While Waters' later years were marred by ill-health, he found time to work with many young white musicians such as **Keith Richards**, **Johnny Winter**, Paul Butterfield and The Band, all of whom had been influenced to some extent by his work. To this day, his former backing group still tours as The Legendary Blues Band, which is for once accurate.

BRUCE WATSON

Born: March 11th 1961, Timmins, Ontario, Canada.

■ **Gibson Les Paul; ESP.**

Big Country's twin guitar sound was founded in Scotland in 1981 when **Stuart Adamson** left The Skids to form the band with childhood chum Watson (who had moved to Scotland while still young) and a rhythm section of Tony Butler and Mark Brzezicki. They were teamed with producer Steve Lillywhite and came up with the novel, swirling 'bagpipe sound' for the two guitars, later emulated by other Scottish bands such as The Waterboys and Simple Minds. Their debut *The Crossing* (1983) featured titles like the anthemic 'In A Big Country' and 'Fields Of Fire'. The guitar work of both Adamson and Watson has given the group a distinct identity, and after a two year hiatus they returned with *Buffalo Skinners* (1993).

DOC WATSON

Born: Arthel Watson, March 3rd 1923, Deep Gap, North Carolina, US.

■ **Martin; Gallagher.**

Watson, blind from birth, was a fine flat-picker in the style of **Grady Martin**, **Merle Travis** and **Dan Reno** and an accomplished fingerstylist. His instruction manuals are significant introductions to the traditional flat-picking styles of the Appalachians.

He spent many years in obscurity assimilating different styles of picking and finally achieved recognition during the folk boom of the early-1960s. Throughout the 1950s Watson played with a string of pop groups, performing covers of hit songs, until in 1960 he came to the attention of producer Ralph Rinzler who was organizing the Folkways sessions that would result in *Old Time Music At Clarence Ashley's*. These recordings were enthusiastically received, and Watson became an immediate fixture on New York's Greenwich Village club circuit, and then went on to appear at Newport Folk Festivals.

The following year Watson was signed to Vanguard where he remained for the better part of the decade. In 1965 he joined forces with his son **Merle Watson**, cutting albums of duets such as *Doc Watson And Son* (1965) and the fine *Southbound* (1966). Object lessons in instrumental virtuosity, they drew their material from blues, Appalachian ballads and traditional English and American folk songs. In 1971 Doc was the catalyst for The Nitty Gritty Dirt Band's important country-rock epic *Will The Circle Be Unbroken*? Doc and Merle went on to record *Then And Now* (1973) and *Two Days In November* (1974), both Grammy winners, and in 1980 Doc cut *Reflections* with **Chet Atkins**, but in 1985 Merle was killed in a farming accident and as a consequence Doc decided to retire.

JOHNNY GUITAR WATSON

Born: February 3rd 1935, Houston, Texas, US.

■ **Gibson ES335.**

Watson has since 1952 been one of the more idiosyncratic Texan performers, and echoes of his influence resound in the work of artists like **Steve Miller**. Watson has managed to transcend fashion, with even his mid-1970s ventures into disco territory proving worthwhile.

After moving to Los Angeles in 1950 he was signed to a succession of independent labels and was dubbed 'Guitar' Watson by Joe Bihari of the Modern label. Although major chart success eluded him, he built up a strong reputation with his performances on the club circuit where he employed such novel and avant-garde techniques as playing the guitar with his teeth and using feedback.

Throughout the 1960s Watson toured with R&B singer Larry Williams, moving into his disco phase with *Listen* (1973), *I Don't Want To Be Alone Stranger* (1976), *Ain't That a Bitch?* (1976) which included 'I Need It', and *A Real Mother For Ya* (1977). Although in recent years he has recorded less and less, he still plays the Los Angeles club circuit and has worked with **Frank Zappa** on occasions.

MERLE WATSON

Born: February 8th 1949, Deep Gap, North Carolina, US.
Died: October 23rd 1985, Lenoir, North Carolina, US.

■ **Gallagher; Martin D-18; Dobro resonator.**

With his father **Doc Watson**, Merle cut a string of albums of duets – *Doc Watson And Son* (1965), *Southbound* (1966), *Home Again* (1967), *Then And Now* (1973) and *Two Days In November* (1974) – that were object lessons in instrumental virtuosity, the material derived from blues, Appalachian ballads and traditional English and American folk songs. Merle was an adept flat-picker, like his father, but also displayed a keen ability on dobro slide. Merle's death in a farming accident had the effect of cutting short his father's career as well.

CHUCK WAYNE

Born: Charles Jagelka, February 27th 1923, New York, New York, US.

■ **D'Angelico.**

After playing a variety of gigs and pursuing different jobs Wayne finally landed a position with jazz bandleader Woody Herman in 1946. Although short-lived this led to a job with blind pianist George Shearing's 'cool' quintet in 1949, where Wayne's guitar was prominently featured. For the next three years Wayne worked a tough schedule with Shearing and, despite later session work, Wayne's work with Shearing remains his most satisfying and, arguably, it coincided with Shearing's most creative phase. In later years both Shearing and Wayne tended to

indulge themselves in flashy playing, or that which would pay the rent – in Wayne's case this meant working sessions for NBC.

STAN WEBB

Born: February 3rd 1946, Birmingham, England.

■ **Gibson Les Paul.**

As a bright young British blues band in the late-1960s, Chicken Shack, like The Groundhogs, found themselves among overwhelming competition: Fleetwood Mac, **John Mayall**'s Bluesbreakers and even Jethro Tull. Chicken Shack had many redeeming features, not only the immaculate vocals of Christine Perfect (later of Fleetwood Mac) on tracks like 'I'd Rather Go Blind', but also Webb's slide guitar work that echoed the enthusiasm and affection implicit in **Elmore James**' best work. Where others went off to pursue more lucrative avenues, Webb, like **Tony McPhee** of The Groundhogs, stuck to the blues. In over 20 years his style has changed little, but it retains a buoyant bonhomie that is irresistible, and there are few who have propped up the British and European club scene as faithfully as Webb.

JIMMIE WEBSTER

Born: US.

■ **Gretsch.**

Webster spent most of his working life playing in jazz big bands such as those of Count Basie, Jimmy Lunceford and Woody Herman. Although his rhythm work was as good as it gets, Webster toured as a soloist periodically, and worked as a part-time demonstrator for the Gretsch guitar company, being partly responsible for the design of their White Falcon model of 1955 and helping to encourage **Chet Atkins** to become involved in a series of instruments.

BERT WEEDON

Born: Herbert Weedon, May 10th 1920, London, England.

■ **Hofner Committee; Guild 'signature'; Yamaha.**

Bert Weedon was one of the first British guitarists to recognize the guitar's potential as a solo instrument, and one of the country's top session players of the 1950s.

His career started with Mantovani, Ted Heath and Cyril Stapleton's popular orchestras, until in 1956 he led his own quartet. Considerable session work for records and radio followed during the latter half of the 1950s and early-1960s, and those with whom Weedon worked included arranger Norrie Paramor, Frank Sinatra, Nat 'King' Cole, Judy Garland, Paul Robeson, Cliff Richard, Billy Fury, Marty Wilde, Adam Faith and Tommy Steele. He did have solo hits for a couple of years with 45s like his cover of The Virtues' arrangement of **Arthur Smith**'s 'Guitar Boogie Shuffle' (1959). Many years later he confounded all expectations when *22 Golden Guitar Greats* (1976) sold over a million copies in Britain, proving that the name Bert Weedon still conjured awe and respect.

Perhaps Weedon's most influential contribution to guitar playing was his instructional manual *Play In*

A Day which formed the basis for the careers of hundreds of teenage strummers, including **Hank Marvin**, **Keith Richards** and **Mark Knopfler**, and which still sells today. The Guild guitar company issued a Bert Weedon model in the mid-1960s.

BOB WEIR

Born: Robert Hall, October 16th 1947, San Francisco, California, US.

■ **Gibson ES335; Gibson ES345; Gibson SG; Ibanez 'signature'; Yairi 'signature'; Modulus Graphite 'signature'.**

When a band has a lead guitarist of the stature of **Jerry Garcia**, and a rhythm section of the quality of Phil Lesh, Bill Kreutzmann and Mickey Hart, who needs a rhythm guitarist? The answer is The Grateful Dead. Hence Bob Weir.

Nowhere is Weir's impact more pronounced than on albums like *Workingman's Dead* and *American Beauty* (1970), where the Dead's songs and structure had become the whole point of the exercise. Although they have recorded dozens of albums since their debut in 1967, the Dead have managed to remain aloof from the chicanery of the record industry, and turned themselves into their own personalized cottage industry. Weir formed his own outfit, Bobby & The Midnites, for informal gigs – although admittedly the idea of 'formality' at a Grateful Dead concert is too bizarre to countenance.

ERIC WEISSBERG

Born: 1939, New York, New York, US.

■ **Martin; Fender Telecaster; Gibson ES345.**

The Greenbriar Boys were formed in 1958 in New York by guitarist/banjoist Weissberg, fiddler John Herald, mandolinist Ralph Rinzler and Bob Yellin. In 1962 they recorded *Greenbriar Boys* for Elektra, but changed labels to Vanguard (which had also signed Doc Watson) where they cut albums like *Ragged But Right* (1964) and *Better Late Than Never* (1967). The lineup of the group was usually in a state of flux, and Weissberg was the only member to forge a significant solo career, via session work with Judy Collins and Tom Rush, and playing banjo to Steve Mandel's guitar on 'Dueling Banjos' (featured in the movie *Deliverance* and based on 'Feuding Banjos' by **Don Reno** and **Arthur Smith**). Weissberg still does session work and plays the East Coast club circuit.

BRUCE WELCH

Born: November 2nd 1941, Bognor Regis, Sussex, England.

■ **Fender Stratocaster; Fender Jazzmaster; Burns Marvin; Martin.**

Such was the assertiveness of **Hank Marvin**'s lead guitar lines in The Shadows that Welch's wonderfully clean and metronomic rhythm work on their 1960s hits is often overlooked. It was therefore fortunate that Welch had the ear of an arranger and the perspective of a producer, in which role he later performed sterling work with Cliff Richard that helped revitalize the singer's career in the 1970s.

Waf-Wel

PAUL WELLER

Born: Paul John William Weller, May 25th 1958, Woking, Surrey, England.

■ *Rickenbacker 330, Rickenbacker 12-string; Rickenbacker 320; Fender Telecaster.*

Of all the musicians to emerge in the British new wave of the late-1970s, Weller's reputation is least tarnished and most likely to endure long after Sex Pistols vocalist John Lydon has been written off. Weller has been able to combine the political rhetoric of singer Billy Bragg and the fly-on-the-wall observation of The Kinks' Ray Davies with a brisk line in neat tunes and deft, punchy chords that owe allegiance to early Who. Proving that age doesn't have to wither all, Weller's later work with The Style Council and his solo work, especially *Wild Wood* (1993), has shown him growing older gracefully while retaining the brio and passion of his earlier years. The guitar work on The Jam's early singles provided triumphant bursts of energy, recalling some of **Pete Townshend**'s and **Dave Davies**' wilder work.

KENNY WERTZ

Born: US.

Kenny Wertz was at the heart of the bluegrass revival in the early-1970s. Formerly a member of The Country Gentlemen and The Flying Burrito Brothers, he played on the latter's excellent live *Last Of The Red Hot Burritos* (1971) before forming Country Gazette with Byron Berline (fiddle), Roger Bush (bass), **Herb Pedersen** (banjo/guitar, vocals) and Roland White (guitar/mandolin, vocals). Their debut *Traitor In Our Midst* (1972) contained some of the most authentic recreations of bluegrass heard outside of Kentucky, although their rock'n'roll approach won them few admirers in bluegrass circles. By 1977 Wertz had returned to session work on the West Coast.

LESLIE WEST

Born: Leslie Weinstein, October 22nd 1945, New York, New York, US.

■ *Gibson Les Paul Junior; Steinberger M.*

West and bassist Felix Pappalardi formed Mountain in 1970 in the image of Cream, and while exciting (*Nantucket Sleighride* and *Flowers Of Evil* 1971) they were ultimately derivative, with West showing little imagination. After the group foundered, Pappalardi was replaced by Jack Bruce and the group became West Bruce & Laing (with drummer Corky Laing). Bruce quickly realized that his compadres lacked creative verve and departed after two studio records and a live album. After the split in 1974 West's career became increasingly erratic, his last reported venture being with Laing and ex-Uriah Heep bassist Mark Clarke in a revived, short-lived Mountain.

RICKY WEST

Born: Richard Westwood, May 7th 1943, Dagenham, Essex, England.

■ *Fender Jaguar.*

When West and The Tremeloes backed singer Brian Poole they made a couple of fine reworkings of R&B classics like The Contours' 'Do You Love Me?' and The Isley Brothers' 'Twist & Shout' (1963), with West a confident and lively lead player. After Poole left for a solo career The Tremeloes recorded a string of gentle hits such as 'Here Comes My Baby' and the ghastly 'Silence Is Golden', their soft harmonies and competent instrumentation winning them a large MOR audience.

SPEEDY WEST

Born: Wesley Webb West, January 25th 1924, Springfield, Missouri, US.

■ *Fender 1000.*

During the 1940s and 1950s, pedal-steel guitarist Speedy West was one of country's most sought-after session musicians. His career started at 13, but after World War II he moved to the West Coast where he worked with Hank Penny and Spade Cooley, establishing his credentials as one of the most inspired and innovative players on the circuit. Over the next five years he worked with country artists such as **Merle Travis**, Hank Thompson, Tex Williams, Tex Ritter and Slim Whitman. Among his most influential work among fellow guitarists was *Two Guitars: Country Style*, one of a number of stunning duets with **Jimmy Bryant** recorded for Capitol in the 1950s. The two made regular TV appearances that helped popularize electric guitars.

BUKKA WHITE

Born: Booker T Washington White, November 12th 1906, Houston, Mississippi, US. Died: February 26th 1977, Memphis, Tennessee, US.

■ *National resonator.*

White was one of the beneficiaries of the revival of interest in the blues in the 1960s, having spent years in obscurity. His career had started during the 1920s when he hoboed around the southern states, playing juke joints and the like. After spending time as a boxer and a baseball pitcher, he recorded briefly for Vocalion ('Shake 'em On Down') until he was imprisoned for assault, and while in prison he recorded two songs for the Library Of Congress.

On his release White recorded sides like 'Parchman Farm Blues', 'Where Can I Change My Clothes' and 'District Attorney Blues', trenchant insights into the penal system made more resonant by his heavily percussive slide guitar. After the war White settled in Memphis with his cousin **BB King**, but was inactive until 1963 when he was discovered by **John Fahey** who introduced him to the burgeoning festival and college circuit. In the years leading up to his death he recorded little, but *The Complete Sessions 1930-1940* is a fine testament to his lyrical facility and abrasive guitar work.

CLARENCE WHITE

Born: June 7th 1944, Lewiston, Maine, US. Died: July 14th 1973, California, US.

■ *Martin D-28; Fender Telecaster; Martin D-18.*

White was a fine flat-picker who, as well as **Doc Watson**, helped establish the style, and White's influence is still heard today in the work of bluegrass artists like **Tony Rice**.

White was also one of the prime movers in The Byrds' shift to a more authentic country sound – as on *Sweetheart Of The Rodeo* (1968) – and was a founder member of The Kentucky Colonels, one of the first progressive bluegrass outfits to emerge in the 1960s.

White was raised in California with his two brothers Roland and Eric, with whom he formed The Country Boys. By 1961 the group had evolved into The Kentucky Colonels, the lineup being completed by Roland (mandolin), Roger Bush (bass), Billy Ray Latham (banjo) and Leroy Mack (dobro).

In 1966, after recording *Kentucky Colonels* and several earlier albums (hard to find at the time of writing), White left the group to form Nashville West with Gene Parsons, recording an eponymous album that is considered one of the earliest examples of country-rock. White joined The Byrds in 1968 and remained with them until 1973, cutting among others *Dr Byrd & Mr Hyde* (1969) and *Untitled* (1970), as well as the classic *Sweetheart*.

He also did outside sessions, including Joe Cocker's first album (1969), Randy Newman's *12 Songs* (1970), and Arlo Guthrie's *Last Of The Brooklyn Cowboys* (1972), and invented with Gene Parsons the Parsons-White B-Bender, a device for altering the pitch of solidbody guitar strings by preset intervals to simulate pedal-steel effects.

Shortly after reforming The Kentucky Colonels in 1973 White, loading his van after a gig, was killed by a drunken driver – a shocking waste of a great guitarist whose influence will be felt for many years to come. A good and sensitive compilation of his best recordings is well overdue. At the time of writing the Fender and Collings guitar companies were planning to market White 'signature' instruments.

JOSH WHITE

Born: February 11th 1915, Greenville, South Carolina, US. Died: September 5th 1969, Manhasset, New York, US.

Like **Jesse Fuller**, White was an all-round entertainer who, having learned his trade on the streets during the 1930s, developed a repertoire that comprised blues, folk songs, spirituals and children's songs. By the 1950s, he had moved to New York where his versatility led him into cahoots with radical folk singers such as Cisco Houston and Pete Seeger. This, with the progressive militancy of the civil rights movement during the 1960s, caused many to comment disparagingly about his performances for white audiences. What was forgotten, however, was his ability to introduce authentic black music to the white middle classes, with an appealingly direct guitar style in tow.

MARK WHITE

Born: April 1st 1961, Sheffield, Yorkshire, England.

Formed by vocalist Martin Fry, ABC were one of the smoothest purveyors of glistening pop songs in the early-1980s, and their playful 12-inch single 'The

Wei-Whi

Look Of Love' (1982) developed the idea of different treatments of one song over a long playing time. Guitarist White in collaboration with Fry contributed most of the group's material, including 'Poison Arrow', 'The Look Of Love' and 'All Of My Heart' and best heard on their startlingly fresh and assured debut *The Lexicon Of Love* (1982), produced by Trevor Horn. White was seldom required to extend himself as Fry's voice and the production were the key elements, but his slick playing undoubtedly aided the group in its pursuit of stylish, glossy pop.

ROBERT WHITE

Born: US.

■ **Gibson L5CES.**

The Motown house band included guitarists White and **Joe Messina** alongside the staggering basslines of James Jamerson, plus drummer Benny Benjamin and keyboardist Earl Van Dyke. There were others, but these men provided the real sound of Motown behind any singer who happened along, creating chugging, liquid backbeats that fell perfectly.

SNOWY WHITE

Born: England.

■ **Gibson Les Paul; Fender Stratocaster.**

After a spell with Pink Floyd's road band in the late-1970s and with Thin Lizzy for *Chinatown* (1980) and two more early-1980s albums, White confounded all expectations by achieving some success in his solo career. Admittedly, 'Bird Of Paradise' (1983) sounded more like **David Gilmour** than did Gilmour himself, but it didn't stop the song from becoming a pleasant relief from the plethora of techno bands that populated the early-1980s. Albums such as *White Flames* (1983) and *Snowy White* (1985) performed well, but the influence of Gilmour was pervasive.

TONY JOE WHITE

Born: July 23rd 1943, Oak Grove, Louisiana, US.

■ **Fender Stratocaster.**

For a brief spell in the late-1960s White was the prime practitioner of 'swamp rock' which, despite his abilities as a writer and guitarist, failed to catch on. In Texas, White had formed Tony & The Twilights, before moving to Nashville in 1968 and cutting *Black And White* (1969). Produced by Billy Swan it included 'Polk Salad Annie', a churning urn of burning funk. Apart from 'Groupie Girl' the follow-ups failed to raise the public's pulse, despite their artistic merits, and gradually White edged towards obscurity, although fine producers such as Tom Dowd and Jerry Wexler tried to arrest the decline. Through much of the 1980s his career was sedate, but in the 1990s White issued the creditable *Closer To The Truth* (1991) and *The Path Of A Decent Groove* (1993).

KEITH WHITLEY

Born: July 1st 1954, Sandy Hook, Kentucky, US. Died: May 9th 1989, Nashville, Tennessee, US.

Whitley is a rare example of a bluegrass musician who made it to the top without compromising his enthusiasm. A competent guitarist by the age of six, he was broadcasting on a local radio in West Virginia when he was nine. In 1971 he joined **Ricky Skaggs** in Ralph Stanley's Clinch Mountain Boys where both made their debut on *Cry From The Cross: A Tribute To The Stanley Brothers*.

Remaining with Stanley until 1977, Whitley went on to join JD Crowe's New South as lead vocalist before gaining a recording contract in Nashville in 1983. His *Hard Act To Follow* (1984) set the tone for his career, combining well-crafted guitar work with a considered repertoire.

LA To Miami (1986) got to the heart of 'new country' with songs that included 'Miami My Amy', 'Ten Feet Away', 'Homecoming 63' and 'Hard Livin'. Traditional in style but contemporary in feel, Whitley's songs bridged the gap between the young turks and the old school. By the late-1980s Whitley had become one of country's finest prospects, but his blossoming career was tragically ended by alcoholic poisoning.

CHARLIE WHITNEY

Born: John Whitney, June 24th 1944, Leicester, England.

■ **Gibson double-neck.**

Family emerged in the British 'progressive' era of the 1960s with the credentials to become one of the finest such groups. Vocalist Roger Chapman sounded as if he toned his vocal cords with sandpaper, hornman Jim King could honk like King Curtis, and guitarist Whitney had a blues grounding that he applied to inventive thematic work. These three helped make *Music In A Doll's House* (1968) and *Family Entertainment* (1969) two of the finest offerings to appear in the post-psychedelic euphoria. That the group failed to survive was partly due to the later absence of King, whose meaty sax solos provided the ideal counterpoint to Chapman's vocals and Whitney's guitar work. Whitney and Chapman continued in a variety of projects after Family split in 1973, notably Streetwalkers, but they lacked the variety and imagination that Family had in their heyday.

DANNY WHITTEN

Died: November 18th 1972.

When Whitten died, **Neil Young** lost his best foil. Whitten's melodic lines complemented Young's plangent riffs and machine-gun phrases, and his supportive work on Young's *Everybody Knows This Is Nowhere* (1969, eg 'Cinnamon Girl') or *After The Gold Rush* (1970, eg 'Southern Man') still takes some beating. To get to grips with just how good a guitarist Whitten was, one has to listen to Crazy Horse albums such as *Crazy Horse* (1970) and *Loose* (1971) where Whitten's lean lines show lessons learned from Young in phrasing, but possess a resigned insight (as on Whitten's song 'I Don't Want To Talk About It', and 'I'll Get By'). Whitten was an under-achiever, no doubt, but Young's tribute to him, 'The Needle And The Damage Done' (on *Harvest* 1972), speaks more eloquently than any anti-drug tirade in the press.

WALLY WHYTON

Born: England.

On BBC radio Whyton's shows have helped introduce British audiences to bluegrass, western swing, 'new country', honky tonk, Tex-Mex and many other strains of country music that are now accepted as part of the landscape. His own recording career in the 1950s as guitarist and mainman with the skiffle group The Vipers (including Whyton's song 'Don't You Rock Me Daddy-O', later covered by **Lonnie Donegan**) attracted less attention than it deserved. But Whyton's championing of country music and roots guitarists on a network still not exactly free from conservatism is worthy of note.

JOHN WILLIAMS

Born: April 24th 1941, Melbourne, Australia.

■ **Fleta; Smallman; Ovation; Gibson RD Artist.**

Williams is one of the foremost classical guitarists to have emerged since World War II. His family moved to London in the early-1950s, and he soon began studying with Segovia in Italy. He made his London concert debut in 1958, soon afterwards playing in the US and Japan. Composer/conductor Andre Previn dedicated his Guitar Concerto to Williams.

Williams recorded a series of exciting and revealing duets with **Julian Bream**, *Together* (1971), *Together Again* (1974) and *Live* (1978). And while **Julian Bream** forged closer ties with modernism in the shape of specially written pieces by comtemporary composers, Williams formed in 1979 the classical-rock fusion outfit Sky, an idea interesting in theory than practice. A later flirtation by Williams, *Concerto For Guitar And Jazz Orchestra* (1987), was much better, proving that he can tackle such meetings in the right circumstances.

In general, Williams' willingness to absorb jazz, pop and other strains of music into his own is notable, given that the classical music world is more insular than most, and his recording of *Music Of Barrios* in the 1980s did much to focus attention on South American and Latin guitar music in general and that of Agustin Barrios in particular.

For Williams' most influential work it is necessary to look to *Plays Spanish Music* (1970). This caused many to hear the work of Rodrigo and Villa-Lobos with fresh ears, prompting a run on pieces by these composers from other guitarists keen to prove their virtuosity. Rodrigo's *Concierto De Aranjuez* has now been recorded by virtually every classical guitarist, but Williams' interpretations are among the finest. A good introduction to Williams' large studio output is the two-CD reissue of some fine 1968 recordings as *Guitar Concertos* (1989).

MASON WILLIAMS

Born: July 24th 1936, Abilene, Texas, US.

■ **Cordova.**

'Classical Gas' was a massive hit for Williams in 1968, and followed his long career on the club circuit and as a songwriter. It featured his classically-inflected guitar arpeggios against an orchestrated backdrop, and has since become a party piece for many an electric guitarist asked to 'get out the acoustic'. Since 'Gas' Williams has worked on sessions and as a poet, an author and a concept artist.

RICHARD WILLIAMS

Born: 1951, Kansas City, Kansas, US.

Kansas were one of those featureless bands that emerged in the 1970s, and after lengthy touring and a number of gold albums the group split up with various of their number becoming born-again Christians. Guitarist Williams reformed the group in 1986 with Dixie Dregs' **Steve Morse** on board. The ensuing *Power* eschewed the jazz-rock connotations of their earlier efforts and moved to a funkier, heavier sound.

JAMES WILLIAMSON

Born: US.

Williamson joined Iggy Pop in The Stooges in 1970, replacing Bill Cheatham. Although the group had passed their peak as a unit and broke up shortly after, Williamson remained with Iggy and they cut *Raw Power* (1973) together on the instigation of David Bowie. This record, in common with The New York Dolls debut, was way ahead of its time, with Williamson's dazzling solos and insistent riffing underscoring Iggy's nihilism, as on 'Search And Destroy' and 'Penetration'. Two more albums emerged, *Metallic KO* (1974) and *Kill City* (1978), foreshadowing heavy metal.

PETE WILLIS

Born: February 16th 1960, Sheffield, England.

■ Hamer Standard.

It was unfortunate for Willis that he was shifted out of Def Leppard just as they were beginning to hit the big time. Willis, while not the most original of heavy metal guitarists, was fundamental to the group's early sound, owing much to the blues-based rock of Led Zeppelin. His contribution to the self-financed EP *Getcha Rocks Off* (1979) was the authentic voice of British heavy metal, where the accent was on thunderous chords delivered at breakneck speed and at a deafening volume.

When producer Robert 'Mutt' Lange appeared on the scene to take over the production chores on their second album, *High'n'Dry* (1981), British fans and Willis were not at all enthusiastic about the glossy high-tech sound that Lange was introducing. By the time they had started to cut *Pyromania* (1983) Willis was on the way out, and **Phil Collen** was on the way in. In recent years Willis has played with Roadhouse, who do pretty much what Def Leppard did before Lange got his hands on them.

JIMMY WILSEY

Born: James Calvin Wilsey, US.

■ Fender Stratocaster.

Wilsey is best known as the man who eerily intoned the wonderfully glass-like guitar backdrops to Chris

Isaak's 'Wicked Game' (used on the soundtrack of *Wild At Heart*) and 'Blue Hotel'. Isaak's unaffected hybrid draws from country, rockabilly and rock'n'roll to create an atmosphere of half-remembered fragments, while Wilsey's guitar work happily leans on the spare, echoed twang of **Duane Eddy**.

AL WILSON

Born: July 4th 1943, Boston, Massachusetts, US.
Died: September 3rd 1970, Los Angeles, California, US.

When slide guitarist Wilson formed Canned Heat with **Henry Vestine**, Wilson had already acquired a reputation for an obsession with the blues, which had culminated in playing with Son House on his comeback album *Father Of The Folk Blues*.

Initially Canned Heat – named after a 1928 recording by bluesman **Tommy Johnson** – were diligent rather than inspired, bearing similarities to **Peter Green**'s Fleetwood Mac. *Boogie With Canned Heat* (1968) changed all that, featuring Wilson's delicate vocals and hypnotic slide on the group's classic take of Jim Oden's 'On The Road Again'. *Livin' The Blues* (1969), a live double album, was regarded as self indulgent by many, but hindsight has proved it to be miles ahead of its contemporaries, with Wilson's and Vestine's playing on 'Parthenogenesis' echoing the free flowing experimentation more readily associated with The Grateful Dead. By the early-1970s, having played the festival circuit and achieved more commercial success with 'Goin Up Country', they were recording with **John Lee Hooker** (*Hooker 'n' Heat* 1971), but in 1970 Wilson was found dead from a drugs overdose in vocalist Bob Hite's back yard.

CARL WILSON

Born: December 21st 1946, Los Angeles, California, US.

■ Fender Stratocaster; Gibson Firebird; Gibson Les Paul Junior; Epiphone Riviera XII; Rickenbacker 12-string; Gibson ES335.

While Brian Wilson of The Beach Boys was justly credited with much of the musical inspiration for the group, guitarist Wilson contributed the snappy licks that punctuated their ornate harmonies. Even in this area Wilson was given little credit, as session guitarists like **Glen Campbell** were often reckoned to be behind these solos. Carl is the sole surviving member of the Wilson brothers in the group today and his guitar work on stage varies little from the sound on the records, despite in some cases the songs having been first recorded over 30 years ago.

CINDY WILSON

Born: February 28th 1957, Athens, Georgia, US.

The B-52s' quirky combination of funk, punk and rock 'n' roll made them hard for audiences to define. While Cindy and Ricky Wilson's guitar work provided the rhythmic thrust to this curious hybrid, it took the group some years to take off, but they eventually came to enjoy cult status on the college circuit with albums like *Wild Planet* (1980) and *Whammy!* (1983) until 'Love Shack' (1989), produced by Nile

Rodgers, thrust them into the mainstream. After Ricky's death from cancer in 1986 Cindy undertook the guitar chores. She left the band in 1992.

DON WILSON

Born: February 10th 1937, Tacoma, Washington, US.

■ Fender Jazzmaster; Fender Stratocaster; Mosrite; Aria 'signature'.

Rhythm guitarist Wilson and lead guitarist **Bob Bogle** have remained in The Ventures since the group's formation in 1959. During that time, the lineup has undergone inevitable change, but Wilson and Bogle remain at the core of one of the most influential instrumental combos of all time. They are one of the most popular groups in Japan, and consequently albums like *Live In Japan* (1977) and *Pops In Japan '81* sell by the truckload.

NANCY WILSON

Born: March 16th 1954, San Francisco, California, US.

■ Gibson; Ovation; Fender Stratocaster; Washburn.

During the 1980s Heart, fronted by vocalist Ann Wilson and guitarist Nancy, were one of the most successful purveyors of glossy AOR pop. Despite their derivative material, Nancy's guitar work, often strengthened by that of Howard Leese, cleverly combined metallic style riffs with the delicacy of folk, best heard on *Heart* (1985) and *Bad Animals* (1987). By 1991 Ann and Nancy had broadened their scope by forming a spin-off acoustic group, The Lovemongers.

MICHAEL WILTON

Born: February 22nd 1962, Seattle, Washington, US.

■ ESP custom.

Queensryche were formed in the early-1980s and have become one of the finest metal bands around with Geoff Tate's immaculate vocals complementing Wilton's and **Chris DeGarmo**'s strident guitar work. Their first album *The Warning* (1984) failed to live up to expectation, but *Rage For Order* (1986) showed the group in full control with 'Gonna Get Close To You', among others, illustrating the distinctiveness of their style. *Operation Mindcrime* (1988) was an Orwellian concept album, lacking in finesse, but *Empire* (1990) included 'Silent Lucidity', 'Best I Can' and 'Jet City Woman', all serving to confirm the status of Queensryche as one of the brightest, least bombastic outfits of their type.

BO WINBERG

Born: March 27th 1939, Gothenburg, Sweden.

■ Fender Stratocaster.

Bo Winberg remained at the heart of The Spotnicks since their formation in the late-1950s and, incredibly, the group was still going in the late-1980s. With a bright instrumental style that owed more to The Ventures and The Tornados than The Shadows, The Spotnicks updated such popular anthems as 'Hava Nagila', and even cut a version of The Tornados' 'Telstar' as The Shy Ones. Like The Ventures, the group has continued to make albums, for example *Love Is Blue* (1988), with some regularity.

JOHNNY WINTER

Born: John Dawson Winter, February 23rd 1944, Leland, Mississippi, US.

■ **Gibson Firebird; IMC Lazer; Erlewine 'signature'.**

Although Winter's career has been erratic, he is a superior guitarist with technique and feel honed into a personal blues/rock'n'roll-based style. He cut *The Progressive Blues Experiment* (1969) which opened the door for a spate of heavy blues-rock albums by a host of notably inferior imitators, and *Second Winter* (1970) built his reputation with storming versions of 'Johnny B Goode' and 'Highway 61 Revisited', among others. Throughout the 1970s and 1980s his career was hindered by drug problems, but by the 1990s he had started to work with the Chicago-based Alligator label, recording *Let Me In* (1991) and *Jack Daniels Kind Of Day* (1992).

STEVE WINWOOD

Born: Stephen Philip Winwood, May 12th 1948, Birmingham, England.

■ **Fender Stratocaster; Gibson Les Paul; Ovation.**

Better known for his expertise on keyboards and as soulful vocalist, Winwood has demonstrated a facility with most instruments and is a fine, underrated guitarist, and with The Spencer Davis Group (1963-67) his lean phrases on the guitar owed more to **Jimmy Nolen** than **Eric Clapton**. In Traffic (1967-74) and, briefly, with Blind Faith in 1969, his guitar work was subordinated to keyboards (notably Hammond organ). But when **Dave Mason** left Traffic in 1969 Winwood took over as guitarist and illustrated not only his economy but also his eloquence. Nowhere was this more apparent than on *John Barleycorn Must Die* (1970, started as Winwood solo) and *The Low Spark Of The High-Heeled Boys* (1971).

After Traffic finally ground to a halt Winwood started a solo career, and his output has been short in volume but high in quality, especially *Arc Of A Diver* (1980) but also *Back In The High Life* (1986) and *Roll With It* (1988) underlining his continuing abilities as a composer. Now a major league performer, quality is Winwood's key – and he has no need to record for its own sake.

LAURIE WISEFIELD

Born: 1953, England.

■ **Fender Stratocaster; Gibson Les Paul Junior.**

At the peak of Wishbone Ash's fame, **Ted Turner** got religion and left the group in 1974. His replacement was Wisefield, who had been a member of Home (a band of whom great things were expected, but which failed to materialize). With **Andy Powell**, Wisefield continued on stage where Turner had left off, duelling lead lines blazing through the group's lengthy pieces as their popularity in the US continued on an upward spiral, even if their studio albums – *Locked In* (1976), *New England* (1977)

and *Just Testing* (1979) – were unadventurous. Consequently, live albums began to take precedence over the studio affairs. That changed in 1987 when Turner rejoined for *Nouveau Calls*. Still working and big in Japan, they have become stalwarts of the international live circuit and show little sign of letting up.

MAC WISEMAN

Born: May 23rd 1925, near Waynesboro, Virginia, US.

■ **Martin D-28.**

One of the finest bluegrass singers and guitarists, Mac Wiseman has dedicated his musical career to the preservation of the old-time songs from the Shenandoah Valley, Virginia. His career has fallen into three main areas: as lead vocalist in **Lester Flatt** & Earl Scruggs's Foggy Mountain Boys; a spell with Bill Monroe's Blue Grass Boys; and his solo career. While his solo career provided him with hits such as 'Shackles And Chains', ''Tis Sweet To Be Remembered', 'Jimmy Brown The Newsboy', 'Ballad Of Davy Crockett' and 'Love Letters In The Sand', he elevated the profile of bluegrass and old-time music during the 1960s and 1970s by touring college campuses and festivals, contributing to the renewal of interest in traditional country music. Around the same time he proved his value as a guitarist, relying on the older thumb-pick-assisted bluegrass style, cutting *On The South Bound* and *Lester'n'Mac* (1969) with Flatt. At the time of writing Wiseman still runs an annual bluegrass festival in Kentucky.

WIZ

Born: Darren Brown, England.

Mega City 4 are one of a number of British thrash bands whose bright, chirpy tunes could help them to survive. Ever since their debut *Tranzophobia* (1989), the group have relied on Wiz's songs and guitar work, which have steadily become more accomplished. *Magic Bullets* (1993) cleverly developed a veneer of sophistication while retaining the untutored energy of their debut.

BOBBY WOMACK

Born: March 5th 1944, Cleveland, Ohio, US.

■ **Fender Telecaster.**

Womack has for almost three decades been at the core of the development of soul, from his earliest associations with Sam Cooke until the present day.

In 1959, with his brothers Cecil, Curtis, Harris and Friendly, he formed The Womack Brothers (they later became The Valentinos) and started to tour on the gospel circuit where he met Sam Cooke, who recruited him as a guitarist in his touring band. After releasing 'Lookin For A Love' and 'It's All Over Now' their promising joint career was interrupted by the death of Cooke in 1964.

Womack started to work as a session guitarist at Chips Moman's American studios and then at Fame in Muscle Shoals, where he worked with artists like Wilson Pickett, King Curtis and Clarence Carter. With Pickett he forged a significant alliance, writing songs

like 'I'm a Midnight Mover' and contributing much of the guitar incidentals. His solo career meanwhile was picking up momentum, and albums like *Live* (1970) illustrated the depth and range of his voice and his steely guitar chops.

In 1971 Womack played guitar with Sly & The Family Stone, appearing on the seminal *There's A Riot Goin' On*, but through much of the 1970s his work was patchy. Then he cut *The Poet* (1981) and *The Poet II* (1981), two of the best recent examples of what soul is all about, combining the gutbucket emotion of gospel and the earthy abrasiveness of R&B. While later albums have reverted to the inconsistency of former years, Womack is a survivor, a fine player capable of serving an ace at any time.

JOSEPH WONG

Born: Joseph Arthur Wong, Trinidad.

Formed in Brooklyn by keyboardist/vocalist Randy Muller in 1968 as Dynamic Soul, the group became Brass Construction in 1975. While the lineup was variable, guitarist Wong and Muller were the constant factors. Their debut *Brass Construction* (1975) established them as one of the leading exponents of jazz-oriented funk. Although as you might imagine the brass section dominated, Wong's Caribbean rhythms gave the group's sound more variation than most of the funk outfits of the time and enabled them to grace the disco era with some style. Despite dwindling sales in recent years their reputation has been enhanced by the remix trend, and they have been electronically sampled with almost as much frequency as James Brown.

RON WOOD

Born: June 1st 1947, London, England.

■ **Fender Stratocaster; Fender Telecaster; Zemaitis; Tokai Strat-style.**

Throughout Wood's career he has played the foil – for **Jeff Beck**, for singer Rod Stewart, and for **Keith Richards**. Although he has often been overshadowed as a player and a personality, Wood's boundless enthusiasm and lack of interest in the spotlight has made him an ideal catalyst.

His career started in a London band called The Birds, who based their repertoire on covers of R&B and Motown material. By the time they split up he was enlisted by Beck for The Jeff Beck Group, initially as guitarist, then as bassist. When the group disbanded in 1969, Wood and Rod Stewart formed The Faces with three former members of The Small Faces. With The Faces, Wood's cheerful slide work on albums like *First Step* (1970), *Long Player* (1971) and *A Nod's As Good As A Wink* (1971) illustrated an uncluttered style and a dislike of technique for its own sake.

After Stewart's departure for a solo career Wood joined The Rolling Stones in 1975, replacing **Mick Taylor**. Although the Stones are constantly chided simply for still being there, the energies of Richards abetted by Wood ensure that the juggernaut keeps rolling, and their ability to whack out good singles ('Start Me Up', 'Under Cover Of The Night', 'Harlem

WIN-WOO

Shuffle' and 'Rock And A Hard Place') and albums (*Some Girls* 1978, *Steel Wheels* 1989) just when they have been consigned to the scrap heap make them an institution well worth preserving.

ROY WOOD

Born: Ulysses Adrian Wood, November 8th 1946, Birmingham, England.

■ **Fender Stratocaster; Fender Jaguar.**

An idiosyncratic writer and effortless creator of pastiche, Wood's immense talent has been overlooked for some years – often because no one knows quite how or where to bracket him.

Throughout the 1960s Wood appeared with a variety of local Birmingham bands until he formed The Move, working alongside guitarist **Trevor Burton**. One of the finest and most underrated groups of the psychedelic era, The Move benefitted from Wood's cute pop songs and rhythm guitar, both combining energy with gentle allusions to rock's recent past.

Although the group later turned into The Electric Light Orchestra and **Jeff Lynne** moved in, the contrasting musical appetites of Wood and Lynne caused Wood to leave and set up Wizzard, and great pop singles like 'Ball Park Incident' (1972), 'See My Baby Jive' (1973) and 'Angel Fingers' (1973) ensued. Since the mid-1970s Wood has ploughed his own furrow with scant regard for other musical activity.

TERRY WOODS

Born: Ireland.

Vocalist Gay Woods and guitarist Terry were founder members of British folk-rock group Steeleye Span. Terry had been in the Irish folk band Sweeney's Men before joining Steeleye, but he didn't stay long, remaining only for the group's debut *Hark! The Village Wait* (1970). Thereafter with Gay he formed The Woods Band, playing traditional Irish folk music. He briefly retired from the music industry to work in a plastics factory, but in 1987 was recruited to join Irish trad/folk/punk band The Pogues, most recently contributing to *Waiting For Herb* (1993).

BOB WOOTTON

Born: US.

After **Luther Perkins** died in a fire in 1969 his replacement in country-pop singer Johnny Cash's band was Wootton. The touring schedule of the Johnny Cash roadshow remains as intensive as ever it was, and Wootton has shown himself a worthy successor.

LINK WRAY

Born: Lincoln Wray, May 2nd 1930, Fort Bragg, North Carolina, US.

■ **Gibson SG; Gibson Les Paul; Danelectro.**

One of the seminal rock'n'roll guitarists, Wray and his group The Wraymen (bassist Shorty Horton and drummer Doug Wray) cut the epochal 'Rumble' in 1958. Its frenetic, distorted tone in a sea of echo was

hugely influential, and **Pete Townshend** was among many to cite it as an inspiration – later hits like 'Rawhide' and 'Jack The Ripper' sounded sophisticated by comparison. While Wray spent much of the 1960s in obscurity, he returned in the 1970s with a string of albums including *Be What You Want* (1973) and *Stuck In Gear* (1976) that replicated the vibrant, earthy qualities of 'Rumble'. Since the late-1970s he has partnered rockabilly revivalist Robert Gordon, on *Fresh Fish Special* (1978) among others. Still recording – most recently *Indian Child* (1993) – Wray has continued to do what he wants and when he wants.

DENNY WRIGHT

Born: England.

■ **Gretsch Country Gentleman.**

Through much of the early-1960s Wright worked in skiffle/country singer Johnny Duncan's Blue Grass Boys ('Last Train To San Fernando'), but as the skiffle craze faded Wright started to play with **Diz Disley** and violinist Stéphane Grappelli, among others. He still appears on the British club circuit.

JIMMY WYBLE

Born: January 25th 1922, Port Arthur, Texas, US.

■ **Fender; Guild Johnny Smith (later).**

As a member of the key western swing group, Bob Wills & His Texas Playboys, Wyble and fellow guitarist Cameron Hill were in the 1940s trailblazers in the use of electric guitars as twin lead instruments in a popular band. Wyble left Wills later in the decade (replaced by **Junior Barnard**) and worked in Los Angeles as a studio musician for film companies. Wyble also studied classical guitar with **Laurindo Almeida** and toured with jazz vibes player Red Norvo's quintet and the Benny Goodman Orchestra.

ZAKK WYLDE

Born: January 14th 1967, New Jersey, US.

■ **Gibson Les Paul.**

When Wylde joined vocalist Ozzy Osbourne's metal band in 1988 he filled a void that had existed in the group since **Randy Rhoads**' death. Although Wylde has acquitted himself well during that time he is, despite his abilities, treading a well-beaten path. It could set Wylde in good stead for slightly more ambitious projects in the future.

ED WYNNE

Born: England.

Wynne has been close to the heart of neo-psychedelic group Ozric Tentacles ever since their inception in 1982. During that time a protracted touring schedule and shifts of personnel have militated against a productive recording career, but this has established them primarily as a live act, alongside albums like *Erp Land* (1990) and *Jurassic Shift* (1993), with Wynne's guitar work owing some allegiance to first-time-around hippies like **Steve Hillage**.

NEAL X

Born: September 11th 1960, England.

■ **Gibson ES295.**

With a playing style best described as **Marc Bolan** with two broken fingers, Neal teamed with Generation X bassist Tony James to form the vastly over-publicized Sigue Sigue Sputnik in 1984. After two poor albums *Flaunt It* (1984) and *Dress For Excess* (1989) they split. Since then Neal has worked with Stiv Bators, **Johnny Thunders** and **Hotei**, performing with the latter on *Guitarrhythm III* (1992) alongside **Chris Spedding**, Mike Edwards and hornman Andy Mackay and intimating that the best is yet to come.

ZAL YANOVSKY

Born: Zalman Yanovsky, December 19th 1944, Toronto, Ontario, Canada.

The departure of Yanovsky from The Lovin' Spoonful brought a summary end to the hit making skills of the band. Although John Sebastian was the songsmith, Yanovsky's prowess as an arranger and guitarist paid dividends. Formerly a member of The Mugwumps with Denny Doherty and Cass Elliott (later of The Mamas & The Papas), Yanovsky lent atmosphere and ambience to Sebastian compositions such as 'Do You Believe In Magic?', 'Did You Ever Have To Make Up Your Mind?', 'Daydream', 'Rain On The Roof', 'Summer In The City', 'Nashville Cats' and 'Darling Be Home Soon'. In 1967 he left the group under a cloud and resurfaced temporarily for *Alive And Well In Argentina* (1970). In 1980 Yanovsky and the rest of the group reunited for a cameo appearance in **Paul Simon**'s movie *One Trick Pony*.

NARCISO YEPES

Born: November 14th 1927, Lorca, Spain.

■ **Ramirez; Bernabe; Fleta (all 10-string).**

Not only is Yepes one of the more significant Spanish classical guitarists to emerge in the wake of **Segovia**, his unusual use of a special 10-string instrument (with four extra low-tuned strings) since the early-1960s is unprecedented. He made his concert debuts in Europe in 1950 and the US in 1964. While it is unsurprising that his interpretations of Spanish pieces indicate a depth of understanding, his readings of Domenico Scarlatti's Sonatas and Vivaldi's Concerti possess a lightness of touch that shames many who have attempted to make these pieces their own. He has also composed film music.

ANGUS YOUNG

Born: March 31st 1959, Glasgow, Scotland.

■ **Gibson SG Standard.**

Through the apparently simple expedient of constant touring AC/DC have become one of the world's most successful heavy metal outfits. Although his guitar work is solid, he has a wide range of crowd pleasing ploys up his sleeve that render a high level of inventiveness superfluous, although a listen to tracks like 'Ride On' from *Dirty Deeds...* (1976) show what

WOO-YOU

he's capable of. On stage he's known for his shorts and schoolboy cap, and his high-energy sallies to the stage's apron always inspire whoops of delight and joy from the audience. Albums such as *Back In Black* (1980), *For Those About To Rock* (1981) and *The Razor's Edge* (1990) have been steady and effective rather than awe-inspiring.

NEIL YOUNG

Born: November 12th 1945, Toronto, Ontario, Canada.

■ *Gibson Les Paul; Gibson J200; Martin; Gretsch.*

Young belongs to a very small coterie of artists (including Bob Dylan, Van Morrison, **Elvis Costello** and **Joni Mitchell**) whose reputation vindicates whatever direction their music takes. His guitar playing is wonderfully negligent of 'rules', and often has the supreme ability to sound as if it is just about to collapse into a heap of feedback and broken strings.

From his earliest days in Buffalo Springfield, Young's iconoclastic songwriting has underscored all his output – this was partly the reason for the souring of his relationship with **Stephen Stills**. However, his career can also be read as a quest to find another guitarist off whom he could spark ideas.

Everybody Knows This Is Nowhere (1969) and *After The Gold Rush* (1970) had him teamed memorably with **Danny Whitten**; Crazy Horse's Frank Sampedro proved a worthy foil for Young on *Rust Never Sleeps* (1979), *Ragged Glory* (1990) and the magnificently live and noisy *Weld* (1991); and more recently a tour with Booker T & The MGs featuring **Steve Cropper** has shown Young's intuitive solos to be as forceful and strident as ever.

While the standard of his electric guitar work is what Young will probably always be judged by, some of *Live Rust* (1979) and *Unplugged* (1993) showed him echoing earlier songs through a variety of acoustic picking styles. Young's advantageous disregard for fashion predicates his own course. Long may he run.

REGGIE YOUNG

Born: Reginald Grimes Young, 1937, Caruthersville, Missouri, US.

■ *Gibson L5CES; Fender Telecaster; Fender Stratocaster.*

Formerly a member of bassist Bill Black's Combo, Young was a member of the house band at Sun studios in Memphis with Tommy Cogbill (bass), Bobby Emmons (keyboards) and Gene Chrisman (drums). In 1964 when producer Chips Moman left Stax to set up American studios, his first move was to lure Young and the rest of the crew over to form the nucleus of the studio band. Young remained with Moman for the remainder of the decade, and thereafter he commuted between Nashville and Memphis as a session guitarist. Neat and without overt embellishment, the guitar work of Young is similar to that of **Steve Cropper**. Young's recordings include Elvis Presley's 'Suspicious Minds' and 'In The Ghetto' (1969), Dobie Gray's 'Drift Away' (1973), Neil Diamond's 'Sweet Caroline' (1970) and Dusty Springfield's 'Son Of A Preacher Man' (1968).

RUSTY YOUNG

Born: February 23rd 1946, Los Angeles, California, US.

■ *Sho-Bud.*

Though Poco were formed out of the remnants of Buffalo Springfield, their main musical influence was The Byrds. Their closest counterparts The Eagles pursued a parallel and far more successful course, The Eagles' songwriting capabilities far exceeding those of the inconsistent Poco. In Young, Poco had a steel guitarist who became not only the common denominator through the group's different incarnations but also, eventually, an accomplished vocalist and writer. Despite the erratic quality of the group's output, a string of albums over the years including *Good Feelin' To Know* and *Crazy Eyes* (1973), *Head Over Heels* (1975), *Rose Of Cimarron* (1976), *Indian Summer* (1977) and, belatedly, *Legacy* (1989) established them as a great country-rock band and Young as a fine steel guitar player.

FRANK ZAPPA

Born: Francis Vincent Zappa, December 21st 1940, Baltimore, Maryland, US. Died: December 4th 1993, Los Angeles, California, US.

■ *Gibson SG; SG-style custom; Fender Stratocaster.*

While Zappa's output was prodigious in volume and his approach to music uncompromisingly cerebral, his guitar work has been melodic, lyrical and fluent, demonstrating an economy of phrasing if not overall quantity that was in stark contrast to his propensity for verbose, indulgent lyrics that oscillated between the unpalatable and the anachronistic.

Impervious to the machinations of the record industry and the thoughts of press or critics, Zappa picked his way through 20th century musical styles and adapted them to his own schemes.

Zappa's guitar work was influenced early on by **Johnny Guitar Watson** and **Guitar Slim**, and later by the modal/drone aspects of Indian music, and was always recognizable: at length on stage, prodding at the corners of the harmonic possibilities, or concise and melodic on a studio track. He stored miles of live and unreleased tape at home, often incorporating and combining old solos into new work. He produced dozens and dozens of albums, but just some of those recommended for their guitar work are *Cruisin' With Ruben & The Jets* (1968), *Hot Rats* (1970), *Waka Jawaka* (1972), *One Size Fits All* (1975), *Zoot Allures* (1976), *Studio Tan* (1978), and one of several guitar-solo-only collections, the delightfully titled *Shut Up 'n' Play Your Guitar* (1984).

ATTILA ZOLLER

Born: Attila Cornelius Zoller, June 13th 1927, Visegard, Bosnia-Herzegovina.

■ *Framus 'signature'; Hofner 'signature'.*

Raised in a fiercely musical environment, Zoller's father was a music teacher and conductor and his sister a violinist and pianist. Attila took violin lessons from the age of four and trumpet at nine, followed by six years in his school orchestra. After World War II,

he took up the guitar and played the Budapest club circuit, developing a style that was a synthesis of the styles of **Charlie Christian** and **Django Reinhardt**. In 1948 Zoller moved to Vienna and thence to New York in 1959, where he toured with bassist Oscar Pettiford, with drummer Kenny Clarke and with saxman Bud Shank. Later, Zoller recorded *Zo-Ko-Ma* (1968) with Lee Konitz (sax) and Albert Mangelsdorff (trombone), and in the 1980s cut a fine trio album *Common Cause* (1982) with Ron Carter (bass) and Joe Chambers (drums), as well as the solo *Conjunction*. Like Reinhardt, Zoller has evolved a unique style that is informed by the gypsy guitarists of Europe alongside bebop and free jazz influences.

BILLY ZOOM

Born: US.

■ *Gretsch Silver Jet.*

A punkish outfit of some repute, X were formed by Zoom, Exene Cervenka (vocals), John Doe (bass) and Mick Basher (drums). Spotted by former Doors keyboardist Ray Manzarek, who produced the group's first two albums *Los Angeles* (1980) and *Wild Gift* (1981), they combined elements of punk, rockabilly and the blues to create a biting synthesis. Zoom's robust chording on *Wild Gift* possessed greater energy than most of the band's counterparts. However, while *Big Black Sun* (1982) was an excellent piece of work, the individual band members became sidelined by solo projects, dissipating the focus of X. After two further albums, *More Fun In The New World* (1983) and *Ain't Love Grand* (1985), Zoom left to concentrate on solo projects... which have failed to materialize.

ZOOT HORN ROLLO

See BILL HARKLEROAD

Main entries in the A-Z text are indicated with **bold** page numbers.

Illustrated features are indicated with *italic* page numbers.

'The' is excluded from group names in the index: for example, The Action are listed as Action. A number as part of a group name is treated as a word; for example, 10cc can be found listed at the place for 'ten'.

Tony Bacon (editor) *Rock Hardware* (Blandford 1981)

Tony Bacon, Paul Day *The Fender Book* (Balafon 1992)

Tony Bacon, Paul Day *The Gibson Les Paul Book* (Balafon 1993)

Tony Bacon, Paul Day *The Ultimate Guitar Book* (Dorling Kindersley 1991)

Anthony Baines (editor) *Musical Instruments Through The Ages* (Penguin 1961)

Chuck Berry *The Autobiography* (Faber 1990)

Alan Betrock *Girl Groups: The Story of a Sound* (Delilah 1982)

Stanley Booth *Rhythm Oil* (Cape 1990)

Ian Carr et al *Jazz: The Essential Companion* (Paladin 1987)

Ray Charles with David Ritz *Brother Ray* (Dial 1978)

Donald Clarke (editor) *The Penguin Encyclopedia of Popular Music* (Penguin 1990)

Nick Cohn *AwopBopaLooBopLopBamBoom* (Paladin 1972)

Tony Cummings *The Sound of Philadelphia* (Methuen 1975)

Fred Dellar et al *The Illustrated Encyclopedia of Country Music* (Salamander 1977)

Willie Dixon *I Am The Blues* (Quartet 1989)

Michael Erlewine, Scott Bultman *All Music Guide: The Best CDs, Albums & Tapes* (Miller Freeman 1992)

Leonard Feather *Encyclopedia of Jazz* (Da Capo 1960)

Pete Frame *The Complete Rock Family Trees* (Omnibus 1993)

Gillian Gaar *She's A Rebel* (Blandford 1993)

Paul Gambaccini et al *British Hit Albums* (GRR 1988)

Paul Gambaccini et al *British Hit Singles* (GRR 1992)

Nelson George *The Death of Rhythm & Blues* (Omnibus 1988)

Nelson George *Where Did Our Love Go? The Rise and Fall of the Motown Sound* (Omnibus 1985)

Charlie Gillett *Making Tracks: Atlantic Records and the Growth of A Multi-Million Dollar Industry* (Souvenir 1974)

Charlie Gillett *The Sound of the City* (Souvenir 1970)

Hugh Gregory *The Soul Music A-Z* (Blandford 1991)

Hugh Gregory *Who's Who In Country Music* (Weidenfeld & Nicholson 1993)

Charlotte Greig *Will You Still Love Me Tomorrow?* (Virago 1989)

Peter Guralnick *Feel Like Going Home* (Omnibus 1981)

Peter Guralnick *Listener's Guide to The Blues* (Blandford 1982)

Peter Guralnick *Sweet Soul Music* (Virgin 1986)

Phil Hardy, Dave Laing *Faber Companion To 20th-Century Popular Music* (Faber 1990)

Gerri Hirshey *Nowhere To Run* (Macmillan 1984)

Ian Hoare et al *The Soul Book* (Methuen 1975)

Barney Hoskyns *Say It One More Time for the Broken Hearted: The Country Side of Southern Soul* (Fontana 1987)

Terry Hounsome *Rock Record 4: The Directory of Rock Albums and Musicians* (Record Researcher 1991)

Steve Howe with Tony Bacon *The Steve Howe Guitar Collection* (Balafon 1993)

Patrick Humphries *Meet On The Ledge: A History of The Fairport Convention* (Eel Pie 1982)

Leroy Jones *Black Music* (William Morrow 1968)

Allan Kozinn et al *The Guitar: The History, The Music, The Players* (Columbus 1984)

Colin Larkin (editor) *Guinness Encyclopedia of Popular Music* (Guinness 1993)

Mark Lewisohn *Complete Beatles Chronicle* (Pyramid 1992)

Mark Lewisohn *Complete Beatles Recording Sessions* (Hamlyn 1990)

Greil Marcus *Mystery Train* (Omnibus 1979)

Dave Marsh *The Heart of Rock and Soul* (Penguin 1989)

Bill Millar *The Coasters* (Star Books 1974)

Bill Millar *The Drifters* (Studio Vista 1971)

Norman Mongan *The History of the Guitar in Jazz* (Oak 1983)

Charles Shaar Murray *Cross Town Traffic* (Faber 1989)

Stuart Nicholson *Ella Fitzgerald* (Gollancz 1993)

David Ritz *Divided Soul: The Life of Marvin Gaye* (Grafton 1986)

Charles Sawyer *BB King: The Authorised Biography* (Blandford 1981)

Irwin Stambler *Encyclopedia of Pop Rock & Soul* (St James Press 1974)

Maurice J Summerfield *The Classical Guitar: Its Evolution, Players & Personalities Since 1800* (Ashley Mark 1991)

Maurice J Summerfield *The Jazz Guitar: Its Evolution and its Players* (Ashley Mark 1978)

Nick Tosches *Country: Living Legends & Dying Metaphors in America's Biggest Music* (Secker & Warburg 1986)

Nick Tosches *The Unsung Heroes of Rock'n'Roll* (Secker & Warburg 1989)

Paul Trynka (editor) *The Electric Guitar* (Virgin 1993)

Alan Warner *Who Sang What in Rock'n'Roll* (Blandford 1990)

Richard Williams *The Sound of Phil Spector: Out Of His Head* (Abacus 1974)

MAGAZINES

Various back issues of the following titles were consulted during research:

Acoustic Guitar; Beat Instrumental/Monthly; Guitar Magazine; Guitar Player; Guitar World; Guitarist; International Musician; Making Music; Music UK; One Two Testing; Record Collector; Sound International; Vintage Guitar Magazine.

HUGH GREGORY

Books of this nature don't happen without extensive guidance and assistance from all sorts of different people and record companies. I have been very fortunate in having had at my disposal the enthusiasm and knowledge of Tony Bacon and Nigel Osborne of Balafon, and they have always been positive and constructive in their suggestions.

Furthermore, I would like to thank the following who have offered words of wisdom and enthusiasm:

Ace Records, Mike Auldridge, Catrina Barnes (FBM), Stuart Booth, Chris Briggs (Compulsion), Dave Bulmer (Celtic Music), Pam Byers (Ken Fritz Management), Martin Carthy, Richard Cook (Verve Jazz), Bob Cotton (Fit Vision), Sarah-Jane Coxon, Michael Deacon (BMG Classics), Myles Evans (Topic Records), Christopher Fagg, Graham Fletcher (Fit Vision), Keren Greenwell (MCA), Brenda and Oliver Gregory, Monty Hitchcock Management, Allegra Huston, Sophie Jefferies (Harold Holt Management), Howard Jones (Sheridan's), Tim Lihoreau (New Note Distribution), Irving Mildener (Clayman & Co), Jonathan Morrish (Sony UK), Kay Mumford (Fit Vision), Lorne Murdoch (MCPS), National Sound Archive, Tim Noakes, Thierry Pannetier (EMI), Chrissy Pierce, Andy Richmond (Silvertone Records), Caffy St Luce (Hall Or Nothing), Martin Satterthwaite (Country Music Association), George Scott (Fit Vision), See For Miles Records, Lucy Stacey (EMI), Phil Straight (Warner Brothers), Judith Weaterton (Arista), Steve Webbon (Beggars Banquet Records), Richard Wootton (Manor House), Neal X.

BALAFON

The publishers would like to thank Charles Alexander, Ralph Baker, Johnny Black, Seamus Brady at the Acoustic Centre, Gary Cooper, Paul Day, Caroline Field, Tony Mitchell, John Morrish, Ian Purser, Ray Ursell and Visuel 7.